# Parallel Architectures for Artificial Neural Networks

## Paradigms and Implementations

*N. Sundararajan*
*P. Saratchandran*

School of Electrical and Electronic Engineering,
Nanyang Technological University,
Singapore, 639798.

IEEE
COMPUTER
SOCIETY

Los Alamitos, California

Washington • Brussels • Tokyo

**Library of Congress Cataloging-in-Publication Data**

Sundararajan, N.
    Parallel architectures for artificial neural networks: paradigms
and implementations / N. Sundararajan, P. Saratchandran.
        p.   cm.
    Includes bibliographical references and index.
    ISBN  0-8186-8399-6
    1.  Neural networks (Computer science)        2.  Parallel processing
(Electronic computers)      3.  Computer architecture.
I. Saratchandran, P.    II. Title.
QA76.87.S86 1998
006.3 ' 2—dc21

                                                        98-22934
                                                        CIP

IEEE Computer Society Press Order Number BP08399
Library of Congress Number 98-22934
ISBN 0-8186-8399-6

*Additional copies may be ordered from:*

| | | |
|---|---|---|
| IEEE Computer Society Press | IEEE Service Center | IEEE Computer Society |
| Customer Service Center | 445 Hoes Lane | Watanabe Building |
| 10662 Los Vaqueros Circle | P.O. Box 1331 | 1-4-2 Minami-Aoyama |
| P.O. Box 3014 | Piscataway, NJ 08855-1331 | Minato-ku, Tokyo 107-0062 |
| Los Alamitos, CA 90720-1314 | Tel: +1-732-981-1393 | JAPAN |
| Tel: +1-714-821-8380 | Fax: +1-732-981-9667 | Tel: +81-3-3408-3118 |
| Fax: +1-714-821-4641 | mis.custserv@computer.org | Fax: +81-3-3408-3553 |
| Email: cs.books@computer.org | | tokyo.ofc@computer.org |

Publisher: Matt Loeb
Developmental Editor: Cheryl Baltes
Advertising/Promotions: Tom Fink

## Dedication

To
my grandparents/parents,
my wife Saraswathi,
and daughters Sowmya and Sripriya

       N. Sundararajan

To
my parents,
my wife Jaya,
and children Para and Hemanth

       P. Saratchandran

To
our teachers and students,
who have all taught and inspired us

       N. Sundararajan
       P. Saratchandran

# List of Contributors

## Introduction

**P. Saratchandran**
School of Electrical Engineering,
Nanyang Technological University
Singapore

**N. Sundararajan**
School of Electrical Engineering,
Nanyang Technological University
Singapore

**Jim Torresen**
Department of Computer and Information Science,
Norwegian University of Science and Technology
Norway

## A Review of Parallel Implementations of Backpropagation Neural Networks

**Jim Torresen**
Department of Computer and Information Science,
Norwegian University of Science and Technology
Norway

**Olav Landsverk**
Department of Computer Systems and Telematics,
Norwegian University of Science and Technology
Norway

## Part I: Analysis of Parallel Implementations

**R. Arularasan**
School of Electrical Engineering,
Nanyang Technological University
Singapore

**Shou King Foo**
School of Electrical Engineering,
Nanyang Technological University
Singapore

**George Kechriotis**
Thinking Machines, Inc.,
Cambridge, Massachusetts

**Elias S. Manolakos**
Communications and Digital Signal Processing (CDSP),
Center for Research and Graduate Studies
Electrical and Computer Engineering Department,
Northeastern University
Boston, Massachusetts

**Stylianos Markogiannakis**
Brigham and Women's Hospital,
Anesthesia Foundation
Boston, Massachusetts

**P. Saratchandran**
School of Electrical Engineering,
Nanyang Technological University
Singapore

**N. Sundararajan**
School of Electrical Engineering,
Nanyang Technological University
Singapore

## Part II: Implementations on a Big General-Purpose Parallel Computer

**Jim Torresen**
Department of Computer and Information Science,
Norwegian University of Science and Technology
Norway

**Shinji Tomita**
Department of Information Science,
Kyoto University
Japan

## Part III: Special Parallel Architectures and Application Case Studies

**Krste Asanović**
Department of Electrical Engineering and Computer Sciences,
University of California, Berkeley
International Computer Science Institute
Berkeley, California

**James Beck**
Department of Electrical Engineering and Computer Sciences,
University of California, Berkeley
International Computer Science Institute
Berkeley, California

**Beat Flepp**
Swiss Federal Institute of Technology (ETH),
Switzerland

**Yoshiji Fujimoto**
Department of Applied Mathematics and Informatics,
Faculty of Science and Technology
Ryukoko University
Japan

**Jean-Luc Gaudiot**
Department of Electrical Engineering,
University of Southern California
Los Angeles, California

**Walter Guggenbühl**
Swiss Federal Institute of Technology (ETH),
Switzerland

**Anton Gunzinger**
Swiss Federal Institute of Technology (ETII),
Switzerland

**David Johnson**
International Computer Science Institute,
Berkeley, California

**Brian Kingsbury**
Department of Electrical Engineering and Computer Sciences,
University of California, Berkeley
International Computer Science Institute
Berkeley, California

**Michael Kocheisen**
Swiss Federal Institute of Technology (ETH),
Switzerland

**Nelson Morgan**
Department of Electrical Engineering and Computer Sciences,
University of California, Berkeley
International Computer Science Institute
Berkeley, California

**Urs A. Müller**
Swiss Federal Institute of Technology (ETH),
Switzerland

**Soheil Shams**
Hughes Research Laboratories - Systems,
Malibu, California

**Patrick Spiess**
Swiss Federal Institute of Technology (ETH),
Switzerland

**John Wawrzynek**
Department of Electrical Engineering and Computer Sciences,
University of California
Berkeley, California

# Preface

## Purpose and Goals

As artificial neural network (ANN) applications move from laboratories to the practical world, the concern about reducing the time for the learning and recall phases becomes very real. Parallel implementation schemes offer an attractive way of speeding up both these phases of ANNs. Although much progress has taken place on the subject of parallel implementation of various ANN paradigms, the work relating to this has not been been explored comprehensively in a single publication; rather it is scattered in various conference proceedings and journal publications, some of which are even outside the field of neural networks. This motivated us to present the parallel implementation aspects of all major ANN models in a single book, which can then serve as a good reference to all those involved in the research and application of this area of neural networks.

The book also aims to provide details of implementations on various processor architectures (ring, torus, and others) built on different hardware platforms ranging from large general-purpose parallel computers to custom-built multi-instructions multi-data (MIMD) machines using transputers and digital signal processors (DSPs). We believe that such a book will promote fruitful research in the interdisciplinary area of parallel processing and neural networks.

The book consists of several self-contained chapters, each authored by experts who have actually performed the implementations covered in their respective chapters. The authors provide results of their work, which in some cases are as yet unpublished.

The book is aimed at graduate students and researchers working in the area of artificial neural networks and parallel computing. It can be used by educators at the graduate level to illustrate the use and methods of parallel computing for ANN simulation. Because the mathematical analyses are lucid we feel it can also serve as a good reference book for the practitioners in this field.

## An Overview

Because the aim of the book is to provide both analysis and experimental results of parallel implementations (of different ANN models) on various hardware platforms, we have divided the book broadly into three parts each providing analysis and implementations on a class of related hardware. As parallel simulation of ANN is the topic of the book, a detailed discussion on the parallel processing aspects of neural networks is given in Chapter 1. This chapter also describes the different ANN models used in the rest of the book for parallel implementation.

As multilayer feedforward network with backpropagation (BP) learning is the most popular of all ANN models, Chapter 2, preceding the three parts, provides a comprehensive review of the various forms of parallelism and a survey of different parallel implementations of BP.

Part I of the book mainly concentrates on the theoretical analysis of parallel implementation schemes on MIMD message-passing machines. It consists of four chapters providing detailed analysis of parallelism for BP, real-time recurrent learning (RTRL), and adaptive resonance theory (ART1).

Part II describes the details of the parallel implementation of BP neural networks on a general-purpose, large, parallel computer. Analysis and results from extensive studies on the Fujitsu AP1000 parallel computer are discussed.

Part III consists of four chapters each describing a specific special-purpose parallel neural computer configuration. They also provide application case studies on practical implementation of some of the ANN models discussed in Chapter 1. Our overall conclusions and predictions of future trends are presented in Chapter 12.

## Organization of the Book

The first two chapters of Part I, Chapters 3 and 4, deal with parallel mapping of multilayer feed-forward neural networks with BP learning on a homogeneous and heterogeneous processor array in a ring topology. The authors, Dr. P. Saratchandran, Dr. N. Sundararajan, Mr. R. Arularasan, and Mr. Foo Shou King, from Nanyang Technological University, Singapore, have addressed the issue of finding the optimal mapping (to find the minimal training time) *using theoretical means* without actually connecting the hardware and running simulations. By developing rigorous mathematical models of the parallel BP running on the hardware, the authors find the optimal solution to the mapping problem for both network-based and training-set parallelism. Using benchmark problems, they have also validated their theoretical models with experimental results using an array of transputers.

Chapter 5 deals with parallel implementation of recurrent neural networks. Written by Prof. Elias Manolakos from the Northeastern University, Boston, this chapter covers in detail the parallel implementation of a fully recurrent neural network on a transputer-based multiprocessor system with a real-time recurrent learning algorithm used for training. This chapter shows that the computationally intensive sequential RTRL algorithm can be transformed into an equivalent parallel algorithm realized in a ring topology that can be matched to a variety of target architectures, ranging from application specific very large scale integration (VLSI) arrays to general-purpose multiprocessor systems. Efficient implementation of the RTRL algorithm on a ring of 19 transputers is discussed and the speedup verified both analytically and experimentally.

Chapter 6, also by Prof. Manolakos and his coworkers from Boston, contains some recently developed results on parallel implementation of ART1 networks. They describe a newly developed parallel algorithm for ART1 that can be mapped on MIMD processor networks and is also suitable for VLSI implementation.

In Part II, Chapter 7 covers the implementations of BP neural networks on large parallel computer systems. Dr. Jim Torresen of Norwegian University of Science and Technology, Norway, and Shinji Tomita of Kyoto University, Japan, have been working in this area using the big Fujitsu AP1000 machine for their studies. They consider the problem of mapping the backpropagation training of real neural applications onto large parallel systems, and they discuss a parallel mapping scheme of neural training that adapts the configuration to the neural application. Also, a heuristic for selecting the best mapping scheme, combining all degrees of parallelism, which minimizes the total training time, is developed in this chapter. The mapping scheme is tested on the general-purpose, parallel computer AP1000, which is a message passing MIMD computer with a two-dimensional torus network of processing elements containing a maximum of 512 processing elements. The results indicate that the training speed can be reduced from hours to minutes if the parallel system is used instead of a single-processor workstation. Moreover, the flexible mapping, which adjusts the configuration to the given neural application, may result in a training speed several hundred percent faster than a fixed mapping.

Part III of the book discusses parallel implementations on special-purpose processor architectures and computing devices that are dedicated for ANN simulation.

Chapter 8 in Part III discusses special architectures called the toroidal lattice architecture (TLA) and the planar lattice architecture (PLA) as massively parallel architectures of neurocomputers for large-scale neural network simulations. Proposed by Prof. Yoshiji Fujimoto from Ryukoko University, Japan, the discussion indicates that the performance of these architectures are almost proportional to the number of node processors and they adopt the most efficient two-dimensional processor connections to be implemented by the wafer scale integration (WSI) technology. Prof. Fujimoto also discusses the implementation of the TLA using transputers for BP as well as Hopfield networks, including the details of parallel processor configurations and the load balance algorithm and evaluation of its performance on problems like the traveling salesman problem (TSP) and the identity mapping problem (IM).

Chapter 9 deals with an implementation method that exploits the maximum amount of the parallelism form of neural computation without enforcing stringent conditions on the neural network interconnection structures for achieving high implementation efficiency. In this chapter, Prof. Jean-Luc Gaudiot of the University of Southern California and Dr. Soheil Shams of the Hughes Research Laboratory, California, propose a new reconfigurable parallel processing architecture called the dynamically reconfigurable extended array multiprocessor (DREAM) Machine and an associated mapping method for implementing neural networks with regular interconnection structures. Examples of BP and Hopfield networks are used to demonstrate the efficiency of the mapping method and also of the DREAM Machine architecture on implementing diverse interconnection structures.

In Chapter 10, Patrick Spiess and his group from ETH, Switzerland, discuss the architecture, implementations, and applications of a DSP-based parallel high-performance computer system named MUSIC (multiprocessor system with intelligent communication). This system consists of an array of up to 63 processing elements, distributed memory, and a ring communication network. The performance for backpropagation learning featuring continuous weight update (on-line learning) is up to 330 million connection updates per second, which outperforms even the fastest conventional supercomputers.

The last chapter in Part III, Chapter 11, describes a special-purpose parallel neural computer called SPERT-II developed by Krste Asanovic and his coworkers at the International Computer Science Institute, Berkeley, California. SPERT-II is based on T0, a custom fixed-point vector microprocessor and serves as an attached processor to a standard workstation host. These systems have been used primarily to speed neural network training for speech recognition work, and results based on this work are presented in this chapter.

The book concludes with Chapter 12, which summarizes the work reported in the earlier chapters and provides some overall conclusions and future directions in this field.

## Acknowledgments

Undertaking and completing a project like this would not have been possible without the support and encouragement of many individuals. First and foremost, we wish to thank all the contributors, who readily agreed to participate in this work, for providing the material in a timely manner. Without their support this book would not have materialized.

Next, we want to thank our doctoral student Foo Shou King who helped us to organize the contributions from authors all over the world with different word processing software and different hardware platforms from PC to Macintosh. He brought them together to the nice world of LaTeX so as to bring a common standard to this volume. We also hereby acknowledge the countless hours he spent with us in compiling this volume while doing his research work.

We wish to record our thanks to Dr. Cham Tao Soon, president of Nanyang Technological University, for providing an excellent academic environment in which we could undertake and succeed in an endeavor like this.

We are grateful to Prof. Er Meng Hwa, dean of the School of Electrical and Electronic Engineering, for his support and encouragement during this project. We also wish to thank Prof. Soh Yeng Chai, head of the Division of Control and Instrumentation, for his support during this project.

We owe a debt of gratitude to the anonymous reviewers who provided valuable comments in the preliminary stages of this project, most of which have been incorporated in the book.

Finally, we extend our thanks to Mr. Bill Sanders and Ms. Cheryl Baltes of the IEEE Computer Society Press, California, for their constant support and help during this project.

# Contents

**1  Introduction**                                                                 **1**

N. SUNDARARAJAN, P. SARATCHANDRAN, JIM TORRESEN

1.1   Parallel Processing for Simulating ANNs . . . . . . . . . . . . . . .      1
   1.1.1   Performance Metrics . . . . . . . . . . . . . . . . . .      2
   1.1.2   General Aspects of Parallel Processing . . . . . . . . . . .      2
1.2   Classification of ANN Models . . . . . . . . . . . . . . . . . . .      5
1.3   ANN Models Covered in This Book . . . . . . . . . . . . . . . . .      5
   1.3.1   Multilayer Feed-Forward Networks with BP Learning . . . .      7
   1.3.2   Hopfield Network . . . . . . . . . . . . . . . . . . . .     13
   1.3.3   Multilayer Recurrent Networks . . . . . . . . . . . . . .     15
   1.3.4   Adaptive Resonance Theory (ART) Networks . . . . . . . . .     16
   1.3.5   Self-Organizing Map (SOM) Networks . . . . . . . . . .     17
   1.3.6   Processor Topologies and Hardware Platforms . . . . . . . .     18

**2  A Review of Parallel Implementations of Backpropagation Neural Networks**   **25**

JIM TORRESEN, OLAV LANDSVERK

2.1   Introduction . . . . . . . . . . . . . . . . . . . . . . . . . . .     25
2.2   Parallelization of Feed-Forward Neural Networks . . . . . . . . . . .     25
   2.2.1   Distributed Computing for Each Degree of BP Parallelism . . .     26
   2.2.2   A Survey of Different Parallel Implementations . . . . . . .     29
   2.2.3   Neural Network Applications . . . . . . . . . . . . . . .     49
2.3   Conclusions on Neural Applications and Parallel Hardware . . . . . . .     54

**I   Analysis of Parallel Implementations**                                       **65**

**3  Network Parallelism for Backpropagation Neural Networks on a
Heterogeneous Architecture**                                                       **67**

R. ARULARASAN, P. SARATCHANDRAN, N. SUNDARARAJAN, SHOU KING FOO

3.1   Introduction . . . . . . . . . . . . . . . . . . . . . . . . . . .     67
3.2   Heterogeneous Network Topology . . . . . . . . . . . . . . . . .     69
3.3   Mathematical Model for the Parallelized BP Algorithm . . . . . . . .     70
   3.3.1   Timing Diagram for the Parallelized BP Algorithm . . . . . .     70
   3.3.2   Prediction of Iteration Time . . . . . . . . . . . . . . .     75
3.4   Experimental Validation of the Model Using Benchmark Problems . . .     76
   3.4.1   Benchmark Problems Used for Validation . . . . . . . . . .     76
   3.4.2   Validation Setup and Results . . . . . . . . . . . . . . .     76
3.5   Optimal Distribution of Neurons Among the Processing Nodes . . . . .     79

| | | |
|---|---|---|
| 3.5.1 | Communication Constraints | 79 |
| 3.5.2 | Temporal Dependence Constraints | 80 |
| 3.5.3 | Memory Constraints | 81 |
| 3.5.4 | Feasibility Constraints | 82 |
| 3.5.5 | Optimal Mapping | 82 |
| 3.6 | Methods of Solution to the Optimal Mapping Problem | 83 |
| 3.6.1 | Genetic Algorithmic Solution | 83 |
| 3.6.2 | Approximate Linear Heuristic (ALH) Solution | 86 |
| 3.6.3 | Experimental Results | 87 |
| 3.7 | Statistical Validation of the Optimal Mapping | 88 |
| 3.8 | Discussion | 91 |
| 3.8.1 | Worthwhileness of Finding Optimal Mappings | 91 |
| 3.8.2 | Processor Location in a Ring | 94 |
| 3.8.3 | Cost-Benefit Analysis | 96 |
| 3.8.4 | Optimal Number of Processors for Homogeneous Processor Arrays | 97 |
| 3.9 | Conclusion | 100 |
| A3.1 | Theoretical Expressions for Processes in the Parallel BP Algorithm | 101 |
| A3.1.1 | Computation Processes | 101 |
| A3.1.2 | Communication Processes | 104 |
| A3.2 | Memory Constraints | 105 |
| A3.2.1 | Storing the Training Set | 105 |
| A3.2.2 | Storing the Neural Network Parameters | 105 |
| A3.2.3 | Overall Memory Requirement | 106 |
| A3.3 | Elemental Timings for T805 Transputers | 106 |

## 4 Training-Set Parallelism for Backpropagation Neural Networks on a Heterogeneous Architecture

111

SHOU KING FOO, P. SARATCHANDRAN, N. SUNDARARAJAN

| | | |
|---|---|---|
| 4.1 | Introduction | 111 |
| 4.2 | Parallelization of BP Algorithm | 112 |
| 4.2.1 | Process Synchronization Graph | 114 |
| 4.2.2 | Variable Synchronization Graph | 117 |
| 4.2.3 | Predicting the Epoch Time | 117 |
| 4.3 | Experimental Validation of the Model Using Benchmark Problems | 119 |
| 4.4 | Optimal Distribution of Patterns Among the Processing Nodes | 120 |
| 4.4.1 | Communication Constraints | 121 |
| 4.4.2 | Temporal Dependence Constraints | 121 |
| 4.4.3 | Memory Constraints | 122 |
| 4.4.4 | Feasibility Constraints | 123 |
| 4.4.5 | Feasibility of Pattern Assignments | 123 |
| 4.4.6 | Feasibility of Waiting | 123 |
| 4.4.7 | Optimal Mapping | 123 |
| 4.5 | Genetic Algorithmic Solution to the Optimal Mapping Problem | 124 |
| 4.5.1 | Experimental Results | 125 |
| 4.6 | Statistical Validation of the Optimal Mapping | 125 |
| 4.7 | Discussion | 126 |
| 4.7.1 | Worthwhileness of Finding Optimal Distribution | 126 |
| 4.7.2 | Processor Location in a Ring | 127 |
| 4.8 | Conclusion | 128 |

4.9   Process Decomposition . . . . . . . . . . . . . . . . . . . . . .   129
4.10  Memory Requirements . . . . . . . . . . . . . . . . . . . . . .   130
    4.10.1  Storing the Network Parameters . . . . . . . . . . . .   130
    4.10.2  Storing the Training Set  . . . . . . . . . . . . . . . .   130
    4.10.3  Memory Required for the Forward Pass of the Backpropagation   130
    4.10.4  Memory Required for the Backward Pass of the Backpropagation   131
    4.10.5  Temporary Memory Storage during Weight Changes Transfer  .   131
    4.10.6  Overall Memory Requirement . . . . . . . . . . . . . . .   131

## 5  Parallel Real-Time Recurrent Algorithm for Training Large Fully Recurrent Neural Networks                                                        135

ELIAS S. MANOLAKOS, GEORGE KECHRIOTIS

5.1   Introduction . . . . . . . . . . . . . . . . . . . . . . . . . . .   135
5.2   Background . . . . . . . . . . . . . . . . . . . . . . . . . . .   136
    5.2.1   The Real-Time Recurrent Learning Algorithm  . . . . . . .   136
    5.2.2   Matrix Formulation of the RTRL Algorithm . . . . . . . .   139
5.3   Parallel RTRL Algorithm Derivation . . . . . . . . . . . . . .   140
    5.3.1   The Retrieving Phase . . . . . . . . . . . . . . . . . .   140
    5.3.2   The Learning Phase . . . . . . . . . . . . . . . . . . .   143
5.4   Training Very Large RNNs on Fixed-Size Ring Arrays  . . . . .   149
    5.4.1   Partitioning for the Retrieving Phase . . . . . . . . . . .   149
    5.4.2   Partitioning for the Learning Phase  . . . . . . . . . . .   150
    5.4.3   A Transputer-Based Implementation . . . . . . . . . . .   150
5.5   Conclusions . . . . . . . . . . . . . . . . . . . . . . . . . .   154

## 6  Parallel Implementation of ART1 Neural Networks on Processor Ring Architectures                                                                  157

ELIAS S. MANOLAKOS, STYLIANOS MARKOGIANNAKIS

6.1   Introduction . . . . . . . . . . . . . . . . . . . . . . . . . . .   157
6.2   ART1 Network Architecture . . . . . . . . . . . . . . . . . .   158
6.3   Serial Algorithm  . . . . . . . . . . . . . . . . . . . . . . . .   161
6.4   Parallel Ring Algorithm . . . . . . . . . . . . . . . . . . . . .   164
    6.4.1   Partitioning Strategy . . . . . . . . . . . . . . . . . . .   169
6.5   Experimental Results . . . . . . . . . . . . . . . . . . . . . .   170
    6.5.1   The MEIKO Computing Surface System  . . . . . . . . .   170
    6.5.2   Performance and Scalability Analysis . . . . . . . . . . .   171
6.6   Conclusions . . . . . . . . . . . . . . . . . . . . . . . . . .   173

## II  Implementations on a Big General-Purpose Parallel Computer                                                                   183

## 7  Implementation of Backpropagation Neural Networks on Large Parallel Computers                                                                   185

JIM TORRESEN, SHINJI TOMITA

7.1   Introduction . . . . . . . . . . . . . . . . . . . . . . . . . . .   185
7.2   Hardware for Running Neural Networks . . . . . . . . . . . . .   186
    7.2.1   Fujitsu AP1000 . . . . . . . . . . . . . . . . . . . . . .   186
    7.2.2   Neural Network Applications Used in This Work  . . . . . .   187

7.2.3    Experimental Conditions in This Work . . . . . . . . . . . . .   188
7.3   General Mapping onto 2D-Torus MIMD Computers . . . . . . . .   188
    7.3.1    The Proposed Mapping Scheme . . . . . . . . . . . . . .   189
    7.3.2    Heuristic for Selection of the Best Mapping . . . . . . . . .   196
    7.3.3    Summary . . . . . . . . . . . . . . . . . . . . . . . . .   201
7.4   Results on the General BP Mapping . . . . . . . . . . . . . . . .   201
    7.4.1    Nettalk . . . . . . . . . . . . . . . . . . . . . . . . . .   201
    7.4.2    Sonar Target Classification . . . . . . . . . . . . . . . .   216
    7.4.3    Speech Recognition Network . . . . . . . . . . . . . . .   221
    7.4.4    Image Compression . . . . . . . . . . . . . . . . . . . .   221
7.5   Conclusions on the Application Adaptable Mapping . . . . . . . . .   225

## III   Special Parallel Architectures and Application Case Studies   231

## 8   Massively Parallel Architectures for Large-Scale Neural Network Computations   233

YOSHIJI FUJIMOTO

8.1   Introduction . . . . . . . . . . . . . . . . . . . . . . . . . . .   233
8.2   General Neuron Model . . . . . . . . . . . . . . . . . . . . . .   235
8.3   Toroidal Lattice and Planar Lattice Architectures of Virtual Processors .   237
8.4   The Simulation of a Hopfield Neural Network . . . . . . . . . . . .   237
    8.4.1    The Simulation of an HNN on TLA . . . . . . . . . . . .   238
    8.4.2    The Simulation of an HNN on PLA . . . . . . . . . . . .   241
8.5   The Simulation of a Multilayer Perceptron . . . . . . . . . . . . .   242
8.6   Mapping onto Physical Node Processors from Virtual Processors . . . .   245
8.7   Load Balancing of Node Processors . . . . . . . . . . . . . . . .   250
8.8   Estimation of the Performance . . . . . . . . . . . . . . . . . .   251
8.9   Implementation . . . . . . . . . . . . . . . . . . . . . . . . .   255
8.10  Conclusions . . . . . . . . . . . . . . . . . . . . . . . . . .   259
A8.1  Load Balancing Mapping Algorithm . . . . . . . . . . . . . . . .   261
A8.2  Processing Time of the NP Array . . . . . . . . . . . . . . . . .   263

## 9   Regularly Structured Neural Networks on the DREAM Machine   271

SOHEIL SHAMS, JEAN-LUC GAUDIOT

9.1   Introduction . . . . . . . . . . . . . . . . . . . . . . . . . . .   271
9.2   Mapping Method Preliminaries . . . . . . . . . . . . . . . . . .   272
    9.2.1    Neural Network Computation and Structure . . . . . . . . .   272
    9.2.2    Implementing Neural Networks on the Ring Systolic Architecture   274
    9.2.3    System Utilization Characteristic of the Mapping onto the Ring Systolic Architecture . . . . . . . . . . . . . . . . . . .   276
    9.2.4    Execution Rate Characteristics of the Mapping onto the Ring Systolic Architecture . . . . . . . . . . . . . . . . . . .   277
    9.2.5    Mapping Multilayer Neural Networks onto the Ring Systolic Architecture . . . . . . . . . . . . . . . . . . . . . . . .   278
    9.2.6    Deficiencies of the Mapping onto the Ring Systolic Architecture   278
9.3   DREAM Machine Architecture . . . . . . . . . . . . . . . . . .   279

9.3.1   System Level Overview . . . . . . . . . . . . . . . . . . . .   279
9.3.2   Processor-Memory Interface . . . . . . . . . . . . . . . . .   280
9.3.3   Implementing a Table Lookup Mechanism on the DREAM Machine . . . . . . . . . . . . . . . . . . . . . . . . . .   281
9.3.4   Interprocessor Communication Network . . . . . . . . . . .   282
9.4   Mapping Structured Neural Networks onto the DREAM Machine . . .   283
9.4.1   General Mapping Problems . . . . . . . . . . . . . . . . .   283
9.4.2   The Algorithmic Mapping Method and Its Applicability . . . .   284
9.4.3   Using Variable Length Rings to Implement Neural Network Processing . . . . . . . . . . . . . . . . . . . . . . . . . .   285
9.4.4   Implementing Multilayer Networks . . . . . . . . . . . . .   287
9.4.5   Implementing Backpropagation Learning Algorithms . . . . .   288
9.4.6   Implementing Blocked Connected Networks . . . . . . . . .   289
9.4.7   Implementing Neural Networks Larger Than the Processor Array   291
9.4.8   Batch-Mode Implementation . . . . . . . . . . . . . . . . .   291
9.4.9   Implementing Competitive Learning . . . . . . . . . . . . .   292
9.5   Implementation Examples and Performance Evaluation . . . . . . . .   293
9.5.1   Performance Metric . . . . . . . . . . . . . . . . . . . . .   294
9.5.2   Implementing Fully Connected Multilayer Neural Networks . .   294
9.5.3   Implementing a Block-Connected Multilayer Neural Network .   295
9.5.4   Implementing a Fully Connected Single Layer Network . . . .   295
9.6   Conclusion . . . . . . . . . . . . . . . . . . . . . . . . . . . . .   297

10 High-Performance Parallel Backpropagation Simulation with On-Line Learning   303
URS A. MÜLLER, PATRICK SPIESS, MICHAEL KOCHEISEN, BEAT FLEPP, ANTON GUNZINGER, WALTER GUGGENBÜHL.

10.1   Introduction . . . . . . . . . . . . . . . . . . . . . . . . . . . .   303
10.2   The MUSIC Parallel Supercomputer . . . . . . . . . . . . . . . .   304
10.2.1   System Hardware . . . . . . . . . . . . . . . . . . . . . .   304
10.2.2   System Programming . . . . . . . . . . . . . . . . . . . .   306
10.3   Backpropagation Implementation . . . . . . . . . . . . . . . . . .   306
10.3.1   The Backpropagation Algorithm . . . . . . . . . . . . . .   306
10.3.2   Parallelization . . . . . . . . . . . . . . . . . . . . . . .   307
10.4   Performance Analysis . . . . . . . . . . . . . . . . . . . . . . . .   310
10.4.1   A Speedup Model . . . . . . . . . . . . . . . . . . . . .   311
10.4.2   Loss Factors . . . . . . . . . . . . . . . . . . . . . . . .   311
10.4.3   Performance Results . . . . . . . . . . . . . . . . . . . .   312
10.5   The NeuroBasic Parallel Simulation Environment . . . . . . . . . .   312
10.5.1   Implementation . . . . . . . . . . . . . . . . . . . . . . .   313
10.5.2   An Example Program . . . . . . . . . . . . . . . . . . . .   314
10.5.3   Performance versus Programming Time . . . . . . . . . . .   316
10.6   Examples of Practical Research Work . . . . . . . . . . . . . . . .   316
10.6.1   Neural Networks in Photofinishing . . . . . . . . . . . . .   316
10.6.2   The Truck Backer-Upper . . . . . . . . . . . . . . . . . .   327
10.7   Analysis of RISC Performance for Backpropagation . . . . . . . . .   333
10.7.1   Introduction . . . . . . . . . . . . . . . . . . . . . . . .   334
10.7.2   Linearization of the Instruction Stream . . . . . . . . . . .   334
10.7.3   Reduction of Load/Store Operations . . . . . . . . . . . . .   335
10.7.4   Improvement of the Internal Instruction Stream Parallelism . . .   336

10.7.5 Results . . . . . . . . . . . . . . . . . . . . . . . . . 338
10.8 Conclusions . . . . . . . . . . . . . . . . . . . . . . . . . . . 339

## 11 Training Neural Networks with SPERT-II        345

KRSTE ASANOVIĆ, JAMES BECK, DAVID JOHNSON, BRIAN KINGSBURY,
NELSON MORGAN, JOHN WAWRZYNEK

11.1 Introduction . . . . . . . . . . . . . . . . . . . . . . . . . . 345
11.2 Algorithm Development . . . . . . . . . . . . . . . . . . . 346
11.3 T0: A Vector Microprocessor . . . . . . . . . . . . . . . . . 347
11.4 The SPERT-II Workstation Accelerator . . . . . . . . . . . . 349
11.5 Mapping Backpropagation to SPERT-II . . . . . . . . . . . 351
11.6 Mapping Kohonen Nets to SPERT-II . . . . . . . . . . . . 355
11.7 Conclusions . . . . . . . . . . . . . . . . . . . . . . . . . . 357

## 12 Concluding Remarks        365

N. SUNDARARAJAN, P. SARATCHANDRAN

12.1 Future Trend . . . . . . . . . . . . . . . . . . . . . . . . . . 367

# List of Tables

1.1 ANN Models and their parallel implementations. . . . . . . . . . .    19

2.1 Advantages and disadvantages of different chip technologies. . . . . .    46

2.2 Parallel general-purpose computer mappings of BP training. A mapping is implemented on the computer unless "M" is indicated in the leftmost column. An "M" indicates that a theoretical model of the system is used.    47

2.3 Transputer implementations of BP. An "M" in the leftmost column indicates that a theoretical model of the system is used. . . . . . . . . . .    48

2.4 BP neurocomputer implementations. . . . . . . . . . . . . . . . .    48

2.5 Performance of neural network training. $\mu$ is the weight update interval, and FP is the floating point precision. The horizontal lines separate general-purpose computers, transputer systems, and neurocomputers, respectively. . . . . . . . . . . . . . . . . . . . . . . . . . . . .    49

2.6 Neural network applications using feed-forward neural networks. A reference to the data set is given if it is freely available. (P) indicates that a preprocessing network is used in front of the FF-NN inputs. . . . . . .    53

2.7 Freely available data training sets. . . . . . . . . . . . . . . . . . .    53

3.1 Comparison of theoretical and experimental times per iteration for different heterogeneous processor networks for the 252-126-252 Encoder problem. . . . . . . . . . . . . . . . . . . . . . . . . . . . . . . .    79

3.2 Comparison of theoretical and experimental times per iteration for different heterogeneous processor networks for the 203-120-28 Nettalk problem. . . . . . . . . . . . . . . . . . . . . . . . . . . . . . . . .    79

3.3 Optimal mapping from the two solution methods for the Encoder problem. Processor network used is TYPE-1. . . . . . . . . . . . . . . . . . .    87

3.4 Optimal mapping from the two solution methods for the Encoder problem. Processor network used is TYPE-2. . . . . . . . . . . . . . . . . . .    88

3.5 Optimal mapping from the two solution methods for the Encoder problem. Processor network used is TYPE-3. . . . . . . . . . . . . . . . . . .    88

3.6 Optimal mapping from the two solution methods for the Nettalk problem. Processor network used is TYPE-1. . . . . . . . . . . . . . . . . . .    88

3.7 Optimal mapping from the two solution methods for the Nettalk problem. Processor network used is TYPE-2. . . . . . . . . . . . . . . . . . .    91

3.8 Optimal mapping from the two solution methods for the Nettalk problem. Processor network used is TYPE-3. . . . . . . . . . . . . . . . . . .    91

3.9 Optimal time per iteration (ms) from the two solution methods for the Encoder problem. . . . . . . . . . . . . . . . . . . . . . . . . . .    91

3.10 Optimal time per iteration (ms) from the two solution methods for the Nettalk problem. . . . . . . . . . . . . . . . . . . . . . . . . . .    94

3.11   Total time for training for the optimal and nonoptimal neuron distributions for the Encoder problem on a TYPE-1 network. Training converged after 302,400 iterations. ............................... 94

3.12   Total time for training for the optimal and nonoptimal neuron distributions for the Encoder problem on a TYPE-2 network. Training converged after 302,400 iterations. ............................... 94

3.13   Total time for training for the optimal and nonoptimal neuron distributions for the Encoder problem on a TYPE-3 network. Training converged after 302,400 iterations. ............................... 95

3.14   Total time for training for the optimal and nonoptimal neuron distributions for the Nettalk problem on a TYPE-1 network. Training converged after 130,000 iterations. ............................... 95

3.15   Total time for training for the optimal and nonoptimal neuron distributions for the Nettalk problem on a TYPE-2 network. Training converged after 130,000 iterations. ............................... 95

3.16   Total time for training for the optimal and nonoptimal neuron distributions for the Nettalk problem on a TYPE-3 network. Training converged after 130,000 iterations. ............................... 95

3.17   Optimal time per iteration (ms) for the three processor networks for the Encoder and Nettalk problems. ...................... 96

3.18   Reduction in the training time per iteration accruing from alternate choices. ............................................ 96

A3.19 Timings for elemental operations for T805-20 and T805-25 Transputers.   107

4.1   Comparison of theoretical and experimental times per epoch for the three-processor networks for the Encoder problem. ............. 120

4.2   Optimal time per epoch (sec) from the GA method for the Encoder and Nettalk problems. ...................................... 125

4.3   Total time taken for training using the two heuristic and GA pattern distributions for the Encoder problem on CONFIG-3. Convergence was reached after 15,200 epochs. ........................... 127

5.1   Number of multiplications, additions, and sigmoid function evaluations per step of the sequential RTRL algorithm. .............. 139

6.1   Optimal Configurations for the Extended Ring. Entries have the format $P_1 + P_2$ where $P_1$ ($P_2$) is the number of processors assigned to F1 (F2) layers that resulted to faster execution, and $P = P1 + P2$. ....... 171

6.2   Optimal Configurations for the Palindrome Ring. Entries have the format $P_1 + P_2$ where $P_1$ ($P_2$) is the number of processors assigned to F1 (F2) layers that resulted to faster execution, and $P = P1 + P2$. ....... 171

7.1   BP applications used for measuring training performance. ....... 187

7.2   Timing on AP1000 ($ns$), including loading from and storing to cache. .   199

7.3   Time measured for operations in implemented programs on AP1000 ($ns$).   204

7.4   The data on Nettalk convergence used for estimation. ......... 213

9.1   Performance comparison of the variable-size ring mapping versus the fixed-size ring mapping based on the MCPS metric. .......... 297

9.2   Performance comparison of the variable-size ring mapping versus the fixed-size ring mapping based on the optimality ratio. ......... 297

10.1   MUSIC system technical data for a 19-inch rack system. . . . . . . . .   305
10.2   Comparison of backpropagation implementations. . . . . . . . . . .   313
10.3   Performance and programming time. . . . . . . . . . . . . . . . .   316
10.4   Summary of the first series of experiments. MSE stands for the mean
       squared error. . . . . . . . . . . . . . . . . . . . . . . . . . .   319
10.5   Summary of the second series of experiments. . . . . . . . . . . .   319
10.6   Time required for the training of 248 neural networks. . . . . . . .   322
10.7   Performance comparison of different feature preprocessing. . . . . .   324
10.8   Detailed analysis of the classification rates and their impact on the color
       correction. . . . . . . . . . . . . . . . . . . . . . . . . . . .   326
10.9   Time required for the training of 39 neural networks. . . . . . . . .   326
10.10  Training setup. . . . . . . . . . . . . . . . . . . . . . . . . . .   329
10.11  Comparison of total training times. . . . . . . . . . . . . . . . .   330
10.12  Comparison of the computation times and programming cost. . . . . .   332
10.13  Comparison of backpropagation performance. . . . . . . . . . . .   338
10.14  Comparing the Assembler and the C version on the PowerPC 601. . . .   339

11.1   Performance Evaluation for Selected Net Sizes. . . . . . . . . . . .   354
11.2   Performance of SPERT-II KSOFM forward pass on real-world networks.   356
11.3   Performance of SPERT-II on the EPFL benchmark for KSOFM training
       for all 30,000 training patterns. The neighborhood is updated after every
       100 patterns with the initial radius, $R_0$, set to half the grid dimensions.
       The other training parameters are $\alpha_0 = 0.1$, $K_\alpha = 0.0025$, and $K_R =$
       0.02. . . . . . . . . . . . . . . . . . . . . . . . . . . . . . .   357

# List of Figures

1.1 Processor topologies for simulating ANNs. . . . . . . . . . . . . . . 4

1.2 A Taxonomy of ANN Models. . . . . . . . . . . . . . . . 6

1.3 A two-weight layer feed-forward neural network. . . . . . . . . . . 7

1.4 The sigmoid function $f(\alpha) = \dfrac{1}{1 + e^{-\alpha}}$. . . . . . . . . . . 8

1.5 The number of floating point operations for weight accumulation and update for block updates, $F_{lbb}$, and for pattern updates, $F_{lbp}$. . . . . . . . 12

1.6 A Hopfield Network of $N$ neurons. . . . . . . . . . . . . . . . 14

1.7 Kohonen's SOM network. . . . . . . . . . . . . . . . . . . 18

2.1 Training set parallelism for learning the English alphabet. . . . . . . 27

2.2 Mapping of the weight matrices for pipelining. . . . . . . . . . . 27

2.3 Pipelining of the training patterns. . . . . . . . . . . . . . . . 27

2.4 Neuron parallelism, also called vertical slicing. . . . . . . . . . . 28

2.5 Synapse parallelism. . . . . . . . . . . . . . . . . . . . . 29

2.6 Combined neuron parallelism and pipelining in Symult S2010. . . . . 33

2.7 Piped-mesh implementation. . . . . . . . . . . . . . . . . . 35

2.8 A ring of size $N_2$ embedded into a longer ring of size $N_1$. . . . . . . 36

2.9 Cascaded systolic ANN. . . . . . . . . . . . . . . . . . . . 36

2.10 Systolic design for feed-forward networks with layers of different sizes. 37

2.11 A transputer ring topology combining training-set parallelism and pipelining. . . . . . . . . . . . . . . . . . . . . . . . . . . . 40

2.12 The output weight matrix: the weights required by processing element 1 are circled. . . . . . . . . . . . . . . . . . . . . . . . . 42

2.13 Block diagram of the RENNS Module. . . . . . . . . . . . . . . 43

2.14 The CNAPS architecture, consisting of processing nodes (PNs) connected together by three global buses. A sequencer chip controls the flow of data and commands on the buses. . . . . . . . . . . . . . . . . . . 44

2.15 The MY-NEUPOWER computer architecture. . . . . . . . . . . . 44

2.16 The SYNAPSE-1 neurocomputer. . . . . . . . . . . . . . . . 45

2.17 The SNAP-64 architecture. . . . . . . . . . . . . . . . . . . 45

2.18 Schematic drawing of the Nettalk network. . . . . . . . . . . . . 50

3.1 Processor array connected in a ring configuration. . . . . . . . . . 69

3.2 Network partitioning for a heterogeneous array of processors. . . . . 71

3.3 Timing diagram for steps 1 and 2 of the parallelized BP on a three-processor network. . . . . . . . . . . . . . . . . . . . . . . . . . . 72

3.4 Timing diagram for one iteration of the parallelized BP on a three-processor network. The dotted line from "Start" to "End" indicates the path used for $t_{iter-3}$ in Equation 3.1. . . . . . . . . . . . . . . . . . . 73

3.5    TYPE-1, TYPE-2, and TYPE-3 networks. S and F denote slow and fast processors, respectively. . . . . . . . . . . . . . . . . . . . . . . . . . . . 78

3.6    Steps involved in the GA algorithm. . . . . . . . . . . . . . . . . . . 84

3.7    Two-point crossover. . . . . . . . . . . . . . . . . . . . . . . . . . . 86

3.8    Distribution of iteration time for the Encoder problem for TYPE-1, TYPE-2, and TYPE-3 processor networks. . . . . . . . . . . . . . . . . . . . . 89

3.9    Distribution of iteration time for the Nettalk problem for TYPE-1, TYPE-2, and TYPE-3 processor networks. . . . . . . . . . . . . . . . . . . . . 90

3.10   Mean $\pm 3\sigma$ for the Encoder problem for various sample sizes for TYPE-1, TYPE-2, and TYPE-3 processor networks. . . . . . . . . . . . . . . . 92

3.11   Mean $\pm 3\sigma$ for the Nettalk problem for various sample sizes for TYPE-1, TYPE-2, and TYPE-3 processor networks. . . . . . . . . . . . . . . . 93

3.12   Time per iteration for various numbers of T805-20 processors for the Encoder and Nettalk benchmark problems. . . . . . . . . . . . . . . . . 98

3.13   Speedups for various numbers of T805-20 processors for the Encoder and Nettalk benchmark problems. . . . . . . . . . . . . . . . . . . . . . 99

4.1    Training-set parallelism for a heterogeneous array of processors. . . . 113

4.2    Processor synchronization graph for the parallelized BP on a three-processor network. . . . . . . . . . . . . . . . . . . . . . . . . . . . . 115

4.3    Variable synchronization graph for the parallelized BP on a three-processor network. Only the process names for processor 1 are shown. . . . . . . 118

4.4    Processor configurations used in the validation experiments. S and F denote slow and fast processors, respectively. . . . . . . . . . . . . . . 120

4.5    Distribution of epoch time for the Encoder problem for configuration CONFIG-1. The symbol $(X)$ indicates the epoch time from the GA solution. . . . . . . . . . . . . . . . . . . . . . . . . . . . . . . . . . . . . 126

4.6    *Mean* $\pm$ $3\sigma$ of epoch time for the Encoder problem for configuration CONFIG-1. . . . . . . . . . . . . . . . . . . . . . . . . . . . . . . . . . 127

5.1    (a) A fully recurrent neural network with $n = 3$ units (oval nodes) and $m = 2$ input nodes (square nodes). Only some weights are shown in the figure. Target values can be specified for any one of the neuron units. (b) An equivalent representation, where every dark dot corresponds to a synapse with a strength weight. . . . . . . . . . . . . . . . . . . . . . . 137

5.2    (a) The DG for the consecutive matrix-vector multiplication. The schedule hyperplanes are shown with dashed lines. (b) The structure of the DG node. (c) The ring SFG. . . . . . . . . . . . . . . . . . . . . . . . . . . 142

5.3    Distributed memory ring array implementation for the retrieving phase. 143

5.4    (a) DG for consecutive matrix-matrix multiplication. Solid lines depict data dependencies on the $(i, k)$ planes. Dashed lines depict dependencies between planes. Not all dependencies are shown for clarity. (b) The structure of the DG node. . . . . . . . . . . . . . . . . . . . . . . . . . 145

5.5    DG for the recursive updating of the $\{P_{ij}\}$ terms. . . . . . . . . . . . 146

5.6    Two-dimensional SFG for the recursive updating of the $\{P_{ij}\}$ terms. . 147

5.7    Distributed memory ring implementation for the learning phase. . . . . 148

5.8    The DG for the retrieving phase when $\hat{n} = n \cdot k = 9$, $\hat{m} = 2$, and $n = 3$. Thick vertical dashed lines indicate block boundaries. Light dashed lines correspond to equitemporal hyperplanes. . . . . . . . . . . . . . . . . . 151

5.9    (a) The structure of the FIFO queue on the return link and the activation buffers within the three PEs. (b) Snapshot of PE activities during the first 12 schedule time periods of the retrieving phase. Each $y$ element currently used is encircled. . . . . . . . . . . . . . . . . . . . . . . . . . .    152

5.10   SFG for the learning phase when $\hat{n} = n \cdot k = 9$, $\hat{m} = 2$, and $n = 3$.    .    153

6.1    Schematic representation of ART1 subsystems and connections. . . . .    159

6.2    Flowchart of the ART1 serial algorithm. . . . . . . . . . . . . . .    161

6.3    Extended ring architecture. $F1_i$ ($F2_i$) denote neurons on F1 (F2) layer, respectively. . . . . . . . . . . . . . . . . . . . . . . . . . .    164

6.4    Schematic view of the ring parallel algorithm. . . . . . . . . . . . .    168

6.5    Palindrome ring architecture with bidirectional communications. . . .    170

6.6    Relative speedup versus the number of processors allocated (A) on layer F2, and (B) on layer F1. . . . . . . . . . . . . . . . . . . . . .    174

6.7    Execution time versus the number of processors and problem size. (A) Extended ring. (B) Palindrome. . . . . . . . . . . . . . . . . . . .    175

6.8    Speedup versus problem size. (A) Extended ring. (B) Palindrome. . . .    176

6.9    Speedup versus the number of processors and problem size. (A) Extended ring. (B) Palindrome. . . . . . . . . . . . . . . . . . . . . .    177

7.1    The AP1000 architecture. . . . . . . . . . . . . . . . . . . . . . .    186

7.2    BP mappings with training-set and node parallelism. . . . . . . . . .    190

7.3    BP mappings including training-set parallelism, pipelining, and node parallelism. H indicates processors training the hidden layer, while O indicates processors training the output layer. . . . . . . . . . . . . . . .    191

7.4    (a) Summing the weight change matrices before weight update in a system of 16 vertical cells. (b) Broadcasting the summed weight change matrices back to each cell. . . . . . . . . . . . . . . . . . . . . . . . . .    193

7.5    Parallel BP training algorithm running in each cell, combining training-set parallelism and neuron parallelism. . . . . . . . . . . . . . . . .    194

7.6    Distribution of training pattern A, B, C,. . . . . . . . . . . . . . .    195

7.7    Pipelined mapping of BP with flexible assignment of cells to each layer.    195

7.8    An extension of the mapping in Figure 7.3, where the number of cells used for synapse parallelism for each layer is assigned according to the computation load. . . . . . . . . . . . . . . . . . . . . . . . . . .    196

7.9    Training-session parallelism and neuron parallelism combined. . . . .    196

7.10   Heuristic in pseudocode for selecting the best parallel mapping of BP onto a 2D-torus computer. . . . . . . . . . . . . . . . . . . . . . . . .    198

7.11   MCUPS performance for different combinations of neuron and training-set parallelism running the Nettalk application with 120 hidden neurons on a 8 x 8 cell configuration. $N_{NP} = 1, 2, 4$, and 8. . . . . . . . . . .    202

7.12   MCUPS performance for different combinations of neuron and training-set parallelism on a 16 x 16 cell configuration. $N_{NP} = 2, 4, 8$, and 16. .    203

7.13   MCUPS performance for different combinations of neuron and training-set parallelism on a $16 \times 32$ cell configuration. $N_{NP} = 4, 8$, and 16. . . .    203

7.14   Training speed for Nettalk network plotted as a function of the number of processors. . . . . . . . . . . . . . . . . . . . . . . . . . . . .    204

7.15   Speedup of the best configuration compared to the implementation with the largest $N_{NP}$ value; that is the $(C_x, C_y)$. . . . . . . . . . . . . . .    204

7.16   Deviation of estimate against measured time for the 64 cell configuration for different weight update intervals. . . . . . . . . . . . . . . . . .    205

7.17 Deviation of estimate against measured time for the 512 cell configuration for different weight update intervals. . . . . . . . . . . . . . . . . . . 205

7.18 Comparing the fastest configuration for 64, 256 and 512 processing elements to estimated values for a weight update interval equal to 906. . . . 206

7.19 The number of $N_{NP}$ values used in Figure 7.18. . . . . . . . . . . . . 206

7.20 Estimated training performance for the Nettalk application for three different weight update intervals, $\mu$. . . . . . . . . . . . . . . . . . . . . . 207

7.21 Estimated training performance for Nettalk application for three different weight update intervals, $\mu$. . . . . . . . . . . . . . . . . . . . . . . . 208

7.22 Comparison of the maximum performance of the flexible configuration to the $(C_x, C_y)$ configuration (named 2APC), for $\mu = 906$. . . . . . . . . 209

7.23 Maximum possible training speed on AP1000. . . . . . . . . . . . . . 210

7.24 Percentage of characters that are not trained for various weight update intervals. . . . . . . . . . . . . . . . . . . . . . . . . . . . . . . . . . 210

7.25 The best learning rate ($\eta$) for each investigated weight update interval. The curve plots the derived rule. . . . . . . . . . . . . . . . . . . . . . 211

7.26 Number of iterations needed to obtain convergence with $E_\% < 5\%$ as the stopping criteria. . . . . . . . . . . . . . . . . . . . . . . . . . . . . . 211

7.27 Plotting of $\frac{1-\alpha}{\eta}$. . . . . . . . . . . . . . . . . . . . . . . . . . . . . 212

7.28 Convergence of Nettalk, logarithmic plot. A vertical line is plotted for $n$ = 20. . . . . . . . . . . . . . . . . . . . . . . . . . . . . . . . . . . . . 213

7.29 Comparing measured and estimated values of $N(\mu)$. . . . . . . . . . . 214

7.30 The sensitivity of the learning rate ($\eta$) on the convergence for epoch versus pattern learning. . . . . . . . . . . . . . . . . . . . . . . . . . . . . . . 215

7.31 Error computed during training compared to error computed after each iteration (epoch) for $\mu = 906$. . . . . . . . . . . . . . . . . . . . . . . 216

7.32 Comparing $E_\% < 5\%$ and $E_\% < 10\%$ error criteria. . . . . . . . . . . 217

7.33 Total training time for Nettalk running on 512 cells, using 120 hidden units. . . . . . . . . . . . . . . . . . . . . . . . . . . . . . . . . . . . . 217

7.34 Total training time for Nettalk running on 256 cells, using 120 hidden units. . . . . . . . . . . . . . . . . . . . . . . . . . . . . . . . . . . . . 218

7.35 Total training time for Nettalk running on 64 cells, using 120 hidden units. 218

7.36 The percentage of patterns that have $E_p > 0.04$, for learning sonar return classification. . . . . . . . . . . . . . . . . . . . . . . . . . . . . . . . 219

7.37 The best learning rate $\eta$ for each of the investigated weight update intervals. The curve plots the derived rule. . . . . . . . . . . . . . . . . . . 220

7.38 Number of iterations required to obtain convergence, that is, $E_p \leq 0.04$ for all training patterns. . . . . . . . . . . . . . . . . . . . . . . . . . . 221

7.39 Number of iterations needed to reach a stopping criteria of 5% error. . 222

7.40 The relation between $\mu$ and $k_e$, where $P$ is the total number of patterns in the training set. . . . . . . . . . . . . . . . . . . . . . . . . . . . . . . 222

7.41 Training performance on 512 processors for speech recognition network. $N_{NP} = 2, 4, 8,$ and 16. . . . . . . . . . . . . . . . . . . . . . . . . . . 223

7.42 MCUPS performance for different combinations of neuron and training-set parallelism on a 16 x 32 processor configuration training a compression network. . . . . . . . . . . . . . . . . . . . . . . . . . . . . . . . 223

7.43 MCUPS performance for different combinations of neuron and training-set parallelism on a 16 x 16 processor configuration training a compression network. . . . . . . . . . . . . . . . . . . . . . . . . . . . . . . . 224

7.44 MCUPS performance for different combinations of neuron and training-set parallelism on an $8 \times 16$ processor configuration training a compression network. . . . . . . . . . . . . . . . . . . . . . . . 224

7.45 MCUPS performance for different combinations of neuron and training-set parallelism on an $8 \times 8$ processor configuration training a compression network. . . . . . . . . . . . . . . . . . . . . . . . . 224

7.46 Training speed for image compression network plotted as function of the number of processors. . . . . . . . . . . . . . . . . . . . . . . 225

7.47 Speedup of the best configuration compared to the $(C_x, C_y)$ configuration. . . . . . . . . . . . . . . . . . . . . . . . . . . . . . 225

8.1 A general neuron model and a general neural network. . . . . . . . . 235
8.2 Virtual processors with the toroidal lattice architecture. . . . . . . . 238
8.3 Virtual processors with the planar lattice architecture. . . . . . . . . 239
8.4 Processing flow for the MLP simulation. . . . . . . . . . . . . . . 240
8.5 Data flow in the calculations of activations on the TLA. . . . . . . . 240
8.6 Data flow in the calculations of activations on the PLA. . . . . . . . 241
8.7 Processing flow for the MLP simulation. . . . . . . . . . . . . . . 242
8.8 (a) Data flow during the activation forward propagation. . . . . . . . 243
8.8 (b) Data flow during the error backpropagation. . . . . . . . . . . . 243
8.8 (c) Data flow during the weight updating. . . . . . . . . . . . . . . 244
8.9 The row and column partitions. . . . . . . . . . . . . . . . . . . . 246
8.10 Node processors with the TLA. . . . . . . . . . . . . . . . . . . . 247
8.11 Node processors with the PLA. . . . . . . . . . . . . . . . . . . . 248
8.12 VPs in partitioned rectangular region assigned to an NP. . . . . . . . 249
8.13 The VP matrix for an MLP with three layers. . . . . . . . . . . . . 251
8.14 Homogeneously or methodically arranged rectangular subregions in VP matrices. . . . . . . . . . . . . . . . . . . . . . . . . . . . . . 252
8.15 The subdivision of VPs for the permutations and partitions. . . . . . 253
8.16 The result of row and column permutations for load balancing. . . . . 253
8.17 VPs in the partitioned rectangular region assigned to the NP of the position (1,2) after permutations. . . . . . . . . . . . . . . . . . . . 254
8.18 Implementation of the TLA on a Transputer array. . . . . . . . . . . 256
8.19 Process control and data flow in an NP for the forward propagation. . 257
8.20 Time chart of process executions in an NP for the forward propagation. 257
8.21 The experimental performance of the TLA Transputer array. . . . . . 259

9.1 Common neural network interconnection structures. . . . . . . . . . 273
9.2 Mapping a fully connected neural network onto a ring systolic processing array. . . . . . . . . . . . . . . . . . . . . . . . . . . . . . 275
9.3 The top-level design of the DREAM Machine. . . . . . . . . . . . . 280
9.4 Processor and memory detail diagram. Associated with each data value in the local memory of each PE is a switch setting values to configure the communication topology of the machine. . . . . . . . . . . . . . 281
9.5 Mapping neurons to PEs and constructing a computation path between the PEs. . . . . . . . . . . . . . . . . . . . . . . . . . . . . . . 284
9.6 Using the reconfigurable switches of the DREAM Machine to construct circular rings on the processing array. . . . . . . . . . . . . . . . . 286
9.7 A 1-D variable length ring architecture using simple switches. . . . . 287
9.8 An embedded ring structure containing a ring of size $N_1$ and another of size $N_2$. . . . . . . . . . . . . . . . . . . . . . . . . . . . . . . 288

9.9 A blocked structured neural network utilizing three disjoint blocks between the input and hidden layers and its associated mapping on three processing rings. . . . . . . . . . . . . . . . . . . . . . . . . . . . . 290

9.10 Memory locations of synaptic weights on the inputs of neuron $i$. . . . . 293

9.11 A neural network structure for image compression and decompression with a regularly blocked structure. . . . . . . . . . . . . . . . . . . . . 296

9.12 The ring structure associated with the image compression and decompression network of Figure 9.11. . . . . . . . . . . . . . . . . . . . . . 296

10.1 Overview of the MUSIC hardware. . . . . . . . . . . . . . . . . . . 305

10.2 A two-layer perceptron. . . . . . . . . . . . . . . . . . . . . . . . 307

10.3 Layer partitioning of a multilayer perceptron. . . . . . . . . . . . . . 308

10.4 Weight partitioning . . . . . . . . . . . . . . . . . . . . . . . . . . 309

10.5 Speedup comparison for updating the weights of a layer with 100 neurons. 310

10.6 Speedup: (a) without losses (linear speedup), (b) considering the loss factor $\alpha$, and (c) considering both loss factors, $\alpha$ and $\beta$. The diamonds represent real measurements. . . . . . . . . . . . . . . . . . . . . . . . . 312

10.7 The pages of a book appear white even if illuminated with the yellowish light of a lightbulb, but they would appear yellowish in an uncorrected photograph. . . . . . . . . . . . . . . . . . . . . . . . . . . . . . . 317

10.8 Overview of a conventional correction system. . . . . . . . . . . . . 318

10.9 Dimensions of the best neural network of the second series of experiments. . . . . . . . . . . . . . . . . . . . . . . . . . . . . . . . . . 319

10.10 The performance of the best network for the correction of color photos (229 inputs, 55, 15, and 5 node in the hidden layers and 3 output nodes). About 12 weeks of CPU time on a 30-processor MUSIC system were required to reach this result, which is approximately equivalent to 3 years CPU time on a Sun SPARCstation 10. . . . . . . . . . . . . . . . . . 321

10.11 Arrangement of the results according to different picture classes. Left: Color correction. Right: Brightness correction. The classes (listed in alphabetic order) are backlight shot, beach/water, bulb light, bulb-light overcorrection, color dominant, density dominant, flash, member of a series, neon light, portrait/skin, snow, special flash, start of series, and vegetation. The exact assignment of the classes is confidential. . . . . . . 321

10.12 Illustration of the difficulty of defining serial pictures. Do all pictures contain the same motif? . . . . . . . . . . . . . . . . . . . . . . . . 323

10.13 Color distribution of the pixels projected on the k1/k2 color plane. (a) and (b) the color distribution of two similar photographs of a baby. (c) the color distribution of a house in the mountains. The color histograms are built by counting the number of pixels belonging to each sector. When building the difference of the histograms of (a) and (b), the histograms will annihilate each other. This is not the case if the difference between the histogram of (c) and one of (a) or (b) is taken. . . . . . . . . . . 325

10.14 Start position of the truck. . . . . . . . . . . . . . . . . . . . . . . 327

10.15 The emulator and controller neural networks. . . . . . . . . . . . . . 328

10.16 Information flow through the controller and emulator networks during a training run. . . . . . . . . . . . . . . . . . . . . . . . . . . . . . . 329

10.17 Performance examples of (a) an untrained, (b) a partially trained, and (c) a well-trained controller network. With the untrained controller, the truck crashes after only a few steps. . . . . . . . . . . . . . . . . . . . . . 330

10.18 Driving around obstacles. . . . . . . . . . . . . . . . . . . . . 332
10.19 Diagram of the remote-controlled system. . . . . . . . . . . . . . . 333
10.20 Photo of the truck model with ultrasonic transducers. . . . . . . . . . 333
10.21 Unrolling of the innermost loop of a perceptron forward path simulation. 335
10.22 Unrolling of the outer loop of a perceptron forward path simulation. . . 336
10.23 Examples in pseudo Assembly code to demonstrate scheduling. . . . . 337
10.24 Innermost loops of the forward path of the reference C code. . . . . . . 338

11.1 Block diagram of T0 microarchitecture. . . . . . . . . . . . . . . . . 349
11.2 SPERT-II System Organization. . . . . . . . . . . . . . . . . . . . 350
11.3 SPERT-II Software Environment. . . . . . . . . . . . . . . . . . . . 350
11.4 Performance evaluation results for on-line backpropagation training of three-layer networks, with equal numbers of units in the input, hidden, and output layers. The workstations perform all calculations in single precision IEEE floating point, whereas SPERT-II uses 16-bit fixed-point weights. . . . . . . . . . . . . . . . . . . . . . . . . . . . . . . . 353
11.5 Photograph of T0 on board. . . . . . . . . . . . . . . . . . . . . . 359
11.6 Photograph of top of SPERT-II board. . . . . . . . . . . . . . . . . 360
11.7 Photograph of bottom of SPERT-II board. . . . . . . . . . . . . . . . 361

# Chapter 1

# Introduction

**N. Sundararajan**
**P. Saratchandran**
School of Electrical and Electronic Engineering,
Nanyang Technological University,
Singapore
**Jim Torresen**
Department of Computer and Information Science,
Norwegian University of Science and Technology,
Norway

Artificial Neural Network (ANN) is a discipline that draws its inspiration from the incredible problem-solving abilities of nature's computing engine, the human brain, and endeavors to translate these abilities into computing machines which can then be used to tackle difficult problems in science and engineering. The field of ANN itself is very broad, attracting researchers from such diverse disciplines as neuroscience, engineering, physics, computer science, and biology. The eclectic nature of this field has given rise to several paradigms each purporting to emulate some functional capabilities of the brain. From an application standpoint all these paradigms have their strengths and weaknesses. Each perform very well in solving certain problems but are not appropriate for others.

However, all ANN paradigms involve a learning phase in which the neural network is trained with a set of examples of a problem. The trained network is then used in a real environment to solve instances of the problem not contained in the examples. This is known as the recall phase. The learning phase usually takes a large amount of computing time for all but simple toy problems. For practical problems where the training data is large, training times of the order of days and weeks are not uncommon on serial machines [1–3]. This has been the main stumbling block for ANN's use in real-world applications and has also greatly impeded its wider acceptability.

The problem of large training time can be overcome either by devising faster learning algorithms or by implementing the existing algorithms on parallel computing architectures. Improving the learning algorithm per se is an active area of research [4, 5], but this book focuses on the latter approach of parallel implementation. The good thing about this approach is that an improved fast learning algorithm can be further speeded up by parallel implementation.

## 1.1 Parallel Processing for Simulating ANNs

An ANN consists of an enormous number of massively interconnected nonlinear computational elements (neurons). Each neuron receives inputs from other neurons, performs a weighted summation, applies an activation function to the weighted sum, and outputs its results to other neurons in the network. Simulation of an ANN comprises simulation of the learning phase and the recall phase. Parallel processing of neural network simulations has attracted much interest during the past years. The learning and recall of neural networks can be represented mathematically as linear algebra functions that operate on vectors and matrices [6]. Thus, standard parallelization schemes can be exploited for both. However, the focus of parallel neural simulations has been more on the learning phase, which is the most computation-intensive part of neuroprocessing.

Parallel architectures for simulating neural networks can be subdivided into general purpose parallel computers and neurocomputers. Neurocomputers are designed as boards and systems for high-speed ANN simulations [7]. Neurocomputers can be classified as general purpose or special purpose [8]. A general-purpose neurocomputer is programmable and is capable of supporting a large range of neural network models, whereas a special-purpose neurocomputer implements one neural model in dedicated hardware. The latter benefits from higher *speed* than the former. Most neurocomputers are based on processing elements computing in parallel. A survey by Solheim [9] lists about 80 different digital neural hardware projects. However, only 20 of these proposed architectures have been implemented. These systems are designed and built by either research institutes or commercial companies.

### 1.1.1  Performance Metrics

Two metrics are commonly used for the speed of neural network simulations. Performance during training is measured in connections updates per second (CUPS). This accounts for the number of weights updated per second. For the recall phase performance, connections per second (CPS) are used, which describe the number of weight multiplications in the forward pass per second.

According to Crowl [10], presentation of parallel performance can be easily and unintentionally distorted. To avoid this, he suggests presenting the elapsed time as opposed to the speedup where possible. The use of speedup to define performance is limited by the lack of consensus for speedup definition. Crowl is of the opinion that many machines sacrifice sequential performance for parallel scalability, which gives rise to overestimated speedup. Linear speed (that is, solutions per time unit) is visually similar to speedup and may be used instead. CPS and CUPS measure linear speed by connections computed or updated per second.

The CUPS measure is sensitive to several factors.[1] When the number of neurons is large, the computation grains become large, which in most cases improve performance compared to that obtained from a small number of neurons. However, if the network is too large to be stored in main memory, the training slows down.

### 1.1.2  General Aspects of Parallel Processing

A parallel computer usually consists of a number of processing elements (PEs). Each processing element consists of a processor and memory.[2] The memory can either be on the processing chip or on separate chip(s). Recently, neural circuits have been produced containing several PEs on a single chip. Because the processing elements may have to

---

[1]For example, in the case of multilayer networks with backpropagation, inclusion of the momentum term increases the speed of convergence. But, there are more computations per iteration, leading to reduced CUPS performance. Also, the output layer has less backward error computation than the hidden layer. Thus, if more hidden layers are added to a network, the CUPS performance will be reduced.

[2]The name *processing element* was originally used for simple elements in SIMD computers, but today it is also used for the more complex elements in MIMD computers.

exchange data with their neighbors, a communication module may be required for each PE.

A number of topologies exist for interconnecting PEs [11]. The most common are shown in Figure 1.1: broadcast bus, ring, array, 2-D mesh, 2-D toroidal mesh (2D-torus), 3-D mesh, and hypercube. 1-D systems have a much lower optimal processor count than 2-D and 3-D systems [7, 12]. This means that much finer grained parallel processing can be realized by using a multidimensional topology.

Designers of parallel programs should be aware of Amdahl's law, which states in essence that the improvement of overall system performance attributed to the speeding up of one part of the system is limited by the fraction of the job that is not speeded up [13].

Parallel computers can be classified according to Flynn's classification, based on the number of simultaneous instruction and data streams [14]:

**SISD** (single instruction stream single data stream): A sequential computer with a single CPU.

**SIMD** (single instruction stream multiple data streams): A single program controls multiple execution units.

**MISD** (multiple instruction streams single data stream): Systolic arrays with pipelined execution.

**MIMD** (multiple instruction streams multiple data streams): Computers with more than one processor and the ability to execute more than one program simultaneously. Computers in this category are also called multiprocessors or multicomputers depending on shared or distributed memory, respectively.

A special execution mode of MIMD has been defined:

**SPMD** (single programs operating on multiple data streams): The same program is downloaded onto all the processing elements. The processors are usually performing the same operations but on different parts of the data [15].

Several different methods are used for interprocessor communication. The two major switching methods for communication [14] are the following :

**Circuit Switching.** A physical path is established between the source and the destination before the message is sent. SIMD machines frequently use circuit switching.

**Packet Switching.** A message is split into fixed or flexible-sized packets. Each packet is routed through the interconnection network independent of other packets. As such, packets may take different routes through the network. MIMD machines are usually based on packet switching.

Two major concerns in parallel *implementations* are the following:

**Load Balancing.** To minimize idle time, it is necessary to keep the processors active. Each processor should be given an equivalent computation load.

**Communication.** To maximize the time processors perform computation, communication should be minimized. Moreover, the communication should be distributed as evenly as possible over all the communication links [16].

As the number of processors increases, these factors become more dominating. One of the purposes of the work presented in this book is to show how fixed mappings of neural

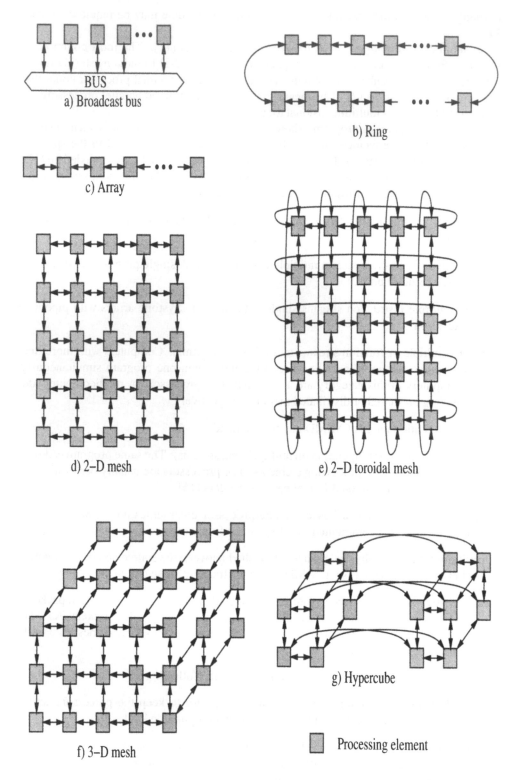

a) Broadcast bus

b) Ring

c) Array

d) 2–D mesh

e) 2–D toroidal mesh

f) 3–D mesh

g) Hypercube

Processing element

FIGURE 1.1. Processor topologies for simulating ANNs (from [11]).

networks to large parallel systems can be weakened by these problems. Another purpose is to propose solutions to minimize these problems.

The computation grain size is an important factor in load balancing [17]. Grain size determines the basic program segment chosen for parallel processing [18]. *Fine*-grained parallelism means that the computation is spread over a number of small tasks; for *coarse*-grained parallelism, however, the tasks are substantially larger. Some computers are suited for coarse-grained computation (such as message-passing MIMD computers), whereas others are designed for fine-grained computation (massively parallel SIMD computers, for example).

Complexity modeling is theoretically a way to specify the upper bound on a program's running time. It is specified by the "big-oh" notation. For an input size $n$, $\mathcal{O}(n^2)$ means that there are positive constants $c$ and $n_0$, such that for $n$ equal to or greater than $n_0$, the running time for a program is $T(n) \leq cn^2$.

## 1.2    Classification of ANN Models

Research on artificial neural networks can be traced back to the 1940s, when McCulloch and Pitts published their pioneering paper [19] describing the properties of a simple binary threshold type of artificial neuron that has both excitatory and inhibitory inputs. When connected as a network, these neurons could compute any logical (Boolean) function. This, together with Donald Hebb's discovery that learning in biological neurons occurs through synaptic growth, triggered the development of several artificial neural computing models in the 1950s. The most notable among the early models was the perceptron [20]. During the early 1960s, researchers presented convincing demonstrations using the perceptron model [21]. But in the late 1960s, Minsky and Papert uncovered severe restrictions in the learning capabilities of the perceptron model [22]. Very little research emerged during the next 15 years, although stalwart researchers like Stephen Grossberg, Teuvo Kohonen, James Anderson, Bernerd Widrow, David Willshaw, Amari, and a few others continued to develop various ANN models and learning algorithms. The major thrust of their work was in the area of associative content-addressable memory in which sufficiently similar inputs become associated with one another. Finally, in 1986, Rumelhart and colleagues introduced the learning algorithm for the multilayer perceptron network, called backpropagation (BP) [23]. This initiated a remarkable increase in neural network research resulting in an explosion of network architectures and learning algorithms.

Because the number of learning algorithms and architectures in the ANN literature is large, diverse, and growing, it is impossible to come up with a single classification scheme that can capture all the essential traits of all these paradigms. A possible classification scheme based on the type of learning (supervised/unsupervised/hybrid), architecture of the network (feed-forward/recurrent), and the connectivity employed for the neurons (such as multilayer, competitive, adaptive resonance theory) is shown in Figure 1.2. The learning algorithms presented in Figure 1.2 have wide popularity but by no means are the only ones to be found in the ANN literature.

## 1.3    ANN Models Covered in This Book

The ANN models for which parallel implementation is discussed in this book are enclosed in shaded boxes in Figure 1.2. A brief description of each of these models follows.

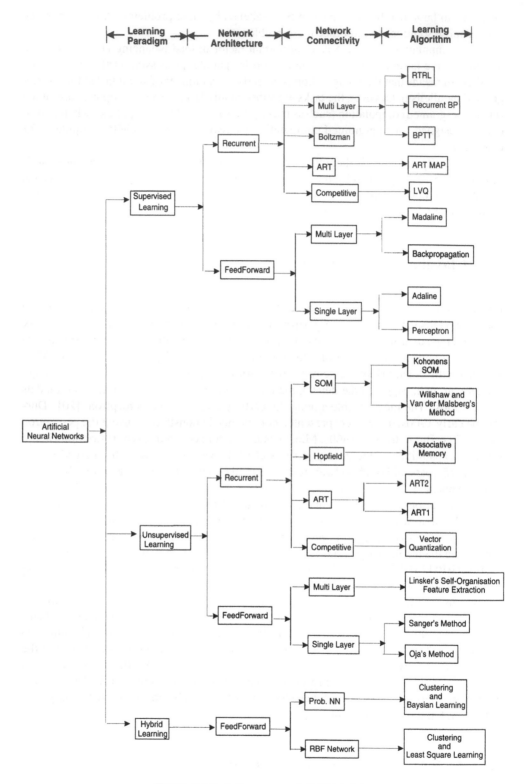

FIGURE 1.2. A Taxonomy of ANN Models.

### 1.3.1 Multilayer Feed-Forward Networks with BP Learning

A two-layer[3] feed-forward network is shown in Figure 1.3. The network is called fully connected, because there are all-to-all connections between two adjacent neuron layers. The number of neurons (also called units) in each layer is $N_i$, $N_h$, and $N_o$ for the input, hidden, and output neuron layers, respectively. The network can be extended to any number of layers; however, because most applications use two-weight layers, the description here has been restricted to two-layer networks. The BP learning phase for a pattern consists of a forward phase followed by a backward phase. The main steps are as follows:

1. Initialize the weights to small random values.

2. Select a training vector pair (input and the corresponding output) from the training set and present the input vector to the inputs of the network.

3. Calculate the actual outputs - this is the *forward phase*.

4. According to the difference between actual and desired outputs (error), adjust the weights $W_o$ and $W_h$ to reduce the difference - this is the *backward phase*.

5. Repeat from step 2 for all training vectors.

6. Repeat from step 2 until the error is acceptably small.

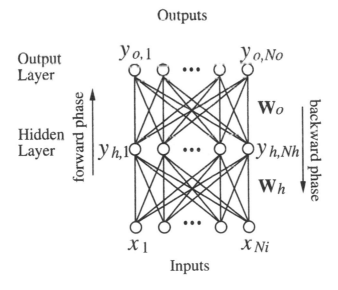

FIGURE 1.3. A two-weight layer feed-forward neural network.

The weight updating scheme used is called *learning by pattern (lbp)* or on-line weight update, and it updates the weights after *each* training pattern has been presented. Experiments have shown this update method, which is stochastic gradient descent [24], converges faster than the total gradient descent, which updates the weights after all training patterns have been presented. However, only the latter method, called *learning by epoch (lbe)*, has

---

[3]In this section, the word *layer* refers to the number of layers of weights in the network. This is equal to the number of layers of neurons, when excluding the input neuron layer.

been proved to converge.[4] An intermediate method is called *learning by block (lbb)* and it updates the weights after a certain number of patterns have been presented.

*1.3.1.1   A Detailed Description of the BP Learning Algorithm.*   In the forward phase the hidden layer weight matrix $W_h$ is multiplied by the input vector $X = (x_1, x_2, \dots, x_{N_i})^T$, to calculate the hidden layer output

$$y_{h,j} = f(\sum_{i=1}^{N_i} w_{h,ji} x_i - \theta) \tag{1.1}$$

where $w_{h,ji}$ is the weight connecting input unit $i$ to unit $j$ in the hidden neuron layer.[5] The $\theta$ is an offset termed bias incorporated into the training algorithm by a weight connected to +1 for each neuron [21]. This bias-weight is trained like an ordinary weight.

The function $f$ is a nonlinear activation function. Normally the S-shaped sigmoid function

$$f(\alpha) = \frac{1}{1 + e^{-\alpha}} \tag{1.2}$$

is used. It compresses the output value to lie in $< 0, 1 >$, as shown in Figure 1.4. Moreover, the function is differentiable, which is a demand of the training algorithm.

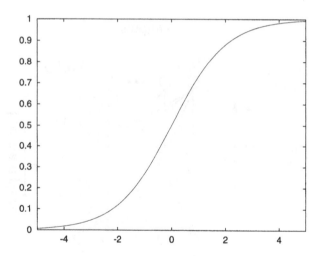

FIGURE 1.4. The sigmoid function $f(\alpha) = \dfrac{1}{1 + e^{-\alpha}}$.

The output from the hidden layer, $y_{h,j}$, is used to calculate the output of the network, $y_{o,k}$

$$y_{o,k} = f(\sum_{j=1}^{N_h} w_{o,kj} y_{h,j} - \theta). \tag{1.3}$$

---

[4]However, the number of training set presentations required for convergence has no known theoretical bound.

[5]To distinguish the different neuron layers, the indices $i$, $j$, and $k$ are used for indexing the input, hidden, and output neuron layers, respectively.

The error measure $E_p$ for a training pattern $p$ is given by

$$E_p = \frac{1}{2} \sum_{k=1}^{N_o} (d_{p,k} - y_{p,o,k})^2. \tag{1.4}$$

The overall error measure for a training set of $P$ patterns is

$$E = \sum_{p=1}^{P} E_p. \tag{1.5}$$

In the following expressions, the pattern index $p$ has been omitted on all variables to improve clarity. In the backward phase the target, $d$, and output, $y_o$, are compared and the difference (error) is used to adapt the weights to reduce the error.

The error used to update the weights can be shown [23] to be

$$\delta_{o,k} = y_{o,k}(1 - y_{o,k})(d_k - y_{o,k}). \tag{1.6}$$

Similar to computing the output delta error, the hidden delta error value for neuron $j$ is

$$\delta_{h,j} = y_{h,j}(1 - y_{h,j}) \sum_{k=1}^{N_o} \delta_{o,k} w_{o,kj}. \tag{1.7}$$

The error is not explicitly given and is computed based on the impact of the fan-in of the output delta errors. To perform steepest descent in the weight space, the weight changes become

$$\Delta w_{o,kj} = \eta \delta_{o,k} y_{h,j} \tag{1.8}$$

$$\Delta w_{h,ji} = \eta \delta_{h,j} x_i \tag{1.9}$$

where $\eta$ is the learning rate coefficient.

If learning by pattern is applied, the output layer weights are changed to $w'_{o,kj}$

$$w'_{o,kj} = w_{o,kj} + \eta \delta_{o,k} y_{h,j}. \tag{1.10}$$

The hidden layer weights are updated accordingly

$$w'_{h,ji} = w_{h,ji} + \eta \delta_{h,j} x_i. \tag{1.11}$$

The training continues for each vector in the training set until the error for the entire set becomes acceptably small.

Instead of updating the weights after each training pattern presentation, they can be updated less frequently by using learning by block. For updates after $\mu$ patterns have been presented, Equations 1.10 and 1.11 become 1.12 and 1.13:

$$w'_{o,kj} = w_{o,kj} + \eta \sum_{p=p'+1}^{p'+\mu} \delta_{p,o,k} y_{p,h,j} \tag{1.12}$$

$$w'_{h,ji} = w_{h,ji} + \eta \sum_{p=p'+1}^{p'+\mu} \delta_{p,h,j} x_{p,i}. \tag{1.13}$$

The total number of training patterns is $P$ and $\mu \leq P$. Learning by block is well suited to parallelization, but as shown by Paugam–Moisy [25], the convergence rate declines as $\mu$ gets larger. Therefore, an appropriate value for $\mu$ needs to be chosen. When $\mu = P$, the scheme is called learning by epoch.

The error measure in Equation 1.5 is dependent on $N_o$ and $P$. Thus, large numbers for $N_o$ and $P$ result in a large value for the overall error $E$. An alternative measure for the overall error is the root mean square error (RMSE) given by

$$E_{RMSE} = \sqrt{\frac{1}{PN_o} \sum_{p=1}^{P} \sum_{k=1}^{N_o} (d_{p,k} - y_{p,o,k})^2}. \tag{1.14}$$

As stated, no proven convergence for the backpropagation algorithm exists,[6] and therefore, the word *convergence* is defined as reaching a predetermined stopping criteria [25].

*1.3.1.2 Momentum.* To obtain true gradient descent requires infinitesimal small changes of the weights. This is obtained by selecting a small value for the learning rate. However, we want to choose as large a learning rate as possible without leading to oscillation,[7] because experiments show that this offers the most rapid learning [23]. To increase the learning rate and avoid oscillation, a momentum can be included. Rumelhart and colleagues proposed to add a fraction, equal to $\alpha$, of the previous weight update value to the current weight change [23]

$$\Delta w_{o,kj}(p+1) = \eta \delta_{o,k}(p+1) y_{h,j}(p+1) + \alpha \Delta w_{o,kj}(p) \tag{1.15}$$

where $p$ is the training pattern index. The weights are then updated

$$w_{o,kj}(p+1)' = w_{o,kj}(p) + \Delta w_{o,kj}(p+1). \tag{1.16}$$

Similarly, Sejnowski and Rosenberg [26] proposed a smoothing term, $\alpha$

$$\Delta w_{o,kj}(p+1) = \alpha \Delta w_{o,kj}(p) + (1-\alpha)\delta_{o,k}(p+1) y_{h,j}(p+1). \tag{1.17}$$

The smoothing makes it less necessary to scale the learning rate according the weight update interval

$$w_{o,kj}(p+1)' = w_{o,kj}(p) + \eta \Delta w_{o,kj}(p+1). \tag{1.18}$$

The equations for updating of the hidden weights can be similarly derived. The term $\alpha$ is normally set to around 0.9.

*1.3.1.3 The Effect of the Weight Update Interval.* It is shown for one neural application by Paugam–Moisy that less frequent weight updates during training reduces the convergence rate. That is, the decrease in error per training iteration is smaller. The network classified patterns into three classes. To avoid unstable behavior during training, the learning rate had to be reduced when the weight update interval was increased. The reason for this can be explained by network paralysis [21]. Adding weight changes for many training vectors together may result in large weight change values. This may lead to large weight

---

[6] An exception is learning by epoch, but still there is no bound in the number of training iterations required.

[7] The error is not constantly decreasing but is oscillating between large and small error values without reaching convergence.

values if the learning rate is not reduced. Large weights can lead to large output values to be input to the nonlinear function. The derivative of the function, which is used for computing the delta error, approaches zero for large values. This results in a very small change in the weights, and the training can come to a virtual standstill.

A special case of learning by pattern is *delayed weight update* in which the weights are updated for pattern $p$ *after* the forward pass for the next pattern, $-p + 1$, has been computed. This method may be used for weight updating when the computation of each layer is distributed over different processors. The delta weight change values are small compared to the weights and thus the convergence should be very close to the convergence of ordinary pattern weight updates.

For some neural application experiments learning by pattern updating results in a stagnation of the error that does not occur for learning by epoch updating. The quick-propagation (quickprop) algorithm, proposed by Fahlman [27], is based on learning by epoch. That is, all training vectors are applied before the new weights are computed. Thus, training set parallelism can be used in parallel implementation of quickprop without leading to any reduction in the convergence rate.

The redundancy in large training sets slows down the convergence of learning by epoch-based algorithms according to Møller [28]. Accumulating redundant gradient weight vectors implies redundant computation. This is not a problem if the weights are updated after each training vector. In fact, redundancy has a positive effect in the beginning of the training. However, simulations show that a conjugate gradient training algorithm— based on epoch learning— which is more efficient in the end of training even though there is redundancy in the training set. Thus, a learning by block approach is proposed, where the block size varies throughout training. Because the redundancy is dependent on the problem, the block size has to be selected by estimation. For each iteration the block size that leads to a confident decrease in the total error of the training set is determined. Simulation using Nettalk [26] shows that the training starts with a very small block size and ends by updating weights only two or three times per epoch.

*1.3.1.4 Learning Performance.* The number of floating point operations used for weight updating for learning by pattern differs from the number for learning by block/epoch. In this section, expressions will be derived to show the difference in computation between the different weight update strategies [29]. The expressions are based on a serial execution of the training program. On a parallel computer, additional time is used for communication. The Nettalk application with number of neurons $N_i = 203$, $N_h = 120$, $N_o = 26$, and $P = 5,438$ training patterns is used here to illustrate the difference. The Nettalk training uses the Sejnowski momentum (Equations 1.17 and 1.18) for weight update. The number of floating point operations used for *lbp* weight updating is then 6 per weight, leading to a total number for one training iteration

$$F_{lbp} = 6P(N_i + N_o)N_h \tag{1.19}$$
$$= 6 \times 5,438(203 + 26)120 = 896,617,440. \tag{1.20}$$

For *lbb* the number of floating point operations for weight accumulation and updating—
2 and 5, respectively— is found from Equations 1.12, 1.13, 1.17, and 1.18. This leads to a
total floating point operation count of

$$F_{lbb} = 2P(N_i + N_o)N_h + 5 \left\lceil \frac{P}{\mu} \right\rceil (N_i + N_o)N_h \tag{1.21}$$

$$= (2P + 5 \left\lceil \frac{P}{\mu} \right\rceil)(N_i + N_o)N_h \tag{1.22}$$

$$= (2 \cdot 5,438 + 5 \left\lceil \frac{5438}{\mu} \right\rceil)(203 + 26)120 \tag{1.23}$$

$$= 298,872,480 + \frac{1}{\mu}747,181,200. \tag{1.24}$$

The first expression in Equation 1.21 represents the weight accumulation and the latter
represents weight updating. The number of operations for weight accumulation is less
than for weight update. Thus, if the weights are infrequently updated we get $F_{lbp} > F_{lbb}$.
Figure 1.5 shows the number of floating point operations for weight accumulation and
update for different weight update intervals, $\mu$.

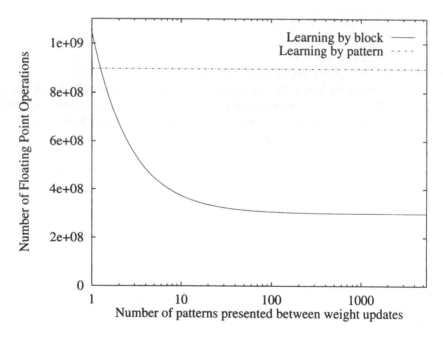

FIGURE 1.5. The number of floating point operations for weight accumulation and update for block
updates, $F_{lbb}$, and for pattern updates, $F_{lbp}$.

The update method learning by epoch uses a smaller number of operations than learning by pattern if the block size is larger or equals two, that is, $\mu \geq 2$.

Where learning by block/epoch is used, CUPS is given by the number of weight-change
values computed per second. That is, the number of weights *updated* is excluded when the
CUPS value is calculated. However, the time for weight update is not excluded. Thus,
only the number of weights *accumulated* per epoch is used for computing the CUPS value,
which is like omitting the second expression in Equation 1.21.

To measure how well a feed-forward neural network has learned, a separate test set should be used in addition to the training set. The available vectors should be partitioned into disjoint sets: learning set and test set. It is preferable that several different test sets are included. The test set should include a representative selection of patterns; for example, for pattern classification, the test set should contain vectors from all classes. The network is trained by the training set and then tested using the test set. The test set or a separate acceptance set is used as an acceptance set for the network.

**Variants of the BP Algorithm.** During recent years, several variants of BP learning have been proposed, such as quick propagation and conjugate gradient method. A comparison of learning algorithms for feed-forward networks by Nesvik [30] showed that some of the new algorithms were less sensitive to the selection of the learning parameters.

### 1.3.2 Hopfield Network

The Hopfield network is a single layer recurrent network that embodies the idea of storing information as the stable states of a dynamically evolving network configuration. Using an energy function in terms of the connection weights and outputs of the neurons, Hopfield showed [31, 32] how such networks can be used to solve specific problems in associative memory and combinatorial optimization. Two versions of the Hopfield network exist: discrete and continuous valued. The discrete Hopfield network is used as associative memory, whereas the continuous Hopfield network is used for combinatorial optimization.

*1.3.2.1 Discrete Hopfield Network.* In this network the neurons can only have two states as their output. The *on* state is represented by +1 and the *off* state is represented by minus 1. A network with $N$ neurons is shown in Figure 1.6. The state of the network is given by the vector $\mathbf{Y} = [y_1, \ldots, y_i, \ldots, y_N]^T$, where $y_i$ denotes the output of neuron $i$, which can only be $\pm 1$. The output of neuron $i$ is given by

$$y_i = sgn(\sum_{j=1}^{N} w_{ij}y_j - \theta_i)$$ (1.25)

where $sgn$ is the signum function, $w_{ij}$ is the weight connecting neuron $i$ and $j$, $w_{ii}$ is zero, and $\theta_i$ is a fixed threshold value. If the argument of the signum function is zero, then the output of neuron $i$ remains unchanged. As an associative network, the operation of Hopfield network has two phases: the storage phase and the retrieval phase.

*1.3.2.2 Storage Phase.* In this phase the network is trained to memorize the patterns it has to recall later. These patterns are known as prototype patterns or fundamental memories of the network. Training the network is a one-shot operation as the connection weights are directly computed from the following equation:

$$w_{ij} = \frac{1}{N} \sum_{p=1}^{m} \eta_i^p \eta_j^p$$ (1.26)

where $\eta_i^p$ and $\eta_j^p$ are the $i^{th}$ and $j^{th}$ elements of the prototype pattern $\eta^p$ and $m$ is the number of prototype patterns the network has to memorize. Once computed, the weights are kept fixed. Note from Equation 1.26 that weights $w_{ij}$ and $w_{ji}$ are the same. The weight matrix $[W]$ for the network is thus symmetric.

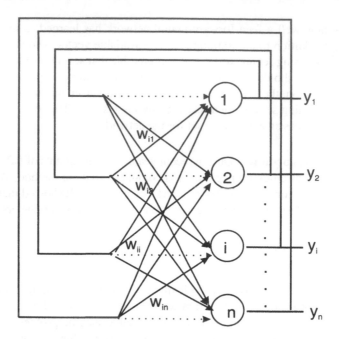

FIGURE 1.6. A Hopfield Network of $N$ neurons.

*1.3.2.3   Retrieval Phase.*   In this phase the network is presented with a pattern that differs from the prototype patterns. Usually it is an incomplete or noisy version of one of the prototype patterns. The state of the network then evolves according to the following difference equation:

$$\mathbf{Y}(k+1) = sgn(\mathbf{W}\,\mathbf{Y}(k) - \Theta) \qquad (1.27)$$

where $\mathbf{Y}$ is the output vector and $\mathbf{W}$ is the symmetric weight matrix. The vector $\Theta = [\theta_1, \ldots, \theta_i, \ldots, \theta_N]^T$ is the threshold vector and $k$ is the iteration index. Starting with the input pattern vector, the outputs are updated recursively according to Equation 1.27 until the network settles to a stable state. The updating of the outputs could be synchronous or asynchronous. In synchronous updating, the outputs for all neurons— that is, $y_i(k+1)$; $i = 1, \ldots, N$— are computed simultaneously at each iteration index. This is also called the parallel mode of operation. In asynchronous updating, $y_i(k+1)$; $i = 1, \ldots, N$ are computed sequentially in some random order. In an iteration, if neurons are selected randomly one by one and their outputs are computed sequentially, then it is known as simple asynchronous updating. If groups of neurons are selected randomly and updated synchronously within the group and sequentially between groups, then it is called general asynchronous dynamics. Note that in simple asynchronous dynamics the neuron updating is always sequential and random whereas in general asynchronous dynamics neuron updating is parallel within a group and serial between groups. However, all neurons must be updated once in each iteration. If the neurons are updated according to the simple asynchronous dynamics, then the Hopfield network will always converge to a stable state. If the neurons are updated synchronously then the network will always converge to a stable state or a limit cycle of length 2 or less [33].

*1.3.2.4   Energy Function.*   Hopfield used an energy function to prove convergence of the network when simple asynchronous updating is used for the network outputs. The energy function $E(k)$, assuming the threshold vector $(\Theta)$ to be zero, is given by

$$E(k) = -\frac{1}{2} \sum_{i=1}^{N} \sum_{j=1}^{N} w_{ij} y_i(k) y_j(k). \tag{1.28}$$

As the network evolves according to the dynamics of Equation 1.27, the energy $E(k)$ can only decrease or stay unchanged at each update. This is because the change $\Delta E(k)$ due to a change in the output $y_i$ can only be zero or negative [33]. Eventually the network will converge to a (local) minimum energy state because $E$ is bounded from below. The local minimum points in the energy landscape correspond to the prototype patterns stored in the storage phase. The maximum number of patterns a Hopfield network of $N$ neurons can store is approximately equal to $0.15N$ [31].

*1.3.2.5  Continuous Hopfield Network.*   The continuous version of the Hopfield network is obtained from the discrete version by replacing the signum function by a sigmoid function in equation 1.25. The neuron outputs are then continuous in the range 0 to 1 and the outputs of all neurons are updated simultaneously and continuously. Because the outputs are continuous valued and they change continuously, the dynamics of the network can be described by a set of simultaneous nonlinear differential equations as [32]

$$\tau_i \frac{dy_i}{dt} = -y_i + f(\sum_{j=1}^{N} w_{ij} y_j) \quad i = 1, \ldots, N \tag{1.29}$$

where $\tau_i$ is a time constant and $f(.)$ is the sigmoid function. Because the weight matrix is symmetric, the solution $y_i(t)$ to the previous equations will always converge to a fixed point as guaranteed by the Cohen-Grossberg theorem [34].

The behavior of the network can then be shown to minimize an energy function as in the case of discrete Hopfield network. Hopfield (1984) used the energy function

$$E = -\frac{1}{2} \sum_{i=1}^{N} \sum_{j=1}^{N} w_{ij} y_i\, y_j + \sum_{i=i}^{n} \int_{0}^{y_i} f^{-1}(y) dy$$

and showed that $\frac{dE}{dt} \leq 0$ for all $t$. It is this property of the Hopfield network that makes it suitable for solving problems in optimization. If a combinatorial optimization problem can be expressed as minimizing an energy function, then a Hopfield network can be used to find the optimal (or suboptimal) solution for that problem. The real difficulty is in mapping the objective function of the optimization problem subject to various constraints into a single energy function. Once the energy function is found, then the weights of the network can be found by relating the terms of the energy function to those of the general form. Hopfield and Tank [35] showed how a continuous Hopfield network can be used to solve the classic Traveling Salesman Problem for 10 cities.

### 1.3.3   Multilayer Recurrent Networks

Single-layer recurrent networks, such as the Hopfield network, with symmetric connection weights, are guaranteed to converge to stable states and, hence, are not suitable for learning temporal sequences of patterns. If the connection weight matrix in a recurrent network is made assymetric, then the resulting network can converge to stable states or exhibit limit cycles or chaos. Such networks can be used for generating, recognizing, and storing temporal sequences of patterns with applications in speech recognition, time series prediction, identification and control of nonlinear dynamic systems, and so on. [36]. The dynamics of assymetric recurrent networks have been studied widely and many training algorithms, which are modified forms of backpropagation, have been proposed [37–42]. The real-time recurrent learning algorithm by Williams and Zipser [41] is perhaps the most popular among these because of its ability to train the network on-line as the input patterns are presented sequentially in time.

### 1.3.3.1 *Real-Time Recurrent Learning.*

In real-time recurrent learning (RTRL) the weights can be incremented on-line or at the end of the whole input sequence. Because on-line updating is possible, the RTRL algorithm can deal with input sequences of arbitrary length and does not require memory proportional to the length of input sequence. The cost function to be minimized is given by $E_{tot}(t_0, t_f)$

$$E_{tot}(t_0, t_f) = \frac{1}{2} \sum_{t=t_0}^{t=t_f} \sum_k [E_k(t)]^2 \tag{1.30}$$

where $t = t_0, \ldots, t_f$ is the time domain of interest. $E_k(t)$ is the error for neuron $k$ at time $t$ and is the difference between the desired output $d_k(t)$ and the actual output $y_k(t)$ of the neuron $k$ at time $t$. If no desired output is specified for neuron $k$ at time $t$, then $E_k(t)$ will be set to zero.

$$E_k(t) = \begin{cases} d_k(t) - y_k(t) & \text{if } d_k(t) \text{ is defined,} \\ 0 & \text{otherwise.} \end{cases}$$

Gradient descent is used to adjust the weights of the network. The gradient of $E_{tot}(t_0, t_f)$ separates in time

$$\frac{\partial}{\partial w} E_{tot}(t_0, t_f) = \frac{1}{2} \frac{\partial}{\partial w} \sum_k [E_k(t_0)]^2 + \ldots + \frac{1}{2} \frac{\partial}{\partial w} \sum_k [E_k(t_f)]^2.$$

Therefore, the total weight increment for any weight becomes the sum of the weight increments calculated at times $t_0, t_1, \ldots, t_f$. The weights can be updated at the end of the sequence at $t = t_f$, but a better procedure is to keep updating them at each time step $t_0, t_1$ and so on. The resulting algorithm is called the real-time recurrent learning because the weights are updated in real time as the input sequence is presented. The method avoids the need for large storage requirement of long input sequences and works especially well if the learning rate is small.

## 1.3.4 Adaptive Resonance Theory (ART) Networks

One of the interesting properties of the human brain is its ability to learn new facts continually without forgetting previously learned facts. It is thus flexible (plastic) enough to learn new facts yet rigid (stable) enough to keep irrelevant facts from washing away the old facts. An artificial neural network trying to exhibit this property should have a high degree of stability with respect to what has been learned, yet it should be adaptive enough to learn new facts on a continuous basis. However, it is not easy for an ANN to have both a high degree of stability and plasticity as these two characteristics conflict. Grossberg calls this the *stability-plasticity dilemma*, and the ART networks (ART1, ART2, ARTMAP) were developed by Carpenter and Grossberg [43–46] in an attempt to solve this stability-plasticity problem. The simplest form of ART network is the ART1 network, which is designed to work for binary (0/1) inputs only. Extension of ART1 to handle both binary and continuous valued inputs is achieved in ART2. Both ART1 and ART2 are unsupervised competitive learning networks. ARTMAP is a modification of ART2 and is a supervised competitive learning network.

The ART1 network consists of an input layer and an output layer that are fully connected to each other. An input pattern vector $X$ is applied and the output neuron that has the largest net input is picked as the winner; that is, if the winning neuron is $r$, then

$$\frac{W_r \cdot X}{\beta + \Sigma_j w_{jr}} > \frac{W_i \cdot X}{\beta + \Sigma_j w_{ji}} \text{ for all } i \tag{1.31}$$

where $W_r$ and $W_i$ are the weight vectors of the output neurons $r$ and $i$, respectively, and the symbol "·" means scalar product. $\beta$ is a small positive constant and $w_{jr}$ and $w_{ji}$ are the $j$th component of $W_r$ and $W_i$ respectively. Note that dividing by $\Sigma_j w_{jr}$ and $\Sigma_j w_{ji}$ normalizes the weight vectors $W_r$ and $W_i$ and $\beta$ is included merely to break the ties in selecting the winner.

The weight vector $W_r$ of the winning neuron is then tested for its similarity with the input pattern $X$. The similarity measure ($s_r$) for the weight vector $W_r$ is computed as the ratio of the number of 1s overlapping in $X$ and $W_r$ to the total number of 1s in $X$. If $s_r \geq \rho$, where $\rho$ is a threshold called the "vigilance" parameter, then $W_r$ is considered to be sufficiently similar to $X$. If $W_r$ is sufficiently similar to $X$, then resonance is said to occur between the input and output and the resonating output neuron becomes a "committed" neuron. The weight vector of the resonating neuron $r$ is then moved closer to $X$ by changing to zeros the 1s in $W_r$ for which the corresponding components in $X$ are zeros.

If $W_r$ is not sufficiently similar to $X$ (that is, $s_r < \rho$), then the winning neuron $r$ is "disabled" or withdrawn from the competition. A new winner is then found using Equation 1.31 from among the output neurons that are not disabled and is tested for resonance with the input vector $X$. If the input vector does not resonate with any of the output neurons, then an "uncommitted" output neuron is picked (even though it did not resonate) and its weight vector made equal to the input vector to provide resonance with the input. If none of the output neurons resonate with the input vector and no uncommitted output neurons are left, then the input pattern is rejected implying that the network has reached its capacity. The ART1 network runs entirely autonomously without needing any external control or sequencing signals and the architecture is entirely parallel.

### 1.3.5 Self-Organizing Map (SOM) Networks

The SOM network [47] is a simplified model of the feature-to-local region mapping done in the human brain. The basic idea is that inputs that are close to each other according to some metric in the input space should be mapped to output neurons that are spatially close together. This is known as topology preservation and is an important aspect of feature mapping in the brain. The architecture of SOM network consists of a two-dimensional array of neurons with each neuron connected to all input nodes. Further, all the neurons also have lateral connections to each other. The strength of lateral connections follow a "Mexican-Hat" function [48]. By involving a neighborhood function to achieve the effect of the Mexican-Hat lateral interactions, Kohonen devised a SOM network in which no lateral connections exist. Figure 1.7 shows the basic architecture of Kohonen's SOM network. There are $n$ input units and the weight connecting input units to the output neuron $i$ is denoted by the vector $W_i$. When an input pattern $X$ is applied, each output neuron computes the Euclidean distance between the input vector and the weight vector of that neuron. Competitive learning rule is then used and the neuron whose weight vector is closest to the

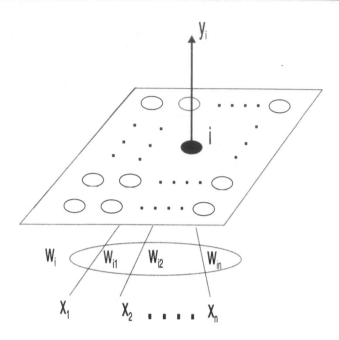

FIGURE 1.7. Kohonen's SOM network.

input vector is chosen as the winner; that is, if the winning neuron is $r$, then

$$\|X - W_r\| = \min_i \|X - W_i\| \text{ for all } i. \tag{1.32}$$

The network learns by changing appreciably the weights of the winning neuron and its neighbors by dragging their weight vectors toward the input pattern $X$, whereas those far away from the winning neurons experience little change to their weights. This is how the topology preservation is achieved. The weight update equation is given by

$$W_i^{new} = W_i^{old} + \alpha \, N(i, r) \, (X - W_i) \text{ for all } i. \tag{1.33}$$

The function $N(i, r)$ is called the neighborhood function, and its value is 1 for $i = r$ and falls off as the distance between the neurons $r$ and $i$ increases. $\alpha$ is the learning rate. The range of $N(i, r)$ and the value of $\alpha$ are reduced gradually as learning progresses. A common choice for $N(i, r)$ is

$$N(i, r) = \exp\left(-\|d_i - d_r\|^2 / (2\sigma^2)\right) \tag{1.34}$$

where $d_i$ and $d_r$ are vectors indicating the positions of neurons $i$, $r$, and $\sigma$ is a width parameter that controls the range of $N(i, r)$ and is gradually decreased as learning proceeds.

### 1.3.6  Processor Topologies and Hardware Platforms

This book deals with parallel mapping of the ANN models described in Section 1.3 on various hardware platforms and processor topologies. Details of the hardware platforms, topologies, and the mapping scheme employed are described in the appropriate chapters. Table 1.1 presents an overview.

| ANN Model | Processor Topology | Hardware Details |
|---|---|---|
| Multilayer Feed-Forward Network | Two-Dimensional Torus | Fujitsu AP1000 (MIMD) (Chapter 7) |
| | Ring | DSPs—MUSIC Machine (MIMD) (Chapter 10) |
| BP Learning | Ring | Transputers (Heterogeneous MIMD) (Chapters 3 and 4) |
| | Two-Dimensional Lattice | DREAM Machine (SIMD) (Chapter 9) |
| | Vector Microprocessor | Spert–II Machine (Chapter 11) |
| Hopfield Network | Toroidal Lattice and Planar Lattice | Transputers (MIMD) (Chapter 8) |
| | Two-Dimensional Lattice | DREAM Machine (SIMD) (Chapter 9) |
| Recurrent BP Network | Ring | Transputers (MIMD) (Chapter 5) |
| Adaptive Resonance Theory Network | Ring | Transputers (MIMD) (Chapter 6) |
| Self-Organizing Map (SOM) | Vector Microprocessor | Spert–II Machine (Chapter 11) |

TABLE 1.1. ANN Models and their parallel implementations.

# References

[1] H. Drucker and Y. Le Cun, "Improving generalization performance using double backpropagation," *IEEE Transactions on Neural Networks*, vol. 3, no. 6, pp. 991–997, 1992.

[2] Y. Le Cun, et. al., "Backpropagation applied to handwritten zip code recognition," *Neural Computation*, vol. 1, no. 4, pp. 541–551, 1989.

[3] A. Waibel, "Consonant recognition by modular construction of large phonetic time-delay neural networks," *Advances in Neural Information Processing Systems*, pp. 215–223, 1989.

[4] C. J. Sheng Ma and J. Farmer, "An efficient EM-based training algorithm for feedforward neural networks," *Neural Networks*, vol. 10, no. 2, pp. 243–256, 1997.

[5] P. B. S. Osowski and M. Stodolaki, "Fast second order learning algorithms for feedforward neural networks and its applications," *Neural Networks*, vol. 9, no. 9, pp. 1583–1596, 1996.

[6] R. W. Means, "High speed parallel hardware performance issues," in *IEEE International Conference on Neural Networks (ICNN'94)* (S. K. Rogers, ed.), pp. 10–16, June 28–July 2 1994.

[7] L. E. Atlas and Y. Suzuki, "Digital systems for artificial neural networks," *IEEE Circuits and Devices Magazine*, pp. 20–24, Nov. 1989.

[8] P. Treleven, *Neurocomputers*. Research Note 89/8, Department of Computer Science, University College London, January 1989.

[9] J. G. Solheim, *The RENNS approach to neural computing*. PhD thesis, Norwegian Institute of Technology, In preparation.

[10] L. A. Crowl, "How to measure, present and compare parallel performance," *IEEE Parallel & Distributed Technology*, vol. 2, no. 1, pp. 9–25, 1994.

[11] L. Utne, *Design of a reconfigurable neurocomputer Performance analysis by implementation of recurrent associative memories*. PhD thesis, Norwegian Institute of Technology, 1995. ISBN 82-7119-793-2.

[12] P. Ienne, "Quantitative comparison of architectures for digital neuro-computers," in *Proc. of IEEE Int. Conference on Neural Networks*, pp. 1987–1990, 1993.

[13] K. Asanovic, J. Beck, J. Feldman, N. Morgan, and J. Wawrzynek, "Designing a connectionist network supercomputer," *International Journal of Neural Systems*, vol. 4, pp. 317–326, December 1993. ISSN: 0129-0657.

[14] K. Hwang and F. A. Briggs, *Computer architecture and parallel processing*. McGraw-Hill Book Company, 5th ed., 1989.

[15] N. Morgan, et. al., "The ring array processor (RAP): A multiprocessing peripheral for connectionist applications," *Journal of Parallel and Distributed Computing*, vol. 14, 1992. Special Issue on Neural Networks.

[16] M. E. Azema-Barac, *A generic strategy for mapping neural network models on transputer-based machines*, pp. 244–249. IOS Press, 1992. In: Transputing in Numerical and neural network applications, G.L. Reijns and J. Luo, Eds.

[17] D. B. Davidson, "A parallel processing tutorial," *IEEE Antennas and Propagation Society Magazine*, pp. 6–19, April 1990.

[18] K. Hwang, *Advanced Computer Architecture: Parallelism, Scalability, Programmability*. McGraw-Hill, Inc., 1993.

[19] W. S. McCulloch and W. Pitts, "A logical calculus of the ideas imminent in nervous activity," in *Neurocomputing: Foundations and research* (Anderson and Rosenberg, eds.), ch. 2, pp. 18–28, The MIT Press, 1988. Reprint of the "Bulletin of Mathematical Biophysics", 1943.

[20] R. F., *Principles of Neurodynamics*. Spartan Books, New York, 1962.

[21] P. D. Wasserman, *Neural Computing – Theory and Practice*. Van Nostrand Reinhold, 1989.

[22] M. Minsky and S. Papert, *Perceptrons*. The MIT Press, 1969.

[23] D. E. Rumelhart, G. E. Hinton, and R. J. Williams, "Learning internal representation by error propagation," in *Parallel Distributed Processing*, vol. 1, pp. 318–362, The MIT Press, 1986.

[24] B. Widrow and S. D. Stearns, *Adaptive Signal Processing*. Englewood Cliffs, N.J.: Prentice-Hall, 1985.

[25] H. Paugam-Moisy, "Parallel neural computing based on neural network duplicating," in *Parallel algorithms for digital image processing, computer vision and neural networks* (I. Pitas, ed.), ch. 10, pp. 305–340, John Wiley & Sons, 1993.

[26] T. J. Sejnowski and C. R. Rosenberg, "Parallel networks that learn to pronounce English text," *Complex Systems*, vol. 1, pp. 145–168, 1987.

[27] S. Fahlman, "Faster-learning variations on back-propagation," in *Proc. of the 1988 Connectionist Models Summer School*, Carnegie-Mellom University, 1988.

[28] M. Møller, "Supervised learning on large redundant training sets," *Int. Journal of Neural Systems*, vol. 4, no. 1, pp. 15–25, 1993. World Scientific Publishing Company.

[29] J. Torresen, *Parallelization of Backpropagation Training for Feed-Forward Neural Networks*. PhD thesis, Norwegian University of Science and Technology, 1996. ISBN 82-7119-906-4.

[30] G. O. Nesvik, *An empirical study of selected learning algorithms for feed-forward neural networks*. PhD thesis, Norwegian Institute of Technology, 1993. ISBN 82-7119-548-4.

[31] J. Hopfield, "Neural networks and physical systems with emergent collective computational abilities," in *Proceedings of National Academy of Science*, vol. 79, (USA), pp. 2554–2558, 1982.

[32] J. Hopfield, "Neurons with graded response have collective computations properties like those of two-state neurons," in *Proceedings of National Academy of Science*, vol. 81, (USA), pp. 3088–3092, 1984.

[33] S. Haykin, *Neural Networks: A Comprehensive Foundation*. New York: MacMillan College Publishing Co, 1994.

[34] M. Cohen and S. Grossberg, "Absolute stability of global pattern information and parallel memory storage by competitive neural networks," *IEEE transaction of Systems, Man and Cybernetics*, vol. 13, pp. 815–826, 1983.

[35] J. J. Hopfield and D. W. Tank, "Neural computations of decisions in optimzation problems," *Biological Cybernetics*, vol. 52, pp. 141–152, 1985.

[36] D. Patterson, *Artificial Neural Networks, Theory and Aplications*. Prentice Hall, 1995.

[37] F. Pineda, "Generalization of backpropagation to recurrent neural networks," *Phys. rev. Letters*, vol. 59, pp. 2229–2232, 1987.

[38] L. Almedia, "Backpropagation in non-feedforward networks," in *Neural Computing Architecture* (I. Aleksander, ed.), pp. 74–91, North Oxford Academic, London, 1989.

[39] P. Werbos, "Generalization of backpropagation with application to a recurrent gas market model," *Neural Networks*, vol. 1, pp. 339–356, 1988.

[40] A. Robison and F. Fallside, "Static and dynamic error propagation networks with applications to speech coding," in *Neural Information Processing Systems* (D. Z. Anderson, ed.), pp. 632–641, American Institute of Physics, New York, 1988.

[41] R. J. Williams and D. Zipser, "A learning algorithm for continually learning fully recurrent neural networks," *Neural Computations*, vol. 1, pp. 270–280, 1989.

[42] B. Pearlmutter, "Learning state space trajectories in recurrent neural networks," *Neural Computations*, vol. 1, pp. 263–269, 1989.

[43] G. Carpenter and S. Grossberg, "A massively parallel architecture for a self-organizing neural pattern recognition machine," *Computer Vision, Graphics and Image Processing*, vol. 37, pp. 54–115, 1987.

[44] G. Carpenter and S. Grossberg, "ART2: Self-organizing of stable category recognition codes for analog input patterns," *Applied Optics*, vol. 26, pp. 4919–4930, 1987.

[45] G. Carpenter and S. Grossberg, "The ART of adaptive pattern recognition by self-organizing neural networks," *IEEE Computer*, vol. 21, pp. 77–88, March 1988.

[46] G. Carpenter and S. Grossberg, *Pattern Recognition by Self-organizing Neural Networks*. MIT Press, Cambridge, Mass, 1991.

[47] T. Kohonen, *Self-Organization and Associative Memory*. Springer-Verlag, Berlin, 3rd ed., 1989.

[48] A. K. J.Hertz and R. Palmer, *Introduction to the Theory of Neural Computation*. Addison Wesley, Reading, MA, 1991.

# Chapter 2

# A Review of Parallel Implementations of Backpropagation Neural Networks

**Jim Torresen**
**Olav Landsverk**
Department of Computer and Information Science
Norwegian University of Science and Technology, Norway
e-mail: jimtoer@idi.ntnu.no

## 2.1   Introduction

In Chapter 1 we reviewed the different ANN paradigms, their learning characteristics, and other factors. Because feed-forward neural networks with backpropagation learning is the most widely used configuration, we deal with this paradigm in more detail in this part of the book. Because the backpropagation learning for a bigger network with a large training set takes a long time (in terms of days), it becomes imperative to look at parallel implementation schemes to reduce this large training time. Before a detailed study of this can be undertaken, it is worthwhile to survey the different parallel implementation schemes for BP networks that exist in the literature indicating their strengths and weaknesses. This is the main theme of this chapter. Because the implementations depend very much on the type of parallelism used, the type of processor networks and the topology, brief descriptions and definitions of these terms are given in the beginning of the chapter. Next, a survey of the different parallel implementations are described along with special-purpose hardware built for these schemes. Finally, the chapter concludes with descriptions of the different applications where parallel implementations have been used successfully.

## 2.2   Parallelization of Feed-Forward Neural Networks

Before we start discussing parallel implementation schemes, it is useful to define the basic terminology along with the different types of parallelism possible for BP neural networks.

**Training Set.**   Consists of a number of training patterns, each given by an input vector and the corresponding output vector.

**Network Size.**   A network of $N_i$ input units, $N_h$ hidden units, and $N_o$ output units is for short written $N_i \times N_h \times N_o$. Note that the word *network* is used for neural network in this study, not for processor topology network. The latter use of the word will be explicitly stated.

**(Training) Iteration.**   Denotes *one* presentation of the whole training set.

**Weight Updating Strategies.**   Three different approaches are used:

- *Learning by pattern (lbp)* updates the weights after *each* training pattern has been presented.

- *Learning by block (lbb)* updates the weights after a subset of the training patterns has been presented.

- *Learning by epoch (lbe)* updates the weights after all patterns have been presented (that is, one training iteration).

**Weight Update Interval.** The number of training patterns that is presented between weight updates is termed $\mu$. For *lbp*, $\mu = 1$, whereas for *lbe* $\mu = P$, where $P$ is the number of training patterns in the training set.

The BP algorithm reveals four different kinds of parallelism, as described in [1, 2].

**Training session parallelism** starts training sessions with different initial training parameters on different processing elements.

**Training set parallelism** splits the training set across the processing elements. Each element has a local copy of the complete weight matrix and accumulates weight change values for the given training patterns. The weights are updated using *lbb/lbe*.

**Pipelining** allows the training patterns to be "pipelined" between the layers, that is, the hidden and output layers are computed on *different* processors. While the output layer processor calculates output and error values for the present training pattern, the hidden layer processor processes the *next* training pattern. The forward and backward phase may also be parallelized in a pipeline. Pipelining requires a delayed weight update or *lbb/lbe*.

**Node parallelism** computes the neurons within a layer in parallel (named *neuron parallelism*). Further, the computation within each neuron may also run in parallel (Nordström [1] names this *weight* or *synapse* parallelism). In this method, the weights can be updated using *lbp*.

**MCUPS** Performance during training is measured in Million Connections Per Second (MCUPS).

### 2.2.1 Distributed Computing for Each Degree of BP Parallelism

This section first describes training set parallelism. Then the other main parallel degree, network partitioning, is detailed by describing pipelining and node parallelism.

*2.2.1.1 Training Set Parallelism.* Training set parallelism is also called *data parallelism* because the training set is partitioned, not the training program. An example is given in Figure 2.1 for training of the English alphabet.

Each processing element (PE) has a local copy of the complete weight matrices and accumulate weight change values for the given training patterns. The neural network weights must be consistent across all the PEs, thus weights are updated in a global operation (learning by block/epoch). The weight change values of each PE are summed and used to update the local weight matrices.

*2.2.1.2 Pipelining.* In pipelining, the different weight layers are computed in different PEs as illustrated in Figure 2.2. Figure 2.3 shows a pipelining example. First, the hidden layer processor computes output values of training pattern (a). The output processor reads

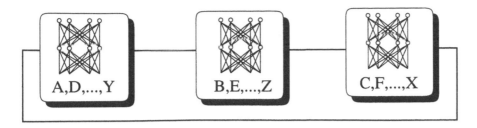

FIGURE 2.1. Training set parallelism for learning the English alphabet.

the values and computes output and error values of (a). The hidden processor concurrently processes the next training pattern (b). Then, it reads the hidden error for (a) and both processors accumulate the weight change values for (a). This method interleaves the forward phase with the backward phase. A further extension is to execute the two training phases in parallel [3].

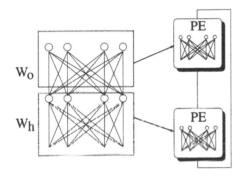

FIGURE 2.2. Mapping of the weight matrices for pipelining.

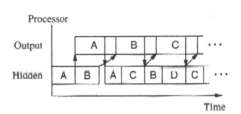

FIGURE 2.3. Pipelining of the training patterns.

### 2.2.1.3 Node Parallelism.

Node parallelism contains two subdegrees of network parallelism: neuron parallelism and synapse parallelism. The parallel mapping schemes, which use a mixture of these two, are named *node parallel methods*. Next, each of the two subdegrees are explained.

**Neuron Parallelism.** The most common way to parallelize a feed-forward network is by using neuron parallelism, also called vertical slicing. The example in figure 2.4 applies the principle to three processing elements.

All incoming weights to one hidden and one output neuron are mapped to each PE. That is, each PE stores all the incoming weights to the neuron assigned to that PE. The network slicing corresponds to storing one row of the weight matrix in each PE. The output of the neurons is computed by the matrix-vector product:

$$\begin{bmatrix} y_{L,1} \\ y_{L,2} \\ y_{L,3} \end{bmatrix} = \begin{bmatrix} w_{L,11} & w_{L,12} & w_{L,13} \\ w_{L,21} & w_{L,22} & w_{L,23} \\ w_{L,31} & w_{L,32} & w_{L,33} \end{bmatrix} \begin{bmatrix} x_1 \\ x_2 \\ x_3 \end{bmatrix} \qquad (2.1)$$

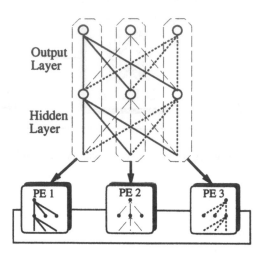

FIGURE 2.4. Neuron parallelism, also called vertical slicing.

where

$$L = \{\text{Layer} \mid \text{Layer} \in \{h, o\}\}.$$

First, the value of one hidden neuron is computed in each PE. Then, each PE exchanges the values, for example, over a ring bus, and continues by computing the value of the output neuron. The hidden layer error is computed based on the output error. This can be formulated as a vector-matrix product

$$\begin{bmatrix} \delta'_{h,1} & | & \delta'_{h,2} & | & \delta'_{h,3} \end{bmatrix} = \begin{bmatrix} \delta_{o,1} \\ \delta_{o,2} \\ \delta_{o,3} \end{bmatrix} \begin{bmatrix} w_{o,11} & w_{o,12} & w_{o,13} \\ w_{o,21} & w_{o,22} & w_{o,23} \\ w_{o,31} & w_{o,32} & w_{o,33} \end{bmatrix}. \tag{2.2}$$

Because the weights are stored in row order, the sum of products is computed by adding partial products. However, a more effective summation could be achieved if the weights were stored in column order. Thus, some implementations store the weights twice, both by row order for forward pass and column order for backward pass. Either duplicated weight updates [4, 5] or communication of the weights [6] is by this method required. The former has been shown to be the most efficient [6].

If the number of neurons in a layer is larger than the number of PEs, each PE computes more than one neuron from each layer.

**Synapse Parallelism.** Instead of mapping the rows of the weight matrices to each PE, the columns may be mapped. In synapse parallelism, each PE computes a partial sum of the neuron output as indicated in Figure 2.5.

The computation is more fine grained than for neuron parallelism. The subresults from each PE have to be added and broadcast to all PEs before the next layer can be computed. The advantage is that the hidden layer error can be computed without communication:

$$\begin{bmatrix} \delta_{h,1} & | & \delta_{h,2} & | & \delta_{h,3} \end{bmatrix} = \begin{bmatrix} \delta_{o,1} \\ \delta_{o,2} \\ \delta_{o,3} \end{bmatrix} \begin{bmatrix} w_{o,11} & w_{o,12} & w_{o,13} \\ w_{o,21} & w_{o,22} & w_{o,23} \\ w_{o,31} & w_{o,32} & w_{o,33} \end{bmatrix}. \tag{2.3}$$

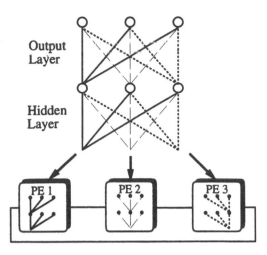

FIGURE 2.5. Synapse parallelism.

Thus, some implementations use neuron parallelism in the first layer and synapse parallelism in the second layer. The two degrees can be combined for both weight layers, as is described in Section 2.2.2.3 [7].

*2.2.1.4  Dimension of Each Parallel Degree.*   Each parallel degree has an inherent limitation given by the following:

- Training-set parallelism. The number of patterns in the training set

- Pipelining: The number of weight layers

- Neuron parallelism: The number of hidden units and output units

- Synapse parallelism: The number of input units and hidden units

Thus, this indicates the maximum number of processing elements that can be assigned to each degree of parallelism.

### 2.2.2  A Survey of Different Parallel Implementations

Many mappings of BP onto parallel computers have been proposed and implemented, for both general purpose and special purpose computers. In this section, a description of the published work surveyed by the authors of this chapter is presented. As far as possible, both the architecture and the parallel implementation are described.

Mapping neural network models onto parallel architectures may be categorized into two general groups: heuristic mapping and algorithmic mapping [8]. Most of the proposed mappings are of the heuristic kind. They are generated by trial and error based on knowledge about the algorithm and the target machine. The algorithmic technique relies on a systematic approach to the implementation. The work by Fujimoto and colleagues [9, 10] and Kumar and colleagues [11] belong to the algorithm mapping category. Moreover, some theoretical studies of parallel algorithms have been made, which are described in Section 2.2.2.3. The majority of other surveyed mappings assign PEs according to the number of elements in a single degree of parallelism, for example, the number of neurons. The same mapping is used for all kinds of neural applications. However, only a few networks and training sets will run optimally on a fixed mapping. What ought to be considered is this: What degree of parallelism should be included and how many PEs should be assigned for each of them to minimize the total training time? In Chapter 7, these issues are addressed.

*2.2.2.1 General Purpose Computer Implementations.* In this section, BP neural network simulations on various general purpose machines are described. A summary of the degrees of parallelism used and performance results are given in Section 2.2.2.9 and 2.2.2.10, respectively.

**MasPar MP-1.** MP-1 is a massively parallel SIMD computer from MasPar Computer Corporation. A variant of the mesh topology connects PEs to their eight nearest neighbors horizontally, vertically, and diagonally. In addition to nearest neighbor communication, a global router allows any PE to send data to any other PE. However, the communication bandwidth is much larger for the nearest neighbor communication than for the global router. A fully configured system consists of a $128 \times 128$ array of PEs. Several node-parallelism-based implementations have been made for the machine. Chin and colleagues made a node parallel implementation where the weights are ordered so that one (or more if available) column of PEs corresponds to a single neuron [12]. For a $256 \times 128 \times 256$ neural network, based on the results from smaller systems, 10 MCUPS is estimated for a 16K PE array [13].

Node parallelism and training-set parallelism are combined in [14] for a $64 \times 64$ system. Each row of the array of PEs is assigned a copy of the network. Within each row neuron parallelism is used for computing the activation values of the hidden neurons. Then, synapse parallelism is used for computing the output activation values. A master processor adds the partial sums together and computes the output error. The error values for the hidden layer can then be computed by neuron parallelism. A network of 128 input neurons, 64 hidden neurons, and 16 output neurons achieved a maximum performance of approximately 12 MCUPS for 1,536 training patterns. The weights were updated by learning by epoch.

A neural network simulator, Stuttgart Neural Network Simulator (SNNS), has been developed at the University of Stuttgart [15]. It is a portable software tool used to generate, test, and visualize ANNs. Many different learning algorithms have been implemented. A parallel SNNS kernel for multilayer feed-forward networks runs on MasPar MP-1216, which is the 16K PEs version of the MasPar computer. Two mappings are proposed based on a combination of training set and neuron parallelism. The first scheme assigns one PE to each vertical slice of the feed-forward network, which includes one neuron from each layer. The number of necessary PEs is equal to the number of neurons in the largest layer, except the input layer. Further, as many multiple copies as possible of the neural network are made to utilize all the PEs. The Nettalk network with 120 hidden units was trained in 41 MCUPS (downloading time for training patterns from the host was not accounted for).

One of the biggest problems identified was the overhead for downloading the training patterns from the host to the parallel system. To avoid a single PE storing the remaining input values for an input layer greater than the other layers, the second implementation assigned the number of PEs equal to the largest number of neurons in *any* layer. A performance measure (including downloading time for the training patterns) for Nettalk was 17.6 MCUPS. Fewer networks can be trained in parallel and more PEs become idle for networks with the largest number of neurons in the input layer.

A third prototype that combined training-set parallelism and node parallelism gained slightly better peak performance than the second implementation. However, in this method, a variation in the number of neurons in each layer leads to dummy weight values in some of the PEs. The results from all three schemes demonstrate a performance dependence on the number of neurons in each layer. An unequal number of neurons in each of the layers reduces the performance.

**IBM GF11.** IBM GF11 is an experimental SIMD machine with 566 processors interconnected by a Benes network.[1] BP has been implemented on this machine using training-set parallelism [17]. The weight changes are summed by a binary tree processor configuration. To reduce the memory latency time, a *subset* of the weights are stored in SRAM. In this case, several patterns are processed on these weights before a new subset of weights is loaded into SRAM as opposed to finishing one training vector before a new one is input. Nettalk with 60 hidden units and a training set of 12,022 patterns (epoch update) learned at 900 MCPS (no measure for CUPS was given) on 356 processors. A ring summing algorithm achieved the highest performance for 128 processors of 222 MCPS, confirming the limitation of processors connected by a single ring.

**Hypercube Machines.** Simulation of BP-trained neural networks on NCube/4[+] is reported by Kerckhoffs [5]. NCube/4[+] is a 4-dimensional hypercube machine with 16 processing elements. Larger systems of 128 and 1,024 PEs are available. A PE can communicate with other PEs by use of asynchronous Direct Memory Access (DMA). The implementation distributes the neurons in each layer between the PEs of the hypercube. A comparison was made between single weight storage and double weight storage for the output layer. For the double weight storage, the forward pass uses neuron parallelism— Equation 2.1— while the backward pass uses synapse parallelism— Equation 2.3. The same double weight storage scheme is employed for MUSIC, see Section 2.2.2.6. The drawback of this method is that the weights are stored and updated twice. Thus, the results show roughly equivalent communication time, but less computation time for the single weight storage scheme. The peak performance is 0.19 MCUPS. For synapse parallelism, the broadcast time has been shown to increase linearly for an NCube size from 1 to 128 [18]. It is concluded in the paper that the effect of reducing the training time by this parallel implementation is minimal.

The hypercube computer Intel iPSC/860 is capable of being configured with up to 128 Intel i860 processors. A node parallel implementation of BP on a 32 PE version of the iPSC/860 is given in [19]. The network is partitioned vertically, that is, all input neurons and at least one hidden unit is mapped to each PE. Each PE computes the output value of its assigned hidden neurons (neuron parallelism). Then, each PE computes a part of the output value based on the assigned hidden units (synapse parallelism). Thus, the only communication required in the forward pass is to sum the partial sums of the output units. For the Nettalk application with 80 hidden units, 11 MCUPS was reported. The weights were updated for every 2,000 training vectors.

**Connection Machines.** Singer reviewed five different ANN implementations on the connection machine (CM-1 and CM-2[2]) [2]. The most sophisticated of those is developed by Zhang [21] for the CM-2. This is a massively parallel SIMD computer with between 16K and 64K processors, each consisting of a one bit processing unit and 8KB or 32KB local memory. Moreover, every 32 processors share one floating point unit. The parallel BP

---

[1] A multistage switching network that can perform all possible connections between inputs and outputs. Conflicts in the use of switches or communication links are solved by rearranging connections [16].

[2] CM-2 is the same architecture as CM-1 with some added features, such as floating point accelerators and larger local memory [20].

algorithm combines neuron parallelism and training-set parallelism. An implementation published by Rosenberg and Blelloch assigns one processor for each neuron in the network and two processors for each weight [3]. This is an inefficient processor assignment and they suggest an improved algorithm using one processor per weight and no separate processor for each neuron. Further, to avoid only processors with weights from one layer to be active at each time, pipelined computation of the training patterns as described in Section 2.2.1.2, is suggested.

BP for CM-5 is presented in [22]. The CM-5 consists of 544 PEs, each a 33 MHz SPARC-2 chip with its own 32 Mbyte memory. The mapping is based on node parallelism, where the input and output neurons are evenly distributed over all processors. To use the Control Network for adding operation and avoiding message passing communication, *all* the hidden neurons are mapped to each processor. Each processor computes a part of each hidden neuron sum in parallel synapse parallelism. The partial results are summed and the sum is sent to *all* PEs. Then, each processor performs the sigmoid function. This is said to be the only redundant computation in the scheme. For the output layer, the PEs compute the outputs in parallel. No communication is needed because all hidden layer outputs are readily available in every processor. The implementation was tested on protein tertiary structure prediction with a network of 257 input neurons, 256 hidden neurons, and 131,072 output neurons. For 512 processors a performance of 76 MCUPS was obtained. For a CM-5 with 32 PEs, the Nettalk network (80 hidden units) learned at 18.33 MCUPS using a batch implementation [23].

Kumar and associates [11] proposed a hybrid scheme using node and training set parallelism for hypercube architectures. The node parallel scheme is called *checkerboarding*. This method makes all-to-all broadcast unnecessary, because only communication within rows or columns is needed. The processors are partitioned into clusters. A cluster forms a hypercube and contains one copy of the network. Each cluster contains different training patterns. The method makes it possible to vary the number of processors assigned to node parallelism against those assigned to training-set parallelism. Theoretical expressions for the total training time were derived based on the cost of computation and communication. The computation cost was based on time per weight per pattern, whereas communication cost was based on start-up time and per-word time for communication. The effect of changing the weight update interval is not considered. The expressions are used to compare the model to simpler schemes. A nonoptimized version of the hybrid method performed over 50 MCUPS for a $1024 \times 256 \times 64$ neural network on a 256 processor CM-5.

**Warp.** The Warp machine consists of a linear array of 10 PEs called cells. Each cell can communicate with its left and right neighbors in the array. In a much cited paper, Pomerleau and associates proposed several BP mapping algorithms onto the Warp computer [24]. In the first implementation, columns of weights were stored in each cell, synapse parallelism, whereas in the second implementation, training-set parallelism was used. As only a 32 Kword[3] memory is available in each cell, weights are in the latter implementation, pumped through the array from a central cluster memory. Nine cells compute the forward and backward pass, whereas the 10th is reserved for updating the weights. Each weight is used for all the training patterns in a cell before the next weight is received. For the Nettalk network, the performance was measured to be 17 MCPS (CUPS measurement is not reported), which was the fastest performance reported at that time. The synapse parallel implementation was much slower.

---

[3]Each word is 4 bytes.

**Supercomputers.** Supercomputers are an alternative to parallel computers in providing high-speed computation. Supercomputers consist of one or a few complex processing elements. They usually consist of multiple functional units, vector registers, and a highly pipelined processor. BP training has been implemented on the Fujitsu VP-2400/10 vectorial supercomputer [25]. The computer was programmed using an extended FORTRAN77 compiler. A high degree of vectorization is reported. The Nettalk network trained at 60 MCUPS.

**Symult S2010.** Symult S2010 is a computer with 16 processors. It is a mesh-connected message-passing parallel computer with dedicated hardware for wormhole routing. An interesting BP mapping is described in [26], which combines neuron parallelism and pipelining. The processors are connected by a ring bus as shown in Figure 2.6.

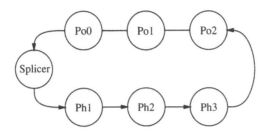

FIGURE 2.6. Combined neuron parallelism and pipelining in Symult S2010 (from [26]).

In this example the three lower processors are designated for the hidden layer, whereas the processors in the upper row are assigned to the output layer. The splicer processor composes messages of training vectors, one vector per message, which are sent to the first element of the pipeline, Ph1. Each message progresses through the pipeline and at each processor, activation values, are computed and added to the received activation values, which are sent on to the next processor on the ring. After a message has passed all Ph processors, each Po processor in the ring computes its output activation values based on the received hidden activation values. Moreover, the output processors compute the output error values, which are also passed through the pipeline. The splicer includes the error values in the training vector messages to be used for computing weight change in each hidden processor. The weights are updated by learning by epoch. An expression for estimating the best number of processors for each layer is derived based on the number of neurons in each layer and the ratio between computing one hidden layer connection versus one output connection. The method has a reduced amount of communication. A disadvantage of this method is that the time for filling the pipeline is proportional to the number of processors. Moreover, to avoid using old weights after a weight update, the pipeline needs to be refilled.

**Fujitsu AP1000.** AP1000 is a general purpose message passing computer designed by Fujitsu. A thorough description of neural network implementations on this computer will be given in Chapter 7. Thus, only summary information is included in the end of this chapter.

*2.2.2.2 Interconnected Workstations.* For mapping BP training onto workstations, background workload has to be considered. A detailed study of both static and dynamic mapping algorithms is reported in [27]. In the dynamic case, the neurons are remapped as the workload changes.

### 2.2.2.3   Research by Use of Models of Parallel Machines.

In this section, schemes that have not been implemented on a real system are described.

**Data-Driven Systems.**   Data-driven computation is based on asynchronous parallel execution of computations, which may be represented by directed graphs. A processor instruction is executed based on the availability of its data operands. Q-x is a floating point data-driven processor. A message-passing multiprocessor is able to be configured of up to 1,024 processors. The processors are interconnected by a 2D-torus communication network. Processing and storage in the processor is carried out as packets flowing through elastic pipelines. A description of the mapping of BP onto the architecture is reported in [28]. The scheme is based on combining neuron parallelism and training-set parallelism, similar to [21]. That is, one row of PEs compute one copy of the network. The neurons are distributed among the processors in a row by vertical slicing of the network. Performance is evaluated by using a system simulator for training an image compression $256 \times 128 \times 256$ network. For 64 processors, 44 MCUPS was predicted.

**Mesh Topology.**   A fine-grain BP algorithm using node parallelism for mesh-connected multiprocessors is proposed in [7]. It combines neuron and synapse parallelism, that is, each cell computes a partial sum for a single neuron. The weight matrices are divided into rectangular blocks or submatrices that are distributed among the cells. The method is similar to the checkerboard partitioning method [29], described in the section on CM-5 implementations. The forward phase of the parallel BP algorithm can be illustrated by using a simple, fully connected network of four input, four hidden, and four output neurons and a system of four cells. The weight matrices are partitioned into submatrices and multiplied by the input vectors $\mathbf{X}_L$ as follows:

$$\begin{bmatrix} y_{L,1} \\ y_{L,2} \\ y_{L,3} \\ y_{L,4} \end{bmatrix} = \left[ \begin{array}{cc|cc} w_{L,11} & w_{L,12} & w_{L,13} & w_{L,14} \\ w_{L,21} & w_{L,22} & w_{L,23} & w_{L,24} \\ \hline w_{L,31} & w_{L,32} & w_{L,33} & w_{L,34} \\ w_{L,41} & w_{L,42} & w_{L,43} & w_{L,44} \end{array} \right] \begin{bmatrix} x_{L,1} \\ x_{L,2} \\ x_{L,3} \\ x_{L,4} \end{bmatrix}$$

$$= \begin{bmatrix} W_{L,11} & W_{L,12} \\ W_{L,21} & W_{L,22} \end{bmatrix} \begin{bmatrix} X_{L,1} \\ X_{L,2} \end{bmatrix} \qquad (2.4)$$

where
$$L = \{\text{Layer} \mid \text{Layer} \in \{h, o\}\}.$$

The mapping scheme can be effective if the network matches the architecture in a way that divides matrices and vectors into *equal* parts for each processing element. If not, some of the processors may become idle. Although communication is minimized in the method, the communication overhead will still be large for most real neural networks and parallel machines because the computation grains become too small.

A theoretical study of implementing pipelining of training patterns on a mesh topology is given in [30]. The method is based on assigning a dedicated mesh to each layer, as indicated in Figure 2.7. The hidden layer is computed by $p \times q$ PEs, and $q \times r$ PEs compute the output layer as indicated in the figure. The data for the hidden units are transmitted from the left to the right mesh. Theoretical expressions for transmission count and computation

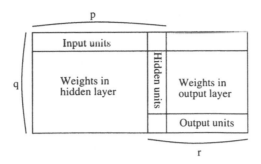

FIGURE 2.7. Piped-mesh implementation (from [30]).

count are derived and used to estimate the optimal number of neurons per PE. For a 1,024 $\times 128 \times 128$ network, six neurons per PE ($u$) is found to be optimal and therefore

$$u = \left\lceil \frac{N_i}{p} \right\rceil = \left\lceil \frac{N_h}{q} \right\rceil = \left\lceil \frac{N_o}{r} \right\rceil \qquad (2.5)$$

where $N_i$, $N_h$ and $N_o$ are the number of neurons in each layer as defined in Section 1.3.1.

A framework for implementing neural networks on massively parallel machines is proposed by Azema-Barac [31]. The model formalizes a speedup for the different degrees of neural network parallelism on the given parallel machine. Derived expressions for one training iteration are made based on the grain of parallelism[4] and the communication overhead. It is not specified how to estimate or measure the communication overhead. Moreover, the accuracy of the method is not substantiated. Further, the effect of weight update interval on the convergence is not considered. The distribution scheme is designed for node parallelism, training-set parallelism, and a combination of these two.

The target machine for implementing the scheme has been DAP 600 (distributed array processor). This is a SIMD machine with $64 \times 64$ PEs, each interconnected to its four nearest neighbors. One of the few results given is based on a digit recognition application [32]. A speedup of 50 over a Sparc station is reported.

**2D-Lattice Topology.** A proposed reconfigurable machine, called dynamically reconfigurable extended array multiprocessor (DREAM), is presented in [33] for implementation of neural networks. It is classified as a SIMD machine and the PEs are arranged on a 2-D lattice, that is, each PE is connected to eight of its closest neighbors through programmable switches. Multiple rings of various lengths can be mapped onto the machine. An *embedded* ring structure is proposed for the case of uneven neuron layers in a multilayer network. For a network of $N_l$ and $N_{l-1}$ neurons in layer $l$ and $l-1$, respectively, the ring size is set to $\max\{N_l, N_{l-1}\}$. If $N_{l-1} > N_l$, the shorter ring of length $N_l$ is embedded into the ring of length $N_{l-1}$ as shown in Figure 2.8. The shorter ring of size $N_2$ is embedded into the ring of size $N_1$. The weight matrices are partitioned vertically (synapse parallelism), and the output of a neuron is computed by accumulating partial sums from each PE. First, $N_{l-1}$ cycles are used for computing the layer $l-1$ outputs. Second, a shortened version of the ring, equal to the $N_l$, is used for the next layer. Thus, the ring size is dynamically changed as the computation moves from layer to layer. If the number of neurons is larger than the number of PEs, time-multiplexing is used for creating virtual PEs.

---

[4]The number of neurons assigned to each processor.

The results presented in the paper are from analytical estimation and not real implementations. Chapter 9 thoroughly describes the DREAM machine architecture.

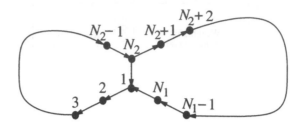

FIGURE 2.8. A ring of size $N_2$ embedded into a longer ring of size $N_1$ (from [33]).

**Hypercube Topology.** A theoretical study of the mapping of a tree structure onto a hypercube topology is proposed in [34]. The trees are used to communicate elements. One tree is used to broadcast a value from a root to all the leaves and another tree is used to sum values from the leaves into a root. $\mathcal{O}(\log N)$ time is required, where $N$ is the size of the largest layer. The scheme is based on node parallelism, similar to the one described in the section on Mesh Topology presented earlier [7]. Pipelining of the patterns is also included.

**Systolic Array Design.** A programmable systolic array is proposed in [35] for a wide variety of artificial neural networks. Very large scale integration (VLSI) is the target architecture for the mapping. A data *dependency graph* (DG) is used to express the recurrence and parallelism associated with the neural network algorithm. The graph is mapped onto a proposed ring systolic array using one ring for each weight layer. The weights for one output neuron, that is, one row of the weight matrix, are mapped to one systolic element, as shown in Figure 2.9. Thus, both the learning and recall phase share the same storage and processing hardware. Input elements are rotated across each ring array.

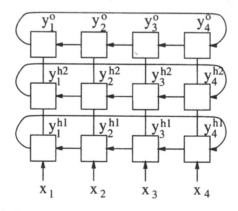

FIGURE 2.9. Cascaded systolic ANN (from [35]).

The proposed systolic design is efficient when the sizes of the different layers are approximately equal. To make the design applicable for multilayer networks of different sizes, the number of systolic elements assigned to each layer may be varied. Each weight layer is mapped to a number of systolic elements equal to the number of rows or columns, depending of which is smallest in number. A two-layer neural network with configuration $3 \times 9 \times 4$ is used in the paper, and the design is shown in Figure 2.10. The hidden weight matrix is vertically partitioned, and one column of weights is stored in each systolic element of the lower PE row. The output weight matrix is partitioned horizontally and stored in the upper PE row. This approach minimizes the number of PEs needed.

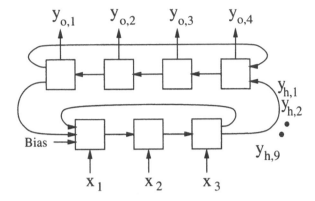

FIGURE 2.10. Systolic design for feed-forward networks with layers of different sizes (from [35]).

First, the forward pass starts by residing the inputs $\{x_i, i = 1, 2, 3\}$ at the corresponding PEs in the first layer. The bias values are pipelined one by one into the array from the leftmost PE. Each bias input initiates an accumulation operation where the product $w_{h,ji}x_i$ is added at the $i$-th PE. The complete hidden neuron element $y_{h,j}$ is output at the rightmost PE after three accumulation operations. The nine hidden neuron elements are sequentially pumped into the upper array of PEs and used for computing the output layer elements $y_{o,k}$. After the nine elements $y_{h,j}$ have passed the four upper PEs, the output $y_{o,k}$ is ready at the $k$-th PE. In a similar way, the backward phase is computed.

A more general mathematical formulation, covering the mapping of a wide range of ANNs to ring systolic arrays, is presented by the same authors in [36, 37]. However, a single ring is used and one layer is computed at a time. The design assumes that all the neuron layers are of uniform size. Further, a systolic mapping where each PE stores a row of the hidden weight matrix and a column of the output weight matrix is presented in [38, 39]. The PEs are connected by a ring bus. Each input element is sequentially input to the upper PEs. The method is extended by using learning by epoch, which allows pipelining of the training patterns in rectangular arrays of PEs.

**SIMD Mesh-Connected Machine Implementations.** A fine-grain node parallel mapping is proposed in [8, 40]. Although claims are made that the method is applicable to various SIMD machines, the details are given for the systolic/cellular array processor (SCAP). However, no implementation results are reported. The scheme is based on a graph-theoretic approach and has no requirement for fully interconnected layers. If the total number of neurons and weights in the network is less than or equal to the number of available processors, then each neuron and each weight is mapped to a separate processor. The input elements are then sent to the processors storing the weights to be multiplied. A transformation scheme is given for transforming the weight matrix between row and column major order. In the opposite case, where the number of available processors is less than the total number of neurons and weights, the data is stored in a global memory. The size of the local memory is very limited. Thus, the processor array is operating on subarrays from the global memory. The essential data movement operations are realized by embedding a Benes network.

### 2.2.2.4 FPGA Implementations.

Field programmable gate arrays (FPGAs) have recently become an alternative to full custom VLSI design. FPGA is reasonably priced and makes the development cycle shorter in comparison to VLSI. However, the flexibility leads to less performance and functionality per unit area of silicon. To fully utilize the flexibility of the FPGA technology it should be used with run-time reconfiguration. This is exploited in the RRANN (Run-time Reconfiguration ANN) system [41]. That is, the BP algorithm is divided into sequentially executed stages: At run-time only one stage is configured on the FPGA at a time. Because only one stage is used at any given time, more hardware resources are available for each stage. In the system, six neurons are mapped to each FPGA (XC3090). Results show that to achieve a higher performance than that achieved by a non-run-time reconfigurable system, more than 22 FPGAs need be used. This is due to the reconfiguration overhead.

A system for the feed-forward recall-phase is presented in [42]. Each hidden and output neuron is implemented in 2 FPGAs (XC3042) connected to an EPROM. The EPROM contains a lookup table for the sigmoid activation function. A network with five input units, four hidden units, and two output units executes at 4 MCPS. They conclude that the size and speed of the system can be greatly improved by using higher density FPGAs. An experimental project called REMAP consists of building an entire computer using only FPGA and memory [43]. It is based on bit-serial processing elements with SIMD control. The PEs are designed for neural computation. A full-scale prototype (256PEs) can run in 10 MHz.

Because one of the main bottlenecks in implementing ANNs in FPGAs is the multiplication operation, the circuitry devoted to multiplication must be significantly reduced, according to Bade and Hutchings [44]. This can be accomplished in two ways: by reducing the number of multipliers or by reducing the complexity of the multiplier. Bade and Hutchings have proposed to use bit-serial stochastic computing to reduce the circuitry necessary for multiplication, that is, to represent signal values as long bit streams according to the statistical distribution of 1s in the bit stream. Then, multiplication can be implemented as a bit-wise Boolean ("and") operation, which is implemented as a lookup table. Because FPGAs are normally based on lookup tables, this scheme is very efficient. The system can process 181K patterns per second (recall phase). This is regardless of the network size. The drawback of the method is that learning is difficult due to lack of precision.

### 2.2.2.5 Transputer Implementations.

A transputer chip contains a microprocessor, memory, and ports for communication. The most commonly used transputer is the INMOS T800.

An analysis of a transputer system shows that for a fully or randomly connected neural network, the topology of the processor network only has a small, constant effect on the iteration time [45]. An expression for the optimal number of processors is derived. Communication overhead is shown to be a major limiting factor in the efficiency of implementation on transputers.

Yoon and Nang [46] have shown that hypercube networks have less communication time complexity than mesh networks for backpropagation training. Thus, as the number of processing elements involved increases, the performance of hypercube mapping outpace the mesh mapping. The model was verified by implementations on a transputer system.

In [47], a neural specification language is defined. The purpose is to parallelize neural networks automatically based on a high-level language. The parallelizing scheme only considers neuron parallelism. The approach scales acceptably for a system of 13 transputers, when the network consists of a large number of neurons.

**Transputers Interconnected by Mesh or 2D-Torus Network.** Fujimoto and colleagues have proposed a load-balanced mapping of the BP and Hopfield neural networks onto both a toroidal lattice architecture (TLA) [10] and a planar lattice architecture (PLA) [9]. A TLA is a one-way directed 2D-torus network, whereas a PLA is a bidirectional mesh network. Both schemes are based on mapping a single weight to a virtual processor. Thus, the method uses node parallelism, that is, both neuron and synapse parallelism. The matrix of virtual processors is partitioned into submatrices, each of which is mapped to a real transputer processor. Before the partitioning, the rows and columns in the virtual matrix are permuted so that each submatrix contains an equal amount of computation (multiply accumulate and sigmoid computation).

A feed-forward network of $256 \times 64 \times 256$ neurons is used in the work. The performance for a 16 transputer system interconnected by a PLA is estimated to be slightly higher than that achieved on a TLA interconnected system. An implementation on TLA is learned at 0.6 MCUPS. The conversion rate from MFLOPS to MCUPS is roughly estimated to 1/40 in the worst case. The proposed schemes are proved to exhibit almost linear performance with respect to the number of processors when expanded for large-scale neural networks. The processor topologies are planned implemented in wafer scale integration (WSI) technology. See Chapter 8 for further details.

The research reported in [48] considers each layer of the network as a stage of a pipeline. Theoretical expressions for the performance of an implementation of pipelining and node parallelism on a 2D-torus transputer system is given. The weight matrices are divided into $Q x Q$ blocks, where $Q$ represent the number of PEs in a row or column. The matrix-vector product is obtained by broadcasting the input elements along columns and accumulating subresults in the rows. This is similar to the *checkerboard* partitioning presented earlier. However, in this work, little is said about the implementation of pipelining on the computer.

Results from a 16 transputer system show that for a three-neuron-layer network, the time usage for the pipelined and the nonpipelined implementation was almost identical. Preliminary experiments show that the pipelining algorithm, using delayed weight update, seems to converge in the same way as the nonpipelined algorithm, updated after each training pattern. It is concluded that pipelining increases the computation load versus communication per processor and enables the computation to be more evenly distributed throughout the network. Thus, pipelining is preferable because the overhead of its operation is negligibly small.

**Transputers Connected by a Ring.** A thorough study of training-set parallelism on a ring of 32 T800 transputers is undertaken by Paugam-Moisy [49]. Each transputer is assigned an equal number of training patterns, and different block sizes are tested for learning by block. For a classification application (described in Section 1.3.1.3) the total training time is computed for different weight update intervals (see Section 7.3.2). A block size in the range $(192, 384)$ is found to be optimal. A model is also made for estimating the time for one training iteration, and estimation of the number of iterations needed for convergence is undertaken (see Section 7.3.2.3).

A transputer ring topology is presented in [50]. The idea is to combine training-set parallelism and pipelining. A three-layer network is mapped onto 15 PEs as shown in Figure 2.11. Each shaded box represents one network cluster. One PE is assigned for each layer within a cluster. No performance results are given.

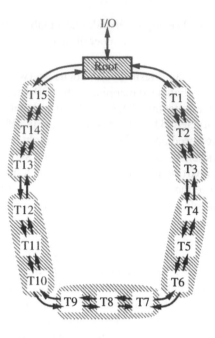

FIGURE 2.11. A transputer ring topology combining training-set parallelism and pipelining.

The MEIKO Computing Surface is a reconfigurable parallel computer based on the T800 INMOS transputer. A mapping scheme of BP onto this system is given in [51]. The mapping scheme combines node and training-set parallelism. The method implies that a subset of the rows of the hidden weight matrix and subset of the columns of the output weight matrix are stored in each processor. In this way, no communication between processors is needed until the partial results from each PE is to be summed to compute the activation of the output layer. This is done by a *master* processor. The number of processors that can be efficiently used by using only node parallelism and learning by pattern, is 20. For a larger number of processors, the performance is only marginally increased. A performance of 8 MCUPS is reported for a $512 \times 256 \times 64$ network, when training-set parallelism is included and the PEs are connected by a $3 \times 40$ mesh. A similar mapping is used on the MP-1 [14].

Transputers connected in a pipelined ring topology were used for training set parallelism by Foo in [52, 53]. An administrative transputer distributes the training set evenly among the other processors in the pipe. For weight update, each pipe processor receives weight changes and errors from its upstream neighbor, adds its own weight changes and errors to these, and passes the new values to the downstream neighbor. Thus, the last downstream processor will hold the overall weight change and the total error. After computing the new weight values it propagates them back through the pipe. Simulations show that for small networks the serial implementation outperforms the parallel implementations. An analytic expression for the training time per iteration is derived. However, the scheme does not consider the effect of the weight update frequency on the convergence. The weight change summing seems to be leaving processors idle, even though an improvement is proposed. In that case, the downstream transputers are assigned a larger number of training patterns [54]. Using this latter scheme, 1.54 MCUPS is reported for Nettalk using 53 T805-20 transputers.

**Transputer Tree.** Several implementations on nine transputers are reported in [55]. Both fully connected network and the extension of shared weights–receptive fields (SW–RF) network are used. The latter network is beneficial for shift-invariant feature extraction and improves the generalization properties.

The best performance for the SW–RF network (almost linear) is seen when the transputers are connected in a tree and use training-set parallelism. However, the problem of slow convergence due to learning by epoch is mentioned. Another implemented scheme combines node parallelism and pipelining. The parallel processing speedup approaches a value of six for the largest input image size. For a fully connected network the speedup is higher, which is explained by an increased utilization of the allocated processors. However, the SW–RF neural network showed better generalization properties.

**Transputer Hypercubes.** Training-set parallelism for hypercubes made up of transputers is studied in [56]. An $\mathcal{O}(\log n)$ step algorithm for summing the weight change matrices is proposed. To enable it to use all the communication channels in the cube concurrently, the weight matrix is split into $\log n$ parts, where $n$ is the number of processors. Each part is summed along one axis at a time. The redundant summation in every two PEs is eliminated by doing half of the summation in each PE and exchanging the results. For a small training set, the described optimizing methods improves the speedup. However, for a training set of 512 samples or more, the difference in speedup is marginal.

The study is restricted to hypercubes of dimension 1, 2, and 3. Moreover, the weight update interval is not considered. The application used was speech recognition.

A training-set parallel scheme is reported in [57] for training a Time Delay Neural Network (TDNN) for speech recognition. The convergence in the number of iterations varied for different weight update frequency. However, with no favor for frequent weight updates. Sixteen transputers showed a speedup factor of 8.8 over a VAX 3600.

**Summary of Transputer Techniques.** Much published work has been undertaken in this area. Communication seems to be a bottleneck in large systems. Some of the implementations depend on using a master processor, which limits the scalability. In many of the projects, training-set parallelism is employed (see Table 2.3 later in this chapter). However, with a few exceptions [49, 57], experiments on the effect of the weight update frequency on the total convergence time has not been reported.

*2.2.2.6 Digital Signal Processor (DSP) Based Systems.* MUSIC (MUlti Signal processor system with Intelligent Communication) is a DSP-based parallel system with distributed memory. A system of 45 PEs with a peak performance of 2.7 GFLOPS [6] is implemented. Each PE consists of a DSP (Motorola 96002), up to 8 Mbyte of Video RAM (VRAM), up to 1 Mbyte of SRAM and an FPGA communication controller. Each board consists of three PEs controlled by a transputer, which also interfaces the PEs to the host computer. Inter-PE communication is by a pipelined ring. A dynamic load balancing scheme is implemented, where the operating system distributes data according to each PE's computation in the previous step. An implementation of BP based on standard neuron parallelism is used, where one network layer is computed after the other. However, to be able to compute the hidden delta error without using partial sums, each PE stores a local copy of the weights needed to compute the error. For a network of two weight layers, this only applies to the output weight layer. This double weight storage was also used in the NCube/4+ mapping described earlier. The machine is outlined in more detail in Chapter 10.

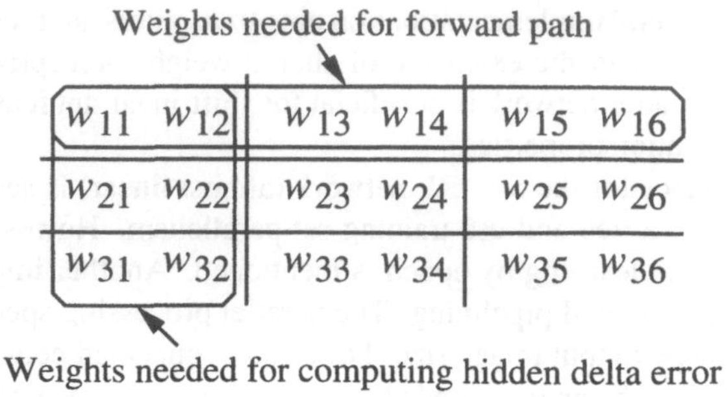

Weights needed for forward path

| $w_{11}$ $w_{12}$ | $w_{13}$ $w_{14}$ | $w_{15}$ $w_{16}$ |
|---|---|---|
| $w_{21}$ $w_{22}$ | $w_{23}$ $w_{24}$ | $w_{25}$ $w_{26}$ |
| $w_{31}$ $w_{32}$ | $w_{33}$ $w_{34}$ | $w_{35}$ $w_{36}$ |

Weights needed for computing hidden delta error

FIGURE 2.12. The output weight matrix: the weights required by processing element 1 are circled.

Figure 2.12 shows the submatrices of the output weights stored in PE 1 for a network of three output neurons. The horizontal slice is used to compute the forward pass, whereas the vertical slice is used to compute the delta error for the hidden layer. To avoid communicating the weights, each processor updates both weight subsets individually. Thus, each weight will be updated twice. Muller and associates have claimed that this implementation is faster than computing partial sums of the hidden layer delta error. A performance of 203 MCUPS is reported. In [58], Solheim has compared several neuron-based mapping schemes and found that storing the weights twice is not beneficial, except for small networks.

RAP (ring array processor) is a neurocomputer designed for continuous speech recognition at the International Computer Science Institute, Berkeley, California [59]. The machine is a DSP-based system with a low-latency ring interconnecting the PEs. Each PE consists of a TMS 320C30 DSP, and has 4 to 16 Mbyte DRAM and 256 Kbyte of local memory. FPGAs were used for the interprocessor ring and the memory controllers. Four interconnected PEs are contained on each board. To speed up the computation, a library of matrix-oriented assembly language routines were written. A working system of 40 PEs was used in the experiments. For a network with 128 neurons in each layer, the learning speed for a vertically sliced feed-forward network was 57.3 MCUPS. Recall speed was 211.1 MCPS.

Based on the experiences of designing RAP, the CNS-1 (Connectionist Network Supercomputer-1) was designed [60]. It is proposed to supply orders of magnitude more computing capability than RAP. Custom designed VLSI digital processing nodes for neural network calculations are connected in a mesh topology and operate independently in a MIMD style. This is different from RAP, which uses standard, commercially available components. The initial system will be built with 128 processing nodes and a total of 4 GB distributed storage. The processor consists of a scalar CPU, a vector coprocessor running at 125 MHz, and hardware for communication, which are all comprised in a single chip. A PE consists of the processor chip and DRAM memory, minimizing the board area required per processor. The goal is that the minimum configuration should perform recall at 100 GCPS and learning should in the worst case be one-fifth of the recall speed.

*Sandy* is a ring-based neurocomputer developed by Fujitsu [61, 62]. The system is based on TMS320C30, and the PEs are connected by a ring bus. The mapping of BP training is by neuron parallelism, that is, vertical slicing. A prototype has been built, running Nettalk learning at 42 MCUPS.

RENNS (REconfigurable Neural Network Server) is a DSP-based parallel computer designed at the Norwegian University of Science and Technology (NTNU). It is a flexi-

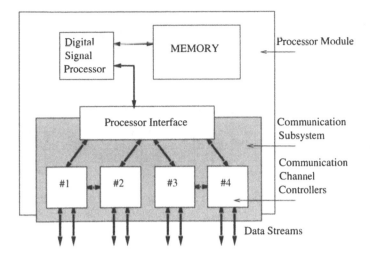

FIGURE 2.13. Block diagram of the RENNS Module.

ble, general-purpose neurocomputer designed to experiment with adapting the hardware to the problem at hand. One of the differences to general-purpose parallel computers is the flexibility of the communication network. An in depth description of the system is given in [58, 63, 64]. The computer is operative with 15 processing elements, called processing modules (PMs). Each consists of a processor module and a communication subsystem. A block diagram of the RENNS module is shown in Figure 2.13. The RENNS communication subsystem is implemented in field programmable gate arrays (FPGAs), thus it can be reconfigured in-system to meet different requirements from ANN algorithms.

Several training algorithms for different neural networks models have been implemented on the RENNS system. Several different parallel implementations of self-organizing feature maps (SOM) have been constructed by Myklebust [63, 65–69]. Solheim has implemented several backpropagation learning programs based on neuron parallelism [58, 70, 71]. Torresen has implemented a BP program combining neuron parallelism and pipelining in a flexible way [25 (in Chapter 7)]. Utne has implemented variants of the Hopfield network [64].

*2.2.2.7 Commercially Available Digital Neurocomputers.* During recent years several neurocomputers have approached the market. They are all designed in digital technology,[5] and most of them are general-purpose machines. To obtain high performance they consist of custom-designed VLSI circuits, some of them with reduced floating point precision. The neurocomputers presented in this section all provide both learning and recall.

One of the first commercially available VLSI neural implementations to offer on-chip learning was the CNAPS-1064 (Connected Network of Adaptive Processors) chip from Adaptive Solutions, Inc. [72, 73]. Low cost is emphasized for inclusion in commercial applications. Each PE was made as small as possible to maximize the number of PEs on a single chip. The chip contains a parallel array of 64 PEs, called processing nodes (PNs), configured for SIMD operation, as depicted in Figure 2.14. The CNAPS Server II offers from 64 to 512 PNs.

---

[5]The authors have not seen information about commercial machines using other technologies.

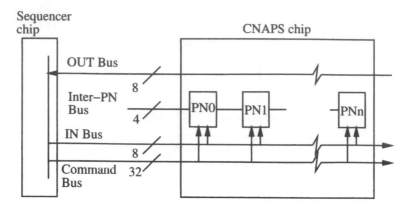

FIGURE 2.14. The CNAPS architecture, consisting of processing nodes (PNs) connected together by three global buses. A sequencer chip controls the flow of data and commands on the buses.

Each processor is a simple digital signal processor with 4 Kbyte of local memory. Each chip can compute 960 million multiply-accumulate operations per second. The weights can be 1, 8, or 16 bits. Multiple chips can be connected and are controlled by a single sequencer chip. The mapping of the feed-forward network is by neuron parallelism, that is, one or more neuron(s) is computed in each PN. Neurons from different layers may either be mapped to the same PN or separate PNs. The Nettalk network learned more than 40 times faster on a CNAPS chip than on a Sun SparcStation.

A similar chip is designed by Hitachi and included into its MY-NEUPOWER neuro-computer [74]. One chip consists of eight digital microprogrammable PEs, each of which includes local memory for on-chip learning. The machine has been shown to learn at a maximum speed of 1.26 GCUPS. Thirty-two neural chips are placed on each neural board. Two neural boards are connected by a bus, which interconnects all the processing elements. This makes a total of 512 processing elements. The weights are either 8 or 16 bits. The digital processing elements operate in SIMD mode, as depicted in Figure 2.15. Performance measurements show that the computer can learn 100 to 1,000 times faster than a workstation.

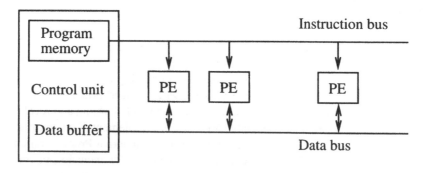

FIGURE 2.15. The MY-NEUPOWER computer architecture.

SYNAPSE-1 (SYnthesis of Neural Algorithms on a Parallel Systolic Engine) is a general-purpose neurocomputer developed by Siemens AG [75, 76]. The design of the computer is shown in Figure 2.16.

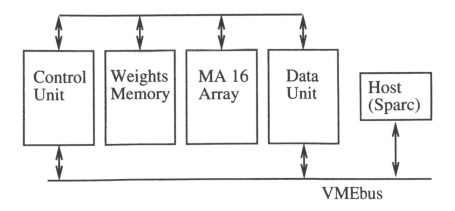

FIGURE 2.16. The SYNAPSE-1 neurocomputer.

It consists of four separate boards. The intensive parts of the neural computation are undertaken in the MA16 array, whereas nonintensive computation is performed by the data unit. The design differs from many others by storing the weights on a separate board. The MA16 array is a two-dimensional systolic array of ASIC neural signal processors (MA16s) arranged in two rows of four columns. Each MA16 consists of a linear systolic array of four processing modules. A local memory is connected to each MA16 for storing intermediate results. The weight resolution default is 16 bits. A programming language, called nAPL (neural algorithms programming language), is defined for the computer. The SYNAPSE-1 has proved to be 8,000 times faster than a Sun SparcStation 2 for computation of one layer of neurons. The peak performances of the CNAPS server and the SYNAPSE-1 are stated to be similar. However, SYNAPSE-1 needs less additional hardware for running large applications.

The SNAP (SIMD numerical array processor) system is designed by HNC for speeding up neural network applications [77, 78]. It is based on a general-purpose chip, HNC100, designed with a SIMD systolic linear array of four processors, each of which implements 32-bit floating-point arithmetic operations. Figure 2.17 shows the layout of the SNAP

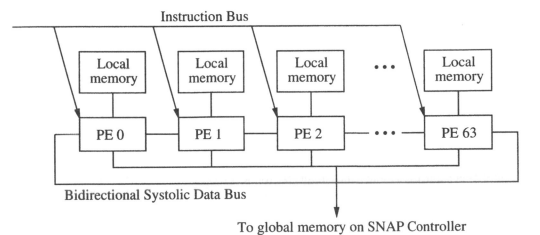

FIGURE 2.17. The SNAP-64 architecture.

system. Each PE contains a local memory of 512 Kbyte. All the PEs are controlled by a single instruction from the external controller. Each PE is connected to a triple-ported global memory for communication to the host processor or peripherals. The global data bus allows data in the global memory to be broadcast to all PEs at the same time. Alternatively, data in a single PE can be broadcast. The SNAP system comprises one to four boards, each with four HNC chips, making a total of 16 to 64 SNAP processing elements in the linear ring array. The largest system of 64 PEs provides 2.56 GFLOPS. A feed-forward network with 512 neurons in each layer learned at 302 MCUPS on the system of 64 PEs, whereas 64 neurons in each layer learned at 76.6 MCUPS [79].

**General Remarks.** Except for SYNAPSE-1, all the systems operate in SIMD mode. The PEs are made as simple as possible to include as many as possible on a single chip. The BP parallelization scheme is based on neuron parallelism. It is interesting to note that synapse parallelism has not been of interest so far.

An important issue when designing a neurocomputer is the I/O interface. Research applications on neurocomputers have in some cases performed a thousand times slower than peak performance due to I/O limits [60].

*2.2.2.8 Other Technologies.* The survey of BP implementations have been for digital target architectures. However, work is also continuing into the use of other technologies like analog and optoelectronics. These are based, respectively, on analog voltage levels and light for signal representation. Because these technologies are not yet commercialized, this study does not include a survey. Description of the many proposals for VLSI implementations (both digital and analog) has also been omitted here. Many of these are only "paper projects" that have not yet been implemented in silicon.

A survey by Nordström and Svensson on the parallel implementation of neural network includes descriptions of some special-purpose neural hardware systems [1].

A survey by Hirai looks at hardware implementations of neural networks in Japan [80]. Several characteristics of neural chips are listed in Table 2.1.

TABLE 2.1. Advantages and disadvantages of different chip technologies (from [80]).

|  | Advantages | Disadvantages |
|---|---|---|
| Analog | Compact<br>High speed | Susceptible to process-parameter variation<br>Susceptible to noise<br>Lacks scalability<br>The precision of synaptic weights is limited<br>Difficult to make modifiable synapses |
| Optoelectronics | Large fan-in and fan-out<br>Modifiable synapses possible | Optoelectronic and electro-optic transformation<br>Susceptible to noise and parameter variation |
| Digital | High precision<br>High scalability<br>Modifiable synapses | Large circuit size |

The digital approach is currently the best solution to implement neural networks with high precision, even though the circuit size for neural networks becomes larger than for the other approaches. The scalability of digital chips allows many chips to be easily connected. To attain scalability, many analog chips employ a 1-bit digital output. Hirai concludes that for special-purpose use, which does not require high precision, analog internal circuits with digital output is the best solution. For general-purpose use and where high precision is required, the digital approach is the best. Another opinion [81] is that often it is desirable to process analog sensor/actuator data without conversion to digital form. Moreover, for reasons of speed or integration a number of tasks require hardware (preferably analog) implementation [82].

One of the benefits of custom design is that the designer can limit the precision to that required by the neural algorithm. However, how much the precision can be reduced is limited. Franzi reported that for fixed point representation, the neural learning only converged in a few cases [83].

Garth [82] gave the following reasons for why so few commercial systems implementing neural networks in hardware have emerged:

- Hardware solutions are often poorly equipped to accept modification to algorithms as they arise due to the trade-off between efficiency and flexibility.

- Difficulties in providing a complete solution. External pre- and post-processing may obviate many of the advantages of the neural chip.

- Many chips achieve much of their speedup by severely restricting the precision in the number of bits. These restrictions may affect the performance of the network.

There seems to be an inverse proportional relation between performance speed and reconfigurability. By making special-purpose chips it is impossible to gain both high speed and reconfigurability. Neural chips often lack flexibility and scalability, compared to the general-purpose computer simulation of neural networks.

The design choice between analog and digital technology may depend on whether the research goal is biological modeling or making a programmable research tool [60]. Moreover, a theoretical high speed is useless if the machine is not flexible enough to do what the user requires.

TABLE 2.2. Parallel general-purpose computer mappings of BP training. A mapping is implemented on the computer unless "M" is indicated in the leftmost column. An "M" indicates that a theoretical model of the system is used.

| Computer | Number of PEs | Tr. Set Parallelism | Pipelined | Neuron Parallelism | Synapse Parallelism | Mapping |
|---|---|---|---|---|---|---|
| AP1000 [17 (in Chapter 7)] | 512 | x | x | x | | H |
| AP1000 [19 (in Chapter 9)] | 512 | x | | x | | A |
| CM-2 [21] | 64K | x | | x | | H |
| CM-2 [3] | 16K | | | x | x | H |
| CM-5 [22] | 512 | | | x | x | H |
| CM-5 [23] | 32 | x | | x | x | H |
| CM-5 [11] | 256 | x | | x | x | A |
| DAP 600 [32] | 4,096 | x | | x | x | |
| DREAM [33] (M) | | | | | x | A |
| GF-11 [17] | 356 | | | | | H |
| Hypercube (M) [34] | | | x | x | x | A |
| Intel iPSC/860 [19] | 32 | | | x | x | H |
| Mesh (M) [30] | | | x | x | x | A |
| MP-1 [14] | 4,096 | x | | x | x | H |
| MP-1 [12] | | | | x | x | H |
| MP-1 [15] | 16K | x | | x | | H |
| NCube/4+ [5] | 16 | | | x | | H |
| Q-x system (M) [28] | 64 | x | | x | | H |
| SCAP (M) [8, 40] | | | | x | x | A |
| Systolic array (M) [35] | | | x | x | x | A |
| Warp [24] | 10 | x | | | | H |

*2.2.2.9 Summary of the Parallel Mapping Schemes.* The degrees of parallelism used in parallel schemes on general purpose architectures are listed in Table 2.2. Neuron parallelism is most often used, while pipelining is rarely used. Table 2.3 indicates the parallel

TABLE 2.3.  Transputer implementations of BP. An "M" in the leftmost column indicates that a theoretical model of the system is used.

| Computer | Number of PEs | Tr. Set Parallelism | Pipelined | Neuron Parallelism | Synapse Parallelism | Mapping |
|----------|---------------|---------------------|-----------|--------------------|--------------------|---------|
| TLA/PLA [10] | 16 | | | x | x | A |
| 2D-torus [48] | 16 | | x | x | x | H |
| Ring (M) [50] | 15 | x | x | | | A |
| Ring [51] | 80 | x | | x | x | A |
| Ring (M) [52, 53] | | x | | | | H |
| Ring [49] | 32 | x | | | | H |
| Tree [55] | 9 | x | | | | H |
| Hypercube [56] | 8 | x | | | | H |
| Hypercube [57] | 16 | x | | | | H |

TABLE 2.4.  BP neurocomputer implementations.

| Computer | Number of PEs | Tr. Set Parallelism | Pipelined | Neuron Parallelism | Synapse Parallelism | Mapping |
|----------|---------------|---------------------|-----------|--------------------|--------------------|---------|
| CNAPS [72, 73] | 512 | | | x | | |
| MUSIC [6] | 45 | | | x | | H |
| MY-NEUPOWER [74] | 512 | | | x | | |
| RAP [59] | 40 | | | x | | H |
| Sandy [62] | 256 | | | x | | H |
| SNAP [79] | 256 | | | x | | H |

mapping schemes used for transputer technologies. Training-set parallelism is often used, probably to minimize the communication bottleneck of transputer systems. For neurocomputers, only implementations employing neuron parallelism are yet published, as shown in Table 2.4. However, few implementations for these computer architectures have been reported.

The majority of parallel *implementations* in the undertaken survey are of the heuristic kind, as shown in Table 2.2. The assignment of processors to each degree of parallelism does not change according to the network size and training set size. This represents a problem because only a few neural network applications will train near optimum for fixed implementations.

The proposed algorithmic mappings are, with a few exceptions [10, 11, 51], only theoretical studies. Moreover, some sophisticated methods are suggested but only implemented on small systems, such as 16 transputers [10].

*2.2.2.10  Summary of the Performance.*  The training performance of the parallel backpropagation implementations presented in Section 2.2.2 are listed in Table 2.5.  Performance is measured in CUPS.

The Nettalk network has been used in many of the reports. However, the commercial neurocomputer companies seem to avoid using this benchmark. Because different networks are used to measure the learning speed, direct comparison between them is not possible. Also, the comments in Section 1.3.1.4 regarding the CUPS measure should be borne in mind when comparing the results. The performance is highly dependent on the degree of optimization of the program code [86]. The double loops can be organized so that the data variables can be kept in fast memory. To optimize speed, the code must be written in assembly language.

TABLE 2.5. Performance of neural network training. $\mu$ is the weight update interval, and FP is the floating point precision. The horizontal lines separate general-purpose computers, transputer systems, and neurocomputers, respectively.

| Computer | Number of PEs | Network Size | $\mu$ | FP | MCUPS |
|---|---|---|---|---|---|
| Sun-3 [19] | 1 | Nettalk | 1 | 32 | 0.034 |
| NCube/4+ [5] | 16 | Optimal network | 1 | 32 | 0.19 |
| Sun SparcStation 10 [84] | 1 | | 1 | 32 | 1.1 |
| Alpha Station [84] | 1 | | 1 | 32 | 3.2 |
| CM-2 [85] | 16K | Nettalk (60) | 1 | | 2.8 |
| Cray 2 [22] | 4 | $257 \times 256 \times 131,072$ | 1 | 32 | 10[1] |
| iPSC/860 [19] | 32 | Nettalk (80) | 2,000 | 32 | 11 |
| MP-1 [14] | 4,096 | $128 \times 64 \times 16$ | 1,536 | 32 | 12 |
| IBM RISC/6000 550 [86] | 1 | $1000 \times 1000 \times 1$ | 1,000 | 32 | 17.6 |
| Cray X-MP [22] | 4 | $257 \times 256 \times 131,072$ | 1 | 32 | 18[1] |
| CM-5 [23] | 32 | Nettalk (80) | lbb | 32 | 18.33 |
| CM-2 [21] | 65,536 | Nettalk (80) | 4,096 | 32 | 40 |
| Cray Y-MP [22] | 2 | $257 \times 256 \times 131,072$ | 1 | 32 | 40[1] |
| MP-1216 [15] | 16,384 | Nettalk (120) | lbb | 32 | 41 |
| Q-x system [28] | 64 | $256 \times 128 \times 256$ | 8,192 | 32 | 44[1] |
| CM-5 [11] | 256 | $1024 \times 256 \times 64$ | lbe | 32 | 50 |
| Fujitsu VP-2400/10 [25] | 1 | Nettalk (60) | 1 | 32 | 60 |
| CM-5 [22] | 512 | $257 \times 256 \times 131,072$ | 1 | 32 | 76 |
| AP1000 [19 (in Chapter 7)] | 512 | Nettalk(120) | 906 | 32 | 86 |
| CM-2 [87] | 64k | $128 \times 128 \times 128$ | 65,536 | 32 | 350 |
| TLA [10] | 16 | $256 \times 64 \times 256$ | 1 | 32 | 0.6 |
| Transputers [54] | 53 | Nettalk (60) | 1,500 | 32 | 1.54 |
| MEIKO [51] | 120 | $512 \times 256 \times 64$ | 30 | 32 | 8 |
| Sandy [62] | 32 | Nettalk (60) | 1 | 32 | 42 |
| Cellular arch. [88] | 4,175 | Nettalk (60) | 1 | 16 | 51.5[1] |
| SNAP [79] | 64 | $64 \times 64 \times 64$ | | 32 | 76.6 |
| RAP [59] | 40 | $640 \times 640 \times 640$ | 1 | 32 | 102 |
| MUSIC [6] | 45 | | 1 | 32 | 203 |
| SNAP [79] | 64 | $512 \times 512 \times 512$ | | 32 | 302 |
| Sandy [62] | 256 | Optimal network | 1 | 32 | 567 |
| MY-NEUPOWER [74] | 512 | Optimal network | | 16 | 1,260 |
| CNAPS [72,73] | 512 | $1,900 \times 500 \times 12$ | 1 | 16 | 2,379[1] |

[1]The performance has been estimated or simulated (not measured).

### 2.2.3  Neural Network Applications

To efficiently utilize parallel processing for speeding up neural network training, we should be aware of which types of networks and training sets are used in today's neural applications. This section provides a survey of neural network applications. Mainly large applications, where parallel processing is of interest, will be described. Feed-forward neural network (FF-NN) with a single hidden layer is assumed unless otherwise stated.

Two of the main contributors to the neural network research, Widrow and Rumelhart, recently published a paper called "Neural Networks: Applications in Industry, Business and Science" [89]. They list a wide variety of commercial applications for neural networks. The increase in commercial products in past years is partly explained by the availability of an increasingly wider array of dedicated hardware. Many of the products have to be cheap to be of commercial interest.

#### 2.2.3.1  Speech.

**Speech Recognition.**  Several research groups are working on the difficult task of continuous speech recognition. Promising results using neural networks are described in [90]. However, the network and training set need to be large. For recognizing 300 sentences (speaker independently), the system achieved 4 to 5 percent error, which is competitive with statistically based systems. For a larger recognition problem, the error for the neuralnetwork system became twice that of the best mainstream system. However, the mainstream system is larger than the neural-network-based system. As the speech networks get larger they tend more toward networks that are not fully connected [60]. This is in the form of fully connected subnets.

**Speech Synthesis.**  Nettalk is a two-layer feed-forward network that transforms text to phonemes[6] using 203 input units, 60 to 120 hidden units, and 26 output units [91]. The input to the network is a series of seven consecutive letters from one of the training words, as seen in Figure 2.18.

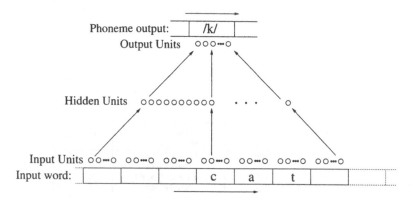

FIGURE 2.18. Schematic drawing of the Nettalk network.

The central letter is the one for which the phonetic output is to be produced. The three letters on each side of central character help to determine the pronunciation. The input word is scrolled through the window of seven letters so that each letter, one after another, is placed in the center of the window. The network can be used for continuous text or a dictionary of words. For the latter approach, the words are moved through the window individually. Thus, empty letters are added in front of and after the input word, as seen in Figure 2.18. For a 1,000-word training set, a 98-percent correct transformation was reported. The training set is freely available and is often used as a benchmark.

### 2.2.3.2  Image Processing.

**Satellite Images.**  Remote sensing is of interest for agricultural, environmental, and weather-control applications. For some of these it is necessary to identify human-made structures like roads or residential areas. Wolfer has shown that neural networks can be used to extract roads in raw Landsat TM images [92].

**Face Recognition.**  High order neural networks have been used for human face recognition [93]. The network consists of a preprocessing network followed by a feed-forward network with one or two hidden layers. Four image planes, each of $16 \times 16$ elements are input to the network. The originally proposed network had to be reduced to make computer simulations possible on an i486 personal computer. The recognition rate varied according to the transforming (scaling and rotation) of the input image. In the best case, over 96 percent of the transformed training patterns were classified correctly.

---

[6]Elementary speech sounds.

**Medical Imaging.** Much research is published within the field of medical imaging [94]. Molecular biology is one area in which neural networks often outpace traditional tried methods. However, in most other areas, neural networks have not yet been shown to outperform statistical techniques. A feed-forward neural network used for cancer cell classification is described in [95]. A classification accuracy of as high as 96.8 percent was obtained. The method is based on using extracted features from the raw image as input to the network.

McKenna investigated analyzes of smears for cervical cancer [96]. Eighty features were derived from the Fourier spectrum of each $256 \times 256$ pixel image and used as input to the network. The classification rate was 92.9 percent, higher than the 91.3 percent achieved by the Bayesian classifier[7]. One hidden layer resulted in better performance than two hidden layers. The classification rate achieved by using the neural network was, for all experiments, higher than that acheived by using the Bayesian classifier. A second experiment indicated that images of higher resolution improved the classification rate.

Blood vessel detection in angiograms has been shown to obtain a superior 92 percent classification performance by using BP trained networks, compared to 68 percent and 83 percent for Bayesian maximum likelihood classifier (MLE) and iterative ternary classification (ITC), respectively [97]. Including more hidden layers was shown not to result in a performance improvement.

**Object Inspection.** Object recognition is one of the key problems in factory automation. Kang [98] proposed a system for inspection of objects moving down a conveyor belt based on a feed-forward neural network. A correct recognition of 94 percent was obtained for the two objects used in the experiments.

Onda and colleagues [99] designed a neural system for identifying metal welding defects. The average identification rate is 75 percent, reported to be approximately equivalent to that obtained by expert engineers. Training of the network required about three hours on their neuroboard-based system.

Shiotani and associates [100] showed that a FF-NN can be used to speed up the recognition of overlapping plant cell objects. The neural network directs the movement of a window to place an object of interest within the window. Afterward, a template matching system is used to check the located object.

**Road and Obstacle Recognition.** Tsinas described a vision system for real-time recognition of traffic situations [101]. Separate FF-NNs are used for recognizing the driving lane and obstacles on the lane, respectively. The time for processing an image of a road scene varied between 0.1 s and 0.65 s on a 486 PC running at 50 MHz. Recognition of 2 minutes of real time video recording reported the one obstacle present and produced one false alarm.

**Image Compression.** Multilayer neural networks can be used to transform image data into compressed data by reducing the spatial redundancy [102]. The number of neurons in the hidden layer is chosen to be smaller than in the input and output layer. Thus, the output of the hidden layer is a compressed image, and the output layer decompresses the image. In order to increase the generalization properties, the image is dived into blocks. By dividing the original image into $8 \times 8$ pixel blocks and using an adaptive compression ratio according to the complexity of each block, Cho and associates obtained a 25:1 compression ratio [103]. However, they reported higher ratios by use of self-organizing maps.

---

[7]Statistical pattern recognition.

**Optical Character Recognition.**   Recognition of characters in printed documents seems to be almost error free, whereas handwritten characters still make recognition prone to errors. In the work of Diep, the network recognizes multisize and multifont printed characters successfully [104]. Garis achieved handwritten writer-independent digit recognition of 92 percent [105]. The network consists of a preprocessing network followed by a single hidden-layer network. However, combining two neural networks, one that inputs the digit image and one that inputs the contour of the digits, resulted in 97.8 percent correct recognition [106].

**Recognizing Paper Bills and Coins.**   Automatic recognition of paper bills and coins is an important issue for vending machines and within the banking industry. Error-free recognition of Japanese or US paper currency is proposed by Takeda and Omatu [107]. To reduce the size of the network, a technique called *random masks* is used. Some parts of the scanned input are covered using random masks. The sum of the pixels not covered is used as input to one input unit. Other masks are used for the other input units. The masks used in the training of the network are also applied when the network is used for recognition. This method implies that the number of weights in the network can be reduced to one-tenth of the original number without increasing the recognition error.

A coin classification system can be based on several different kinds of sensors – acoustic and weight based, used as inputs to a FF-NN. A system of this kind used for the recognition of British coins obtained an accuracy rate of 100 percent [108].

### 2.2.3.3   Miscellaneous Applications.

**Weather Prediction.**   Weather prediction normally involves computations using approximations of complex mathematical models. The prediction models require detailed information of the areas to be studied. Carpintero and associates [109] used adaptive time-delay neural networks for local, short-term weather forecasting. The input is METOSAT images and local information about temperature, pressure, speed and wind direction, and visibility. Promising predictions of temperature and wind speed were obtained, although no comparison with traditional methods was undertaken.

Rainfall prediction using a neural network with two hidden layers is presented in [110]. Infrared-light and visible-light images from geostationary meteorological satellite (GMS) are used as input data. An average classification accuracy of approximately 90 percent is reported.

**Sonar Return Classification.**   Gorman and associates [111, 112] used feed-forward neural network to the classification of sonar returns from two underwater targets, a metal cylinder and a similar shaped rock. The network classification performance was shown to be better than that of trained human listeners. The network uses one hidden layer and 60 continuous-valued input units. The best performance was achieved in the case of 24 hidden units. However, this was only slightly better than that achieved with only 12 hidden units. Two output units were used, where (1, 0) represented a return signal from a metal cylinder, and (0, 1) represented a return signal from a rock. A set of 208 returns (111 cylinder returns and 97 rock returns) were used in the experiments.

### 2.2.3.4 Commercial Products.

**Magnetic Character Reader.** Verifone has developed the Onyx check reader, which does magnetic-ink character recognition (MICR) of the digits on the bottom of checks. The company claims 99.6 percent accuracy even with checks that are crumpled or overwritten [113]. The character reader uses a custom chip designed by Synaptics. The chip combines a retina-like optical sensor with a neural network.

**Financial Forecasting.** By training a neural network to mimic a market, its prediction can be used to guide investments. As described by Hammerstrom [113], many companies are secretly using neural networks for various financial tasks. However, little information is available on their methods and results, because neural networks have demonstrated an outstanding performance. A system mentioned in the article was tried for two months with a $10 million investment. The performance was 2.8 percent above benchmarked performance.

**Process Control.** Neural networks are ideal for process control because they can build predictive models of the process directly from multidimensional data collected from sensors [113]. The networks need history, which is often abundant, and not theory, which is often absent. Thus, neural networks are well-suited for predicting, controlling, and optimizing industrial processes.

TABLE 2.6. Neural network applications using feed-forward neural networks. A reference to the data set is given if it is freely available. (P) indicates that a preprocessing network is used in front of the FF-NN inputs.

| Application | Data Set | Network Size $(I \times H \times 0)$ | No of Tr. Pat. |
|---|---|---|---|
| Blood vessel detection in angiograms [97] | | $121 \times 17 \times 2$ | 75 |
| Cancer cell classification [95] | | $3,600 \times 20 \times 1$ | 467 |
| Coin recognition [108] | | $259 \times 5 \times 6$ | |
| Handwritten digit recognition (P) [105] | [114] | $32 \times 15 \times 10$ | 2,000 |
| Image compression [103] | | $64 \times 8, 6, 4 (\times 64)$ | |
| Location of plant cells in images [100] | | $100 \times 15 \times 10$ | 52;67;69 |
| Nettalk text to phonemes [91] | [115] | $203 \times 60 - 120 \times 26$ | 5,438 |
| Object detector [101] | | $961 \times 50 \times 1$ | 50 |
| Object inspection [98] | | $4,096 \times 64 \times 2$ | |
| Optical character recognition [104] | | $3,000 \times 20 \times 94$ | 94 |
| Optical character recognition [104] | | $2,500 \times 100 \times 94$ | 1,128 |
| Papanicoloau smear cell classification [96] | | $80 \times 6 \times 1$ | 702 |
| Paper currency recognition [107] | | $128 \times 64 \times 12$ | |
| Road classifications in satellite images [92] | | $56 \times 20 \times 1$ | 552 |
| Speech recognition [90] | | $234 \times 1,000 \times 61$ | 1,300,000 |
| Speech recognition [90] | | $351 \times 4,000 \times 61$ | 6,000,000 |
| Welding defect identification [99] | | $15 \times 10 \times 9$ | 1,024 |

TABLE 2.7. Freely available data training sets.

| Data Set | Number of Elements per Pattern | Number of Patterns |
|---|---|---|
| 26 capital letters, 20 different fonts [116] | 16 units | 20,000 |
| Isolated handwritten digits (49 writers) [114] | $32 \times 32$ pixels | 3,471 characters |
| Nettalk corpus [115] | 29 per character | 20,008 English words |
| Sonar return data [117] | 60 units | 208 |

*2.2.3.5   Summary of Applications.*    Table 2.6 lists a summary of backpropagation applications. As far as possible, variations in the network structure are indicated. Some freely available training sets are given in Table 2.7.

*2.2.3.6   Do Neural Network Applications Need Parallel Hardware?*    From the survey in the previous section, at least two common characteristics of many applications are noticeable. They indicate that the ANNs are quite different from the complex organization of the human brain. First, the networks are small enough to be trained and applied on a computer with a single processor. Only in a few instances has parallel processing been used. The survey concentrated on large networks, thus many other applications using small networks have been omitted. Second, the output neuron layer often consists of a small number of neurons. The latter indicates that allocation of many processors for computing the output layer is unnecessary.

Several researchers have reported the need for selection of good feature vectors to make the network smaller and executable on their serial computers. They demonstrate that the same level of performance can be obtained as when using larger networks. Reports about improved performance by using larger neural network are few. Mainly all are based on a single hidden weight layer. Most of the published applications are from academic work. Because commercial companies rarely publish in scientific conferences, many commercial applications probably exist that are not described here.

It is obvious that some of the neural network applications require parallel processing; for example, for speech recognition this is required both for training of the network and for recognition of real-time speech when the network is applied. However, many applications can be successfully implemented without parallel hardware. This may also be necessary for a product to be marketable, such as for control applications in consumer products. However, it is still possible for parallel processing to be used to reduce the *training time* of an application.

## 2.3   Conclusions on Neural Applications and Parallel Hardware

Section 2.2.3.6 reported that few researchers studying neural network applications were using parallel processing. Section 2.2.2, reported that researchers making parallel programs and hardware for neural computing have mainly been running one or a few benchmark programs, for example, Nettalk. In addition, for some instances only the maximum obtainable performance is reported. This is usually based on a large, nonrealistic-sized network.

To make parallel computers more accessible to application developers, a standardized neural network language is needed. Several languages have been proposed, for example, PYGMALION [118], without leading to frequent employment.

It would seem that parallel processing will be employed in the future for applications that need fast real-time performance, such as speech recognition and image processing applications. A market for special-purpose hardware for sensor and control applications will also exist. These assumptions are supported by the fact that the number of *hardware-*related papers submitted to neural network conferences is said to be dropping. However, the remaining papers are principally about sensor and control applications.

Few experiments have been undertaken to see if a larger and more complex neural network together with a larger number of training patterns can gain a better application performance, that is, recognition rate, than the neural models used today. Parallel processing seems to be the tool to make such experiments possible. If it becomes a success, it may make artificial neural networks the number-one method for many applications, as neural networks today are striving to show better performance than traditional methods.

# References

[1] T. Nordstrom and B. Svensson, "Using and designing massively parallel computers for artificial neural networks," *Journal of Parallel and Distributed Computing*, vol. 14, pp. 260–285, March 1992.

[2] A. Singer, "Implementation of artificial neural networks on the Connection Machine," *Parallel Computing*, vol. 14, pp. 305–315, Summer 1990.

[3] C. Rosenberg and G. Blelloch, "An implementation of network learning on the Connection Machine.," in *Connectionist Models and their Implications.* (D. Walz and J. Feldman, eds.), pp. 329–340, Ablex, Norwood, NJ, 1988.

[4] H. Yoon, J. H. Nang, and S. Maeng, "Parallel simulation of multilayered neural networks on distributed-memory multiprocessors," *Microprocessing and Microprogramming*, vol. 29, pp. 185–195, 1990.

[5] E. Kerckhoffs, F. Wedman, and E. Frietman, "Speeding up backpropagation training on a hypercube computer," *Neurocomputing*, vol. 4, pp. 43–63, 1992.

[6] U. Muller, B. Baumle, P. Kohler, A. Gunzinger, and W. Guggenbuhl, "Achieving supercomputer performance for neural net simulation with an array of digital signal prosessors," *IEEE Micro*, pp. 55–65, October 1992.

[7] T. Yukawa and T. Ishikawa, "Optimal parallel back-propagation schemes for mesh-connected and bus-connected multiprocessors," in *Proc. of IEEE Int. Conference on Neural Networks*, pp. 1748–1753, 1993.

[8] W.-M. Lin, V. K. Prasanna, and K. W. Przytula, "Algorithmic mapping of neural network models onto parallel SIMD machines," *IEEE Transactions on Computers*, vol. 40, pp. 1390–1401, December 1991. ISSN: 0018-9340.

[9] Y. Fujimoto, "An enhanced parallel planar lattice architecture for large scale neural network simulation," in *Proc. of Int. Joint Conference on Neural Networks*, vol. 2, (San Diego), pp. 581–586, 1990.

[10] Y. Fujimoto, N. Fukuda, and T. Akabanc, "Massively parallel architecture for large scale neural network simulation," *IEEE Trans. on Neural Networks*, vol. 3, pp. 876–887, November 1992.

[11] V. Kumar, et. al., "A scalable parallel formulation of the back propagation algorithm for hypercubes and related architectures," *IEEE Trans. on Parallel and Distributed Systems*, vol. 5, pp. 1073–1090, October 1994.

[12] G. Chinn, et. al., "Systolic array implementations of neural nets on the MasPar MP-1 massively parallel processor," in *Proc. of Int. Joint Conference on Neural Networks*, vol. II, pp. 169–173, 1990.

[13] K. A. Grajski, *Parallel Digital Implementations of Neural Networks*, pp. 51–76. PTR Prentice Hall, 1993. In Neurocomputing using the MasPar MP-1.

[14] A. d' Acierno and R. Vaccaro, "A parallel implementation of the back-propagation or errors learning algorithm on a SIMD parallel computer," in *Proceedings of Int. Conference on Artificial Neural Networks*, pp. 1074–1077, 1993.

[15] Andreas Zell, et. al., "Problems of massive parallelism in neural network simulation," in *Proc. of IEEE Int. Conference on Neural Networks*, pp. 1890–1895, 1993.

[16] K. Hwang, *Advanced Computer Architecture: Parallelism, Scalability, Programmability*. McGraw-Hill, Inc., 1993.

[17] M. Witbrock and M. Zagha, "An implementation of backpropagation learning on GF11, a large SIMD parallel computer," *Parallel computing*, vol. 14, pp. 329–346, 1990.

[18] S. Tang, M. J. Niccolai, and M. W. Bringmann, "A model for the execution of a neural network upon a multiprocessor," in *Proc. of the Fifth Workshop on Neural Networks: Academic/Industrial/NASA/Defene*, pp. 259–262, 1993.

[19] D. Jackson and D. Hammerstrom, "Distributing back propagation networks over the Intel iPSC/860 hypercube," in *Proc. of Int. Joint Conference on Neural Networks*, vol. I, pp. 569–574, 1991.

[20] L. W. Tucker and G. G. Robertson, "Architecture and Applications of the Connection Machine," *Computer*, vol. 21, pp. 26–38, Aug. 1988.

[21] X. Zhang, "The backpropagation algorithm on grid and hypercube architectures," *Parallel Computing*, vol. 14, pp. 317–327, Summer 1990.

[22] X. Liu and G. L. Wilcox, "Benchmarking of the CM-5 and the Cray machines with a very large backpropagation neural network," in *Proc. of IEEE Int. Conference on Neural Networks*, vol. 1, pp. 22–27, 1994.

[23] J. Adamo and D. Anguita, "Object oriented design of a BP neural network simulator and implementation on the Connection Machine (CM-5)," tech. rep., International Computer Science Institute, September 1994. TR-94-46.

[24] D. A. Pommerleau, et. al., "Neural network simulation at warp speed: How we got 17 million connections per second," in *Proc. of IEEE Int. Conference on Neural Networks*, 1988.

[25] E. Sànchez, S. Barro, and C. Regueiro, "Artificial neural networks implementation on vectorial supercomputers," in *Proc. of IEEE Int. Conference on Neural Networks*, (Orlando, FL), pp. 3938–3943, June 28 - July 2, 1994.

[26] W. Allen and A. Saha, "Parallel neural-network simulation using back-propagation for the ES-kit environment," in *Proc. of 1989 Conference Hypercubes, Concurrent Computers and Application*, pp. 1097–1102, 1989.

[27] L.-C. Chu and B. W. Wah, "Optimal mapping of neural-network learning on message-passing multicomputers," *Journal of Parallel and Distributed Computing*, vol. 14, pp. 319–339, 1992.

[28] A. M. Alhaj and H. Terada, "Exploiting parallelism in neural networks on a dynamic data-driven system," *IEICE Trans. on fundementals*, vol. E76 A, pp. 1804–1811, October 1993.

[29] V. Kumar, A. Grama, A. Gupta, and G. Karypis, *Introduction to parallel computing*, ch. 5. Benjamin-Cummings, 1993.

[30] Y. Suzuki and L. Atlas, "A comparison of processor topologies for a fast trainable neural network for speech recognition," in *Proc. IEEE Intl. Conference on Acoustics, Speech and Signal Processing, Glasgow*, May 1989.

[31] M. E. Azema-Barac, "A conceptual framework for implementing neural networks onto massively parallel machines," in *6th International Symposium on Parallel Processing (IPPS)*, (IEEE Press), pp. 527–530, 1992.

[32] M. E. Azema-Barac, "Neural network implementations and speed-up on massively parallel machines," *Microprocessing and microprogramming*, vol. 35, pp. 747–754, 1992.

[33] S. Shams and J.-L. Gaudiot, "Implementing regularly structured neural networks on the DREAM machine," *IEEE Trans. on Neural Networks*, vol. 6, pp. 407–421, March 1995.

[34] Q. Malluhi, M. Bayoumi, and T. Rao, "A parallel algorithm for neural computing," in *Proc. of World Congress on Neural Networks*, vol. 2, pp. 563–569, 1994.

[35] S. Y. Kung, "Parallel architectures for artificial neural nets," in *IEEE International Conference on Systolic Arrays* (K. Bromley, S -Y. Kung, and E. Swartzlander, eds.), pp. 163–174, IEEE Computer Society Press, 1988.

[36] S. Y. Kung and J. N. Hwang, "A unified systolic architecture for artificial neural networks," *Journal of Parallel and Distributed Computing*, vol. 6, pp. 358–387, 1989.

[37] S. Y. Kung and J. N. Hwang, "A unifying algorithm/architectures for artificial neural networks," in *Proc. of International Conference on Acoustics, Speech and Signal Processing*, vol. 4, pp. 2505–2508, 1989.

[38] S.-Y. Kung and W.-H. Chou, "Parallel Digital Implementations of Neural Networks," in *Mapping of neural networks onto VLSI array processors* (K. W. Przytula and V. K. Prasanna, eds.), ch. 1, pp. 3–49, PTR Prentice Hall, 1993.

[39] S. Kung, *Digital Neural Networks*. PTR Prentice Hall, 1993.

[40] K. W. Przytula, V. K. Prasanna, and W.-M. Lin, "Parallel implementations of neural networks," *Journal of VLSI Signal Processing*, vol. 4, pp. 111–123, May 1992.

[41] J. G. Eldredge and B. L. Hutchings, "RRANN: The run-time reconfiguration artificial neural network," in *Proc. of the IEEE Custom Intergrated Circuits Conference*, pp. 77–80, 1994.

[42] N. M. Botros and M. Abdul-Aziz, "Hardware implementation of an artificial neural network using field programmable gate arrays," *IEEE Trans. on Industial Electronics*, vol. 41, pp. 665–667, December 1994.

[43] A. Linde, T. Nordstrom, and M. Taveniku, "Using FPGAs to implement a recon-figurable highly parallel computer," in *Selected papers from: Second International workshop on Field-Programmable Logic and Applications (FPL'92)*, pp. 199–210, Springer-Verlag, 1992.

[44] S. L. Bade and B. L. Hutchings, "FPGA-based stochastic neural networks – Imple-mentation," in *Proc. of IEEE Workshop on FPGAs for custom computing machines*, pp. 189–198, 1994.

[45] J. M. J. Murre, "Transputers and neural networks: An analysis of implementation constraints and performance," *IEEE Trans. on Neural Networks*, vol. 4, pp. 284–292, March 1993.

[46] H. Yoon and J. H. Nang, "Multilayer neural networks on distributed-memory multi-processors," in *INNC*, pp. 669–672, 1990.

[47] I. Cloete and J. Ludik, "Parallelization of artificial neural networks on transputers," in *Proc. of the International Conference on Parallel Computing '91*, pp. 367–373, Elsevier Science Publishers B.V., 1992.

[48] A. Petrowski, G. Dreyfus, and C. Girault, "Performance analysis of a pipelined backpropagation algorithm," *IEEE Trans. on Neural Networks*, vol. 4, pp. 970–981, November 1993.

[49] H. Paugam-Moisy, "Parallel neural computing based on neural network duplicat-ing," in *Parallel algorithms for digital image processing, computer vision and neu-ral networks* (I. Pitas, ed.), ch. 10, pp. 305–340, John Wiley & Sons, 1993.

[50] S. Zickenheimer, M. Wendt, B. Klauer, and K. Waldschmidt, "Pipelining and paral-lel training of neural networks on distributed-memory multiprocessors," in *Proc. of IEEE Int. Conference on Neural Networks*, vol. 4, pp. 2052–2057, 1994.

[51] A. d' Acierno and R. Vaccaro, "The back-propagation learning algorithm on parallel computers: A mapping scheme," in *Proc. of Sixth Italian Workshop Neural Nets WIRN VIETRE – 93*, (Salerno), pp. 249–254, 1994.

[52] S. K. Foo, et. al., "A theoretical study of training set parallelism for backpropagation networks on a transputer array," in *Proc. of World Congress on Neural Networks*, vol. 2, pp. 519–524, 1994.

[53] S. K. Foo, P. Saratchandran, and N. Sundararajan, "Comparison of parallel and se-rial implementation of feedforward neural networks," *Journal of Microcomputer Applications*, vol. 17, pp. 83–94, January 1995.

[54] S. K. Foo, P. Saratchandran, and N. Sundararajan, "Analysis of training set paral-lelism for backpropagation neural networks," *Int. Journal of Neural Systems*, vol. 6, pp. 61–78, March 1995.

[55] K. Diakonikolaou, S. Kollias, D. Kontoravdis, and A. Stafylopatis, "Implementa-tion of neural network learning strategies on a transputer-based parallel architec-ture," in *Parallel and Distributed Computing in Engineering Systems. Proc. of the IMACS/IFAC International Symposium*, pp. 365–370, North-Holland, June 1991. ISBN: 0 444 89276 1.

[56] W. K. King, G. Pieroni, D. M. Barreca, and B. Zupan, "A fast implementation of the back-propagation algorithm," in *Proc. of Sixth Itallan Workshop Neural Nets WIRN VIETRE – 93*, (Salerno), pp. 218–226, 1994.

[57] D. M. Weber, "Parallel implementation of time delay neural networks for phoneme recognition," in *Proc. of IEEE Int. Conference on Neural Networks*, pp. 1583–1587, 1993.

[58] J. G. Solheim, *The RENNS approach to neural computing*. PhD thesis, Norwegian Institute of Technology, In preparation.

[59] N. Morgan, et. al., "The ring array processor (RAP): A multiprocessing peripheral for connectionist applications," *Journal of Parallel and Distributed Computing*, vol. 14, 1992. Special Issue on Neural Networks.

[60] K. Asanovic, J. Beck, J. Feldman, N. Morgan, and J.Wawrzynek, "Designing a connectionist network supercomputer," *International Journal of Neural Systems*, vol. 4, pp. 317–326, December 1993. ISSN: 0129-0657.

[61] Hideki Kato, et. al., "A parallel neurocomputer architecture with ring registers," in *Proc. of an international conference organized by the IPSJ to commemorate the 30th anniversary*, pp. 233–240, 1990.

[62] H. Yoshizawa and K. Asakawa, "Highly parallel architecture for back-propagation using a ring register data path," *Fujitsu Sci. Tech. J*, pp. 227–233, September 1993.

[63] G. Myklebust, *Implementations of an unsupervised neural network model on an experimental multiprocessor system*. PhD thesis, Norwegian Institute of Technology, 1996. ISBN 82-7119-893-9.

[64] L. Utne, *Design of a reconfigurable neurocomputer Performance analysis by implementation of recurrent associative memories*. PhD thesis, Norwegian Institute of Technology, 1995. ISBN 82-7119-793-2.

[65] G. Myklebust, J. Solheim, and J. Greipsland, "Self organizing maps on a reconfigurable computer," in *Proceedings of the Sixth International Conference on Signal Processing Applications and Technology*, Oct. 1995.

[66] G. Myklebust and J. G. Solheim, "Parallel Self-organizing Maps for actual applications," in *Proceedings of the IEEE International Conference on Neural Networks*, Dec. 1995.

[67] G. Myklebust, J. G. Solheim, and E. Steen, "Speeding up small sized Self Organizing Maps for use in visualization of multispectral medical images," in *Eighth IEEE Symposium on Computer-Based Medical Systems*, (Lubbock, Texas), pp. 103–110, IEEE Computer Society Press, June 1995.

[68] G. Myklebust, J. G. Solheim, and E. Steen, "Wavefront implementation of Self Organizing Maps on RENNS," in *International Conference on Digital Signal Processing*, (Limassol, Cyprus), pp. 268–273, 1995.

[69] G. Myklebust, J. G. Solheim, and J. Tørresen, "Parallel implementations of self organizing maps on RENNS," in *Proceedings of The Norwegian Neural Network Seminar*, SINTEF Instrumentation, Dec. 1994. Report no. STF31 S94026, ISBN 82-595-8893-5.

[70] J. G. Solheim and G. Myklebust, "RENNS - an experimental computer system with a reconfigurable interconnection network," in *Proceedings of the First International Workshop on Parallel Processing (IWPP '94)*, (Bangalore, India), pp. 205–210, Tata McGraw Hill, Dec. 1994.

[71] J. G. Solheim and G. Myklebust, "RENNS - a Reconfigurable Computer System for Artificial Neural Networks," in *Proceedings of first IEEE International Conference on Algorithms and Architectures for Parallel Processing, Brisbane, Australia*, pp. 197–206, Apr. 1995.

[72] D. Hammerstrom, "A VLSI architecture for high-performance, low cost, on-chip learning," in *Proc. of Int. Joint Conference on Neural Networks*, vol. 2, pp. 537–542, 1990.

[73] D. Hammerstrom, "CNAPS - 1064 Digital parallel processor," 1992. Product information AR800A, Adaptive solutions, Inc.

[74] Yuji Sato, et. al., "Development of a high-performance, general purpose neurocomputer composed of 512 digital neurons," in *Proc. of Int. Joint Conference on Neural Networks*, pp. 1967–1970, 1993.

[75] U. Ramacher, et. al., "Multiprocessor and memory architecture of the neurocomputer SYNAPSE-1," in *Proc. of World Congress on Neural Networks*, vol. 4, pp. 775–778, 1993.

[76] U. Ramacher, W. Raab, J. Anlauf, U. Hachmann, and M. Weßeling, "SYNAPSE-1 – a general-purpose neurocomputer," tech. rep., SIEMENS AG, Feb. 1993.

[77] R. W. Means, "High speed parallel hardware performance issues," in *IEEE International Conference on Neural Networks (ICNN'94)* (S. K. Rogers, ed.), pp. 10–16, June 28–July 2 1994.

[78] R. W. Means and K. P. Qing, "Parallel image, signal and neural network processing with HNC's vision processor (ViP) and HNC's SIMD numerical array processor (SNAP)," in *Int. parallel processing symposium (IPPS)*, 1993.

[79] SNAP – SIMD Numerical Array Processor, "High-performance parallel computing," 1994. Product information, Technology Development Division, HNC.

[80] Y. Hirai, "Hardware implementations of neural networks in Japan," *Neurocomputing*, vol. 5, pp. 3–16, 1993.

[81] A. F. Murray, "Analogue neural VLSI: Issues, trends and pulses," in *Artificial Neural Networks* (I. Aleksander and J. Taylor, eds.), vol. 2, pp. 35–43, Elsevier Science Publishers B.V., 1992.

[82] S. C. J. Garth, "To simulate or not to simulate...," in *Artificial Neural Networks* (I. Aleksander and J. Taylor, eds.), vol. 2, pp. 1397–1403, Elsevier Science Publishers B.V., 1992.

[83] E. Franzi, "Neural accelerator for parallelization of back-propagation algorithm," *Microprocessing and Microprogramming*, vol. 38, pp. 689–696, 1993.

[84] U. A. Muller, "A high performance neural net simulation environment," in *Proc. of IEEE Int. Conference on Neural Networks*, (Orlando), pp. 1–4, 1994.

[85] G. Blelloch and C. R. Rosenberg, "Network learning on the Connection Machine," in *Proc. of IJCAI87*, pp. 323–326, 1987.

[86] D. Anguita, G. Parodi, and R. Zunino, "An efficient implementation of BP on RISC-based workstations," *Neurocomputing*, vol. 6, pp. 57–65, 1994.

[87] A. Singer, "Exploiting the inherent parallelism of artificial neural networks to achieve 1300 million interconnects per second," in *Proc. of International Neural Networks Conference*, (Paris, France), pp. 656–660, July 9-13 1990.

[88] B. Faure and G. Mazare, "A cellular architecture dedicated to neural net emulation," *Microprocessing and Microprogramming*, vol. 30, pp. 249–256, August 1990.

[89] Bernard Widrow, et. al., "Neural networks: Applications in industry, business and science," *Communication of ACM*, vol. 37, pp. 93–105, March 1994.

[90] N. Morgan, "Using a million connections for continous speech recognition," in *Proc. of Int. Conference On Neural Network Processing*, pp. 1439–1444, October 1994.

[91] T. J. Sejnowski and C. R. Rosenberg, "Parallel networks that learn to pronounce English text," *Complex Systems*, vol. 1, pp. 145–168, 1987.

[92] James Wolfer, et. al., "Robust multispectral road classificatiuon in Landsat thematic mapper imagery," in *Proc. of World Congress on Neural Networks*, vol. 1, pp. 260–268, 1994.

[93] R. Foltyniewicz and S. Skoneczny, "An improved high order neural network for invariant recognition of human faces in gray scale," in *Proc. of World Congress on Neural Networks*, vol. 1, pp. 587–592, 1994.

[94] J. N. Weinstein, "Neural networks in the biomedical sciences: A survey of 386 publications since the beginning of 1991," in *Proc. of World Congress on Neural Networks*, vol. 1, pp. 121–126, 1994.

[95] Y. Hu, et. al., "Neural network based cancer cell classification," in *Proc. of World Congress on Neural Networks*, vol. 1, pp. 416–421, 1994.

[96] S. J. McKenna, et. al., "High-resolution classification of Papanicoloau smear cells using back-propagation neural networks," in *Proceedings of Int. Conference on Artificial Neural Networks*, pp. 907–910, 1993.

[97] R. Nekovei and Y. Sun, "Back-propagation network and its configuration for blood vessel detection in angiograms," *IEEE Trans. on Neural Networks*, vol. 6, pp. 64–72, January 1995.

[98] Y.-I. Kang, "Creation of an inpection system combining backpropagation networks and image processing system," in *Proc. of Int. Conference On Neural Network Processing*, pp. 174–179, 1994.

[99] H. Onda, "Neural network application to welding defect identification," *FUJITSU Sci. Tech. Journal*, vol. 29, pp. 271–277, September 1993.

[100] Shigetoshi Shiotani, et. al., "Fast recognition of overlapping targets using neural networks," in *Proc. of Int. Conference On Neural Network Processing*, (Seoul), pp. 614–619, 1994.

[101] L. Tsinas and V. Graefe, "Coupled neural networks for real-time road and obstacle recognition by intelligent road vehicles," in *Proc. of Int. Joint Conference on Neural Networks*, (Nagoya, Japan), 1993.

[102] N. Sonehara, et. al., "Image data compression using a neural network model," in *Proc. of Int. Joint Conference on Neural Networks*, vol. 2, (Washington, D.C.), pp. 35–40, 1989.

[103] K. B. Cho, et. al., "Image compression using multi-layer perceptron with block classification and SOFM coding," in *Proc. of World Congress on Neural Networks*, vol. 3, pp. 26–31, 1994.

[104] T. A. Diep and H. I. Avi-Itzhak, "A neural network approach to high accuracy optical character recognition," in *Proc. of World Congress on Neural Networks*, vol. 3, pp. 76–86, 1994.

[105] M. D. Garris, "Methods for enhancing neural network handwritten character recognition," in *Proc. of Int. Joint Conference on Neural Networks*, vol. 1, pp. 695–700, July 1991.

[106] A. Thepaut and Y. Autret, "Handwritten digit recognition using combined neural networks," in *Proc. of Int. Joint Conference on Neural Networks*, pp. 1365–1368, 1993.

[107] F. Takeda and S. Omatu, "High speed paper currency recognition by neural networks," *IEEE Trans. on Neural Networks*, vol. 6, pp. 73–77, January 1995.

[108] M. D. Emmerson and R. I. Damper, "Determining and improving the fault tolerance of multilayer perceptrons in a pattern-recognition application," *IEEE Trans. on Neural Networks*, vol. 4, pp. 788–793, September 1993.

[109] A. Carpintero, et. al., "Weather forecasting with adaptive time-delay neural networks: A case study," in *Proc. of Int. Conference On Neural Network Processing*, pp. 842–846, 1994.

[110] T. Chen and M. Takagi, "Rainfall prediction of geostationary meteorological satellite images using artificial neural network," in *Int. Geoscience and Remote Sensing Symposium*, vol. 3, pp. 1247–1249, 1993.

[111] R. P. Gorman and T. J. Sejnowski, "Analysis of hidden units in a layered network trained to classify sonar targets," *Neural networks*, vol. 1, pp. 75–89, 1988.

[112] R. P. Gorman and T. J. Sejnowski, "Learned classification of sonar targets using a massively parallel network," *IEEE Trans. on acoustics, speech and signal processing*, vol. 36, no. 7, pp. 1135–1140, 1988.

[113] D. Hammerstrom, "Neural networks at work," *IEEE Spectrum*, vol. 30, no. 6, pp. 26–32, 1993.

[114] N. I. of Standards and Technology, "*fl3* subset of the NIST Special Database 1, obtainable from sequoyah.ncsl.nist.gov in pub/databases/data/."

[115] T. J. Sejnowski, "NETtalk corpus." from ftp.idiap.ch in pub/benchmarks/neural/nettalk.tar.Z.

[116] D. J. Slate, "Letter image recognition data, obtainable from ics.uci.edu in pub/machine-learning-database/letter-recognition," 1991.

[117] T. J. Sejnowski, "Sonar, mines vs. rocks." obtainable from ftp.idiap.ch in pub/benchmarks/neural/sonar.data.Z.

[118] P. Trealeaven and R. Rocha, "Towards a general-purpose neurocomputing system," in *Silicon Architectures for Neural Nets. Proceedings for the IFIP WG 10.5 Workshop*, pp. 167–177, North Holland, November 1991. ISBN: 0-444-89113-7.

# Part I

# Analysis of Parallel Implementations

# Chapter 3

## Network Parallelism for Backpropagation Neural Networks on a Heterogeneous Architecture

**R. Arularasan**
**P. Saratchandran**
**N. Sundararajan**
**Shou King Foo**
School of Electrical Engineering,
Nanyang Technological University,
Singapore

### 3.1 Introduction

Backpropagation (BP) [1] is one of the most widely used training algorithms for multi-layer neural networks. However, the BP algorithm is computationally intensive and training times on the order of days and weeks are not uncommon for this algorithm on serial machines [2,3]. As a result, considerable interest has been focused on studying parallel implementations [4–7] and efficient mappings of this algorithm [8,9] on a variety of parallel machines.

Two main paradigms are used for parallelizing the BP algorithm. They are the network-based parallelism, and the training-set parallelism [10]. In network-based parallelism, the neural network is partitioned and distributed among the processing nodes. The common approach to partitioning is through the so-called vertical slicing [11–13] of the network. Each processor then simulates a vertical slice (that is, groups of neurons belonging to different layers) of the neural network over the whole training set. In training-set parallelism the training patterns are partitioned and distributed over the processors (that is, the training set is sliced and one slice is assigned to each processor while keeping a complete copy of the whole neural network in each processing node). A study of training-set parallelism on a heterogeneous transputer network in a ring topology is presented in the Chapter 4 as a sequel to this discussion.

Network-based parallelism uses *on-line learning,* in which the weights are updated after each pattern; training-set parallelism uses *batch learning,* in which the weights are updated after all the patterns are presented. The advantage of on-line learning is faster convergence, especially for problems with a large training set that possess redundant information. Further it is the only choice if all the training examples are not available, at the start of the training and continuous adaptation to a stream of training patterns is required. Batch learning is in general slow in overall convergence, but if all the patterns are available batch learning can be useful to avoid mutual interference of the weight changes due to different patterns. For a detailed discussion of the advantages and disadvantages of on-line and batch learning schemes, see Chapter 3 in [14].

In this study, network-based parallelism is used as the paradigm for mapping the BP onto a heterogeneous processor network in a ring configuration. Heterogeneous networks consist of processors of different speed, memory, and cost. They offer a very powerful environment for high-performance computing and are becoming increasingly popular as a parallel computing medium [15]. However, heterogeneous processing presents a number of challenges not found in traditional high-performance parallel machines. Because different processors run at different speeds, mapping an algorithm onto a heterogeneous network requires a very informed approach. The BP algorithm using network-based parallelism is known to have a high communication overhead [16], and this makes it rather difficult to distribute the neural network among the various processors so that no processor idles too long waiting for interprocess communication. The usual practice of equally dividing the neurons in each layer among the processors will be inefficient as faster processors will take less time to finish their computations and will have lengthy waiting periods before data transfer to and from the slower processors. Any arbitrary allocation could result in a severe load imbalance and consequently negate the potential high computational performance to be gained from the heterogeneous network. Thus the need for a sound analysis of the allocation problem cannot be over emphasized. But such analyses require a mathematical model of the BP running on heterogeneous hardware. In the literature on parallel implementation of BP, a rigorous mathematical model of the hardware is often missing. The general practice has been to study the performance of various mappings from experimental results. The shortcomings of such purely experimental approaches are that (1) they are very time consuming and (2) they restrict evaluations to only those hardware resources available to the experimenter. A good theoretical model allows evaluation of alternate mapping strategies and processor configurations without the need to perform costly experiments. A theoretical model is also essential to find the *optimal* mapping of a neural network on a given processor configuration. This motivated us to develop a rigorous mathematical model of the BP running on a heterogeneous processor network and use the model to obtain optimal mappings for various benchmark problems.

The objective of the study is thus twofold. The first goal is to develop a mathematical model for a heterogeneous network and obtain, for any given mapping of the neural network, an expression for the time for a training iteration in terms of the timings for elemental computation and communication operations of the different processors. The next goal is to address the issue of finding the optimal mapping to minimize the time for a training iteration for a neural network on a given heterogeneous processor network. Time for a single iteration is chosen as the objective for the minimization because parallel mappings can only reduce the time per training iteration and not the total number of iterations required for the overall convergence of the BP algorithm. The number of iterations required for convergence depends on the parameters of the BP, such as the learning rate, momentum rate, and so on.

The mathematical model is developed by analyzing the computations and communications that each processor needs to perform in a training iteration and decomposing these operations into elemental computing and communication operations. An expression for the time for an iteration can then be derived in terms of the timings for the elemental computation and communication operations. Finding the optimal mapping requires finding the optimal allocation of neurons to the processors so as to minimize the time for an iteration. Analysis of the expression for the time per iteration shows that the optimal allocation problem for the heterogeneous processor network is a nonlinear mixed integer optimization (NLMIO) problem. Two solution strategies for the optimization problem is considered. The first one uses a genetic algorithm (GA) approach to directly solve the NLMIO problem. The second method approximates the NLMIO problem to a linear mixed integer optimization problem and then uses a heuristic method to solve it. The optimal distributions from the two methods are obtained for the Encoder [17] and Nettalk [18] benchmark problems on a number of heterogeneous networks. The time for an iteration corresponding to the optimal distribution is then obtained from the heterogeneous networks. It turns out that both methods need more or less same time to obtain their solutions, and the resulting optimal iteration times are also very similar. A Monte Carlo study is then carried out to statistically verify the proximity of these solutions to the global optimum for the NLMIO problem. The mean and standard deviation for iteration times obtained from the Monte Carlo study on several sample sizes are compared with the optimal iteration times obtained from the GA and approximate linear heuristic (ALH) methods. The results show the optimal iteration time to be more than $3\sigma$ lower than the sample mean. This indicates that the optimal solutions obtained from the two methods are quite close to the global optimum.

The real benefit of obtaining the optimal distribution is investigated by looking at the time taken to solve the NLMIO problem in the context of the overall training time. The overall training time from the optimal mapping is compared with that of several heuristic mappings, and savings in training time accruing from optimal mapping is found to be considerably more than the extra time needed to solve the NLMIO problem.

Finally, the theoretical model is used for homogeneous processor arrays to find the optimal number of processors for the Encoder and Nettalk benchmark problems. It is found that the optimal number of processors is neural network dependent.

The chapter is organized as follows. Section 3.2 describes the processor topology used in the study. Section 3.3 deals with the parallelization of the backpropagation training algorithm. A mathematical model for the parallelized BP is developed and an expression for the time for a training iteration of the parallelized algorithm is derived in this section. Experimental verification of the model is performed in Section 3.4 on heterogeneous networks rigged in the laboratory using transputers of different speed and memory as processing elements. Section 3.5 analyzes the issue of optimal distribution of the neural network among the various processors to give minimum training time. It is shown that finding the optimal distribution is an NLMIO problem. Section 3.6 describes the two solution strategies and provides experimental results for iteration times from heterogeneous processor networks for the Encoder and Nettalk benchmark problems. The Monte Carlo study and its results are discussed in Section 3.7. Section 3.8 looks at the time taken to find the optimal distribution and discusses the worthwhileness of obtaining the optimal solution in the context of overall training time. The section also looks at the effect of processor location on the optimal iteration time. The section also offers a cost-benefit analysis using the theoretical model, and presents the optimal number of processors for homogeneous processor arrays. Section 3.9 summarizes the overall conclusions from the study.

## 3.2 Heterogeneous Network Topology

The heterogeneous processor network used in this study is a message-passing multiprocessor ring network. The ring configuration is shown in Figure 3.1.

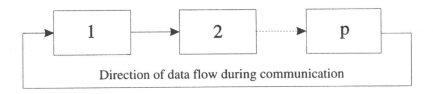

FIGURE 3.1. Processor array connected in a ring configuration.

It comprises a set of processors of different computation power and local (external) memory, and a set of communication links connecting these processors. The processor itself consists of a processing unit, on-chip memory, and a set of communication channels through which it can communicate with other processors. It is assumed there is no background workload on any of the processors. The computation power of a processor is characterized by the execution times for elemental computation operations, which in the case of this study include arithmetic and logic operations. The processor interconnection network uses the point-to-point configuration, and interprocessor message passing is carried out through synchronized communications. The time taken to transfer a message of $m$ words between two neighboring processors is given by

$$t_{comm} = t_{comm-init} + m\ t_{word}$$

where $t_{comm}$ is the total time for the transfer, $t_{comm-init}$ is the initialization time for a single transfer, and $t_{word}$ is the time to transfer one word. Note that the all-to-all broadcast operation commonly employed in the vertical partitioning method [13] cannot be used here as the processors are heterogeneous and communications and computations can overlap in the network used in this study.

## 3.3   Mathematical Model for the Parallelized BP Algorithm

This section presents the mathematical model for the network-based parallel BP algorithm implemented on heterogeneous processor arrays. Section 3.3.1 describes the computation and communication steps involved in executing one iteration of the parallelized BP algorithm on a heterogeneous processor network. The sequence of events that occurs are shown with the help of a timing diagram. Section 3.3.2 shows the expression for the time for an iteration of the BP algorithm.

### 3.3.1   Timing Diagram for the Parallelized BP Algorithm

As network-based parallelism with vertical partitioning is used as the parallelizing method, each processor will have some neurons from each layer of the neural network. But because of heterogeneity, the number of neurons contained in each processor will in general be different from the others. Figure 3.2 shows such a mapping. In this implementation, processors hold the incoming and outgoing weights of the hidden and output layer neurons that reside in them. Such a scheme is used in [11, 12] for a homogeneous processor network to improve the speed of the forward and backward passes of BP. In the forward pass, each processor computes the activations for the neurons contained in it. In order to do this it is necessary to have the activation values of all neurons from the previous layer. This means each processor has to transfer the activations (of its neurons) of each layer to all other processors once these have been computed. Because the processor network is heterogeneous, all processors will not complete their computations at the same time, and this causes processors to wait before sending data to or receiving data from their neighbors. A similar reaction occurs while calculating the *deltas* during the backward pass of the BP algorithm.

In this study, neural networks with a single hidden layer are considered, as most applications of neural networks use such networks. Extension of the model to cover neural networks with multiple hidden layers is straightforward.

Neurons from the input layer are not partitioned among the processors as they do not perform any computations, thus all the processors have a copy of all the input neurons and input training patterns. Only hidden and output neurons are partitioned. As the output

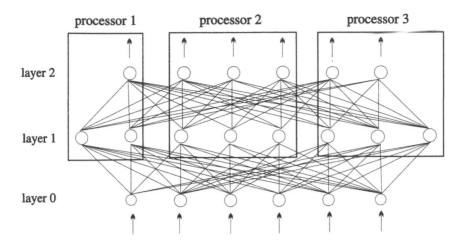

FIGURE 3.2. Network partitioning for a heterogeneous array of processors.

neurons are partitioned, each processor stores only the output patterns associated with the neurons residing in it.

The following steps are involved in executing one iteration of the parallelized back-propagation algorithm.

1. The processors calculate the activations for the hidden layer neurons residing in them. Because the processors are heterogeneous, it cannot be assumed that they finish this computation all at the same time.

2. Each processor needs the activations of all the hidden neurons of the neural network before it can commence the next computation. Hence it sends the activations of its neurons to all the other processors as soon as these have been computed. Because this is true for all the processors, the total number of communication steps required at worst is $n * \lceil \frac{n}{2} \rceil$, where $n$ is the number of processors in the network. Note that in the case of a homogeneous network with equal neuron allocation this can be performed by a single all-to-all broadcast requiring $(n - 1)$ communication steps. Only in the ideal load balancing case would such a situation occur for the heterogeneous network.

3. Once the activations of all the hidden neurons are received, each processor calculates the output values for all the output layer neurons residing in it. This completes the forward pass of the algorithm.

4. The backward pass involves calculation of the delta values. All processors calculate the deltas for the output neurons residing in them.

5. All processors send these delta values to all other processors. As in the case with activations, this can take up to $n * \lceil \frac{n}{2} \rceil$ communication steps.

6. The processors calculate the deltas for all the hidden neurons residing in them as soon as they have received the deltas for all the output neurons.

7. Finally, the processors calculate the weight increments and update the incoming and outgoing weights for those neurons that reside in them.

This completes one iteration of training for the parallel BP. Note that processors may experience waiting times in between the various steps. As an example, a timing diagram for step 1 and step 2 along with the possible waiting times, are shown in Figure 3.3 for a three-processor heterogeneous network.

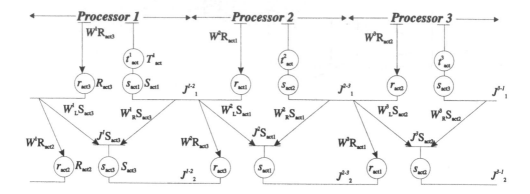

FIGURE 3.3. Timing diagram for steps 1 and 2 of the parallelized BP on a three-processor network.

The circles in the figure represent processes. The time taken for the execution of a process is indicated inside the circle. Thus $T_{act}^1$, $T_{act}^2$, and $T_{act}^3$ are the processes that compute the activations of the hidden layer neurons in processors 1, 2, and 3 respectively (that is, step 1) and $t_{act}^1$, $t_{act}^2$, and $t_{act}^3$ are the execution times needed by these processes. Because the network is heterogeneous, these processes will not finish their execution all at the same time. In step 2, the processors send and receive the activations computed in step 1 to each other. In Figure 3.3, the sending and receiving processes are indicated by capital $S$'s and $R$'s, and their execution time is represented by lowercase $s$'s and $r$'s. Various waiting times occur in the processors as they commence step 2. For example, $W^1 R_{act3}$ is the time the process $R_{act3}$ in processor 1 has to wait before receiving the activations from processor 3. Thus, the process $R_{act3}$ cannot commence together with $T_{act}^1$, even though communication and computing processes can run concurrently in our network. This is because processor 1 can only receive the activation values after processor 3 has completed $T_{act}^3$. The magnitude of this waiting will depend on $t_{act}^3$. Likewise $S_{act3}$ in processor 1 can only start (that is, send the activation received from processor 3 to processor 2) after $R_{act3}$ and $S_{act1}$ are completed. In this case, $S_{act3}$ can only occur after $R_{act3}$ because the activations from processor 3 have to be received before they can be sent out to processor 2. $S_{act3}$ also has to wait for the completion of $S_{act1}$ because it can only use the output channel after $S_{act1}$ has finished using it. This causes $S_{act3}$ to wait for the completion of $R_{act3}$ and $S_{act1}$. $W_L^1 S_{act3}$ is the waiting time because of noncompletion of $S_{act1}$ and $W_R^1 S_{act3}$ is the waiting time because of noncompletion of $R_{act3}$. This is indicated in Figure 3.3 by the temporal junction $J^1 S_{act3}$. The process $R_{act2}$ in processor 1 can commence only when $S_{act2}$ in processor 3 is ready. The waiting $R_{act2}$ experiences is $W^1 R_{act2}$. Similar waiting intervals occur for processes in processors 2 and 3 as well.

Note that step 2 involves the exchange of data (activations) between the processors. For a homogeneous processor network with equal neuron allocation, an all-to-all broadcast where the receiving and sending in each processor occurs concurrently can be used. Here the same broadcast principle is used, but the receiving and sending processes in each processor need not occur together because of processor heterogeneity or load imbalance.

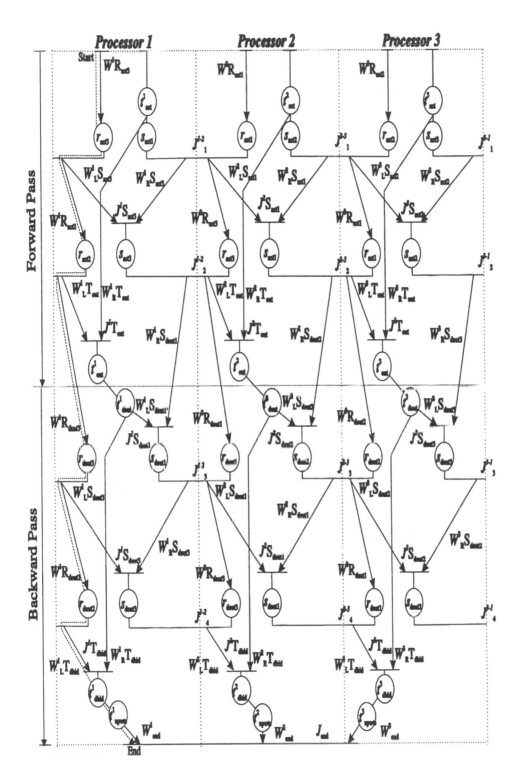

FIGURE 3.4. Timing diagram for one iteration of the parallelized BP on a three-processor network. The dotted line from "Start" to "End" indicates the path used for $t_{iter-3}$ in Equation 3.1.

A timing diagram which shows all the seven steps together with all the possible waiting times that can take place during a single iteration, is shown in Figure 3.4 for a three-processor network. To avoid too many symbols, Figure 3.4 does not contain process names, but these are obvious from the execution time indicated inside the circles. Arrows indicate waiting times that may be incurred by the processes pointed to by them. $J$'s indicate temporal junctions showing precedence relationships. The temporal junctions are characterized by a horizontal line with one or more processes connecting to it from below and one or more processes connecting to it from above. The meaning of the temporal junction is as follows: The processes connected to the horizontal bar from below can start only after the completion of all the processes connected to the horizontal bar from above. The junctions without arrows pointing toward the horizontal line indicate interprocessor communications, which are always synchronized. The $W_L$'s and the $W_R$'s on the left and right arrows pointing to a junction indicate the possible waiting times, that may be incurred by the processes connected to the junction from below. In an actual running, one of the two waiting times will be zero. The $W$'s directly pointing to a process indicate the possible waiting times that may be incurred by that process. The detailed explanation of the symbols in Figure 3.4 is as follows:

- $t^i_{act}$: The time needed to execute the process $T^i_{act}$, which computes the activations of the hidden layer neurons residing in processor $i$.

- $t^i_{out}$: The time needed to execute the process $T^i_{out}$, which computes the outputs of the output layer neurons residing in processor $i$.

- $t^i_{dout}$: The time needed to execute the process $T^i_{dout}$, which computes the deltas of the output layer neurons residing in processor $i$.

- $t^i_{dhid}$: The time needed to execute the process $T^i_{dhid}$, which computes the deltas of the hidden layer neurons residing in processor $i$.

- $t^i_{upwts}$: The time needed to execute the process $T^i_{upwts}$, which computes weight increments and updates the weights residing in processor $i$.

- $s_{acti}$ : The communication time needed by the process $S_{acti}$ to send the activations computed in processor $i$.

- $s_{douti}$: The communication time needed by the process $S_{douti}$ to send the deltas of the output layer neurons computed in processor $i$.

- $r_{acti}$: The communication time needed by the process $R_{acti}$ to receive the activations computed in processor $i$.

- $r_{douti}$: The communication time needed by the process $R_{douti}$ to receive the deltas of the output layer neurons computed in processor $i$.

- $W^i X$: The waiting time that may be incurred by the process $X$ in processor $i$.

- $W^i_L X$, $W^i_R X$: The waiting times from the left and right arrows of temporal junctions. The possible waiting time that may be incurred by the process $X$ in processor $i$ is either the waiting time coming from the left (that is, $W^i_L X$) or the waiting time coming from the right (that is, $W^i_R X$).

- $W^i_{end}$: The time processor $i$ spends waiting for the other processors to reach the end of the iteration.

- $J^i X$: The intraprocessor temporal junctions in processor $i$. The process $X$ can start only after the completion of the processes connected to the junction from left and right.

- $J_k^{i-j}$: The interprocessor temporal junctions between processors $i$ and $j$. The subscript $k$ denotes the $k$-th interprocessor temporal junction between the processors $i$ and $j$.

- $J_{end}$: The junction indicating the end of the iteration.

In the mathematical model, each of the computing and communication processes are expressed in terms of their basic operations. This is done by writing the functionality of the processes in pseudocodes and finding out the various basic operations required from those codes. The timings expressions for the various processes are shown in Appendix A3.1 in terms of elemental operations. The elemental operations are shown in Appendix A3.3.

### 3.3.2 Prediction of Iteration Time

Time for an iteration is the time taken to traverse down from the "Start" to the "End" in the timing diagram following any path. This can be calculated once the times for the various processes and the various waiting intervals are known. Because the waiting times are dependent on the times taken by the various computing and communicating processes, they can be worked out once the times for these processes are known. Following the path sketched in Figure 3.4 the equation for the time for an iteration for a three-processor heterogeneous network ($t_{iter-3}$) can be written as follows:

$$
t_{iter-3} = \sum_{k=2}^{3} [W^1 R_{actk} + r_{actk} + W^1 R_{doutk} + r_{doutk}]
$$
$$
+ W_L^1 T_{dhid} + t_{dhid}^1 + t_{upwts}^1 + W_{end}^1. \tag{3.1}
$$

Extension of Equation 3.1 for a heterogeneous network with $n$ processors is conceptually straightforward. In an $n$ processor network, for a similar path taken as in Figure 3.4, there would be only extra receiving processes and its associated waiting times. For a complete exchange of data between the processors, processor 1 has to receive data from all other processors, that is, from processors 2 to $n$. Thus, the resulting expression for $t_{iter-n}$ is given by

$$
t_{iter-n} = \sum_{k=2}^{n} [W^1 R_{actk} + r_{actk} + W^1 R_{doutk} + r_{doutk}]
$$
$$
+ W_L^1 T_{dhid} + t_{dhid}^1 + t_{upwts}^1 + W_{end}^1. \tag{3.2}
$$

Although the execution times of only a few computing and communication processes appear explicitly in Equation 3.2, the execution times of all the rest of the computing and communication processes are present implicitly in the expression through the waiting times ($W$'s). For example, to calculate the waiting time $W^1 R_{actn}$, knowledge of the time taken by the process $T_{act}^n$ is required. Thus, for a large processor network, the computation of $t_{iter-n}$ becomes tedious as more communication and computation processes and waitings are involved, and these have to be resolved first before the value of $t_{iter-n}$ can be found.

## 3.4 Experimental Validation of the Model Using Benchmark Problems

In this section theoretical iteration times obtained from Equation 3.2 are compared with iteration times experimentally obtained for a number of heterogeneous processor networks rigged in our laboratory using different models of transputers[1] on the Encoder and Nettalk benchmark problems. These benchmark problems are discussed in Section 3.4.1. The validation test setup and results are discussed in Section 3.4.2.

### 3.4.1 Benchmark Problems Used for Validation

The benchmark problems considered in this study are the Encoder [17] and Nettalk [18] problems.

The Encoder problem is made up of both an encoder and a decoder combined together. The general neural network structure of such a problem is $N$-$X$-$N$, where $N$ is the number of input and output neurons present and $X$ is the number of hidden neurons. $X$ is normally smaller than $N$ so as to perform some encoding or compression effect. The input and output patterns of the encoder is normally binary in nature unless stated otherwise. For an Encoder problem with configuration $N$-$X$-$N$, the number of training patterns used is normally $N$ unless specified otherwise. That is, there will be $N$ input patterns and $N$ output patterns. Each of the input-output neurons will take values 0 or 1. The Encoder problem is chosen because of its popularity and flexibility. A 252-126-252 Encoder network is used in this study.

In the Nettalk problem, a neural network is trained to produce proper phonemes, given a string of letters as input. The input is a seven-lettered English word. Unary encoding is used. Thus, for each of the seven letter positions in the input, the network has a set of 29 input neurons: one for each of the 26 letters in English and three for punctuation characters. Thus, there are $29 \times 7 = 203$ input neurons in all. The number of neurons from the hidden layer can vary from 0 to 120. The output of the network uses a distributed representation for the phonemes. There are 21 output neurons representing various articulatory features such as voicing and vowel height. Each phoneme is represented by a distinct binary vector over this set of 21 units. Sejnowski's [18] Nettalk neural network has five additional output neurons that encode stress and syllable boundaries. Thus, there are a total of 26 output neurons and the network has a 203-X-26 neuron structure where $X$ can vary from 0 to 120. In our network there are seven instead of five output neurons that encode stress and syllable boundaries for a finer encoding and 120 hidden layer neurons. Thus the structure of the network becomes 203-120-28.

### 3.4.2 Validation Setup and Results

The transputer is a multicomputer building block and a network of transputers is an MIMD machine because each transputer is separately programmable. The transputer models employed in our processor networks used for validation are the T805-20 (20 MHz) and the T805-25 (25 MHz). The timings for elemental computing and communication operations for these processors are measured using methods described in [19] and are given in Table A3.19 in Appendix A3.3.

In the first set of validation experiments, the time for an iteration was found for a 252-126-252 Encoder network with 252 input patterns and 63,504 connections on three different heterogeneous processor networks each having ten T805-20 (20 MHz) and four

---

[1]Freund and Sunderam [15] referred to such networks as mixed-mode heterogeneous processing networks.

T805-25 (25 MHz) transputers. For each processor network, two neuron distributions are considered. Details of the experiments are as follows:

**EXP-1(enc).** In this experiment the slow processors are followed by the fast processors in the ring as shown in Figure 3.5(a). This processor network will be referred as TYPE-1 network for the rest of the chapter. The time for an iteration from theory and experiment are obtained for the following two neuron distributions.

> *DIST-1(enc).* In this case the fast processors are allocated more neurons, than the slow processors. However, among the fast and slow processors equal distribution is followed. Thus the slow processors have seven hidden layer neurons and 16 output layer neurons, and the fast processors have 14 hidden layer neurons and 23 output layer neurons residing in them.

> *DIST-2(enc).* In this case neurons are allocated in proportion to the relative speeds of the processors. So fast processors will have proportionately more neurons residing in them than the slow ones. The leftover neurons after such an allocation are distributed among the fast processors. The slow processors are all thus allocated eight hidden and 16 output neurons. Two of the fast processors are allocated 11 hidden and 23 output neurons, and the other two fast processors are allocated 12 hidden and 23 output neurons

**EXP-2(enc).** In this experiment, the slow processors are interposed with the fast processors as shown in Figure 3.5(b). This processor network will be referred as TYPE-2 network for the rest of the chapter. The experimental and theoretical time per iteration are calculated for the same distributions DIST-1(enc) and DIST-2(enc) used in EXP-1(enc).

**EXP-3(enc).** In this experiment, the slow and fast processors are intermingled in a random way as shown in Figure 3.5(c). This processor network will be referred as TYPE-3 network for the rest of the chapter. Here too the experimental and theoretical times per iteration are calculated for DIST-1(enc) and DIST-2(enc) mappings.

Table 3.1 shows the theoretically predicted and experimentally obtained iteration times for the three experiments described. The last column of the table shows the difference between the theoretical and experimental iteration times expressed as a percentage of the experimental value:

$$\text{Difference} = \frac{t_{iter-n}^{experimental} - t_{iter-n}^{theoretical}}{t_{iter-n}^{experimental}} 100\%.$$

where, *Difference* is the percentage difference between the theoretical and experimental times per iteration, and $t_{iter-n}^{theoretical}$ and $t_{iter-n}^{experimental}$ are the theoretical and experimental times per iteration.

In the second set of validation experiments, the time for an iteration is found for a 203-120-28 Nettalk network on TYPE-1, TYPE-2, and TYPE-3 heterogeneous processor networks. Details of the experiments are as follows:

**EXP-1(net).** In this experiment, TYPE-1 network is used. The time for an iteration from theory and experiment are obtained for the following two neuron distributions.

> *DIST-1(net).* In this case the fast processors are allocated more hidden neurons than the slow processors. However, among the fast and slow processors equal distribution is followed. As there only 28 output neurons, equal distribution of

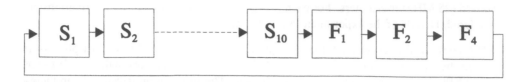

(a) TYPE-1 Network

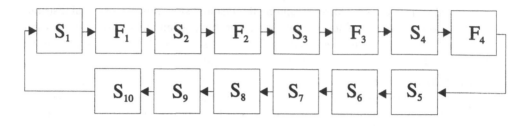

(b) TYPE-2 Network

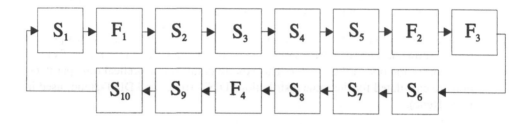

(c) TYPE-3 Network

FIGURE 3.5. TYPE-1, TYPE-2, and TYPE-3 networks. S and F denote slow and fast processors, respectively.

output neurons is followed. Thus, the slow processors have six hidden layer neurons and two output layer neurons, and the fast processors have 15 hidden layer neurons and two output layer neurons residing in them.

*DIST-2(net).* In this case neurons are allocated in proportion to the relative speeds of the processors. Therefore fast processors will have proportionately more neurons residing in them than the slow ones. The leftover neurons after such an allocation are distributed among the fast processors. The slow processors are all thus allocated eight hidden and one output neurons. Two of the fast processors are allocated 10 hidden and four output neurons, and the other two fast processors are allocated 10 hidden and five output neurons.

**EXP-2(net).** In this experiment, TYPE-2 network is used. The experimental and theoretical times per iteration are calculated for the same distributions DIST-1(net) and DIST-2(net) used in EXP-1(net).

**EXP-3(net).** In this experiment, TYPE-3 network is used. Here too the experimental and theoretical times per iteration are calculated for DIST-1(net) and DIST-2(net) mappings.

TABLE 3.1. Comparison of theoretical and experimental times per iteration for different heterogeneous processor networks for the 252-126-252 Encoder problem.

| Type of Network | Mapping used | Time for an iteration (ms) | | Difference (%) |
|---|---|---|---|---|
| | | Theoretical | Experimental | |
| TYPE-1 | Dist-1(enc) | 220.0 | 223.7 | 1.7 |
| | Dist-2(enc) | 198.1 | 204.3 | 3.0 |
| TYPE-2 | Dist-1(enc) | 220.0 | 223.9 | 1.7 |
| | Dist-2(enc) | 198.0 | 202.3 | 2.1 |
| TYPE-3 | Dist-1(enc) | 219.9 | 223.9 | 1.8 |
| | Dist-2(enc) | 198.1 | 202.3 | 2.1 |

TABLE 3.2. Comparison of theoretical and experimental times per iteration for different heterogeneous processor networks for the 203-120-28 Nettalk problem.

| Type of Network | Mapping used | Time for an iteration (ms) | | Difference (%) |
|---|---|---|---|---|
| | | Theoretical | Experimental | |
| TYPE-1 | DIST-1(net) | 84.4 | 88.0 | 4.1 |
| | DIST-2(net) | 65.9 | 68.0 | 3.1 |
| TYPE-2 | DIST-1(net) | 84.4 | 86.4 | 2.3 |
| | DIST-2(net) | 65.9 | 68.4 | 3.7 |
| TYPE-3 | DIST-1(net) | 84.4 | 86.4 | 2.3 |
| | DIST-2(net) | 65.9 | 68.2 | 3.4 |

Table 3.2 shows the theoretically predicted and experimentally obtained iteration times for all three experiments described. The last column of the table shows the difference between the theoretical and experimental iteration times expressed as a percentage of the experimental value.

The results in Tables 3.1 and 3.2 show that the theoretical predictions of the iteration times are close to the experimental times and thus validate the model.

## 3.5 Optimal Distribution of Neurons Among the Processing Nodes

In the preceding section, a mathematical model was developed and validated that allows the prediction of the iteration time for a given mapping of a neural network. This section will address the problem of finding the *optimal* mapping for a neural network on a given heterogeneous processor network using the preceding mathematical model. The objective is to find the assignment of neurons to processors so as to minimize the time for an iteration without violating any of the constraints imposed by the processor network and the neural network. The time for an iteration is given by Equation 3.2. The various constraints that need to be satisfied are described next.

### 3.5.1 Communication Constraints

These constraints are due to the type of communication used for interprocessor message passing in the processor network. In this study, interprocessor message passing uses synchronized communications, which means that a processor cannot send data to another unless the other processor is ready to receive it. In Figure 3.4 an interprocessor junction $J_k^{i-j}$ indicates the time at which the $k$-th data transfer from processor $i$ to processor $j$ is completed. Figure 3.4 shows that at junction $J_1^{1-2}$, the time at which processor 1 completes sending data to processor 2 is $t_{act}^1 + s_{act1}$, and the time at which processor 2 completes receiving data from processor 1 is $W^2 R_{act1} + r_{act1}$. These two times must be equal as interprocessor communications are always synchronized. Hence at junction $J_1^{1-2}$ the following equality must hold:

$$t_{act}^1 + s_{act1} = W^2 R_{act1} + r_{act1}$$

where $t_{act}^1$ is the time taken by the process $T_{act}^1$, $s_{act1}$ and $r_{act1}$ are times taken by the communication processes $S_{act1}$, $R_{act1}$, and $W^2 R_{act1}$ is the waiting time incurred by the process $R_{act1}$ in processor 2. Likewise, equality constraints at all other interprocessor junctions can be formulated. For the processor $i$ in an $n$ processor network, these constraints can be expressed in a compact matrix form as

$$A_1^i = B_1^i \tag{3.3}$$

where

$$A_1^i = \begin{bmatrix} (t_{act}^i + s_{acti}) \\ (W_R^i S_{actj} + s_{actj}) \\ (W_R^i S_{doutk} + s_{doutk}) \end{bmatrix}, \quad B_1^i = \begin{bmatrix} (W^m R_{acti} + r_{acti}) \\ (W^m R_{actj} + r_{actj}) \\ (W^m R_{doutk} + r_{doutk}) \end{bmatrix},$$

and $j$, $k$, and $m$ are given by[2]

$$ring(i-1,n) \leq j \leq ring(i-(n-2),n),$$
$$ring(i,n) \leq k \leq ring(i-(n-2),n),$$
$$m = ring(i+1,n).$$

### 3.5.2 Temporal Dependence Constraints

These constraints occur mainly because communication and computation can overlap in the processor network used in this study. In the timing diagram, every intraprocessor temporal junction creates a constraint. For example, at $J^1 S_{act3}$ in Figure 3.4, the following equality must hold:

$$W^1 R_{act3} + r_{act3} + W_L^1 S_{act3} = t_{act}^1 + s_{act1} + W_R^1 S_{act3}.$$

Similarly constraints at all the other intraprocessor junctions can be formulated. Again, for any processor $i$ these constraints can be expressed in a compact matrix form[3] as

$$A_2^i = B_2^i, \tag{3.4}$$
$$A_3^i = B_3^i, \tag{3.5}$$
$$A_4^i = B_4^i, \tag{3.6}$$

---

[2]The ring function is defined as

$$ring(x,n) = \begin{cases} n & \text{if } x - \lfloor \frac{x}{n} \rfloor n = 0, \\ n - \lfloor \frac{x}{n} \rfloor n & \text{if } x - \lfloor \frac{x}{n} \rfloor n \neq 0. \end{cases}$$

[3]Matrix constraint $A_3^i = B_3^i$ only exists if there are four or more processors. These constraints can be seen from the timing diagram for four or more processors.

where

$$A_2^i = \left[ \begin{array}{c} (W^i R_{actj} + r_{actj} + W_L^i S_{actj}) \\ (W^i R_{doutj} + r_{doutj} + W_L^i S_{doutj}) \end{array} \right],$$

$$B_2^i = \left[ \begin{array}{c} (t_{act}^i + s_{acti} + W_R^i S_{actj}) \\ (W_L^i T_{out} + t_{out}^i + t_{dout}^i + W_L^i S_{douti} + s_{douti} + W_R^i S_{doutj}) \end{array} \right],$$

and

$$j = ring(i-1,n).$$

$$A_3^i = \left[ \begin{array}{c} (W^i R_{actj} + r_{actj} + W_L^i S_{actj}) \\ (W^i R_{doutj} + r_{doutj} + W_L^i S_{doutj}) \end{array} \right],$$

$$B_3^i = \left[ \begin{array}{c} (W_L^i S_{actk} + s_{actk} + W_R^i S_{actj}) \\ (W_L^i S_{doutk} + s_{doutk} + W_R^i S_{doutj}) \end{array} \right],$$

and $j$ and $k$ are given by

$$ring(i-2,n) \leq j \, ring(i-(n-2),n),$$
$$k = ring(j+1,n).$$

$$A_4^i = \left[ \begin{array}{c} (\sum_{m=1}^{(n-1)} [W^i R_{actq} + r_{actq}] + W_L^i T_{out}) \\ (\sum_{m=1}^{(n-1)} [W^i R_{doutq} + r_{doutq}] + W_L^i T_{dhid}) \\ (W^i R_{actj} + r_{actj} + W_L^i T_{out} + t_{out}^i + t_{dout}^i + W_L^i S_{douti}) \\ (W^i R_{doutj} + r_{doutj} + W_L^i T_{dhid} + t_{dhid}^i + t_{upwts}^i + W_{end}^i) \end{array} \right],$$

$$B_4^i = \left[ \begin{array}{c} (t_{act}^i + W_R^i T_{out}) \\ (W_L^i T_{out} + t_{out}^i + t_{dout}^i + W_R^i T_{dhid}) \\ (W_L^i S_{actk} + s_{actk} + W_R^i S_{douti}) \\ (W_L^i S_{doutk} + s_{doutk} + W_L^j T_{dhid} + t_{dhid}^j + t_{upwts}^j + W_{end}^j) \end{array} \right],$$

and $j$, $k$ and $q$ are given by

$$j = ring(i+1,n),$$
$$k = ring(i+2,n),$$
$$q = ring(i-m,n).$$

### 3.5.3 Memory Constraints

Because each processor has fixed local memory, the number of neurons that can reside in a processor is limited. This results in the following constraint for processor $i$:

$$M_{pat}^i + M_{net-param}^i < M_{tot}^i \tag{3.7}$$

where $M_{pat}^i$ is the memory (in bytes) needed to store the training patterns and $M_{net-param}^i$ is the memory needed to store the parameters (activations, deltas, and so forth) for the slice of the network resident in processor $i$. $M_{tot}^i$ is the external memory of processor $i$. Details of the derivation of Equation 3.7 is given in Appendix A3.2.

### 3.5.4 Feasibility Constraints

Feasibility constraints include the feasibility of assignments and the feasibility of waitings.

*3.5.4.1 Feasibility of Neuron Assignments.* These constraints require that the number of neurons assigned to the processors from each layer must be nonnegative integers and their sum must equal the total number of neurons in that layer in the neural network. So for every layer $l$ of the neural network (except the input layer),

$$\sum_{i=1}^{n} N_l^i = N_l^{tot}, \tag{3.8}$$

$$N_l^i \geq 0, \text{ for all } l. \tag{3.9}$$

Here $N_l^i$ is the number of neuron allocated to processor $i$ from layer $l$, and $N_l^{tot}$ is the total number of neurons in the neural network from layer $l$. $l$ ranges from 1 (hidden layer) to 2 (output layer). Note that the input layer is not partitioned and every processor has a copy of all the input neurons.

*3.5.4.2 Feasibility of Waitings.* The intraprocessor waiting times must be nonnegative:

$$W^i X \geq 0 \tag{3.10}$$

$$W_L^i X \geq 0 \tag{3.11}$$

$$W_R^i X \geq 0 \tag{3.12}$$

$$W_{end}^i \geq 0. \tag{3.13}$$

### 3.5.5 Optimal Mapping

Finding the optimal distribution of neurons, that is, $N_l^i$, among the processors to minimize the time for an iteration ($t_{iter-n}$ in Equation 3.2) subject to the constraints given by Equations 3.3 to 3.13, is a nonlinear mixed integer optimization (NLMIO) problem:[4]

$$\min_{N_l^i, W} \{t_{iter-n}\}, \quad 1 \leq i \leq n; \ 1 \leq l \leq 2 \tag{3.14}$$

subject to

$$A_k^i = B_k^i, \ 1 \leq k \leq 4$$

$$M_{pat}^i + M_{net-param}^i < M_{tot}^i$$

$$\sum_{i=1}^{n} N_l^i = N_l^{tot}$$

$$N_l^i \geq 0$$

$$W^i X \geq 0$$

$$W_L^i X \geq 0$$

$$W_R^i X \geq 0$$

$$W_{end}^i \geq 0.$$

---

[4]The problem is nonlinear because of the presence of the product of two $N_l^i$'s (decision variables) and mixed because $N_l^i$'s must be integers, but the $W^i X$'s, $W_{end}^i$'s, $W_L^i X$'s, and $W_R^i X$'s can be real numbers.

NLMIO problems are known to be NP complete [20] and their solution normally takes enormous computing time. In our NLMIO problem the decision variables are the neuron allocations for the hidden layer and output layer for each processor ($N_l^i$) and the various waiting intervals ($W$'s). A network with $n$ processors will have a total of $(6 \ n^2 - n)$ decision variables, out of which $(2 \ n)$ variables must take integer values and the rest can have real values. The number of constraints are $(10 \ n^2 - 2 \ n + 1)$. It is very clear that the complexity of the allocation problem is too overwhelming to attempt an exhaustive search.

## 3.6 Methods of Solution to the Optimal Mapping Problem

In this section two suboptimal approaches to solving the NLMIO problem are considered. These are the genetic algorithmic solution and the approximate linear heuristic solution methods.

### 3.6.1 Genetic Algorithmic Solution

In this case the nonlinear objective function of Equation 3.2 is minimized directly using a genetic algorithmic approach. Genetic algorithms are powerful search methods that mimic natural evolution and have been established as a viable technique for optimization across a variety of disciplines [21]. The GA used in this study is a slightly modified form of the simple GA used by Holland [22, 23]. The modification is in the way the chromosomes are encoded. Each element of the population (chromosome) represents a solution, that is, an allocation of neurons among the processors. The chromosomes are not encoded as binary strings; instead they are encoded as integer strings where each integer is an allele value. Thus the chromosome is encoded as $N_1^1 N_2^1 N_1^2 N_2^2, \ldots, N_1^n N_2^n$. Further, after every recombination the allele values are normalized to ensure that the constraints on neuron assignments described in Section 3.5.4.1 are not violated. The basic steps in our GA are the same as that of the simple genetic algorithm [24] as shown in Figure 3.6.

A description of the various components of the GA used in the optimization problem is described next.

*3.6.1.1 Initial Population.* GA begins to find an optimal solution from a set of randomly generated chromosomes. These chromosomes form the initial population. Half of the chromosomes or solutions are randomly generated from a uniform distribution centered at equal allocation. The spread on either side of the center for the uniform distribution is taken to be half the equal allocation. Each element of the chromosome or allele is generated one by one. The first allele corresponding to $N_1^1$ is generated as shown:

$$N_1^1 = trunc(\frac{N_1^{tot}}{n}) + random(-\frac{N_1^{tot}}{2 \ n}, +\frac{N_1^{tot}}{2 \ n})$$

where the $trunc(x)$ function returns the truncated value of the fractional argument $x$, and the $random(x, y)$ function returns a random integer value from a uniform distribution between $x$ and $y$. The $N_1^2$ allele is generated next with the equal allocation recalculated using the remaining number of neurons from layer 1 and the remaining number of processors that are to be allocated as shown:

$$N_1^2 = trunc(\frac{N_1^{tot} - N_1^1}{n - 1}) + random(-\frac{N_1^{tot} - N_1^1}{2 \ (n - 1)}, +\frac{N_1^{tot} - N_1^1}{2 \ (n - 1)}).$$

If all the neurons from a layer have been assigned, the remaining processors will be assigned zero neurons for that layer. Likewise, the rest of the alleles are assigned a value randomly.

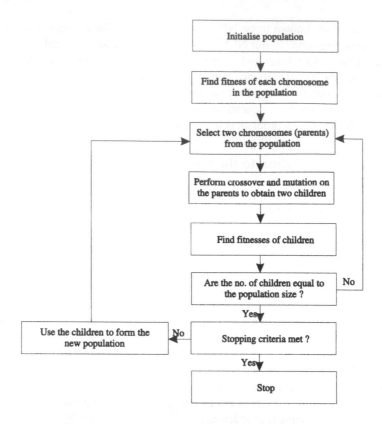

FIGURE 3.6. Steps involved in the GA algorithm.

A quarter of the chromosomes in the initial population are randomly generated from a uniform distribution. Again, the alleles are generated one by one. The first allele, $N_1^1$, is generated as shown:

$$N_1^1 = random(1, N_1^{tot}).$$

The allele $N_1^2$ is generated next by taking into account the number of neurons already assigned to processor one, as shown:

$$N_1^2 = random(1, N_1^{tot} - N_1^1).$$

If all the neurons from a layer have been assigned, the remaining processors are assigned zero neurons for that layer. The other alleles are generated in a similar manner.

The rest of the chromosomes from the initial population are also randomly generated from a uniform distribution. But now, the alleles are generated starting from the end of the chromosome. This is to give the alleles from the end of chromosome large values. Thus first the allele, $N_1^n$, is generated as shown:

$$N_1^n = random(1, N_1^{tot}).$$

Next, $N_1^{n-1}$ is generated as shown:

$$N_1^{n-1} = random(1, N_1^{tot} - N_1^n).$$

If all the neurons from a layer have been assigned, the remaining processors will be assigned zero neurons for that layer. The other alleles are generated in a similar manner.

Note that the initial population is generated randomly without violating neuron assignment constraints. The population size (number of chromosomes in the population) used is 1,000.

*3.6.1.2 Fitness.* The fitness of a chromosome or solution is related to the objective of using GA. In the case of this study, the GA is used to find a solution having a minimum time per iteration. Thus the fitness of a chromosome indicates its quality. The higher the fitness value, the better are the neuron assignments encoded in the chromosome. Thus fitness values are inversely proportional to the time per iteration. But this would result in chromosomes having a large variation in fitness values. To overcome this problem, the fitness values are mapped between 0 and 1 by using the serial time per iteration, $t_{iter-1}$, as a reference. The fitness value is computed from the time per iteration as follows:

$$fitness = \frac{t_{iter-1} - t_{iter-n}}{t_{iter-1}}.$$

The fitness value of a chromosome is used by the selection process, which is described next.

*3.6.1.3 Parent Selection.* The purpose of parent selection in GA is to give more reproductive chances, on the whole, to those population members that are more fit. This study uses the tournament selection scheme [25] to choose two parent chromosomes from the population. According to this scheme, a fixed number (known as tournament size) of chromosomes are randomly picked from the population and the fittest among them is identified as a parent. This procedure of randomly picking a fixed number of chromosomes and identifying the best is repeated to obtain the second parent. The tournament selection scheme was chosen instead of the more popular roulette wheel [21] scheme based on a comparison study [26] for a similar problem, which showed tournament selection producing faster convergence. The tournament size used is 100. After selection, recombination operators are applied to the parents to produce chromosomes different from them. Crossover and mutation operators are two important recombination operators, which are discussed next.

*3.6.1.4 Crossover Operator.* Crossover operators exchange genetic material between parents. Two-point crossover, in which there are two crossover sites in each chromosome and recombination between two chromosomes takes place by exchanging alleles between the crossover points with some probability, is used in this study. This is shown in Figure 3.7. The probability of crossover used is 0.8. Note that two-point crossover will not introduce differences for alleles where both parents have the same value. Crossover acts to combine building blocks (schemata) of good solutions from diverse chromosomes.

*3.6.1.5 Mutation.* The mutation operator introduces new genetic structures in the population that are unrelated to any previous genetic structure of the population. In this study the uniform mutation scheme is used. In this scheme each gene in a chromosome is given a chance to undergo mutation with some probability. If an allele with a value of $N_j^i$ is chosen for mutation, a random integer is obtained from a uniform distribution between $-\frac{N_j^i}{2}$ and $+\frac{N_j^i}{2}$ and is added to the old allele value. The mutation probability used is 0.1.

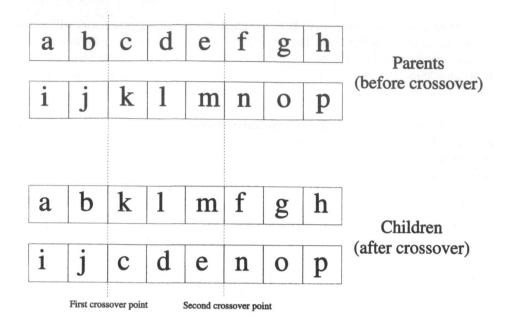

FIGURE 3.7. Two-point crossover.

*3.6.1.6 Normalization.* Crossover and mutation recombination operators change the allele values of the chromosomes without regard to the neuron assignment constraints. Thus after each recombination operation, the new children chromosomes are normalized to satisfy the neuron assignment constraints, as described next.

The total value of all alleles corresponding to each layer is accumulated. Note that this total may be different from the actual number of neurons from that layer in the neural network. A proportional fraction of neurons are assigned back to each allele based on their previous value, as shown:

$$a_l^{new} = \frac{a_l^{old}}{a_l^{tot}} \, N_l^{tot} \tag{3.15}$$

where $a_l^{new}$ and $a_l^{old}$ are the new and old allele values for layer $l$, respectively, $a_l^{tot}$ is the sum of all alleles for layer $l$, and $N_l^{tot}$ is the total number of neurons from layer $l$ in the neural network. The fractional $a_l^{new}$ values are truncated and the remaining neurons are added to the alleles corresponding to layer $l$, one at a time starting from the allele with the largest truncation.

*3.6.1.7 Stopping Criterion.* A good stopping criterion is needed to make the algorithm convergent and avoid a situation where the best solution is obtained in one generation and lost in the next, never to reappear. In this study the GA simulation is stopped if no better solution (chromosome) is found for the next 200 generations.

### 3.6.2 Approximate Linear Heuristic (ALH) Solution

In this case the nonlinear objective function of Equation 3.2 and the constraint Equations 3.3 to 3.13 are approximated to linear functions, and the resulting linear mixed integer optimization problem is solved using a heuristic method. The approximate linear objective function is obtained by neglecting the nonlinear terms in the original objective function and is given by

$$\tilde{t}_{iter-n} = \sum_{k=2}^{n} [W^1 R_{actk} + r_{actk} + W^1 R_{doutk} + r_{doutk}]$$

$$+ W_L^1 T_{dhid} + t_{dhid}^1 + \tilde{t}_{upwts}^1 + W_{end}^1. \quad (3.16)$$

In the preceding equation, the term $\tilde{t}_{upwts}^i$ is the linear approximated time needed to update weights in processor $i$ and the expression is given in Appendix A3.1. All the other terms in Equation 3.16 are same as those in the original objective function of Equation 3.2 as they do not have any nonlinear components. Similarly, $t_{upwts}^i$, $M_{wts}^i$, and $M_{\Delta wts}^i$ are linearized and replaced by $\tilde{t}_{upwts}^i$, $\tilde{M}_{wts}^i$, and $\tilde{M}_{\Delta wts}^i$, respectively in all the constraint equations of 3.3 to 3.13. $M_{wts}^i$ and $M_{\Delta wts}^i$ are the amount of memory needed to store the weight and weight changes values in processor $i$. These linearized expressions are given as Equation A3.23 in Appendix A3.1 and Equations A3.32 and A3.33 in Appendix A3.2.

In the heuristic approach, all integer constraints are relaxed and the resulting linear optimization problem is solved using the Simplex method. The resulting solution will have fractional neuron allocations to the various processors. To obtain integer solutions, all noninteger allocations from the Simplex [27] are first truncated to their integer values. The effect will be that all processors will have integer neuron allocations. However, the effect of truncation will be that the total number of neurons allocated to the processor network will be less than the total neurons in the neural network, thus violating the feasibility constraints of Equation 3.8. This is solved by allocating the remaining neurons to the processors, starting from those that had the largest truncation.

### 3.6.3 Experimental Results

In this section optimal mapping for the three heterogeneous processor networks shown in Figure 3.5 are obtained using the GA and the ALH methods. The benchmark problems considered are the 252-126-252 Encoder and the 203-120-28 Nettalk problems. Tables 3.3 to 3.8 show the optimal mapping of hidden and output layer neurons in TYPE-1, TYPE-2, and TYPE-3 networks for the Encoder and Nettalk problems resulting from the ALH and GA methods.

TABLE 3.3. Optimal mapping from the two solution methods for the Encoder problem. Processor network used is TYPE-1.

| Solution | Layer | Processor Description | | | | | | | | | | | | |
|---|---|---|---|---|---|---|---|---|---|---|---|---|---|---|
| Method | | S | S | S | S | S | S | S | S | S | F | F | F | F |
| ALH | Hidden | 8 | 9 | 9 | 8 | 8 | 8 | 8 | 8 | 8 | 8 | 11 | 11 | 11 | 11 |
| | Output | 16 | 16 | 17 | 17 | 17 | 17 | 17 | 17 | 17 | 17 | 21 | 21 | 21 | 21 |
| GA | Hidden | 8 | 8 | 8 | 9 | 9 | 8 | 8 | 8 | 8 | 8 | 11 | 11 | 11 | 11 |
| | Output | 18 | 18 | 18 | 15 | 14 | 18 | 17 | 18 | 18 | 18 | 20 | 20 | 20 | 20 |

Tables 3.9 and 3.10 show the time for an iteration corresponding to optimal mapping for the three processor networks for the Encoder and Nettalk problems, respectively. The solution times given in the tables for GA are the average iteration times over several runs with each run using a different initial population. This is because GAs are sensitive to initial conditions and without multiple replications of the experimental conditions one cannot make a good case about their performance. Tables 3.9 and 3.10 show that the time for an iteration corresponding to the mappings obtained from the two methods are close to each

TABLE 3.4. Optimal mapping from the two solution methods for the Encoder problem. Processor network used is TYPE-2.

| Solution Method | Layer | Processor Description | | | | | | | | | | | | | |
|---|---|---|---|---|---|---|---|---|---|---|---|---|---|---|---|
| | | S | F | S | F | S | F | S | F | S | S | S | S | S | S |
| ALH | Hidden | 8 | 11 | 9 | 11 | 9 | 11 | 8 | 11 | 8 | 8 | 8 | 8 | 8 | 8 |
| | Output | 17 | 21 | 16 | 21 | 16 | 21 | 17 | 21 | 17 | 17 | 17 | 17 | 17 | 17 |
| GA | Hidden | 8 | 11 | 8 | 10 | 8 | 10 | 9 | 10 | 9 | 9 | 9 | 8 | 9 | 8 |
| | Output | 18 | 20 | 18 | 22 | 16 | 22 | 16 | 21 | 16 | 16 | 16 | 18 | 16 | 17 |

TABLE 3.5. Optimal mapping from the two solution methods for the Encoder problem. Processor network used is TYPE-3.

| Solution Method | Layer | Processor Description | | | | | | | | | | | | | |
|---|---|---|---|---|---|---|---|---|---|---|---|---|---|---|---|
| | | S | F | S | S | S | S | F | F | S | S | S | F | S | S |
| ALH | Hidden | 8 | 11 | 8 | 8 | 8 | 8 | 11 | 11 | 9 | 9 | 8 | 11 | 8 | 8 |
| | Output | 17 | 21 | 17 | 17 | 17 | 17 | 21 | 21 | 16 | 16 | 17 | 21 | 17 | 17 |
| GA | Hidden | 8 | 11 | 8 | 9 | 9 | 8 | 10 | 10 | 9 | 9 | 8 | 10 | 9 | 8 |
| | Output | 18 | 20 | 18 | 15 | 14 | 18 | 23 | 23 | 15 | 15 | 18 | 22 | 15 | 18 |

other. Further, both methods took similar time to find their optimal solutions. Although the solutions obtained from GA and ALH are similar, it is not known whether these solutions are indeed close to the (global) optimum for the NLMIO problem. This is investigated in the next section using a statistical approach.

## 3.7 Statistical Validation of the Optimal Mapping

A Monte Carlo simulation study is carried out to find out the proximity of the solutions obtained in Section 3.6.3 to the global optimal solution. According to the Monte Carlo method used in this study, a large number of neuron allocations are randomly generated from a uniform distribution for the heterogeneous processor networks (for the benchmark problems), and the iteration times corresponding to each of the random allocation are experimentally obtained. The sample sizes in the study varied from 100 to 1,300, and for each sample size the mean and standard deviation for the iteration time was obtained. These are then compared with the iteration times obtained from the GA and ALH solutions. If the iteration time from these solutions are close to the global minimum, then they should lie *far* below the sample mean for all trials.

Figures 3.8 and 3.9 shows the distribution of the iteration time for the Encoder and Nettalk problems, respectively, when the sample size is 1,000 for TYPE-1, TYPE-2, and TYPE-3 heterogeneous processor networks. The symbol (×) in the figure points to the iteration time from the GA mapping. Because the iteration time from ALH and GA are very close to each other, we have shown only the GA solutions in Figures 3.8 to 3.11.

TABLE 3.6. Optimal mapping from the two solution methods for the Nettalk problem. Processor network used is TYPE-1.

| Solution Method | Layer | Processor Description | | | | | | | | | | | | | |
|---|---|---|---|---|---|---|---|---|---|---|---|---|---|---|---|
| | | S | S | S | S | S | S | S | S | S | S | F | F | F | F |
| ALH | Hidden | 8 | 8 | 8 | 8 | 8 | 8 | 8 | 8 | 8 | 8 | 10 | 10 | 10 | 10 |
| | Output | 2 | 2 | 2 | 2 | 2 | 2 | 2 | 2 | 2 | 2 | 2 | 2 | 2 | 2 |
| GA | Hidden | 8 | 8 | 8 | 8 | 8 | 8 | 8 | 8 | 8 | 8 | 10 | 10 | 10 | 10 |
| | Output | 2 | 2 | 2 | 2 | 2 | 2 | 2 | 2 | 2 | 2 | 2 | 2 | 2 | 2 |

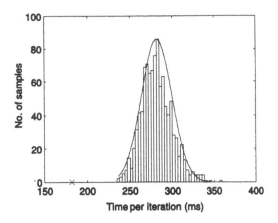

(a) TYPE-1 Processor Network

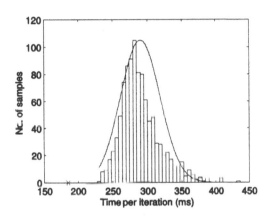

(b) TYPE-2 Processor Network

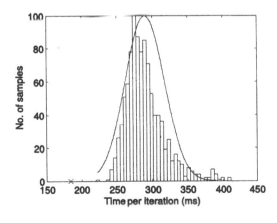

(c) TYPE-3 Processor Network

FIGURE 3.8. Distribution of iteration time for the Encoder problem for TYPE-1, TYPE-2, and TYPE-3 processor networks.

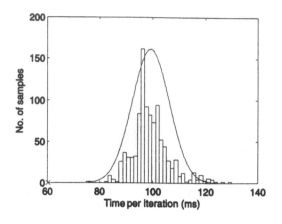

(a) TYPE-1 Processor Network

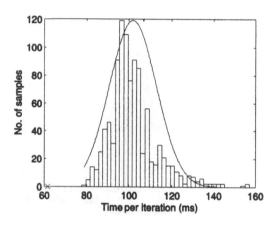

(b) TYPE-2 Processor Network

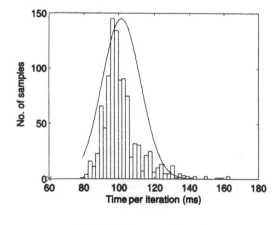

(c) TYPE-3 Processor Network

FIGURE 3.9. Distribution of iteration time for the Nettalk problem for TYPE-1, TYPE-2, and TYPE-3 processor networks.

TABLE 3.7. Optimal mapping from the two solution methods for the Nettalk problem. Processor network used is TYPE-2.

| Solution Method | Layer | Processor Description | | | | | | | | | | | | | |
|---|---|---|---|---|---|---|---|---|---|---|---|---|---|---|---|
| | | S | F | S | F | S | F | S | F | S | S | S | S | S | S |
| ALH | Hidden | 8 | 10 | 8 | 10 | 8 | 10 | 8 | 10 | 8 | 8 | 8 | 8 | 8 | 8 |
| | Output | 2 | 2 | 2 | 2 | 2 | 2 | 2 | 2 | 2 | 2 | 2 | 2 | 2 | 2 |
| GA | Hidden | 8 | 10 | 8 | 10 | 8 | 10 | 8 | 10 | 8 | 8 | 8 | 8 | 8 | 8 |
| | Output | 3 | 3 | 2 | 3 | 2 | 2 | 1 | 1 | 2 | 2 | 1 | 2 | 2 | 2 |

TABLE 3.8. Optimal mapping from the two solution methods for the Nettalk problem. Processor network used is TYPE-3.

| Solution Method | Layer | Processor Description | | | | | | | | | | | | | |
|---|---|---|---|---|---|---|---|---|---|---|---|---|---|---|---|
| | | S | F | S | S | S | S | F | F | S | S | S | F | S | S |
| ALH | Hidden | 8 | 10 | 8 | 8 | 8 | 8 | 10 | 10 | 8 | 8 | 8 | 10 | 8 | 8 |
| | Output | 2 | 2 | 2 | 2 | 2 | 2 | 2 | 2 | 2 | 2 | 2 | 2 | 2 | 2 |
| GA | Hidden | 8 | 10 | 8 | 8 | 8 | 8 | 10 | 10 | 8 | 8 | 8 | 10 | 8 | 8 |
| | Output | 2 | 2 | 2 | 2 | 2 | 2 | 2 | 2 | 2 | 2 | 2 | 2 | 2 | 2 |

Figures 3.10 and 3.11 show the mean $\pm 3\sigma$ for the iteration time for various sample sizes. Figures 3.10 and 3.11 show the iteration time corresponding to GA is always more than three standard deviations ($3\sigma$) lower than the sample means. This indicates that the optimal solutions are quite close to the global minimum.

## 3.8 Discussion

The results from the previous sections show that GA and ALH are suitable for solving the NLMIO problem for optimal neuron distributions and their solutions are quite close to the optimal solutions. Because these methods need a finite amount of time to converge to their solution, any judgement on the merit of using them can be made only after the question of the *overall* reduction in time accruing from these optimal mappings has been addressed in the context of total training time.

### 3.8.1 Worthwhileness of Finding Optimal Mappings

Although the results in Section 3.7 show the GA and the ALH solutions to be quite close to the *global optimal* iteration time, they do not provide any information about the time taken by these methods to find their solution. Because the whole objective of finding the optimal distribution is to obtain a lower training time than any other nonoptimal distributions, it is important to investigate whether the time taken to find the optimal allocation itself might offset any reduction in training time accruing from the use of the optimal allocation.

TABLE 3.9. Optimal time per iteration (ms) from the two solution methods for the Encoder problem.

| Type of Processor Network | Method of Solution | |
|---|---|---|
| | ALH | GA |
| TYPE-1 | 186.4 | 182.6 |
| TYPE-2 | 184.1 | 185.5 |
| TYPE-3 | 184.1 | 183.8 |

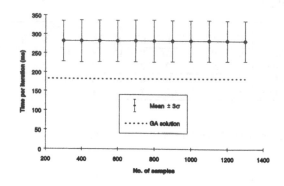

(a) TYPE-1 Processor Network

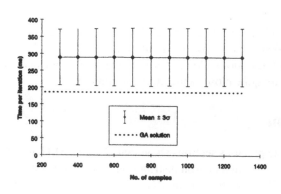

(b) TYPE-2 Processor Network

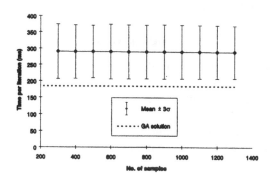

(c) TYPE-3 Processor Network

FIGURE 3.10. Mean $\pm 3\sigma$ for the Encoder problem for various sample sizes for TYPE-1, TYPE-2, and TYPE-3 processor networks.

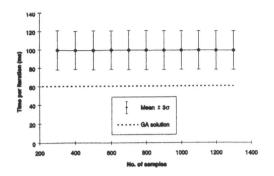

(a) TYPE-1 Processor Network

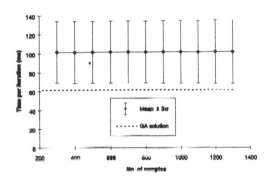

(b) TYPE-2 Processor Network

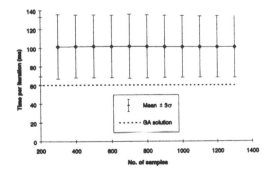

(c) TYPE-3 Processor Network

FIGURE 3.11. Mean $\pm 3\sigma$ for the Nettalk problem for various sample sizes for TYPE-1, TYPE-2, and TYPE-3 processor networks.

TABLE 3.10. Optimal time per iteration (ms) from the two solution methods for the Nettalk problem.

| Type of Processor Network | Method of Solution | |
|---|---|---|
| | ALH | GA |
| TYPE-1 | 59.5 | 60.2 |
| TYPE-2 | 59.5 | 61.6 |
| TYPE-3 | 59.5 | 60.1 |

TABLE 3.11. Total time for training for the optimal and nonoptimal neuron distributions for the Encoder problem on a TYPE-1 network. Training converged after 302,400 iterations.

| Allocation Technique | Time Taken to Obtain Allocation (mins) | Time Taken for Training (mins) | Total Time Taken (mins) |
|---|---|---|---|
| DIST-1 | 0 | 1,109 | 1,109 |
| DIST-2 | 0 | 998 | 998 |
| GA | 11 | 920 | 931 |
| ALH | 8 | 939 | 947 |

Hence, the training time for the optimal allocation was compared with that of nonoptimal allocations where the training time for optimal allocation included the time taken to search and find the solution. Tables 3.11 to 3.16 show the total training time taken by the two solution methods and two nonoptimal allocations for the Encoder and Nettalk benchmark problems for the TYPE-1, TYPE-2, and TYPE-3 heterogeneous, processor networks.

Tables 3.11 to 3.16 show that the reduction realized in training time using the optimal allocations more than compensates the extra time needed to find them. The relatively small reductions obtained for the examples in Tables 3.11 to 3.16 are due to the relatively small difference in the processor speeds (20 MHz and 25 MHz) in the heterogeneous networks used. The reductions from optimal mapping will be more pronounced for processor networks with greater heterogeneity.

### 3.8.2 Processor Location in a Ring

Section 3.6 discussed the optimal solution corresponding to a *given* processor configuration in the ring network. Because the processor network is heterogeneous, an obvious question

TABLE 3.12. Total time for training for the optimal and nonoptimal neuron distributions for the Encoder problem on a TYPE-2 network. Training converged after 302,400 iterations.

| Allocation Technique | Time Taken to Obtain Allocation (mins) | Time Taken for Training (mins) | Total Time Taken (mins) |
|---|---|---|---|
| DIST-1 | 0 | 1,109 | 1,109 |
| DIST-2 | 0 | 998 | 998 |
| GA | 10 | 935 | 945 |
| ALH | 4 | 928 | 932 |

TABLE 3.13. Total time for training for the optimal and nonoptimal neuron distributions for the Encoder problem on a TYPE-3 network. Training converged after 302,400 iterations.

| Allocation Technique | Time Taken to Obtain Allocation (mins) | Time Taken for Training (mins) | Total Time Taken (mins) |
|---|---|---|---|
| DIST-1 | 0 | 1,108 | 1,108 |
| DIST-2 | 0 | 998 | 998 |
| GA | 11 | 926 | 937 |
| ALH | 5 | 928 | 933 |

TABLE 3.14. Total time for training for the optimal and nonoptimal neuron distributions for the Nettalk problem on a TYPE-1 network. Training converged after 130,000 iterations.

| Allocation Technique | Time Taken to Obtain Allocation (mins) | Time Taken for Training (mins) | Total Time Taken (mins) |
|---|---|---|---|
| DIST-1 | 0 | 183 | 183 |
| DIST-2 | 0 | 143 | 143 |
| GA | 11 | 130 | 141 |
| ALH | 5 | 129 | 134 |

TABLE 3.15. Total time for training for the optimal and nonoptimal neuron distributions for the Nettalk problem on a TYPE-2 network. Training converged after 130,000 iterations.

| Allocation Technique | Time Taken to Obtain Allocation (mins) | Time Taken for Training (mins) | Total Time Taken (mins) |
|---|---|---|---|
| DIST-1 | 0 | 183 | 183 |
| DIST-2 | 0 | 143 | 143 |
| GA | 7 | 133 | 140 |
| ALH | 4 | 129 | 133 |

TABLE 3.16. Total time for training for the optimal and nonoptimal neuron distributions for the Nettalk problem on a TYPE-3 network. Training converged after 130,000 iterations.

| Allocation Technique | Time Taken to Obtain Allocation (mins) | Time Taken for Training (mins) | Total Time Taken (mins) |
|---|---|---|---|
| DIST-1 | 0 | 183 | 183 |
| DIST-2 | 0 | 143 | 143 |
| GA | 8 | 130 | 138 |
| ALH | 3 | 129 | 132 |

is whether optimal iteration time for a different arrangement of processors within the ring can be still shorter. If this is so, then the solution presented in Section 3.6 will be of only limited value. The effect of processor location on the performance of the ring network can be analyzed from the results of Tables 3.9 and 3.10, which show the optimal iteration times for the three processor networks. Taken together these results indicate that locations of the processors do not have any great effect on the performance, and the optimal iteration time will be nearly the same for all processor configurations in a ring topology. Table 3.17 shows this succinctly.

TABLE 3.17. Optimal time per iteration (ms) for the three processor networks for the Encoder and Nettalk problems.

| Processor | Optimal Iteration Time | |
|---|---|---|
| Network | Encoder | Nettalk |
| TYPE-1 | 182.6 | 60.2 |
| TYPE-2 | 185.5 | 61.6 |
| TYPE-3 | 183.8 | 60.1 |

### 3.8.3  Cost-Benefit Analysis

From time to time almost all project managers face the problem of deciding whether to procure, within the available budget, a small number of expensive but fast processors *or* a larger number of relatively slow but less expensive processors for a given application. Theoretical analysis that can predict the relative benefit from the different choices would be a very valuable tool in such cases for making an informed procurement decision.

The analyses presented in Sections 3.3, 3.5, and 3.6 can be used for such a cost-benefit analysis, as shown by the following example.

*3.8.3.1  Example.*  This example considers a heterogeneous network with 20 T805-20 transputers and 10 T805-25 transputers connected in a ring. Assume that a decision whether to procure 10 fast processors *or* 20 slow processors has to be made based on the reduction in the training time to be realized. Assume the application is to train a 32768-1024-32768 neural network. Using the GA approach presented in Section 3.6.1, the training times per iteration for the two cases are calculated theoretically and shown in Table 3.18. The table shows that the slow processor option would yield greater reduction

TABLE 3.18. Reduction in the training time per iteration accruing from alternate choices.

| Type of Choice | Iteration Time (sec) | % Reduction Over Existing Setup |
|---|---|---|
| Existing Setup | 88.8 | 0.0 |
| Procure 10 fast processors | 67.0 | 24.5 |
| Procure 20 slow processors | 59.6 | 32.9 |

in training time for the application considered. So a decision based on reduction of training time alone would favor the procurement of slow processors.

### 3.8.4 Optimal Number of Processors for Homogeneous Processor Arrays

In this section the theoretical model is used for homogeneous processor arrays to find the optimal number of processors for the Encoder and Nettalk benchmark problems. For a homogeneous processor array, the optimal allocation would be an equal allocation of all the neurons, which would result in balanced loads in all the processors. For a balanced load, computations in every processor would take the same amount of time to complete. As a result, the receiving and sending phases in each processor would occur together, resulting in an all-to-all broadcast. Thus, there would be no waitings in the processors. Extra neurons assigned to the processors would ruin the load balance and cause waitings, but this cannot be helped if the total number of neurons are not divisible by the number of processors.

The theoretical time per iteration was obtained for the 252-126-252 Encoder and 203-120-28 Nettalk problems for variously sized homogeneous processor networks. For each processor array, an equal or almost equal allocation of neurons is used. For example, for a five processor network, the neurons in the Encoder network can be allocated as $\begin{smallmatrix} 26 & 25 & 25 \\ 50 & 50 & 50 \end{smallmatrix}$ $\begin{smallmatrix} 25 & 25 \\ 51 & 51 \end{smallmatrix}$ or $\begin{smallmatrix} 25 & 25 & 25 & 25 & 26 \\ 50 & 50 & 50 & 51 & 51 \end{smallmatrix}$. The time per iteration is 522.6 ms and 524.5 ms for the first and second allocation, respectively. Thus, an allocation where the total number of hidden and output neurons in each processor is almost equal is better. Using the allocation scheme with a smaller time per iteration described earlier, the time per iteration corresponding to each processor array size is graphically shown in Figure 3.12 for the Encoder and Nettalk problems, respectively.

Figures 3.12(a) and 3.12(b) show that the minimum time per iteration is obtained using 126 and 148 processors for the Encoder and Nettalk problems, respectively. The optimum number of processors for the Encoder network is intuitive because using more than 126 processors would result in some processors not having any hidden neurons. But the optimal number of processors for the Nettalk problem is not intuitive, as a 148 processor array would result in processors having only a hidden or output neuron.

Figure 3.12 also shows that using more processors than the optimum results in a higher time per iteration. As more processors are used, the computation time in each processor decreases but the communication time increases. Thus, the increase in the communication time is more than the decrease in the computation time for processor arrays having more than the optimal number of processors. The opposite is true for processor arrays having fewer processors than the optimal value. Speedup ratios also show the performance of variously sized processor arrays. The speedup ratio is calculated as shown:

$$Speedup = \frac{t_{iter-1}}{t_{iter-n}}.$$

For a processor array with $n$ processors, the ideal speedup would be $n$. But this ideal value is not achievable because a message-passing processor array has to communicate to exchange data. This becomes an overhead. Furthermore, in the case of the parallel BP implementation discussed in this study, some computations are duplicated in the processor array[5]. The speedup for variously sized processor array for the Encoder and Nettalk problem is shown in Figure 3.13. The figure shows that the speedup decreases as more processors than the optimum are added to the processor array. The maximum speedup is obtained using the optimum number of processors. The increase in speedup also decreases for every processor added to the processor array having fewer than the optimum number of

---

[5]Some weights are duplicated in the processor array. Thus, the updating of these weights are duplicated.

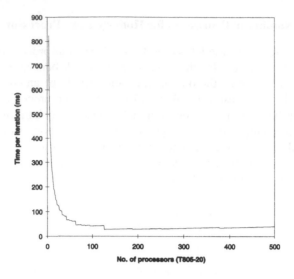

(a) Encoder Benchmark Problem

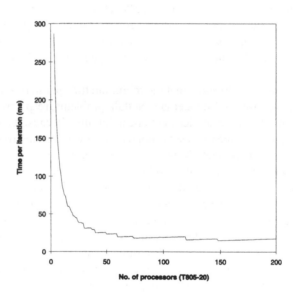

(b) Nettalk Benchmark Problem

FIGURE 3.12. Time per iteration for various numbers of T805-20 processors for the Encoder and Nettalk benchmark problems.

processors. Thus, a cost-benefit analysis can be made using a similar speedup graph before the purchase of extra processors.

Figures 3.12 and 3.13 show that the performance of the various processor arrays is almost a step function. This is due to the fact that the number of neurons is not always divisible by the number of processors. When there is an unequal number of neurons in each processor there is a load imbalance causing waitings in the processors, and there is a stepped increase in performance when there are equal numbers of neurons in each processor.

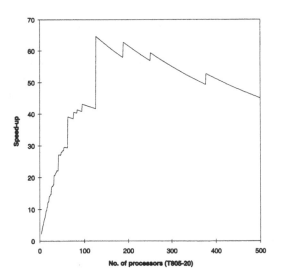

(a) Encoder Benchmark Problem

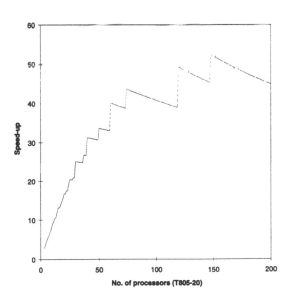

(b) Nettalk Benchmark Problem

FIGURE 3.13. Speedups for various numbers of T805-20 processors for the Encoder and Nettalk benchmark problems.

## 3.9 Conclusion

This chapter presented a detailed analysis of network-based parallel implementation of BP learning on a heterogeneous processor network in ring topology. A mathematical model for the parallel BP running on the heterogeneous network was developed and experimentally validated. Using the model the problem of finding the optimal mapping of neural networks was studied and was shown to result in a nonlinear mixed integer optimization problem. Genetic algorithms and ALH method were used and shown to be viable methods for solving the optimization problem. Using a Monte Carlo method, the iteration times from the optimal mappings were shown to be $3\sigma$ lower than the mean iteration times for several sample sizes. This implies that the optimal solutions are very close to the global optimal solutions. Because these methods takes a finite amount of time to solve the nonlinear mixed integer optimization, their usefulness must be assessed in the context of net reduction in *total* training time before pronouncing their merits. This has been done in the study by comparing the total training time from these optimal allocations with that of two nonoptimal allocations that do not require finding the optimal solution. From the results obtained for benchmark problems we conclude that the GA and the ALH optimal mappings do produce sufficient reduction in total training time to warrant their use. We further conclude from the results that the locations of processors do not have any significant impact on the performance of a heterogeneous ring network. The mathematical model and the analyses presented in this study have also been shown to assist in procurement decisions based on cost-benefit analysis. Finally, the optimum number of processors for a homogeneous processor array was found for the Encoder and Nettalk benchmark problems.

Although all the experimental results were given for heterogeneous transputer networks, the model and the analyses put forward are applicable for any message-passing multiprocessor heterogeneous network.

# Appendices

## A3.1 Theoretical Expressions for Processes in the Parallel BP Algorithm

Theoretical expressions to predict the time for all the computation and communication processes in processor $i$ are given here.

### A3.1.1 Computation Processes

In any processor $i$, computational processes are required for calculating activations ($T_{act}^i$), outputs ($T_{out}^i$), deltas for the output ($T_{dout}^i$), and hidden neurons ($T_{dhid}^i$) and finally for updating the weight values ($T_{upwts}^i$). Theoretical expressions to predict the execution time for these processes in terms of the elemental timings of the processor $i$ are derived next. This is done by writing the functionality of these processes in pseudocodes and finding out the various elemental operations required from them.

*A3.1.1.1 $T_{act}^i$.* This process calculates the activation values for the hidden neurons residing in processor $i$. The pseudocodes for $T_{act}^i$ are as follows:

```
/* nodep[1] is the number of neurons assigned from   */
/* layer 1 to processor i. 1 is 0 for input layer, 1 */
/* for hidden layer and 2 for output layer.          */
/* z[1][j] is the activation of neuron j in layer 1  */
/* in processor i.                                   */
for (j=0; j<nodep[1]; j++)

    /* initialization of z[1][j] is done here before  */
    /* the computations occur                         */

    for (k=0; k<nodep[0]; k++)
       z[1][j]+=(w[1][j][k]*z[0][k]);         (a)
    /* calculate sigmoid value */
    z[1][j] = sigmoid(z[1][j]);               (b)
```

It can be seen from the pseudocodes that the computation operations are those in lines (a), (b), and the *'for'* loop statement. The type of operations performed in lines (a) and (b) are multiplication ($*$), compound addition ($+ =$), and the *sigmoid*.[6] The number of times these three operations are performed is nodep[0]$\times$nodep[1], nodep[0]$\times$nodep[1], and nodep[1], respectively. Thus, an expression for the time to execute the process $T_{act}^i$

---

[6] $sigmoid(.) = \frac{1}{1+exp-(.)}$, is considered as a single computation operation here as this operation is used repeatedly in the BP algorithm. The *sigmoid* computation time, $t_{sig}^i$ includes the assignment of the *sigmoid* value to the variable on the left of the equal sign, i.e. $z[1][j]$.

can be written in terms of the timings for the three operations $*$, $+ =$, *sigmoid*, and the *for* loop as

$$
\begin{aligned}
t_{act}^i = {} & (t_m^i + t_{saa}^i) * (nodep[0] * nodep[1]) \\
& + t_{sig}^i * nodep[1] \\
& + t_{loop}^i * (nodep[0] * nodep[1]).
\end{aligned} \tag{A3.17}
$$

In Equation A3.17, $t_{act}^i$ is the time taken to execute the process $T_{act}^i$. $t_m^i, t_{saa}^i, t_{sig}^i$ are the timings for the three operations $*$, $+ =$, *sigmoid*, and $t_{loop}^i$ is the time for the loop operation in processor $i$. If these elemental timings are known, then Equation A3.17 can be used to theoretically predict the time for $T_{act}^i$. Using a similar approach, theoretical expressions to predict the time for all the computation and communication processes can be derived as shown in the rest of this appendix.

If $N_l^i$ is the number of neurons residing in processor $i$ from layer $l$ and $N_l^{tot}$ is the total number of neurons in the neural network from layer $l$, Equation A3.17 can be written as shown:[7]

$$
t_{act}^i = t_{sig}^i \, N_1^i + (t_{loop}^i + t_m^i + t_{saa}^i)\,(N_1^i \, N_0^{tot}). \tag{A3.18}
$$

*A3.1.1.2* $T_{out}^i$. The pseudocode for the computation of output values for output neurons residing in processor $i$ is the same as shown in the computation of activation values of the hidden layer neurons above. Again, the time for the computation is the sum of the for loop timings and the computation time for lines (a) and (b). Line (a) consists of a multiplication $(t_m^i)$ and a compound addition and assignment $(t_{saa}^i)$, that is, $+ =$ . Line (c) contains a sigmoid value computation $(t_{sig}^i)$. Line (a) is computed $N_2^i \, N_1^{tot}$ times, and line (b) is computed $N_2^i$ times. Thus, the total time for calculating the output values for the output neurons in processor $i$ is

$$
t_{out}^i = t_{sig}^i \, N_2^i + (t_{loop}^i + t_m^i + t_{saa}^i)\,(N_2^i \, N_1^{tot}). \tag{A3.19}
$$

*A3.1.1.3* $T_{dout}^i$. This process calculates the delta values for the output neurons residing in processor $i$. The pseudocodes for $T_{dout}^i$ are as follows:

```
for (i=0; i<nodep[2]; i++)

   /* out_pattern is the desired output pattern */
      delta[2][i] = (out_pattern[cur_pattern_no][i]-z[2][i])
                   * (z[2][i]*(1.0-z[2][i]);
```

Time for calculating the delta values for the output neurons is the sum of the time for the $N_2^i$ for loops and the time for computation of delta. The delta computation involves a multiplication and assignment $(t_{ma}^i)$, two subtractions $(2\,t_s^i)$, and a multiplication $(t_m^i)$. The delta computation occurs for $N_2^i$ times. Thus the total time is

$$
t_{dout}^i = N_2^i \, (t_{loop}^i + 2\,t_s^i + t_m^i + t_{ma}^i). \tag{A3.20}
$$

*A3.1.1.4* $T_{dhid}^i$. This process calculates the delta values for the hidden neurons residing in processor $i$. The pseudocodes for $T_{dhid}^i$ are as follows:

---

[7]Note that $nodep[l] = N_l^i$, and because the input neurons are not partitioned, $nodep[0] = N_0^i = N_0^{tot}$.

```
for (j=0; j<nodep[1]; j++)

   /* Initialization of delta value delta[1][j] */
   /* is done here before computation            */

   /* Computation of partial delta values */
   /* nonode[1] is the total number of     */
   /* neurons from layer 1 in the neural   */
   /* network                              */
   for (k=0; k<nonode[2]; k++)
       delta[1][j] + = (delta[2][k]*w[2][k][j]);   (a)
    /* Computation of delta value */
    delta[1][j]*=(z[1][j]*(1.0-z[1][j]);           (b)
```

The time for computing the deltas is the sum of the for loop timings and the computation times corresponding to lines (a) and (b). Line (a) involves a multiplication ($t_m^i$) and a compound addition and assignment += ($t_{saa}^i$). Line (b) involves a subtraction ($t_s^i$), multiplication ($t_m^i$) and a compound multiplication and assignment ($t_{sma}^i$), *=. Line (a) is executed $N_1^i N_2^{tot}$ times and line (b) is executed $N_1^i$ times. There are $N_1^i N_2^{tot}$ for loops. Thus, the total time is

$$t_{dhid}^i = (t_s^i + t_m^i + t_{sma}^i) N_1^i + (t_{loop}^i + t_m^i + t_{saa}^i) (N_1^i N_2^{tot}) \qquad (A3.21)$$

*A3.1.1.5* $T_{upwts}^i$. This process calculates and updates all the input and output weight values of hidden and output layer neurons residing in processor $i$. The pseudocodes for $T_{upwts}^i$ are as follows:

```
for (i=0; i<=1; i++)
{
  /* update all input weight values */
  for (j=0; j<nodep[i+1]; j++)
    for (k=0; k<nonode[i]; k++)
    {
      /* calculate change of input weights of neurons */
      dw = alpha*delta[i+1][j]*z[i][k]
           + beta*old_dw[i+1][j][k];               (a)
      /* update weight */
      w[i+1][j][k]+= dw;                           (b)
      /* store old change in weight value */       (c)
      old_dw[i+1][j][k] = dw;
    }
  if (i!=0) /* update all other output weight values */
    for (j=nodep[2]; j<nonode[2]; j++)
      for (k=0; k<nodep[1]; k++)
      {
       /* calculate change of output weights of nodes */
       dw = alpha*delta[2][j]*z[1][k]
            + beta*old_dw[2][j][k];                (d)
       /* update weights */
       w[2][j][k]+= dw;                            (e)
```

```
        /* store old change in weights */                    (f)
        old_dw[2][j][k] = dw;
    }
}
```

Each processor stores input and output weights. Computations corresponding to lines (a), (b), and (c) are for the update of all input weights of neurons from the hidden and output layers residing in processor $i$. Lines (d), (e), and (f) are for the update of output weights of neurons from the hidden layer that are not part of the input weights already updated in lines (a), (b), and (c). Lines (a) and (d) consist of a multiplication and assignment ($t_{ma}^i$), an addition ($t_a^i$), and two multiplications $2\,t_m^i$. Lines (b) and (e) involve a compound addition and assignment $t_{saa}^i$. Lines (c) and (f) consist of an assignment ($t_{ass}^i$). Lines (a), (b), and (c) are executed $N_0^{tot}\,N_1^i + N_1^{tot}\,N_2^i$ times and there are $N_0^{tot}\,N_1^i + N_1^{tot}\,N_2^i$ corresponding *for* loops. Lines (d), (e), and (f) are executed $N_1^i\,\{N_2^{tot} - N_2^i\}$ times and there are $N_1^i\,\{N_2^{tot} - N_2^i\}$ corresponding *for* loops. There are also two outermost *for* loops corresponding to two layers of weight values in the neural network. Thus, the time taken to update the weights in processor $i$ is

$$
\begin{aligned}
t_{upwts}^i = \; & 2\,t_{loop}^i \\
& + (t_{loop}^i + t_{ma}^i + t_a^i + 2t_m^i + t_{saa}^i + t_{ass}^i) \\
& \cdot (N_0^{tot}\,N_1^i + N_1^{tot}\,N_2^i) \\
& + (t_{loop}^i + t_{ma}^i + t_a^i + 2t_m^i + t_{saa}^i + t_{ass}^i) \\
& \cdot (N_1^i(N_2^{tot} - N_2^i)).
\end{aligned}
\tag{A3.22}
$$

The expression for $t_{upwts}^i$ is nonlinear as it has the terms $N_1^i\,N_2^i$. This nonlinear term comes because the weights connecting the hidden and output layer neurons residing in the same processor are not duplicated as incoming and outgoing. Linearization of Equation A3.22 can be done by ignoring this term, which then implies that these weights are duplicated as incoming and outgoing. The linearized time for weight update, $\tilde{t}_{upwts}^i$, is given by

$$
\begin{aligned}
\tilde{t}_{upwts}^i = \; & 2\,t_{loop}^i + (t_{loop}^i + t_{ma}^i + t_a^i + 2t_m^i + t_{saa}^i + t_{ass}^i) \\
& \cdot (N_0^{tot}\,N_1^i + N_1^{tot}\,N_2^i) \\
& + (t_{loop}^i + t_{ma}^i + t_a^i + 2t_m^i + t_{saa}^i + t_{ass}^i) \\
& \cdot (N_1^i N_2^{tot}).
\end{aligned}
\tag{A3.23}
$$

Equation A3.23 is used when the ALH method is used to find the optimal mapping in Section 3.6.2.

### A3.1.2  Communication Processes

Communication processes are needed to send and receive data from one processor to another. The data transferred between processors are the activations and deltas of the hidden and output layer neurons, respectively.

*A3.1.2.1  $S_{acti}$ and $R_{acti}$.*  These are the sending and receiving processes for the activations from the hidden layer. Because interprocessor communications are synchronized and the data received is same as the data sent, the time needed for $S_{acti}$ and $R_{acti}$ would have to be same, that is, $s_{acti} = r_{acti}$, and

$$
s_{acti} = t_{comm-init} + N_1^i\,t_{word}
\tag{A3.24}
$$

where $t_{comm-init}$ and $t_{word}$ are the communication initialization time for a single transfer and the time required to transfer one word, respectively.

*A3.1.2.2 $S_{douti}$ and $R_{douti}$.* These are the sending and receiving processes for the deltas of the output layer neurons. As in the case with activations, the sending and receiving time must be equal, that is, $s_{douti} = r_{douti}$, and

$$s_{douti} = t_{comm-init} + N_2^i\, t_{word}. \tag{A3.25}$$

## A3.2 Memory Constraints

In network-based parallelism each processor has to keep a complete copy of the training set as well as the slice of the neural network allocated to it. Because each processor has a fixed local memory (1 Mbyte, 2 Mbyte, 4 Mbyte, and so on), there is a limit to the number of neurons and training patterns that a processor can hold. In this appendix we examine the memory requirement on the processors for implementing the parallelized backpropagation algorithm.

### A3.2.1 Storing the Training Set

Memory is needed to store all training patterns. Corresponding to each input (training) pattern is a desired output pattern. Because the input neurons are not partitioned, a copy of all the input patterns are stored in every processor, but only output patterns corresponding to the output neurons residing in the processor need to be stored. If $N_0^{tot}$ is the total number of neurons in the input layer of the neural network, $N_2^i$ the number of neurons in the output layer residing in processor $i$ and $r$ is the number of bytes required to store a floating point number, then to store each training pattern $r(N_0^{tot} + N_2^i)$ bytes of memory is required. The memory required in processor $i$ to store all the patterns ($P_{tot}$) in the training set will be $M_{pat}^i$ which is given by

$$M_{pat}^i = P_{tot}\, r\, (N_0^{tot} + N_2^i). \tag{A3.26}$$

### A3.2.2 Storing the Neural Network Parameters

The neural network parameters that each processor needs to store are the relevant neuron activations, outputs, deltas, weights, and weight changes. Because each processor needs the activations of all the hidden neurons of the network, the number of bytes required to store these are

$$M_{act}^i = r\, N_1^{tot} \tag{A3.27}$$

where $N_1^{tot}$ is the total number of hidden neurons. Only outputs of output neurons residing in processor $i$ is stored. Thus, memory bytes required to store the outputs are

$$M_{out}^i = r\, N_2^i. \tag{A3.28}$$

In the case of deltas, a processor $i$ needs the deltas of all the output neurons to compute the deltas of those hidden neurons residing in it. Thus, the memory required will be

$$M_{del}^i = r\, (N_1^i + N_2^{tot}). \tag{A3.29}$$

For the weights, each processor stores the incoming and outgoing weights of hidden layer neurons and only incoming weights of output layer neurons residing in it. However, the weights connecting the neurons within the same processor are not duplicated as incoming and outgoing. Thus, the number of weights that need to be stored in processor $i$ will be $(N_0^{tot} \, N_1^i + N_1^{tot} \, N_2^i) \, + N_1^i \, (N_2^{tot} - N_2^i)$. The memory required for these weights is $M_{wts}^i$ where

$$M_{wts}^i = r \, \{(N_0^{tot} \, N_1^i + N_1^{tot} \, N_2^i) \, + N_1^i \, (N_2^{tot} - N_2^i)\}. \qquad \text{(A3.30)}$$

The memory requirements for weight changes are same as those for weights and can be written as

$$M_{\Delta wts}^i = r \, \{(N_0^{tot} \, N_1^i + N_1^{tot} \, N_2^i) \, + N_1^i \, (N_2^{tot} - N_2^i)\}. \qquad \text{(A3.31)}$$

Using similar arguments as in A3.1.1.5 for linearization, linear equations for $M_{wts}^i$ and $M_{\Delta wts}^i$ can be written as

$$\tilde{M}_{wts}^i = r \, \{(N_0^{tot} \, N_1^i + N_1^{tot} \, N_2^i) \, + N_1^i \, N_2^{tot}\}. \qquad \text{(A3.32)}$$

$$\tilde{M}_{\Delta wts}^i = r \, \{(N_0^{tot} \, N_1^i + N_1^{tot} \, N_2^i) \, + N_1^i \, N_2^{tot}\}. \qquad \text{(A3.33)}$$

Equations A3.32 and A3.33 are used in the ALH method of Section 3.6.2. The total memory requirement for storing the network parameters is the sum of Equations A3.27, A3.28, A3.29, A3.30, A3.31, and is given by $M_{net-par}^i$ where,

$$M_{net-par}^i = M_{act}^i + M_{out}^i + M_{del}^i + M_{wts}^i + M_{\Delta wts}^i. \qquad \text{(A3.34)}$$

### A3.2.3 Overall Memory Requirement

The overall memory requirement for any processor is the sum of $M_{pat}^i$ and $M_{net-par}^i$. This must be less than the external memory, $M_{tot}^i$, of the processor $i$:

$$M_{pat}^i + M_{net-param}^i < M_{tot}^i. \qquad \text{(A3.35)}$$

## A3.3 Elemental Timings for T805 Transputers

The time taken by the T805-20 and the T805-25 transputers for various elemental operations used in C language are given in Table A3.19. The timings in Table A3.19 are more accurate than those in [28] as these are obtained from experiments that mimicked more closely the run time entourage of BP.

TABLE A3.19. Timings for elemental operations for T805-20 and T805-25 Transputers.

| Type of Operation | Symbol Used | Time Taken ($\mu secs$) | |
|---|---|---|---|
| | | T805-20 | T805-25 |
| *for* loop | $t_{loop}$ | 1.67 | 1.30 |
| $a = b * c$ | $t_{ma}$ | 4.73 | 3.83 |
| $a * b$ | $t_m$ | 1.70 | 1.33 |
| $a* = b$ | $t_{sma}$ | 4.76 | 3.83 |
| $a = b - c$ | $t_{sa}$ | 4.76 | 3.83 |
| $a - b$ | $t_s$ | 1.61 | 1.27 |
| $a- = b$ | $t_{ssa}$ | 4.74 | 3.83 |
| $a = b + c$ | $t_{aa}$ | 4.74 | 3.83 |
| $a + b$ | $t_a$ | 1.69 | 1.33 |
| $a+ = b$ | $t_{saa}$ | 4.76 | 3.83 |
| $a = b$ | $t_{ass}$ | 3.44 | 2.78 |
| $a = sigmoid(b)$ | $t_{sig}$ | 73.5 | 58.70 |
| $t_{comm-init}$ | $t_{comm-init}$ | 22.8 | 22.8 |
| $t_{word}$ | $t_{word}$ | 2.30 | 2.30 |

# References

[1] D. E. Rumelhart, G. E. Hinton, and R. J. Williams, "Learning internal representations by error propagation," *Nature*, vol. 323, pp. 533–536, 1986.

[2] Y. Le Cun, et. al., "Backpropagation applied to handwritten zip code recognition," *Neural Computation*, vol. 1, no. 4, pp. 541–551, 1989.

[3] A. Waibel, "Consonant recognition by modular construction of large phonetic time-delay neural networks," *Advances in Neural Information Processing Systems*, pp. 215–223, 1989.

[4] Y. Fujimoto, N. Fukuda, and T. Akabane, "Massively parallel architectures for large scale neural network simulations," *IEEE Transactions on Neural Networks*, vol. 3, pp. 876–888, November 1992.

[5] S. W. Aiken, M. W. Koch, and M. W.Roberts, "A parallel neural network simulator," in *Proceedings of the ICNN International Conference on Neural Networks*, vol. 2, (San Diego, California), pp. 611–616, 1990.

[6] R. Battiti and A. Colla, "Parallel learning strategies on the emma-2 multiprocessor," in *Aritificial Neural Networks: Proc. ICANN-91* (T. Kohonen, et. al., ed.), vol. 2, pp. 1493–1500, Elsevier Science Publishers B.V. (North Holland), 1991.

[7] S. Kung and W.-H. Chou, "Mapping of neural networks onto vlsi array processors," in *Parallel Digital Implementation of Neural Networks* (K. Przytula and V. K. Prasanna, eds.), pp. 3–49, Englewood Cliffs, New Jersey: Prentice Hall International Inc, 1993.

[8] X. Zhang, et. al., "An efficient implementation of the backpropagation algorithm on the Connection Machine," *Advances in Neural Information Processing Systems*, vol. 2, pp. 801–809, 1990.

[9] L.-C. Chu and B. W. Wah, "Optimal mapping of neural-network learning on message-passing multicomputers," *Journal of Parallel and Distributed Computing*, vol. 14, pp. 319–339, 1992.

[10] M. Witbrock and M. Zagha, "Back-propagation learning on the IBM GF11," in *Parallel Digital Implementations of Neural Networks* (K. W. Przytula and V. K. Prasanna, eds.), ch. 3, pp. 77–104, Englewood Cliffs, NJ: PTR Prentice Hall, 1993.

[11] H. Yoon, J. H. Nang, and S. R. Maeng, "Parallel simulation of multilayered neural networks on distributed-memory multiprocessors," *Microprocessing and Microprogramming*, vol. 29, pp. 185–195, July 1990.

[12] F. Baiardi, R. Mussardo, R. Serra, and G. Valastro, "Feedforward layered networks on message passing parallel computers," *Second Italian Workshop on Parallel Architectures and Neural Networks*, pp. 212–222, 1990.

[13] V. Kumar, S. Shekhar, and M. B. Amin, "A scalable parallel formulation of the back-propagation algorithm for hypercubes and related architectures," *IEEE Transaction on Parallel and Distributed Computing*, vol. 5, pp. 1073–1090, October 1994.

[14] A. Cichocki and R. Ubehauen, *Neural Networks for Optimization and Signal Processing*. UK: John Wiley & sons, 1993.

[15] R. Freund and V. Sunderam, "Guest editor's introduction," *Journal of Parallel and Distributed Computing - Special issue on Heterogenous Processing*, no. 21, pp. 255–256, 1994.

[16] G. Richards, "Implementation of backpropagation on a transputer array," in *Developments in Occam* (J. Kerridge, ed.), pp. 173–179, Amsterdam: IOS Press, 1988.

[17] S. Fahlman, "An empirical study of learning speed in backpropagation networks," CMU-CS-88-162, Carnegie Mellon University, School of Computer Science, Pittsburgh, USA, 1988.

[18] T. J. Sejnowski and C. R. Rosenberg, "Parallel networks that learn to pronounce English text," *Complex Systems*, vol. 1, pp. 145–168, 1987.

[19] R. Arularasan, P. Saratchandran, and N. Sundararajan, "Timings for elemental operations in parallel c on t805 transputers," technical report eee/csp/9501, Nanyang Technological University, Nanyang Avenue, Singapore 639798, February 1995.

[20] A. Schrijver, *Theory of Linear and Integer Programming*. John Wiley & Sons, 1986.

[21] D. E. Goldberg, *Genetic Algorithms*. Addison Wesley, 1987.

[22] J. H. Holland, *Adaption in Natural and Artificial Systems*. Ann Arbor: The University of Michigan Press, 1975.

[23] L. Davis, ed., *Handbook of Genetic Algorithms*. New York: Van Nostrand Reinhold, 1991.

[24] M. Srinivas and L. M. Patnaik, "Genetic algorithms: A survey," *IEEE Computer*, pp. 17–26, June 1994.

[25] K. Deb and D. E. Goldberg, "A comparative analysis of selection schemes used in genetic algorithms," in *Foundations of Genetic Algorithms*, pp. 69–93, San Mateo, California: Morgan Kaufmann Publishers, 1991.

[26] S. K. Foo, P. Saratchandran, and N. Sundararajan, "Genetic algorithms based pattern allocation schemes for parallel implementations of backpropagation neural networks," technical report eee/csp/9502, Nanyang Technological University, Nanyang Avenue, Singapore 639798, May 1995.

[27] H. M. Salkin and K. Mathur, *Foundations of Integer Programming*. Elsevier Science Publishers B.V. (North-Holland), 1989.

[28] S. K. Foo, P. Saratchandran, and N. Sundararajan, "Analysis of training set parallelism for backpropagation neural networks," *International Journal of Neural Systems*, vol. 6, no. 1, pp. 61–78, 1995.

# Chapter 4

# Training-Set Parallelism for Backpropagation Neural Networks on a Heterogeneous Architecture

**Shou King Foo**
**P. Saratchandran**
**N. Sundararajan**
School of Electrical and Electronic Engineering,
Nanyang Technological University,
Singapore

## 4.1  Introduction

This study is a sequel to Chapter 3, which analyzes the issues relating to the network-based parallelism of the backpropagation algorithm (BP) onto a heterogeneous multiprocessor ring architecture. This sequel emphasizes training-set parallelism of the backpropagation algorithm. The heterogeneous processor network used is the same as that used in Chapter 3, which is a a message-passing multiprocessor unidirectional ring.

When the BP is partitioned using training-set parallelism, the entire neural network is placed in each processor while the training patterns are distributed among the processors. Due to this requirement, training-set parallelism can only be implemented efficiently with batch learning, whereas network-based parallelism can be implemented efficiently with on-line learning. In batch learning, the weights are updated after all the patterns are presented to the neural network. This is also known as epoch updating. In on-line learning, weights are updated after each pattern.

For training-set parallelism, communication overhead occurs because of the transfer of weight increments, which take place only at the end of each epoch. For network-based parallelism, communication overhead occurs because of the transfer of activation values and "delta" values during the forward and backward pass, respectively, which take place for every pattern, thus leading to a larger overall communication overhead.

Another difference between network-based parallelism and training-set parallelism is that for network-based parallelism, activation values of neurons present in each processor are broadcasted to the other processors. This step is needed so that each processor will have all the activation values of all the neurons in the previous layer. Because a heterogeneous array is used, the number of neurons present in each processor is different. This means that data packets of different sizes will be broadcasted in network-based parallelism. Contrasting this with training-set parallelism, the weight increments in each processor have to be broadcasted to the other processors and accumulated along the way so that the total weight increments for the epoch will be known in each processor. Because the number of weights present in the neural network is fixed, each processor will be broadcasting the same number of weight increments to other processors. Thus, the data packets of the same size will be broadcasted in training-set parallelism.

In this aspect, we can expect the theoretical model for network-based parallelism to be more complicated than that of training-set parallelism because more synchronization of processes are involved. However, as the transfer of weight increments and accumulations can occur in parallel in training-set parallelism, we can achieve more parallelism between calculations and communications in training-set parallelism.

The approach taken in this study is similar to that taken in Chapter 3. First, we develop a mathematical model to obtain, for any given mapping of the training set, an expression for the training time per epoch in terms of the timings for elemental computation and communication operations of the different processors. In the formulation of the theoretical time per epoch model, a new graphical representation known as process synchronization graph (PSG) is used. The PSG shows in a diagrammatic way the various computing and communication processes and their concurrency during the execution of a single epoch. Also, when the processes in a PSG are replaced by the variables in them, it is transformed to a variable synchronization graph (VSG), which aids in analyzing the parallel programming aspects of the processes and enhances the parallelism between computation and communication processes.

Next, we address the use of the mathematical model for finding the optimal mapping of training patterns to minimize the time for a training epoch for a neural network on a given heterogeneous processor network. One point of interest is that the optimal mapping problem for the heterogeneous processor network is a linear mixed integer programming (MIP) problem. This is in contrast with the network-based parallelism in which the optimal mapping of the neural network turns out to be a nonlinear MIP problem.

The organization of this chapter is as follows. Section 4.2 deals with the parallelization of the backpropagation training algorithm. It shows how a process synchronization graph can be used to develop a mathematical model and obtain an expression for the training time per epoch of the parallelized algorithm. This section also introduces a variable synchronization graph, which aids in the programming aspects of the parallelized algorithms. Experimental verification of the model is performed in Section 4.3 on heterogeneous networks rigged in the laboratory using transputers of different speed and memory. Section 4.4 analyzes the issue of optimal distribution of the patterns among the various processors to give minimum training time. It is shown that finding the optimal distribution is a linear MIP problem. Section 4.5 describes the genetic algorithm (GA) based solution strategy and provides the GA optimal epoch times for different benchmark problems. The benchmark problems chosen are similar to those in Chapter 3, namely, the Encoder [1] and Nettalk [2] benchmark problems. A Monte Carlo study and its results are discussed in Section 4.6. Section 4.7 provides a discussion on the worthwhileness of obtaining the optimal mapping by comparing the optimal epoch times with the epoch times from several heuristic pattern distributions. This section also looks into the effect of processor location on the optimal epoch time in the heterogeneous network. Section 4.8 summarizes the overall conclusions from the study.

## 4.2 Parallelization of BP Algorithm

This section describes the computation and communication steps involved in executing one epoch of the parallelized backpropagation algorithm on the heterogeneous processor network. As training-set parallelism is used as the parallelizing method, each processor will have only a subset of the whole training set and because of heterogeneity, the number of patterns in each processor would in general be different. Figure 4.1 shows such a mapping.

In the figure, $P^1, P^2, \ldots, P^n$ are the number of patterns allocated to the processors $1, 2, \ldots, n$. The processors perform the forward and backward pass of the BP algorithm

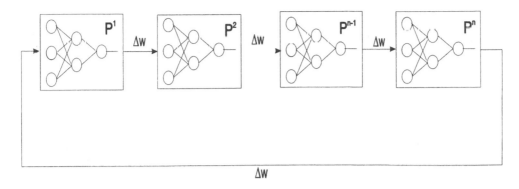

FIGURE 4.1. Training-set parallelism for a heterogeneous array of processors.

on those patterns allocated to them and compute the resulting weight increments ($\Delta w$ s). Each processor then needs the weight increments computed in all the other processors in order to update the weight values. This means each processor has to transfer the weight increments (because of the patterns allocated to it) to all other processors once these have been computed. Because the ring network used is unidirectional, this transfer is effected by the processors sending data to their right neighbor and receiving data from their left neighbor. Because the processor network is heterogeneous, all processors will not complete their computations at the same time and this will cause processors to wait before sending data to and receiving data from their neighbors.

The following steps are involved in executing one epoch of the parallelized backpropagation algorithm.

1. The processors initialize the weight changes for the current epoch to zero.

2. Each processor performs the forward pass and the backward pass of the BP algorithm on the patterns assigned to it and calculates the total weight increment due to these patterns. The quadratic error between the desired and actual outputs is also computed in this step.

3. The processors transfer the weight increments to each other. A set of weight increments includes the set of weight changes and bias changes. In an $n$ processor network, each processor needs to send and receive $n - 1$ weight increments. As the processors in a heterogeneous network cannot be expected to finish step 2 all at the same time, they may experience waiting times before sending and receiving data from their neighbors. The received weight increments are also accumulated so that at the end of the last transfer all processors will have the total weight increments due to the whole training set.

4. The processors update the weight values to obtain the new set of weights for their copy of the neural network. Because, in training-set parallelism, the same neural network is duplicated in all processors, the new weight values will be same in all processors.

5. The processors perform the convergence test and if the algorithm has not converged, iteration continues from step 1.

This completes one epoch of training for the parallel BP. Note that computing and communication processes can overlap in our network as this would enhance parallelism.

The processes needed to carry out steps 1 to 5 with the possible waitings that may occur can be clearly understood through a process synchronization graph. The PSG shows in a diagrammatic way the various computing and communication processes and their concurrency during the execution of a single epoch. It serves as an aid to obtain the mathematical model from which an expression for the time per epoch can be derived.

### 4.2.1 Process Synchronization Graph

The PSG is a modification of the timing diagram [3], communication graph (CG) [4] and the task graph (TG) [5]. Compared to the timing diagram, the PSG can represent not only those processes running in parallel among processors, but also the processes that run concurrently within a processor. Like the CG and the TG, the PSG can also show the temporal precedences among the processes. But unlike CG and TG, when the processes in a PSG are replaced by the variables in them, it is transformed to a variable synchronization graph (VSG), which aids in analyzing the parallel programming aspects of the processes. These include finding the locations of semaphores and maintaining data integrity. Figure 4.2 shows a PSG for the parallel BP on a three-processor heterogeneous ring network and Figure 4.3 shows the corresponding VSG.

In the PSG, circles represent processes and arrows indicate the waiting times that may be incurred by the processes. The time taken to execute a process is indicated inside the circle. For example, $T^1_{\Delta w_0}, T^2_{\Delta w_0}$, and $T^3_{\Delta w_0}$, are the times taken to execute the (computational) processes $\mathcal{P}^1_{\Delta w_0}, \mathcal{P}^2_{\Delta w_0}$, and $\mathcal{P}^3_{\Delta w_0}$, respectively, which initialize the weight increments to zero (step 1). To avoid too many symbols, Figure 4.2 does not show process names beside every circle but these are obvious from the execution time indicated inside the circles. $T^1_{BP}, T^2_{BP}$, and $T^3_{BP}$ are the times taken to compute the weight increments in processor 1, 2, and 3 (step 2). In step 3 the processors transfer the weight increments to each other. The times for these communication processes are indicated by $T^1_{send,1}, T^2_{rec,1}$, and so on. Various waiting times occur in the processors as they commence step 3. For example, $wr^2_1$ is the time the (communication) process $\mathcal{P}^2_{rec,1}$ in processor 2 has to wait before receiving the weight increments from processor 1. Thus, the receiving process cannot commence with the computation processes $\mathcal{P}^2_{\Delta w_0}$ and $\mathcal{P}^2_{BP}$, even though communication and computing processes can run concurrently in our network. This is because the receiving process in processor 2 can commence only when processor 1 is ready to send its weight increments and this is possible only after the completion of $\mathcal{P}^1_{BP}$.

In the PSG, the precedence relationships between the various processes are shown through temporal junctions. These are denoted by $J$'s in Figure 4.2 and are characterized by a horizontal line with one or more processes connecting to it from below and one or more processes connecting to it from above. The meaning of the temporal junction is as follows. The processes connected to the horizontal bar from below can start only after the completion of all processes connected to the horizontal bar from above. Two types of temporal junctions exist. The intraprocessor temporal junctions involve processes within the same processor, and the interprocessor temporal junctions involve processes in different processors. The detailed explanation of symbols in Figure 4.2 are as follows. For all the symbols, subscript $j$ is an index to indicate the $j$-th occurrence of the entity.

- $T^i_{\Delta w_0}$; $1 \leq i \leq n$: Time taken by the $i$-th processor for initializing all the weight increments to zero. The value of $i$ ranges from 1 to $n$ where $n$ is the total number of processor present in the ring topology. For example, in Figure 4.2, $n = 3$.

- $T^i_{BP}$; $1 \leq i \leq n$: Time taken to calculate the weight increments by the $i$-th processor.

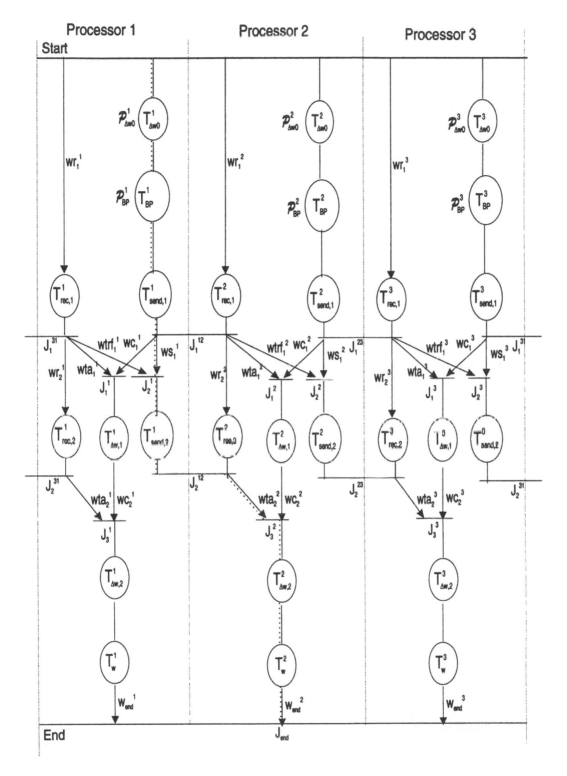

FIGURE 4.2. Processor synchronization graph for the parallelized BP on a three-processor network.

- $T_{send,j}^i$; $1 \le i \le n$, $1 \le j \le (n-1)$: Time taken to send the weight increments over the communication link by the $i$-th processor. The time taken for the "send" operation includes the time needed to initialize a communication process and the time needed to transfer the data.

- $T_{rec,j}^i$; $1 \le i \le n$, $1 \le j \le (n-1)$: Time taken to receive data over the communication link by the $i$-th processor. The time taken for the "receive" operation includes the time needed to initialize a communication process and the time to receive the data.

- $T_{\Delta w,j}^i$; $1 \le i \le n$, $1 \le j \le (n-1)$: This is the time for accumulating the weight increments by the $i$-th processor.

- $T_w^i$; $1 \le i \le n$: Time for updating the weight values in the $i$-th processor.

- $ws_j^i$; $1 \le i \le n$, $1 \le j \le (n-2)$: These are the waiting intervals for the sending process $\mathcal{P}_{send,j}^i$ because the corresponding receiving process (in the $(i+1)$-th processor) is not ready.

- $wr_j^i$; $1 \le i \le n$, $1 \le j \le (n-1)$: These are the waiting intervals for the receiving process $\mathcal{P}_{rec,j}^i$ because the corresponding sending process (in the $(i-1)$-th processor) is not ready.

- $wtrf_j^i$; $1 \le i \le n$, $1 \le j \le (n-2)$: These are the waiting intervals for process $\mathcal{P}_{send,j}^i$. These occur because the weight increments can be sent out to the downstream processor after they have been received from the upstream processor.

- $wta_j^i$; $1 \le i \le n$, $1 \le j \le (n-1)$: These are the waiting time intervals for process $\mathcal{P}_{\Delta w,j}^i$. These occur because the weight increments can only be accumulated only after receiving it.

- $wc_j^i$; $1 \le i \le n$, $1 \le j \le (n-1)$: This is the waiting time experienced by the accumulation process because the previous accumulation is not completed.

- $w_{end}^i$; $1 \le i \le n$: This is the time spent on waiting by process $\mathcal{P}_w^i$ for the completion of $\mathcal{P}_w$s in all the other processors.

- $J_j^i$; $1 \le i \le n$, $1 \le j \le 2n-3$: This is the intraprocessor temporal junctions within processor $i$.

- $J_j^{ab}$; $1 \le j \le n-1$; This is interprocessor temporal junctions involving processor $a$ and $b$.

- $J_{end}$: This junction indicates the end of the epoch.

The PSG, although capable of showing the concurrency and temporal precedence among the processes, cannot be used to analyze (parallel) programming issues such as the sharing/isolation of data areas (that is, buffers) and locations of semaphores. Correct use of these is important to guarantee data integrity and enhance parallelism. A tool that facilitates understanding of these issues is the variable synchronization graph.

A VSG is a modified version of the PSG in which the execution times of the processes are replaced by the names of buffers required by the processes. If two processes can share a buffer, then the corresponding buffers' names in both processes will be the same to indicate sharing. For example, Figure 4.2 shows that the communication process to receive the weight increments, $\mathcal{P}^1_{rec,1}$, and the computing process, $\mathcal{P}^1_{BP}$, can run concurrently. However, to maintain data integrity, these processes must hold their weight increments in separate buffers. The same applies between $\mathcal{P}^1_{rec,2}$ and $\mathcal{P}^1_{BP}$. However, the processes $\mathcal{P}^1_{\Delta w_0}$ and $\mathcal{P}^1_{BP}$ can share a buffer to hold their data because the two processes are not concurrent. Information of this nature is shown clearly in the VSG.

### 4.2.2 Variable Synchronization Graph

In the VSG of Figure 4.3, the subscripts indicate the buffer number and the superscripts indicate the processor number. Thus $\Delta w^1_1 = 0$ means buffer 1 in processor 1 is initialized to zero.[1] $BP^i$ refers to computed weight increments, and these are held in the same buffer used for initialization. The symbol '$\Rightarrow S^i$' means "sent to processor $i$" and '$R^i \Rightarrow$' means "received from processor $i$." So $R^3 \Rightarrow \Delta w^1_2$ means the weight increments received from processor 3 are held in buffer 2 in processor 1. The accumulation is indicated by "$+ =$." Thus $\Delta w^1_1 + = \Delta w^1_3$ means the content of buffer 3 is accumulated to the content of buffer 1 where the buffers are all in processor 1.

From the VSG diagram we can see that to implement all the parallelism shown in the PSG of Figure 4.2, four buffer areas are needed in each processor and these hold the weight increments and weight values. Further, we can see that in any processor $i$, buffer 1 is shared among the processes $\mathcal{P}^i_{\Delta w_0}$, $\mathcal{P}^i_{BP}$, $\mathcal{P}^i_{send,1}$, $\mathcal{P}^i_{\Delta w,1}$, and $\mathcal{P}^i_{\Delta w,2}$, whereas buffer 2 is shared among the processes $\mathcal{P}^i_{rec,1}$ and $\mathcal{P}^i_{send,2}$. Buffers 3 and 4 are exclusive to processes $\mathcal{P}^i_{rec,2}$ and $\mathcal{P}^i_w$, respectively. Such information is useful at the programming stage of parallel algorithms. If the (local) memory available in the processor is not sufficient to hold four buffer areas, it then implies that all the parallelism in the PSG cannot be implemented due to resource limitations. The thing to do in such a case would be to redesign the PSG with reduced parallelism to reflect resource availability.

VSG can also show implementation aspects of the intraprocessor temporal junctions of the PSG. These junctions indicate the required temporal precedences between processes. Semaphores provide a good mechanism to enforce these precedences and in the VSG a semaphore symbol is located at each of these junctions. The processes linked to a temporal junction share the semaphore located at that junction, for example, $S^1_3$ is the semaphore used to implement the temporal junction $J^1_3$ and is shared by the processes $\mathcal{P}^1_{rec,2}$, $\mathcal{P}^1_{\Delta w,1}$, and $\mathcal{P}^1_{\Delta w,2}$. Thus, from the VSG diagram we can tell the number of semaphores needed and their locations in each processor to correctly implement the temporal precedences shown in the PSG.

### 4.2.3 Predicting the Epoch Time

A mathematical model for the parallel BP running on the processor network can be obtained by expressing the computing and communication processes of the PSG in terms of the basic operations performed in them. This can be done by first writing the functionality of these processes in pseudocodes and then finding out the various basic computing and communication operations required from these codes. If the times taken for these basic operations are known, then the time required to execute the process can be theoretically predicted. As an example, Appendix 4.9 shows how this can be done for the process $\mathcal{P}^i_{\Delta w_0}$.

From the mathematical model, the time for an epoch can be derived. It is the time taken to traverse down from "Start" to "End" in the PSG following any path. This can be calculated once the times for the various processes and the various waiting intervals are known. Because the waiting times are dependent on the times taken by the various

---

[1] $\Delta w$ indicates that this buffer is used to hold weight increments.

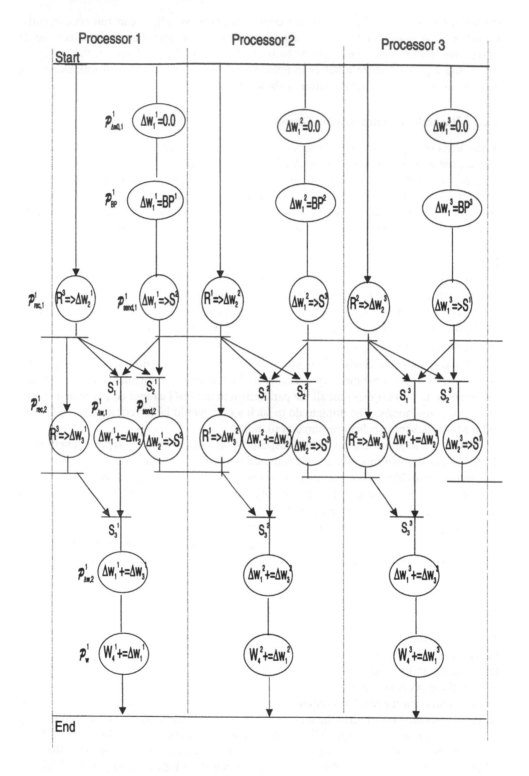

FIGURE 4.3. Variable synchronization graph for the parallelized BP on a three-processor network. Only the process names for processor 1 are shown.

computing and communicating processes, they can be worked out once the times for these processes are known. Following the path sketched in Figure 4.2, the equation for the time for an epoch for a three-processor heterogeneous network ($T_{epoch\_3}$) can be written as,

$$T_{epoch\_3} = T^1_{\Delta w_0} + T^1_{BP} + ws^1_1 + 2T^1_{send,1} + wta^2_2 + T^2_{\Delta w,2} + T^2_w + w^2_{end} \quad (4.1)$$

In Equation 4.1, the term $2T^1_{send,1}$ is used instead of the term $T^1_{send,1} + T^1_{send,2}$ because the time taken to send the weight increments is the same within the same processor. Extension of Equation 4.1 for a heterogeneous network with $n$ processors is conceptually straightforward but tedious in practice. The resulting expression for $T_{epoch\_n}$ is:

$$T_{epoch\_n} = T^1_{\Delta w_0} + T^1_{BP} + \sum_{j=1}^{j=n-2} ws^1_j + (n-1)T^1_{send,1} + wta^2_{n-1}$$
$$+T^2_{\Delta w,n-1} + T^2_w + w^2_{end} \quad (4.2)$$

Although the execution times of only a few computing and communication processes appear explicitly in Equation 4.2, the execution times of all the rest of the computing and communication processes are present implicitly in the expression through the waiting times. Details of the theoretical expressions to predict the execution times for all the communications and computing processes can be found in [6].

## 4.3 Experimental Validation of the Model Using Benchmark Problems

In this section theoretical epoch times obtained from Equation 4.2 are compared with experimentally obtained epoch times for a number of heterogeneous processor networks using different models of transputers [7]. The transputer models used in this processor network are the T805-20 (20 MHz) and the T805-25 (25MHz). The timings for elemental computing and communication operations for these processors are measured using methods described in [8] and are given in Appendix A3.3 of Chapter 3.

The benchmark problem considered in this section is the Encoder [1] problem described in detail in Chapter 3. In the experiments, we varied both the processor configuration and the pattern distributions. The time for an epoch is found for a 256-8-256 Encoder network on three different heterogeneous processor networks each having 10 T805-20 (20MHz) and six T805-25 (25MHz) transputers. The local (external) memory for T805-20 is 1 Mbyte and that for the T805-25 is 2 Mbytes. Details of the processor configurations used in our experiments are as follows:

**Configuration 1.** In this configuration the slow processors are followed by the fast processors as shown in Figure 4.4(a). This processor network will be referred to as the CONFIG-1 network in the rest of the study.

**Configuration 2.** Here, groups of slow processors are interposed with groups of fast processors as shown in Figure 4.4(b). This processor network will be referred to as the CONFIG-2 network in the rest of the study.

**Configuration 3.** Here the slow and fast processors are intermingled in a random way as shown in Figure 4.4(c). This processor network will be referred to as the CONFIG-3 network in the rest of the study.

Time for an epoch from theory and experiment was compared for a number of random pattern allocations. In all cases, theoretically predicted epoch time was within 5 percent of

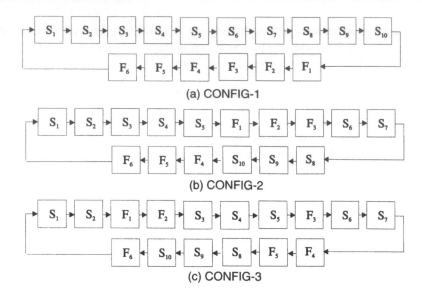

FIGURE 4.4. Processor configurations used in the validation experiments. S and F denote slow and fast processors, respectively.

the experimental time. Table 4.1 presents the theoretically predicted and the experimentally obtained epoch times for two sample pattern distributions. The two distributions are as follows:

**DIST-1.** In this case an equal number of patterns are allocated to all the processors. Thus, each processor is allocated 16 patterns.

**DIST-2.** In this case fast processors are allocated more patterns than the slow ones. Among the fast and slow processors equal distribution is maintained. Thus, the 10 slow ones are allocated 13 patterns each and the 6 fast ones are allocated 21 patterns each.

TABLE 4.1. Comparison of theoretical and experimental times per epoch for the three-processor networks for the Encoder problem.

| Type of Network | DIST-1 | | | DIST-2 | | |
|---|---|---|---|---|---|---|
| | Time for an Epoch (sec) | | Difference | Time for an Epoch (sec) | | Difference |
| | Theoretical | Experimental | % | Theoretical | Experimental | % |
| CONFIG-1 | 2.842 | 2.980 | 4.86 | 2.932 | 3.009 | 2.63 |
| CONFIG-2 | 2.842 | 2.957 | 4.05 | 2.932 | 3.012 | 2.73 |
| CONFIG-3 | 2.842 | 2.965 | 4.33 | 2.932 | 3.019 | 2.97 |

Table 4.1 shows that the theoretically predicted epoch times are close to the experimental times, thus validating our model.

## 4.4 Optimal Distribution of Patterns Among the Processing Nodes

In the previous section, we developed and validated a mathematical model to predict the epoch time for a given distribution of patterns. This section makes use of the time per epoch model to find the *optimal* distribution of the training patterns on a given heterogeneous processor network. The objective is to find the allocation of patterns to processors so as to minimize the time per epoch without violating any of the constraints imposed by the processor network. The time for an epoch is given by Equation 4.2. The various constraints that need to be satisfied are described next.

### 4.4.1 Communication Constraints

These constraints arise because of the synchronized communications used for interprocessor message passing in the processor network. For example, it can be seen at Junction $J_1^{12}$ in Figure 4.2 that the time at which processor 1 completes sending data to processor 2 is $T_{\Delta w_0}^1 + T_{BP}^1 + T_{send,1}^1$, and the time at which processor 2 completes receiving the data from processor 1 is $wr_1^2 + T_{rec,1}^2$. These two times must be equal as interprocessor communications are always synchronized. Hence, at junction $J_1^{12}$, the following equality must hold:

$$T_{\Delta w_0}^1 + T_{BP}^1 + T_{send,1}^1 = wr_1^2 + T_{rec,1}^2.$$

Likewise, equality constraints at all other interprocessor junctions can be formulated and be represented in a compact matrix forms as

$$A_1 X_1 = B_1, \tag{4.3}$$

$$A_2 X_2 = B_2, \tag{4.4}$$

where[2]

$$A_1 = \begin{bmatrix} T_{BP}^i & -1 \end{bmatrix}_{1\times 2}, \quad X_1 = \begin{bmatrix} 1^{il} \\ wr_1^{ring(i+1)} \end{bmatrix}_{2\times 1},$$

$$B_1 = \begin{bmatrix} T_{rec,1}^{ring(i+1)} - T_{send,1}^i - T_{\Delta w_0}^i \end{bmatrix}_{1\times 1}, \quad 1 \le i \le n,$$

and

$$A_2 = \begin{bmatrix} 1 & -1 \end{bmatrix}_{1\times 2}, \quad X_2 = \begin{bmatrix} ws_j^i \\ wr_{ring(j+1)}^{ring(i+1)} \end{bmatrix}_{2\times 1},$$

$$B_2 = \begin{bmatrix} T_{rec,j+1}^{ring(i+1)} - T_{send,j+1}^i \end{bmatrix}_{1\times 1}, \quad 1 \le i \le n, \ 1 \le j \le n-2, \ n \ge 3.$$

### 4.4.2 Temporal Dependence Constraints

These constraints occur mainly because communication and computation can overlap in our processor network. In the PSG, every intraprocessor temporal junction creates a constraint. For example, at junction $J_1^2$ in Figure 4.2, the following equality must hold:

$$T_{\Delta w_0}^1 + T_{BP}^1 + T_{send,1}^1 + wta_1^2 = T_{\Delta w_0}^2 + T_{BP}^2 + T_{send,1}^2 + wc_1^2.$$

Similarly constraints at all the other intraprocessor junctions can be formulated. Again they can be expressed in a compact matrix form as

$$A_3 X_3 = B_3, \tag{4.5}$$

$$A_4 X_4 = B_4, \tag{4.6}$$

---

[2]The ring function is defined as

$$ring(x) = \begin{cases} n & \text{if } x - \lfloor \frac{x}{n} \rfloor n = 0, \\ n - \lfloor \frac{x}{n} \rfloor n & \text{if } x - \lfloor \frac{x}{n} \rfloor n \ne 0. \end{cases}$$

where

$$A_3 = \left[ \begin{array}{cccc} T_{BP}^{ring(i-1)} & -T_{BP}^i & 1 & -1 \end{array} \right]_{1 \times 4}, \quad X_3 = \left[ \begin{array}{c} P^{ring(i-1)} \\ P^i \\ wta_1^i \\ wc_1^i \end{array} \right]_{4 \times 1},$$

$$B_3 = \left[ \begin{array}{c} T_{send,1}^i - T_{send,1}^{ring(i-1)} + T_{\Delta w_0}^i - T_{\Delta w_0}^{ring(i-1)} \end{array} \right]_{1 \times 1}, \quad 1 \le i \le n,$$

and

$$A_4 = \left[ \begin{array}{cccc} 1 & 1 & -1 & -1 \end{array} \right]_{1 \times 4}, \quad X_4 = \left[ \begin{array}{c} ws_j^{ring(i-1)} \\ wta_{ring(j+1)}^i \\ wta_j^i \\ wc_{ring(j+1)}^i \end{array} \right]_{4 \times 1},$$

$$B_4 = \left[ \begin{array}{c} -T_{send,j+1}^{ring(i+1)} + T_{\Delta w,j+1}^i \end{array} \right]_{1 \times 1}, \quad 1 \le i \le n, \ 1 \le j \le n-2, \ n \ge 3.$$

The time taken from "Start" to "End" must be the same for all processors because this is the time for completion of one epoch. So,

$$T_{epoch\_n}^1 = T_{epoch\_n}^i, \quad 2 \le i \le n \tag{4.7}$$

where $T_{epoch\_n}^i$ is the time from "Start" to "End" for the $i$-th processor; that is,

$$T_{epoch\_n}^i = T_{\Delta w_0}^i + T_{BP}^i + (n-1)T_{send,1}^i$$
$$+ \sum_{j=1}^{j=n-2} ws_j^i + T_{\Delta w,n-1}^{ring(i+1)} + T_w^{ring(i+1)} + w_{end}^{ring(i+1)}, \quad 1 \le i \le n. \tag{4.8}$$

### 4.4.3 Memory Constraints

In training-set parallelism, each processor has to keep a complete copy of the neural network as well as the patterns that are allocated to it. Because each processor has a fixed external memory, (1 Mbyte, 2 Mbytes, 4 Mbytes, and so on), there is a limit to the number of network parameters (weights, activations, and so forth) and training patterns that a processor can hold. This results in the following constraints for processor $i$ :

$$r[(n+2)N_w + (n+5)N_{tot} + P^n(N_1 + N_l)] < M^i \tag{4.9}$$

where

- $r$ is the number of bytes required to store a floating point number,

- $N_w$ is the number of weights in the network,

- $N_{tot}$ is the number of neurons (excluding neurons in the input layer) in the network,

- $N_1$ is the number of neurons in the input layer,

- $N_l$ is the number of neurons in the output layer, and

- $M^i$ is the amount of memory (in bytes) available in processor $i$.

Details of the derivations of Equation 4.9 are given in Appendix 4.10.

### 4.4.4 Feasibility Constraints

Feasibility constraints include the feasibility of pattern assignments and the feasibility of waiting.

### 4.4.5 Feasibility of Pattern Assignments

These constraints require that the number of patterns assigned to the processors be non-negative integers and their sum be equal the total number of patterns present in the training set. Therefore,

$$P^k \geq 0, \quad 1 \leq k \leq n \tag{4.10}$$

$$\sum_{k=1}^{k=n} P^k = P_{tot} \tag{4.11}$$

where $P_{tot}$ is the total number of training patterns in the training set.

### 4.4.6 Feasibility of Waiting

All intraprocessor waiting intervals must be nonnegative:

$$W^i \geq 0, \, 1 \leq i \leq n \tag{4.12}$$

where $W^i = \begin{bmatrix} ws^i_j & wr^i_j & wc^i_j & wtrf^i_j & wta^i_j & w^i_{end} \end{bmatrix}^T$.

### 4.4.7 Optimal Mapping

This section discusses how we can find the optimal pattern distribution among the processors so that the time for an epoch ($T_{epoch\_n}$ in Equation 4.2) is minimized. The constraints given by Equations 4.3 to 4.12 can be posed as a linear mixed integer programming (MIP) problem,[3] as given below:

$$\min_{P^i, W^i} : T_{epoch\_n}. \tag{4.13}$$

This is subject to

$$A_j X_j = B_j, \quad 1 \leq j \leq 4$$
$$r[(n+2)N_w + (n+5)N_{tot} + P^n(N_1 + N_l)] < M^i, \quad 1 \leq i \leq n$$
$$\sum_{k=1}^{k=n} P^k = P_{tot}$$
$$T^1_{epoch\_n} = T^i_{epoch\_n}, \quad 2 \leq i \leq n$$
$$P^i \geq 0, \quad 1 \leq i \leq n$$
$$W^i \geq 0, \quad 1 \leq i \leq n.$$

MIP problems are known to be NP complete [9] and their solution normally takes enormous computing time. In our MIP problem, the decision variables are the pattern allocations for each processor ($P^i$) and the various waiting intervals ($W^i$'s). For a network

---

[3]Mixed because $P^i$ must be integers but the $ws^i_j$, $wr^i_j$, $wc^i_j$, $wtrf^i_j$, $wta^i_j$, and $w^i_{end}$ can be real numbers.

with $n$ processors, we will have a total of $5n^2 - 5n$ decision variables out of which $n$ variables must take integer values and the rest can have real values. The number of constraints to be considered are $3n^2 - 3n - 1$. It is very clear that the complexity of the allocation problem is too overwhelming to attempt an exhaustive search. For example, it took 2 days 16 hrs 38 min of VAX 9000 CPU time to completely solve the MIP problem for the encoder benchmark on the CONFIG-3 network using the branch and bound approach [10]. This motivated us to look for suboptimal solutions that are fast and sufficiently close to global optimum.

## 4.5 Genetic Algorithmic Solution to the Optimal Mapping Problem

In this section, we consider a GA-based solution to the MIP problem. The GA considered in this section is similar to that used in Chapter 3. The main difference is in the coding of the chromosomes. In this study, the number of training patterns allocated to each processor will be the allele value for each gene, whereas in Chapter 3 the number of neurons allocated to each processor was the allele value. Further, after every recombination, the allele values are normalized to ensure that the constraints on patterns assignments described in Section 4.4 are not violated. The basic steps in our GA are same as that of the simple genetic algorithm [11], as given here

```
Initialize the population;
Find the fitness of each chromosome in the population;
Repeat
   Select solution chromosomes to form the intermediate
   population;
   Perform crossover and mutation on the intermediate
   population to obtain the next generation;
   Find the fitness of the chromosomes in
   the new generation;
Continue until stopping criterion is met;
```

A brief description of the various components of the GA used in our optimization problem is given as follows. A detailed description can be found in [12].

**Initial population.** Each element of the initial population is a potential solution and consists of a string of integers. The initial population is randomly generated from a uniform distribution centered at equal allocation. The spread on either side of the center for the uniform distribution is taken to be half the equal allocation. Care is taken to ensure that the phenotypic values of the chromosomes of the population do not violate the feasibility constraints on pattern assignment discussed in Section 4.4. The population size used is 150.

**Fitness.** The fitness of a chromosome is defined as the time for an epoch resulting from the pattern allocation in the chromosome.

**Selection.** This study uses the tournament selection scheme [13] to form the intermediate population from the initial population. According to this scheme, a fixed number (known as tournament size) of chromosomes are randomly picked from the initial population and the fittest among them is identified as a member for the intermediate population. This procedure of randomly picking a fixed number of chromosomes and identifying the best is repeated until the desired number of chromosomes is obtained for the intermediate population. We choose the tournament selection scheme instead

TABLE 4.2. Optimal time per epoch (sec) from the GA method for the Encoder and Nettalk problems.

| Type of Processor Network | Benchmark Problem | |
|---|---|---|
| | Encoder | Nettalk |
| CONFIG-1 | 2.705 | 18.822 |
| CONFIG-2 | 2.705 | 18.879 |
| CONFIG-3 | 2.705 | 18.886 |

of the more popular roulette wheel [14] scheme based on a comparison study [15] for a similar problem, which showed tournament selection producing faster convergence. The tournament size used is 50.

**Crossover and mutation.** These are the recombination operators used on the intermediate population to obtain new solutions. Two-point part crossover, in which there are two crossover sites in each chromosome and recombination between two chromosomes takes place by successively switching sides at these sites with some probability, is used in this study. The genes between the two crossover points are normalized to ensure that the sum of allele values tallies with the total number of training patterns. The mutation operator introduces new genetic structures in the population, which are unrelated to any previous genetic structure of the population. We used a uniform mutation scheme in which each gene in a chromosome is given a chance to undergo mutation with some probability. The crossover and mutation probabilities used are 0.75 and 0.1, respectively.

**Stopping criterion.** A good stopping criterion is needed to make the algorithm convergent and avoid a situation where the best solution is obtained in one generation and lost in the next, never to reappear. In this study, we make use of the stopping criterion discussed in [16], which is based on the reduction in the slope of the fitness curve.

### 4.5.1 Experimental Results

In this section optimal mapping for the three heterogeneous processor networks shown in Figure 4.4 are obtained using the GA method. The benchmark problems considered are the 256-8-256 Encoder and the Nettalk text to phoneme problem. The Nettalk problem used this study has 203 input neurons, 30 hidden neurons, 26 output neurons and 2,000 training patterns. Table 4.2 shows the time for an epoch corresponding to GA optimal mapping for the three processor networks for the Encoder and Nettalk problems. The optimal solution times in Table 4.2 are the average of several GA runs with each run using a different initial population. This is because GAs are sensitive to initial conditions, and without multiple replication of the experimental conditions one cannot make a good case about their performance. Although solutions are readily obtained from the GA method, it is not known whether these solutions are indeed close to the (global) optimum for the MIP problem. This is investigated in the next section using a statistical approach.

## 4.6   Statistical Validation of the Optimal Mapping

Similar to Chapter 3, a Monte Carlo simulation study is carried out to find out the proximity of the solutions obtained in Section 4.5.1 to the global optimal solution. In this Monte Carlo simulation, the sample sizes varied from 100 to 500, and for each sample size, the mean and standard deviation for the epoch time was obtained. These are then compared with the epoch times obtained from the GA solutions. If the epoch time from GA is close to the global minimum, then it should lie *far* below the sample mean for all trials.

Figure 4.5 shows the distribution of the epoch time for the Encoder problem when the sample size is 500. The configuration used is CONFIG-1. Similar Gaussian-like distributions were obtained for the other two processor configurations as well. The epoch time from the GA solution is also shown in Figure 4.5.

Figure 4.6 shows the mean$\pm 3\sigma$ for the epoch time for various sample sizes using configuration CONFIG-1. As Figure 4.6 shows, the epoch time from the GA method is always less than the sample's mean time by three standard deviations ($3\sigma$). This implies that the GA optimal solutions must be quite close to the global minimum.

Monte Carlo simulations for Nettalk also showed that the GA solutions are close to the global minimum.

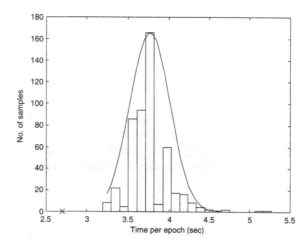

FIGURE 4.5. Distribution of epoch time for the Encoder problem for configuration CONFIG-1. The symbol $(X)$ indicates the epoch time from the GA solution.

## 4.7 Discussion

The previous section showed that GA is a viable method for solving the optimal pattern allocation problem. However, GA takes a finite amount of time to find the optimal solution. This raises the question of whether the time taken by GA to find the optimal solution would itself offset the benefit to be gained from using the optimal allocation. This issue is discussed in this section.

### 4.7.1 Worthwhileness of Finding Optimal Distribution

Although the results in Section 4.5 show that GA solutions are close to the global optimum for the MIP problem, no information is provided about the time taken to find the solution. To investigate the worthwhileness of finding the optimal pattern allocation with GA, the training time for the GA allocation was compared with that of heuristic allocations, where the training time for GA allocation included the time taken to find the optimal solution. Table 4.3 shows the total training time taken by the GA and two heuristic allocations for

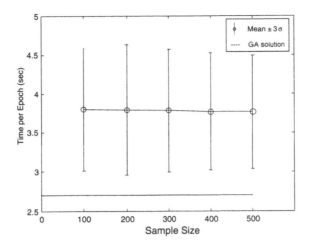

FIGURE 4.6. $Mean \pm 3\sigma$ of epoch time for the Encoder problem for configuration CONFIG-1.

the Encoder benchmark problem on CONFIG-3. The two nonoptimal allocations chosen are DIST-1 and DIST-2, as described in Section 4.3.

TABLE 4.3. Total time taken for training using the two heuristic and GA pattern distributions for the Encoder problem on CONFIG-3. Convergence was reached after 15,200 epochs.

| Distribution | Time to Find the Allocation Time (min) | Training Time (min) | Overall Time (min) |
|---|---|---|---|
| DIST-1 | 0 | 719.97 | 719.97 |
| DIST-2 | 0 | 742.87 | 742.87 |
| GA | 0.820 | 685.52 | 686.34 |

Table 4.3 shows that finding the optimal allocation is a worthwhile exercise as the reduction realized in overall training time more than compensates for the extra time needed to find the optimal solution. The small reduction (5 to 6 percent) in the overall time from GA in Table 4.3 is because of the relatively small difference in the processor speeds in our heterogeneous network and the small size of the training set in the Encoder problem. We feel that for large problems with many thousands of training patterns and processor networks with greater heterogeneity, the reduction in training time from optimal pattern allocations will be more pronounced.

### 4.7.2 Processor Location in a Ring

The effect of processor locations on the performance of the ring can be analyzed from the results of Table 4.2, which indicate that locations of the processors do not have much effect on the performance and the optimal epoch time will vary very little with respect to processor locations in a ring topology. Similar observations were made for network-based parallel mapping in Chapter 3.

## 4.8 Conclusion

This chapter presented a detailed analysis of training-set parallel implementation of back-propagation learning on a heterogeneous processor network in ring topology. A mathematical model for the parallel BP running on the heterogeneous network was developed and experimentally validated. The model was obtained using a process synchronization and a variable synchronization graph. The variable synchronization graph aids in the programming aspects, such as process synchronization and buffers allocation for the parallel BP.

Using the model, the problem of finding the optimal mapping of the training set can be studied and is shown to result in a linear mixed integer optimization problem. Genetic algorithms were used and shown to offer a viable method for solving the MIP problem. Using a Monte Carlo method, the epoch times from the GA optimal mappings were shown to be $3\sigma$ lower than the mean epoch times for several sample sizes. This implies that the GA optimal solutions are very close to the global optimal solutions. These results further indicate that the locations of processors do not have any significant impact on the performance of a heterogeneous ring network.

Although all the experimental results are given for heterogeneous transputer networks, the model and the analysis put forward are applicable for any message-passing multiprocessor heterogeneous network, as was the case for network-based parallelism in Chapter 3.

# Appendices

## 4.9 Process Decomposition

This appendix gives an example of how to decompose a process in terms of its basic operations to obtain the execution time. The process considered is $\mathcal{P}^i_{\Delta w_0}$, which initializes the weight and bias changes.

At the start of an epoch all the weight changes and bias changes have to be initialized to zero to nullify the values existing from the previous epoch. The initialization requires one assignment statement to perform the assign zeros to each of the weight changes and bias changes. The C-like pseudocodes for performing the initialization are as follows.

```
/*initialize the weight changes to zero*/
/*``layer'' is the total number of layers present
(including the input layer)*/
/*Nlayer is the number of neurons in the output layer*/
/*Nlayer-1 is the number of neurons in the layer
before the output layer*/
/*k refers to the layer index*/
/*i refers to the i-th node in the (k + 1)-th layer*/
/*j refers to the j-th node in the k-th layer*/
for (k = 0; k < (layer − 1); k++)
for (i = 0; i < N_{k+1}; i++)
for (j = 0; j < N_k; j++)
Δw[k][i][j] = 0.0;  (a)
/*initialize the bias changes to zero*/
/*for this case and the rest that follows*/
/*k refers to the layer index*/
/*j is the j-th node in the (k + 1)-th layer*/
for (k = 0; k < (layer − 1); k++)
for (j = 0; j < N_{k+1}; j++)
Δbias[k][j] = 0.0;  (b)
```

The pseudocodes show that the computational operations are those in lines (a), (b), and the *for* loop statements. The type of operation performed in lines (a) and (b) is assignment (=).

As shown from the pseudocodes, the total number of weights to be initialized is

$$\sum_{k=0}^{k=layer-2} N_{k+1} \times N_k.$$

This corresponds to $N_w$. Likewise, the total number of biases to initialized is

$$\sum_{k=0}^{k=layer-2} N_{k+1}.$$

This corresponds to $N_{tot}$. Because there are $N_w$ weights and $N_{tot}$ biases in the network, $T^i_{\Delta w_0}$ is given by

$$T^i_{\Delta w_0} = (N_w + N_{tot})(t_{ass} + t_{loop}) \tag{4.14}$$

where $t_{ass}$ represents the elemental operation time for assignment and $t_{loop}$ is the time taken for a "for" loop. The values of $t_{ass}$ and $t_{loop}$ for transputers are given in Appendix C of Chapter 3.

Using a similar approach, theoretical expressions to predict the time for all the computation and communication processes can be derived.

## 4.10  Memory Requirements

This appendix discusses the memory requirement for the processors in the ring network for implementing the parallelized backpropagation algorithm.

### 4.10.1  Storing the Network Parameters

If $r$ is the number of bytes required to store a floating point number, then the amount of memory required to store all the weights and biases in a neural network is

$$r(N_w + N_{tot}) \tag{4.15}$$

where $N_w$ is the number of weights in the network and $N_{tot}$ is the number of neurons (excluding neurons in the input layer) in the network. $N_{tot}$ also corresponds to the number of biases in the neural network.

### 4.10.2  Storing the Training Set

Memory is needed to store the training patterns allocated to a processor. Corresponding to each input (training) pattern is a desired output pattern. If $N_1$ and $N_l$ are the number of neurons in the input and output layer, respectively, to store each training pattern $r(N_1 + N_l)/$ amount of memory is required. The total memory required to store all the $P^i$ patterns allocated to a processor $i$ will be

$$rP^i(N_1 + N_l) \tag{4.16}$$

### 4.10.3  Memory Required for the Forward Pass of the Backpropagation

The forward pass of the backpropagation requires the output value at every neuron and this in turn requires the input value at every neuron. Because there are $N_{tot}$ neurons in the network, the amount of memory required to store these will be

$$r(N_{tot} + N_{tot}) \tag{4.17}$$

### 4.10.4  Memory Required for the Backward Pass of the Backpropagation

During the backward pass of the backpropagation each processor has to store the weight changes, bias changes, and, at each neuron, the errors ("deltas"). The memory required for all these will be

$$r(N_w + N_{tot} + N_{tot}) \tag{4.18}$$

For this implementation, because the momentum term is used in the backpropagation during the updating of the weights, the weights and biases of the previous epoch need to be saved. This requires a memory of

$$r(N_w + N_{tot}) \tag{4.19}$$

### 4.10.5  Temporary Memory Storage during Weight Changes Transfer

As mentioned in Section 4.2.2, because each processor can receive the set of weight changes from the previous process at any time, $n - 1$ sets of temporary weight changes are needed to ensure that there is no crash in data during the transfer. This amount of memory is

$$(n - 1)r(N_w + N_{tot}) \tag{4.20}$$

### 4.10.6  Overall Memory Requirement

The overall memory requirement for each processor is obtained by adding the expressions 4.15 to 4.20, which results in

$$r[(n + 2)N_w + (n + 5)N_{tot} + P^n(N_1 + N_l)] \tag{4.21}$$

# References

[1] S. Fahlman, "An empirical study of learning speed in backpropagation networks," CMU-CS-88-162, Carnegie Mellon University, School of Computer Science, Pittsburgh, USA, 1988.

[2] T. J. Sejnowski and C. R. Rosenberg, "Parallel networks that learn to pronounce English text," *Complex Systems*, vol. 1, pp. 145–168, 1987.

[3] S. K. Foo, P. Saratchandran, and N. Sundararajan, "Optimal distribution of patterns in a heterogeneous array of transputers for backpropagation networks," in *Proceedings of IEEE World Congress on Computational Intelligence 94, WCCI 94*, (Orlando, U.S.A.), June 1994.

[4] U. Carlini and U.Villano, *Transputers and Parallel Architectures: message-passing distributed systems*. Chichester, England: Ellis Horwood Limited, 1991.

[5] H. El-Rewini, T. G. Lewis, and H. H. Ali, *Task Scheduling in Parallel and Distribution Systems*. Englewoods Cliffs, New Jersey: PTR Prentice Hall, 1994.

[6] S. K. Foo, "Parallel mapping of backpropagation learning onto heterogeneous architectures: The training set parallelism approach," EEE/CSP/9602, Nanyang Technological University, Centre for Signal Processing, Nanyang Avenue, Singapore, May 1996.

[7] R. Freund and V. Sunderam, "Guest editor's introduction," *Journal of Parallel and Distributed Computing - Special issue on Heterogenous Processing*, no. 21, pp. 255–256, 1994.

[8] R. Arularasan, "Timings for elemental operations in Parallel C on T805 transputers," eee/csp/9501, Nanyang Technological University, Nanyang Avenue, Singapore, February 1995.

[9] A. Schrijver, *Theory of Linear and Integer Programming*. John Wiley & Sons, 1986.

[10] W. L. Winston, *Operations research: Applications and Algorithms*. An Imprint of Wadsworth Publishing Company, Belmont, California: Duxbury Press, third ed., 1994.

[11] M. Srinivas and L. M. Patnaik, "Genetic algorithms: A survey," *IEEE Computer*, pp. 17–26, June 1994.

[12] S. K. Foo, P. Saratchandran, and N. Sundararajan, "Genetic algorithm based mapping of backpropagation neural networks onto a parallel heterogeneous processor array," *Neural, Parallel and Scientific Computations*, vol. 3, pp. 467–486, 1995.

[13] K. Deb and D. E. Goldberg, "A comparative analysis of selection schemes used in genetic algorithms," in *Foundations of Genetic Algorithms*, pp. 69–93, San Mateo, California: Morgan Kaufmann Publishers, 1991.

[14] D. E. Goldberg, *Genetic Algorithms in Search, Optimization, and Machine Learning*. Addison-Wesley Publishing Co., 1989.

[15] S. K. Foo, P. Saratchandran, and N. Sundararajan, "Genetic algorithms based pattern allocation schemes for training set parallelism in backpropagation neural networks," in *Proceedings of IEEE International Conference on Evolutionary Computing 95, ICEC 95*, vol. 2, (Perth, Western Australia), pp. 545–550, Nov 1995.

[16] S. K. Foo, P. Saratchandran, and N. Sundararajan, "Applications of genetic algorithm for parallel implementation of backpropagation neural networks," in *Proceedings of International Symposium on Intelligent Robotic Systems, ISIRS 95*, (Bangalore, India), pp. 76–79, Nov 1995.

# Chapter 5

# Parallel Real-Time Recurrent Learning Algorithm for Training Large Fully Recurrent Neural Networks

**Elias S. Manolakos***
Communications and Digital Signal Processing (CDSP),
Center for Research and Graduate Studies,
Electrical and Computer Engineering Department,
409 Dana Building, Northeastern University,
Boston, Mass. 02115
**George Kechriotis**
Thinking Machines, Inc.,
245 First Street,
Cambridge, Mass. 02142

## 5.1 Introduction

Fully *recurrent neural networks* (RNNs), the most general case of neural networks with feedback in which every neuron unit may be connected to itself and any other unit in the network, can realize dynamical systems of arbitrary complexity. RNNs have at least the representational power of Fourier decomposition. One can use a pair of units to build an oscillator of arbitrary frequency; furthermore, using the first $n$ terms of a function's Fourier decomposition it is possible to find analytically a set of weights of a recurrent neural network with $2n + 1$ neurons that generates this approximation [1].

The RNNs are nonlinear dynamical systems that exhibit a rich and complex dynamical behavior. They have shown the ability to learn state space trajectories and follow limit cycles of dynamical systems [1] to encode sequential structures for learning simple grammar rules [2], to emulate a Turing machine for parenthesis balancing [3], to behave as finite automata [4], or learn the structure of interconnection networks [5].

Among many applications of RNNs here we just mention speech processing [6–8], equalization of linear and nonlinear communication channels using trained or blind adaptation [9–11], nonlinear systems identification and control [12,13], and chaotic time series modeling and prediction [14,15]. In [16] it has been shown that there is a direct correspondence between the Volterra series representation of a nonlinear dynamical system and an RNN. Specifically, given any nonlinear dynamical system there exists a finite-sized RNN whose first and second-order Volterra kernels are equal to those of the given system.

Several algorithms have been proposed for training fully recurrent neural networks [17]. *Backpropagation through time* (BPTT) implements a forward simulation (unfolding) of the network from time $t_0$ to $t_1$ and then a backward error propagation from $t_1$ to $t_0$. BPTT cannot be used in real time, and it imposes constraints on the type of patterns that

---

*To whom all correspondence should be addressed. This work has been partially supported by the Defense Advanced Project Research Agency under grant MDA 972-93-1-0023 monitored by the Air Force Office of Scientific Research.

135

the network can learn. To use BPTT some a priori knowledge of the maximum time interval for which a pattern is presented to the RNN is necessary.

On the other hand, the *real-time recurrent learning* (RTRL) algorithm proposed by Williams and Zipser [3, 18] can be used to update the weights of the RNN on-line, while sequences are being presented. The ability to do continuous processing frees it from any requirement for a fixed or even bounded epoch length, as opposed to BPTT. However, the computational complexity of the RTRL is much larger than that of BPTT; for a network of $n$ units the number of computations required per iteration belongs to $O(n^4)$. Therefore, training large-sized RNNs requires using some form of parallel processing.

In this chapter, we systematically develop a parallel algorithm that can be realized efficiently on a ring topology and is capable of performing the two alternating phases (retrieving and learning) of the RTRL using the same resources. Because the RTRL is nonlocal, in the sense that every neuron should have access to an error vector depending on all the other neurons and to all the weights in the network [3, 18], we have transformed the RTRL to an equivalent algorithm with only localized data dependencies. Then, using linear space-time mapping, we translated the localized algorithm into a ring parallel processing system that requires only near-neighbor communications. Such a system can be implemented as a dedicated very large scale integration (VLSI) array architecture or embedded into a larger granularity general-purpose parallel machine.

The rest of this chapter is organized as follows: In Section 5.2 we describe the sequential RTRL algorithm and introduce a convenient matrix formulation. In Section 5.3 we show how the matrix operations of the retrieving and the learning phase of the RTRL can be mapped to a ring topology with as many processors as the number of neuron units. In Section 5.4 we present a scheme for partitioning large RNN training problems into subproblems that can be allocated to a fixed-sized ring of processors and maintain high efficiency. Furthermore, we briefly comment on the efficiency of a Transputer-based implementation. Finally, in Section 5.5 we conclude by summarizing our findings and pointing to issues that deserve further investigation.

## 5.2 Background

### 5.2.1 The Real-Time Recurrent Learning Algorithm

In this section we describe the discrete-time RTRL algorithm. For a more detailed treatment of this and other algorithms proposed for the RNN training, see [3, 17]. Assume that the network consists of $n$ fully connected semilinear units and $m$ input units; an example of such a network with $n = 3$ and $m = 2$ is shown at Figure 5.1.

Let $w_{ij}[t]$ be the weight (synapse strength) of the connection from the $j$-th to the $i$-th unit at time (iteration) $t$. The accumulated input to the $k$-th unit at time $t + 1$ is given by the weighted average of the activations $y_l[t]$ of all the other units in the network and the external inputs $x_l^{net}[t]$ at the previous time instant:

$$s_k[t + 1] = \sum_{l=1}^{n} w_{kl}[t]y_l[t] + \sum_{l=1}^{m} w_{k,n+l}[t]x_l^{net}[t]. \tag{5.1}$$

If we define, as in [17], $\mathbf{x}[t] \in \mathbf{R}^{n+m}$ to be the column vector whose $k$-th element is given by

$$x_k[t] = \begin{cases} y_k[t], & \text{if } k \le n, \\ x_{k-n}^{net}[t], & \text{if } k > n, \end{cases} \tag{5.2}$$

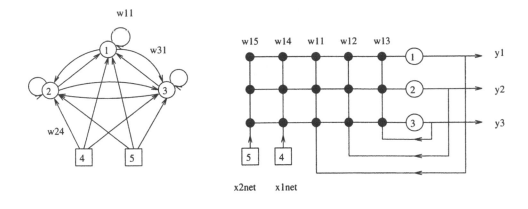

(a)                                                                    (b)

FIGURE 5.1. (a) A fully recurrent neural network with $n = 3$ units (oval nodes) and $m = 2$ input nodes (square nodes). Only some weights are shown in the figure. Target values can be specified for any one of the neuron units. (b) An equivalent representation, where every dark dot corresponds to a synapse with a strength weight.

and $\mathbf{W}[t] \in \mathbf{R}^{n \times (n+m)}$ to be the weight matrix with elements $w_{ij}[t]$, then we can rewrite the previous equation in vector form as follows:

$$s[t + 1] = \mathbf{W}[t]\mathbf{x}[t]. \tag{5.3}$$

The output of the $k$-th neuron is then given by

$$y_k[t + 1] = f(s_k[t + 1]) \tag{5.4}$$

and in vector notation

$$\mathbf{y}[t + 1] = f(\mathbf{s}[t + 1]) \tag{5.5}$$

where $f(\cdot)$, is usually the *sigmoid* nonlinearity $f(x) = \frac{1}{1+e^{-x}}$. Assume, without loss of generality, that for every unit in the network a desired value $d_k[t]$ at time $t$ is specified. We define the *error vector* $\mathbf{e}[t + 1] \in \mathbf{R}^n$ as the column vector whose $k$-th element is given by

$$e_k[t + 1] = d_k[t + 1] - y_k[t + 1], \quad k = 1, 2, \ldots, n. \tag{5.6}$$

The *network error* at time $t$ is then defined as

$$J[t] = -\frac{1}{2} \sum_{k=1}^{n} e_k^2[t] \tag{5.7}$$

and the *overall network error* over a time period $[t_1, t_2]$ is defined as

$$J^{total}[t_1, t_2] = \sum_{t=t_1}^{t_2} J[t].$$

The *gradient* of the scalar function $J^{total}$ with respect to the weights over a time interval $[t_1, t_2]$ is given by the sum of the corresponding gradients of the errors at every time instant:

$$\nabla_W J^{total}[t_1, t_2] = \sum_{t=t_1}^{t_2} \nabla_W J[t].$$

In order to maximize the cost function $J^{total}$ (that is, to minimize the square error), the weights are changed along a constant positive multiple of the performance measure gradient:

$$\Delta w_{ij}[t_2] = \alpha \frac{\partial J^{total}[t_1, t_2]}{\partial w_{ij}[t_1]} \tag{5.8}$$

$$w_{ij}[t_2] = w_{ij}[t_1] + \Delta w_{ij}[t_2] \tag{5.9}$$

where, $i = 1, 2, \ldots, n$ and $j = 1, 2, \ldots, n + m$. Now let us define, as in [17], the terms

$$p_{ij}^k[t] = \frac{\partial y_k[t]}{\partial w_{ij}[t_1]} \tag{5.10}$$

$k = 1, 2, \ldots, n$ and $t \in [t_1, t_2]$. This quantity measures the *sensitivity of the output* of the $k$-th neuron at time $t$ to a small change in the value of $w_{ij}$. The effect of such a change is taken into account over the entire trajectory from $t_1$ to $t$, while at the same time the initial state, the inputs and the rest of weights are assumed to remain fixed. Then, using Equations 5.7, 5.6, and 5.10, one can get that

$$\frac{\partial J[t]}{\partial w_{ij}[t_1]} = \sum_{k=1}^{n} e_k[t] p_{ij}^k[t]. \tag{5.11}$$

Differentiating Equations 5.1 and 5.4 for the network dynamics yields

$$p_{ij}^k[t+1] = f'(s_k[t+1]) \left( \sum_{l=1}^{n} w_{kl}[t] p_{ij}^l[t] + \delta_{ik} x_j[t] \right) \tag{5.12}$$

where $\delta_{ik}$ is the Kroneker delta and $x_j[t]$ is defined in Equation 5.2. If the activation function $f(\cdot)$ is the sigmoid nonlinearity, then it holds that

$$f'(s_k[t+1]) = y_k[t+1] \cdot (1 - y_k[t+1]). \tag{5.13}$$

Furthermore, if the initial state of the network has no functional dependence on the weights, it holds that

$$p_{ij}^k[t_1] = \frac{\partial y_k[t_1]}{\partial w_{ij}[t_1]} = 0. \tag{5.14}$$

Therefore the RTRL algorithm consists of the following steps:

1. *Forward Step.* (Matrix-vector multiplication) For every neuron $k$ compute $y_k[t+1]$, from the weights $w_{kj}[t]$, the previous outputs $y_l[t]$ and the net inputs $x_l^{net}[t]$, using Equations 5.1 and 5.4.

2. *Error Vector Computation.* For every neuron $k$ compute $e_k[t+1]$, from $d_k[t+1]$ and $y_k[t+1]$, using Equation 5.6.

3. *Updating of Sensitivity Terms.* Compute $p_{ij}^k[t+1]$ from $w_{ij}[t]$, $p_{ij}^k[t]$, $y_k[t]$, $x_k^{net}[t]$, and $y_k[t+1]$, using Equations 5.12 and 5.13.

4. *Gradients Computation.* Compute $\frac{\partial J[t+1]}{\partial w_{ij}[t]}$, from $e_k[t+1]$ and $p_{ij}^k[t+1]$, using Equation 5.11.

TABLE 5.1. Number of multiplications, additions, and sigmoid function evaluations per step of the sequential RTRL algorithm.

| RTRL Step | Multiplications | Additions | Sigmoids |
|---|---|---|---|
| 1 | $n(n+m)$ | $n(n+m-1)$ | $n$ |
| 2 | 0 | $n$ | 0 |
| 3 | $n^2(n+m)(n+1)+n$ | $n^2(n+m)(n-1)+n(m+n)+n$ | 0 |
| 4 | $n(n+m)n$ | $n(n+m)(n-1)$ | 0 |
| 5 | $n(n+m)$ | $n(n+m)$ | 0 |

5. *Weights Updating.* Compute $w_{ij}[t+1]$, from $w_{ij}[t]$ and $\frac{\partial J[t+1]}{\partial w_{ij}[t]}$, using Equations 5.8 and 5.9.

If we assume that the network consists of $n$ fully connected neuron units, $m$ external inputs, and that target outputs are specified for all units, then the number and type of operations performed at each one of the RTRL steps are summarized in Table 5.1.

If $T_A$, $T_M$ and $T_F$ are the times required for a single addition, multiplication, and sigmoid function evaluation correspondingly, then the total computational time for a single iteration of the RTRL algorithm can be expressed as follows:

$$T_{seq} = [n^4 + n^3m + 2n^2 + n(2m+1)] \cdot T_A + \\ [n^4 + n^3(m+2) + n^2(2m+2) + n(2m+1)] \cdot T_M + n \cdot T_F. \tag{5.15}$$

As we can see from Equation 5.15, during each time iteration we have to perform $O(n^4)$ additions and $O(n^4)$ multiplications. Note that using RTRL the weights of the RNN can be updated either after each time iteration or after a fixed number of iterations. In the former case (that does not correspond to gradient descent) an input pattern is presented and steps 1 and 2 are performed (*retrieving phase*). Then the sensitivities are calculated and the weights are updated (steps 3,4, and 5— *the learning phase*). In the latter case, the weights are updated (step 5) only after a prespecified number of input patterns have been presented to the network. Because the updating of sensitivity terms (step 3), which is the most time-consuming operation, cannot be avoided, the computational complexity of the latter case is only slightly smaller than that of the former.

## 5.2.2 Matrix Formulation of the RTRL Algorithm

As we have already shown, the retrieving phase can be realized as consecutive matrix-vector multiplications interleaved with nonlinear activation function evaluations (Equations 5.3 and 5.5). In order now to express Equation 5.12, that is, in the heart of the learning phase, in matrix form we can rearrange the sensitivity terms $\{p_{ij}^k\}$ into a column vector $\mathbf{p}^k$, and the elements $\{w_{ij}\}$ of the weight matrix $\mathbf{W}$ into another vector $\mathbf{w}$ with the same structure,

$$\mathbf{p}^k = [\, p_{11}^k p_{12}^k \cdots p_{1,n+m}^k \mid p_{21}^k p_{22}^k \cdots p_{2,n+m}^k \mid \cdots \mid p_{n,1}^k p_{n,2}^k \cdots p_{n,n+m}^k \,]^T \tag{5.16}$$

$$\mathbf{w} = [\, w_{11} w_{12} \cdots w_{1,n+m} \mid w_{21} w_{22} \cdots w_{2,n+m} \mid \cdots \mid w_{n,1} w_{n,2} \cdots w_{n,m+n} \,]^T \tag{5.17}$$

where $\mathbf{p}^k$ and $\mathbf{w}$ belong to $\mathbf{R}^{(n^2+nm)\times 1}$. Furthermore, let $\mathbf{P} \in \mathbf{R}^{(n^2+nm)\times n}$ be the matrix composed of the column vectors $\{\mathbf{p}^k\}$, that is, $\mathbf{P} = [\mathbf{p}^1\mathbf{p}^2 \ldots \mathbf{p}^n]$. Similarly, let us define

$$\mathbf{X} = \begin{bmatrix} \mathbf{x} & & & \\ & \mathbf{x} & & \\ & & \ddots & \\ & & & \mathbf{x} \end{bmatrix} \in \mathbf{R}^{(n^2+nm)\times n} \tag{5.18}$$

where the column vector $\mathbf{x}$ is defined in Equation 5.2 and

$$\mathbf{F} = \begin{bmatrix} f'_1 & & \\ & \ddots & \\ & & f'_n \end{bmatrix} = \begin{bmatrix} y_1 \cdot (1 - y_1) & & \\ & \ddots & \\ & & y_n \cdot (1 - y_n) \end{bmatrix}. \tag{5.19}$$

Then, the recursive Equations 5.12 and 5.14 of the learning phase become

$$\mathbf{P}[t_1] = \mathbf{0} \tag{5.20}$$

$$\mathbf{P}[t + 1] = (\mathbf{P}[t] \cdot \mathbf{W}_1^T[t] + \mathbf{X}[t]) \cdot \mathbf{F}[t + 1] \tag{5.21}$$

where $\mathbf{W}_1$ is the $n \times n$ submatrix formed by the first $n$ columns of matrix $\mathbf{W}$. Moreover, assuming that the weights are updated after every iteration (as usually the case with the RTRL), the incremental weight changes vector $\Delta\mathbf{w}$ is given by

$$\Delta\mathbf{w}[t + 1] = \alpha\mathbf{P}[t + 1] \cdot \mathbf{e}[t + 1] \tag{5.22}$$

and

$$\mathbf{w}[t + 1] = \mathbf{w}[t] + \Delta\mathbf{w}[t + 1]. \tag{5.23}$$

Therefore, the learning phase can be realized as a consecutive matrix–matrix multiplication form.

## 5.3 Parallel RTRL Algorithm Derivation

To derive systematically an efficient parallel implementation of the two alternating phases of the RTRL algorithm, we can utilize linear space-time mapping techniques like the canonical mapping methodology (CMM) [19] introduced by S.Y. Kung. Using CMM, data *broadcasting* can be translated to pipelining, leading to the formulation of an equivalent locally recursive algorithm (LRA). The LRA can be represented by an acyclic *dependencies graph* (DG), where a vertex corresponds to a computation and a directed arc to a data dependence (precedence relationship between computations). If every node is thought of as a processor, the DG corresponds to the finest granularity array architecture for the constructed LRA. By choosing a *projection* direction vector $\vec{d}$ and a time *schedule* vector $\vec{s}$, we can derive a *signal flow graph* (SFG) of lower dimensionality than the DG. The SFG provides a behavioral model for a coarser-grain parallel implementation.

### 5.3.1 The Retrieving Phase

The system dynamics during the retrieving phase can be formulated as a multiplication of a nonsquare matrix $\mathbf{W}$ by a vector $\mathbf{x}$ (Equation 5.3), followed by a nonlinear activation function evaluation (Equation 5.4). After the system has been successfully trained, that is, the total square error has been minimized, the neural network's operation consists solely of consecutive retrieving phases, in which we present an input pattern we let propagate through the network and compute the activation of the output units.

In order to formulate an efficient coarse grain-parallel algorithm for implementing consecutive iterations of the retrieving phase on a ring of only $n$ processing elements (PEs), we should cascade appropriately many instances of the DG for matrix-vector multiplication (corresponding to one iteration of the retrieving phase). Therefore, we need to "align" the directions of propagation of the input and output data for each DG instance so that they are not orthogonal to each other. For the case of a square weight matrix and a vector consisting only of external inputs (as with feed-forward neural net), Hwang and Kung [20] have shown how to exploit this idea and derive a ring systolic array. In our case, $\mathbf{W}$ is an $n \times (n + m)$ weights matrix and the vector to multiply with consists of the external inputs $\mathbf{x}^{net}[t]$ concatenated with the $\mathbf{y}[t]$ vector of neuron activations. This leads to a slightly different DG, but following a similar procedure we obtain a modified ring architecture for the retrieving phase of the RTRL.

The DG when $n = 3$, $m = 2$ is shown in Figure 5.2(a). The oval nodes (see Figure 5.2(b)), model a simple multiply-accumulate (MAC) operation and the square ones model the computation of the nonlinear activation function. As in [20], we have rearranged the placement of the $\{w_{ij}\}$ elements so that the outputs $y_i[t + 1]$, $i = 1, 2 \ldots n$ can become inputs to an exact replica of the same DG (corresponding to the next iteration of the retrieving phase). So DG instances can be "stacked" along the $j$ direction, whereas there are always only $n$ nodes in every DG row (along the $i$ direction). To construct such a DG structure, elements of the the $i$-th row of matrix $\mathbf{W}$, $i = 1, 2, \ldots n$, are first placed on the corresponding nodes of the $i$-th column of the DG; then these weight elements are circularly shifted up by $i - 1$ positions. As we can see in Figure 5.2(a), the leftmost node of DG row $j$ is connected to the rightmost node of row $j + m + 1$. This arrangement differs from that in [20] where the leftmost DG node in each row is connected to the rightmost node of the *next* row. Another difference is that the $x_i^{net}$ variables enter the DG from the right-side copies of the same DG can now be cascaded from the top down, with the inputs and outputs perfectly interfaced, leading to a thin and tall DG structure (with $K(n+m+1)$ rows but only $n$ columns).

If this DG is "collapsed" along the vertical direction $j$ (projection vector $\vec{d} = [i, j]^T = [0, 1]^T$) and the schedule $\vec{s} = \vec{d} = [0, 1]^T$ (default schedule) is used, the SFG of 5.2(c) is derived. The projection direction and equitemporal hyperplanes are shown at Figure 5.2(a). The corresponding distributed memory ring architecture is shown in Figure 5.3. In this figure it is assumed that each PE has an output $y$-buffer, and only the number of additional buffers in the spiral (return) communication link are shown explicitly. The ring operation can be better understood by an example ($n = 3$, $m = 2$), detailing the computation and communication actions performed by every PE on the ring during each schedule time period $t_s$.

• At $t_s = 1$, the internal accumulator of every PE is set to zero. The computations $y_1 w_{11}$, $y_2 w_{22}$, and $y_3 w_{33}$ are performed by the three PEs ($n$ in general), and the results are stored to the internal accumulators. At the same time every PE transmits its corresponding $y$ input data token to the neighboring PE in a *left circular* fashion, that is, PE$_3$ sends $y_3$ to PE$_2$ and PE$_1$ sends $y_1$ to the first buffer on the spiral link.

• At time $t_s = 2$, all PEs receive their input values from the right neighbor. Especially PE$_3$ (PE$_n$ in general) receives the external input $x_1^{net}$ from the upper horizontal link. The computations $y_2 w_{12}$, $y_3 w_{23}$, $x_1^{net} w_{34}$ are performed by the three PEs and the results are again accumulated. Every PE transmits its input data token to the left neighbor in a left circular fashion.

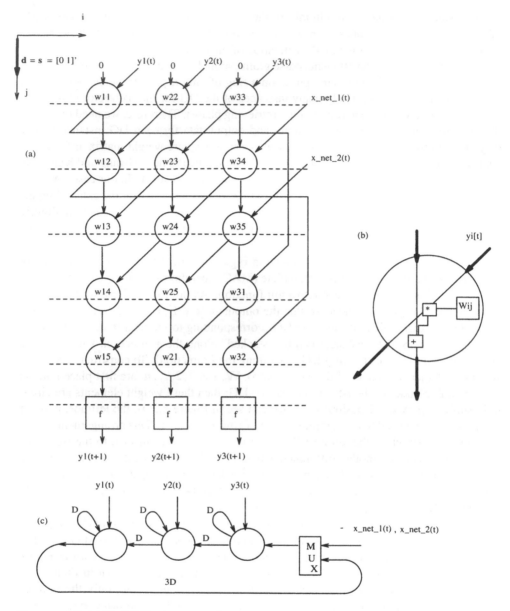

FIGURE 5.2. (a) The DG for the consecutive matrix-vector multiplication. The schedule hyperplanes are shown with dashed lines. (b) The structure of the DG node. (c) The ring SFG.

- At time $t_s = 3$, PE$_3$ receives $x_2^{net}$ from outside. (In general, PE$_n$ receives inputs from outside during schedule time periods $2, \ldots m+1$). All PEs perform a multiply-accumulate function, while they transmit the input data to the left.

. . .

- At the end of period $t_s = 5$, the accumulator of each PE$_i$ contains the corresponding net input $s_i[t + 1]$, $i = 1, 2, \ldots n$.
- At time $t_s = 6$, PE$_i$ computes the new activation through the evaluation of the nonlinear function $y_i[t + 1] = f(s_i[t + 1])$, $i = 1, 2, \ldots n$.

As it has become clear, during the *retrieving* phase, every unit activation $y_i[t]$, $i = 1, \ldots, n$ and every external input $x_i^{net}[t]$, $i = 1, \ldots, m$ will pass from all the PEs in the ring. Because these values will be needed to the PEs during the *learning* phase, every PE stores them in a $(n + m)$-size local memory. In addition, $PE_i$ has to store locally an $i$-th row of the $\mathbf{W}$ weights matrix, so that the total storage requirements for each PE during the retrieving phase is $O(n + m)$ memory locations.

Assuming that one communication (per link) and one MAC computation (DG node execution) can be completed within a schedule time period (step), this scheme requires $n+m+1$ steps per time iteration of the retrieving phase. More precisely, if $T_A$, $T_M$, and $T_F$ are as defined before, and $T_C$ is the time needed for a point-to-point data communication, then assuming that communications can be performed concurrently with computations, the parallel time for the retrieving phase can be expressed as follows:

$$T_{par}(retrieving) = (n + m) \cdot \max(T_A + T_M, T_C) + T_F. \tag{5.24}$$

Note that if the PE cannot perform communication and computation concurrently, the $max$ operator in Equation 5.24 has to be replaced with the sum $T_A + T_M + T_C$.

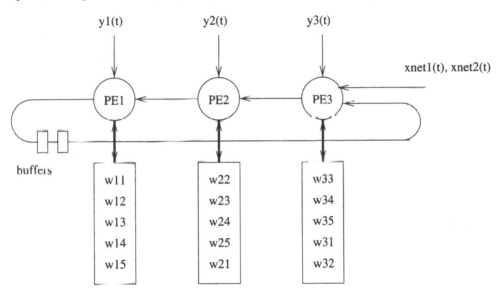

FIGURE 5.3. Distributed memory ring array implementation for the retrieving phase.

### 5.3.2 The Learning Phase

The derivation of the ring implementation for the retrieving phase was a straightforward extension of the ideas presented in [20] and [21]. However, the matching of the learning phase steps in the same ring array is a more challenging and important problem, because most of the computational work in the RTRL algorithm is spent in that phase. As discussed in Section 5.2, by rearranging the sensitivities $\{p_{ij}^k\}$ into an $[n(n + m) \times n]$ matrix $\mathbf{P}$, the update over a time trajectory can be expressed as *consecutive* steps of the form

$$\mathbf{P}[t + 1] = (\mathbf{P}[t] \cdot \mathbf{W}_1^T[t] + \mathbf{X}[t]) \cdot \mathbf{F}[t + 1] = \tilde{\mathbf{P}}[t + 1] \cdot \mathbf{F}[t + 1] \tag{5.25}$$

where $\mathbf{W}_1[t]$ is the principal $n \times n$ submatrix of $\mathbf{W}[t]$ and $\mathbf{X}[t]$ is a sparse and $\mathbf{F}[t + 1]$ is a diagonal matrix. Therefore, let us start by deriving the DG for consecutive matrix-matrix multiplication.

The multiplication of an $N \times K$ matrix $\mathbf{A}$ by an $K \times M$ matrix $\mathbf{B}$ can be expressed as $c_{ij} = \sum_{k=1}^{K} a_{ik} b_{kj}$, for $i = 1, \dots, N$ and $j = 1, \dots, M$. However, in our particular case it has the form

$$\mathbf{C}[t + 1] = \mathbf{C}[t] \cdot \mathbf{B}.$$

Therefore, it is essential to align the direction of arrival of the input data matrix $\mathbf{A}$ (here $\mathbf{C}[t]$) with that of the output matrix $\mathbf{C}$ (here $\mathbf{C}[t + 1]$) so that multiple copies of the DG can be cascaded before the overall structure is projected to a one-dimensional array. So we now need to rearrange the placement of the elements of matrix $\mathbf{B}$. Assuming that all three matrices belong to $\mathbf{R}^{3 \times 3}$, the corresponding DG is shown at Figure 5.4. In this figure, matrix $\mathbf{B}$ is loaded at the DG plane $i = 0$, and its $j$-th column is circularly shifted up (in the $j$ direction) by $j - 1$ positions. Although the resulting DG is not totally localized (due to the presence of the spiral communication arcs), the direction of inputs $\mathbf{A}$ (entering from the bottom) and outputs $\mathbf{C}$ (exiting from the top) is the same and thus many consecutive DG instances can be cascaded.

Similarly, the DG for the calculation of the product $\mathbf{P}[t] \cdot \mathbf{W}_1^T$ is shown in Figure 5.5, where the $\{P_{ik}[t + 1]\}$ correspond to the intermediate results and not to the final values of the updated $\mathbf{P}$ matrix elements. Choosing the projection direction $\vec{d} = [i, j, k]^T = [1, 0, 0]^T$ and the default schedule $\vec{s} = \vec{d} = [1, 0, 0]$, we obtain the two-dimensional SFG in Figure 5.6. To obtain a one-dimensional ring array, we project once more along the direction $\vec{d} = [j, k]^T = [1, 0]^T$, and we choose again the default schedule $\vec{s} = \vec{d} = [1, 0]^T$. The resulting architecture is shown at Figure 5.7.

The ring implementation can be better understood by discussing the case in Figure 5.7. So let $n = 3, m = 2$ (hence $\mathbf{W}_1^T \in \mathbf{R}^{3 \times 3}$) and $P_{ij}$ denote the $ij$-th element of matrix $\mathbf{P}[t]$, where $i = 1, 2, \dots 15$ (in general, $i = 1, 2, \dots n(n + m)$) and $j = 1, 2,$ and 3 (in general, $j = 1, 2, \dots, n$). During iteration $t + 1$ of the RTRL algorithm, the array operations associated with the learning phase, at every schedule time period are described as follows ($t_s$ is initialized to 1 for the discussion):

- At time $t_s = 1$, the target value $d_k[t + 1]$ is available to every $PE_k$ and the error $e_k[t + 1] = d_k[t + 1] - y_k[t + 1]$ is locally computed for $k = 1, 2, \dots n$.

- At time $t_s = 2$, $PE_k$ performs $e_k[t + 1] := \alpha e_k[t + 1]$, where $\alpha$ is the step of the gradient descent algorithm (learning rate) in Equation 5.8.

- At time $t_s = 3$, the differences $1 - y_k[t + 1]$ is computed at $PE_k$, $k = 1, 2 \dots n$.

- At time $t_s = 4$, the previously computed difference is multiplied by $y_k[t + 1]$ at $PE_k$, $k = 1, 2 \dots n$, to form the partial derivatives of the activation function $f_k'[t + 1]$.

Note that during the preceding four scheduling periods, no interprocessor communication is required and all PEs compute in parallel. The following $n^2(n + m)$ scheduling periods involve the calculation of the matrix multiply-accumulate operation $\tilde{\mathbf{P}}[t+1] = \mathbf{P}[t] \cdot \mathbf{W}_1^T + \mathbf{X}[t]$. During each one of these steps a scalar MAC of the form $AC := AC + P \times w$ is performed at each PE and the operands $P$ are circulated around the ring. The addition of the block diagonal matrix $\mathbf{X}[t]$ to the product $\mathbf{P}[t] \cdot \mathbf{W}_1^T$ can be handled by initializing appropriately the accumulators in every PE. Specifically,

- At time $t_s = 5$, $P_{11}, P_{12}$, and $P_{13}$ are introduced at $PE_1, PE_2$, and $PE_3$, respectively, and products $P_{11}w_{11}, P_{12}w_{22}$, and $P_{13}w_{33}$, are computed and stored in an accumulator of each PE. The accumulator is initialized to $AC := x_1[t]$ at $PE_1$, and to $AC := 0$ in all other PEs. Note that all $\{x_k[t]\}$s are available because they have

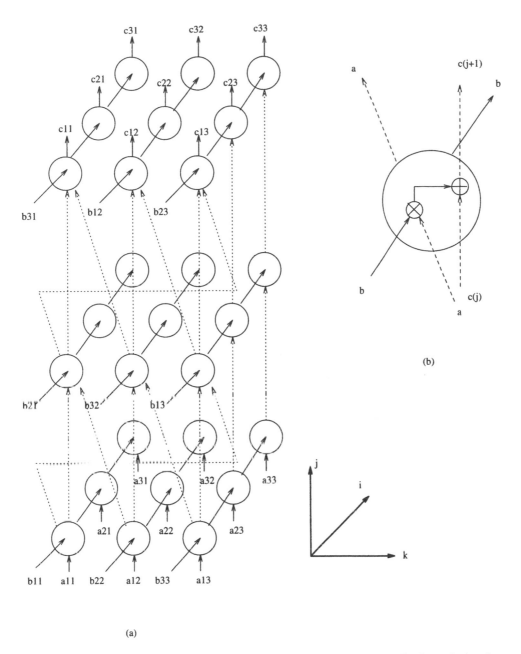

(a)

FIGURE 5.4. (a) DG for consecutive matrix-matrix multiplication. Solid lines depict data dependencies on the $(i, k)$ planes. Dashed lines depict dependencies between planes. Not all dependencies are shown for clarity. (b) The structure of the DG node.

traveled once around the ring and are stored to every PE during the retrieving phase. At the same time, $P_{11}$ is transmitted to $PE_3$, $P_{12}$ to $PE_1$, and $P_{13}$ to $PE_2$ in a left circular fashion.

- At time $t_s = 6$, the products $P_{12}w_{12}$, $P_{13}w_{23}$, and $P_{11}w_{31}$ are computed and added to the previous values of the accumulators. $P_{12}$, $P_{13}$, and $P_{11}$ are transmitted once more in a left circular fashion.

145

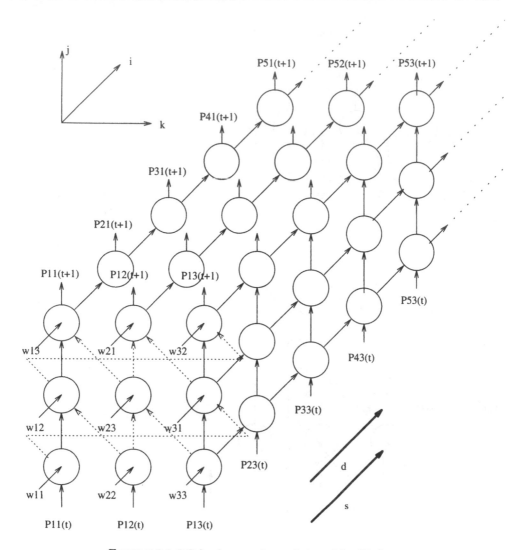

FIGURE 5.5. DG for the recursive updating of the $\{P_{ij}\}$ terms.

- At the end of the scheduling period $t_s = 7$, ($t_s = n + 4$ in general), the values $P_{11}[t]$, $P_{12}[t]$, and $P_{11}[t]$, have traveled once around the ring and the partial results of $\tilde{P}_{11}[t + 1]$, $\tilde{P}_{12}[t + 1]$, and $\tilde{P}_{13}[t + 1]$ have been computed in processors, $PE_1$, $PE_2$, and $PE_3$, respectively. Also, notice that in every PE the weights involved in the computations are fetched in a circular manner.

- At time $t_s = 8$, $P_{21}$, $P_{22}$ and $P_{23}$ are introduced at $PE_1$, $PE_2$, and $PE_3$, respectively, and the products $P_{21}w_{11}$, $P_{22}w_{22}$, and $P_{23}w_{33}$ are computed in $PE_1$, $PE_2$, and $PE_3$. The accumulator of $PE_1$ is now initialized to $AC := x_2[t]$, whereas the accumulators of the other PEs are again initialized with zeros.

After $n$ more time steps, (that is, at the end of the scheduling period $2n + 4$), the partial results of $\tilde{P}_{21}[t + 1]$, $\tilde{P}_{22}[t + 1]$, and $\tilde{P}_{23}[t + 1]$ have been computed in $PE_1$, $PE_2$, and $PE_3$, respectively. Therefore, in general, after $n^2(n + m) + 4$ time steps, the matrix $\tilde{\mathbf{P}}[t + 1] = (\mathbf{P}[t] \cdot \mathbf{W}_1^T[t] + \mathbf{X}[t])$ has been computed, and its $(i, k)$-th element is stored in $PE_k$.

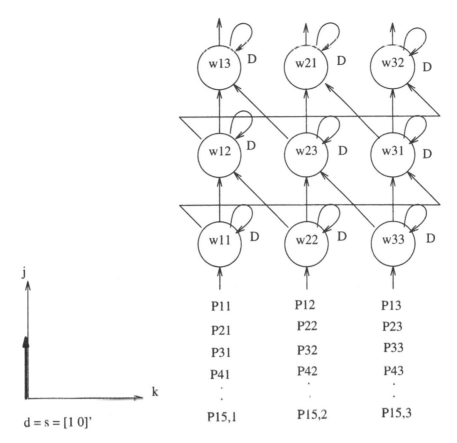

FIGURE 5.6. Two-dimensional SFG for the recursive updating of the $\{P_{ij}\}$ terms.

In this scheme, each processor stores one column of the matrix $\mathbf{Ps}$ as well as one column of $\mathbf{W}_1^T$. This accounts for storage requirements in the order of $n(n+m)+n$ memory locations per PE. Note that during the computation of the matrix-matrix product every $P_{il}[t]$ value has passed through every processor in the ring (all-to-all broadcast). Every $PE_k$, $k = 1, 2, \ldots n$ stores in its local memory the values

$$\{P_{il}[t], l = 1, \ldots n, \quad i = (n+m)(k-1)+1, \ldots, (n+m)k\},$$

to be used in the steps to be described next. This accounts for an additional $(n-1)(n+m)$ local memory requirement per PE.

- During the next $n(n+m)$ time steps, the sensitivity terms

$$\left\{ P_{ik}[t+1] = \tilde{P}_{ik}[t+1] \cdot f_k'[t+1] \right\}, i = 1, 2, \ldots n(n+m)$$

are computed in the corresponding $PE_k$, $k = 1, 2, \ldots n$. Now the whole matrix $\mathbf{P}[t+1]$ has been updated, and its $k$-th column is stored locally in $PE_k$. During the first $n$ steps of this phase, and while the processors compute sensitivities, the scaled error values $e_k[t]$, $k = 1, 2, \ldots n$, produced during the previous RTRL iteration in $PE_k$, $k = 1, 2, \ldots n$, respectively, circulate around the ring so that each PE gets to know all of them (all-to-all broadcast).

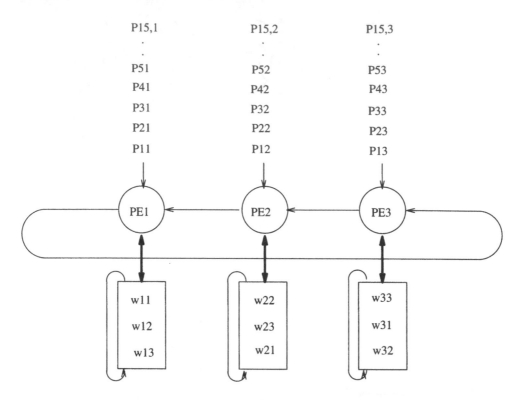

FIGURE 5.7. Distributed memory ring implementation for the learning phase.

- During the next $n(n+m)$ time steps and in each $PE_k$, $k = 1, 2, \ldots n$, all the synaptic weights locally stored are updated as follows:

for $j = 1, 2, \ldots (n+m)$ do
$\quad i = (k-1)(n+m) + j$
$\quad w_{kj}[t+1] := w_{kj}[t] + \sum_{l=1}^{n} P_{il}[t]e_l[t]$
end for

Because the corresponding sensitivity and scaled error $\{e_l[t],\ l = 1, 2, \ldots n\}$ terms are available to $PE_k$, there is no need for interprocessor communications during this phase.

This scheme requires $n^2(n+m) + 2n(n+m) + 4$ periods for updating all the weights of $\mathbf{W}$, assuming that one multiply-accumulate operation per PE and one point-to-point communication per PE link can be completed in one schedule time period. Moreover, if as in the previous section, $T_A$, $T_M$, and $T_C$ is the time required for a single addition, multiplication, and communication, respectively, and communications can occur in parallel with a computation, an estimate of the time needed per learning phase iteration of the RTRL parallel algorithm on a MIMD ring architecture is given by

$$
\begin{aligned}
T_{par}(learning) = {} & n^2(n+m) \cdot max(T_A + T_M, T_C) \\
& + n \cdot max(T_M, T_C) \\
& + ((n(n+m) + 2) + n(n+m-1)) \cdot T_M \\
& + (n(n+m) + 2) \cdot T_A
\end{aligned}
\tag{5.26}
$$

If we define the *efficiency* of the parallel system with $n$ processors as the ratio $T_{acq}/nT_{pur}$, then from Equations 5.15, 5.26, and 5.24 we see that as the number of neurons (and consequently the number of processors) increases, the efficiency converges to

$$E_\infty = \frac{T_A + T_M}{\max(T_A + T_M, T_C)} \tag{5.27}$$

From Equation 5.27 we see that in order to achieve the maximum theoretical efficiency of unity, the point-to-point communication time $T_C$ has to be less than the time required for one multiply-accumulate (MAC) operation $T_A + T_M$. In case that the PEs cannot handle near-neighbor communications in parallel with floating point computations, the *max* operator in Equation 5.27 has to be replaced with the *sum* operator, and the efficiency will be upper bounded by $\frac{T_A + T_M}{T_A + T_M + T_C}$.

## 5.4 Training Very Large RNNs on Fixed-Size Ring Arrays

So far we have shown how we can map recurrent neural network processing to a distributed memory ring array architecture with as many processors as the number of neurons. In practice, however, there is always a problem much larger than the size of the available parallel machine. So we would like to be able to map a neural network of arbitrary size to a fixed size architecture. Moreover, as the number of the neurons increases, it becomes not only impractical but also inefficient to use equally large rings. It is, therefore, essential to derive an efficient *partitioning scheme*, which allows large problems to be divided into smaller subproblems of the same type that can be allocated on a fixed and smaller size architecture. In this section we show how an RNN with $\hat{n} = k \cdot n$ neuron units can be mapped to a ring of only $n$ PEs.

To map systematically an algorithm to a smaller size array, the dependencies graph (DG) is partitioned into blocks. To allocate the partitioned DG to the array, we may choose either the number of blocks or the block size to match the number of available processors. In the former case, each block is mapped into one PE that sequentially executes all DG nodes of the block; this scheme is called *locally sequential globally parallel* (LSGP) [19]. In the latter case, nodes within a block are executed concurrently by the processors, but the blocks themselves are executed the one after the other; this method is called *locally parallel globally sequential* partitioning (LPGS). We use here the LSGP method that provides better balancing between communications and computations.

### 5.4.1 Partitioning for the Retrieving Phase

For an RNN with $\hat{n}$ neurons and $\hat{m}$ external inputs, where $\hat{n} = n \cdot k$ and $\hat{n} >> \hat{m}$, the DG associated with the matrix-vector multiplication, which is in the core of the retrieving phase, is partitioned into $n$ blocks each one of size $(nk + \hat{m}) \times k$. An example of the partitioned DG for the case $\hat{n} = 9$, $n = 3$, $k = 3$, and $\hat{m} = 2$ is shown in Figure 5.8. The RNN modeled in Figure 5.8 is to be mapped to a ring array of $n = 3$ processors. Each PE serially executes the nodes of the corresponding block. The projection direction remains the same (that is, $\vec{d} = [1 \ 0]^T$). A sufficiently slow linear schedule is to be found so that at any time instant there is at most one PE (out of $n$) executing computations pertaining to a block. At the same time the linear systolic schedule chosen has to be optimal, that is, the $\vec{s}$ that achieves minimal *pipelining period* $\alpha = \vec{s}\vec{d}$ given $\vec{d}$ [19]. In this context, the smallest possible $\alpha$ will be equal to the number of SFG nodes that will be assigned to a PE after the projection. In Figure 5.8, $k = 3$ SFG nodes are assigned to each one of the $n = 3$ PEs after the space mapping, and the $\vec{s} = [1 \ 3]^T$ used satisfies $\vec{s}\vec{d} = \alpha = 3$, hence it is optimal.

In Figure 5.9(a) we see that a FIFO queue is used in the return link, whose size is equal to $\hat{m} + k$ (5 in the example). Each PE uses $k = 3$ memory buffers to hold the previous activation values $y_i[t]$ that are circulated in the ring. A complete circulation corresponds to an iteration of the RTRL retrieving phase. Because of the simple linear schedule used, a regular control strategy is sufficient for handling the stream of operations in every PE. At every schedule time instant a PE uses the contents of a buffer as the operand to multiply with the associated weight and then moves them to the buffer in the left. The first (leftmost) memory buffer in each PE, after it has been used, is sent to the left neighbor or to the FIFO on the return link. Every PE also uses a number of buffers equal to the block size $k$ to accumulate partial results that at the end form the new activation values. In Figure 5.9(b) a snapshot of the PE activities corresponding to the first 12 schedule time periods (equitemporal hyperplanes in the DG of Figure 5.8) is provided. Interprocessor communications are now needed only every $k = 3$ time steps, thus reducing the associated overhead of the parallel implementation.

### 5.4.2 Partitioning for the Learning Phase

A similar LPGS scheme can be used for the learning phase as well. The DG for the learning phase is first projected along the $i$ direction resulting in the two-dimensional SFG shown in Figure 5.10. The SFG for consecutive matrix-matrix multiplication is now partitioned into $n = 3$ blocks, and each block is allocated to a PE. The same schedule $\vec{s} = \begin{bmatrix} 1 & 3 \end{bmatrix}^T$ is used, and it results to optimal $\alpha$ as before. In the resulting ring array, the structure of the PEs is the same as for the retrieving phase, the only difference being that now the number of buffers in the return link is equal to the block size because no external inputs are entering the array during this phase.

The example presented here can easily be generalized for any size $\hat{n} = k \cdot n$ RNN. A sufficiently slow schedule satisfying the requirement that at every time instant a PE executes at most one computation (DG node) is $\vec{s} = \begin{bmatrix} 1 & k \end{bmatrix}^T$. In the example presented, point-to-point communication between two PEs is needed only every third scheduling period ($k = 3$). This is especially desirable when communications are relatively slow. If the speed of MAC computations is as usual larger than the speed of a point-to-point message passing, then matching the algorithm to a smaller size ring provides balancing and results to a better utilization of the available resources.

If a RNN of size $\hat{n} = k \cdot n$ is mapped to a ring array of $n$ PEs, at the limit (where $\hat{n}$ become very large), the efficiency approaches

$$\lim_{n,k} E = \lim_{n,k} \frac{(nk)^4 (T_A + T_M)}{n(nk)^3 \cdot \max(k(T_A + T_M), T_C)} = \lim_{n,k} \frac{(T_A + T_M)}{\max((T_A + T_M), \frac{T_C}{k})} = 1 \tag{5.28}$$

meaning that even when the communication is slow, we can achieve linear speedup if we partition the RTRL algorithm and map it to a sufficiently smaller array. For every particular implementation platform it is necessary to find the appropriate partitioning factor $k$ that achieves optimal efficiency.

### 5.4.3 A Transputer-Based Implementation

In this section we briefly summarize the results of a prototype implementation of the parallel RTRL algorithm on a Transputer-based Meiko multiprocessor machine. A detailed description of the implementation and a thorough discussion of the results is provided in [22].

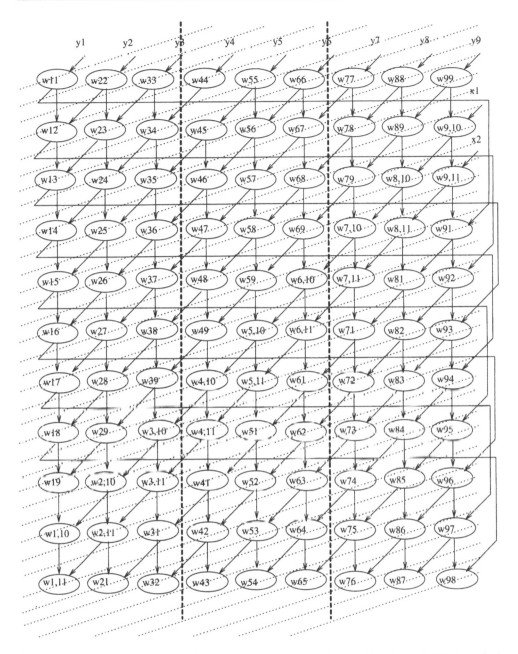

FIGURE 5.8. The DG for the retrieving phase when $\hat{n} = n \cdot k = 9$, $\hat{m} = 2$, and $n = 3$. Thick vertical dashed lines indicate block boundaries. Light dashed lines correspond to equitemporal hyperplanes.

The T-800 Transputer is a microprocessor fabricated by INMOS that can be used as a building block for large MIMD parallel processing systems. Each T-800 chip has four bidirectional links supporting bit-serial point-to-point communications with four near neighbors at a data rate up to 20 Mbits/sec. Each link has its own autonomous interface and can operate concurrently with the CPU. The T800 chip uses a 20 MHz clock and is equipped with a floating point unit (FPU) sustaining about 1 MFLOPS. In addition, each T-800 has 4 Kbytes of on-chip static RAM and 4 Mbytes of dynamic RAM external local memory.

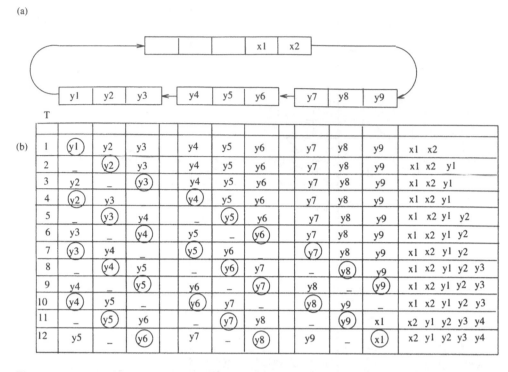

FIGURE 5.9. (a) The structure of the FIFO queue on the return link and the activation buffers within the three PEs. (b) Snapshot of PE activities during the first 12 schedule time periods of the retrieving phase. Each $y$ element currently used is encircled.

The parallel RTRL algorithm was coded in Occam-2, a programming language that supports the model of communicating sequential processes [23] on a Meiko Computing Surface CS-1400 system consisting of five four-Transputer boards. The 20 processors of the system can be connected through the backplane to create arbitrary topologies, and a Sparc-2 host is used for monitoring program execution and handling external I/O. We constructed various rings with up to 19 processors (one T800 was assigned to control the ring and to provide buffering between the active processors and the host).

RNNs of several sizes were trained via the parallel RTRL. Although Transputers are known to exhibit fast point-to-point latency, their FPU is very slow relative to more recent processors. The experimentally measured point-to-point communication latency was about five times larger than the floating point MAC time, and therefore the maximum attainable efficiency is severely limited when the number of processors is equal to the number of neuron units of the RNN. For example, in such a case an efficiency of only 0.22 can be achieved when using 12 or more Transputers. However, as we showed in the previous section, when communication is slower than computation and asynchronous communications are supported, the efficiency of the parallel system can be improved by allocating a large number of neurons per processor subject to the available memory per processor. For example, by mapping five neurons to each processor, a speedup of 9.5 was achieved with 19 processors. Also, with 5 processors and 16 neurons allocated per processor, the efficiency can be as high as 0.65. The partitioned implementation is highly scalable because the work per processor can be increased without increasing proportionally the communication overhead.

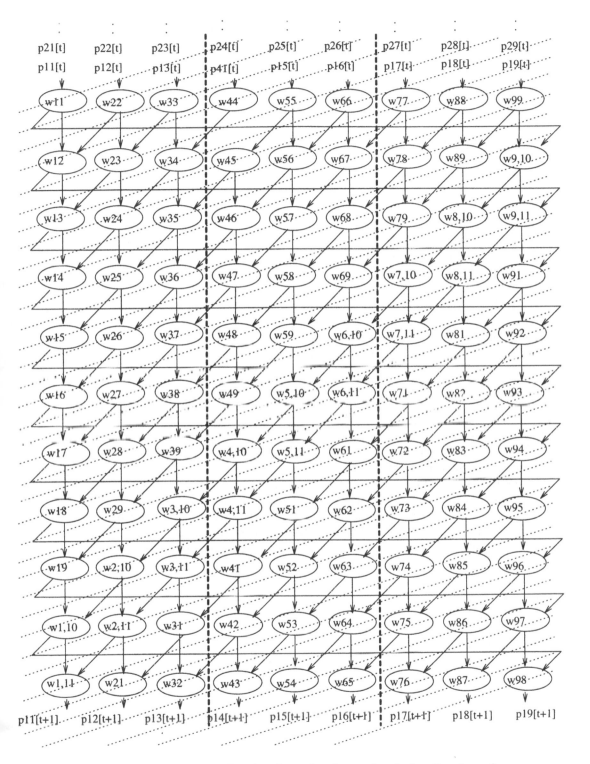

FIGURE 5.10. SFG for the learning phase when $\hat{n} = n \cdot k = 9$, $\hat{m} = 2$, and $n = 3$.

## 5.5 Conclusions

We have shown how the real-time recurrent learning algorithm for training fully recurrent neural networks can be mapped efficiently to a distributed memory ring multiprocessor architecture. In recent years, RNNs have proved useful in a wide range of applications using dynamical systems modeling, prediction, and temporal pattern recognition. However, the large computational complexity of training algorithms limits the use of large models required to handle complex problems. With the emergence of parallel MIMD multiprocessors as a better price/performance alternative to traditional vector supercomputers, the interest in efficient parallel algorithm/architecture combinations for simulating large neural network models has grown substantially.

The RTRL algorithm is computationally very expensive. In this chapter we systematically used space-time mapping techniques, originally proposed for translating sequential algorithms with static dependencies to VLSI arrays, in order to derive a parallel RTRL realization on a ring topology. The ring architecture was selected because it is simple to construct using fine-grain VLSI embedded processors, but also because it is simple to embed into networks of powerful microprocessors.

We have shown how the efficiency of the parallel implementation depends on the ratio of the point-to-point communication latency to the MAC computation time of the nodes, and we have proposed a partitioning method that allows the implementation of real-time recurrent learning for large RNNs in a fixed-sized ring configuration. Partitioning the RTRL algorithm into smaller blocks using the LSGP method has not only the desired property of generality but also facilitates the balancing of communications with computations, which improves efficiency.

The Transputer-based ring array we experimented with can access up to 4 Mbytes $\times$ number of processors of distributed memory with a bandwidth that is directly proportional to the number of processors. This is probably one of the main advantages of the distributed memory system over conventional workstations. When the number $n$ of neurons in the RNN grows, the memory requirements grow as fast as $O(n^3)$. For the largest RNN we were able to simulate in the array (19 PEs x 8 neurons/PE = 152 neurons), the storage requirements were in the order of 80 Mbytes. Having to access directly large amounts of memory for every iteration of the RTRL makes the sequential algorithm very slow on a single CPU machine. It is interesting to note that for the case of 152 neurons, our 19 T-800 array was 15 times faster than a SPARC-2-based SUN workstation.

One of the advantages of using a systematic parallelization methodology is that if using a ring is not providing adequate speed to an application, it is straightforward to construct a mesh array implementation with $O(n^2)$ processors. This will reduce the number of the parallel time to $O(n^2)$. Of course, achieving high efficiency on the mesh will be a more challenging task because we will have to face the well-known trade-off of lower efficiency versus higher parallel running time. A complete *iso-efficiency* analysis [24] for different parallel processing algorithm/architecture combinations needs to be performed before the optimal parallel system is derived.

# References

[1] B. A. Pearlmutter, "Learning state space trajectories in recurrent neural networks," *Neural Computation*, vol. 1, no. 2, pp. 263–269, 1989.

[2] D. Servan-Schreiber, A. Cleermans, and J. L. McClelland, "Encoding sequential structure in simple recurrent networks," tech. rep., Carnegie-Mellon, 1988.

[3] D. Z. R. J. Williams, "Experimental analysis of the real-time recurrent learning algorithm," *Connection Science*, vol. 1, no. 1, 1989.

[4] C. L. Giles, C. Miller, D. Chen, G. Sun, and Y. Lee, "Learning and extracting finate state automata using second-order recurrent neural networks," *Neural Computation*, vol. 4, pp. 393–405, 1992.

[5] G. Goudreau and C. Giles, "Using recurrent neural networks to learn the structure of interconnection networks," tech. rep., University of Maryland, 1994.

[6] A. Robinson, "An application of recurrent nets to phone probability estimation," *IEEE Transactions on Neural Networks*, vol. 5, no. 3, pp. 298–305, 1994.

[7] T. Robinson, "A real-time recurrent error propagation network word recognition system," *ICASSP Int. Conference Accoustics, Speech and Signal Proc*, vol. 1, pp. 617–620, 1992.

[8] R. L. Watrous and L. Shastri, "Learning phonetic features using connectionist networks: An experiment in speech recognition," tech. rep., University of Pennsylvania, 1986.

[9] G. Kechriotis, E. Zervas, and E. S. Manolakos, "Using recurrent neural networks for adaptive communication channel equalization," *IEEE Trans. on Neural Networks*, vol. 5, pp. 267–278, March 1994.

[10] G. Kechriotis, E. Zervas, and E. Manolakos, "Using recurrent neural networks for blind equalization of linear and nonlinear communication channels," in *MILCOM, IEEE Conference on Military Communications*, October 1992.

[11] G. Kechriotis, *Feedback Neural Networks in Digital Communications: Algorithms, Architectures and Applications*. PhD thesis, Dep. Elec. Eng., Notheastern University, Boston, MA, June 1994.

[12] K. S. Narendra and K. Parthasarathy, "Identification and control of dynamical systems using neural networks," IEEE Trans. on Neural Networks, vol. 1, no. 1, pp. 4–27, 1990.

[13] G. V. Puskorius and L. A. Feldkamp, "Neurocontrol of nonlinear dynamical systems with Kalman filter trained recurrent networks," *IEEE Trans. on Neural Networks*, vol. 5, no. 2, pp. 279–298, 1994.

[14] G. Kechriotis and E. Manolakos, "Using neural networks for nonlinear and chaotic signal processing," in *ICASSP Int. Conference Accoustics, Speech and Signal Proc*, vol. 1, pp. 465–496, April 1993.

[15] Y. Murakami and M. Sato, "A recurrent network which learns chaotic dynamics," in *Proc. Third Australian Conference on Neural Networks*, 1992.

[16] N. Z. Hakim, J. J. Kaufman, G. Gerf, and H. E. Meadows, "Volterra characterization of neural networks," in *Proc. IEEE Asilomar Conference on Signals, Systems and Computers*, pp. 1128–1132, November 1991.

[17] R. J. Williams and D. Zipser, "Gradient-based learning algorithms for recurrent networks," in *Back-propagation : Theory, Architectures and Applications* (Y. Chauvin and D. E. Rumelhart, eds.), Hillsdale, NJ: Erlbaum Publ., 1991.

[18] R. J. Williams and D. Zipser, "A learning algorithm for continually running fully recurrent neural networks," *Neural Computation*, vol. 1, pp. 270–280, 1989.

[19] S. Y. Kung, *VLSI Array Processors*. Prentice Hall Inc., 1988.

[20] J. Hwang and S. Kung, "Parallel algorithms / architectures for neural networks," *Journal of VLSI Signal Processing*, vol. 1, pp. 221–251, 1989.

[21] J. Hwang and S. Kung, "A unified systolic architecture for artificial neural networks," *Journal of Parallel and Distributed Computing, Special Issue on Neural Networks*, pp. 358–387, April 1989.

[22] G. Kechriotis and E. S. Manolakos, "Training fully recurrent neural networks on a ring transputer array," *Microprocessors & Microsystems*, vol. 18, pp. 5–11, January 1994.

[23] C. A. R. Hoare, *Communicating Sequential Processes*. U.K.: Prentice Hall International, 1985.

[24] V. Kumar, A. Grama, A. Gupta, and G. Karypis, *Introduction to Parallel Computing, Design and Analysis of Algorithms*. Benjamin, Cummings, 1994.

# Chapter 6

# Parallel Implementation of ART1 Neural Networks on Processor Ring Architectures

**Elias S. Manolakos***
Communications and Digital Signal Processing (CDSP),
Center for Research and Graduate Studies,
Electrical and Computer Engineering Department,
409 Dana Building, Northeastern University,
Boston, Mass. 02115, USA
**Stylianos Markogiannakis**
Brigham and Women's Hospital,
Anesthesia Foundation,
Boston, Mass. 02115

## 6.1  Introduction

The *adaptive resonance theory* (ART) was originally developed by Grossberg and Carpenter as an attempt to model the way biological organisms learn and behave. During the last 10 years, Grossberg and his group have proposed a number of specific architectures to account for the different types of input (analog versus binary) as well as to recognize and adapt mechanisms that would also be consistent with physiological findings. In their work, the originators of ART also made efforts to model psychological mechanisms encountered in living species, such as selective attention.

All ART architectures are basically extensions or enhancements of the ART1 neural network [1,2]. For example, ART2 [3,4] is an extension that can accommodate analog inputs in addition to binary ones. ART3 [5] incorporates a model of the chemical synapse mechanism of physiological neurons as a way to address the computational needs of the searching mechanism.

Fuzzy ART [6] borrows elements from fuzzy set theory in order to work with arbitrary sequences of analog or binary input patterns. Finally, ARTMAP [7] utilizes two ART modules linked together by an associative learning network to provide a supervised learning mechanism that can be used to predict one pattern, given another.

In this chapter, we will consider only ART1 [1,2] neural networks, in which inputs and outputs are binary and the learning mode is unsupervised. ART1 networks form clusters of binary input data patterns and can create new classes without affecting the storage or recall of already existing classes. They learn by "following the leader"— that is, after the formation of a class, a new one is generated only if the distance of the presented pattern from all existing clusters exceeds a threshold controlled by the so-called *vigilance* parameter.

---

*To whom all correspondence should be addressed. This work has been partially supported by the Defense Advanced Project Research Agency under contract F49620-93-1-0490, which is monitored by the Air Force Office of Scientific Research.

An interesting feature of ART1 networks is that, in their operation, the learning and recall phases are not separate. In fact, these phases do not alternate in time, as they do in most neural network models under supervised training. ART1 networks, for the duration of their operation, perform both phases concurrently.

Although the ART1 networks are considered to be the first truly potent self-organizing pattern recognition networks, they have certain drawbacks. For instance, even a small change in the value of the vigilance parameter can have a great impact on the classification process. Also, they are not suited for raw data processing due to spatial distortions of the patterns. On the other hand, they are very good high-level classifiers and with proper preprocessing they can be effective in categorical perception.

ART neural networks, in many of their forms, have been found useful in numerous applications in diverse scientific and engineering disciplines such as: image processing [8–15], speech processing [9, 16–19], temporal pattern recognition [20], decision making [21], neurobiology [22], classical conditioning [23–25], control [26–28], diagnostics [29, 30], knowledge processing [31, 32], telecommunications [33], and radar image detection [34, 35].

Neural networks are inherently parallel systems and ART1 networks are no exception. The ART1 algorithm can be parallelized and as a consequence applications that involve pattern matching or feature extraction can greatly benefit from such an implementation. In this chapter, we introduce a ring parallel algorithm and present its implementation. The neurons in the different layers of an ART1 network are fully connected. The challenge is to find a way to implement efficiently the required logical full connectivity in an architecture where each processor is physically connected to only a few neighbors. The architecture we considered here is the ring because it can be easily realized in very large scale integration (VLSI) or embedded into more complex, commonly used processor networks such as the two-dimensional mesh and the hypercube [36]. Furthermore, ring parallel algorithms have been developed for many other neural network models [37].

The rest of this chapter is organized as follows: Section 6.2 provides a brief overview of the operation of ART1 networks. Section 6.3 describes the steps of the fast learning ART1 algorithm [1, 38]. They lead to the steady state solution of the differential equations governing the dynamic behavior of the neurons. Section 6.4 describes, in detail, the corresponding ring algorithm and emphasizes the modifications needed to construct a distributed realization. Partitioning schemes are introduced, for allocating processes to physical processors, to allow the simulation of large-size ART1 networks on fixed-size processor arrays. Section 6.5 presents experimental results obtained from a Transputer-based implementation, followed by a discussion on how the speedup is changing when the number of processors is increasing in relation to the problem size. Finally, in Section 6.6, we conclude by outlining some related work in progress.

## 6.2 ART1 Network Architecture

To achieve a network that has both plasticity and learning stability, Carpenter and Grossberg [1, 2] proposed an architecture composed of three interacting components: the gain control subsystem, the orienting subsystem, and the attentional subsystem. The gain control subsystem stabilizes system operation and primes the network to receive expected patterns. The orienting subsystem is invoked when the network encounters a new pattern and shuts down any attempt to continue poor matching with old categories. The attentional subsystem performs the actual pattern recognition and consists of two layers. The first layer, called F1, has as many neurons as the binary digits in the input pattern. The second layer, called F2, has at least as many neurons as the number of the clusters that are

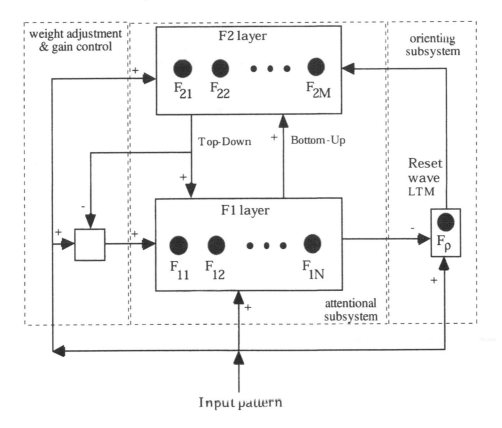

FIGURE 6.1. Schematic representation of ART1 subsystems and connections.

needed (or expected) to be formed. The neurons of the first layer are fully connected with the neurons of the second layer and vice versa. In addition, the neurons on the F2 layer are laterally fully connected and these connections are *inhibitory*, in contrast to all the other connections across layers that are *excitatory*. The connections from one layer to the other are weighted and the weights constitute the *long-term memory* (LTM) of the system. The activities of the neurons for each particular pattern constitute the short-term memory (STM) of the system [1]. The overall architecture of the ART1 network is depicted in Figure 6.1.

The operation of the network can be briefly described as follows: Upon introduction of a data pattern to the inputs of the F1 layer, STM activity is generated to the output of the F1 layer. Each neuron is *activated* if its input is above a desired threshold and its output is generated from a nonlinear thresholder, which in this study is a hard delimiter. The STM activity on the F1 layer is multiplied with the corresponding bottom-up (BU) LTM connection weights before it is introduced to the inputs of the F2 layer. Due to the presence of STM activity of the F1 layer, the neurons of the F2 layer are activated and because a winner-take-all competition is taking place on F2, only one neuron will "fire." The output of the "winner" neuron is multiplied by the corresponding top-down (TD) LTM weights and the result is fed back as an additional input to the F1 neurons contributing to the requirements of the "2/3 rule" [1].

At this point, if there is a significant mismatch between the bottom-up and top-down inputs to the F1 layer, the STM activity pattern of the orienting subsystem, driven by the newly updated STM activity of the F1 layer, will create a nonspecific reset signal to the F2 layer. The neuron on F2 that was declared the winner will become inactive and will remain suppressed for the rest of the period that the same input pattern is presented as the input to F1. Now, another neuron has the chance to win the competition taking place on F2, and present its cluster representative pattern to the orienting subsystem. The search continues until a neuron in F2 is found that does not create a considerable mismatch with the input pattern, in which case the orienting subsystem remains quiet, *resonance* is achieved, and the LTM weights are adjusted to incorporate the input pattern to the cluster represented by the winning neuron on F2.

A closer look at Figure 6.1 reveals the requirements for a neuron on either F1 or F2 to be activated. There are three input paths to each neuron, and at least two of them need to be active for the neuron to become active; this is referred to as the *2/3 rule* [1]. In particular, a neuron on F1 receives input (1) from the input pattern (2) from F2 (feedback), and (3) from the gain control subsystem (nonspecific input). Upon presentation of a pattern, the gain control subsystem provides the second input needed by the neurons on F1 to become active. Once that happens, it triggers activity on the F2 layer. This activity is fed back to the F1 layer disengaging the gain control system and providing in its place the second input needed by the F1 neurons to remain active. It is apparent now that a template matching is taking place between the input pattern and the TD weight vector originating from the winning neuron of the F2 layer.

As Figure 6.1 shows the neuron $F_\rho$ of the orienting subsystem is receiving an excitatory stimulus from the input pattern itself and inhibitory stimulus from the immediate output of the F1 layer. Initially, the two stimuli cancel each other and $F_\rho$ remains quiet. After new activation emerges from F2, the modified activity of F1 (because of F2's influence) will deviate from that because of the input pattern. The inhibitory and excitatory connections now will differ, and if this difference is significant (exceeding the vigilance threshold) a reset wave will be issued to the neurons of F2. If, on the other hand, the modified activity on F1 is similar to the input pattern itself, then resonance is achieved and the LTM learning process continues uninterrupted.

A similar process is taking place on layer F2. Upon introduction of an input pattern, the neurons on F2 are receiving activity from the gain control subsystem (becoming primed or "subliminary active"). When the activity of the F1 layer is propagated up through the BU weights, F2 neurons receive the additional input needed and become active. Now, because the lateral connections on the F2 layer are inhibitory, only one neuron on F2 will survive the competition and present its template (encoded in its TD weights) to the F1 layer. Again, if resonance is achieved, the winning F2 neuron will remain active and the weight adjustments will take place to incorporate the input pattern into its cluster. If resonance is not achieved, the inhibitory reset signal will shut down this neuron and trigger a new competition cycle among the other neurons on F2.

The initialization of the weights is such that, at the beginning, the first pattern activates all the neurons on F2. In situations in which many neurons on F2 have the same activation, only one is selected to fire.[2] The top-down weights are initialized with values ranging from zero to one and during learning they may change to zero or one depending on whether the receiving neuron on F1 is inactive or active during resonance respectively. Once a weight is set to zero, it will retain its value. On the other hand, the bottom-up weights are initialized in a way that guarantees minimum activation for all neurons on F2 [2]. Their values are in the interval $[0, 1]$ and during learning may change to strengthen the association of the input pattern with the winning cluster to which it belongs. Furthermore, if an input pattern does not belong to any of the formed clusters (all vigilance tests fail) and the capacity of the network is exceeded (all neurons on F2 are committed), then no learning takes place for

---

[2]Without loss of generality, we can choose the F2 neuron in the group with the lowest index.

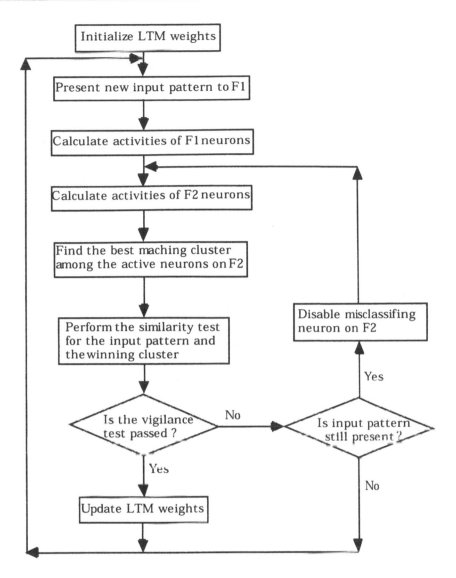

FIGURE 6.2. Flowchart of the ART1 serial algorithm.

the duration of the presentation of that input pattern (epoch). The operation of the ART1 neural network is summarized by the flowchart shown in Figure 6.2.

## 6.3 Serial Algorithm

The differential equations that govern the operation of a neuron $k$ on layer F1 or F2 have the form [1, 38]

$$\varepsilon \dot{x}_k = -x_k + (1 - A_1 x_k)J_k^+ - (B_1 + C_1 x_k)J_k^-$$

where $A_1, B_1$, and $C_1$ are appropriately chosen constants, $J_k^+$ is an excitatory input, and $J_k^-$ is an inhibitory input. In particular for neuron F1$_k$, the total excitatory input $J_k^+$ is given by

$$J_k^+ = I_k + D_1 I_k' + B_1 G$$

161

where $D_1$ is constant and $I'_k$ is the input to F1$_k$ due to the feedback from the winner F2 neuron. Also, for neurons on F1 the inhibitory term, $J_k^-$, is set to 1. The output $G$ of the gain control subsystem that is used for the application of the 2/3 rule can be described by

$$G = \begin{cases} 1 & \text{if } I_k \neq 0 \text{ and } I'_k = 0 \ \forall \text{ neurons } F1_k \in F1, \\ 0 & \text{otherwise.} \end{cases}$$

Here we follow the *fast learning* model [1,38], in which it is assumed that the patterns remain present at the input for a sufficiently long time so that all state variables reach their steady state values. In this case, the activity of the winning neuron on F2 (because we have a winner-take-all competition) is the weighted sum of the activities of neurons on F1 multiplied by the BU LTM weights. Furthermore, the weight updates also reach their asymptotic values.

In the sequel we summarize the corresponding serial algorithm so that the parallel algorithm of the following section can also be understood.

**Step 1: Initialization.** The network weights and the constants $A_1, B_1, C_1, D_1$, and $L_1$ are initialized. The matrices **W** (bottom-up LTM weights), and **V** (top-down LTM weights) are of size $M \times N$ and $N \times M$, where $N$ ($M$) is the number of neurons on layer F1 (F2), respectively, and each matrix is initialized with identical entries:

$$\mathbf{W} = \left[ \frac{L_1}{L_1 - 1 + N} \right], \tag{6.1}$$

$$\mathbf{V} = \left[ \frac{B_1 - 1}{D_1} \right]. \tag{6.2}$$

In addition, the vigilance parameter is set:

$$0 < \rho < 1 \tag{6.3}$$

as well as the constants

$$A_1 \geq 0, \ C_1 \geq 0, \ D_1 \geq 0, \ L_1 > 1, \ \max\{D_1, 1\} < B_1 < D_1 + 1.$$

When these conditions hold, they can ensure stable, fast learning.

**Step 2: Compute the Activations of F1 Neurons.** A binary input vector **I** is presented to the input nodes. F1 neuron activities $\{x_{1i}, \ i = 1, 2, \ldots N\}$ are calculated as follows:

$$x_{1i} = \frac{I_i}{1 + A_1(I_i + B_1) + C_1}. \tag{6.4}$$

**Step 3: Compute the Output of F1 Neurons.**

$$s_{1i} = h(x_{1i}) = \begin{cases} 1 & x_{1i} > 0, \\ 0 & x_{1i} \leq 0, \end{cases} \tag{6.5}$$

where $\mathbf{s_1}$ is the F1 output vector after applying the hard delimiter $h(\cdot)$.

**Step 4: Compute the Activations of F2 Neurons.** All activations of the F2 neurons $\{x_{2j}, j = 1, 2, \ldots M\}$ are computed as follows:

$$x_{2j} = \sum_{i=1}^{N} W_{ji} s_{1i} \tag{6.6}$$

where $W_{ji}$ is the BU LTM weight from neuron F1$_i$ to neuron F2$_j$.

**Step 5: Compute the Output of F2 Neurons.** Only the winning F2 neuron produces a nonzero output:

$$s_{2j} = \begin{cases} 1 & x_{2j} = \max_{k}\{x_{2k}\} \text{ for } k = 1, 2, \ldots, M, \\ 0 & \text{otherwise,} \end{cases} \tag{6.7}$$

where $s_2$ is the F2 layer output vector. We will assume that the winning node is F2$_J$, so $s_{2J}=1$ and $s_{2k} = 0 \ \forall \ k \neq J, \ k \in [1, M]$.

**Step 6: Compute the Contribution of F2 to F1 Activity.** Propagate the output from F2 back to F1 and calculate the net inputs from F2 to the F1 units:

$$I'_i = \sum_{j=1}^{M} V_{ij} s_{2j} = V_{iJ} \tag{6.8}$$

where $V_{ij}$ is the TD LTM weight from neuron F2$_j$ to neuron F1$_i$, and $I'$ is the contribution of the F2 layer to the activity of F1 layer neurons.

**Step 7: Update Activity of F1 Neurons.** Calculate the new activities of F1 neurons as follows:

$$x_{1i} = \frac{I_i + D_1 I'_i - B_1}{1 + A_1 (I_i + D_1 I'_i) + C_1}. \tag{6.9}$$

**Step 8: Update Outputs of F1 Neurons.** Determine the new output values $\{s_{1i}\}, i = 1, 2, \ldots N$ of the F1 neurons using a hard delimiter nonlinearity as in step 3.

**Step 9: Perform the Vigilance Test.** The similarity test for the (currently) winning neuron $J$ is performed as follows:

$$\frac{|s_1|}{|I|} = \frac{\sum_{i=1}^{N} s_{1i}}{\sum_{i=1}^{N} I_i}. \tag{6.10}$$

If $|s_1|/|I| < \rho$, mark F2$_J$ as inactive, zero the outputs of F2 neurons, and go back to step 2 using the same input pattern, if still present. If $|s_1|/|I| \geq \rho$, continue.

**Step 10: Bottom-up LTM Weights Update.** Update only the bottom-up weights into neuron F2$_J$ that won the competition in F2— that is, update the weights in the $J$-th row of matrix **W** as follows:

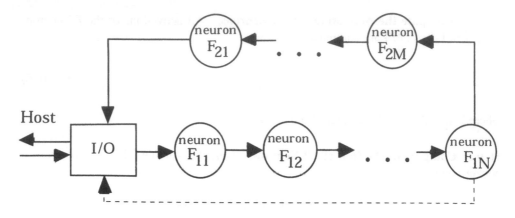

FIGURE 6.3. Extended ring architecture. $F1_i$ ($F2_i$) denote neurons on F1 (F2) layer, respectively.

$$W_{Ji} = \begin{cases} \frac{L}{L_1 - 1 + |s_1|} & \text{if } F_{1i} \text{ is active,} \\ 0 & \text{if } F_{1i} \text{ is inactive.} \end{cases} \tag{6.11}$$

**Step 11: Top-down LTM Weights Update.** Update the top-down weights from $F2_J$ to all the F1 neurons— that is, CQS update the $J^{th}$ column of matrix $\mathbf{V}$ as follows:

$$V_{iJ} = \begin{cases} 1 & \text{if } F_{1i} \text{ is active,} \\ 0 & \text{if } F_{1i} \text{ is inactive.} \end{cases} \tag{6.12}$$

**Step 12: Completion of Epoch.** Restore all inactive F2 units and return to step 2 starting with a new input pattern presentation.

## 6.4 Parallel Ring Algorithm

The parallel algorithm that we developed is suitable for the ring topology shown in Figure 6.3. Each processing element (PE) in the ring models a neuron of layer F1 or F2 and locally holds a vector with the corresponding LTM weights of connections terminating to this neuron and originating from each one of the neurons on the opposite layer. Every PE can communicate directly only with the two nearest neighbor PEs in the ring. There is a split (dashed line) of the ring at the PE that simulates the last neuron of layer F1 ($F_{1N}$), which is used for all the communications among neurons in F1 that do not concern the neurons of F2. Therefore, data tokens may travel around the whole ring, or just the first (lower) part of it, depending on the kind of communication pattern that it is necessary to implement at each step of the algorithm.

The parallel algorithm requires one pass around the whole ring (complete circulation) to find an initial candidate class for classifying the given input pattern. This is followed by a circulation around the short (lower) ring in order to check if the initial candidate class passes the vigilance test. If the candidate class chosen turns out not to resonate with the pattern, an additional pass around the short (lower) ring is needed to check the next candidate, and this process will be repeated until the similarity (vigilance) test is passed or all classes have been checked unsuccessfully. Finally, a pass is needed in order to update the LTM weights of the F2 neuron that resonated with the input pattern.

During the first pass, the input pattern is provided from the host and the resulting activations of the F1 layer are circulating so that each node on F2 learns the activation of all the nodes on F1. The inner product of these activations with the locally stored BU LTM weights produces (after passing from the nonlinearity) the F2 neuron activation. This pass is completed by circulating the produced activations of the F2 layer back to all the nodes of F1 where they are stored in each node. At this point, a node on F1 can locally search for the winning F2 neuron and use the winner's index to update its own activation (due to feedback from F2). The updated F1 activation needs to be distributed to the other F1 nodes, for the application of the vigilance test, and this is implemented using the lower ring. The local search and the F1 activations distribution cycle is repeated as many times as needed, until the correct class is found—that is, locked to a particular F2 neuron with index $J$. At that point, each F1 node can update locally its TD weight connection from $F2_J$. Finally, once resonance has been achieved, the new F1 activations and the winning F2 neuron's index $J$ are distributed to the F2 layer so that node $F_{2J}$ can update its BU LTM weights.

In the sequel we provide the single program multiple data (SPMD) pseudocode describing the computation and communication operations performed *concurrently* by PEs assigned either to the F1 or to the F2 parts of the ring, simulating neurons in the corresponding ART1 layers. At every step a PE assigned to a layer executes serially a set of actions, but it is operating in parallel with all other PEs in the ring. PEs are synchronized by exchanging messages that may be formed by concatenating more than one piece of information.[3] When needed, we will assume that the host that controls the ring acts as a source and sink of messages. The pseudocode is meant to be self explanatory but some comments have also been inserted wherever needed.

### Step 1: Initialization.

```
Every neuron F1_j, j=1,2, ... ,N, set
A1≥0, C1≥0, D1≥0
    max{D1,1}<B1<D1+1
    L1>1
    0<ρ≤1                    /* Init constants, Eq. 6.3 */
    For k=1 to M
  v[k]:=(B1-1)/D1            /* Init local TD weights vector,
                                Eq. 6.2 */
Every neuron F2_j, j=1,2, ...  M, do
    For k=1 to N
        w[k]:=L1/(L1-1+N)  /* Init local BU weights vector,
                                Eq. 6.1 */
```

### Step 2: Pattern Presentation, Activity on F1 Layer.

```
msg = < I>                    /* where I is the binary
                                input pattern vector */
Every neuron F1_i, i=1,2, ... ,N, do
    input:=msg.from.previous
    msg.to.next:=input
    x1:=input[i]/(1+A1*(input[i]+B1)+C1) /* Eq. 6.4 */
```

---
[3]The notation msg $=< a, b, \dots >$ will be used in that case.

```
        If x1>0 then s1:=1
              else s1:=0            /* Eq. 6.5 */
```

**Step 3: Activity on F2 Layer.**

```
Every neuron F1ᵢ, i=1,2, ... ,N
msg:=<s1,i>                      /* Form the message */
Do i-1 times                     /* i is index of F1 neuron */
        msg.to.next:=msg
        msg:=msg.from.previous
    msg.to.next:=msg

Every neuron F2ⱼ, j=1,2, ... ,M
    x2:=0
    Do N times
        msg:=msg.from.previous
        msg.to.next:=msg
        i:=msg[2]                /* recover index of
        s1s[i]:=msg[1]              sending F1 PE */
                                 /* store received
                                    F1 PE's activity */

        x2:=x2+s1s[i]*w[i]   /* Eq. 6.6 */
```

**Step 4: Feedback of F2 Activation to F1.**

```
Every neuron F2ⱼ, j=1,2, ... ,M
    msg:=<x2,j>
    Do M-j times
        msg.to.next:=msg
        msg:=msg.from.previous
    msg.to.next:=msg
Every neuron F1ᵢ, i=1,2, ... ,N
    Do M times
        msg:=msg.from.previous
        msg.to.next:=msg
        j:=msg[2]            /* recover index of
                                sending F2 PE */
        x2s[j]:=msg[1]    /* store received
                             PE's activity */
```

**Step 5: Search for the Winner of F2.**

```
Every neuron F1ᵢ, i=1,2, ... ,N, do
    Find J such that x2s[J] >  x2s[k],  k=1,2,...,M
/* J is the index of the neuron winning F2 competition */
    s2:=v[J]                        /* s2 is I' of Eq. 6.8 */
```

**Step 6: Update Activities on F1.**

```
Every neuron F1ᵢ, i=1,2, ... ,N, do
    x1:=(input[i]+D1*s2-B1)/(1+A1*(input[i]+D1*s2)+C1)
                                      /* Eq. 6.9 */
    If x1>0 then s1:=1
            else s1:=0               /* Eq. 6.5 */
```

**Step 7: Vigilance Test (Using Short Lower Ring).**

```
Every neuron F1ᵢ, i=1,2, ... ,N
    msg:=<s1>
    /* Compute the bit sum of current pattern */
    Isum:= number_of_bits(input[])
    Ssum:=0
    Do N times
          msg.to.next:=msg
          msg:=msg.from.previous
          Ssum:=Ssum+msg[1]          /* Ssum = |s₁|
                                        of Eq. 6.10 */

    If ρ*Isum > Ssum then            /* Eq. 6.10 */
          x2s[J]:=0
          go back to Step 5
    else
          go to Step 8
```

**Step 8: Update Top-down Weights.**

```
Every neuron F1ᵢ, i=1,2, ... ,N, do
    If s1<>0 then v[J]:=1
            else v[J]:=0             /* Eq. 6.12 */
    If i=N then                      /* neuron F1N sends
          msg:=<Ssum,J>                 Ssum and J to F2M */
          msg.to.next:=msg
    msg:=<s1,i>
    Do i-1 times
          msg.to.next:=msg
          msg:=msg.from.previous
    msg.to.next:=msg

Every neuron F2ⱼ, j=1,2, ... ,M, do
    msg:=msg.from.previous
    Ssum:=msg[1]
    J:=msg[2]
    msg.to.next:=msg

    Do N times                       /* receive modified
          msg:=msg.from.previous        F1 activity */
          s1s[i]:=msg[1]
          i:=msg[2]
          msg.to.next:=msg
```

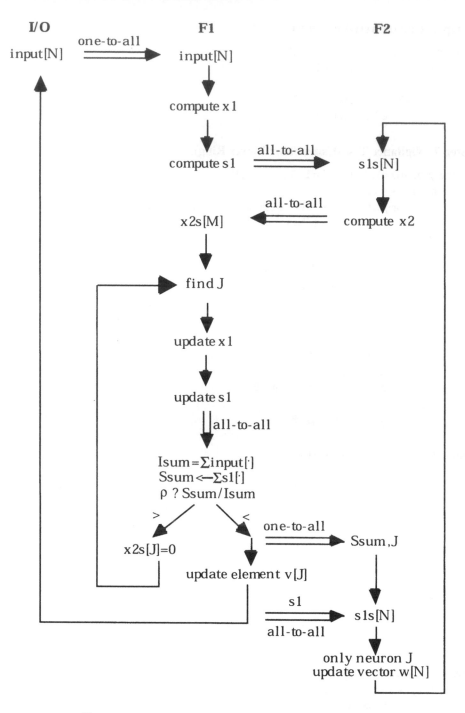

FIGURE 6.4. Schematic view of the ring parallel algorithm.

**Step 9: Update Bottom-up Weights.**

```
Neuron F2ⱼ (winner) only, do
    For i:=1 to N
        If s1s[i]<>0 then
                w[i]:=L1/(L1-1+Ssum)     /* Eq. 6.11 */
        else
                w[i]:=0
```

**Step 10: Completion of Epoch**

```
        Return to Step 2 with a new input pattern.
```

Figure 6.4 summarizes pictorially the exchange of data and the updating of variables involved in the parallel algorithm described, as seen from the point of view of concurrent processes simulating the operation of F1 and F2 neurons. Steps that involve communication between processes are marked with $\Longrightarrow$, and the regular sequential flow of operation is denoted with vertical simple arrows. I/O is a process that controls the ring and provides the input and output interface with the host environment. A vector held locally by a process is denoted by $X[K]$, where $K$ is the number of elements in the vector. In particular, input[N] denotes the binary input pattern vector, s1s[N] the vector of F1 neuron activations received by an F2 neuron, and x2s[M] the vector of F2 neuron activations received by an F1 neuron.[4]

One-to-all broadcast corresponds to the distribution of a single token generated by a process in a layer to all the neuron processes of the other layer. All-to-all broadcast is the communication primitive in which every neuron sends one token to all other neurons in the other (or the same) layer. For example, if information flows from F1 to F2, the semantics are such that the primitive does not complete before each F2 process has collected exactly one token from every F1 process in the ring.

### 6.4.1 Partitioning Strategy

Up to this point we have assumed that each neuron is simulated by one processing element, but this may not always be feasible because of a lack of resources. Therefore, partitioning of the problem is required in order to simulate arbitrarily large neural networks with a fixed number of physical processors. There are two ways that we can partition the logical ring. We could map a number of near-neighbor processes from both layers, F1 and F2, to the same physical processor, or we could allocate neighboring processes from only F1 (or F2) to a processor.

The second scheme was found to be more efficient in the Transputer-based implementation, as described in the next section. Partitioning of an arbitrary large problem is therefore implemented by allocating neuron processes of the F1 (F2) layer equally among the processors assigned to simulate the F1 (F2) layer in order to maintain load balancing when the dimensions of the two layers change. Scalable and efficient implementations can be obtained if the amount of local computations (that is proportional to the number of simulated neurons per processor) is increased to the point that it balances the relatively slower interprocessor communications. Such an allocation is always possible when the chosen partitioning scheme is used, as will be explained in the next section.

---

[4]The only exception to the rule is that v[J] is not a vector with $J$ elements, but just the $J$-th element of vector **v**.

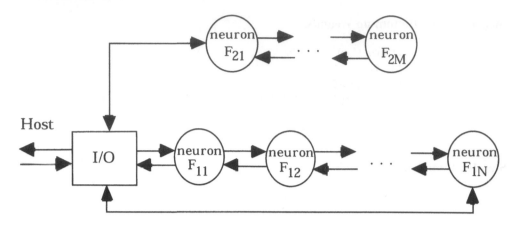

FIGURE 6.5. Palindrome ring architecture with bidirectional communications.

Pipelining is essential in minimizing communication overhead in all-to-all broadcast primitives. In the extended ring architecture of Figure 6.3, partial results generated at the F1 nodes that could become immediately available to nodes at F2 have to travel all the way to neuron $F1_N$ before they can reach any neuron in F2. Also, if we view the ring as a pipeline, it may be emptied before new tokens become available and ready to travel around the ring.

These inefficiencies can be avoided if a ring with bidirectional communication links (called "palindrome" here) is used. In this way, partial results that emerge in one layer and need to become available in the other layer can start traveling as soon as possible in the opposite direction than the tokens that generate them. Thus, partial results can arrive at the consuming layer faster due to the better utilization of the communication links. The palindrome ring architecture is shown in Figure 6.5. The ring algorithm remains essentially the same except for minor modifications in the control flow of information. Moreover, the same partitioning strategy can be applied.

## 6.5  Experimental Results

### 6.5.1  The MEIKO Computing Surface System

The logical ring architectures described in the previous section were realized on a Meiko Computing Surface [39] CS-1400 system consisting of an array of 32 T-800 INMOS Transputers. The Transputers are organized in eight boards of four processors fully connected through the backplane. Therefore, a variety of Transputer network topologies can be realized under software control. A Sparc host is used to monitor program execution and for handling external I/O.

The T800 Transputer [40] is a microprocessor fabricated by INMOS that can be used as a building block for large multiple instruction multiple data (MIMD) parallel processing systems. Each T-800 chip can communicate with four near neighbors through four bidirectional links supporting bit-serial point-to-point communications. The links are capable of passing 1.8 Mbytes per second in one direction, and 2.4 Mbytes per second in both directions simultaneously. Each link interface is autonomous and can operate concurrently with the central processing unit. The minimum clock cycle is 33ns and there is a floating point unit on chip sustaining about 1 Mflops. Each T800 has 4 Kbytes of on-chip static

TABLE 6.1. Optimal Configurations for the Extended Ring. Entries have the format $P_1 + P_2$ where $P_1$ ($P_2$) is the number of processors assigned to F1 (F2) layers that resulted to faster execution, and $P = P1 + P2$.

| Extended | | Total Number of Processors (P) | | | | | | | |
|---|---|---|---|---|---|---|---|---|---|
| F1 Size (N) | Connections | 2 | 6 | 10 | 14 | 18 | 22 | 26 | 29 |
| 35 | 1,820 | 1+1 | 4+2 | 6+4 | 9+5 | 12+6 | 15+7 | 19+7 | 18+11 |
| 70 | 3,640 | 1+1 | 4+2 | 7+3 | 10+4 | 14+4 | 15+7 | 19+7 | 24+5 |
| 105 | 5,460 | 1+1 | 5+1 | 8+2 | 11+3 | 14+4 | 15+7 | 19+7 | 23+6 |
| 140 | 7,280 | 1+1 | 5+1 | 8+2 | 11+3 | 14+4 | 18+4 | 21+5 | 24+5 |
| 175 | 9,100 | 1+1 | 5+1 | 8+2 | 12+2 | 15+3 | 18+4 | 22+4 | 23+6 |

TABLE 6.2. Optimal Configurations for the Palindrome Ring. Entries have the format $P_1 + P_2$ where $P_1$ ($P_2$) is the number of processors assigned to F1 (F2) layers that resulted to faster execution, and $P = P1 + P2$.

| Palindrome | | Total Number of Processors (P) | | | | | | | |
|---|---|---|---|---|---|---|---|---|---|
| F1 Size (N) | Connections | 2 | 6 | 10 | 14 | 18 | 22 | 26 | 29 |
| 35 | 1,820 | 1+1 | 4+2 | 7+3 | 9+5 | 12+6 | 14+8 | 19+7 | 20+9 |
| 70 | 3,640 | 1+1 | 5+1 | 7+3 | 10+4 | 13+5 | 18+4 | 19+7 | 20+9 |
| 105 | 5,460 | 1+1 | 5+1 | 8+2 | 11+3 | 14+4 | 18+4 | 22+4 | 22+7 |
| 140 | 7,280 | 1+1 | 5+1 | 8+2 | 11+3 | 15+3 | 19+3 | 22+4 | 25+4 |
| 175 | 9,100 | 1+1 | 5+1 | 8+2 | 11+3 | 15+3 | 19+3 | 22+4 | 26+3 |

RAM and 4 Mbytes linearly addressed external dynamic RAM as local memory accessed at a rate of about 40 Mbytes per second.

The parallel algorithm was coded in Occam-2 [41], an elegant simple concurrent programming language that supports the model of communicating sequential processes [42]. In Occam-2, processes are the application building blocks and can be considered as independent units communicating through channels that support synchronous message passing with blocking. If the two processes that need to exchange information are allocated to the same processor, then communication is realized through synchronized local memory accesses that are invisible to the programmer.

### 6.5.2 Performance and Scalability Analysis

To compare the performance of the two ring architectures (of Figures 6.3 and 6.5) and study how it scales as both the number of processors and the problem size are increasing, we conducted a large number of experiments. Each reported time measurement was observed when executing a given task using a fixed number of processors.

A task consisted of learning exactly $M = 26$ patterns. Each bit pattern was different and was generated by repeating a pattern-specific template having 35 bits. The figures of merit (speedup and parallel running time) are reported as a function of the number of weighted connections between the F1 and F2 layers that is equal to $2MN$. For example, if each one of the $M = 26$ input patterns of a task has length $N = 2 \times 35 = 70$ bits, then the number of connections of the corresponding ART1 network is 3,640. The configurations (number of processors assigned to layer F1 and F2 neuron processes) that led to minimum execution time, given the total number of available processors and pattern length, are provided in Tables 6.1 and 6.2 for the extended ring and palindrome architectures, respectively.

The entries in these tables suggest that most of the computational power should be offered to the processes that realize the function of the F1 layer. Figure 6.6A confirms that this is the case. The question we addressed in this particular experiment was how the computations relate to communications so to suggest efficient allocation strategies of neuron processes to physical processors for each layer. The $M = 26$ different input patterns we used had all length equal to $N = 175$ bits.

To study layer F2 allocation, we dedicated 15 processors to layer F1, while varying the number of processors allocated to F2. The relative speedup factor, plotted on Figure 6.6, was calculated as the ratio of the time needed to complete the task when allocating a single processor to the F2 to the time needed to complete the same task when using a larger number of processors for F2 (always keeping to 15 the number of processors working on F1). As Figure 6.6A shows, the communication overhead becomes apparent very early, and negligible, if any, speedup improvement is obtained by increasing the number of processors allocated to F2 beyond three to four processors.[5]

To study layer F1 allocation, we dedicated three processors to F2 and varied the number of processors assigned to F1. The behavior of layer F1 is completely different than that of F2, as demonstrated by Figure 6.6B, as the relative speedup is increasing almost linearly with the number of processors working on F1. With the machine we used, we could not reach a speedup plateau (as it easily happened with the F2 layer). For this experiment, and after assigning 25 processors to F1 (seven neuron processes per processor), it seems that the communication overhead still remains well hidden and the relative speedup keeps rising.

The time measurements for both the extended and the palindrome ring architectures, and for all problem sizes we considered (always using the optimal configurations of Tables 6.1 and 6.2) are shown in the three-dimensional plots of Figure 6.7. The base-2 logarithm of the time (in $\mu$sec) spent to complete a task by the parallel and the serial algorithms is provided. A task consisted of three presentations (epochs) of exactly $M = 26$ patterns of bit-size $N$ to an ART1 network with $N$ F1 and $M$ F2 neurons, that is, having $2MN$ weighted connections. The observed behavior is consistent with the one expected by highly parallelizable algorithms. For a fixed problem size (number of connections) and as the overall number of processors increases, the parallel running time is rapidly decreasing.

Speedup curves as a function of the problem size for both the extended and the palindrome architecture are provided in Figure 6.8. The speedup was calculated as the ratio of the time needed to complete a task by mapping all the processes of the F1 and F2 layers to one processor over the time needed to complete the same task by mapping the processes of F1 and F2 on a larger number of processors (always following the allocation schemes shown on Tables 6.1 and 6.2). From the curves of Figure 6.8, it is evident that a speedup close to the theoretical maximum value can be achieved. Some speedup variability is observed for large rings that can be attributed to the physical characteristics of the machine and the underlying interconnection network (communications between near-neighbor processors in the same board or in different boards through the crossbar switch of the backplane). These minor fluctuations seem to diminish as the problem size increases.

Another view of the speedup for both the extended and the palindrome ring architectures and for the same configurations and problem sizes considered in Figure 6.7, is provided by Figure 6.9. From these three-dimensional plots, it is clear that the algorithm is scalable because it exhibits almost linearly increasing speedup with the number of processors and for all problem sizes considered.

---

[5]The observed speedup factor fluctuations have probably to do with the utilization of the on-chip cache in every case.

By comparing the figures of merit for the extended and the palindrome rings, we conclude that the extended ring architecture performs slightly better. Although the argument for the development of the palindrome ring was better pipeline utilization, this expectation did not materialize in the system we used. The main reason seems to be that although the Transputers have separate interface hardware for each physical link, introducing bidirectional communications does not double their communication throughput.[6] This is because the communication protocol inserts acknowledgment packages that have to share the same links with the data.

The time measurements for the serial algorithm were obtained by mapping all concurrent processes of the ring algorithm to one physical processor. This is not the optimal serial algorithm implementation because message-passing communications (with blocking) over logical channels are implemented by the compiler using semaphores and are slower than regular shared memory accesses. However, the same strategy was used for mapping multiple processes to every processor in the distributed algorithm. Whatever optimization could have been applied to make the serial algorithm faster would also be applicable to the code running in each processor of the distributed implementation. For ease of programmability, we used the same Occam-2 source code and in every run we changed only the placement part of it (allocating processes to processors).

## 6.6 Conclusions

In this chapter, we introduced a parallel algorithm for simulating large size ART1 neural networks on ring architectures. The algorithm was shown to be highly parallelizable and exhibit very good scalability properties.

It is evident from the performance results that the point-to-point latency, and not the bandwidth, is the important parameter for optimizing communications. Furthermore, the partitioning strategy plays a very important role in determining the overall performance. Because of the nature of the ART1 algorithm, allocation of processes to processors should be done independently along layers F1 and F2. This choice facilitates pipelining and provides the freedom to allocate additional resources to F1 processes that can exploit them without introducing long communication paths between the smaller number of F2 processes.

We are currently investigating the use of ART1 networks as soft pattern matching mechanisms in computer vision, focusing currently on the classical stereo correspondence problem. Although this work is still in progress, preliminary results using synthetic binocular images are encouraging. A parallel implementation is also targeted [43].

Also of interest is the formulation of similar algorithms for ART2 and ART3 neural networks and their extensions to similar structures, such as the adaptive bidirectional associative memories (BAM) [44, 45].

---

[6]Only a 33 percent increase in throughput is observed when links are used bidirectionally.

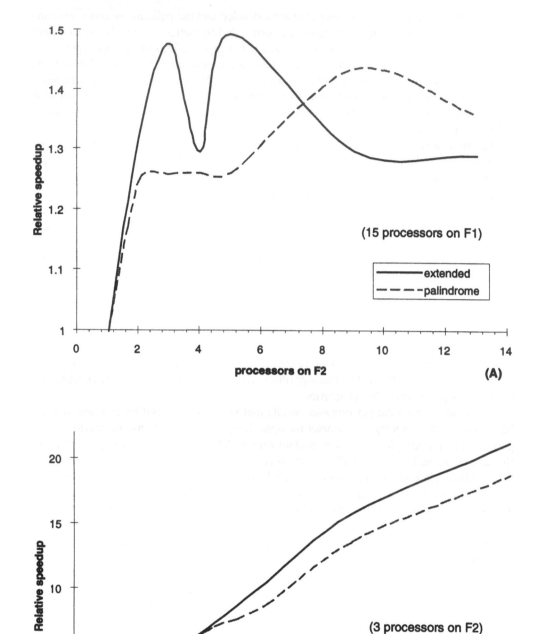

FIGURE 6.6. Relative speedup versus the number of processors allocated (A) on layer F2, and (B) on layer F1.

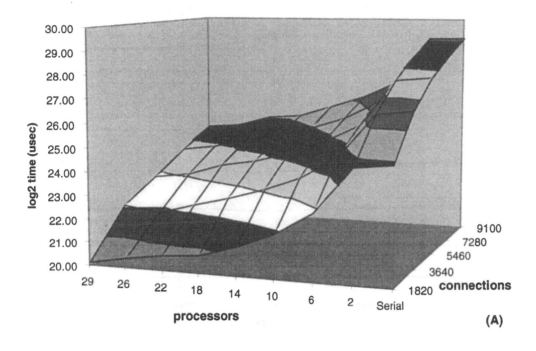

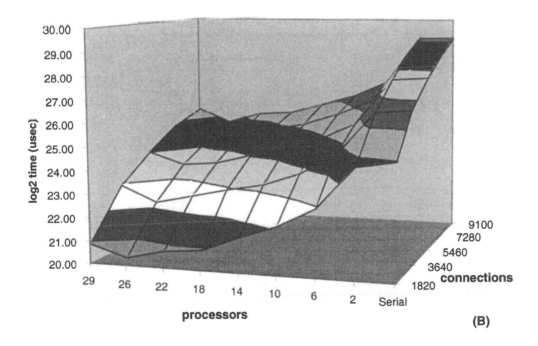

FIGURE 6.7. Execution time versus the number of processors and problem size. (A) Extended ring.
(B) Palindrome.

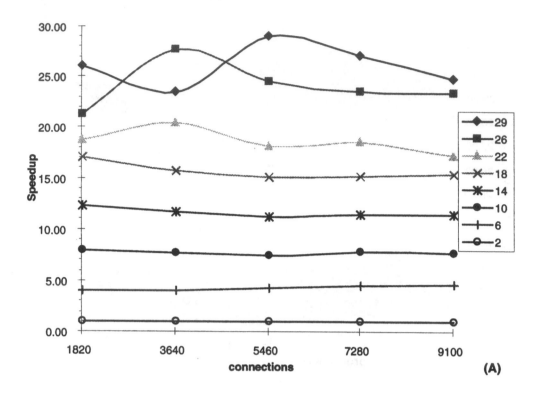

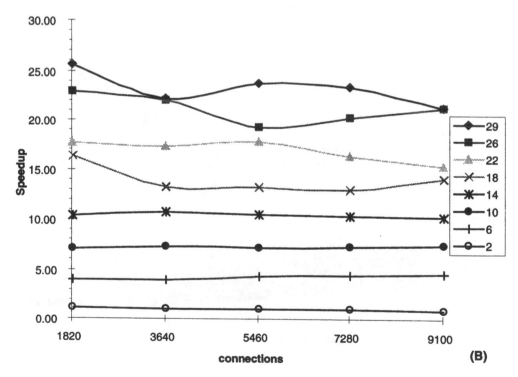

FIGURE 6.8. Speedup versus problem size. (A) Extended ring. (B) Palindrome.

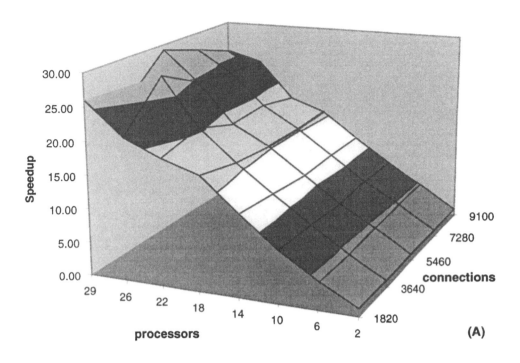

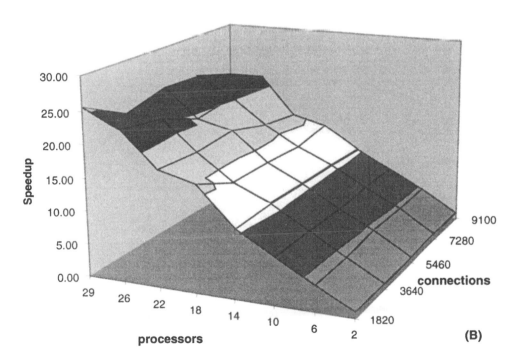

FIGURE 6.9. Speedup versus the number of processors and problem size. (A) Extended ring. (B) Palindrome.

# References

[1] G. Carpenter and S. Grossberg, "A massively parallel architecture for a self- organizing neural pattern recognition machine," *Computer Vision, Graphics, and Image Processing*, vol. 37, pp. 54–115, 1987.

[2] G. Carpenter and S. Grossberg, "The ART of adaptive pattern recognition by a self-organizing neural network," *Computer*, vol. 21, pp. 77–88, March 1988.

[3] G. Carpenter and S. Grossberg, "ART2: Self-organization of stable category recognition codes for analog input patterns," in *Procceedings of the IEEE First International Conference on Neural Networks*, pp. 727–736, 1987.

[4] G. Carpenter and S. Grossberg, "ART2: Self-organization of stable category recognition codes for analog input patterns," *Applied Optics*, vol. 26, pp. 4919–4930, 1987.

[5] G. Carpenter and S. Grossberg, "ART3: Hierarchical search using chemical transmitters in self-organizing pattern recognition architectures," *Neural Networks*, vol. 3, pp. 129–152, 1990.

[6] S. Grossberg, D. Rosen, and G. Carpenter, "Fuzzy ART: Fast stable learning and categorization of analog patterns by an adaptive resonance system," *Neural Networks*, vol. 4, pp. 759–771, 1991.

[7] S. Grossberg, J. Raynolds, and G. Carpenter, "ARTMAP: Supervised real-time learning and classification of nonstationary data by a self-organizing neural network," *Neural Networks*, vol. 4, pp. 565–588, 1991.

[8] G. Carpenter and S. Grossberg, "Assosiative learning, adaptive pattern recognition, and cooperative decision making by neural networks," in *Proceedings of the SPIE*, vol. 634, pp. 218–247, 1986.

[9] S. Grossberg, *The Adaptive Brain: Vols. I and II*. New York: Elsevier Science Publishers, 1986.

[10] S. Grossberg, "Cortical dynamics of three-dimensional form, color and brightness: Parts i and ii," *Perception and Psychophysics*, vol. 41, pp. 87–158, 1987.

[11] S. Grossberg and E. Mingolla, "Neural dynamics of perceptual grouping: Textures, boundaries, and emergent segmentations," *Perception and Psychophysics*, vol. 38, pp. 141–171, 1985.

[12] P. Rak and S. Kolodzy, "Invariant object recognition with the adaptive resonance (ART) network," *Neural Networks Supplement: INNS Abstracts*, vol. 1, p. 43, 1988.

[13] I. Kadar, et. al., "An approach to restoration and recovery problems using parallel hierarchical neural networks," *Neural Networks Supplement: INNS Abstracts*, vol. 1, p. 449, 1988.

[14] J. Zmuda., "Target recognition using adaptive resonance neural networks," *Neural Networks Supplement: INNS Abstracts*, vol. 1, p. 478, 1988.

[15] G. Carpenter and S. Grossberg., "Invariant recognition of cluttered scenes by a self-organizing ART architecture: Cort-x boundary segmantation," *Neural Networks*, vol. 2, no. 3, pp. 169–181, 1989.

[16] S. Grossberg, D. Stork, and M. Cohen, "Recent developments in a natural model of real-time speech analysis and synthesis," in *Proceedings of the IEEE First International Conference on Neural Networks*, vol. 6, (San Diego), pp. 443–454, 1987.

[17] S. Grossberg, "The adaptive self-organization of serial order in behavior: Speech, language and motor control," in *Pattern Recognition by Humans and Machines* (E.Schwab and H. Nusbaum, eds.), pp. 187–294, Boston: Academic Press, 1986.

[18] S. Grossberg and G. Stone, "Neural dynamics of attention switching and temporal-order information in short-term memory," *Memory and Cognition*, vol. 14, pp. 452–468, 1986.

[19] S. Grossberg and G. Stone, "Neural dynamics of word recognition and recall: Attentional priming, learning, and resonance," *Psychological Review*, vol. 93, pp. 46–74, 1986.

[20] C. Marchette, D. Sung, and C.-H. Priebe, "Temporal knowledge: Recognition and learning of time-based patterns," *Neural Networks Supplement: INNS Abstracts*, vol. 1, p. 317, 1988.

[21] S. Grossberg and W. Gutowski, "Neural dynamics of decision making under risk: Affective balance and cognitive-emotional interactions," *Psychological Review*, vol. 94, p. 300, 1987.

[22] J. Banquet., "Connectionist theories, art and cognitive potentials," *Neural Networks Supplement: INNS Abstracts*, vol. 1, p. 159, 1988.

[23] S. Grossberg, "Processing of expected and unexpected events during conditioning and attention: A psychological theory," *Psychological Review*, vol. 89, pp. 529–572, 1982.

[24] S. Grossberg and D. Levine, "Neural dynamics and attentionally modulated pavlovian conditioning: Blocking, interstimulus interval, and secondary reinforcement," *Applied Optics*, vol. 26, pp. 5015–5030, 1987.

[25] S. Grossberg and N. Schmajuk, "Neural dynamics and attentionally modulated pavlovian conditioning: Conditioned reinforcement, inhibition, and opponent processing," *Psychobiology*, vol. 15, p. 195, 1987.

[26] T. Ryan and C. Winter, "Variations on adaptive resonance," in *Proceedings of the IEEE First International Conference on Neural Networks*, vol. 2, (San Diego), pp. 767–776, 1988.

[27] C. Winter, "An adaptive network that flees pTrcuit," *Neural Networks Supplement: INNS Abstracts*, vol. 1, p. 367, 1988.

[28] C. Winter, C. Turner, and T. Ryan, "Dynamic control of an artificial neural system: The property inheritance network," *Applied Optics*, vol. 26, pp. 4961–4971, 1987.

[29] T. Ryan, C. Winter, and C. Turner, "Tin: A trainable inference network," in *Proceedings of the IEEE First International Conference on Neural Networks*, vol. 2, (San Diego), pp. 777–786, 1987.

[30] P. McDuff and R. Simpson, "An adaptive resonating diagnostics system," in *AUTOTESTCON*, 1989.

[31] S. Leven, "Sam: A triune extension to the ART model," in *Third Annual Symposium on Networks in Brain and Computer Architectures*, 1988.

[32] S. Leven and Y. Yoon, "Dynamic schemas, expert systems, and ART," *Neural Networks Supplement: INNS Abstacts*, vol. 1, p. 455, 1988.

[33] T. John, "Multistate information filtering using cascaded neural networks," in *International Workshop in Applications of Neural Networks in Communications (IWANNT '93)*, (Princeton, New Jersey), pp. 245–251, 1993.

[34] D. Levine and P. Penz, "ART1,5– A simplified adaptive resonance network for classifying anolog data," in *Second International Joint Conference on Neural Networks*, vol. 2, (Washington, D.C.), pp. 639–642.

[35] M. Cohen and S. Grossberg, "Neural dynamics of speech and language coding: Developmental programs, perceptual grouping, and competition for short term memory," *Human Neurobiology*, vol. 5, pp. 1–22.

[36] V. Kumar, A. Grama, A. Gupta, and G. Karypis, *Introduction to Parallel Computing*. Benjamin Cummings, 1994.

[37] J. Hwang and S. Y. Kung, "Parallel algorithms/architectures for neural networks," *Journal of VLSI Signal Processing*, pp. 221–251, 1989.

[38] J. A. Freeman and D. M. Skapura, *Neural Networks: Algorithms, Applications, and Programming Techniques*. Addison-Wesley Publishing Company, Inc., 1991. ISBN 0-201-51376-5.

[39] *Hardware reference manual*. Bristol, U.K., 1988.

[40] *The Transputer databook*. Bristol, U.K., 1989.

[41] *Occam 2 Reference manual*, 1988.

[42] C. A. R. Hoare, "Communicating sequential processes," *Communications of the ACM*, vol. 21, pp. 666–677, August 1978.

[43] S. Markogiannakis, "The ART of depth recovery from stereo," Master's thesis, ECE Dept. Northeastern University, Boston, 1997. In progress.

[44] B. Kosko, "Adaptive bidirectional associative memories," *Applied Optics*, vol. 26, pp. 4947–4960, 1987.

[45] B. Kosko, "Bidirectional associative memories," *IEEE Transactions on Systems, Man, and Cybernetics*, vol. 18, pp. 42–60, 1988.

# Part II

# Implementations on a Big General-Purpose Parallel Computer

# Chapter 7

# Implementation of Backpropagation Neural Networks on Large Parallel Computers

**Jim Torresen**
Department of Computer and Information Science
Norwegian University of Science and Technology, Norway
e-mail: jimtoer@idi.ntnu.no
**Shinji Tomita**
Department of Information Science
Kyoto University, Japan

## 7.1   Introduction

This chapter considers the problem of mapping the backpropagation training of real neural applications onto large parallel systems. Many parallel neural training programs have been implemented, but most are tested on none or few real applications. The programs tested for large neural networks usually show better performance than what is obtainable for real neural networks, which are usually small. On parallel systems with few processing elements, many mapping schemes are able to run efficiently. However, as the number of processors increases, the problem of communication overheads and uneven load becomes more prominent. Based on the inherent degrees of parallelism in the training algorithm, it is possible to suggest an efficient mapping, which minimizes the problems. This chapter proposes a parallel mapping of neural training, which adapts the configuration to the neural application.

A popular way of implementing backpropagation networks on a parallel machine is to partition the training set and have the processing elements train different patterns in parallel. This method inhibits updating the weight values after each pattern presentation. Experiments reported here show a linearly increasing number of iterations needed for convergence as the weights are less frequently updated. This fact cannot be omitted in the mapping strategy. Thus, we suggest a heuristic for selecting the best mapping scheme, combining all degrees of parallelism, according to what minimizes the total training time.

The mapping scheme is tested on the general-purpose, parallel computer Fujitsu AP1000. This is a message-passing MIMD computer with a two-dimensional torus network of processing elements. The largest system contains 512 processing elements. Fujitsu offers the computer for free to registered users (for a limited number of hours each month). The computer is accessed over the Internet and programmed using the C programming language.

The results indicate that the training speed can be reduced from hours to minutes if the parallel system is used instead of a single processor workstation. Moreover, the flexible mapping, which adjusts the configuration to the given neural application, may result in a training speed several hundred percent faster than a fixed mapping. (This is by using the general-purpose computer AP1000, not a specialized neurocomputer.)

## 7.2 Hardware for Running Neural Networks

This section presents the parallel computer used in this study for implementing the back-propagation training algorithm. In addition, conditions for the experiments are discussed.

### 7.2.1 Fujitsu AP1000

Fujitsu AP1000 is a general-purpose message-passing MIMD computer with distributed memory [1]. Figure 7.1 depicts the architecture. The AP1000 processing element is called a *cell* and consists of a SPARC CPU, an FPU (floating point unit), a message-passing unit, 128 Kbyte cache, and 16 Mbyte local memory. The largest available system consists of 512 cells.[1] The cells are connected by three different communication networks as seen in the figure. First, the cells are interconnected by bidirectional channels in a two-dimensional

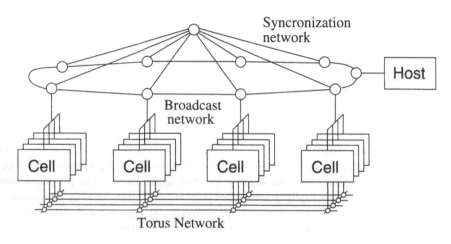

FIGURE 7.1. The AP1000 architecture.

torus network. Communication is by packet switching and packets are routed from source to destination using the wormhole routing switching method. As such, the path length has little effect on communication time. Second, there is a broadcast network for bidirectional communication with the host—a Sun 4 workstation running the UNIX operating system. Third, there is a network for fast synchronization. The computer can be programmed using either FORTRAN or C programming languages. The languages are enhanced for doing communication and so on.

The AP1000 is accessible over the Internet, without any fee, to registered users in Japan and other areas overseas from the *Fujitsu Parallel Computing Research Facilities* (FPCRF, Kawasaki, Japan). Several versions of the computer are available: 64, 128, 256, and 512 cells. Through an Open Use program, each user group can reserve any of the computers for up to 20 hours each month. In this research, we mainly used a 64-cell version located at Kyoto University in Japan, and we obtained the results for larger systems by running the programs at FPCRF. A similar facility, with a 128-cell system, is available at the Imperial College in London.

*7.2.1.1 Programming the System.* To use the AP1000 computer, at least two programs are required: a host program running on the host computer and one or more cell pro-

---

[1]Organized as 32 rows by 16 columns of cells.

grams. The host program configures the cells by using a command—a call to a library function— which specifies the number of cells in the $x$ and $y$ dimensions. Cell *program(s)* are downloaded to all cells by a single command. The host can communicate with cells by broadcasting to all or addressing a specific cell.

A library of global reduction functions is available in the programming language to calculate the absolute maximum, absolute minimum, or the sum of data in all cells or in cells in the same column or row of the 2D-torus network. The functions operate on single variables, not arrays. A scatter/gather data function can be used to communicate data between all cells and the host. Each cell receives or sends only the portion of the data specified.

A performance analysis tool is available, which shows the activity of each cell during run time. A trace function is also available to plot the activity of cells in a selected time interval. Support for more detailed timing information is also available.

*7.2.1.2 Neural Network Implementations.* Only one published work is known, except for those by the authors of this chapter, on parallel neural network implementations on AP1000. Kuga and associates have implemented a neuron parallel implementation by vertical slicing of the feed-forward network [2]. Thus, each PE contains a slice of the network. Three different methods for all-to-all communication are compared. First, one-to-one communication is used. Second, messages are rotated in horizontal and vertical rings. Third, the sending PE is located in the center of the torus and messages are propagated through parallel routes to the other PEs. The methods are compared for the recall phase for the case of an equal number of neurons in each layer. Results are expressed in terms of speedup for each of the methods. The second method, broadcasting by rotation, obtained the highest speedup. The difference in speedup for the methods increases as the number of PEs increases (256 neurons per layer are used).

## 7.2.2 Neural Network Applications Used in This Work

In this work realistic figures for network size are used by analysis of real world applications. The applications used in the experiments in this work are listed in Table 7.1.

TABLE 7.1. BP applications used for measuring training performance.

| Application | Network Size | # Training Patterns |
|---|---|---|
| Nettalk [3] | $203 \times 120 \times 26$ | 5,438 |
| Character recognition (a X11 font set) | $40 \times 30 \times 26$ | 26 |
| Image compression [4] | $64 \times 4\text{–}16 \times 64$ | 4,096 |
| Speech recognition [5] | $256 \times 64\text{–}1024 \times 64$ | 4,096 |
| Sonar target classification [6, 7] | $60 \times 24 \times 2$ | 208 |

Nettalk, which has been used in performance testing of both general-purpose computers [8–14] and neurocomputers [15, 16], is regarded as a benchmark for comparing computers running the BP algorithm. However, some differences in the number of hidden units and weight updating frequency exist. In this work, Nettalk is used as the main benchmark. An increased variation in the number of hidden units has been included in the experiments to obtain more general results.

### 7.2.3 Experimental Conditions in This Work

The implementations were first debugged and tested for a small character recognition problem. The training performances were then measured using randomly generated training patterns on networks with size equal to real applications. Bias was not explicitly implemented but was assumed to be one of the input units and one of the hidden units set to "1." Because of the large cell memory, the *whole* training set can be stored in the cells, thus downloading is only needed initially. This means that the downloading time is very short, compared to the total training time, and is omitted from the time measurements.

The weight matrices are updated according to the following equations:[2]

$$\Delta w_{o,kj}(p + 1) = \alpha \Delta w_{o,kj}(p) + (1 - \alpha)\delta_{o,k}(p + 1)y_{h,j}(p + 1) \tag{7.1}$$

and

$$w_{o,kj}(p + 1)' = w_{o,kj}(p) + \eta \Delta w_{o,kj}(p + 1). \tag{7.2}$$

As the main purpose of these experiments has not been to show the computer speed, little time has been used on program code optimization.

## 7.3 General Mapping onto 2D-Torus MIMD Computers

The topic of this section is to make a mapping of BP onto a parallel processor, which minimizes the total training time of *any* BP application. Most real implementations of BP are based on a heuristic with a fixed assignment of processors to each involved degree of parallelism. However, the different kinds of applications— neural network structure and training set— require different mappings in order to obtain minimum training time. Thus, the performance of these fixed implementations are highly application dependent. In many publications on parallel BP mappings, performance is only measured for, at most, one real application. For instance, some select a nonrealistic network, usually large, that runs near optimally on the parallel machine, without reporting the performance of real applications. Also, when training-set parallelism is used, the weight update frequency is usually not considered.

In this section a general mapping scheme, which includes all degrees of parallelism, is proposed. It is a heuristic for mapping feed-forward neural networks near optimally onto a 2D-torus MIMD computer. The assignment of cells to each degree of parallelism is done according to the given neural network and training set. That is, the method selects the appropriate mapping according to the given application. The method will run on any number of processors available in today's parallel computers. However, the mapping's main advantage is for the case of a large number of processors. Small networks and training sets in particular can run more efficiently on larger parallel systems.

Today's technology allows more logic to be placed on a given circuit area. It is, therefore, expected that tomorrow's technology will allow a larger number of processors on a single circuit and that parallel systems will consist a of larger number of processors. Massively parallel computers will be more available than the few presently available machines. These massively parallel systems can overcome the limit of sequential program execution by several orders of magnitude if the parallel algorithms can scale efficiently.

The main interest here is to minimize the *total* training time. Thus, it is impossible to omit the selection of a proper weight update interval when training-set parallelism is used.

---

[2]Same as Equations 1.17 and 1.18 of Chapter 1.

Few of the published mapping methods address the issue of total training time, which is a topic of this study. To obtain high speedup on a highly parallel computer, previous work has shown that the issue is to combine *multiple* degrees of parallelism [17]. Whereas the previous work was on fixed combinations of the degrees of parallelism, the new scheme allows arbitrary combinations of training-set parallelism, pipelining, and node parallelism.

Some mapping strategies (for example, [13,18]) are based on assigning one processing element to each neuron. In this way, the utilization of the parallel computer depends on the neural network. This assignment requires a certain number of available processors, and a possibility of processors being idle exists. A better approach is to base the mapping on the number of available processors and then ask how the different degrees should be combined to utilize, in the best way, the available processors. That is, to combine the different parallel BP training dimensionalities in the way that minimizes the total training time. This is the underlying idea of the mapping that will be presented next. This scheme has been named *application adaptable* mapping. Parts of this work are published in [19–21].

### 7.3.1 The Proposed Mapping Scheme

The proposed mapping aims to obtain the best possible load balance between the processing cells for *any* neural network application. Hence, the number of processors assigned for each degree of parallelism is made to be changeable. The mapping will be presented first in a version without pipelining and second in a version including pipelining. Further, some improvements will be given.

The first part of the proposed mapping is shown in Figure 7.2 and consists of a set of possible system configurations. Each configuration combines node and training-set parallelism. Within each dotted rectangle, node parallelism is used. The box within the figure indicates the mapping of the elements for node parallelism. Neuron parallelism is represented within each row of processors. Synapse parallelism is achieved in the vertical dimension. This scheme is based on an ordinary parallelization of matrix-vector multiplication, as described in Section 2.2.2.3 [22]. The lower part of the figure gives a selection of the number of training-set partitions versus processors assigned to neuron parallelism. Correspondingly, in the left-hand part of the figure, the choice in ratio between training-set parallelism and synapse parallelism is shown. This illustrates the flexibility to adjust the parallel configuration to both the neural network size and training-set size.

The mapping can be extended by including pipelining, that is, by making one processing element box in the figure into one O–H pair as shown in Figure 7.3. The processors marked **H** compute the hidden layer part, while the output layer part is computed by the processors marked **O**. This scheme combines all degrees of BP parallelism except training-session parallelism. The efficiency of including pipelining depends on the number of processors and the number of neurons in each layer. This was illustrated in [17].

Below each processor configuration in the figures, the number of training-set partitions $N_{TSP}$ and the number of processors for node parallelism $N_{NP}$ are given – $(N_{TSP}, N_{NP})$. For Figure 7.2 the relation between them can be expressed by

$$N_{TSP} = \frac{C_x C_y}{N_{NP}} \tag{7.3}$$

where $C_x$ and $C_y$ are the number of cells in the horizontal and vertical dimension, respectively, in the 2D-torus array.[3] If pipelining is included we get

$$N_{TSP} = \frac{C_x C_y}{2N_{NP}}. \tag{7.4}$$

---

[3]For the largest available AP1000 with 512 cells, $C_x = 16$ and $C_y = 32$.

189

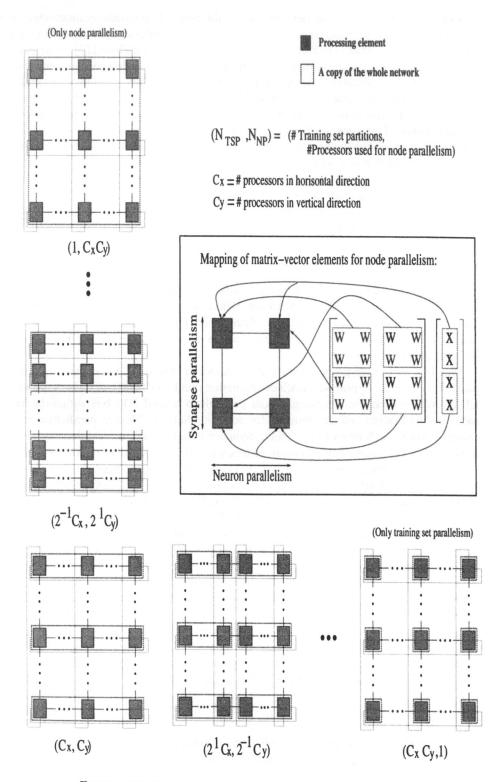

FIGURE 7.2. BP mappings with training-set and node parallelism.

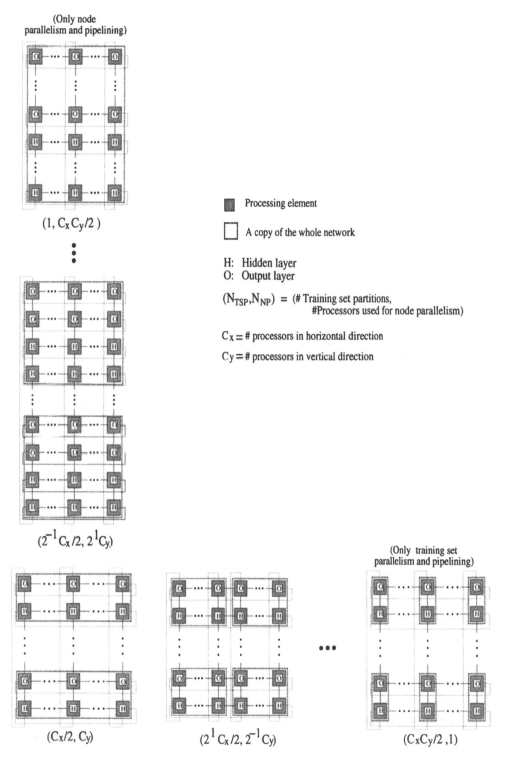

FIGURE 7.3. BP mappings including training-set parallelism, pipelining, and node parallelism. H indicates processors training the hidden layer, while O indicates processors training the output layer.

For a given weight update interval, a larger number of training-set partitions imply fewer training pattern computations on each processor between weight updates.

One problem of the mapping scheme is network contention, that is, several cells send messages concurrently to the same link. However, the communication time on AP1000 is reasonable also when network contention exists. It is approximately doubled if five messages are on the same channel, indicating that much time is spent within each cell for communication overhead and less on the physical transfer of data [23].

### 7.3.1.1 *Optimizing the Weight Update.*

As described earlier, convergence rate improves when weights are updated frequently, and, as such, it is important to minimize the weight update time. To prevent weight updating from becoming a bottleneck in large systems, a $(\log_2 C_y - 1)$ step summing technique is proposed for summing weight change matrices in the vertical dimension. This method requires $C_y \in \{4, 8, 16, 32\}$ for AP1000. The summing algorithm is illustrated in Figure 7.4a [24].

The summing starts in the leftmost column in the figure. Hidden layer cells send their matrices to cells to the south of where the cells themselves are located, whereas output layer cells send to cells to their north. The receiving cell adds its local weight change matrix to the received matrix and then forwards the summed matrix. The solution is called *edge summing*, because the matrices are summed in the northmost cell and southmost cell for the output and hidden layer, respectively. In the given system, only three steps are required for summing the eight weight change matrices. Then, the summed matrices are broadcasted, in the opposite direction of summing, to the cells. After each cell receives the summed weight matrix, it *updates* its local weight matrix.

The same summing method can be used for the mapping without pipelining [25]. The number of summing steps becomes $(\log_2 C_y)$. Thus, one more step of summing is needed. However, for the pipelining method additional overheads are incurred due to filling the pipeline after new weights are computed.

### 7.3.1.2 *The Implemented Mapping.*

To be able to evaluate the benefit of a parallel backpropagation algorithm that can vary the amount of each degree of parallelism, the lower part of Figure 7.2— configuration $(C_x, C_y)$ to $(C_x C_y, 1)$— was implemented on AP1000. Hence, the system can be configured to an even amount of neuron and training-set parallelism, just training-set parallelism, or an *intermediate* configuration. The latter implies that there will be conflicts in the communication.

Comparison of the configurations $(C_x, C_y)$ and $(C_x C_y, 1)$ has been undertaken in earlier work [17]. These are popular methods for parallelizing BP training. However, the training speed will probably be limited compared to that obtainable by using a flexible configuration.

Pseudocode for the implementation is given in Figure 7.5. The distribution of the training patterns is as indicated in Figure 7.6. The number of training vectors assigned to each network partition is calculated as shown in Figure 7.5 and stored in the variable MaxPattern.

### 7.3.1.3 *Improvements of the Mapping.*

According to the survey of neural applications in Section 2.2.3, the neural network is often irregular in number of neurons in each layer. Further, the number of neurons in the output layer is often small. This section suggests ways to further improve the mapping with regard to these circumstances.

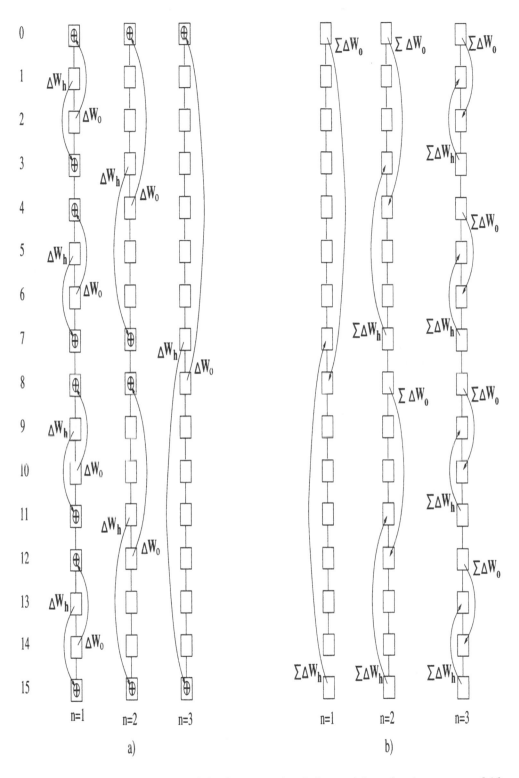

FIGURE 7.4.  (a) Summing the weight change matrices before weight update in a system of 16 vertical cells. (b) Broadcasting the summed weight change matrices back to each cell.

BackPropagation_GeneralMap()
**begin**

$n_h = \left\lfloor \frac{N_h}{N_{NP}} \right\rfloor$;

$n_o = \left\lfloor \frac{N_o}{N_{NP}} \right\rfloor$;

$\mu_c = \left\lfloor \frac{\mu}{N_{TSP}} \right\rfloor$; { Weight update interval }

LookUp(MyCellId_x MyCellId_y);

Read learning parameters from the host;

Initialize weights;

**if** (MyCellId_y $\left\lfloor \frac{C_x}{N_{NP}} \right\rfloor$ + $\left\lfloor \frac{\text{MyCellId\_x}}{N_{NP}} \right\rfloor$) < ($P$ **mod** $N_{TSP}$) **then**

    MaxPattern = $\left\lfloor \frac{P}{N_{TSP}} \right\rfloor$ + 1;

**else**

    MaxPattern = $\left\lfloor \frac{P}{N_{TSP}} \right\rfloor$;

Read training patterns from the host;

**while** *trainend* = 0 **do begin**

    *totalerror* = *0*;

    **for** $p$ = 1 **to** MaxPattern **do begin**

    { Forward phase }

        Compute $n_h$ hidden outputs, $\mathbf{y}_h$;

        Multiply $\mathbf{y}_h$ by the corresponding weights $\mathbf{W}_o$

        for $\mathbf{y}_o'$ partial output values;

        **for** $c$ = 1 **to** $C_x - 1$ **do**

            Send_receive_multiply_add($n_h$ hidden elements);

        Compute sigmoid function for the $n_o$ outputs, $\mathbf{y}_o$;

    { Backward phase }

        Compute $n_o$ elements of delta error $\delta_o$ and sum of *error*

        from the $n_o$ outputs;

        *error* = SumError(x-dimension, *error*);

        { Global reduction function }

        **if** error > $e$ **then**

            totalerror = totalerror +1;

        Compute $N_h$ partial $\delta_h$ values; { Hidden delta error }

        **for** $c$ = 1 **to** $C_x - 1$ **do**

            Send_receive_add($n_h$ elements of $\delta_h$);

        Accumulate_weight_changes;

        **if** ($p$ **mod** $\mu_c$) = 0 **then**

            Update_weights;

    **end;** SetStatus(*totalerror* > 0);

    Update_weights;

    **if** GetStatus = 0 **then**

        *trainend* = *1*;

    **end;**

**end;**

FIGURE 7.5. Parallel BP training algorithm running in each cell, combining training-set parallelism and neuron parallelism.

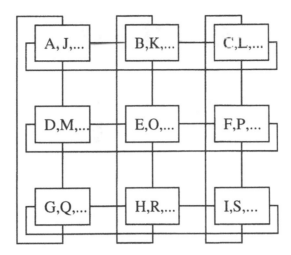

FIGURE 7.6. Distribution of training pattern A, B, C,....

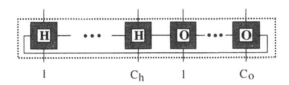

FIGURE 7.7. Pipelined mapping of BP with flexible assignment of cells to each layer.

**Few Output Units.** To train a network efficiently when it consists of only a few output layer units, the number of processors assigned to the output layer computation should be reduced.

Figure 7.7 shows a possible pipelined mapping scheme. This scheme can be combined with the one presented in Figure 7.2 to include pipelining. The dotted rectangle in Figure 7.7 represents one dotted rectangle in Figure 7.2. For most cases, the number of processors assigned to the hidden layer, $C_h$, will be larger than the number of processors assigned to the output layer, $C_o$. The best configuration can be found by measuring the time for one pass through the training set for different processor assignments. This scheme has been tested on the RENNS neurocomputer [26].

**Improving Load Balance.** The scheme in the left-hand part of Figure 7.3 can be improved on load balance, as depicted in Figure 7.8. A larger number of rows is assigned (synapse parallelism) to the hidden layer with respect to the output layer. This scheme maps *large* feed-forward networks efficiently, whereas *small* networks should be trained by the method presented in the previous section. Both methods make the implementation adjustable to the computation load in the different layers.

*7.3.1.4 Training Session Parallel Scheme.* The convergence of BP is highly dependent on the various parameters, such as learning rate, initial weights, and number of hidden units. Moreover, a hierarchical network may need the training of several different networks. Thus, a training-session parallel scheme can be an interesting alternative, where

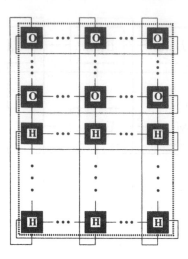

FIGURE 7.8. An extension of the mapping in Figure 7.3, where the number of cells used for synapse parallelism for each layer is assigned according to the computation load.

networks train in parallel with different initial training parameters. In Figure 7.9 a combination of training-session parallelism and neuron parallelism is proposed.

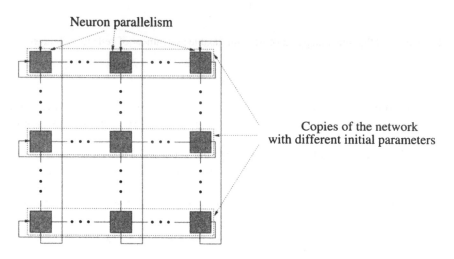

FIGURE 7.9. Training-session parallelism and neuron parallelism combined.

This approach can train using learning by pattern. The method can be implemented as an iterative improvement scheme, where results from using different learning parameters are compared. The best ones are selected and combined for the next training session.

### 7.3.2  Heuristic for Selection of the Best Mapping

Before running a neural application, the mapping giving the shortest possible total training time has to be selected. First, the best initial training parameters— weights, learning rate, and so on— have to be found. Then, for each mapping the total training time for a set of weight update intervals has to be predicted. The total training time is given by

$$T_{total}(\mu) = T_{1it}(\mu)N(\mu) \tag{7.5}$$

where $T_{1it}(\mu)$ is the time for one training iteration and $N(\mu)$ is the number of iterations needed for convergence, given a weight update interval $\mu$. $T_{1it}$ can be found either by estimation or by running each of the possible mappings for one training iteration. $N(\mu)$ can be estimated in several different ways, although a general method is not yet derived. The mapping giving the smallest possible $T_{total}$ is selected and the corresponding $\mu$-value is used.

The heuristic is formulated in pseudocode in Figure 7.10. It covers all steps to make a near optimal mapping of BP onto a 2D-torus computer. It evaluates all possible mappings and picks the best one for a set of $\mu$-values. In step 1, some initialization of the parameters has to be done. In step 2, the performance of the mappings in Figure 7.2 and 7.3 is estimated for some given weight update intervals. The *best* configuration for each given weight update interval is found. In step 3, the number of training iterations needed is estimated for the given weight update intervals. Combining the results of steps 2 and 3 gives us, in step 4, the best weight update interval and the corresponding best configuration. That is, the total training time is minimized. The heuristic is described in more detail in the next section.

The heuristic is based on the one given in [27] for selecting the best weight update interval according to the total training time. However, the mapping used is a fixed implementation based on training-set parallelism. Also, experimental rules on convergence rates are deduced from a small application using synthetic data.

*7.3.2.1 Selection of Backpropagation Parameters.* Several papers have shown that back propagation parameter setting is of major importance for improving the convergence rate. The number of hidden neurons, initial weight values, the learning rate ($\eta$), a momentum term ($\alpha$), and the weight update interval all influence the convergence rate. Both Sato [28] and Higashino [29] found from experiments that the number of training iterations $N$ is proportional to $(1 - \alpha)/\eta$ within the region in which a stable convergence is obtained. Thus, it is desirable that $\eta$ takes as large a value as possible and $\alpha$ is as near to 1 as possible. The convergence rate can be accelerated by adaptively adjusting $\eta$ and $\alpha$ during training, as shown in [30–32].

One of the problems of backpropagation is that it has a tendency to get trapped in the local minima. Different approaches have been suggested to overcome this problem. One is to use genetic algorithms (GA), which search a large parameter space. However, this means longer training time. GA has been used in experiments for improving BP in several ways:

- Avoid local minima by adjusting the weights by GA, either initially [33] or during training [34].

- Adjust learning rate and momentum term during training [34].

- Find the optimal neuron interconnections by adding and deleting connections between neurons in the same and different layers [35].

Because the topic of initial parameters is covered in many papers, it is not included in this chapter. Still, the learning parameters are very important for the convergence rate. For each application used in this research, the best parameters have been searched for.

1. Find optimal initial weights, number of hidden neurons, learning rate, and momentum value.

2. For the given neural network, training set, and computer architecture, estimate the performance for one iteration using the algorithm *Best_Map()*. Find the best mapping $M[\mu_i]$ for each of the weight update intervals $\mu_1, \mu_2, \ldots, \mu_n$, and store the time for one iteration, $T_{1it}[\mu_i]$.

*Best_Map()*
**begin**
**for** $\mu = \mu_1, \ldots, \mu_n$ **do**
    Min_time_1it$[\mu] = \infty$;
{ Pipeline not included/included }
**for** pipeline= 0 **to** 1 **do**
    { Examine each mapping }
    **for** config= 0 **to** ($\log_2 (C_x \cdot C_y)$ – pipeline) **do**
    **begin**

        nodepar= $2^{\text{config}}$;
        { From Equation (7.3) and (7.4) }
        trainpar= $(C_x \cdot C_y)$ **div** (nodepar $\cdot$ $2^{\text{pipeline}}$);
        **for** $\mu = \mu_1, \ldots, \mu_n$ **do begin**
            time = *Estimate_time_1_iteration*(pipeline,nodepar,
            trainpar,$\mu$);
            { Perf. impr. by reducing no of cells? }
            **while** (time can be reduced) **do**
                try reducing number of cells, update time;
            **if** (time < Min_time_1it$[\mu]$) **then**
                { Store new map. as the best }
                *update_M*(pipeline,nodepar,trainpar,$\mu$);
        **end;**
      **end;**
    **end;**

3. Estimate the number of iterations needed, $N[\mu_i]$, for $\mu_1, \mu_2, \ldots, \mu_n$ equal to those in step 2.

4. Pick $\mu_m$ so that

$$T_{total}[\mu_m] = T_{1it}[\mu_m]N[\mu_m] \quad m = 1, \ldots, n$$

becomes minimized.

5. Configure the system by $M[\mu_m]$ and update the weights for every $\mu_m$ pattern.

FIGURE 7.10. Heuristic in pseudocode for selecting the best parallel mapping of BP onto a 2D-torus computer.

*7.3.2.2 Estimation of Execution Time.* The execution time can be estimated based on the count of floating point instructions and time for communication. A similar approach is used in [14] to estimate neural network performance on CM-2. The accuracy of the method is dependent on various aspects, such as idle time and cache misses. However, if the accuracy is acceptable, the method of estimation is to be preferred instead of measuring real execution time, because less computation is needed.

The *Best_Map()* algorithm in Figure 7.10 examines all the possible mappings described. First, the performance using all cells available is estimated. For large systems, using fewer cells may give better performance. Thus, a test on this issue has been included. The *Estimate_time_1_iteration()*-function will be explained below.

**Timing Data.** In Table 7.2, the floating point performance and communication timing of the AP1000 is presented [23]. The given timing is for basic operations like adding floating point variables. In a real program, overhead will be added for additional instructions— for example, for addressing. Thus, when estimating the performance based on the number of floating point operations, this overhead is omitted. The compiler is assumed to generate code that optimally utilizes the arithmetic units in the processor. However, the result can still be of interest to estimate the theoretically maximum obtainable performance.

In the result section (Section 7.4.1.2), average timing for floating point operations measured in the real program will be used for estimation. In addition to predicting execution time, the estimation method makes it possible to determine the optimal number of processors. This is probably much larger than the number of PEs in any of the available systems.

TABLE 7.2. Timing on AP1000 ($ns$), including loading from and storing to cache [23].

| | | |
|---|---|---|
| $t_{add}$ | 442 | Time to add floats sequentially. |
| $t_{mul}$ | 442 | Time to multiply floats sequentially |
| $t_{mul+add}$ | 646 | Time for alternating multiply and add of floats. |
| $t_{load/store}$ | 880 | Time for loading or storing when cache miss occurs. |
| $t_{sigmoid}$ | 7,500 | Time to compute $1/(1 + e^{-x})$. |
| $t_{comm}(B)$ | $16,700 + 175B$ | Communication time for sending $B$ bytes between cells. |
| $t_g(C)$ | $6,000 + 16,000 \log_2(C)$ | Time for global reduction function (for example, $x.fsum$) for $C$ cells. |
| $t_{cont}(B, n)$ | $T_{cont}(B, n)$ | Network contention; communication time when $n$ messages of size $B$ are sent between cells. See [23]. |

**Time Estimation.** Next, the time used for one iteration will be estimated for the implementation described in Section 7.3.1.2. First, the basic time units are computed. Time to compute output of the hidden layer is determined:

$$T_{Fh} = n_h(N_i t_{mul+add} + t_{sigmoid}). \tag{7.6}$$

Time to compute output of the output layer is determined:

$$T_{Fo} = n_h n_o t_{mul+add}$$
$$+ (N_{NP} - 1)(t_{comm}(n_h) + n_h n_o t_{mul+add}) + n_o t_{sigmoid}. \tag{7.7}$$

Time to compute the output layer error is determined:

$$T_{Boe} = n_o(t_{add} + t_{mul+add} + t_{mul} + t_{mul+add})$$
$$+ (N_{NP} - 1)(t_{comm}(1) + t_{add}). \tag{7.8}$$

Time to compute the hidden layer error is determined:

$$T_{Bhe} = N_h n_o t_{mul+add}$$
$$+ (N_{NP} - 1)(t_{comm}(n_h) + n_h t_{add}) + n_h(t_{mul+add} + t_{mul}). \quad (7.9)$$

Time to accumulate the output layer weight change is determined:

$$T_{Woa} = N_h n_o t_{mul+add}. \quad (7.10)$$

Time to accumulate the hidden layer weight change is determined:

$$T_{Wha} = N_i n_h t_{mul+add}. \quad (7.11)$$

Time to update the hidden and output layer weights is determined:

$$T_{Wupd} = \log_2(C_y)(max\{t_{comm}(N_i n_h), t_{comm}(N_h n_o)\} \quad (7.12)$$
$$+ max\{N_i n_h t_{add}, N_h n_o t_{add}\}) + t_{comm}(N_i n_h) + t_{comm}(N_h n_o) \quad (7.13)$$
$$+ k(\frac{C_x}{N_{NP}} - 1)(t_{comm}(N_i n_h) + N_i n_h t_{add}$$
$$+ t_{comm}(N_h n_o) + N_h n_o t_{add}) \quad (7.14)$$
$$+ 3N_i n_h t_{mul+add} + 3N_h n_o t_{mul+add}. \quad (7.15)$$

Expressions 7.12 and 7.13 represent the vertical summing of the cell array, followed by the horizontal summing in Expression 7.14. The constant $k$ compensates for the additional overhead, due to communication conflicts (contention). Its value will be given in the result section. The final Expression 7.15 adds the weight update time. Except for $T_{Wupd}$, the units are computed for *one* training pattern.

Based on these units it is possible to get an estimate of the time needed for one whole training iteration:

$$T_{it}(\mu) = P_c(T_{Fh} + T_{Fo} + T_{Boe} + T_{Bhe} + T_{Wha} + T_{Woa}) + \left\lceil \frac{P}{\mu} \right\rceil T_{Wupd}$$

where $P$ is the total number of training patterns, and $P_c$ is the number of patterns in each cell.

### 7.3.2.3 Convergence Estimation.

One of the major problems of BP training is to decrease the number of iterations needed to train an application. Much work is published on this topic. However, estimation for training time is seldom reported.

At least three approaches are possible. The first approach is to use existing formulas [27, 28] for estimation of $N(\mu)$. These are based on specific applications and compute the number of iterations needed based on the learning rate. Because these have been tested only for a few applications, they may be inaccurate in general. A bound on the probabilistic rate of convergence of feed-forward networks trained to estimate a smooth function is detailed in [36].

A second approach is outlined in [21, 37] and explained in the result section. It is based on running the algorithm for a few iterations— for various weight update intervals— and based on the initial error, the total number of iterations $N(\mu)$ used for convergence is estimated. A formula is derived for the convergence of Nettalk, based on the convergence after 25 initial iterations. By estimating the convergence based on the initial error, any techniques for improving the convergence rate is reflected in the estimation.

A third method, to be detailed later in this chapter, is to use the average ratio of convergence iterations between learning by pattern and learning by epoch.

In the result section, the convergence of several applications will be given. The different convergence estimation methods will be compared. Furthermore, some sensitivity and convergence aspects will be studied.

*7.3.2.4 Modeling the Memory Usage.* In this section, general expressions for the memory needed for the implemented mapping is derived. The memory allocated in each cell for the implementation described in Section 7.3.1.2 is given by

Weight matrices:
$$M_w = 4 \cdot 4(N_i n_h + N_h n_o)$$
$$= 16(N_i \lceil \tfrac{N_h}{N_{NP}} \rceil + N_h \lceil \tfrac{N_o}{N_{NP}} \rceil) \text{ byte}$$

Training patterns:
$$M_p = 4 P_c (N_i + n_o)$$
$$= 4 \lceil \tfrac{P}{N_{TSP}} \rceil (N_i + \lceil \tfrac{N_o}{N_{NP}} \rceil) \text{ byte}$$

Array and data variables:
$$M_d < 10 \text{ Kbyte}$$

Program memory:
$$M_p = 250 \text{ Kbyte}$$

The factor of 4 in the expressions is due to floating point variables requiring 4 bytes of memory. The expressions are given as maximum values. In the case of noneven distribution of the neurons to cells, some cells may allocate less memory. These expressions can be used to show how the memory requirement for each cell is reduced for an increasing number of cells.

### 7.3.3 Summary

This section has described a general mapping scheme, which includes all the inherent parallel degrees of the backpropagation algorithm. The mapping is flexible and combines the different degrees so that the total training time can be minimized.

To select the best implementation, a heuristic is given. This estimates the training time for the possible configurations. These estimates are used together with convergence estimates for different weight update intervals to select the best configuration and weight update interval.

In the next section, a subset of the mapping scheme will be tested. Moreover, the estimation of execution time and convergence of real neural applications will be studied.

## 7.4 Results on the General BP Mapping

In this section, one part of the mapping scheme proposed in the previous section is evaluated through experiments on AP1000. The implementation is described in Section 7.3.1.2. The applications Nettalk, sonar classification, speech recognition, and image compression are used in the experiments. Training speed for different network sizes and processor configurations are given. For the two first applications the convergence for different weight update frequencies are studied. The mapping that minimizes the total training time for the parallel program is determined for Nettalk. Results from estimation of execution time will also be given.

### 7.4.1 Nettalk

In this section, the Nettalk neural network application is used in the experiments. The section consists of four parts. First, the training speed is evaluated from measurements on the AP1000. Second, the performance is estimated. Third, the convergence is tested and analyzed. Finally, the minimum total training time is determined. The training set consists of 1,000 of the most common English words (a total of 5,438 characters). Experiments have been conducted for $\mu = 63; 259; 494; 906; 1,360; 2,719;$ and $5,438$. The best performance reported by Sejnowski and Rosenberg [3] used 120 hidden units and, as such, is chosen for the experiments in this section. Bias was implemented using one of the idle input units (to be used for punctuation and word boundaries for continuous speech) and one of the 120 hidden units.

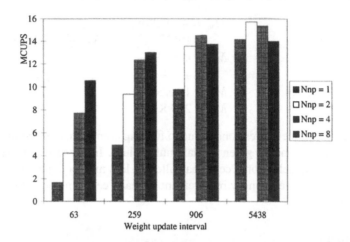

FIGURE 7.11. MCUPS performance for different combinations of neuron and training-set parallelism running the Nettalk application with 120 hidden neurons on a 8 x 8 cell configuration. $N_{NP} = 1, 2, 4,$ and 8.

*7.4.1.1 Training Speed.* Figure 7.11 illustrates the performance of the general BP implementation running the Nettalk application on 64 processors. The figure makes a comparison between the training speed for four different weight update intervals. For each of them, four different configurations are used. The figure shows that it is more important to select the best configuration for small weight update intervals than for large intervals.

The combined solutions achieve better performance than using only training-set parallelism— $N_{NP} = 1$. However, for large weight update intervals, for example, $\mu = 906$ and $\mu = 5438$, smaller $N_{NP}$ values (and thus larger $N_{TSP}$ values) result in performance improvements. This is as expected because infrequent weight updates reduce the total weight update time for an iteration. Thus, a larger number of training-set partitions can train efficiently, and the most efficient configurations are those involving computer network contention— $N_{NP} < 8$. The contention-free mapping, $N_{NP} = 8$, is the most efficient for frequent weight updates.

Results for the 256 cell system are displayed in Figure 7.12. A similar performance as in the 64 cell system is seen, but the weight update interval becomes more significant. Thus, as the number of processors increases, the difference in the fastest training speed for frequent and infrequent weight updates increases. The best performance for $\mu = 5,438$ is more than twice the performance for $\mu = 63$. For the largest available system consisting of 512 processing elements, see Figure 7.13; this difference is almost three. These results are understandable because the number of training-set partitions is large on a system of many processors. Thus, fewer training patterns are trained between weight updates. Further,

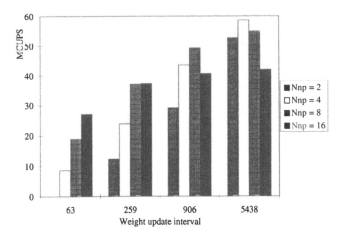

FIGURE 7.12. MCUPS performance for different combinations of neuron and training-set parallelism on a 16 x 16 cell configuration. $N_{NP} = 2, 4, 8$, and 16.

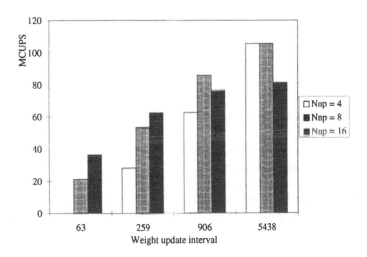

FIGURE 7.13. MCUPS performance for different combinations of neuron and training-set parallelism on a $16 \times 32$ cell configuration. $N_{NP} = 4, 8$, and 16.

more processors are assigned to each partition leading to shorter computation time for each training pattern. Hence, the impact of the weight update becomes more dominant.

A summary of the preceding results are plotted in Figure 7.14, where the maximum performance for 64, 256, and 512 processors is given. The performance on one cell is less than 1 MCUPS, thus the performance scaling is reasonable. This is especially true for large weight update intervals. For the largest system, the best performance for $\mu = 906$ is 86 MCUPS. This Nettalk training speed is faster than those reported by others (see Table 2.5). Because the convergence is not included, other methods may require less total training time.

In Figure 7.15, the performance of the best configuration is compared to the system with the largest $N_{NP}$ value, equal to the $(C_x, C_y)$ configuration. The measure of the speedup between the two configurations is given, that is, the ratio between CUPS perfor-

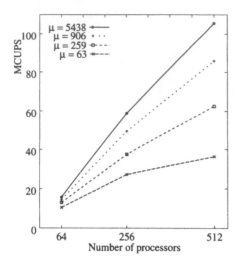

FIGURE 7.14. Training speed for Nettalk network plotted as a function of the number of processors.

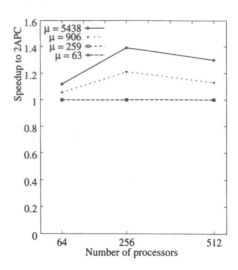

FIGURE 7.15. Speedup of the best configuration compared to the implementation with the largest $N_{NP}$ value; that is the $(C_x, C_y)$.

mances. For $\mu = 63$ and $\mu = 259$, the $(C_x, C_y)$ configuration[4] is the fastest, and thus there is no speedup. For larger $\mu$, the speedup reaches 1.4 in the best case. This means that the performance of the best mapping is 40 percent faster than that of the equal degree of parallelism-based mapping.

### 7.4.1.2 Estimation of the Performance.

The accuracy of the estimation model presented in Section 7.3.2.2 is investigated in this section. The training performance of the flexible mapping is tested using the Nettalk application with 120 hidden units.

The results will state if the estimation method is accurate enough to predict the execution time, compared to using real measurements, for selecting the best mapping for a given neural network application. If the estimation method is accurate, it can also be used to predict the possible performance for larger nonexisting configurations of the parallel machine.

To measure the average time of various operations, several tests were undertaken in the implemented programs. The average timing used for the following estimations are given in Table 7.3.

TABLE 7.3. Time measured for operations in implemented programs on AP1000 ($ns$).

| | | |
|---|---|---|
| $t_{add}$ | 1,280 | Time to add floats sequentially. |
| $t_{mul}$ | 1,400 | Time to multiply floats sequentially. |
| $t_{mul+add}$ | 1,770 | Time for alternating multiplication and addition of floats. |
| $t_{sigmoid}$ | 7,500 | Time to compute $1/(1 + e^{-x})$. |
| $t_{comm}(B)$ | $60,000 + 250B$ | Communication time for sending $B$ bytes between cells. |

---

[4]In the figure it is named two aspects of parallelism combined (2APC).

Early experiments revealed underestimated weight update time, and therefore the constant $k$ (in Expression 7.14) was introduced and set equal to 1.5 in the following experiments. A cache hit prediction has not been implemented in the model as the cache performance analysis on AP1000 showed that the average hit-rate was about $99 \pm 0.5$ percent.

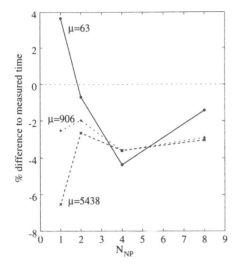

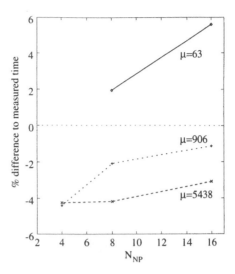

FIGURE 7.16. Deviation of estimate against measured time for the 64 cell configuration for different weight update intervals.

FIGURE 7.17. Deviation of estimate against measured time for the 512 cell configuration for different weight update intervals.

Figure 7.16 and Figure 7.17 show the error profile for the execution time estimates for 64 PEs and 512 PEs, respectively. The estimates are seen to be quite accurate, with an average error of less than 5 percent. For 512, cells the estimated time for the small weight update interval $\mu = 63$ is greater than that measured. For $\mu = 906$ and $\mu = 5,438$, on the other hand, the estimates are less than the measured values. On 64 cells, $\mu$ equal to 64 is also underestimated for some configurations. This is due to more training patterns, compared on 512 cells, computed between weight updates. Hence, the impact of weight update is less for the small system. Therefore, to improve the model, the training time without weight updating must be increased and the weight update time decreased.

The time estimates can be used to calculate the performance in MCUPS. Figure 7.18 compares the estimated and measured performance for the fastest configurations for 64, 256, and 512 PEs, and $\mu = 906$. The $N_{NP}$ values for the fastest mappings are listed in Figure 7.19. The estimated performance is slightly higher than the measured performance. Considering the simplicity of the estimation model, that is, only based on floating point operation count and a simple expression for communication time, the estimation method is fairly good. With this level of accuracy, it is interesting to estimate the performance for larger systems.

Figure 7.20 shows the estimated training performance for systems larger than 512 PEs. The configurations with the highest performance are used in the figure. The weight update interval highly influences the obtainable performance. The real difference in performance for the given weight update intervals is probably smaller, according to the estimation error in Figure 7.17. For $\mu = 63$ the MCUPS value is probably underestimated, whereas for the other it is probably overestimated.

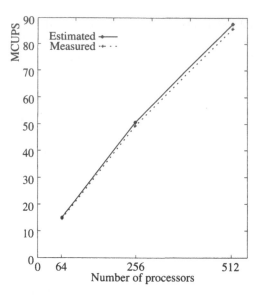

FIGURE 7.18. Comparing the fastest configuration for 64, 256 and 512 processing elements to estimated values for a weight update interval equal to 906.

| Number of processors | $N_{NP}$ |
|---|---|
| 64 | 4 |
| 256 | 8 |
| 512 | 8 |

FIGURE 7.19. The number of $N_{NP}$ values used in Figure 7.18.

The performance for even larger systems are shown in Figure 7.21. Learning by epoch gives a maximum training speed of 3.6 GCUPS, whereas the weight update interval of $\mu = 906$ shows a maximum of 1.3 GCUPS. Both are for 500K cells. Thus, the performance could be at least 10 times faster than that for 512 cells if there were no limitations on the number of cells. This shows the properties of the mapping on a massively parallel computer.

The estimations do not take into account the additional overhead incurred when *few* connections and training vectors are computed by a cell. Thus, the estimates are probably slightly too high for large systems.

Figure 7.22 presents a performance comparison of the fixed $(C_x, C_y)$ configuration—that is, no training-set parallelism in the vertical dimension— with the fastest possible training speed. As the number of PEs increases the gap between the two increases. This emphasizes the importance of application adaptable mapping on large parallel systems.

Using the technical data for AP1000 given in Section 7.3.2.2, we can estimate the maximum theoretical training speed of the available systems, as shown in Figure 7.23. For 64 cells, the measured performance is 36.4 percent of the maximum performance, where $\mu = 906$. The difference in performance on 512 cells is 38.5 percent. Therefore, the implementation could, in the best case, be optimized by a factor of slightly less than three. However, it is anticipated this would require some assembly programming in the code.

This simulation has been tuned to the Nettalk application. A few experiments were undertaken with image compression and speech recognition networks. To obtain accurate estimates, $k$ had to be set to a specific value for each application. Thus, for making a general estimation method, an expression for computing $k$ ought to be developed. This should be based on the network size, because its purpose is to compensate for added overhead (communication conflicts) when large weight change matrices are to be added. In conclu-

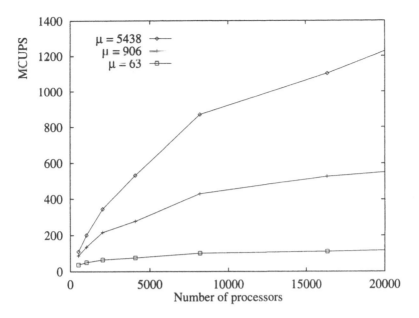

FIGURE 7.20. Estimated training performance for the Nettalk application for three different weight update intervals, $\mu$.

sion, the experiments are promising for using this estimation technique in picking the best parallel configuration for a neural network application.

*7.4.1.3  The Convergence of Nettalk Learning.*  To investigate the convergence rate for different weight update intervals, 1,000 of the most common English words (a total of 5,438 characters) were used. The error function for a training pattern $p$ is equal to Equation 1.4 and is given by

$$E_p(n) = \frac{1}{2} \sum_k (d_{p,k} - y_{p,o,k})^2$$

where $n$ is the training iteration number, $d_{p,k}$ is the target output, and $y_{p,o,k}$ is the output layer output. Rumelhart and associates use the values 0.1 and 0.9 as target values, because the extreme values of 0 or 1 can never be reached [38]. If the error is 0.1 per output unit, the pattern error becomes

$$E_p(n) = \frac{1}{2} \sum_{k=1}^{26} (0.1)^2 = 0.13$$

and this value has been used as a threshold for determining if a pattern is trained or not. Weight change values were accumulated for a pattern $p$ having $E_p(n) > 0.13$, whereas a pattern is trained when $E_p(n) \leq 0.13$. This is a slightly different error measure than reported by Sejnowski and Rosenberg, who measured the error at each individual output neuron. They used a "best guess," which compared the output values to a subset of the training set (52 target vectors). If the vector that had the smallest output error was equal to the training vector, then the vector was considered correctly trained. Both methods

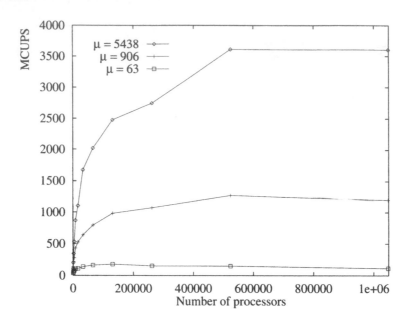

FIGURE 7.21. Estimated training performance for Nettalk application for three different weight update intervals, $\mu$.

decrease the sum of square error function

$$E(n) = \sum_{p=1}^{5438} \sum_{k=1}^{26} (d_{p,k} - y_{p,o,k})^2. \tag{7.16}$$

The error measure used in this research avoids overtraining without a large loss in the load balance of the computation. Because the purpose of these experiments has been to study the relation between weight update interval and convergence and not the performance of the application, a separate test set has not been used. Testing convergence on the training set requires less time than using a test set. Thus, more tests for each weight update interval could in this way be undertaken.

For each weight update interval investigated, the best learning rate $\eta$ was searched for. Between 10 and 15 runs of each weight update interval were performed. These experiments in total required several hundred CPU hours. For a small $\mu$, the best learning rate was equal to 1.5. It had to be decreased for larger values of $\mu$. For larger $\mu$, the convergence was more sensitive to the selection of $\eta$. The best value for the smoothing term $\alpha$ was, after some initial experiments, found to be 0.9. This value was used for all the experiments. Due to this smoothing term, it was possible to keep a fairly large learning rate value even with infrequent weight updates. Bias was also used in the experiments.

Experiments with adaptive learning rate during training and other similar methods to speed up the convergence are not included. This is mainly because it would have required a *much* larger number of experiments to make a fair comparison of the convergence for different weight update intervals.

Figure 7.24 shows the results of the convergence as a percentage (called $E_\%$) of the characters that have not been trained. Each curve represents one weight update interval. Almost without exception, a larger $\mu$ implies a slower reduction in number of nontrained patterns. The percentage of characters not trained went down and stabilized slightly be-

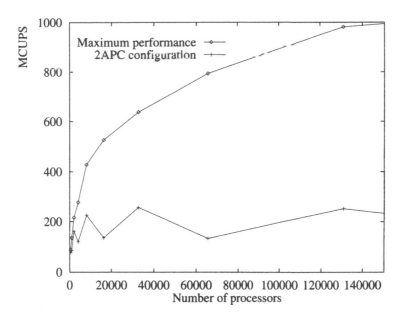

FIGURE 7.22. Comparison of the maximum performance of the flexible configuration to the $(C_x, C_y)$ configuration (named 2APC), for $\mu = 906$.

low 5%. This is due to the representation limitation of the network as mentioned in [3]. Therefore, a network is here regarded as converged, when $E_\% < 5\%$.

Figure 7.25 shows the optimal learning rate, the value resulting in the smallest number of iterations for convergence, for each $\mu$ used in the experiments. Based on these values the following rule is established:

$$\eta(\mu) = 6.0\mu^{-0.5} \tag{7.17}$$

This is comparable to the rule derived by Paugam-Moisy in [27]: $\eta(\mu) = k_1\mu^\alpha$, for the application of classifying patterns into three classes, see Section 1.3.1.3.

The number of iterations required for convergence is given in Figure 7.26. Due to the fairly linear distribution of the points, the least squares method is used to establish the experimental rule

$$N(\mu) = \frac{\mu}{11.5} + 76.4. \tag{7.18}$$

This linear relation between number of training iterations and the weight update interval was also found by Paugam-Moisy. The linear distribution of points tells us that for predicting $N(\mu)$ it is sufficient to estimate the total number of iterations for a few (minimum 2) weight update intervals. These can then be used to find a linear formula for $N(\mu)$.

As mentioned in Section 7.3.2.1 several researchers have found that $N$ is proportional to $\frac{1-\alpha}{\eta}$. Figure 7.27 plots this expression for the learning rates in Figure 7.25. The points are linearly distributed along the least squares fit line. By scaling by the number of iteration for $\mu = 906$, we get

$$N(\mu) = \frac{\mu}{8.43} + 51.2. \tag{7.19}$$

This gives a good estimation for $\mu = 1$ with a number of five iterations fewer than measured. However, the estimates are less precise for larger weight update intervals, for example, for $\mu = 5,438$ a number of 85 iterations more than measured is estimated.

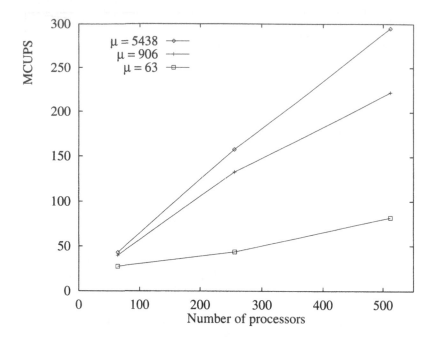

FIGURE 7.23. Maximum possible training speed on AP1000.

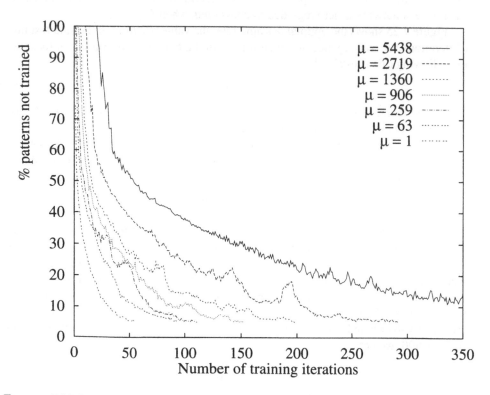

FIGURE 7.24. Percentage of characters that are not trained for various weight update intervals.

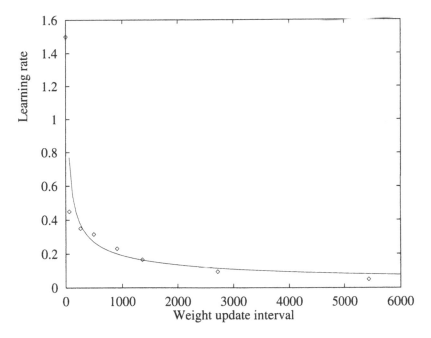

FIGURE 7.25. The best learning rate ($\eta$) for each investigated weight update interval. The curve plots the derived rule.

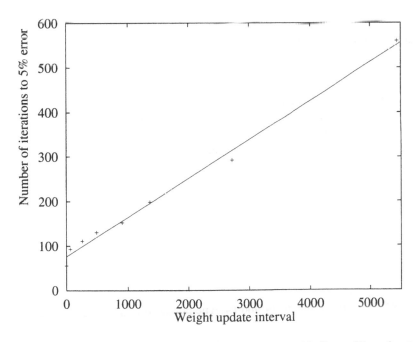

FIGURE 7.26. Number of iterations needed to obtain convergence with $E_\%< 5\%$ as the stopping criteria.

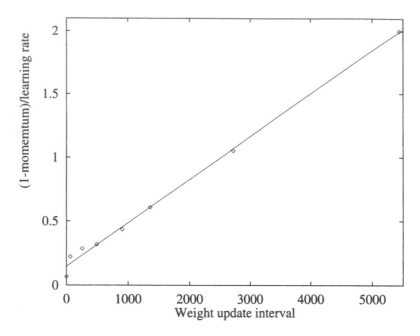

FIGURE 7.27. Plotting of $\frac{1-\alpha}{\eta}$.

In the following it is shown that the total number of iterations needed can be estimated based on the error after a small number of training iterations. By looking at the curves in Figure 7.24, we see that they are of similar form, but have different curvature. To find a curve that estimates each error curve, logarithmic regression can be used to find an expression for each $\mu_i$ of the form

$$E_\%(n) = k_1 n^{k_2} \tag{7.20}$$

where $n$ is the iteration index and $k_1$ and $k_2$ are parameters to be estimated. This requires that the points $(\log n_i, \log E_\%(n_i))$ $\forall i$ are situated on a straight line. Figure 7.28 shows a logarithmic plot of Figure 7.24.

Above 20 iterations, see on the right-hand side of the vertical line in the figure, the curves become more linear for increasing iterations. Thus, regression should be used on this linear part. Several different regression analyses were made to search for a curve describing the error convergence. Equation 7.20 was extended

$$E_\%(n) = k_1(n + k_3)^{k_2} \tag{7.21}$$

by $k_3$, which may be called the offset of the error curve, equal to twice[5] the number of iterations from start of training until $E_\% \leq 95\%$. Equation 7.21 was solved for each $\mu$ for the initial point $(n = 25, E_\%(25))$ and the convergence point ($n$ when $E_\%$ becomes less than 5%, 5) with respect to $k_1$ and $k_2$. The points were given by the registered values during training (see Table 7.4).

The value of $k_2$ was found to be fairly constant for all the weight update intervals and averaged to approximately -1.25. Now $k_1$ can be computed based on *only* the error at

---

[5]Experiments showed a better approximation when using twice the number, compared to using the explicit number.

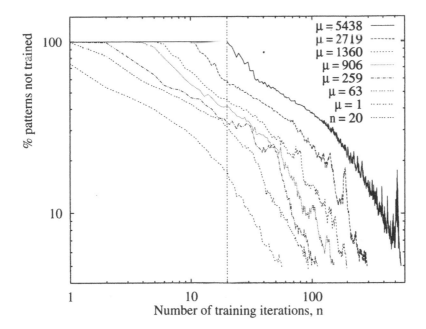

FIGURE 7.28. Convergence of Nettalk, logarithmic plot. A vertical line is plotted for $n = 20$.

TABLE 7.4 The data on Nettalk convergence used for estimation.

| Weight Update Interval ($\mu$) | $k_3$ | $E_\%(25)$ | $n$ when $E_\%(n) < 5$ |
|---|---|---|---|
| 1 | 0 | 12.61 | 56 |
| 63 | 0 | 25.65 | 93 |
| 259 | 4 | 32.86 | 111 |
| 494 | 6 | 32.38 | 130 |
| 906 | 8 | 35.77 | 152 |
| 1,360 | 12 | 41.12 | 198 |
| 2,719 | 22 | 53.51 | 292 |
| 5,438 | 42 | 85.20 | 560 |

$n = 25$ iterations:

$$k_1 = \frac{E_\%(n)}{(n + k_3)^{-1.25}}. \tag{7.22}$$

Furthermore, the total number of iterations is given from Equation 7.21 by

$$N = \left(\frac{5}{k_1}\right)^{1/-1.25} - k_3. \tag{7.23}$$

Figure 7.29, which shows both measured and estimated values of $N(\mu)$, proves the accuracy of the estimation model for this application. However, in general, this accuracy may not be the case. This is a field of research where very little published work using real applications exists. Thus, more studies are required to form a more general framework and to see if it is possible to estimate the convergence in general.

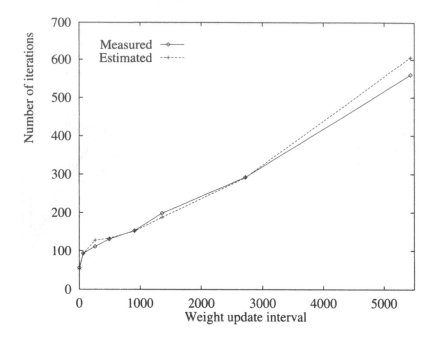

FIGURE 7.29. Comparing measured and estimated values of $N(\mu)$.

**Sensitivity and Convergence Aspects.** The BP algorithm is more sensitive to the selection of the learning rate when the weights are infrequently updated. Figure 7.30 shows the convergence for $\mu = 1$ ( learning by pattern) and $\mu = 5,438$ (learning by epoch). The error $E_\%$ is plotted and the minimum error corresponds to the learning rate, which gives the quickest convergence (that is, $E_\%$ is less than 5 percent). The $x$-axis is logarithmic, and still the epoch learning has a narrower valley in the error curve.

In the training scheme used, a pattern is said to be trained if the error is below a certain threshold. Because the weights are changed during an iteration, there is a risk of trained patterns becoming detrained (that is, of having an error larger than the threshold after the training iteration). Thus, the number of patterns trained correctly may be less than the number counted during an iteration. Figure 7.31 compares the $E_\%$ accumulated *during* each training iteration with $E_\%$ computed for the whole training set *after* each training iteration for $\mu = 906$. Even though the epoch computed error is less stable, the two convergence criteria harmonize well with little difference in the final convergence. Similar results were recorded for other values of $\mu$.

Figure 7.32 shows the convergence when $E_\% < 10\%$. Thirty-one iterations are required before convergence using learning by pattern. In the Nettalk paper [3], the training continued for 30 iterations. As for the $E_\% < 5\%$ convergence criteria, there is a linear relation between the weight update interval and the number of iterations required before convergence.

An interesting aspect is the ratio

$$k_e = \frac{N(P)}{N(1)} \tag{7.24}$$

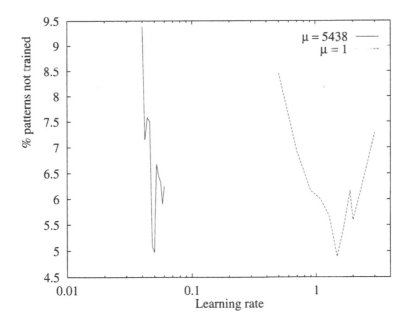

FIGURE 7.30. The sensitivity of the learning rate ($\eta$) on the convergence for epoch versus pattern learning.

where $P$ is the number of patterns in the training set. Then, $N(P)$ represents the number of iterations for learning by epoch. For Nettalk training with 5% error threshold,

$$k_e = \frac{560}{56} = 10. \tag{7.25}$$

For a 10% error threshold this becomes

$$k_e = \frac{359}{31} = 11.58. \tag{7.26}$$

For the least strict threshold (10%), there is a larger difference in the number of iterations for learning by pattern compared to the number for learning by epoch.

*7.4.1.4 Minimizing the Total Training Time.* This section determines the best weight update intervals for running Nettalk on AP1000. By applying Equation 7.5, the total training time is found as the time for one iteration multiplied by the number of iterations used for convergence. Total time calculations are conducted for $\mu = 63; 259; 494; 906; 1,360; 2,719;$ and $5,438$.

The time for one iteration, $T_{1it}$, can be computed from Figures 7.11 through 7.13 (not all $\mu$-values are shown). The number of iterations needed for convergence, $N(\mu)$, is given in Figure 7.26.

For the 512 cell system, the total training time is plotted in Figure 7.33. The best weight update interval is for $\mu = 906$ using the configuration $(N_{TSP}, N_{NP}) = (64, 8)$. Convergence is obtained after 265 seconds. However, there is only a marginal differences in the time for $\mu \in \{259, 494, 906\}$. The slowest training time is for $\mu = 5,438$. Thus, infrequent weight update is not as promising as the MCUPS measure indicates.

Weight changes have not been accumulated for a pattern where the error is sufficiently small to avoid overtraining. Thus, $T_{1it}$ decreases during training as the number of patterns

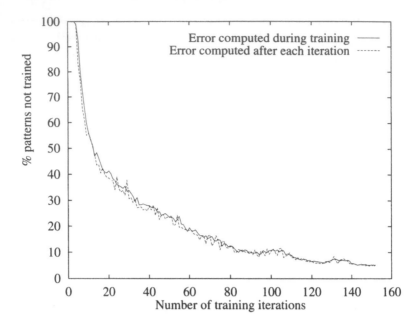

FIGURE 7.31. Error computed during training compared to error computed after each iteration (epoch) for $\mu = 906$.

trained increases. As a constant $T_{1it}$ is used, the $T_{total}$ is larger than the real execution time.

Running the same program, with parallel parts removed, on a SPARC10 workstation using learning by pattern reached convergence after 56 iterations and 115 minutes. This was measured when no other users were active on the computer. AP1000 speedup based on total execution time ($T_{1it}N$) is, therefore, shown to be 26 times. This is a conservative measure, because the decreasing $T_{1it}$ for AP1000 is not accounted for. When the serial program updated the weights for every pattern, the total training time was 236 minutes. This is 54 times slower than training on AP1000. Thus, total training time can be reduced from hours to minutes by using parallel processing.

Total training time for 256 cells and 64 cells are given in Figures 7.34 and 7.35, respectively. As the system gets smaller, more frequent weight updates lead to the shortest training time. This can partly be understood by the number of training-set partitions, as explained in Section 7.4.1.1. In Figure 7.11, the difference in maximum performance for the various $\mu$ values is small compared to Figure 7.13. Combined with the few iterations required for convergence for frequent weight updating, this leads to the shortest total training time for small systems.

### 7.4.2 Sonar Target Classification

This section gives the results of the convergence of the sonar return application, described in Section 2.2.3.3. In the experiments, all the available patterns (208) have been used as a training set. The weights are updated, or accumulated for learning by block, for a pattern where the error is larger than 0.04. That is,

$$E_p(n) > \frac{1}{2}\sum_{k=1}^{2}(0.2)^2 = 0.04.$$

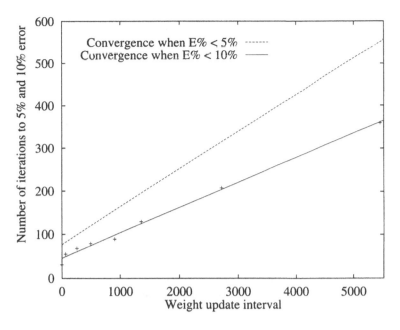

FIGURE 7.32. Comparing $E_\%  < 5\%$ and $E_\% < 10\%$ error criteria.

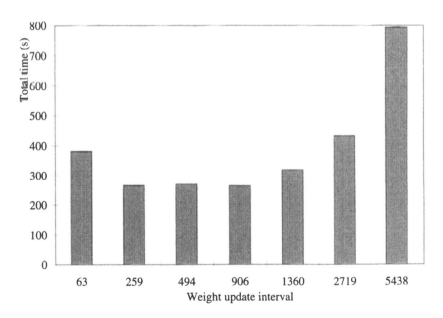

FIGURE 7.33. Total training time for Nettalk running on 512 cells, using 120 hidden units.

This threshold is based on an error of 0.2 on each of the output units, which was used by Gorman and associates [6, 7]. As in their work, the smoothing term was set to 0. The number of hidden units was set to 24, which was reported as giving the best recognition rate on the training set.

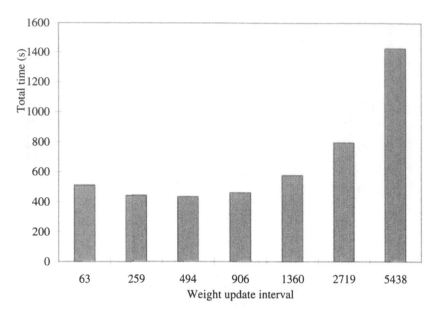

FIGURE 7.34. Total training time for Nettalk running on 256 cells, using 120 hidden units.

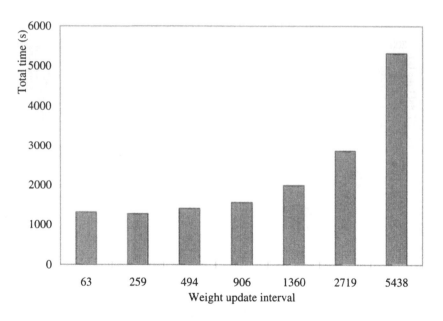

FIGURE 7.35. Total training time for Nettalk running on 64 cells, using 120 hidden units.

### 7.4.2.1 Results on Sonar Target Classification.

The convergence for different weight update intervals is given in Figure 7.36. The $y$-axis represents the percentage of training patterns with $E_p > 0.04$. The results are very similar to Nettalk—a larger weight update interval leads to slower learning. However, the convergence curves are steeper, and it is not possible to use the same logarithmic regression as for Nettalk to estimate the number of training iterations.

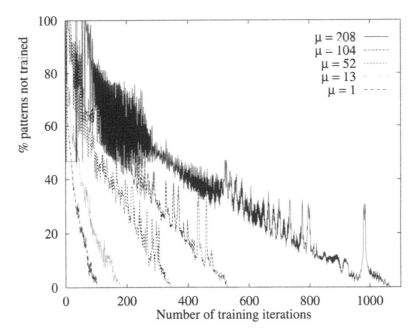

FIGURE 7.36. The percentage of patterns that have $E_p > 0.04$, for learning sonar return classification.

The convergence was very sensitive to small changes in initial weights and other parameters. It was seen that the resolution of floating point variables influenced the convergence rate. Continuous values in the input units, instead of two-level values as in the case of Nettalk, probably make the algorithm more sensitive to the accuracy of the variables.

The best learning rate for each weight update interval is plotted in Figure 7.37. A similar experimental rule to Equation 7.17 is established:

$$\eta(\mu) = 3.0\mu^{-0.5}. \tag{7.27}$$

The total number of iterations until *all* training patterns have reached $E_p \leq 0.04$ during a learning cycle is plotted in Figure 7.38, together with the derived least squares fit of the points:

$$N(\mu) = 106.66 + 4.51\mu. \tag{7.28}$$

The number of iterations required for an error threshold equal to 5 percent of the non-trained patterns is plotted in Figure 7.39. This is equivalent to the error threshold used for Nettalk. The least squares error equation is given by:

$$N(\mu) = 97.04 + 3.88\mu. \tag{7.29}$$

*7.4.2.2 Comparing Sonar Results to Nettalk Results.* In this section, common properties of the two applications are highlighted. The idea is to search for a general way of estimating the number of iterations needed for convergence, $N$, as a function of the weight update interval.

For Nettalk, the learning ratio was found to be $k_e = 10$ for a 5 percent error threshold and $k_e = 11.58$ for a 10 percent error threshold. Correspondingly, for the sonar target

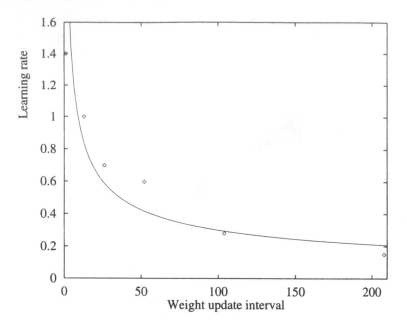

FIGURE 7.37. The best learning rate $\eta$ for each of the investigated weight update intervals. The curve plots the derived rule.

classification (all of the patterns trained), we have:

$$k_e = \frac{1,065}{102} = 10.44. \tag{7.30}$$

For the less strict stopping criteria of 5 percent, $k_e = 11.9$. Thus, $k_e$ is in the 10 to 12 range for both applications. Thus, learning by pattern trains 10 to 12 times faster than learning by epoch. Moreover, a less strict error threshold increases $k_e$. The resemblance between these two applications was not expected, as they are different in both network size and number of training patterns.

This result, of a near constant $k_e$ ratio, will now be used in estimating $N(\mu)$ based on a single result for convergence, $N(1)$. The relation between $\mu$ and the $k$-ratio is illustrated in Figure 7.40. The straight line is assumed according to the earlier shown linear relation between the weight update interval, $\mu$ and $N(\mu)$. The equation for the line passing through the points $(1,1)$— learning by pattern— and $(P, k_e)$— learning by epoch— is given by:

$$k_\mu - 1 = \frac{k_e - 1}{P - 1}(\mu - P) - k_\mu = \frac{k_e - 1}{P - 1}(\mu - P) + 1 \tag{7.31}$$

where $k_\mu$ also can be understood as $N(\mu)/N(1)$. An estimate of the $N(\mu)$ is then given by:

$$N(\mu) = k_\mu N(1). \tag{7.32}$$

For neural training, the application is usually trained several times with different parameters. Therefore, Equation 7.32 can be used for the approximation of $N(\mu)$, after some initial convergence tests, in the heuristic shown in Figure 7.10. To confirm the estimation method, other applications should be tested.

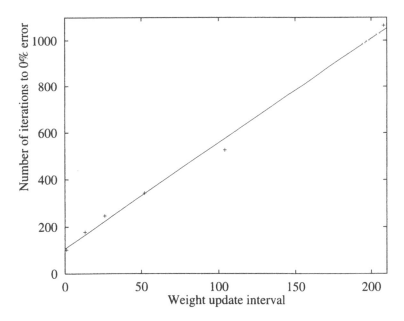

FIGURE 7.38. Number of iterations required to obtain convergence, that is, $E_p \leq 0.04$ for all training patterns.

To set the appropriate learning rate, the previous experimental rules (Equation 7.17 and 7.27) can be formulated in a general approximation rule:

$$\eta(\mu) = k\mu^{-0.5} \tag{7.33}$$

where $k$ is a positive constant less than 10. As the training set gets smaller, the appropriate $k$ value decreases. This is in accordance to the two experiments reported in this chapter.

### 7.4.3 Speech Recognition Network

Figure 7.41 shows the performance for a speech recognition network on 512 processing elements. It was not possible to execute all the configurations because of communication limitations (*ring buffer overflow*). Except for 64 hidden units, the highest training speed is obtained for $N_{NP} = 16$, that is, 16 cells assigned to each copy of the network. For this configuration there is no training-set partition in the horizontal dimension and, therefore, the training speed does not exceed that for the fixed $(C_x, C_y)$ configuration. To further improve the performance, synapse parallelism should probably be introduced because of the size of the network.

### 7.4.4 Image Compression

Image compression requires a small network [4] but implies a large amount of data, both for training and for real-time compression. The performance for a 64 input and 64 output network and 512 cells is given in Figure 7.42 for three different compression ratios. The number of hidden units varied between 4, 8, and 16. A small number of hidden units implies a large compression ratio. The weights were updated for every 512 training patterns. For the smallest network (four hidden units), the performance of the noncontention mapping $(N_{TSP}, N_{NP}) = (32, 16)$ is approximately six times less than that for the best

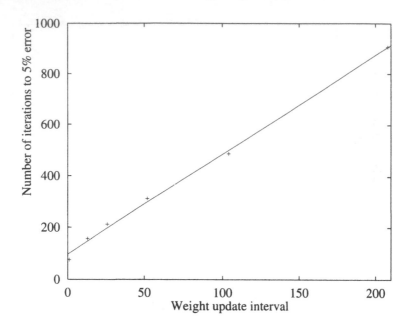

FIGURE 7.39. Number of iterations needed to reach a stopping criteria of 5% error.

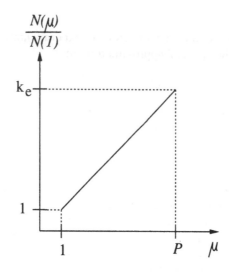

FIGURE 7.40. The relation between $\mu$ and $k_e$, where $P$ is the total number of patterns in the training set.

mapping $(N_{TSP}, N_{NP}) = (128, 4)$. Thus, for small networks a large degree of training-set parallelism is beneficial.

Figure 7.43 shows the performance for 256 cells. In this configuration, $N_{NP} = 4$ also gives the best overall performance. However, for $N_{NP} = 2$, the performance is higher than for $N_{NP} = 8$ (for 8 and 16 hidden units) which is opposite from Figure 7.42.

The performance on 128 processors appears in Figure 7.44. The number of cells in the $y$-dimension (16) and $x$-dimension (8) is half of that in the 512 cell system. The difference

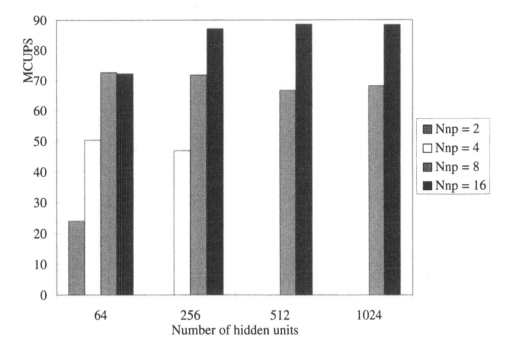

FIGURE 7.41. Training performance on 512 processors for speech recognition network. $N_{NP} = 2$, 4, 8, and 16.

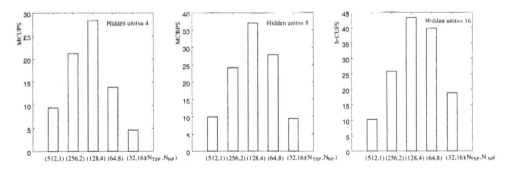

FIGURE 7.42. MCUPS performance for different combinations of neuron and training-set parallelism on a 16 x 32 processor configuration training a compression network.

between the best and worst results is lower than for the larger systems. For 4 and 8 hidden units the maximum learning speed is reached when $N_{NP} = 2$. Thus, assigning fewer processors to each copy of the network is important as the number of cells is reduced. In this way, a large number of training-set partitions can be maintained. The training speed on 64 cells is given in Figure 7.45.

The highest speeds in each of these experiments are plotted in Figure 7.46. The ratio between the highest performance achieved and the performance of the $(C_x, C_y)$ configuration is plotted in Figure 7.47. As shown, a reduction in the number of hidden units leads to larger ratios. For 4 hidden units and 256 processors the difference is a factor of 6.5. This corresponds to 550 percent faster training speed— a considerable difference. The

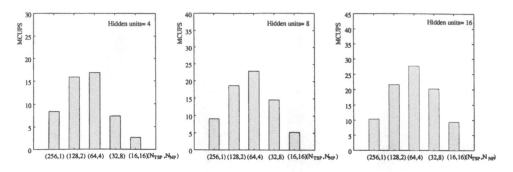

FIGURE 7.43. MCUPS performance for different combinations of neuron and training-set parallelism on a 16 x 16 processor configuration training a compression network.

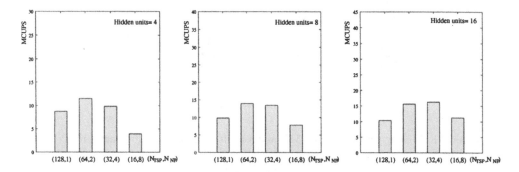

FIGURE 7.44. MCUPS performance for different combinations of neuron and training-set parallelism on an $8 \times 16$ processor configuration training a compression network.

nonlinearity in the curves in the figure can be explained by the difference in configuration. For 128 and 512 processors, $C_y = 2C_x$, whereas for 64 and 256 processors, $C_y = C_x$. Thus, when there are twice the number of processors in the vertical dimension, additional training-set partitions in the horizontal dimension do not give rise to the same increase in performance as for 64 and 256 processors. It can be seen that the scaling in Figure 7.46 would drop dramatically if the $(C_x, C_y)$ configuration had been used. This is especially

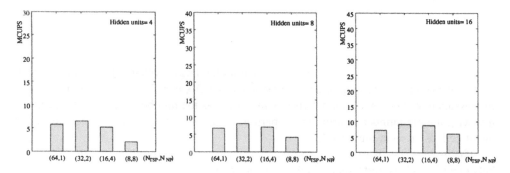

FIGURE 7.45. MCUPS performance for different combinations of neuron and training-set parallelism on an $8 \times 8$ processor configuration training a compression network.

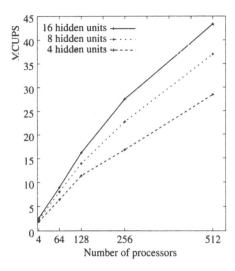

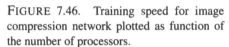

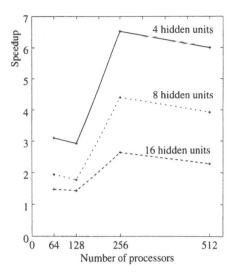

FIGURE 7.46. Training speed for image compression network plotted as function of the number of processors.

FIGURE 7.47. Speedup of the best configuration compared to the $(C_x, C_y)$ configuration.

true for networks with a small number of hidden units, for which the flexible mapping already has a limited scaling.

The primary goal of designing the parallel mapping scheme has been to reduce the neural network training time. However, for image compression a large amount of data will need to be processed for the real-time compression of video frames. The proposed mapping will allow fast compression by compressing different parts of each frame on different copies of the neural network.

## 7.5 Conclusions on the Application Adaptable Mapping

This chapter proposed a near optimal mapping of the backpropagation algorithm onto a parallel computer. Multiple degrees of parallelism were exploited and the influence of the weight update interval on convergence was included in the mapping strategy.

The importance of the flexible implementation depends on the neural application. For Nettalk, 40 percent higher performance than for the $(C_x, C_y)$ configuration was achieved in the best case. For the smaller networks, like image compression networks, the difference in performance was larger— 550 percent in the best case. This highlights the advantages of an *application adaptable* mapping algorithm to reduce training time.

The results also indicate that flexibility becomes more important for parallel computers with a large number of processing elements. This is because most neural network applications require a relatively small neural network size. However, the number of training patterns for training or the amount of data to be processed in the recall phase may be very large. Therefore, on large systems, the number of training-set partitions should be large rather than the number of processors assigned to each subset.

Estimation of execution time, based on the number of floating point operations and communication time estimates, was tested. For the Nettalk application it turned out to be accurate and was used to show that the number of processors for the flexible mapping can be increased almost without limit, resulting in increased performance.

Most other BP implementations published do not consider the weight update interval or the mapping strategy according to the *given* neural network application. The convergence tests of two applications in this chapter indicate a linear relation between the weight update interval and the number of iterations to reach convergence. Learning by epoch is a factor of 10 to 12 times slower than learning by pattern. Even though the speedups indicated by the MCUPS figures are not practically obtainable, the computation of total execution time undertaken shows that parallel processing can drastically reduce training time. This requires that the parallel implementation is flexible and adaptable to the given neural network and training-set.

# References

[1] H. Ishihata, et. al., "Third generation message passing computer AP1000," in *Proc. of the International Symposium on Supercomputing*, pp. 46–55, Nov. 1991.

[2] M. Kuga, Y. Namiuchi, B. Apduhan, and T. Sueyoshi, "Implementation and performance evaluation of a neural network simulator on highly parallel computer AP1000," in *ICPAS*, 1993.

[3] T. J. Sejnowski and C. R. Rosenberg, "Parallel networks that learn to pronounce English text," *Complex Systems*, vol. 1, pp. 145–168, 1987.

[4] K. B. Cho, et. al., "Image compression using multi-layer perceptron with block classification and SOFM coding," in *Proc. of World Congress on Neural Networks*, vol. 3, pp. 26–31, 1994.

[5] N. Morgan, "Using a million connections for continous speech recognition," in *Proc. of Int. Conference On Neural Network Processing*, pp. 1439–1444, October 1994.

[6] R. P. Gorman and T. J. Sejnowski, "Analysis of hidden units in a layered network trained to classify sonar targets," *Neural networks*, vol. 1, pp. 75–89, 1988.

[7] R. P. Gorman and T. J. Sejnowski, "Learned classification of sonar targets using a massively parallel network," *IEEE Trans. on acoustics, speech and signal processing*, vol. 36, no. 7, pp. 1135–1140, 1988.

[8] J. Adamo and D. Anguita, "Object oriented design of a BP neural network simulator and implementation on the Connection Machine (CM-5)," tech. rep., International Computer Science Institute, September 1994. TR-94-46.

[9] G. Blelloch and C. R. Rosenberg, "Network learning on the Connection Machine," in *Proc. of IJCAI87*, pp. 323–326, 1987.

[10] D. Jackson and D. Hammerstrom, "Distributing back propagation networks over the Intel iPSC/860 hypercube," in *Proc. of Int. Joint Conference on Neural Networks*, vol. I, pp. 569–574, 1991.

[11] D. A. Pommerleau, et. al., "Neural network simulation at warp speed: How we got 17 million connections per second," in *Proc. of IEEE Int. Conference on Neural Networks*, 1988.

[12] E. Sànchez, S. Barro, and C. Regueiro, "Artificial neural networks implementation on vectorial supercomputers," in *Proc. of IEEE Int. Conference on Neural Networks*, (Orlando, FL), pp. 3938–3943, June 28 - July 2, 1994.

[13] Andreas Zell, et. al., "Problems of massive parallelism in neural network simulation," in *Proc. of IEEE Int. Conference on Neural Networks*, pp. 1890–1895, 1993.

[14] X. Zhang, "The backpropagation algorithm on grid and hypercube architectures," *Parallel Computing*, vol. 14, pp. 317–327, Summer 1990.

[15] B. Faure and G. Mazare, "A cellular architecture dedicated to neural net emulation," *Microprocessing and Microprogramming*, vol. 30, pp. 249–256, August 1990.

[16] H. Yoshizawa and K. Asakawa, "Highly parallel architecture for back-propagation using a ring register data path," *Fujitsu Sci. Tech. J*, pp. 227–233, September 1993.

[17] J. Torresen, S. Mori, H. Nakashima, S. Tomita, and O. Landsverk, "Parallel back propagation training algorithm for MIMD computer with 2D-torus network," in *Proceedings of International Conference On Neural Information Processing (ICONIP'94), Seoul, Korea*, vol. 1, pp. 140–145, October 1994.

[18] S. Y. Kung, "Parallel architectures for artificial neural nets," in *IEEE International Conference on Systolic Arrays* (K. Bromley, S.-Y. Kung, and E. Swartzlander, eds.), pp. 163–174, IEEE Computer Society Press, 1988.

[19] J. Torresen, H. Nakashima, S. Tomita, and O. Landsverk, "General mapping of feed-forward neural networks onto an MIMD computer," in *Proc. of IEEE Int. Conference on Neural Networks (ICNN'95)*, (Perth, Western Australia), IEEE, 27 November – 1 December 1995.

[20] J. Torresen, *Parallelization of Backpropagation Training for Feed-Forward Neural Networks*. PhD thesis, Norwegian University of Science and Technology, 1996. ISBN 82-7119-906-4.

[21] J. Torresen, "The convergence of backpropagation trained neural networks for various weight update frequencies," *Int. Journal of Neural Systems*, vol. 8, pp. 263–277, June 1997.

[22] T. Yukawa and T. Ishikawa, "Optimal parallel back-propagation schemes for mesh-connected and bus-connected multiprocessors," in *Proc. of IEEE Int. Conference on Neural Networks*, pp. 1748–1753, 1993.

[23] H. Ishihata, "Performance evaluation of the AP1000," in *Proc. of CAP workshop*, pp. N–1–8, 1991.

[24] J. Torresen, S. Mori, H. Nakashima, S. Tomita, and O. Landsverk, "Exploiting multiple degrees of BP parallelism on the highly parallel computer AP1000," in *Fourth International Conference on Artificial Neural Networks (ANN'95)*, (Cambridge, UK), pp. 483–488, IEE, June 1995.

[25] M. Witbrock and M. Zagha, "An implementation of backpropagation learning on GF11, a large SIMD parallel computer," *Parallel computing*, vol. 14, pp. 329–346, 1990.

[26] J. Torresen and J. Solheim, "Implementing backpropagation training on a reconfigurable computer using pipelining of the training patterns," in *Proceedings of International Conference On Neural Information Processing (ICONIP'96), Hong Kong*, vol. 2, pp. 1017–1022, Springer, September 1996.

[27] H. Paugam-Moisy, "Parallel neural computing based on neural network duplicating," in *Parallel algorithms for digital image processing, computer vision and neural networks* (I. Pitas, ed.), ch. 10, pp. 305–340, John Wiley & Sons, 1993.

[28] A. Sato, "An analytical study of the momentum term in a backpropagation algorithm. In Proc. of ICANN–91," in *Artificial Neural Networks* (T. Kohonen, et. al., ed.), vol. 1, pp. 617–622, Elsevier Science Publishers B.V. (North-Holland), 1991.

[29] J. Higashino, et. al., "Numerical analysis and adaption method for learning rate of back propagation," in *Proc. of Int. Joint Conference on Neural Networks*, vol. I, (WASH.DC), pp. 627–630, 1990.

[30] R. Battiti, "Optimizing methods for back propagation: Automatic parameter tuning and faster convergence," in *Proc. of Int. Joint Conference on Neural Networks*, vol. I, (WASH.DC), pp. 593–596, 1990.

[31] J. R. Chen and P. Mars, "Stepsize variation methods for accelerating the back propagation algorithm," in *Proc. of Int. Joint Conference on Neural Networks*, vol. I, (WASH.DC), pp. 601–604, 1990.

[32] T.P. Vogl, et. al., "Accelerating the convergence of the back propagation method," *Biological Cybernetics*, vol. 59, pp. 257–263, 1988.

[33] H. Kitano, "Emperical studies on the speed of convergence of neural network training using genetic algorithms," in *Proceedings 8th JMIT national conference in artificial intelligence*, vol. 2, (Boston MASS), pp. 789–796, 1990.

[34] M. McInerney and A. P. Dhawan, "Use of genetic algorithms with back propagation in training of feed-forward neural networks," in *Proc. of IEEE Int. Conference on Neural Networks*, pp. 203–208, 1993.

[35] S. Oliker, et. al., "Design architectures and training of neural networks with a distributed genetic algorithm," in *Proc. of IEEE Int. Conference on Neural Networks*, pp 199–202, 1993.

[36] D. F. McCaffrey and A. R. Gallant, "Convergence rates for single hidden layer feed-forward networks," *Neural Networks*, vol. 7, no. 1, pp. 147–158, 1994.

[37] J. Torresen, S. Tomita, and O. Landsverk, "The relation of weight update frequency to convergence of BP," in *Proc. of World Congress on Neural Networks (WCNN'95)*, vol. 1, (Washington, D.C.), pp. 679–682, INNS Press, July 1995.

[38] D. E. Rumelhart, G. E. Hinton, and R. J. Williams, "Learning internal representation by error propagation," in *Parallel Distributed Processing*, vol. 1, pp. 318–362, The MIT Press, 1986.

[28] A. Siou, "The statistical study of the speculation term $\beta$ ...

...

...

# Part III

# Special Parallel Architectures and Application Case Studies

# Chapter 8

# Massively Parallel Architectures for Large-Scale Neural Network Computations

**Yoshiji Fujimoto**
Department of Applied Mathematics and Informatics,
Faculty of Science and Technology,
Ryukoko University,
Japan

## 8.1  Introduction

A neurocomputer is an essential tool for the research and development of biological and artificial neural networks and their applications. In the research of a new neuron model, it is necessary to simulate considerable scale of its networks to demonstrate its effectiveness. In the application of neural networks to various fields such as optimization problems, character recognition, speech recognition, robot control, image processing, and natural language processing, the simulation of neural networks with various configurations, parameters, and a large number of learning data is needed. A neurocomputer used for neural network computation should have the following characteristics:

1. Considerable computational power.

2. Sufficient capacity for large-scale neural networks.

3. Sufficient flexibility to handle various neural network configurations.

4. The potential to simulate a variety of neuron models including new models.

A spontaneous solution to the problem of computational power is the parallel architecture of computation associated with the structure of the biological neural networks. The neural network computations are implemented on general-purpose parallel machines, special-purpose parallel neurocomputers, and various kinds of analog and digital hardware in parallel. For example, the neural network computations are implemented on general-purpose parallel machines such as the systolic array machines [1, 2], the Connection Machine [3, 4], the Associative String Processor (ASP) [5], the Distributed Array Processor (DAP) [6], MasPar [7], GF11 [8] and the Transputer Array [9]. On the other hand, special-purpose parallel neurocomputers have been developed such as Neuro-Turbo [10], AAP-2 [11], Sandy/8 [12], GCN [13], CNAPS [14], and REMAP[3] [15]. And, at last, a wafer scale integration (WSI) [16] for the neurocomputer has been developed. As a result, a performance of hundreds of millions of connections per second was obtained. However, in computations of large-scale neural networks with millions of neurons for bringing out biological performance, it was evident that the conspicuous performance degradation

233

exhibited by parallel machines is caused by the data transmission bottleneck between processors. No definite solution has ever been proposed for this performance degradation problem in most of the parallel machines mentioned.

The capacity of neuron cells and connections in a neurocomputer can be increased with augmented memory capacity. However, on a neurocomputer with enhanced parallel architecture, there is the considerable problem of tangled connections between processors. It is treated as a connectivity problem [17] between processors that is constrained by physical implementation and a mapping problem of a neural network connecting graph to a communication graph between physical processors that gives the minimum data transmission between processors [18].

The parallel architecture of a neurocomputer should be independent of the configurations and sizes of the neural networks. To obtain this independence, it is necessary to develop a mapping algorithm from neural network configurations to parallel processor configurations and a load balancing algorithm between processors; and, to minimize the number of transactions between processors as mentioned. How a simulation task of a neural network with various configurations and sizes is divided into subtasks and how they are assigned to physical processors to balance loads are important problems for efficient parallel processing. The load balancing problem is closely related to the dimensions of parallelism. The data partitioning approach [1] and the network partitioning approach [2,3,9] have been tried. The data partitioning approach is dependent on learning algorithms and needs the duplication of stored data. In the network partitioning approach, the number of transactions is also the number of connections between the partial cell sets of the neural network that are partitioned to assign them to physical processors. Partition and assignment problems result in the above-mentioned mapping problem when the number of connections is minimized.

A neurocomputer should support as many types of artificial neural network models [17, 19] as possible, such as the multilayer perceptron (MLP) [20], the Hopfield network [21], the recurrent networks [22], the Boltzmann machine [23], the Neocognitron [24], the adaptive resonance theory (ART II) [25], the reduced coulomb energy (RCE) [26], Kohonen's feature map network [27], and so on. In applications of artificial neural networks, an appropriate artificial neural network model is selected for each application. It should also have the potential to simulate new artificial neural network models. The conventional neural network models are being improved and revised and new models are being created, because artificial neural network models to date are simple and elementary compared with the biological neuron models, such as the Hodgkin-Huxley equation [28] of a neuron cell. That is, the artificial neural network models are under research and development and are not fixed to some typical and definitive neural network models.

In this chapter, we propose a toroidal lattice architecture (TLA) [29–31] and a planar lattice architecture (PLA) [31, 32] as massively parallel architectures for large-scale neural network computations that satisfy the four conditions mentioned. They also give a solution to the problems of the connectivity constraints, the performance degradation caused by the data transmission bottleneck, and load balancing for efficient parallel processing. The processor connections of these architectures are configured in toroidal lattice and complete planar lattice structures that are most efficient for implementation using a wafer scale integration (WSI) and can be expanded to an even greater degree of parallelism. The performance of these architectures is almost proportional to the number of processors. Furthermore, this architecture exhibits great flexibility in simulating the various neural network architectures and a variety of neuron models.

First, we define a general neuron model and split the neuron into synapse and cell functions. Then, we describe virtual processors (VPs), each with the TLA and PLA, and explain how they simulate a Hopfield neural network [21] and an MLP with the backpropagation algorithm [20] as typical neuron models. Next, we show the partitions of VPs, each with the TLA and PLA, to map them onto the physical node processors with the same TLA and PLA, and the permutations to balance the computational loads of the node processors with the mapping algorithm. The system performances of TLA and PLA are estimated and the proportional relation between the performance and the number of node processors is derived.

Finally, a parallel neurocomputer with the TLA is implemented by 16 Transputers. A Hopfield network for the traveling salesman problem and an MLP for the identity mapping (IM) are implemented on the parallel neurocomputer. In the neural network simulations, the performances of approximately 2 million connections per second (MCPS) for the Hopfield network and 600 KCPS for the MLP learning procedure are obtained. It was proven by implementing the TLA on the four different numbers of Transputers that the performance of TLA is almost proportional to the number of node processors.

## 8.2 General Neuron Model

A general model of artificial neurons is shown in Figure 8.1 and is represented by Equations 8.1 and 8.2.

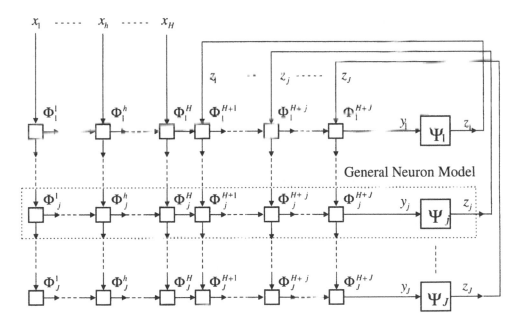

FIGURE 8.1. A general neuron model and a general neural network.

$$y_j = \Phi(\phi(v_1), \phi(v_2), \ldots, \phi(v_i), \ldots, \phi(v_{H+J}))$$
$$= \Phi(\phi(v_i), \Phi(\phi(v_1), \phi(v_2), \ldots, \phi(v_{i-1}), \phi(v_{i+1}), \ldots, \phi(v_{H+J}))) \quad (8.1)$$
$$z_j = \Psi(y_j) \quad (j = 1, 2, \ldots, J) \quad (8.2)$$

where $\mathbf{z} = (z_1, \ldots, z_J)$ is the output vector of neurons, $\mathbf{x} = (x_1, \ldots, x_H)$ is the input vector to the neural network, and $\mathbf{v} = (v_1, \ldots, v_K) = (x_1, \ldots, x_H, z_1, \ldots, z_J)$, $K = H + J$. Though this model is very simple, it represents the essential functions of artificial neuron models. Equation, 8.1, in which $\Phi$ satisfies the associative rule, can be considered to correspond to the function of synapses and dendrites; that is, the weighted accumulation of input pulses from other neurons and sensor such as Equations 8.3 and 8.7, where $w_{i,j}$ is the weight of a connection between neurons or between a neuron and an input. Equation 8.1 can also correspond to other multiply-accumulate operations as in Equation 8.12. Equation 8.2 corresponds to the functions of a cell body: the threshold function, temporal inhibition, and so on. The function $\Psi(y_j)$ is defined by different equations corresponding to the types of artificial neuron models. For example, $\Psi(y_j)$ is the function given by a differential Equation 8.5 and a sigmoid function for the Hopfield model or a sigmoid function (Equation 8.8) for the Perceptron.

**Hopfield Model.**

$$y_j(t) = \sum_{k=1}^{J} T_{k,j}(t) \cdot z_k(t) - x_j(t) = \sum_{i=1}^{K} w_{i,j}(t) \cdot v_i(t) \ (j = 1, 2, \ldots, J) \tag{8.3}$$

where

$$K = 2J, \quad w_{i,j}(t) = 0 \text{ if } i \neq j, \quad w_{j,j} = -1, \quad w_{J+k,j}(t) = T_{k,j}(t), \tag{8.4}$$

$$\frac{d}{dt} u_j(t) \approx u_j(t) - u_j(t-1) = -\gamma \cdot u_j(t) + y_j(t), \tag{8.5}$$

$$z_j(t) = f(u_j(t)) = \frac{1}{1 + e^{-u_j(t)/T}}. \tag{8.6}$$

**Multilayer Perceptron.** (Activation Forward Propagation)

$$y_j(n) = \sum_{i=1}^{K} w_{i,j}(n) \cdot v_i(n), \quad (j = 1, 2, \ldots, J) \tag{8.7}$$

$$z_j(n) = f(y_j(n)) = \frac{1}{1 + e^{-y_j(n)/T}}. \tag{8.8}$$

**Error Backpropagation.**

$$\Delta w_{i,j}(n) = \alpha \cdot \delta_j(n) \cdot v_i(n) \tag{8.9}$$

$$w_{i,j}(n+1) = w_{i,j}(n) + \Delta w_{i,j}(n) + \beta \cdot \Delta w_{i,j}(n-1). \tag{8.10}$$

**<Output Layer>**

$$\delta_j(n) = z_j \cdot (1 - z_j(n)) \cdot (t_j(n) - z_j(n)). \tag{8.11}$$

**<Hidden Layer>**

$$S_j(n) = \sum_{i=1}^{J} \delta_i(n) \cdot w_{k,i}(n), \quad (k = g(j) = H + j, \ H \leq k \leq K) \tag{8.12}$$

$$\delta_j(n) = z_j \cdot (1 - z_j(n)) \cdot S_j(n). \tag{8.13}$$

The basic idea of the general neuron model is that a neuron is split into synapses and a cell body as a unit of simulation. Furthermore, Equation 8.1 can be changed into a recursion formula (Equation 8.14), which corresponds to each synapse function.

$$\Phi^i = \Phi(\Phi^{i-1}, \phi(v_i))$$

where

$$\Phi^i = \Phi(\phi(v_1), \phi(v_2), \dots, \phi(v_i)). \tag{8.14}$$

This recursion formula is applied to Equations 8.3 and 8.7 as shown in Equation 8.15.

$$y_j^i(n) = y_j^{i-1}(n) + w_{i,j}(n) \cdot v_i(n) \text{ or } y_j^i(n) = y_j^{i+1}(n) + w_{i,j}(n) \cdot v_i(n)$$
$$(i = 1, 2, \dots, K, j = 1, 2, \dots, J). \tag{8.15}$$

where $y_j^i(n)$ is a partial accumulation of an active potential.

The accumulation of error levels given in Equation 8.12 is also changed to the recursion formula.

$$S_k^i(n) = S_k^{i-1} + w_{k,i}(n) \cdot \delta_i(n) \text{ or } S_k^i(n) = S_k^{i+1} + w_{k,i}(n) \cdot \delta_i(n),$$
$$(k = 1, 2, \dots, K, \quad j = 1, 2, \dots, J) \tag{8.16}$$

where $S_k^i(n)$ is a partial accumulation of error levels.

The splitting operations make it possible to simulate a neuron with many different processors and to realize a new enhanced parallel processing architecture.

## 8.3 Toroidal Lattice and Planar Lattice Architectures of Virtual Processors

In this section, a TLA and a PLA of virtual processors (VPs) are proposed, as shown in Figure 8.2 and Figure 8.3. The VPs consist of a synapse processor (SP), a cell processor (CP), an input processor (IP), an output processor (OP), and an input/output processor (IOP). The SP has the functions corresponding to the functions of a synapse that are the product-sum operation given in Equations 8.3, 8.7, and 8.12 and the updating operations of its weight given in Equations 8.9 and 8.10. The CP includes the functions of the SP and has the functions corresponding to the activation functions of a cell body such as the threshold functions given in Equations 8.6 and 8.8, the neurodynamic functions given in Equation 8.5, and the error evaluations given in Equations 8.11 and 8.13. The IP, OP, and IOP have communication functions between a host computer and VPs. They receive training data and target data from a host computer, then send the status of the neural network, such as the outputs of cell bodies and connection weights, back to the host computer. VPs on the nodes of a toroidal or planar lattice are arranged as shown in Figures 8.2 and 8.3. CPs are placed on the diagonal of the $J \times J$ square region. The SPs and CPs are each connected to their four nearest neighbors with one-way channels in the TLA and with bidirectional channels in the PLA. In the TLA, each VP on the four edges of the rectangular lattice has a oneway connection to one on the edge of opposite side. Although, in the PLA, the VPs on the edge of the rectangular lattice have no connection to the outside, except IPs, OPs, and IOPs connected to the host computer through a bus line.

## 8.4 The Simulation of a Hopfield Neural Network

The simulation of a Hopfield neural network (HNN) as a typical example of neural networks is described. The simulation of the HNN is executed through the processing flow

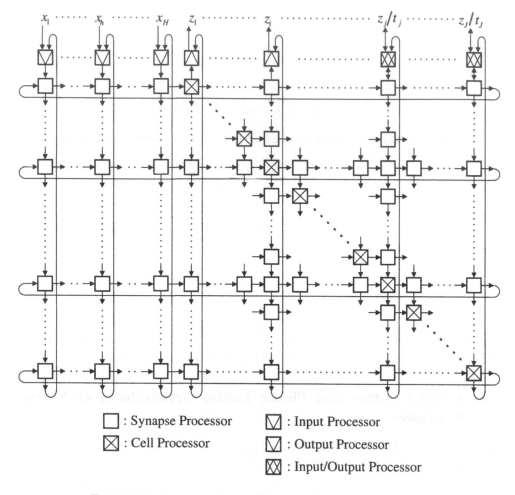

: Synapse Processor     : Input Processor

: Cell Processor     : Output Processor

: Input/Output Processor

FIGURE 8.2. Virtual processors with the toroidal lattice architecture.

shown in Figure 8.4. In the process, the weight calculation process is executed on the host computer. Each weight calculation is different depending on each problem. In an optimization problem, for example, a weight matrix is calculated from an energy function [33].

In this chapter the simulations of the HNN on the TLA and PLA are described.

### 8.4.1 The Simulation of an HNN on TLA

The HNN simulation is performed on the TLA, as shown in Figure 8.4.

1. Initialization

   Each weight to be stored in each SP or CP is transferred from the host computer through the one-way vertical connections of an IP and SPs or connections of an IOP, SPs, and a CP. The output $z_j(t)$ of each CP is initialized at random.

2. Deliveries of input data and CP output data

   Each IP feeds an input datum at time $t$, $v_i(t) = x_i(t)$ received from the host computer and delivers it to the SPs in the same column through the one way vertical

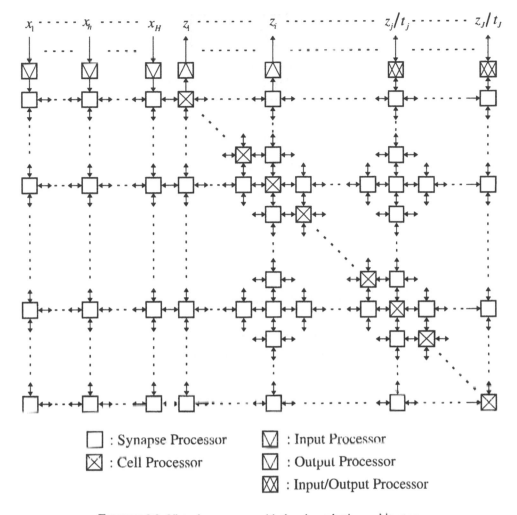

FIGURE 8.3. Virtual processors with the planar lattice architecture.

connections of them. Each CP sends its output downward and delivers it to all SPs on the same column through the one-way round connections of the SPs.

3. Calculations of activations

In this procedure, the product-sum operations given in Equation 8.3 are executed on the SPs and CP through the row, as shown in Figure 8.5.

Each CP sends the initial zero value of the partial accumulation $y_j^{J+j}(t) = 0$ to the right adjacent SP. Each SP receives the partial accumulation $y_j^{i-1}(t)$ from the left adjacent SP or CP and adds the product $w_{i,j}(t) \cdot v_i(t)$ to it. The SP sends the result as the new partial accumulation $y_j^i(t)$ to the right adjacent SP or CP. The product-accumulation operations go along the row and when each CP receives the $y_j^{J+j-1}(t)$ from the left adjacent SP as the action potential $y_j(t)$ in Equation 8.3, the CP performs the approximation of the differential equation (Equation 8.5) and the sigmoid calculation (Equation 8.6) to determine the state value $z_j(t)$ and then stores the result in its memory.

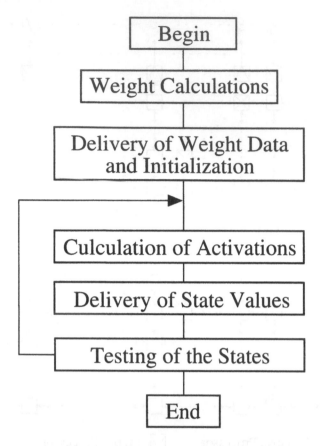

FIGURE 8.4. Processing flow for the MLP simulation.

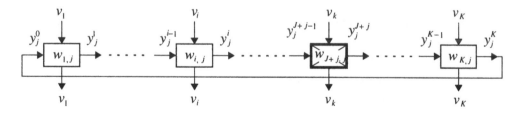

FIGURE 8.5. Data flow in the calculations of activations on the TLA.

4. Monitoring of the network state

Each CP sends the state value $z_j(t)$ to the host computer through the one way round connections of the SPs and an IOP in the same column to report the state of the HNN to the host computer.

Procedures 2 and 4 are repeated until the state of the HNN has fallen into one of attractors that are steady states and limit cycles.

### 8.4.2   The Simulation of an HNN on PLA

The HNN simulation flow on the PLA is the same as that on the TLA, as shown in Figure 8.4.

1. Initialization

   Each weight to be stored in each SP or CP is transferred from the host computer through the vertical downward connections of an IP and SPs or downward connections of an IOP, SPs, and a CP. The output $z_j(t)$ of each CP is initialized at random.

2. Deliveries of input data and CP output data

   Each IP feeds an input datum at time $t$, $v_i(t) = x_i(t)$ received from the host computer and delivers it to the SPs in the same column through the vertical downward connections of them. Each CP sends its output to both upper and lower adjacent SPs. The output is delivered to the SPs of the same column on the upper side of the CP through the upward connections of the SPs and to the SPs of the same column on the lower side of the CP through the downward connections of the SPs.

3. Calculations of Activations

   In this procedure, the product-sum operations given in Equation 8.3 are executed on the SPs and CP through the row, as shown in Figure 8.6.

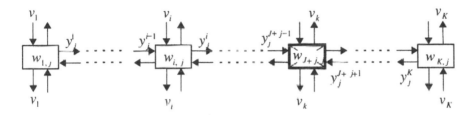

FIGURE 8.6. Data flow in the calculations of activations on the PLA.

In the SPs of both right and left edges, the partial accumulations are initialized at $y_j^1(t) = w_{1,j}(t) \cdot v_1(t)$ and $y_j^K(t) = w_{K,j}(t) \cdot v_K(t)$. Each SP on the left side of the CP receives the partial accumulation $y_j^{i-1}(t)$ from the left adjacent SP and adds the product $w_{i,j}(t) \cdot v_i(t)$ to it. The result $y_j^i(t)$ of the product-sum operation is sent to the right adjacent SP as a partial accumulation. Each SP on the right side of the CP executes the same operation from right to left. These product-accumulation operations are completed when both of the partial accumulations reach the CP. The CP adds both partial accumulations sent from the right and left sides of SPs $y_j^{J+j}(t) = y_j^{J+j-1}(t) + y_j^{J+j+1}(t)$ as the $y_j(t)$ in Equation 8.3. The CP performs the approximation of the differential equation (Equation 8.5) and the sigmoid calculation (Equation 8.6) to determine the state value $z_j(t)$ and then stores the result in its memory.

4. Monitoring of the network state

   Each CP sends the state value $z_j(t)$ to the host computer through the upward connections of the SPs and an IOP in the same column to report the state of the HNN to the host computer.

Procedures 2 and 4 are repeated until the state of the HNN has fallen into one of attractors that are steady states and limit cycles.

## 8.5   The Simulation of a Multilayer Perceptron

The simulation of a multilayer perceptron (MLP) as a typical example of neural networks is described. The simulation of the MLP is executed through the processing flow shown in Figure 8.7. In this section, the procedure for the simulation of the error backpropagation algorithm on the TLA is described, because the simulation on the PLA was described previously [32] in detail.

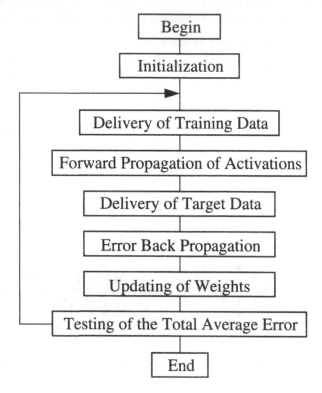

FIGURE 8.7. Processing flow for the MLP simulation.

1. Initialization

   Each weight stored in an SP or CP is initialized at some small random number. The output $z_i(n)$ of each CP is initialized at zero.

2. Deliveries of training data and CP outputs data

   Each IP feeds the $n$-th training data $v_i(n) = x_i(n)$ received from the host computer and delivers it to the SPs and CP in the same column through the connections of them. Each CP sends its output downward and delivers it to all SPs through the round connections on the same column.

3. Forward propagations of activations

   In this procedure which is almost the same as the HNN simulation, the product-sum operations given in Equation 8.15 are executed on the SPs and CP through the row, as shown in Figure 8.8 (a).

   Each CP sends the initial zero value of the partial accumulation $y_j^k(n) = 0$, ($k = g(j)$) to the right adjacent SP. Each SP receives the partial accumulation $y_j^{i-1}(n)$

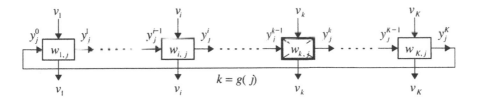

FIGURE 8.8. (a) Data flow during the activation forward propagation.

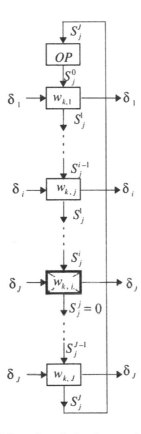

FIGURE 8.8. (b) Data flow during the error backpropagation.

from the left adjacent SP or CP and adds the product $w_{i,j}(n) \cdot v_i(n)$ to it. The SP sends the result as the new partial accumulation $y_j^i(n)$ to the right adjacent SP or CP. The product-accumulation operations go round along the row and when each CP receives the $y_j^{k-1}(n)$ from the left adjacent SP as the active potential $y_j(n)$ in Equation 8.7, the CP performs the sigmoid calculation (Equation 8.8) to determine the activation level $z_j(n)$ and then stores the result in its memory. To propagate activations from the input to the final output layer, procedures 2 and 3 are repeated the same number of times M-1 as the total number of hidden and output layers.

4. Deliveries of target data

Each IOP feeds the target data $t_j(n)$ received from the host computer and delivers it to the CP that belongs to the output layer in the same column through the SPs on the

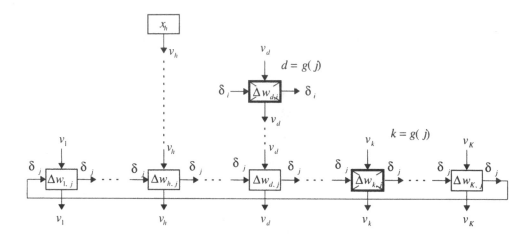

FIGURE 8.8. (c) Data flow during the weight updating.

way. The SPs between the IOP and the CP transfer the target data downward. Each CP in the output layer calculates the initial error $\delta_j(n)$ in Equation 8.11. Each CP in the hidden layers initializes the error $\delta_j(n)$ at zero.

5. Error backpropagations

This procedure is executed vertically in the same way as the forward propagation procedures, as shown in Figure 8.8 (b). Before that, each CP releases its error level $\delta_j(n)$ to all SPs on the same row.

Each CP sends the initial zero value of the partial accumulation $S_j^j(n) = 0$ to the lower adjacent SP. Each SP receives the partial accumulation $S_j^{i-1}(n)$ from the upper adjacent SP or CP and adds it to the product $\delta_i(n) \cdot w_k^i(n)$ $(k = g(j))$. The SP sends the result as $S_j^i(n)$ to the lower adjacent SP or CP. The product-sum operations go round along the column and each CP receives the $S_j^{j-1}(n)$ as the integrated error $S_j(n)$ in Equation 8.12 and the CP performs Equation 8.13 to determine the error level $\delta_j(n)$ then stores the result in its memory.

This procedure is repeated M-2 times to propagate errors from the output layer to the first hidden layer.

6. Updating of weights

As shown in Figure 8.8 (c), each CP delivers the error level $\delta_j(n)$ to the SPs in the same row through the right adjacent SP. Each CP delivers the output $v_k(n) = z_i(n)$, $(k = g(i))$ to the SPs in the same column through the lower adjacent SP. After the delivery, all SPs and CPs calculate the weight changes using Equation 8.9 and update the weights using Equation 8.7.

7. Testing of the total average error

Procedures 2 to 6 are repeated until the average or maximum value of errors between the activation data and the target data becomes less than the small constant.

One important point for the preceding procedures is that the switch-overs between the horizontal and vertical product-sum operations are smoothly executed by the horizontal and vertical data deliveries from the diagonally arranged CPs.

## 8.6  Mapping onto Physical Node Processors from Virtual Processors

The number of VPs with the TLA and the PLA* described in Sections 8.3, 8.4, and 8.5 is proportional to the square of the number of neurons and is quite large. This would not be feasible for millions of neurons. In this section, we attempt to map the VPs onto a feasible number of physical node processors (NP) by partitioning the rectangular lattice. The rows of the rectangular lattice are partitioned into $Q$ ($Q < H + J$) parts and the columns are partitioned into $P$ ($P < J + 1$) parts as shown in Figure 8.9. A physical node processor is assigned to the VPs in each rectangular region formed by the preceding partitions and each physical node processor is connected to its four nearest neighbors with one-way channels in the TLA and bidirectional channels in the PLA in the same manner as the VPs. Consequently, the $P \times Q$ physical node processors form a toroidal lattice, and a planar lattice, as shown in Figure 8.10 and Figure 8.11, respectively. The NPs in the first row are connected to the host computer through a bus line. A microprocessor with data memories and four communication channels can be used as the NP, but it must have a high-speed product-sum operation.

Each NP sequentially executes the functions of the VPs included in the assigned rectangular region, as shown in Figure 8.12. The product-sum operations of the SPs and CPs are integrated into one equation. Equations 8.7 and 8.12 are again changed into Equations 8.17 and 8.18 and Equations 8.19 and 8.20, respectively.

$$B_j^q(n) = \sum_{i=I_{bq}}^{I_{eq}} w_{i,j}(n) \cdot v_i(n), \quad q = 1, 2, \ldots, Q, \ j = 1, 2, \ldots, J \tag{8.17}$$

$$y_j^q(n) = y_j^{q-1}(n) + B_j^q(n) \text{ or } y_j^q(n) = y_j^{q+1}(n) + B_j^q(n) \tag{8.18}$$

where $I_{bq}$ is the beginning column and $I_{eq}$ is the end column in the rectangular region.

$$D_k^p(n) = \sum_{i=J_{bp}}^{J_{ep}} w_{k,i}(n) \cdot \delta_i(n), \quad p = 1, 2, \ldots, P, \ k = g(j),$$

$$1 \le k \le K, \quad j = 1, 2, \ldots, J \tag{8.19}$$

$$E_k^p(n) = E_k^{p-1}(n) + D_k^p(n) \text{ or } E_k^p(n) = E_k^{p+1}(n) + D_k^p(n) \tag{8.20}$$

where $J_{bp}$ is the beginning row and $J_{ep}$ is the end row in the rectangular region.

The partial accumulations in Equations 8.17 and 8.19 are calculated on all NPs simultaneously, and the partial accumulations in Equations 8.18 and 8.20 are calculated through the NPs in the same row and column sequentially.

The procedures on NPs for the error backpropagation algorithm of the MLP are executed in almost the same way as in Section 8.5. The different parts of the activation forward propagation and the error backpropagation are described as follows:

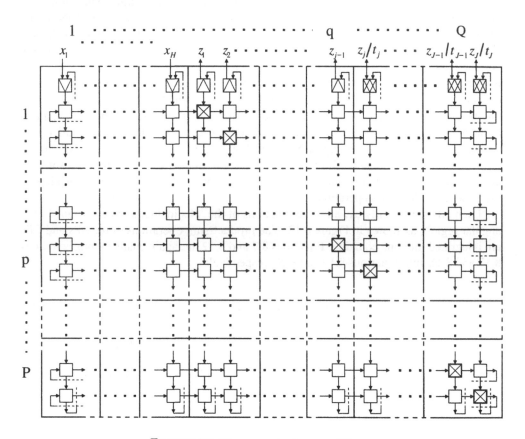

FIGURE 8.9. The row and column partitions.

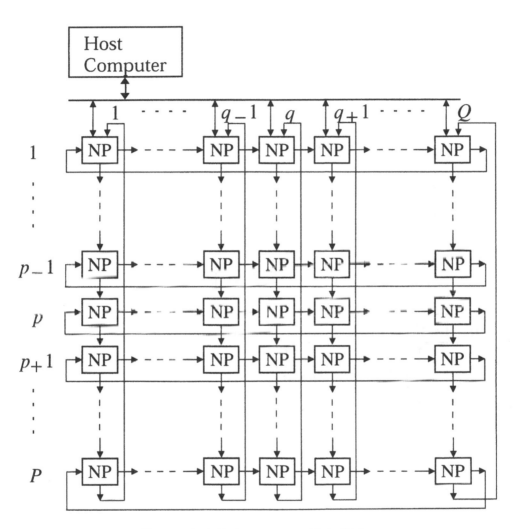

FIGURE 8.10. Node processors with the TLA.

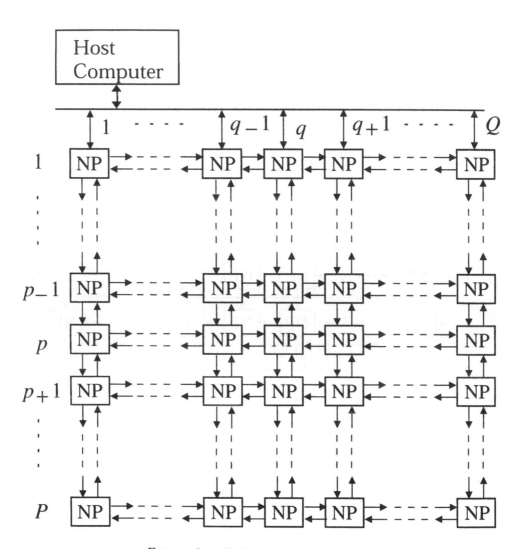

FIGURE 8.11. Node processors with the PLA.

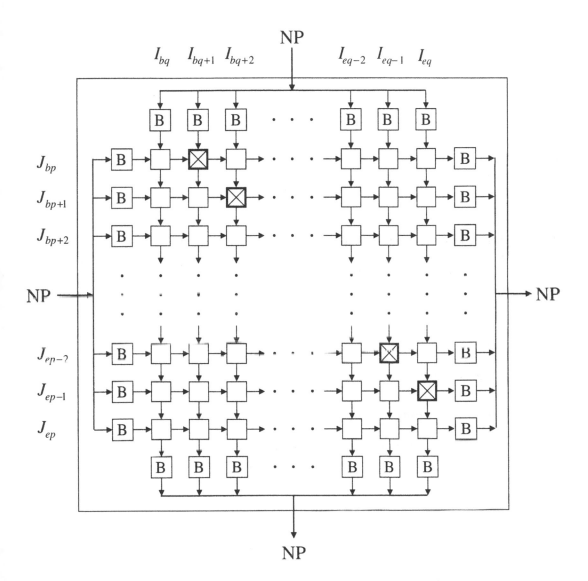

FIGURE 8.12. VPs in partitioned rectangular region assigned to an NP.

1. Forward Propagations of Activations

   Each NP that includes CPs delivers the outputs of the CPs with their column numbers to the NPs on the same column through the one-way round connections on the TLA. Each NP receives the data $v_i(n)$ with its column number "$i$." from the upper adjacent NP and holds it in the $i$-th buffer memory and sends it to the lower adjacent NP with the column number "$i$." All NPs execute the calculations of the partial sums in Equation 8.17 simultaneously.

   Each NP that includes the $j$-th CP sends the partial sum $B_j^r(n)$ with the row number "$j$" as the initial value of the partial accumulation $y_j^r(n)$ to the right adjacent NP. Each NP receives a partial accumulation $y_j^{q-1}(n)$ for the $j$-th CP with the row number "$j$" from the left adjacent NP and adds it to the partial sum $B_j^q(n)$ in Equation 8.18. The NP sends the result with the row number "$j$" as the new one $y_j^q(n)$ to the right adjacent NP. When each NP that includes the $j$-th CP receives the $y_j^{r-1}(n)$ with the row number "$j$" from the left adjacent NP, the NP makes it equal to the active potential $y_j(n)$ given in Equation 8.7 and performs the sigmoid calculation in Equation 8.8 to determine the activation level $z_j(n)$. The result is stored in its memory.

2. Error Backpropagations

   The product sum of the backpropagation calculations given in Equations 8.19 and 8.20 is executed vertically in the same way as the forward propagation calculations by exchanging row and column. Finally, an NP that contains the $j$-th CP executes Equation 8.13 to determine the error level $\delta_j(n)$.

   In this procedure, one remarkable point is that the transmission of partial accumulations of active potentials and error levels can be executed simultaneously during the calculations given Equation 8.17 to Equation 8.20. That is, during the calculation of product sums $B_j^q(n)$, the $q$-th NP can send the data of partial accumulation $y_{j-1}^q$ to the adjacent NP through the direct memory access (DMA) channel.

## 8.7 Load Balancing of Node Processors

The load balancing of NPs is the crucial problem for efficient parallel processing in the simulation of large-scale neural networks. In this section, the row and column permutations of the VP rectangular array before mapping VPs to NPs by the partitions are proposed for the load balancing.

When the VP matrix for the Hopfield network or the MLP is partitioned and assigned to NPs in the TLA and PLA neurocomputer, how we can partition the matrix into submatrices with good load balance is a tangled problem. The main reason is that the computational load of each kind of VP is different. For example, the CP load is about 10 times that of the SP, and the SP with zero weight has no load. Therefore, if we try to partition the original VP matrix, such as the one shown in Figure 8.13 for an MLP, simply, no adequate partition could be found with good load balancing.

To partition the VP matrix equally, a permutation before partitioning is one solution for load balancing. The basic ideas are to permute rows and columns with no effect of Equations 8.17, 8.18, 8.19, and 8.20 by the assumption of the associative rule of Equation 8.1 defining the general neuron model and to distribute to the NPs the rectangular sub-regions obtained by dividing homogeneous or methodically arranged rectangular regions ($h/m$ rectangular region). For examples, six kinds of $h/m$ rectangular regions are shown in Figure 8.14.

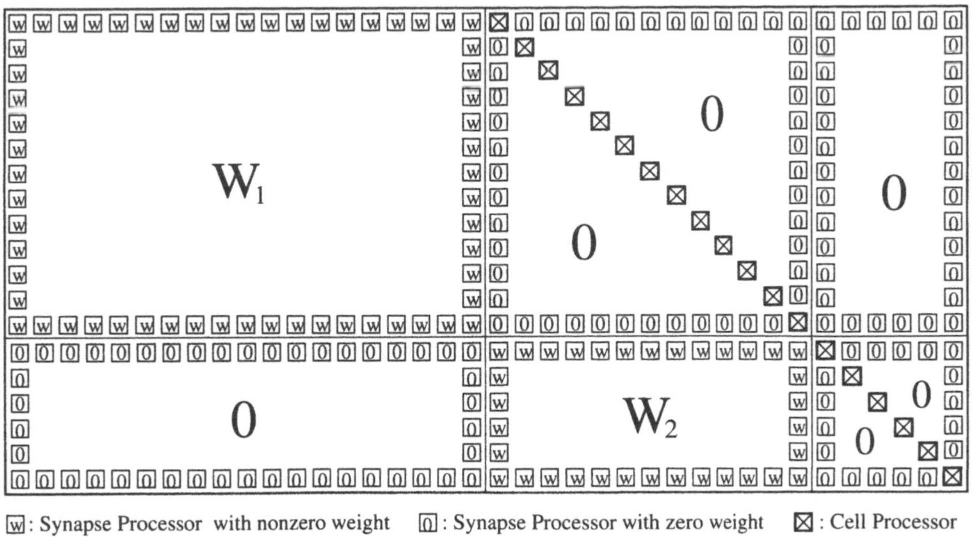

w: Synapse Processor with nonzero weight   n: Synapse Processor with zero weight   ⊠: Cell Processor

FIGURE 8.13. The VP matrix for an MLP with three layers.

The $h/m$ rectangular regions of (a), (b), and (c) are sampled from a matrix of an MLP. The $h/m$ rectangular regions of (d) and (e) are sampled from a matrix of a Hopfield network. The $h/m$ rectangular region of (f) corresponds to local connections in an MLP. The subdivisions of the $h/m$ rectangular regions in a typical matrix of a three-layer MLP are shown in Figure 8.15.

Each $h/m$ rectangular region is divided into $P \times Q$ subregions or $P \times PQ$ subregions. Subregions are rearranged by permutations so that the divided subregions of each $h/m$ rectangular region are equally included in each submatrix assigned to NPs, as shown in Figure 8.16.

By this rearrangement, the matrix can be easily partitioned almost uniformly into submatrices and the VPs included in those submatrices are assigned to NPs as shown in Figure 8.17. Each NP has almost the same number of SPs and CPs, that is, the load of each NP is nearly equal.

Further, the load balancing algorithm is described in Appendix A8.1 as a row and column mapping by permutations and partitions that is a little complicated for reducing differences caused by residuals in partitioning of the rectangular subregions. Even though this algorithm is based on the existence of a homogeneous or methodically arranged rectangular region in a given matrix, it is applicable to nearly all neural network models on the assumption that they have some regularities on their connections.

## 8.8   Estimation of the Performance

Under the load balancing condition, the relation between the performance of these architectures and numbers of neurons, connections, and NPs is derived. Appendix A8.2 shows the derivation of the processing time in one cycle of the error backpropagation algorithm of an MLP for one pair of training and target data on the TLA. In this derivation, for the parallel processing of calculations and inter-NP communications in the activation forward propagation and error backpropagation, the scheduling is described in the next section.

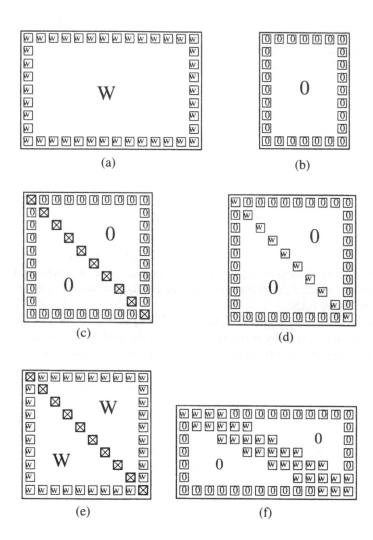

FIGURE 8.14. Homogeneously or methodically arranged rectangular subregions in VP matrices.

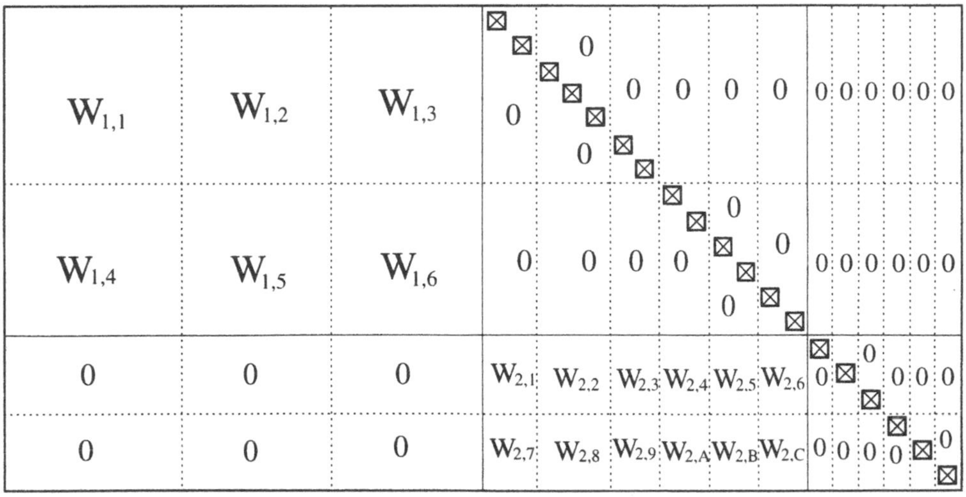

FIGURE 8.15. The subdivision of VPs for the permutations and partitions.

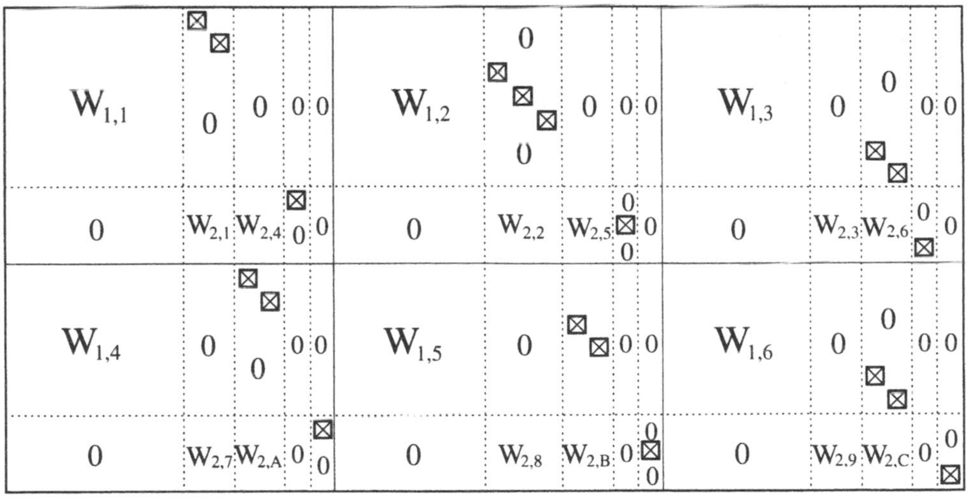

FIGURE 8.16. The result of row and column permutations for load balancing.

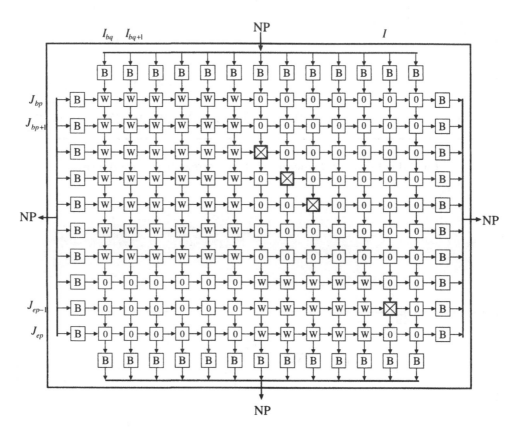

FIGURE 8.17. VPs in the partitioned rectangular region assigned to the NP of the position (1,2) after permutations.

Equation 8.21 gives the upper bound of the one-cycle processing time.

$$T < \frac{N_S}{PQ} \times (\tau_{SF} + \tau_{SB} + \tau_{Su})$$
$$+ \frac{N_C}{PQ} \times (\tau_{CF} + \tau_{CB})$$
$$+ \frac{N_C \times (P + Q - 2) + (N_I + N_O) \times P}{PQ} \times \tau_{ch}$$
$$+ (M \times P + (M - 1) \times Q) \times \tau_{ch}$$
$$+ (M - 1) \times (\tau_{SF} + \tau_{SB} + \tau_{SU} + \tau_{CF} + \tau_{CB}). \tag{8.21}$$

The first and second terms are inversely proportional to the total number of NPs; $P \times Q$ and the third term is inversely proportional to the column or row number of NP array, $P$ or $Q$. In contrast to these terms, the fourth term is the overhead of parallel processing that is proportional to $P$ or $Q$ and the fifth term is constant. However, the first and second terms are dominant for simulations of large-scale neural networks, because the execution times $\tau_{SF} + \tau_{SB} + \tau_{SU}$ and $\tau_{CF} + \tau_{CB}$ are estimated hundreds times of the execution time $\tau_{ch}$, and the value of $N_S/PQ$ and $N_C/PQ$ can be set at considerably greater ones than those of $P$ and $Q$ for large-scale neural networks, for example, hundreds or thousands times of $P$ or $Q$. Furthermore, the execution time $\tau_{ch}$ can be reduced by increasing the channel capacity by a higher transmission rate and higher parallelism. Therefore, the performance that is almost proportional to the number of NPs can be expected in simulations of large-scale neural networks.

## 8.9 Implementation

The TLA neurocomputer system is implemented on 16 Transputers (INMOS T800 processors) in a 4 × 4 NP array with TLA, a root Transputer, and an IBM-PC host, and simulation programs of an MLP and a Hopfield neural network are implemented. The 17 Transputers are assigned as one root processor (RP) and four trunk processors (TP), the NPs on the top row, and the 12 other NPs shown in Figure 8.18. The host computer executes the load balancing algorithm and communicates the network architecture, initial weight matrix, and network active potentials with the RP. It also distributes the submatrices to the NPs through the RP and TPs. The RP is used mainly for communication between the host computer and other NPs. In the simulation of an MLP, the TP has four tasks: holding pairs of input and target data; computing the weighted accumulation of an active potential and an error; communicating the weights of virtual submatrices, partial active potentials, and partial errors with adjacent NPs; and uploading the status of the NPs. Except for holding pairs of input and target data and uploading the status of the NPs, the other NPs play the same role as a TP.

First, the host computer maps the columns and rows of the VP matrix onto those of an NP array to balance loads of NPs by permutations and partitions and sends the VP submatrix configurations to NPs through the RP. Next, the RP delivers the assigned VP submatrix configuration to each NP through a TP. Then, each NP starts neurocomputing on its assigned VP submatrix that is described in the next paragraph in detail. Finally, the computing result is collected and sent to the host computer through the RP and TPs.

The neurocomputing for the forward propagation of an MLP simulation is implemented in each NP as follows. The process control and data flow in an NP for the forward propagation and the time chart of those process executions are shown in Figure 8.19 and Figure 8.20, respectively. There are two types of processes. One is a CPU process such as the

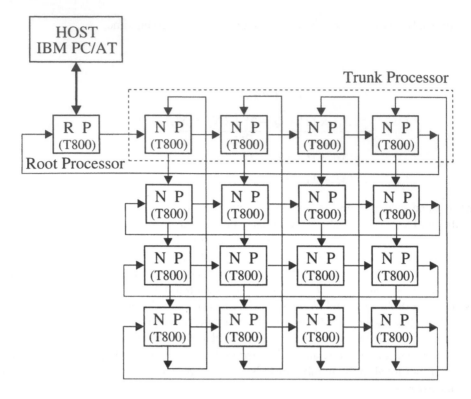

FIGURE 8.18. Implementation of the TLA on a Transputer array.

calculation of product-sums (CPS), the calculation of partial accumulation (CPA), and the calculation of sigmoid function (CSF). The other is an I/O process such as vertical delivery of data (VDD), transferring data (TD), sending initial partial-accumulation (SIPA), receiving a partial accumulation (RPA), and sending a partial-accumulation (SPA). They can be simultaneously executed by a CPU and DMA channels in each NP. The host computer starts the VDD and TD processes. They deliver input data in the calculation of the first hidden layer and transfer outputs of neurons in the calculation of the other layers. When all the data for the next calculations are stored in the data buffer, each NP selects the first row in which a CP of the first hidden layer is included in the NP and executes the CPS process for the selected row. Its result is sent to the right adjacent NP as the initial partial-accumulation value by the SIPA process. Here, the numbers of the first selected rows of the four NPs on the $p$-th row are presented as $r_{p1}(1)$, $r_{p1}(2)$, $r_{p1}(3)$, and $r_{p1}(4)$. Each of four NPs on the $p$-th row has been previously programmed by the host computer to execute the CPS processes for the rows with no CP in the following orders:

- The execution order of the first NP is $[r_{p1}(4), r_{p1}(3), r_{p1}(2)]$.

- The execution order of the second NP is $[r_{p1}(1), r_{p1}(4), r_{p1}(3)]$.

- The execution order of the third NP is $[r_{p1}(2), r_{p1}(1), r_{p1}(4)]$.

- The execution order of the fourth NP is $[r_{p1}(3), r_{p1}(2), r_{p1}(1)]$.

Therefore, when each NP receives the partial accumulation and finishes the CPS process, it can execute the CPA process to get the new partial accumulation by adding the old

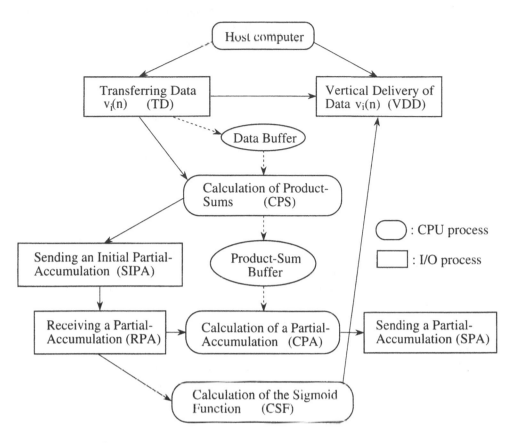

FIGURE 8.19. Process control and data flow in an NP for the forward propagation.

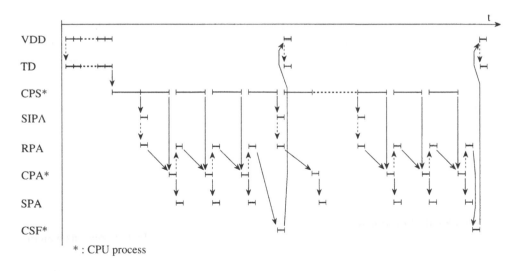

FIGURE 8.20. Time chart of process executions in an NP for the forward propagation.

one and partial product sum and then the SPA process to send it to the right adjacent NP, as shown in Figure 8.20. When each NP receives the partial accumulation of the row in which a CP is included, that partial accumulation is used as the active potential to determine the activation level by the CSF process. When the first processing cycle for the first selected rows is completed, each of the four NPs selects the second row $r_{p2}(1)$, $r_{p2}(2)$, $r_{p2}(3)$, or $r_{p2}(4)$ in which a CP of the first hidden layer is included in the NP and repeats the same processes mentioned. The activation level is delivered to NPs on the same column for the next layer calculation by the VDD and TD processes. When all the rows of the first hidden layer, including a CP, have been selected, the calculations for the first hidden layer are completed. When the outputs of the first hidden layer are delivered vertically to each of 16 NPs, the calculations for the next layer are started. The time chart of Figure 8.20 shows parallel processing of the CPU process and the I/O process clearly. Of course, the 16 Transputers execute the same CPU processes and communication processes with adjacent NPs in parallel.

A Hopfield network for the traveling salesman problem (TSP) and an MLP for the identity mapping (IM) are implemented on the TLA neurocomputer system. This system is able to simulate the Hopfield network to solve the TSP with up to 20 cities and the MLP for the IM of $256 \times 64 \times 256$. It is important to note that the potential number of simulated artificial neurons and connections are only limited by the total memory capacity. In this implementation, the simulation rate on the $4 \times 4$ Transputer array is approximately 2 MCPS for the Hopfield network and 600 KCUPS for the MLP learning procedure. Figure 8.21 shows comparative activation feed-forward propagation and error backpropagation processing performances for several configurations. It was proven by implementing the TLA on the $1 \times 1$, $2 \times 2$, $2 \times 4$, and $4 \times 4$ Transputers array that the performance of TLA is almost proportional to the number of processors. Though the absolute performances are not so high, this indicates the TLA architecture can be expanded for large-scale neural networks.

The performance of the PLA is easily estimated higher than that of the TLA, because the transmission rate of two-way channels between processors of the PLA is higher than that of the TLA. However, the difference between two architectures is considered to be small.

Finally, we try to study the feasibility of the large-scale simulation of MLP neural networks by a parallel neurocomputer with TLA. A target is the high speed simulation of hundreds of billions CUPS for a large-scale MLP with one million neurons and 10 billion connections. The ratio of ten thousand connections per neuron comes from biological information about the human cerebral cortex where the number of synapses connected to a neuron is estimated as 1,000 to 10,000.

First, we have to estimate the learning performance of an NP from its computational power presented by MFLOPS. We got the performance of 0.6 MCUPS using the 16 Transputer T800-20 with the performance of 1.5 MFLOPS. The conversion rate from MFLOPS to MCUPS is roughly estimated to be 1/40 as the worst case. Therefore, if a high-speed microprocessor such as i-860 with the performance of 80 MFLOPS is adopted as an NP, there is a possibility of realizing the performance of more than one hundred billion CUPS by the $256 \times 256$ processor array with the TLA or PLA.

Next, we try to estimate the memory size of an NP, when $256 \times 256$ NPs are available. An SP with a connection has to hold the two weights, present weight and previous weight, and an index for processing sparse connections. Four bytes are needed for the floating point expression of a weight and 2 bytes are needed for the index. The total number of bytes for an SP is 10 bytes. A CP also has to hold the activation level and error level using

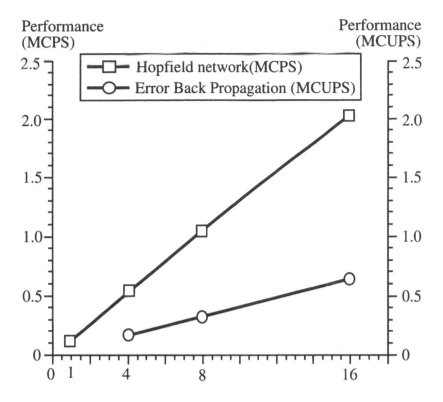

FIGURE 8.21. The experimental performance of the TLA Transputer array.

8 bytes. The total memory size of the neurocomputer is more than 100 billion bytes. Thus, each NP has to have the memory size of more than 2 Mbytes.

## 8.10   Conclusions

The TLA and the PLA, based on a general neuron model, were proposed. They promise enhanced parallel processing and greater expandability of the neurocomputer for high-speed, large-scale simulations of neural networks. They have sufficient flexibility to simulate the various neural network architectures by load balancing algorithm and to simulate a variety of neuron models by programing them on the NPs. The TLA has a topologically planar lattice structure that gives a solution for the connectivity problem. Moreover, the PLA can realize a completely planar lattice structure that is the most efficient for WSI implementation. Although the load balancing algorithm is presented in this chapter for a multilayer neural network, it has great generality and can be easily modified for the other configurations of neural networks such as the configurations with local connections. The performances of these architectures are estimated on parameters such as the numbers of neuron cells, synapses, and NPs, and it is derived that they are almost proportional to the number of NPs.

We developed a prototype of a TLA neurocomputer with the 4×4 Transputers and simulated a Hopfield neural network and a multilayer perceptron; we applied them to the traveling salesman problem and the identity mapping, respectively. This TLA neurocomputer has achieved 2 MCPS in a Hopfield neural network and 600 KCUPS in a backpropagation network using 16 Transputers. Actual proof is given that the performance of the

TLA is almost proportional to the number of processors. Although the absolute performance of 2 MCPS and 600 KCUPS is inadequate because of a Transputer performance of only 1.5 MFLOPS and a small number of processors—16 Transputers— it is concluded that high-speed simulation of more than one hundred billion CUPS for a large-scale MLP neural network with one million neurons and 10 billion connections is feasible using the 256×256 NPs with the 80 MFLOPS of performance and more than 2 Mbytes of memory as the node processors of the TLA or PLA.

In their survey paper [34], Nordström and Sevensson ranked parallel neurocomputers according to the number of processor elements $N$ as follows.

$$\text{Barely parallel: } 2^0 < N < 2^4,$$
$$\text{Moderately parallel: } 2^4 \leq N < 2^8,$$
$$\text{Highly parallel: } 2^8 \leq N < 2^{12},$$
$$\text{Massively parallel: } 2^{12} \leq N.$$

They classified the TLA and PLA in the highly parallel neurocomputer category by the experimental implementation of 16 Transputers. However, the TLA and PLA are architectures exactly suited to massively parallel neurocomputers.

We expect that above-target results will be achieved in the near future because of the improvement of WSI and large-scale integration technologies and our massively parallel architectures.

# Appendices

## A8.1  Load Balancing Mapping Algorithm

The load balancing mapping algorithm from VPs for an M-layer neural network with the TLA or PLA onto NPs with the same TLA or PLA by permutations and partitions is presented with C-like descriptions as follows:

1. Definition

   $N_{Cm}$: the number of neuron cells on the $m$-th layer (the 0-th layer is the input layer).

   $H[m, n]$ $(m = 0, 1, 2, \ldots, M - 1; n = 0, 1, 2, \ldots, PQ - 1)$ : the number of columns included in the $n$-th subregion of the $m$-th layer horizontally.

   $V[m, n]$ $(m = 0, 1, 2, \ldots, M - 1; \ n = 0, 1, 2, \ldots, P - 1)$ : the number of rows included in the $n$-th subregion of the $m$-th layer vertically.

   $h_b[m, n]$: the beginning column number of the $n$-th subregion in horizontal of the $m$-th layer.

   $h_e[m, n]$: the end column number of the $n$-th subregion in horizontal of the $m$ th layer.

   $v_b[m, n]$: the beginning row number of the $n$-th subregion in vertical of the $m$-th layer.

   $v_e[m, n]$: the end row number of the $n$-th subregion in vertical of the $m$-th layer.

   $x, y$: the column number and the low number of a VP, respectively.

   $x'(q)$: the column number of a VP in an NP on the $q$-th column.

   $y'(p)$: the row number of a VP in an NP on the $p$-th row.

2. Preparations of residual adjustments

   /* Initialization. */

   $v.sup = 0; \quad h.sup = 0;$

   /* For column adjustments of the input layer. */

   $b = mod(N_{c0}, P);$
   $\text{for } (h = 0; h < b; h + +)$
   $\quad H[0, h] = N_{C0}/Q + 1;$
   $\text{for } (h = b; h < Q; h + +)$
   $\quad H[0, h] = N_{C0}/Q;$
   $h.sup = h.sup + b;$

/* For row and column adjustments of the cell layers. */

```
for (m = 1; m < M; m++){
    b = mod(N_{Cm}, P);
    for (v = v.sup; v < v.sup + b; v++)
        V[m, v] = N_{Cm}/P + 1;
    for(v = v.sup + b; v < v.sup + P; v++)
        V[m, v] = N_{Cm}/P;
    v.sup = mod(v.sup + b, P);
    for(u = 0; u < P; u++){
        c = mod(V[m, u], Q);
        for (h = h.sup; h < h.sup + c; h++)
            H[m, u × Q + mod(h, Q)] = V[m, u]/Q + 1;
        for (h = h.sup + c; h < h.sup + Q; h++)
            H[m, u × Q + mod(h, Q)] = V[m, u]/Q;
        h.sup = mod(h.sup + c, Q);
    }
}
```

3. Column mapping from the VP array onto the NP array by permutations and partitions.

/* Setting the beginning and end column numbers of subregions*/

$$
\begin{aligned}
&\text{for } (n = 0; n < Q; n++)\{ \\
&\quad h_b[0, n] = \sum_{j=0}^{n-1} H[0, j]; \\
&\quad h_e[0, n] = h_b[0, n] + H[0, n] - 1; \\
&\} \\
&\text{for}(m = 1; m < M; m++)\{ \\
&\quad \text{for } (n = 0; n < PQ; n++)\{ \\
&\quad\quad h_b[m, n] = \sum_{i=0}^{m-1} N_{Ci} + \sum_{j=0}^{n-1} H[m, j]; \\
&\quad\quad h_e[m, n] = h_b[m, n] + H[m, n] - 1; \\
&\quad \} \\
&\}
\end{aligned}
$$

/* The $x$-th column of the VP array is mapped onto the $x'(q)$-th column of the VP subarray in an NP on the $q$-th column of the NP array. */

```
for (q = 0; q < Q; q++){
    for (x = h_b[0, q]; x < h_e[0, q]; x++)
        x'(q) = x - h_b[0, q];
}
for(m = 1; m < M; m++){
    for(j = 0; j < P; j++){
        for (q = 0; q < Q; q++){
            for (x = h_b[m, j × Q + q]; x < h_e[m, j × Q + q]; x++)
                x'(q) = x - h_b[m, j × Q + q] + H[0, q]
```

$$+ \sum_{\substack{i=1 \\ j-1}}^{m-1} \sum_{k=0}^{P-1} H[i, k \times Q + q]$$

$$+ \sum_{k=0}^{j-1} H[m, k \times Q + q];$$

$$\quad \}$$
$$\quad \}$$
$$\}$$

4. Row mappings from the VP array onto the NP array by permutations and partitions.

   /* Setting the beginning and end row numbers of subregions*/

   for $(m = 1; m < M; m + +)\{$
     for $(n = 0; n < P; n + +)\{$
       $$v_b[m, n] = \sum_{i=1}^{m-1} N_{ci} + \sum_{j=0}^{n-1} V[m, j];$$
       $$v_e[m, n] = v_b[m, n] + V[m, n] - 1;$$
     $\}$
   $\}$

   /* The $y$-th row of the VP array is mapped onto the $y'(p)$-th row of the VP subarray in an NP on the $p$-th row of the NP array */

   for $(m = 1; m < M; m + +)\{$
     for $(p = 0; p < P; p + +)\{$
       for $(y = v_b[m, p]; y < v_e[m, p]; y + +)$
       $$y'(p) = y - v_b[m, p] + \sum_{i=1}^{m-1} V[i, p];$$
     $\}$
   $\}$

## A8.2 Processing Time of the NP Array

The processing time of the NP array with the TLA versus the numbers of neuron cells, synapses, and NPs in the simulation of the error backpropagation of an MLP are estimated as follows.

1. Definitions

   $M$: the number of layers of the MLP.

   $N_C$: the total number of neuron cells in the MLP.

   $N_{Ci}$: the total number of neuron cells in the $i$-th layer.

   $N_I$: the total number of inputs of the MLP. ($N_I = N_{C0}$)

   $N_O$: the total number of outputs of the MLP. ($N_O = N_{C(M-1)}$)

   $N_S$: the total number of connections (synapses) in the MLP.

   $N_{Sij}$: the total number of connections from the $i$-th layer to the $j$-th layer.

$\tau_{SF}$: the processing time of the synapse function in the activation forward propagation.

$\tau_{SB}$: the processing time of the synapse function in the error backpropagation.

$\tau_{SU}$: the processing time of the synapse function in the weight updating.

$\tau_{CF}$: the processing time of the cell function in the activation forward propagation.

$\tau_{CB}$: the processing time of the cell function in the error backpropagation.

$\tau_{ch}$: the transfer time of the communication channels in the TLA.

[ ]: Gauss notation.

2. The input data delivery time.

$$T_I < \left( \left[ \frac{N_I}{Q} \right] + 1 \right) \times \tau_{ch} + (P-1) \times \tau_{ch}$$

3. The activation forward propagation time of the $j$-th layer.

$$T_{Fj} \; < \; \left( \left[ \frac{\sum_{i=0}^{j-1} N_{Sij}}{PQ} \right] + 1 \right) \times \tau_{SF} + \left( \left[ \frac{N_{Ci}}{PQ} \right] + 1 \right) \times \tau_{CF} + \tau ch$$

4. The output data delivery time of the $j$-th layer.

$$T_{Oj} < \left( \left[ \frac{N_{Cj}}{PQ} \right] + 1 \right) \times \tau_{ch} \times (P-1)$$

5. The target data delivery time.

$$T_T < \left( \left[ \frac{N_O}{Q} \right] + 1 \right) \times \tau_{ch} + \left( \left[ \frac{N_O}{PQ} \right] + 1 \right) \times \tau_{CB}$$

6. The error data delivery time of the $i$-th layer.

$$T_{Ei} < \left( \left[ \frac{N_{Ci}}{PQ} \right] + 1 \right) \times \tau_{ch} \times (Q-1)$$

7. The error backpropagation time of the $i$-th layer.

$$T_{Bi} < \left( \left[ \frac{\sum_{j=i+1}^{M-1} N_{Sij}}{PQ} \right] + 1 \right) \times \tau_{SB} + \left( \left[ \frac{N_{Ci}}{PQ} \right] + 1 \right) \times \tau_{CB} + \tau_{ch}$$

8. The weight updating time of the $i$-th layer.

$$T_{Ui} < \left( \left[ \frac{\sum_{k=0}^{i-1} N_{Ski}}{PQ} \right] + 1 \right) \times \tau_{SU}$$

9. One cycle time of the error backpropagation algorithm.

$$
\begin{aligned}
T \;=\; & T_I + \sum_{j=1}^{M-1} (T_{Fj} + T_{Oj}) + T_T + \sum_{i=1}^{M-1} (T_{Ei} + T_{Ui}) + \sum_{i=1}^{M-2} T_{Bi} \\
<\; & \frac{N_S}{PQ} \times (\tau_{SF} + \tau_{SB} + \tau_{SU}) \\
& + \frac{N_C}{PQ} \times (\tau_{CF} + \tau_{CB}) \\
& + \frac{N_C \times (P + Q - 2) + (N_I + N_O) \times P}{PQ} \times \tau_{ch} \\
& + (M \times (P + Q) - Q) \times \tau_{ch} \\
& + (M - 1) \times (\tau_{SF} + \tau_{SB} + \tau_{SU} + \tau_{CF} + \tau_{CB}) - \tau_{SB}
\end{aligned}
$$

# References

[1] D. A. Pomerleau, G. L. Gusciora, D. S. Touretzky, and H. T. Kung, "Neural network simulation at warp speed: How we got 17 million connections per second," in *Proceedings of the ICNN*, vol. 2, (San Diego, CA.), pp. 143–150, July 1988.

[2] S. Y. Kung and J. N. Hwang, "Parallel architectures for artificial neural nets," in *Proceedings of the ICNN*, vol. 2, (San Diego, CA.), pp. 165–172, July 1988.

[3] G. Blelloch and C. R. Rosenberg, "Network learning on the Connection Machine," in *Proceedings of the IJCAI*, (Milano, Italy), pp. 323–326, August 1987.

[4] X. Zhang, et. al., "An efficient implementation of the back propagation algorithm on the Connection Machine CM-2," in *Neural Information Processing Systems 2*, pp. 801–809, Denver, CO., 1989.

[5] A. Krikelis and M. Grozinger, "Implementing neural networks with the associative string processor," in *International Workshop for Artificial Intelligence and Neural Networks*, (Oxford), pp. 399–408, 1990.

[6] F. J. Nunez and J. A. B. Fortes, "Performance of connectionist learning algorithms on 2-d SIMD processor arrays," in *Neural Information Processing Systems 2*, pp. 810–817, Denver, CO., 1989.

[7] K. A. Grajski, et. al., "Neural network simulation on the maspar mp-1 massively parallel processor," in *Proceedings of the INNC*, (Paris), p. 673, July 1990.

[8] M. Witbrock and M. Zagha, "An implementation of back-propagation learning on GF11, a large SIMD parallel computer," Tech. Rep. CMU-CS-89-208, Carnegie Mellon University, Computer Science, 1989.

[9] A. Johannet, et. al., "A transputer-based neurocomputer," in *Parallel Programming of Transputer Based Machines: Proceeding of the 7th OCCAM User Group Technical Meeting Grenoble*, (France), pp. 120–127, September 1987.

[10] A. Iwata, et. al., "An artificial neural network accelerator using general purpose 24 bits floating point digital signal processors," in *Proceedings of the IJCNN*, vol. 2, (Washington D.C.), pp. 171–175, June 1989.

[11] T. Watanabe, Y. Sugiyama, T. Kondo, and Y. Kitayama, "Neural network simulation on a massively parallel cellular array processor: Aap-2," in *Proceedings of the IJCNN*, vol. 2, (Washington D.C.), pp. 155–161, June 1989.

[12] H. Kato, et. al., "A parallel neurocomputer architecture towards billion connection updates per second," in *Proceedings of the IJCNN*, vol. 2, (Washington D.C.), pp. 47–50, 1990.

[13] A. Hiraiwa, et. al., "A two level pipe line RISC processor array for ANN," in *Proceedings of the IJCNN*, vol. 2, (Washington D.C.), pp. 137–140, 1990.

[14] D. Hammerstrom, "A VLSI architecture for high-performance, low-cost, on-chip learning," in *Proceedings of the IJCNN*, vol. 2, (San Diego), pp. 537–544, 1990.

[15] B. Svensson and T. Nordstrom, "Execution of neural network algorithms on an array of bit-serial processors," in *The 10th International Conference on Pattern Recognition, Computer architectures for vision and pattern recognition*, vol. 2, (Atlantic City, New Jersey), pp. 501–505, 1990.

[16] M. Yasunaga, et. al., "Design, fabrication and evaluation of a 5-inch wafer scale neural network LSI composed of 576 digital neurons," in *Proceedings of the IJCNN*, vol. 2, (San Diego), pp. 527–535, July 1990.

[17] DARPA, ed., *Neural Network Study*. AFCEA International Press, November 1989.

[18] T. Beynon and N. Dodd, "The implementation of multi-layer perceptrons on transputer networks," in *Parallel Programming of Transputer Based Machines: Proceedings of the 7th OCCAM User Group Technical Meeting*, (Grenoble, France), pp. 108–119, September 1987.

[19] R. P. Lippmann, "An introduction to computing with neural nets," *IEEE ASSP Magazine*, pp. 4–22, April 1987.

[20] D. E. Rumelhart, G. E. Hinton, and R. J. Williams, "Learning internal representations by error propagation," in *Parallel Distributed Processing : Explorations in the Microstructure of Cognition. Vol. 1 : Foundations.*, pp. 318–362, MIT Press, 1986.

[21] J. J. Hopfield, "Neural networks and physical systems with emergent collective computational abilities," in *Proceedings of National Academic Science*, vol. 79, (USA), pp. 2554–2558, 1982.

[22] R. J. Williams and D. Zipser, "Learning algorithm for continually running fully recurrent neural networks," *Neural Computation*, vol. 1, pp. 270–280, 1989.

[23] D. H. Ackley, G. E. Hinton, and T. J. Sejnowski, "A learning algorithm for boltzmann machines," *Cognitive Science*, vol. 9, no. 1, pp. 147–169, 1985.

[24] K. Fukushima and S. Miyake, "Neocognitron: A self-organizing neural network model for a mechanism of pattern recognition unaffected by shift in position," *Biological Cybernetics*, vol. 36, no. 4, pp. 193–202, 1980.

[25] G. A. Carpenter and S. Grossberg, "ART 2: Self-organization of stable category recognition codes for analog input patterns," *Applied Optics*, pp. 4919–4930, December 1987.

[26] D. L. Reilly, L. N. Cooper, and C. Elbaum, "A neural model for category learning," *Biological Cybernetics*, vol. 45, pp. 35–41, 1982.

[27] T. Kohonen, "Automatic formation of topological maps of patterns in a self organizing system," in *Proceedings of the second Scandinavian Conference on Image Analysis*, pp. 214–220, 1981.

[28] A. L. Hodgkin and A. F. Huxley, "A quantitative description of membrane current and its application to conduction and excitation in nerve," *Journal of Physiology*, vol. 117, pp. 500–544, 1952.

[29] Y. Fujimoto and N. Fukuda, "An enhanced parallel toroidal lattice architecture for large scale neural networks," in *Proceedings of the IJCNN*, vol. 2, (Washington D.C.), p. 614, June 1989.

[30] N. Fukuda, Y. Fujimoto, and T. Akabane, "A transputer implementation of toroidal lattice architecture for parallel neurocomputing," in *Proceedings of the IJCNN*, vol. 2, pp. 43–46, January 1990.

[31] Y. Fujimoto, N. Fukuda, and T. Akabane, "Massively parallel architecture for large scale neural network simulations," *IEEE Transaction on Neural Networks*, vol. 3, pp. 876–887, December 1992.

[32] Y. Fujimoto, "An enhanced parallel planar lattice architecture for large scale neural network simulations," in *Proceedings of the IJCNN*, vol. 2, (San Diego), pp. 581–586, June 1990.

[33] J. J. Hopfield and D. W. Tank, "Neural computation of decisions in optimization problems," *Biological Cybernetics*, vol. 52, pp. 141–152, 1985.

[34] T. Nordstrm and B. Svensson, "Using and designing massively parallel computers for artificial neural networks," tech. rep., LULE University of Technology, 1991.

# Chapter 9

# Implementing Regularly Structured Neural Networks on the DREAM Machine

**Soheil Shams**
Hughes Research Laboratories— Systems
3011 Malibu Canyon Road
Malibu, California 90265
Tel: (310) 317-5870
e-mail: shams@maxwell.hrl.hac.com
**Jean-Luc Gaudiot**
Department of Electrical Engineering,
University of Southern California,
Los Angeles, California 90089
Tel: (213) 740-4484
e-mail: gaudiot@usc.edu

## 9.1 Introduction

Neural network models have recently been demonstrated as powerful computational paradigms that can effectively address complex classification and recognition problems. Unlike conventional procedural algorithms that follow a sequential flow, neural computations are performed in a distributed fashion over a large number of simple processing units (called neurons). The number of neurons used in a particular application is generally proportional to the complexity of the problem. High throughput implementations of neural networks are needed in order to expand the use of this technology from small research problems into practical, real-world applications. Because of the wide range of possible neural network models and their rapid evolution, a high degree of implementation flexibility is essential. Among the many methods proposed for implementations of neural networks, programmable parallel computers offer an attractive compromise between high throughput and flexibility. These systems can take advantage of several inherently parallel computational structures available in neural network models to achieve high processing rates [1, 2]. At the same time, the programmability of these systems allows for easy modifications of the various computational and structural parameters of the neural networks being implemented.

Nonetheless, achieving a suitable level of flexibility for implementing the diverse range of neural network models might require costly hardware support for nonlocal and high bandwidth interprocessor communications. A number of architectures have been proposed and developed to efficiently implement neural networks with dense and regular interconnection structures [3–12]. However, the efficiency of these implementations is greatly related to the simplicity and density of the interconnection structures used by the neural networks being implemented.

271

This chapter presents an architecture that offers a high degree of flexibility, required for neural network implementations, while maintaining nearest-neighbor interprocessor connectivity. This architecture, called the Dynamically Reconfigurable Extended Array Multiprocessor (DREAM) Machine, has been specifically designed for implementation of neural networks. The architecture gains a considerable amount of flexibility by allowing for programmability at the level of communication as well as computation. This high degree of programmability enables the architecture to also be efficiently utilized as a general-purpose parallel processor for implementing a wide range of applications involving matrix and vector operations. In this chapter, we will describe a mapping technique that can achieve and maintain high throughput rates for implementing various neural network models on the DREAM Machine. The use of this mapping method will be demonstrated through several examples. It will be shown that this mapping method is applicable to any neural network structure consisting of single or multiple layers of neurons with dense interconnections within blocks of neurons, where a block is defined as a contiguous segment of neurons connected to another contiguous segment of neurons in the neural network structure. Complex neural network structures that can be represented as ensembles of densely connected blocks of neurons can also be efficiently processed. The performance of this architecture is compared to similar systolic implementations and shown to be superior when the size and shape of the interconnection structure does not match the target machine size.

In Section 9.2 we will describe the computational requirements of neural networks and the principal mapping concepts used for their implementation on digital systolic architectures. A description of the DREAM Machine architecture is given in Section 9.3 followed by a detailed discussion of our mapping method in Section 9.4. In Section 9.5 we demonstrate the applicability of the DREAM Machine and the mapping method through several examples. Concluding remarks are given in Section 9.6.

## 9.2 Mapping Method Preliminaries

An understanding of the computational and communicational requirements of neural networks is essential in order to arrive at an efficient method for their implementation. In this section we will describe the principal operations performed by neural network models and describe how these operations can be performed on a ring-connected parallel processing architecture. The fundamental mapping principles described in this section are used as bases for our mapping method on the DREAM Machine architecture.

### 9.2.1 Neural Network Computation and Structure

Artificial neural network models vary significantly in structure and computation. Nevertheless, the basic underlying principle of most models can be summarized as employing a network of simple processing elements called neurons, interconnected via connection links called synapses. The structure of the synaptic interconnection network can vary significantly from model to model and between various applications of each model. For example, a Hopfield network [13] consists of a single layer of neurons with full interconnections between all neurons. The multilayer perceptron network [14] consists of several layers of neurons with interconnections only between adjacent layers and no connections within a layer. The neocognitron network [15] utilizes a rather complex network of connections between a relatively large number of layers (typically between 7 to 11 layers). The connection structure between layers of the neocognitron model is restricted to a few local receptive field regions per neuron. Figure 9.1 depicts several of the basic interconnection structures.

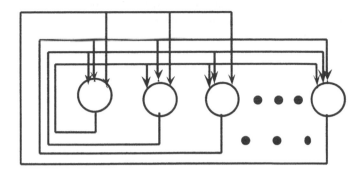

(a) One-Layer Fully Connected Network

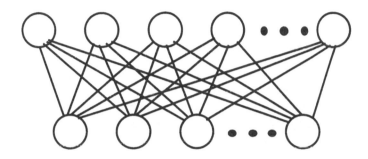

(b) Two-Layer Network

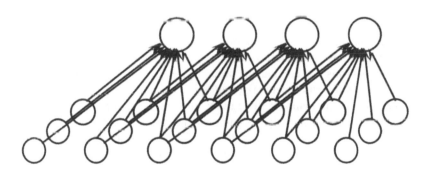

(c) Two-Layer Network with Limited Receptive Field Interconnections

FIGURE 9.1. Common neural network interconnection structures.

Regardless of such large discrepancies in the interconnection structures, the primary operations performed by each synaptic connection and each neuron is basically similar for all neural network models. Each synapse transfers a given value from one neuron to another. The synapse can accordingly modify this value based on some local computation. Commonly, the operation performed by a synapse connecting neuron $j$ to neuron $i$ is to scale the transmitted value according to a weighting parameter $w_{ij}$. An important feature of neural networks is their ability to learn and modify their behavior by varying these synaptic interconnection values according to a specific learning algorithm.

The operation of the neurons in a neural network is formulated as a function of the inputs received over the synaptic connections and the various local parameters of the neuron. The output generated by neuron $i$ can be calculated as

$$a_i = f(u_i + \theta_i) \tag{9.1}$$

where

$$u_i = \sum_{j=1}^{N} w_{ij} a_j \tag{9.2}$$

and $f$ is the neuron transfer function and $\theta$ is the bias value. In these equations, $u_i$ represents the weighted sum of all inputs connected to this neuron $i$. Because the sum operation in Equation 9.2 is performed sequentially using two operand adders, the variable $u_i$ is shown as an accumulator of the partial sum value in the following sections.

### 9.2.2 Implementing Neural Networks on the Ring Systolic Architecture

Implementing neural network models on parallel processing architectures require a method for efficiently mapping neural computations to processing elements (PEs) of the target machine. In general, the objective of this mapping is to distribute the required computation among the PEs of the system such that the amount of interprocessor communication is minimized and at the same time the number of PEs performing useful operations (that is, those operations that directly contribute to the neural network processing) is maximized. Many approaches for mapping neural networks onto parallel SIMD architectures have been proposed [3, 5, 6, 9–12, 16–23]. The performance of any implementation is strongly related to its efficiency in performing the weighted sum operation of Equation 9.2 in a distributed fashion when neuron output values are distributed across the various PEs in the processing array. The implementation of computations requiring data local to the neuron, such as the application of the transfer function to the partial sum value, does not require communication between neurons and can thus be processed efficiently in parallel regardless of the interprocessor communication network topology.

A simple yet efficient mapping strategy for implementing densely connected blocks of neurons can be devised by linearly assigning each neuron to each PE of a ring-connected processing array [6], as shown in Figure 9.2. To simplify the discussion, we describe the mapping for a single block of a two-layer network consisting of only an input and an output layer. The extension of this method to multilayer networks will be addressed later in this section. The basic mapping concept is to assign individual neurons and all of the weights associated with their output synaptic connections to unique processors. The mapping method requires that the PE being assigned the first neuron of the block to be a neighbor of the PE that is assigned the last neuron of the block. This restriction implies construction of a processing ring of size equal to the number of neurons in the input layer. In cases where the number of output layer neurons is greater than the number of neurons in the input layer, the input layer is padded with zero output value neurons so that the input and output layers are of equal size.

For the sake of simplicity, for the moment we will assume that the number of processors in the system is greater than or equal to the number of neurons. Implementing Equation 9.1 for evaluation of neuron $i$ in the output layer requires the output values of all the neurons in the input layer assigned to various processors of the architecture. Because of the inherently serial nature of the addition operation, a path through all the PEs participating in this summation can be constructed by starting the processing at a specific PE and traversing the complete ring, arriving back at the starting PE. Each path is initiated in a different processor and rotates in the same direction around the ring, thus always ensuring that no two paths ever cross the same PE at the same time.

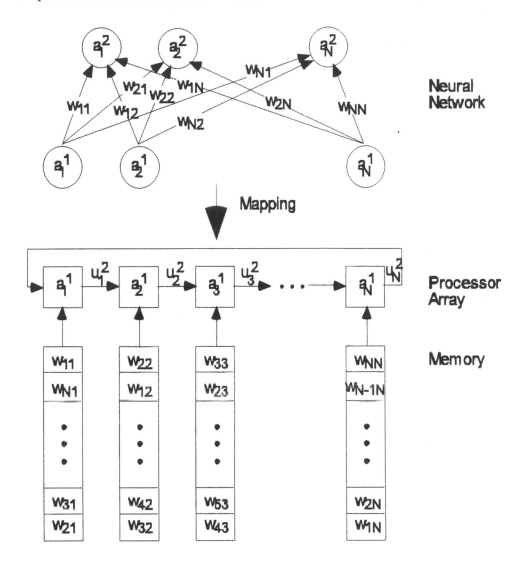

FIGURE 9.2. Mapping a fully connected neural network onto a ring systolic processing array.

At each time step $t$, the product $w_{ij}a_j$ is calculated by the $t$-th PE in the path and added to the partial sum value received from the preceding PE. The partial sum is accordingly modified as $u_i^{t+1} = u_i^t + w_{ij}a_j$ and passed to the next PE in the path. At the completion of the path, the appropriate threshold value $\theta_i$ can be added to the partial sum $u_i$ followed by the application of the transfer function $f$. In this mapping, only a single systolic cycle of each processor is needed by each path to perform the multiply-accumulate operation, therefore multiple paths can utilize the same PE each at a different time. This feature allows for parallel execution of various paths in the network. Similar mapping approaches have been proposed in the literature for implementing neural network models on various parallel processing architectures [6, 12, 19, 22]. The addition operation can be implemented faster by utilizing a binary tree adder structure [8, 23]. However, this scheme requires more hardware than the ring systolic approach and is applicable to fully interconnected neural network structures. Because the objective of our research is to demonstrate the effective use of the DREAM Machine in implementing neural networks with regular but possibly sparse interconnection structures, we will perform a direct comparison with a single approach that assumes full interconnectivity. The ring systolic architecture is selected as this exemplar because it is widely used in several implementations and also because its processing is closely related to our approach on the DREAM Machine.

It should be noted here that most of the computation required by the neural network during the recall phase is functionally identical to the computation of the learning phase. In other words, the same vector-matrix product computation is used for processing both the recall and learning operations. For the sake of simplicity, we present the details of the recall operations. However, specific needs of learning operations are addressed in Sections 9.4.5, 9.4.8, and 9.4.9.

### 9.2.3 System Utilization Characteristic of the Mapping onto the Ring Systolic Architecture

Mapping neural networks onto ring-connected processing arrays is highly efficient when the number of neurons in the network is equal to the number of processors in the processing array. Formally, let $N_t$ represent the number of neurons in layer $l$, and $P$ represent the number of PEs in the processing array. Because $P$ paths are traversed simultaneously with each path performing $P$ operations, the implementation has a potential for performing $P^2$ useful calculations. A two-layer neural network requires $\mu N_l N_{l-1}$ operations where $\mu$ is defined as the interconnection density between layer $l$ and $l-1$ calculated as

$$\mu = \frac{\text{\# of nonzero connections between layer } l \text{ \& } l-1}{N_l N_{l-1}}.$$

Assuming that the number of neurons in each layer of the neural network is less than or equal to the number of PEs in the processing ring, the system utilization factor $\eta$, indicating the ratio of useful operations per total possible operations, can be determined as

$$\eta = \frac{\mu N_l N_{l-1}}{P^2} \tag{9.3}$$

where $\mu N_l N_{l-1}$ is the number of non-zero synaptic connection weights in the neural network. It is apparent that the maximum system utilization ($\eta = 1$) is achieved when $\mu = 100\%$ and $N_l = N_{l-1} = P$.

System utilization, $\eta$, scales linearly with respect to both interconnection density and the ratio of neurons to PEs. Should the number of neurons exceed the number of processors, virtual processors can be created using time multiplexing techniques. In such cases, a single PE can simulate multiple processors by using different consecutive time slices to implement the processing associated with each virtual PE. The general form of the system utilization function for a ring systolic array can thus be written as

$$\eta = \frac{\mu N_l N_{l-1}}{\left\lceil \frac{N_l}{P} \right\rceil \left\lceil \frac{N_{l-1}}{P} \right\rceil P^2} \tag{9.4}$$

where $\lceil N_l/P \rceil$ indicates the number of neurons of layer $l$ assigned to one physical processor.

It can be noticed that the round-off factor introduced by the ceiling function can be minimized by either keeping the number of neurons per layer $N_l$ equal to an integer multiple of the processing array size $P$, or by having the number of PEs being much smaller than the number of neurons in the network. With the round-off effects removed under these conditions, the system utilization will be

$$\eta \approx \mu. \tag{9.5}$$

This result indicates that to ensure good system utilization, regardless of the exact size of the neural network, we require dense interconnections between layers of neurons and a small number of processors. At the same time, we would like to exploit all the available parallelism in the neural network by having a large number of processors. This causes a dilemma in determining a good number of PEs to be used in the system architecture. A large number of processors are required to effectively implement large neural networks, but their use causes great inefficiency for implementing networks with different sizes. In Section 9.4, we show how the DREAM Machine architecture and the associated mapping method can relieve this problem by removing the direct relationship between the number of PEs and the throughput of the system. Thus, the DREAM Machine can be built with a large number of PEs to match the size of large-scale neural networks, without negatively affecting the system performance on implementing smaller-sized neural networks.

### 9.2.4 Execution Rate Characteristics of the Mapping onto the Ring Systolic Architecture

Although system utilization is of interest in evaluating the efficiency of a particular implementation, the primary measure of performance is the execution rate of the implementation. We now analyze the execution rate of the mapping and the effects of processor array size on system throughput. The number of cycles required to process a neural network using the mapping discussed earlier on a ring-systolic architecture is equal to the number of cycles needed to traverse a path (making a complete circle around the processing ring) plus the additional cycles used to implement the neuron activation function. The total time for implementing a single block can be calculated as

$$T_l = \left( \left\lceil \frac{N_l}{P} \right\rceil \left\lceil \frac{N_{l-1}}{P} \right\rceil P k_1 + \left\lceil \frac{N_l}{P} \right\rceil k_2 \right) \tag{9.6}$$

where $k_1$ is the time required to perform a multiply-accumulate operation and $k_2$ is the time required to implement the neuron transfer function. This formula also assumes the use of time-multiplexing multiple neurons on a single PE in cases where the processing array is smaller than the neural network. If $P \geq N_l$ and $P \geq N_{l-1}$, the execution time will be $O(P)$. This implies that it is possible to reduce the execution rate of an implementation by increasing the number of PEs in the system. As the number of neurons in the network increases, we would like to increase the number of PEs to maintain high throughput. Unfortunately, with a large number of processors, the degradational effects of an unequal number of neurons to PEs on the system utilization and throughput is proportionally larger. In Section 9.4, we will outline a method for constructing variable-length rings on the DREAM Machine, which can alleviate a number of these problems by matching the ring size to the problem size.

### 9.2.5 Mapping Multilayer Neural Networks onto the Ring Systolic Architecture

Implementing multilayer neural networks on 1-D ring systolic arrays can also be performed using the mapping technique described earlier by time multiplexing the processing associated with each layer on the processor array. The computation associated with each layer of a neural network can be performed consecutively on the ring array as the data flows from the input layer toward the output layer. This type of implementation leads to an execution time of $O(LP)$, where $L$ is the number of layers in the neural network structure. Pipelining techniques can be used, as proposed in [6], to decrease the execution time back to $O(P)$ given $L$ ring arrays organized in a two-dimensional (2-D) mesh topology. The efficiency of this type of implementation is strongly related to the match between the number of neurons and layers to the size and structure of the processor array. The pipelined mapping method requires the number of layers in the neural network to be equal to the number of rows (that is, pipeline stages) in the processor array. Furthermore, the mapping assumes an equal number of neurons for all the different layers. These are rather strong restrictions on the neural network interconnection structure for efficient implementation.

### 9.2.6 Deficiencies of the Mapping onto the Ring Systolic Architecture

As mentioned previously, a major deficiency in the use of the linear mapping method for implementing neural networks on fixed-size ring systolic architectures is attributed to the strong dependence of the processor array size on the efficiency in implementing varied size neural networks. We have shown through Equation 9.6 that the execution rate of this mapping is $O(P)$ when both the processing array size and neural network size are of the same order of magnitude. This type of scaling characteristic is not well suited for neural network applications because the large number of neurons required for real-world applications will, in turn, require a large number of processors that would finally yield a high execution rate.

If we assume full interconnections between all the neurons of a large real-world network, this mapping would remain viable as it yields maximum utilization. However, current evidence, both from biological examples [24] and artificial neural networks [25], indicate that real-world systems are generally constructed of modular and sparsely interconnected networks. This fact, thus, indicates that the fix-ring mapping method, although useful for relatively small and densely interconnected neural networks, is not suitable as an implementation method for large-scale, general-purpose neural processing.

In addition to the low system utilization characteristics of the fixed-size ring systolic mapping, the processing array interconnection topology is also problematic. The ring systolic architecture utilizes a 1-D interconnection topology, which does not lend itself well to such applications as image processing and vision, where neural networks have extensively been used [15, 26]. A planner topology is a more natural architecture for such applications because the data is structured and manipulated in a 2-D format. In addition, locally connected 2-D planar architectures, such as the mesh, are a more natural match to VLSI implementations than the 1-D topology because of the inherent two-dimensional nature of integrated circuits. A mapping method has been demonstrated for 2-D mesh connected systolic arrays [10]. This mapping utilizes batch-mode processing where different instantiations of a network are mapped onto different rows of a 2-D processor array. Each row of the array is considered as a single 1-D ring of processors employing a mapping similar to the one described earlier. Unfortunately, the method utilizes concurrent execution of multiple networks for speedup and is inefficient in processing only a single network at a time. All of the shortcomings associated with the systolic ring implementation are addressed effectively by the DREAM Machine architecture through the use of novel architectural features and a generalized mapping method.

## 9.3 DREAM Machine Architecture

The DREAM Machine is a parallel processor designed specifically for efficient implementation of neural network models. Due to the considerable amount of diversity in neural network models and the wide range of applications utilizing these models, the DREAM Machine architecture is scalable and offers programmability in both computation and communication operations.

### 9.3.1 System Level Overview

The DREAM Machine can roughly be classified as a single instruction multiple data streams (SIMD) medium- or fine-grain parallel computer. The processing elements (PEs) are arranged on a 2-D lattice where each PE is connected to eight of its closest neighbors through four programmable switches. The top level architecture of the DREAM Machine is depicted in Figure 9.3. The choice of an SIMD execution paradigm for neural computation can be justified by considering that neural network models are built of a homogeneous array of neurons with each neuron performing the same basic operation on different data sets. This type of computation is a perfect match for implementation on SIMD architectures because all processors perform the same computation on their locally stored data. Certain neural network models, such as the adaptive resonance theory (ART) [27] and the neocognitron [15] models, utilize different neuron types in different layers. In general, the number of different neuron types is small (two in the case of ART and neocognitron) and the major operations performed by either type of neurons are the same. Therefore, these models can be effectively implemented by time-multiplexing the operations that are specific for each neuron type without a significant loss in throughput.

In addition to savings gained by having only a single instruction memory for the entire system, through the use of the SIMD execution paradigm the tightly coupled distributed memory structure of the DREAM Machine offers a simple scheme for interprocessor communications. Communication between processors are performed one word at a time requiring only a single instruction cycle. Communication and computation operations can be initiated in parallel by a single instruction. When implementing systolic algorithms, the communication operations can be completely overlapped by computation, consequently achieving very high execution efficiency.

The DREAM Machine system consist of three major units: the host computer, the controller, and the processor array (PA). The DREAM Machine can be viewed as an attached coprocessor of the host computer. The DREAM Machine memory is mapped into the memory space of the host. This feature permits a simple programming interface between the host and the DREAM Machine. The host computer is primarily used for properly formatting the input data, long-term storage of data, and as a visual interface between the operator and the DREAM Machine. The controller interfaces to both the host computer and the PA. The controller unit contains a microprogram memory area that can be accessed by the host. High-level programs are written and compiled on the host and the generated control information is downloaded from the host to the microprogram memory of the controller. The controller broadcasts instruction and address data to the PA during each processing cycle. The processors in the PA perform operations received from the controller on their local data. Each processor can selectively be masked from performing computation based on a mask flag available in each PE. The DREAM Machine architecture allows for condition-

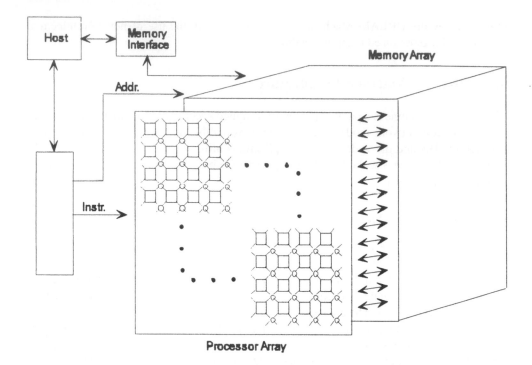

FIGURE 9.3. The top-level design of the DREAM Machine.

ally modifying the status of the mask bit in each processor giving an additional degree of autonomy to each processor.

### 9.3.2 Processor-Memory Interface

Each processor of the DREAM Machine has read/write access to its own local memory area (see Figure 9.4). The memory is kept off chip to allow for simple memory expansion. The size of this local memory area is related to the number of processors in the system and the expected size of the neural network models being implemented on this machine. In our mapping, all the outgoing weight values associated with each neuron are stored in the local memory area of the PE assigned to that neuron. Therefore, the local memory size is a function of the number of connections per neuron. However, if time multiplexing of operations is used to implement neural networks larger than the processor array, the local memory size has to increase proportionally. In a fine-grain architecture, implementing sparsely interconnected neural networks requires a small memory area that is enough to hold the nonzero weight values required by each neuron.

During each processing cycle, the memory location associated with each instruction is broadcasted by the control unit to all the PEs. In this fashion, all of the processors can access a single plane of memory at each time step. The memory access speed is matched with the computation rate of each processor so that each memory access can be completely overlapped with computation. This feature allows for efficient systolic processing.

The microword instruction used by the DREAM Machine contains two distinct fields, one for specifying the memory access and another for specifying the operation to be performed by the processors. The instruction set of this machine consists of the conventional arithmetic, logical, and shift operations (addition, multiplication, AND, OR, left and right shift, and so on). In addition, the DREAM Machine instruction set also supports global broadcasting of data from the controller to all the PEs in the processing array. This is accomplished through the use of an instruction/data bit in the instruction word broadcasted by the controller. If this bit is set to zero, the remaining bits of the instruction word are treated as a single data value. If it is set to one, the remaining bits of the instruction word are decoded and used for their appropriate functions within the PE.

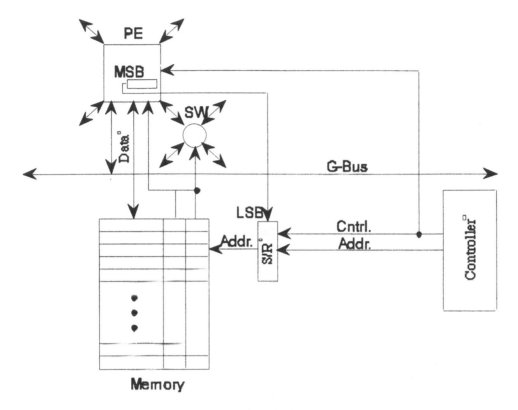

FIGURE 9.4. Processor and memory detail diagram. Associated with each data value in the local memory of each PE is a switch setting values to configure the communication topology of the machine.

### 9.3.3  Implementing a Table Lookup Mechanism on the DREAM Machine

A novel feature of the DREAM Machine architecture is its hardware support mechanism for implementing a variable accuracy lookup table. Neural network models use a variety of nonlinear transfer functions (represented as $f$ in Equation 9.1), such as the sigmoid and the hyperbolic tangent functions, which can be efficiently implemented as a lookup table. Implementation of a table lookup mechanism on a SIMD architecture requires a method for generation/modification of the memory address supplied by the controller based on some local value in each PE. The BLITZEN Machine [28] performs this task by logically ORing the 10 most significant bits of the memory address supplied by the controller, with a local register value. Such a scheme does not offer sufficient flexibility as required for general-purpose neurocomputer design. The accuracy, or level of quantization of the neuron output values tolerated by neural networks can vary significantly (from 2 to 16 bits) between different neural network models and different applications of each model.

To accommodate lookup tables of varying sizes, the DREAM Machine incorporates two shift registers that are used to modify the address supplied by the controller. One shift register is associated with the PE and keeps the data value used for addressing the lookup table. The other shift register is associated with the PE's local memory and is used to modify the address received from the controller (see Figure 9.4). The table lookup procedure is initiated when the controller loads the base address of the table to each of the shift registers associated with each PE's local memory. The offset value is then shifted into this register one bit at the time from the local register in the PE starting from the most significant bit into the least significant bit of the memory address register. The control signals for this shifting operation are generated by the controller and broadcasted to all PEs as part of the microinstruction word. This scheme does require the duplication of the lookup table for each of the PE's local memory area. However, a table of size $2^k$ can be accessed in $k$ time steps by all processors, whereas a conventional approach would require time proportional to the number of PEs in the system.

### 9.3.4 Interprocessor Communication Network

The processors in the PA are arranged on a 2-D lattice with eight nearest-neighbor connections implemented through dynamically reconfigurable switches. The basic switch design is similar to the X-net switch used on other systems, such as the MasPar and the BLITZEN machine [28]. The X-net switch allows for communication between eight nearest-neighbor PEs while only requiring 4 I/O connections to each PE. The communication bandwidth between adjacent PEs are kept equal to the memory access bandwidth to assure efficient systolic processing. The most unique feature of the DREAM Machine architecture is to allow each switch in the interconnection network to be set to a distinct configuration. The switch settings are stored in the local memory of each switch and accessed at the beginning of each processing cycle. The switch memory is 4 bits wide. The first 2 bits are used to select the incoming line, from one of the four processors, and the second half is used to select the outgoing line, again from the four PEs attached to the switch.

The switch memory address is supplied by the controller at each cycle. This design allows for a dynamically changing flow pattern of data through the processing array. In other 2-D connected parallel SIMD architectures, such as the Hughes SCAP [29] and the AMT DAP [30] architectures, all the PEs perform the same communication operation. In the DREAM Machine, one PE can receive data from its north neighbor while another is receiving data from its west neighbor, depending on the local switch settings. This flexibility in interprocessor communication is essential to efficiently implement neural networks with sparse or block structured interconnections, as will be demonstrated in the remainder of this chapter.

A second method of interprocessor communication supported by the DREAM Machine is through a single-bit global bus, called the G-bus, electrically connecting all the PEs together (see Figure 9.4). The principal use of the G-bus is to perform global broadcast communications between processors. The G-bus can be used to efficiently implement competitive neural network models. A number of neural network models, such as the self-organizing feature maps [31] and adaptive resonance theory (ART) [27], utilize various versions of the competitive learning algorithm [32]. Competitive learning requires that the neuron with the maximum activity value be identified. In a distributed system where each neuron is mapped to a different PE, this task might require $O(N)$ time, where $N$ is the number of neurons in the network.

The G-bus is designed as a wired-OR circuit where each PE can pull down the bus by setting a local flag register to zero. The G-bus can thus be used to implement a global minimum or maximum operation in $k$ time steps, where the data to be evaluated is $k$ bits, using the procedure described in [33, 34]. This procedure involves simultaneous broadcasting of the data value over the G-bus by all the PEs one bit at a time starting from the most significant bit. After the broadcast of each bit, all the processors compare their local data value with the wired-OR value on the G-bus. This allows each PE to selectively mask itself out of future broadcasts if another PE in the system has a greater or smaller data value, depending on the min or max function being implemented. A useful side effect of this method for finding the global min/max value is that at the completion of the $k$ processing steps, all the PEs contain the value min/max value. In addition to neural network applications, this feature can be useful in implementing other algorithms, such as genetic algorithms [35], where all the PEs require access to the global min/max cost value.

## 9.4 Mapping Structured Neural Networks onto the DREAM Machine

The mapping method described in Section 9.2 for implementing neural networks on ring connected systolic architectures can be very efficient. We demonstrated that this mapping could achieve 100 percent system utilization and, therefore, a linear speedup factor, given full interconnections between layers of the neural network and a perfect match between the processor ring size and the neural network size. To reduce the effects of the neural network structure on the implementation efficiency, we now propose a generalized version of this mapping method.

In this general mapping approach, neurons are assigned to processors of the parallel architecture as before, except we no longer require linear assignment of neurons to PEs. Because of the commutative nature of the addition operation, the computation paths required for evaluation of the partial sum values $u$ can be constructed without any specific ordering of the processor traversals, as long as each path passes through all the PEs contributing to its partial sum value $u_i$. A small segment of an arbitrarily connected neural network and an example mapping is shown in Figure 9.5. The basic computation performed by each processor in the machine is identical to the one described in Section 9.2. Specifically, a PE holding the output value of neuron $j$ receives the partial sum value $u_i$ from the previous PE in the path. It then adds its contribution $(w_{ij}a_j)$ to the partial sum value $u_i$ and passes the updated partial sum value on to the next PE in the path.

### 9.4.1 General Mapping Problems

Given the processing approach described earlier, the problem of finding efficient mappings can be formulated into two interdependent optimization problems: assignment of neurons to processors and congestion-free scheduling of path traversals. The assignment problem involves generating a permutation that assigns neurons that participate in a common path to processors that are physically close to each other. This will help in generating paths with minimal length. The scheduling problem involves construction of multiple paths, one associated with each neuron being evaluated, through the processing array in such a fashion that no two paths cross the same PE at the same time. A prime objective of this mapping is to construct these paths such that the length of the longest path is minimized.

To efficiently implement this mapping method, the target machine architecture must allow for local autonomy of interconnections between each PE and its neighbors. As described in Section 9.3, the DREAM Machine architecture supports independent and dynamically programmable interprocessor connections, which can be used to efficiently support this mapping method. Finding good solutions for this optimization problem is difficult and compute intensive (solving only the assignment problem has been shown to be

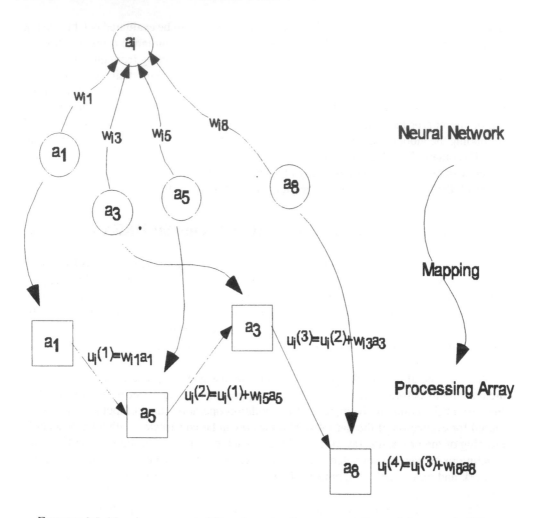

FIGURE 9.5. Mapping neurons to PEs and constructing a computation path between the PEs.

NP-complete [36]). An optimization method for solving this mapping problem has been formulated based on neural computation approaches [1,37]. This approach is applicable to problems with irregular interconnection structures that require high throughput rates and can tolerate the one-time cost associated with the optimization computation.

### 9.4.2    The Algorithmic Mapping Method and Its Applicability

Mapping methods for implementing regularly structured neural network models can take advantage of this regularity and devise a systematic and direct approach for solving the assignment and scheduling problems. In the remainder of this section, we will demonstrate the use of such an algorithmic approach used to arrive at efficient mappings for implementing regularly connected neural networks with dense interconnection structures. The mapping method is applicable to neural network structures with single or multiple layers of neurons where each layer can comprise one or more blocks. The mapping method produces the necessary assignment of neurons to processors and establishes the associated computational paths through the processing array. This is accomplished by employing a processing ring approach, similar to the one described in Section 9.2, for linearly assigning neurons to PEs of the ring and scheduling the paths as complete traversals of the processing ring.

As mentioned previously, a major problem with implementations on 1-D ring architectures is due to the requirement of having an equal number of neurons and processors in the ring. The flexibility in the communication network of the DREAM Machine architecture allows for embedding variable length 1-D rings on the 2-D processor array topology of the machine. With the ability to vary the ring size to match the neural network size, the system throughput can be maintained at a high level compared to the fixed size ring array. With a processing array size of $P$ processors, a ring of size $R$ can simply be embedded onto the 2-D interconnection topology by folding the ring into a snakelike shape. Figure 9.6(a) shows how a ring topology can be created on the DREAM architecture with the ring length less than the number of PEs. Figure 9.6(b) shows how multiple rings of varying lengths can be implemented in parallel on the DREAM Machine architecture.

Of course, one can achieve the same results by inserting a two-pole switch between the PEs of a ring systolic architecture (see Figure 9.7). In this approach, one can vary the ring size to match the number of neurons in the neural network by setting the appropriate switch to select the feedback line. Although this approach is simpler and cheaper (based on the amount of hardware required) to implement than the DREAM Machine scheme, it is considerably less effective in implementing spare and regularly structured neural networks. This is due to a number of factors. First, the architecture of Figure 9.7 is one-dimensional and, thus, exhibits a number of the same deficiencies outlined in Section 9.2.6 for fixed-size ring implementations. Second, the 2-D interconnection structure of the DREAM Machine allows for the construction and parallel execution of multiple rings of different length, as shown in Figure 9.6(b). This feature can be very effectively utilized in implementing neural networks with block-structured interconnection; see Section 9.4.6 for an example. Such structures cannot be implemented on the ring architecture of Figure 9.7. Third, the dynamic and independent reconfigurability of the switches in the DREAM Machine, architecture allows for the construction of irregular flow patterns. This feature is used very effectively in implementing sparse and irregular neural networks [1,37], which cannot be implemented on the architecture of Figure 9.7.

### 9.4.3 Using Variable Length Rings to Implement Neural Network Processing

First let us discuss the use of variable-length processing rings for implementing one- and two-layer neural networks. Let $P$ represent the number of processors in the machine, and define $R_l$ to be the number of PEs in the ring used for computing the neuron output values of layer $l$. For example, in Figure 9.6(a), $P=64$ and $R=59$. We further define $v_l$ as the number of output layer neurons assigned to each PE in the processing ring of length $R_l$, and we define $\omega_l$ as the number of input layer neurons assigned to each PE of the ring. Formally, $v_l$ and $\omega_l$ are defined as

$$v_l = \left\lceil \frac{N_l}{R_l} \right\rceil \tag{9.7}$$

and

$$\omega_l = \left\lceil \frac{N_{l-1}}{R_l} \right\rceil . \tag{9.8}$$

Using this notation, Equation 9.6 (used to calculate the time required for evaluating the output values of neurons in layer $l$) can be rewritten for the variable ring implementation

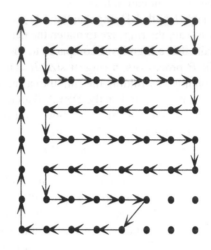

(a) A Single Ring of size 59

(b) Three Disjoint Rings of Different Sizes Executed in Parallel

FIGURE 9.6. Using the reconfigurable switches of the DREAM Machine to construct circular rings on the processing array.

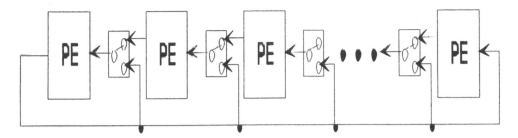

FIGURE 9.7. A 1-D variable length ring architecture using simple switches.

as

$$T_l = (v_l \omega_l R_l K_1 + v_l k_2) \qquad (9.9)$$

where

$$1 \leq R_l \leq P. \qquad (9.10)$$

It can be noticed that this equation is no longer a function of the processor array size; rather the execution time is now dependent on the number of processors used in the ring and the number of neurons assigned to each processor of the ring. For the sake of simplicity, we assume that $N_l \leq R_l$ and $N_{l-1} \leq R_l$ so that $v_l = 1$ and $\omega_l = 1$. Later in this section, we will describe the characteristics of this mapping without this restriction.

### 9.4.4 Implementing Multilayer Networks

For the one- and two-layer neural networks (for example, the Hopfield network [13] and the BAM network [38]), a single ring is sufficient to efficiently implement the network. In the case of multilayer neural networks, where neuron output values are propagated through consecutive layers of the network, a more complicated ring structure can be designed that matches the number of PEs in the ring to the number of neurons in each layer of the network. This is accomplished by dynamically changing the ring size as the computation moves from layer to layer with $R_l = \max\{N_l, N_{l-1}\}$ for each layer $l$. For example, a three-layer neural network with $N_1 > N_2 > N_3$, can be mapped efficiently to a ring structure of length $N_2$ embedded in a longer ring of length $N_1$, as shown in Figure 9.8. In the first $N_1$ cycles of processing, the partial sum values $u$'s are propagated through the large loop of length $N_1$. At the completion of this phase, the final $u$ values for the $N_2$ neurons in the second layer are available in the first $N_2$ PEs of the ring. All the processors can then perform the application of the neuron activation function in unison to evaluate the second layer neuron's output values. Because the large ring of length $N_1$ is folded in such a way that PE #1 and PE #$N_2$ are adjacent to each other, the communication switch between these PEs can be reconfigured to implement a ring of size $N_2$ (see Figure 9.7). After $N_2$ processing cycles, the first $N_3$ PEs in this ring will have the final $u$ values of neurons in the output layer. After the application of the transfer function, the network output values are ready to be stored in memory for further processing or access by the host computer. The total time required to complete the computation of a network with $L$ layers is

$$T = \sum_{l=1}^{L} T_l \qquad (9.11)$$

with $v_l = 1$ and $\omega_l = 1$, and the total time to complete the network computation can be calculated as

$$T = k_1 \sum_{l=2}^{L} R_l + (L-1)k_2. \qquad (9.12)$$

In cases where the number of neurons in one-layer is less than the number of neurons in the next higher layer ($N_{l-1} < N_l$), a similar ring embedding structure can be created. In such cases, layer $l-1$ can be padded with zero-valued neurons in order to make $N_{l-1} = N_l$. This results in creation of only a single ring of size $N_l$ PEs. In general, the ring length needed to implement the processing associated with layer $l$ is

$$R_l = \max(N_l, N_{l-1}) \qquad (9.13)$$

By means of this ring embedding technique, various ring structures can be devised for efficient implementation of each layer in the neural network. A number of different neural network structures and their associated processing rings used for their implementation are illustrated in Section 9.5.

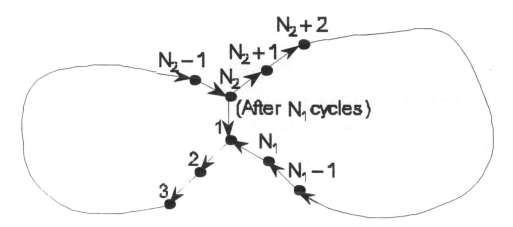

FIGURE 9.8. An embedded ring structure containing a ring of size $N_1$ and another of size $N_2$.

### 9.4.5 Implementing Backpropagation Learning Algorithms

Some neural network learning algorithms, such as error backpropagation [14], require that the error values be calculated and propagated from the output layer back to the input layer after the evaluation of the output layer neurons. This can be implemented using our mapping method by keeping the partial sum values associated in the calculation of the error contributions local in each PE and rotating the neuron activation values through the ring structure. This approach is similar to that described in [10] except that the ring length can now be adjusted to fit the neural network size for increased efficiency and throughput. The construction and traversal of the rings are also performed in the reverse order. That is, the ring of size $R_l$ is traversed followed by the ring of size $R_{l-1}$, and so on. This procedure is continued until processing for layer 2 is completed.

### 9.4.6   Implementing Blocked Connected Networks

In addition to the layered interconnection structures, a number of neural network models use or allow the use of blocked connected interconnection structures. In our treatment here, a block consists of two disjoint sets of neurons with full interconnections between the sets and no connections within neurons of each set. Such interconnection structures are more general than the layered networks because each layer can be represented as being composed of a single block. A more complex structure might utilize several blocks within each layer. We can treat the mapping method described earlier as a single block per layer case and extend this mapping to multiple block per layer structures.

Block structures are commonly used for two reasons. First, block structured networks can be used to perform data fusion by combining the outputs of several disjoint portions of the network. An example of such a structure is shown in Figure 9.9. The second type of block structure is usually employed to perform some type of feature detection using a concept called weight sharing [25]. These networks generally perform a convolution type operation on the previous layer's neurons using the synaptic weights as a mask filter. The interconnection structure of these networks contains many small and overlapping blocks. An example of such a network is the neocognitron model used for invariant object recognition [15].

*9.4.6.1   Implementing Data Fusion Style Structured Networks.*   The simplest case of implementing block connected networks is when each block is completely disjoint from other blocks in the network. In this case, ring structures, such as those described earlier in this section, can be used to process each block on different parts of the processing array. If the blocked structure network is from the class of models used for data fusion, the output of a number of blocks is combined into a single block and possibly processed by additional layers in the neural network (such as the one depicted in Figure 9.9). Let's define $N_l^b$ as the number of neurons in block $b$ of layer $l$ of the network and $R_l^b$ as the length of the processor ring associated with that block. If the output of several blocks of layer $l$ are to be treated as input to layer $l + 1$, processing rings associated with each block of layer $l$ are placed next to one another to form another ring for computation associated with layer $l + 1$. For example, in Figure 9.9 after 200 cycles used for completion of the longest ring, the switch setting between the PEs of adjacent rings will be changed to form a processing ring of size 13. After 13 computation cycles in this configuration, the final neuron values for the output neurons are available in the first three PEs in this ring.

The number of cycles required to implement one-layer of a blocked, connected neural network using this mapping method is

$$T_l = (\tilde{v}_l \tilde{\omega}_l \tilde{R}_l k_1 + \tilde{v}_l k_2) \tag{9.14}$$

where

$$\tilde{v}_l = \max_{b \in B_t} \left\{ v_l^b \right\}, \tilde{\omega}_l = \max_{b \in B_t} \left\{ \omega_l^b \right\}, \text{ and } \tilde{R}_l = \max_{b \in B_t} \left\{ R_t^b \right\}. \tag{9.15}$$

Equation 9.15 represents the set of blocks that comprise layer $l$ of the network. Because multiple blocks are executed concurrently on different processing rings implemented on the machine, the time required to complete the computation associated with all the blocks is equal to the time required to complete the longest ring. Thus, $\tilde{R}_l$ is set equal to the longest ring of the layer. The DREAM Machine's masking capability is used to inhibit the processors in all the rings that have completed their computation before the longest ring is completely traversed. The number of neurons in layer $l$ assigned to each PE of the ring

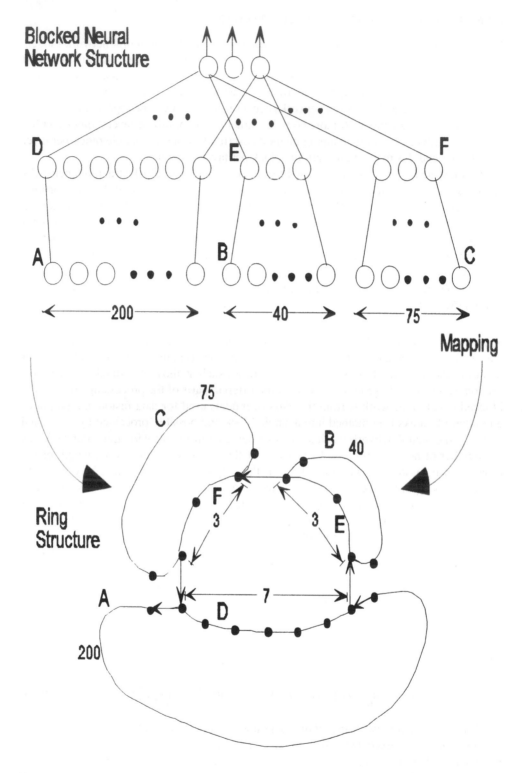

FIGURE 9.9. A blocked structured neural network utilizing three disjoint blocks between the input and hidden layers and its associated mapping on three processing rings.

must be equal, or treated as being equal, for all the different blocks in that layer. This is due to the SIMD execution paradigm used by this mapping. Therefore, $\tilde{v}_l$ and $\tilde{\omega}_l$ are set equal to the largest value of $v_l$ and $\omega_l$, respectively, of all the blocks in layer $l$, as represented in Equation 9.15.

*9.4.6.2 Implementing Feature Detection Style Structured Networks.* A different approach can be taken when implementing block connected structures with overlapping blocks of neurons on the DREAM Machine. In many cases involving structures with overlapping blocks of neurons, a weight-sharing technique is used to create specific feature-detecting neurons [15, 39]. Weight sharing is a concept where all the neurons have input synapses of the same spatial distribution. In other words, all neurons share the same input synapse values connected to different overlapping blocks of neurons. Efficient implementation of such structures can be accomplished by mapping each unique synaptic weight value to a specific PE and storing the corresponding neuron activation values in the local memory of each processor. In this fashion, there is only a single copy of each synaptic weight stored in the processing array and only a few redundant copies of the neuron activation values are stored in the array, depending on the amount of overlap between adjacent blocks. This mapping approach is more efficient when the number of processors in the processing array is close to the number of unique weight values in the neural network.

### 9.4.7 Implementing Neural Networks Larger Than the Processor Array

In the previous discussion, we assumed that there are always enough processors to construct rings of arbitrary size $R_l$. This condition can be satisfied if the number of neurons in the largest layer of the neural network is less than or equal to the processor array size. To formulate the previous mapping technique in a more general fashion, we employ the use of time-multiplexing in creating virtual PEs. The number of virtual PEs that can be implemented is an integer multiple of the processing array size. The formalism given in Equations 9.9 and 9.14, for arriving at the execution rate of this mapping, incorporates the effects of the required virtual PEs through the use of the $v_l$ and $\omega_l$ terms.

The goal of an optimal mapping will be to determine the appropriate values for the $R_l$ values such that the total execution time (given by Equation 9.11) is minimized. Because of the noncontinuities in the execution time equations introduced by the ceiling functions, we cannot directly solve for the best values. In many cases, the network structure can give good hints as to approximate values for the ring sizes. Heuristic techniques, such as simulated annealing [40], can analytically evaluate the execution rate of a specific mapping using Equation 9.11 and can, therefore, be used to arrive at efficient mapping solutions.

### 9.4.8 Batch-Mode Implementation

As described earlier, batch-mode processing is used to simultaneously implement multiple instantiations of a single neural network on a parallel processor. This type of mapping has been extensively used to increase throughput rates for a number of different parallel implementations [10, 12, 20, 23, 41]. Batch-mode processing can be used to improve the system utilization of the mapping method in cases where the number of neurons in the network is smaller than the number of processors in the processor array. The DREAM Machine's processor array can be configured into many small regions of size equal to that of the neural network being implemented. Each of these regions can independently implement the complete network given that input patterns associated with each network are stored locally in each region. This type of processing requires that a number of different input patterns be available to the system before the processing is initiated.

Batch-mode processing can also be used to implement neural network learning algorithms. There are two major disadvantages with using batch-mode learning. The first is due to the lack of models that allow for batch-mode learning. The second problem is associated with the effectiveness of this training approach. In gradient descent-based learning algorithms, such as backpropagation, the mathematically correct algorithm requires weight updates at each step. By using batch-mode learning, true gradient descent is not implemented. Another attribute of this approach is that by combining several weight contributions, the learning process might be slowed proportional to the batch size. Therefore, the speed gained by running multiple networks in parallel is lost by having to increase the number of learning cycles by a factor close to the batch size. In Section 9.5 we will compare a number of different neural network implementations based on their throughput. In these comparisons we will not consider the use of batch-mode processing because of the problems mentioned here.

### 9.4.9 Implementing Competitive Learning

Neural network models utilizing competitive learning algorithms can also be implemented efficiently on the DREAM Machine. These algorithms update the weight values associated with synaptic connections arriving at the inputs of the neuron with the largest activation value, called the winner neuron, in the specific layer. Certain models, such as the self-organizing feature maps [31], also modify the weight values of neurons in a local neighborhood of the winning neuron. In Section 9.3.4 we described how the G-bus could be utilized to efficiently determine the winning neuron. Using the conditional masking instruction, all the PEs, except the one assigned the winning neuron, can be masked out from executing the weight modification procedure. In our mapping the weight values attached to the inputs of the winning neuron are distributed across the different PEs in the ring. Nevertheless, the learning algorithm can be implemented by rotating the mask bit through the PEs of the ring starting from the winner PE. In this fashion, the appropriate weight associated with the winning neuron is modified in the properly enabled processor. This procedure requires $O(R_l)$ time steps, where $R_l$ is the number of neurons in the ring being evaluated.

A more efficient weight-update method can be devised using the local address modification capability of the DREAM Machine (described in Section 9.3.3) and the G-bus. In this approach, the local memory of each processor holds the neuron ID value indicating the neuron's relative location in the ring. The input weights associated with neuron $i$ are stored in memory location (W_$Base+offset$) of the processor assigned neuron $j$, where W_$Base$ represents the base address of the weight memory space and offset is calculated as

$$offset = \begin{cases} j - 1 & \text{if } j \geq i, \\ R_l + j - 1 & \text{if } j < i, \end{cases} \tag{9.16}$$

(see Figure 9.10).

To achieve maximum parallelism in the weight updating phase, after the determination of the winning neuron, the locally stored neuron ID value ($ID_{max}$) is broadcasted to all the PEs in the machine by the controller using the instruction/data broadcast mechanism described in Section 9.3.2. All of the processors can then calculate their corresponding memory offset values according to Equation 9.16. The controller can then load each PEs local address register with W_$Base$ and shift the offset value into this register in $O(\log R_l)$ time steps. At this point, all processors can access the appropriate weight values and perform the update function in unison. For large values of $R_l$, this approach yields a higher

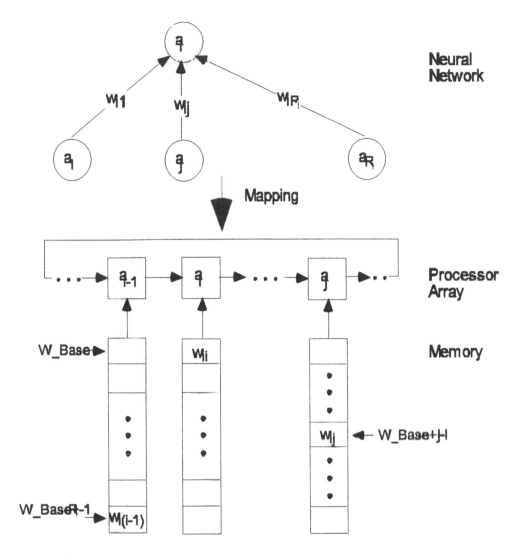

FIGURE 9.10. Memory locations of synaptic weights on the inputs of neuron $i$.

performance requiring only $O(\log R_l)$ steps compared to the earlier method yielding a performance of $O(R_l)$ steps.

## 9.5 Implementation Examples and Performance Evaluation

In this section we demonstrate the performance of the DREAM Machine through the use of several real-world example mappings. We compare this result with that obtained from mapping onto a ring systolic architecture. Because of the nature of the mapping method, other more complex interconnection topologies (hypercube, plain mesh, and others) do not offer additional advantages over the 1-D ring and thus are not included in our evaluation.

### 9.5.1 Performance Metric

A commonly used and quoted measure of implementation performance for neural networks is the million connection updates per second (MCUPS) metric. This measure is calculated by dividing the total number of connections in the neural network by the amount of time required to perform a weight updating procedure on the complete network. The execution time is measured starting from the point where input data is presented to the network through the point where all synaptic weight updates have been completed. The main problem with using this measure is that the weight values can be updated using a number of different learning algorithms, each having different computational requirements.

For evaluating and comparing the performance of our implementation, we will use the less restricting metric based on recall processing only. The metric used here is the million connections per second (MCPS). This measure is evaluated by dividing the number of connections in the network by the total time between the presentation of the input pattern until all the output values are generated. Use of real-world example networks offers a better assessment of the system's ability to efficiently implement varying network structures over the often-quoted peak execution rate.

Optimally, the number of operations that can be performed in parallel with any implementation taking advantage of neuron level parallelism [2] (assigning individual neurons to distinct PEs) is equal to $\min(N_l, N_{l-1})$. The optimum execution rate for implementing the processing associated with layer $l$ can be represented as

$$T_l^* = \frac{N_l N_{l-1}}{\min(N_l, N_{l-1})} = \max(N_l, N_{l-1}). \tag{9.17}$$

A relative measure of performance of any mapping method can be evaluated as a ratio of the mapping's execution rate over the optimal. We have selected three different neural network structures as benchmarks for evaluating our mapping method applied to the DREAM Machine architecture. We use both the MCPS and the percentage of optimality measure in our evaluations.

### 9.5.2 Implementing Fully Connected Multilayer Neural Networks

A commonly used neural network model for comparing relative performances of parallel implementations of neural network is the Nettalk network [42]. Nettalk is a simple three-layer neural network with full interconnections between adjacent layers, which utilizes the backpropagation learning algorithm to produce speech from printed text. The network consists of 203 input neurons, 60 hidden neurons (neurons in the second layer), and 29 output neurons. Using the mapping method described in Section 9.4, we can construct a ring structure (similar to Figure 9.8) with $N_1$=203 and $N_2$=60. Assuming a DREAM Machine architecture with 256 processing elements, the implementation execution rate can be arrived at by using Equations 9.11 and 9.12 to be $T$=263$k_1$+2$k_2$ seconds, where $k_1$ is the time to execute a single systolic cycle of the algorithm and $k_2$ is the time required to perform the table lookup operation.

Because the DREAM Machine architecture allows for memory access, interprocessor data transfer, and arithmetic operations, to be executed in parallel, $k_1$ will be equal to the time required to implement the most time consuming of these three operations. Assuming current technology for the implementation of the DREAM Machine, we can safely assume a value of $k_1$=100ns. Assuming an 8-bit quantization level for the neuron activation function, the time required to implement the table lookup operation will be nine memory access cycles (eight for loading the shift register and one for reading the final value). Allowing for a 50ns memory access time, $k_2$=450ns.

Using these values we arrive at a performance measure of 512 MCPS for implementing the Nettalk network on the DREAM Machine. The implementation of the same neural network model on a fixed-ring systolic array, following the mapping in [43], with a ring size of 256 PEs, will achieve a throughput rate of $512k_1+2k_2$ seconds. Allowing for the same implementation technology and setting $k_1$=100ns and $k_2$=450ns, we arrive at a 267 MCPS throughput rate. This assumes that the ring architecture supports the same type of table lookup mechanism as the DREAM Machine. If the neuron activation value is to be determined analytically, the performance will be further reduced.

The relatively similar execution rate obtained from the fixed-ring mapping and the DREAM Machine mapping is due to the limited degree of parallelism in the Nettalk network and its simple fully interconnected structure. This point becomes evident if we consider the percentage of optimality factor for both implementations. The optimal execution rate for implementing the Nettalk network is $T^*$=$263k_1+2k_2$ seconds. This leads to an optimality factor of 100 percent for the DREAM Machine implementation versus 52 percent for the fixed-ring implementation.

### 9.5.3  Implementing a Block-Connected Multilayer Neural Network

A neural network model that reflects the current trend in structured network design was proposed in [44] for image compression. The structure of this network (shown in Figure 9.11) is a good example of a blocked connected neural network used for data fusion described in Section 9.4.6. This network consists of five layers. The input layer is comprised of eight disjoint blocks of 64 neurons each. Each 64-neuron block in the input layer is fully connected to a unique 8-neuron block in the second layer. All of the 64 neurons in the second layer are fully connected to $n$ neurons in the third layer. The number of neurons in this layer ($n$) determines the amount of compression performed by the network. A symmetrically identical interconnection structure is constructed to decompress the information from the third through the fifth layer.

The ring structure for implementing this network on the DREAM Machine is shown in Figure 9.12. This ring structure operates in two configurations: Configuration 1 contains eight nonintersecting rings of length 32 used for processing layers 2 and 5, thus $\tilde{R}_2 = \tilde{R}_5 = 32$. Configuration 2 is used for processing layers 3 and 4 and consists of a single ring with 64 processors, thus $\tilde{R}_3 = \tilde{R}_4 = 64$. Virtual PEs must be used to implement the required 512 neurons in the input and output layers, because the processor array has only 256 processors. The use of virtual PEs to implement layers 1 and 5 leads to $\tilde{\omega}_2 = \tilde{\omega}_5 = 2$. No other layers require virtual processors and, therefore, $\tilde{\omega}_3 = \tilde{\omega}_4 = 1$ and $\tilde{v}_2 = \tilde{v}_3 = \tilde{v}_4 = \tilde{v}_5 = 1$. Using Equations 9.11 and 9.14, we can calculate the execution time required for implementing this network to be $T$=$256k_1+4k_2$ corresponding to a 598 MCPS throughput, assuming the compression factor ($n$=64). Using a fixed-ring architecture, the expected execution time will be $T$=$1536k_1+4k_2$, yielding a throughput rate of only 105 MCPS.

We can calculate the optimal execution time for this network taking advantage of all the available neuron level parallelism. This leads to a $T^*$=$256k_1+4k_2$ value. We can notice that similar to the Nettalk mapping, the DREAM Machine implementation can achieve a 100 percent level of optimality where the fixed-ring approach yields a performance of 18 percent of optimum.

### 9.5.4  Implementing a Fully Connected Single Layer Network

The peak performance of this implementation can be evaluated by mapping a neural network structure that offers the greatest amount of parallelism. One such network was pro-

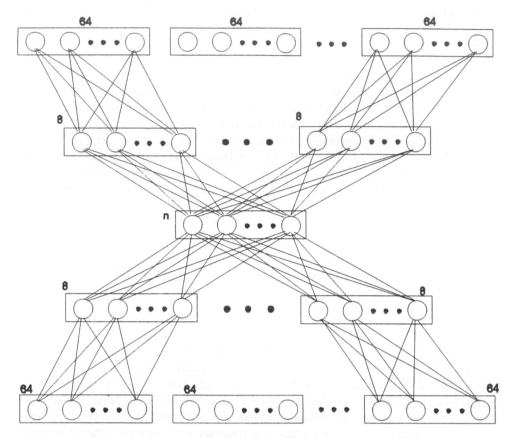

FIGURE 9.11. A neural network structure for image compression and decompression with a regularly blocked structure [44].

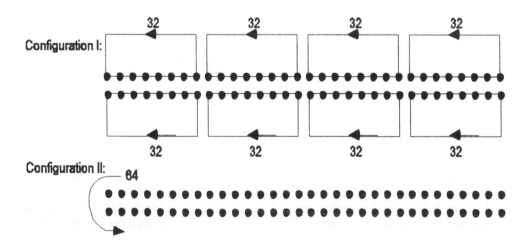

FIGURE 9.12. The ring structure associated with the image compression and decompression network of Figure 9.11.

TABLE 9.1. Performance comparison of the variable-size ring mapping versus the fixed-size ring mapping based on the MCPS metric.

| | Nettalk [42] (MCPS) | Compression Net [44] (MCPS) | Hopfield 30 Cities TSP [13] (MCPS) |
|---|---|---|---|
| Fixed-Size Ring Mapping | 267 | 105 | 1,969 |
| Variable-Size Ring Mapping | 512 | 598 | 2,239 |

TABLE 9.2. Performance comparison of the variable-size ring mapping versus the fixed-size ring mapping based on the optimality ratio.

| | Nettalk [42] (%) | Compression Net [44] (%) | Hopfield 30 Cities TSP [13] (%) |
|---|---|---|---|
| Fixed-Size Ring Mapping | 52 | 18 | 77 |
| Variable-Size Ring Mapping | 100 | 100 | 88 |

posed in [13] where a fully connected neural network is used to solve the traveling salesman problem (TSP). The neural network requires $N^2$ neurons and thus $N^4$ synapses to implement an $N$ city TSP. A 16-city TSP can efficiently utilize all the PEs of the DREAM Machine to arrive at a peak performance of 2,516 MCPS. The same type of performance can be expected from a fixed-ring architecture when implementing this network because the ring size matches perfectly the number of available PEs in the machine. To implement the 30 cities problem described in [13], we can construct a ring of size 225 for processing the required 900 neurons. The amount of time required for each update of the neuron output values can be found via Equation 9.9 to be $T=(4*4*225k_1 + 4k_2) = 361.8\mu s$ or 2,239 MCPS performance. Implementing this network on a 256 element fixed-ring architecture leads to a 1,969 MCPS performance. This illustrates well the capability of the DREAM Machine and the variable ring mapping strategy to maintain a performance close to the peak value for neural network structures with varying sizes.

Tables 9.1 and 9.2 summarize the results of the performance comparisons made in this section.

## 9.6 Conclusion

In this chapter we described a mapping method and a supporting computer architecture for efficient implementation of neural network models with regularly structured interconnections. We described how various features of the DREAM Machine architecture can be used to efficiently implement specific requirements imposed by neural network processing. Examples of these features include support for global min/max operations across all PEs and a mechanism for implementing table lookup operations. The mechanism used for constructing processing rings of arbitrary size (less than the processing array size) was shown to be useful for matching the size of the problem to the architecture. The use of embedded ring structures, described in Section 9.4 and demonstrated in Section 9.5, have outlined the effectiveness of this method in significantly reducing the restrictions on the size and shape of the interconnection structure of multilayer neural networks for efficient and fast processing.

The performance of the DREAM Machine architecture was compared to the ring-connected systolic architecture. Because both architectures use nearest neighbor communications, the extra communication hardware required by the DREAM Machine is only a constant factor greater than the 1-D ring architecture. On the other hand, the execution rate of the fixed ring was shown to be $O(P)$, where $P$ is the number of processors in the network (assuming the number of neurons per layer is always less than $P$). Using the variable ring mapping method on the DREAM Machine, the execution rate of this implementation is $O(\tilde{R}^b)$, where $\tilde{R}^b$ is the size of the largest block in the network. As neural networks continue to be applied to more demanding applications requiring specialized structures for processing various portions of the input data, the number of blocks in a specific neural network will increase but the size of each block should remain relatively small and constant. To exploit all the available parallelism in such networks, the number of processors in the system should increase. The DREAM Machine architecture and the variable ring size mapping method support these demands very efficiently because the execution rate scales are relative to the small and constant $\tilde{R}^b$ value rather than the large and growing processor array size.

## Acknowledgment

We would like to thank the referees for their helpful comments and suggestions on improving and refining this chapter. The first author would like to thank Dr. Scott Toborg for helpful comments on the initial draft of this chapter.

# References

[1] S. Shams, *DREAM Machine—A Platform for Efficient Implementation of Neural Networks with Arbitrarly Complex Interconnection Structures*. PhD thesis, University of Southern California, Los Angeles, CA, 1992.

[2] S. Shams and J.-L. Gaudiot, "Parallel implementations of neural networks." Submitted for publication, Nov. 1992.

[3] A. J. D. Groot and S. R. Parker, "Systolic implementation of neural networks," in *Proceedings of the SPIE, High Speed Computing II* (K. Bromley, ed.), vol. 1058, (Los Angeles), pp. 182–190, 1989.

[4] B. M. Forrest, et. al., "Implementing neural network models on parallel computers," *The Computer Journal*, vol. 30, no. 5, pp. 413–419, 1987.

[5] D. Hammerstorm, "A VLSI architecture for high-performance, low-cost, on-chip learning," in *Proceedings of the International Joint Conference on Neural Networks*, vol. 2, (San Diego), pp. 537–544, 1990.

[6] S. Y. Kung and J. N. Hwang, "A unified systolic architecture for artificial neural networks," *Journal of Parallel and Distributed Computing*, vol. 6, pp. 358–387, 1989.

[7] H. K. Kwan and P. C. Tsang, "Systolic implementation of multi-layer feed-forward neural network with back-propagation learning scheme," in *Proceedings of the International Joint Conference on Neural Networks*, vol. 2, (Washington D.C.), pp. 155–158, 1990.

[8] G. G. Pechanek, S. Vassiliadis, and J. G. Delgado-Frias, "Digital neural emulators using tree accumlation and communication structures," *IEEE Transactions on Neural Networks*, vol. 3, no. 6, pp. 934–950, 1992.

[9] U. Ramacher, J. Beichter, and N. Bruls, "Architecture of a general-purpose neural signal processor," in *Proceedings of the International Joint Conference on Neural Networks*, vol. 1, (Seattle, WA), pp. 443–448, 1991.

[10] S. Shams and K. W. Przytula, "Implementation of multilayer neural networks on parallel programmable digital computers," in *Parallel Algorithms and Architectures for DSP Applications* (M. Bayoumi, ed.), pp. 225–253, Kluwer Acadamic Publishers, 1991.

[11] S. Vassiliadis, G. G. Pechanek, and J. G. Delgado-Frias, "SPIN: A sequential pipelined neurocomputer," in *Proceedings of the IEEE International Conference on Tools for AI*, (San Jose, CA), pp. 74–81, 1991.

[12] X. Zhang, M. McKenna, J. P. Mesirov, and D. L. Waltz, "An efficient implementation of the back-propagation algorithm on the Connection Machine CM-2," in *Advances in Neural Information Processing Systems 2* (D. S. Touretzky, ed.), pp. 801–809, San Mateo, CA, Morgan Kaufmann, 1990.

[13] J. J. Hopfield and D. W. Tank, "Neural computation of decisions in optimization problems," *Biological Cybernetics*, vol. 52, pp. 141–152, 1985.

[14] D. E. Rumelhart, G. E. Hinton, and R. J. Williams, "Learning internal representations by error propagation," in *Parallel Distributed Processing: Explorations in the Microstructure of Cognition* (D. E. Rumelhart and J. McClelland, eds.), vol. 1, pp. 318–364, Cambridge: MIT Press, 1986.

[15] K. Fukushima, "Neocognitron: A hierarchical neural network capable of visual pattern recognition," *Neural Networks*, vol. 1, pp. 119–130, 1988.

[16] G. Blelloch and C. R. Rosenberg, "Network learning on the Connection Machine," in *Proceedings of the 10th Intern. Joint Conference on Artificial Intelligence*, (Milan, Italy), pp. 323–326, 1987.

[17] J. R. Brown, M. M. Garber, and S. F. Venable, "Artificial neural network on a SIMD architecture," in *Proceedings of the Symposium on the Frontiers of Massively Parallel Computations*, pp. 43–47, 1988.

[18] K. A. Grajski, "Neurocomputing using the MasPar MP-1," Tech. Rep. 90-010, Ford Aerospace Corp., 1990.

[19] N. Morgan, et. al., "The RAP: A ring array processor for layered network calculations," in *Proceedings of the International Conference on Appl. Spec. Array Proc.* (J. A. B. F. S. Y. Kung, E. E. Swartzlander and K. W. Przytula, eds.), (Princeton, NJ), pp. 296–308, 1990.

[20] D. A. Pomerleau, G. L. Gusciora, D. S. Touretzky, and H. T. Kung, "Neural network simulation at warp speed: How we got 17 million connections per second," in *Proceedings of the IEEE International Confer. on Neural Networks*, (San Diego), 1988.

[21] V. K. P. Kumar and K. W. Przytula, "Algorithmic mapping of neural network models onto parallel SIMD machines," in *Proceedings of the International Conference on Appl. Spec. Array Proc.* (J. A. B. F. S. Y. Kung, E. E. Swartzlander and K. W. Przytula, eds.), (Princeton, NJ), 1990.

[22] S. Shams and K. W. Przytula, "Mapping of neural networks onto programmable parallel machines," in *Proceedings of the Intern. Symp. on Circuits and Systems*, vol. 4, (New Orleans, LA), pp. 2613–2617, 1990.

[23] M. Witbrock and M. Zagha, "An implementation of back-propagation learning on GF11, a large SIMD parallel computer," *Parallel Computing*, vol. 14, no. 3, pp. 329–346, 1990.

[24] M. A. Arbib, *The Metaphorical Brain 2, Neural Networks and Beyond.* John Wiley & Sons, 1989.

[25] Y. Le Cun, J. S. Denker, and S. A. Solla, "Optimal brain damage," in *Advances in Neural Information Processing Systems 2* (D. S. Touretzky, ed.), pp. 598–605, San Mateo, CA, Morgan Kaufmann, 1990.

[26] S. T. Toborg and K. Hwang, "Cooperative vision integeration through data-parallel neural computations," *IEEE Transactions on Computer*, vol. 40, no. 12, pp. 1368–1379, 1991.

[27] G. A. Carpenter and S. Grossberg, "A massively parallel architecture for a self-organizing neural pattern recognition machine," *Compute Vision, Graphics, and Image Processing*, vol. 37, pp. 54–115, 1987.

[28] D. W. Blevins, E. W. Davis, R. A. Heaton, and J. H. Reif, "BLITZEN: A highly integrated massively parallel machine," *Journal of Parallel and Distributed Computing*, vol. 8, pp. 150–160, 1990.

[29] K. W. Przytula and J. G. Nash, "A special purpose coprocessor for signal processing," in *Proceedings of the 21st Asilomar Conference on Signals, Systems and Computers*, (Monterey, CA), pp. 736–740, 1987.

[30] R. M. Hord, *Parallel Supercomputing in SIMD Architectures*. Boca Raton, CRC Press, 1990.

[31] T. Kohonen, *Self-Organization and Associative Memory*. Springer Series in Information Sciences, Springer-Verlag, second ed., 1987.

[32] B. Kosko, "Unsupervised learning in noise," *IEEE Transactions on Neural Networks*, vol. 1, no. 1, pp. 44–57, 1990.

[33] D. B. Shu, J. G. Nash, M. M. Eshaghian, and K. Kim, "Implementation and application of a gated-connection network in image understanding," in *Reconfigurable Massively Parallel Computers* (H. Li and Q. F. Stout, eds.), Prentice Hall, 1991.

[34] C. C. Weems, *Image Processing on a Content Addressable Array Parallel Processor*. PhD thesis, University of Massachusetts, Amherst, MA, 1984.

[35] D. E. Goldberg, *Genetic Algorithms in Search, Optimization, and Machine Learning*. Addison-Wesley Publishing Co., 1989.

[36] S. H. Bokhari, "On the mapping problem," *IEEE Transactions on Computers*, vol. 30, no. 3, pp. 207–214, 1981.

[37] P. Simic and S. Shams, "Solving the assignment and scheduling problems using cnet," Tech. Rep. CALT-68-1892, California Institute of Technology, 1992.

[38] B. Kosko, "Bidirectional associative memories," *IEEE Transactions on Systems, Man, and Cybernetics*, vol. 18, pp. 49–60, 1988.

[39] Y. Le Cun, et. al., "Handwritten digit recognition with a back-propagation network," in *Advances in Neural Information Processing Systems 2* (D. S. Touretzky, ed.), pp. 396–403, San Mateo, CA, Morgan Kaufmann, 1990.

[40] S. Kirkpatrick, C. D. G. Jr, and M. P. Vecchi, "Optimization by simulated annealing," *Science*, vol. 220, pp. 671–680, 1983.

[41] R. Mann and S. Haykin, "A parallel implementation of kohonen feature maps on the warp systolic computer," in *Proceedings of the International Joint Conference on Neural Networks*, vol. 2, (Washington D.C.), pp. 84–87, 1990.

[42] T. J. Sejnowski and C. R. Rosenberg, "Parallel networks that learn to pronounce English text," *Complex Systems*, vol. 1, pp. 145–168, 1987.

[43] S. Y. Kung and J. N. Hwang, "Systolic architectures for artificial neural nets," in *Proceedings of the IEEE International Conference on Neural Networks*, vol. 2, (San Diego, CA), pp. 165–172, 1988.

[44] A. Namphol, M. Arozullah, and S. Chin, "Higher order data compression with neural networks," in *Proceedings of the International Joint Conference on Neural Networks*, vol. 1, (Seattle, WA), pp. 55–59, 1991.

# Chapter 10

# High-Performance Parallel Backpropagation Simulation with On-Line Learning

**Urs A. Müller**
**Patrick Spiess**
**Michael Kocheisen**
**Beat Flepp**
**Anton Gunzinger**
**Walter Guggenbühl**
Swiss Federal Institute of Technology (ETH),
Switzerland

## 10.1  Introduction

Neural networks are inherently parallel. It, therefore, seems natural to build parallel hardware for their implementation. However, one has to distinguish between the *training phase* and the *recall phase* of a neural network, which pose different requirements to the hardware. In the recall phase, the weights and the structure of the network are fixed and the required computing precision is usually low, typically 8 bits or less. It is, therefore, feasible to build dedicated high-speed and low-cost hardware chips [1]. In the training phase, on the other hand, the adjustment of the weights and sometimes also the structure of the neural network have to be adapted and a higher precision is required. A 32-bit floating point is commonly used. Furthermore, it is often appropriate to investigate several different neural network structures and learning algorithms for the same problem to get the optimal solution. Both the necessary degree of freedom and the higher precision make it infeasible to build dedicated hardware in most cases.

The training phase is also more critical in terms of computing power. A single pattern presentation, including the updating of the weights, requires about three times more operations than the recall phase. In addition, a large amount of training patterns is presented several times. Finally, many training experiments are usually necessary to find a satisfactory solution. For example, let's assume that the development of a certain neural network requires 10 training runs with 100 presentations of 10,000 patterns each. Compared to a single pattern presentation in the recall phase, this requires $3 \times 10 \times 100 \times 10,000 = 30$ million times more operations. In other words, a computer that is able to process 100 patterns per second in the recall phase requires more than three days of CPU time to satisfy the computational demand of the network development!

In terms of computing performance, the training phase is therefore the critical part. We describe the implementation and application of the MUSIC parallel supercomputer for neural networks simulation. The system was developed at the Electronics Laboratory of the Swiss Federal Institute of Technology in Zurich in 1991 and 1992. Since then it has been used for computing intensive simulations in chemistry, physics, digital signal processing, image processing, and neural networks research [2]. It helped to speed up many compute intensive experiments by one to two orders of magnitude compared to modern workstations.

The chapter is organized as follows. Section 10.2 describes the architecture and implementation of the MUSIC system. Section 10.3 compares different parallelization schemes for the backpropagation algorithm and shows how it has been implemented on the MUSIC system. Section 10.4 presents a theoretical performance model and verifies it with real measurements of the backpropagation implementation. Section 10.5 describes the NeuroBasic parallel simulation environment. Section 10.6 reports on two examples of practical research work, which were made possible only through the availability of NeuroBasic and the MUSIC system. Section 10.7 examines trends for future MUSIC generations and compares the backpropagation performance of many new RISC processors. Section 10.8, finally, presents some concluding remarks.

## 10.2  The MUSIC Parallel Supercomputer

The goal of the MUSIC project was to build a fast parallel system and to use it in real-world applications [3]. The key idea of the architecture is to support the collection and redistribution of complete multidimensional data sets by a simple, efficient, and autonomously working communication network realized in hardware. Instead of considering where to send and from where to receive data, each processing element determines which part of the data set it has produced and which other part it wants to receive. A programmer therefore does not have to subdivide data distributions into individual point-to-point transactions. This has the advantage of reducing the complexity for the programmer, lowering the communication latency, and increasing the data throughput by automatically broadcasting data for several recipients in parallel.

### 10.2.1  System Hardware

It is up to the communication hardware to realize the actual data redistribution in the most efficient way in terms of performance, cost, and implementation time. In case of the MUSIC computer, the communication network is a ring (Figure 10.1). Each processing element has a communication interface realized with a XILINX 3090 field-programmable gate array. During communication the data is shifted through a 40-bit wide bus (32 data bits and eight token bits) operated at a 5-MHz clock rate. On each clock cycle, the processing elements shift a data value to their right neighbor and receive a value from their left neighbor. By simply counting the clock cycles, each processing element knows when to copy data from the passing data stream into its local memory and, likewise, when to insert data from the local memory into the ring. The tokens are used to mark invalid data and to determine when a data value has circulated through the complete ring.

Three processing elements are placed on a $9 \times 8.5$-inch board, each of them consisting of a Motorola 96002 floating-point digital signal processor (DSP), 2 Mbyte video (dynamic) memory, 1 Mbyte static memory, and the above mentioned communication controller. The video memory has a parallel port, which is connected to the processor, and a serial port, which is connected to the communication interface. Therefore, data processing is almost not affected by the communication network's activity and communication and processing can overlap in time, allowing more efficient use of the available communication bandwidth. The processors run at 40 MHz with a peak performance of 60 Mflops. Each board further contains an Inmos T425 transputer as a board manager. It is responsible for performance measurements and data communication with the host (a Sun workstation, PC, or Macintosh).

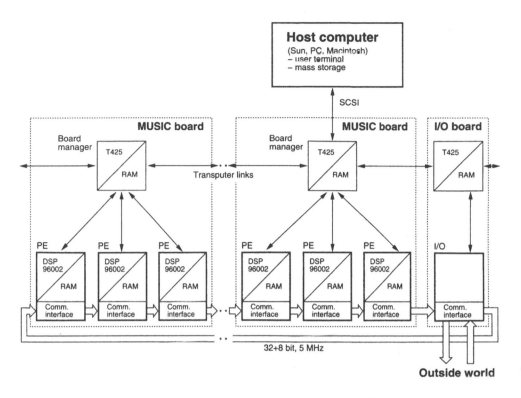

FIGURE 10.1. Overview of the MUSIC hardware.

To provide the fast data throughput required by many applications, special I/O modules (for instance, for real-time video processing applications) can be added that have direct access to the communication bus (see Figure 10.1). A SCSI interface module for four parallel SCSI-2 disks has been built, which allows the storage of huge amount of training data for neural networks. Up to 21 boards (63 processing elements) fit into a standard 19-inch rack resulting in a 3.8-Gflops system. MUSIC's technical data is summarized in Table 10.1.

TABLE 10.1. MUSIC system technical data for a 19-inch rack system.

| | |
|---|---|
| Number of processing elements: | 63 |
| Peak performance: | 3.8 Gflops |
| Floating-point format: | 44-bit IEEE single extended precision |
| Memory: | 180 Mbyte |
| Programming language: | C, Assembler |
| Cabinet: | 19-inch rack |
| Cooling: | forced air cooling |
| Total power consumption: | < 800 Watt |
| Host computer: | Sun workstation, PC, or Macintosh |

To allow the interconnection of multiple MUSIC racks, an optical interface board has been developed [4]. This way, systems of up to 166 processing elements have been successfully operated.

### 10.2.2 System Programming

From the hardware point of view, MUSIC is a multiple instructions multiple data (MIMD) computer. Each processing element is able to execute a different program. However, the programming paradigm most often used is single program multiple data (SPMD), where all processing elements carry out the same program but on different data subsets (data-parallel). Periodically, they synchronize to exchange or redistribute data. The difference to a single instruction multiple data (SIMD) architecture is that the MUSIC processing elements are not synchronized on the instruction level. This allows different program paths to be taken on different processors without the performance degradation that occurs on SIMD computers in such cases.

For programming the communication network only three library functions are necessary: `Init_comm()` to specify the data block dimensions and data partitioning, `Data_ready()` to label a certain amount of data as ready for communication, and `Wait_data()` to wait for the arrival of the expected data (synchronization). Other functions allow the exchange and automatic distribution of data blocks between the host computer and MUSIC and the calling of individual user functions. The activity of the transputers is embedded in these functions and remains invisible to the user.

Data partitioning has the only restrictions of rectangular subsets and a maximum of three-dimensional data sets. Frequently used cases are supported automatically by the system software. This is, for instance, the case for partitioning along a single dimension ($x$, $y$, or $z$). The operating system determines the actual partitioning at run time according to the present number of processing elements. As a result, the compiled code is completely independent of the system size. The basic partitioning method is to divide the data sets into equal pieces (static load balancing). It works well if the processing time is independent of the data. If this is not the case, however, the operating system can change the partitioning dynamically according to time measurements from previous iteration steps (dynamic load balancing).

The standard programming language is C with time-critical parts sometimes written in Assembly language. Writing data-parallel code for MUSIC is not much more difficult than writing sequential code. The major difference is that the data-parallel code works on subsets of the data and has points of synchronization where data is exchanged or redistributed.

## 10.3 Backpropagation Implementation

We will discuss the problem of parallelization on the example of the *multilayer perceptron*. This feed-forward net is one of the most widely used neural network models. It is usually trained using a gradient descent method, which often is a derivative of the standard backpropagation algorithm. The parallelization of backpropagation is presented here as a basic representative for a wide class of training algorithms.

### 10.3.1 The Backpropagation Algorithm

Figure 10.2 shows the structure of a multilayer perceptron. The number of layers in this case is two, but in general it can be arbitrarily large. The input layer (layer 0) is usually not counted because it carries out no computation. The output, $o_j$, of a neuron is computed as

$$o_j = f(a_j) = f\left(\sum_i w_{ji} \cdot o_i\right) \qquad (10.1)$$

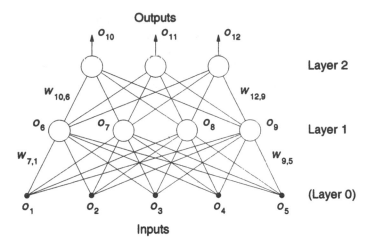

**Outputs**

**Layer 2**

**Layer 1**

**(Layer 0)**

**Inputs**

FIGURE 10.2. A two-layer perceptron.

where $f(\cdot)$ is a sigmoid-like differentiable nonlinear function and $o_i$ are the inputs of the neuron, which are outputs of the neurons in the previous layer.

In the recall phase, the input pattern is forward propagated by applying Equation 10.1 layer by layer to all neurons. For the training phase, we need examples (training patterns) consisting of input patterns and the corresponding target output vectors. A pattern is first forward propagated through the net. The output of the network is then compared with the target vector and the resulting errors, $\delta_j$, of the neurons are backpropagated through the net according to

$$\delta_j = \begin{cases} f'_j(a_j) \cdot (t_j - o_j) & \text{for output neurons,} \\ f'_j(a_j) \cdot \sum_k (w_{kj} \cdot \delta_k) & \text{otherwise.} \end{cases} \qquad (10.2)$$

The index $k$ refers to all neurons that are connected to the output of neuron $j$, and $t_j$ are the elements of the target vector. Note that the computation in forward propagation (Equation 10.1) and backpropagation (Equation 10.2) is very similar but in different directions. After the errors $\delta_j$ are computed, the weights are updated according to

$$w^{\text{new}}_{ji} = w^{\text{old}}_{ji} + \Delta W_{ji} = w^{\text{old}}_{ji} + \eta \cdot \delta_j \cdot o_i. \qquad (10.3)$$

where the constant $\eta$ is the so-called *learning rate*. This is the backpropagation algorithm. A detailed description can be found in [5].

### 10.3.2 Parallelization

Different data sets, and thus different levels of parallelism, are found in a neural network experiment. If one is interested in a series of independent learning experiments, then each processor is able to carry out one or more of the experiments. Many researchers make use of this practice by distributing an experimental series over multiple workstations. It works well if a large number of independent experiments is to be carried out. It is, however, no longer applicable if the results of one experiment are needed to set up a following one.

To parallelize a single training experiment, it is important to distinguish between updating the weights immediately after each pattern presentation (referred to as *continuous weight update*) or accumulating the weight changes, $\Delta w$, over many patterns before making the actual weight updates (referred to as *batch learning*).

Batch learning is easier to parallelize and is frequently reported in the literature [6–9]. The neural network can be replicated on all processing elements and each of them can work on a different subset of the patterns. Periodically the processing elements have to communicate the accumulated weight changes. Most theoretical studies about backpropagation are based on batch learning. On the other hand, it is empirically known that continuous weight update usually converges much faster than batch learning [3]. Especially in research it is therefore important not to be restricted to batch learning only.

A next, deeper level is *parallelization in layer space*, which means computing different layers on different processing elements. To keep all processors busy, the patterns are propagated and backpropagated in a pipelined manner (see, for instance, [10]), which still restricts the implementation to batch learning. This is because in continuous weight update, a propagate/backpropagate cycle must be completed before the next pattern can be presented.

To allow continuous weight update, the parallelization level must go one step further, as realized in the presented implementation: *parallelization in neuron space*. In each iteration step, the output of a specific layer is computed. All processing elements have a local copy of the complete input vector of the layer and compute a subset of its output vector. Afterward, the communication controllers collect the partial vectors and distribute a copy of the assembled vector back to each processing element, which then serves as input for computing the output of the next layer. The backward path looks similar except that, besides computing the errors $\delta_j$, the weights must be updated as well. A welcome side effect of this method is that each processing element needs to store only a subset of the weights in its local memory instead of the complete weight set of a network, as is the case for parallelization in pattern space. The memory of the parallel computer is therefore much more efficiently used. The partitioning of a layer is illustrated in Figure 10.3.

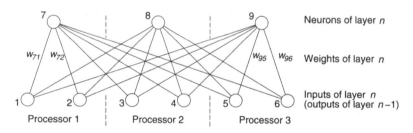

FIGURE 10.3. Layer partitioning of a multilayer perceptron.

One difficulty, however, is given by the fact that on each processing element different weight subsets are needed to forward-propagate the inputs than are needed for backpropagating the errors (compare Figure 10.3). Communicating the updated weights after each propagate/backpropagate cycle is normally not feasible because the number of weights increases nearly with the square of the number of neurons and the communication of weights will saturate the communication. A better method is to let each processing element compute a part of the sum according to the weights stored locally and afterward accumulate the parts globally. This method is used, for example, in [11].

However, to avoid the global accumulation of vectors, which is only efficient with a specialized communication network with a built-in adder, we implemented another method, proposed in [12]. Each processing element has a local copy of two different weight subsets, one needed in the forward path and the other needed in the backward path. Let's assume that the weights of a particular layer are organized in a matrix $[w_{ji}]$, where $j$ denotes a neuron of the layer and $i$ denotes the inputs of that neuron (Figure 10.4). In the forward path, each processing element must compute the outputs of a subset of the neurons in the layer (Figure 10.3) and therefore needs a horizontal slice of the weight matrix. In the backward path, each processing element needs to compute the error $\delta_i$ for a part of the neurons of the preceding layer and thus needs a vertical slice of the same matrix.

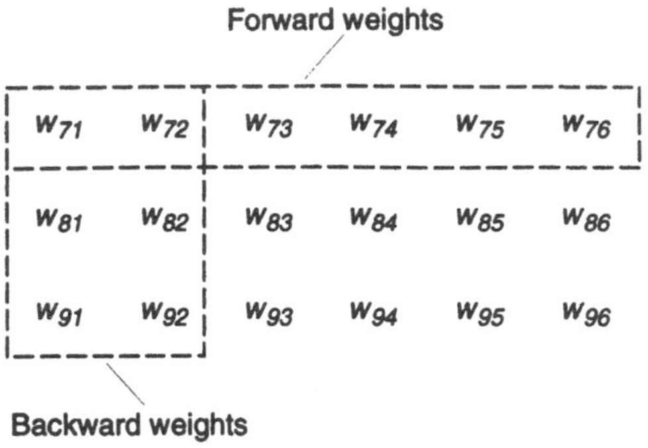

Forward weights

|        |        |        |        |        |        |
|--------|--------|--------|--------|--------|--------|
| $w_{71}$ | $w_{72}$ | $w_{73}$ | $w_{74}$ | $w_{75}$ | $w_{76}$ |
| $w_{81}$ | $w_{82}$ | $w_{83}$ | $w_{84}$ | $w_{85}$ | $w_{86}$ |
| $w_{91}$ | $w_{92}$ | $w_{93}$ | $w_{94}$ | $w_{95}$ | $w_{96}$ |

Backward weights

FIGURE 10.4. Weight subsets of processor 1 corresponding to Figure 10.3.

Each processor locally updates both stored subsets. As an overall consequence, each weight update is carried out twice on different processing elements. This increases the necessary computation by about 30 percent but reduces the communication from $O(n^2)$ to $O(n)$. Furthermore, the additional performance is not required in the first layer because the backpropagation of the error is not needed here. This is important because the first layer is also often the largest one.

This situation can be illustrated with a simple model. We assume that the computing time per connection in the forward and backward path is $t_p$ each, the time for a connection update is $t_w$ and the time needed for communicating a single value is $t_c$. We further concentrate on a specific layer of a net that has $s$ neurons and $s$ inputs. The number of connections of this layer then is $s^2$ (neglecting the bias) and the sum of output and $\delta$ values is $2s$. If the weights are communicated, the total time for one propagate/backpropagate cycle ($t_{comp} + t_{comm}$) on an $n$-processor system is given by

$$t_{tot}(n) = \frac{s^2 \cdot (2t_p + t_w)}{n} + (2s + s^2) \cdot t_c \qquad (10.4)$$

and for updating the weights twice instead of communicating them

$$t_{tot}(n) = \frac{s^2 \cdot (2t_p + 2t_w)}{n} + 2s \cdot t_c . \qquad (10.5)$$

Note, that the communication time in Equation 10.4 increases with the square of the number of neurons, whereas in Equation 10.5 it increases only linearly. For a realistic situation, we assume that $t_w = 2t_p = 2t_c$ (which is a good approximation for the MUSIC implementation) and that $t_c$ is 1 time unit. The performance, measured in number of connection updates per time unit, then results to

$$p(n) = \frac{s^2}{t_{tot}(n)} . \qquad (10.6)$$

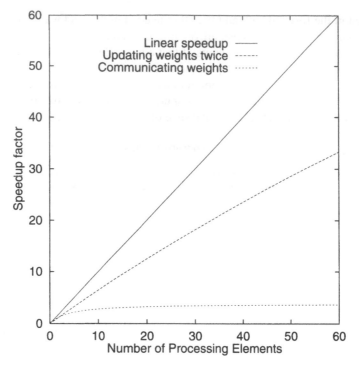

FIGURE 10.5. Speedup comparison for updating the weights of a layer with 100 neurons.

The speedup factors of the two methods are illustrated in Figure 10.5. The speedup factor is the ratio between the execution time on one processing element (without communication) to the execution time on $n$ processing elements. It becomes clear that communicating the weights results in almost no speedup at all.

This situation is not uncommon in a multiprocessor environment. It is often more efficient to compute values multiple times on different processing elements than to communicate them.

## 10.4  Performance Analysis

The parallel performance is limited by various factors of which the computational (peak) performance is only one, as the following example demonstrates.

The number of arithmetical operations per connection update for backpropagation is eight. Two operations are needed in the forward path (Equation 10.1), two in the backward path (Equation 10.2), and four to update each weight twice on different processing elements (Equation 10.3). The computation of the nonlinear function and its derivative is negligible for large networks. The maximum number of connection updates per second a system can compute then is determined by $\frac{1}{8} \cdot peak\ performance$. A 63-processing element MUSIC system, for instance, with 3.8 Gflops peak performance can therefore compute a maximum of 475 MCUPS (million connection updates per second). This is the *computational upper bound*.

However, this is not the only limiting factor. In the MUSIC system, for instance, a processing element can receive a maximum of 20 Mbytes per second. For each neuron, two values have to be broadcasted: the output value in the forward path and the error in the backward path. Considering 4 bytes per value (32-bit floating point), a maximum of 2.5

million neurons per second can be processed. If we assume a perceptron with 150 inputs per neuron, the maximum performance is 375 MCUPS. This is the *communicational upper bound*, which, in this case, is less then the computational upper bound!

### 10.4.1 A Speedup Model

A first-order approximation of the system performance is to take the lower of the two bounds. However, other factors are involved. In general, the total time needed to complete a task on $n$ processing elements, $t_{tot}(n)$, can be subdivided into three parts. A parallel part $t_p$, which decreases linearly with the number of processing elements $n$, a sequential part $t_s$, which is independent of $n$, and a cumulative part $t_\ell$, which even increases with the number of processing elements $n$:

$$t_{tot}(n) = \frac{1}{n}t_p + t_s + nt_\ell. \tag{10.7}$$

The *parallel part $t_p$* is the part of the computation that can be subdivided into smaller pieces assigned to different processing elements (mostly the program loops). The total execution time for the parallel part decreases proportionally to $1/n$. Without taking the other parts into account, the system speedup would be linear.

The *sequential part $t_s$* includes program parts like initialization or loop and communication overhead, which cannot be parallelized. In the backpropagation example, for instance, the time a processing element needs to receive the output values from all neurons of a certain layer is constant and does not decrease with $n$. The total execution time cannot become smaller than $t_s$ and the sequential part therefore limits the maximum possible speedup (Amdahl's law).

The *cumulative part $t_\ell$*, finally, includes any part that increases with the number of processing elements. It is typically found in communication latency between processing elements. Even if this part is small on a single-processor system, it is of increasing importance with a growing numbers of processing elements. It not only limits the maximum achievable speedup but also causes it to decrease again once the optimal number of processing elements is exceeded.

If we set the computing time of a single processing element to approximately $t_p$ (neglecting the sequential overhead in case of having only one processing element), then the total system speedup $s(n)$, including all three parts, results to

$$s(n) = \frac{t_p}{t_{tot}(n)} = \frac{1}{\frac{1}{n}t_p + \frac{t_s}{t_p} + \frac{t_\ell}{t_p}} = \frac{1}{\frac{1}{n} + \alpha + n\beta}. \tag{10.8}$$

### 10.4.2 Loss Factors

The parameters $\alpha$ and $\beta$ in Equation 10.8 represent the loss factors. If they both were zero, then the speedup would be linear: $s(n) = n$. The parameter $\alpha$ causes the speedup to saturate at $s(n \to \infty) = \frac{1}{\alpha}$. The influence of $\beta$ is even worse. It causes the speedup curve, $s(n)$, to have a maximum at $n = \frac{1}{\sqrt{\beta}}$ of

$$s_{max} = s\left(\frac{1}{\sqrt{\beta}}\right) = \frac{1}{\alpha + 2\sqrt{\beta}} \tag{10.9}$$

and after that to decrease again. A more detailed analysis of this can be found in [13]. Figure 10.6 illustrates the speedup for the specific values of $\alpha = 4.9 \cdot 10^{-3}$ and $\beta = 6.9 \cdot 10^{-5}$, which were derived for the backpropagation implementation of a neural network with 900 inputs, 600 hidden neurons, and 30 output neurons on the MUSIC system. Figure 10.6 further contains real measurement points to confirm the accuracy of the speedup model.

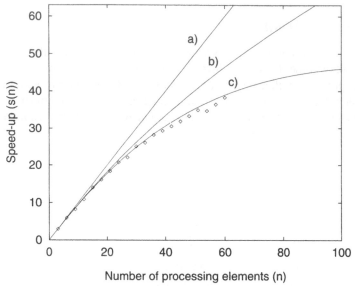

FIGURE 10.6. Speedup: (a) without losses (linear speedup), (b) considering the loss factor $\alpha$, and (c) considering both loss factors, $\alpha$ and $\beta$. The diamonds represent real measurements.

It becomes clear that even though the parameter $\beta$ is much smaller than $\alpha$, it plays an important role in the speedup. This is because its influence is proportional to the number of processing elements (Equation 10.8). This means that the communication latency, which is mostly responsible for $\beta$, is of fundamental importance. It limits the system performance in a way that cannot be corrected by adding or taking more powerful processing elements or by increasing the communication bandwidth.

### 10.4.3 Performance Results

The highest backpropagation speed on the MUSIC computer was reached by using assembly language to implement the kernel of the algorithm. Table 10.2 compares the performance of the MUSIC backpropagation implementation to other results reported in the literature and to own performance measurements on different computers. As far as we know, all examples, except connected network of adaptive processors (CNAPS), are based on floating-point computation. The performance in the forward path is measured in million connections per second (MCPS) and in million connection updates per second (MCUPS) for the learning, including both the forward and the backward path. A short description of most of the systems can be found in [3].

## 10.5 The NeuroBasic Parallel Simulation Environment

The goal of the presented simulation environment is to provide a simple way for neural networks researchers to access MUSIC's parallel processing power. For this purpose, a simple command language has been chosen as the user interface. It is being used to create *neuroobjects*, such as layers or weight sets, and to combine these objects with a given set of *neurofunctions*, such as forward propagation, backward propagation, and weight update.

TABLE 10.2. Comparison of backpropagation implementations.

| System | Number of PEs | Performance | | Continuous Weight Update |
|---|---|---|---|---|
| | | Forward [MCPS] | Learning [MCUPS] | |
| PC (Pentium, 100 MHz)† | 1 | 9.9 | 4.3 | Yes |
| Sun (SuperSPARC II, 85 MHz)† | 1 | 29.6 | 15.0 | Yes |
| Warp [6] | 10 | | 17.0 | No |
| CM-5 [14] | 544 | | 76.0 | No |
| RAP [15] | 40 | 574.0 | 106.0 | Yes |
| NEC SX-3† | 1 | | 130.0 | Yes |
| MUSIC-166* | 166 | 1,015.0 | 500.0 | Yes |
| GF11 [7] | 356 | | 901.0 | No |
| CNAPS [16] (8/16 bit) | 512 | 5,700 | 1,460 | Yes |

* Own measurements.
†No published reference available.

The neurofunctions themselves are implemented parallel in C or Assembly language. The following properties were of primary importance:

- Interactivity

- Ease of learning and using

- Flexibility

- Loops and conditional branches

- Variables.

### 10.5.1 Implementation

Instead of defining a new special-purpose command language, we decided to consider an existing one. The choice was BASIC, which seems to meet the preceding requirements best. It is easy to learn and to use and it is widely spread, flexible, and interactive. A BASIC interpreter, named *NeuroBasic*, has been written that allows the calling of neuro- and other functions running in parallel on MUSIC. From the BASIC level the parallelism is completely invisible. To allocate a new layer with 300 neurons, for instance, one can simply type

```
a = new_layer(300)
```

This creates the layer as a parallel object, distributed on the processing elements, and assigns a handle to the BASIC variable a. We call it layer a. The following command propagates layer a to layer b using the weight set w:

```
propagate(a, b, w)
```

Other functions allow the randomization of weights, the loading of patterns and weight sets, the computation of mean squared errors, and so on. Each instruction can be executed directly by typing it into the command line, or it can be part of a program. The sequence

```
a = new_layer(300)
b = new_layer(10)
w = new_weights(a, b)
```

for example, defines a single-layer perceptron with 300 inputs and 10 outputs being connected with the weights $w$. Larger programs, loops, and conditional branches can be used to construct and train complete neural networks or to automatically run a complete series of experiments where experimental setups depend on the result of previous experiments. The BASIC environment thus allows all kinds of gradations in experimental research, from the interactive programming of small experiments to large, off-line learning jobs.

Note that BASIC is not the programming language for the MUSIC system; it is a high-level command language for the easy control of parallel algorithms. A documented interface between the BASIC level and the parallel hardware allows one to extend the simulation environment with the new one or to modify existing algorithms written in C or Assembly language.

The BASIC interpreter runs on the host computer (see Figure 10.1) allowing easy access to the input/output devices of the host, such as the screen and the keyboard. However, the time needed for interpreting the commands on the host and sending them to the MUSIC system one by one can easily become a bottleneck, as illustrated in the following simple example. Let's assume that 90 percent of the computing time of an experiment run on a workstation can be parallelized and is executed on the attached parallel computer. The other 10 percent is overhead of the command interpreter and remains on the workstation. Let's further assume that the parallel computer is able to speedup its part by a factor of 50 down to 1.8 percent of the original simulation time. The total time then is 10.8 percent of the original time. The overall speedup results to 8.5, which is not even close to the speedup of 50 of the parallel system itself. This, again, is a consequence of Amdahl's law.

The BASIC code is, therefore, not directly interpreted on the host computer. Before execution, it is compiled to a simpler stack-oriented metacode, named b-code, which is downloaded to the MUSIC system and executed by all processing elements in parallel at optimum speed. The compilation phase is not really noticeable to the user because compiling 1,000 source lines takes typically less than a second.

Of course, NeuroBasic is not restricted to the MUSIC system. The same principle can be used for neural networks simulations on conventional workstations, vector computers, or other parallel systems. Furthermore, the parallel algorithms of MUSIC also run on sequential computers. Simulations in NeuroBasic can, therefore, be executed locally on a workstation or PC without modifications.

### 10.5.2 An Example Program

The following example program defines and trains a simple two-layer perceptron. It first creates a network of size 256–100–10 neurons, randomizes the weights, loads the training patterns digits.mat and the target patterns diglbl.mat from disk, and then performs 100 training epochs. Before each epoch the mean squared error mse is measured in a separate forward pass of all training patterns.

```
create_net(100)              ! create net with
                             ! 100 hidden neurons
for k = 1 to 10
test_net()                   ! measure mse
learn_net()                  ! do one training epoch
print "epoch "; k; ":", "error = ";mse,class_rate;" %"
next k
end
rem
rem *** function for creating the network ***
rem =======================================
```

```
deffn create_net(nhidden)
layer0 = new_layer(256)            ! input layer
layer1 = new_layer(nhidden)        ! hidden layer
layer2 = new_layer(10)             ! output layer
weights1 = new_fcw(layer0, layer1, FCW_FIRST)
weights2 = new_fcw(layer1, layer2, FCW_NORMAL)
randomize(weights1, 2.4/256)
randomize(weights2, 2.4/nhidden)
patt = new_patterns(256, 100, FLOAT)! input pat.
targ = new_patterns(10, 100, FLOAT) ! target pat.
load(patt, "digits.mat")           ! load pattern ..
load(targ, "diglbl.mat")           ! ..from disk
evec = new_mse(10)                 ! error vector
eta = 0.0013                       ! learning rate
endfn
rem
rem *** prop/backprop ***
rem =====================
deffn learn_net()
for i = 0 to 99
copy_pattern(patt, i, layer0)! i-th training pattern
fcprop(layer0, layer1, weights1)! forward prop
sqtanh(layer1, 1.1, 1.5)           ! squashing function
fcprop(layer1, layer2, weights2)! forward prop
sqtanh(layer2, 1.1, 1.5)           ! squashing function
net_error(layer2, targ, i, NO_OBJECT)! compute
                                   !net error
sqdtanh(layer2, 1.1, 1.5)    ! mpy by derivative
fcbackprop(layer1, layer2, weights2, eta)! bp/wts upd.
sqdtanh(layer1, 1.1, 1.5)    ! mpy by derivative
fcbackprop(layer0, layer1, weights1, eta)! bp/wts upd.
next i
endfn
rem
rem *** evaluate mean squared error ***
rem ===================================
deffn test_net()
clr_mse(evec)
class_rate = 0
for i = 0 to 99
copy_pattern(patt, i, layer0)! i-th training pattern
fcprop(layer0, layer1, weights1)! forward prop
sqtanh(layer1, 1.1, 1.5)           ! squashing function
fcprop(layer1, layer2, weights2)! forward prop
sqtanh(layer2, 1.1, 1.5)           ! squashing function
net_error(layer2, targ, i, evec)! compute net error
class_rate = class_rate + test_layer(layer2, targ, i)
next i
mse = get_mse(evec)
endfn
```

### 10.5.3 Performance versus Programming Time

Table 10.3 summarizes our experiences in terms of performance improvements and programming times. It compares the performance and the estimated implementation time between a modern workstation (Sun SuperSPARC II, 85 MHz) and MUSIC. Note, however, that this is a comparison between the relatively old MUSIC system (1992) and a modern workstation (1996). At the time the MUSIC system was first used for neural networks research the typical performance gain compared to a workstation of that time was 30 to 60 for programming in C.

TABLE 10.3. Performance and programming time.

| Algorithm | Additional Programming | Speedup |
|---|---|---|
| Backpropagation (C) | × 2 | 7 |
| Backpropagation (Assembler) | × 8 | 33 |
| Cellular neural nets (CNN) | × 3 | 14 |

## 10.6 Examples of Practical Research Work

### 10.6.1 Neural Networks in Photofinishing

Day by day millions of photos are taken by amateur photographers all over the world. The exposed rolls of film are sent to the photo laboratories where they are developed and transferred to paper prints. During this process, called photofinishing, every picture is automatically adjusted in terms of colors and brightness.

This section presents two examples of how neural networks can contribute to enhance the quality of photo correction. In a first series of experiments, different multilayer perceptrons were investigated to perform the task of photo correction. The second series of experiments was dedicated to find a neural network that was able to detect photos with equal motifs in order to guarantee consistent colors. Totally, 287 complete training experiments using a large image database of 30,000 pictures were carried out. The numerous training experiments in conjunction with the large database and large networks required a fast simulation environment. Therefore, NeuroBasic running on the MUSIC parallel computer was used to carry out the experiments. The total CPU time was approximately 14 weeks. If only a workstation would have been available, these experiments would have taken about 3.5 years!

*10.6.1.1 Overview of the Photofinishing Process.* Every year about 60 billion photographs are taken all over the world. To handle this large number of pictures the photofinishing process is automated. Most large photo labs are equipped with fully automated production lines capable of processing several hundred thousand pictures each day, and only the final quality control is performed by humans. However, not only quantity but also quality counts. The primary goal is to optimize the customer's impression of the pictures. Note that this is not equivalent to reproducing the exact colors and gray-levels of the original scene. In other words, an exact reproduction of the true colors will not result in a good-looking picture. To understand this statement one has to take a look into the phenomenon of the human visual perception and the technical aspects of photo processing.

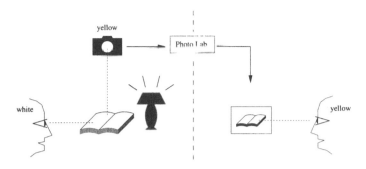

FIGURE 10.7. The pages of a book appear white even if illuminated with the yellowish light of a lightbulb, but they would appear yellowish in an uncorrected photograph.

When taking a picture the photographer's perception is adapted to the current illumination of the scene (Figure 10.7). For example, we perceive the pages of a book in a tungsten-illuminated room as white, even though the tungsten light reflected from the white pages is actually yellowish. An uncorrected photograph therefore shows a book with yellowish pages. This is always the case, even if the picture is viewed under the same lighting conditions as the picture was taken because the visual system of the viewer is calibrated to perceive "real" white as white (such as the back side of the paper print). Therefore, the book pages keep their yellowish color. If we want the white pages to appear white, the picture needs to be corrected.

Another dominant phenomenon of visual perception is brightness adaptation. The human brightness sensitivity is calibrated to a narrow spot in the center of the visual field. When one looks around, the person's sensitivity is constantly readjusted. A camera, on the other hand, has only one global setting for the entire picture. During photo processing this can lead to conflicting situations, especially on pictures with a large contrast like flash or backlight photographies. Optimal correction often requires guessing which are the important parts of the picture.

It becomes obvious that no precise model for the visual perception exists. Therefore, today's correction algorithms include a fair amount of heuristics. Figure 10.8 shows an overview of the algorithm running on a state-of-the-art photo printer by GRETAG Imaging, Inc.[1] The negative is first scanned with a resolution of $26 \times 39$ pixels to obtain the input data for the correction algorithm. In the next step, several features are extracted based on hand-tuned color histograms. The pixels are weighted according to several criteria, such as the pixel locations or the local neighborhood (the exact configuration of the algorithm is proprietary). The features are then used as input for the correction algorithm, which determines the three corrective parameters K0, K1, and K2. These parameters control the color filters of the exposure unit where the picture is transferred from the negative to the paper. By controlling the spectral composition of the exposure light, the colors and brightness of the picture can be adjusted. Note that only global correction is possible, that is, regions on a photo cannot be corrected individually. The correction algorithm was developed using statistical methods applied to a database of more than 30,000 pictures from real production, which includes the optimal correction parameters determined by a human expert.

---

[1]GRETAG Imaging, Inc., Switzerland, is one of the leading manufacturers of photo printers and was a project partner.

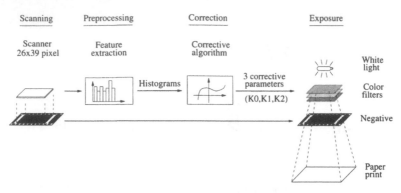

FIGURE 10.8. Overview of a conventional correction system.

### 10.6.1.2  *Color and Gray-Level Correction.*

The lack of a precise visual perception model and the availability of a large example database were the initial motivations for investigating neural networks for photo correction. The first approach was to replace only the correction algorithm (see Figure 10.8) by a neural network. Because the target patterns (the desired correction parameters) are known, a supervised training algorithm, backpropagation, has been selected.

In order to find the best network configuration, two series of experiments with a total of 248 training runs were carried out. The first series was dedicated to explore the optimal size of the neural network. For this purpose, 103 networks of various configurations were trained. The picture database was divided into 27,000 training patterns and 3,000 test patterns. Each pattern of the training set was presented 150 times to the network during the training phase. The input data was limited to 70 out of 229 statistical features (color histograms), the same as are used by the conventional algorithm. These 70 features were designated by an expert to be most relevant. Furthermore, the output of the networks was limited to only one of the three correction parameter, namely K0, to simplify the task for the first experiments. The first networks consisted of just one hidden layer, which was varied from 50 to 1,000 neurons. Their performance, compared to the conventional algorithm, was poor (see Table 10.4).

An improvement was obtained by adding a second hidden layer. The additional layer increased the degree of freedom and therefore the number of experiments considerably. The first hidden layer ranged from 10 to 500 neurons, whereas the the second hidden layer varied from five to 200 neurons. The small networks showed clearly a lack of capacity (too few weights) and the large networks tended to memorize the patterns rather than to generalize (a large gap between the training set and the test set error was observed). The results are summarized in Table 10.4. The best results were obtained with networks of approximately the size 70–20–25–1. However, variations in the number of hidden neurons around that point resulted in only minor changes in the performance. This observation allowed the conclusion that, at least for our task, the network performance is not very sensitive to the exact number of hidden neurons.

To verify the best network configuration, cross validation was used.[2] For that purpose, the database was divided into ten different subsets. Ten networks of the same architecture (70–20–25–1) were trained with nine subsets each leaving out a *different* tenth subset for testing each time. One of the experiments showed a strange behavior: the error of the train-

---

[2] A single test set may be not representative for the database. To make the results more reliable, the experiment is repeated multiple times with a different subset of the database taken as a test set. The results are then averaged.

TABLE 10.4. Summary of the first series of experiments. MSE stands for the mean squared error.

| Network Configuration | Number of Weights | MSE of K0 | |
| --- | --- | --- | --- |
| | | Training Set | Test Set |
| 70–50–1 | 3,601 | 0.041 | 0.102 |
| 70–1000–1 | 72,001 | 0.059 | 0.116 |
| 70–10–5–1 | 771 | 0.074 | 0.081 |
| 70–20–25–1 | 1,971 | 0.044 | **0.052** |
| 70–70–20–1 | 6,411 | 0.043 | 0.058 |
| 70–500–200–1 | 135,901 | 0.014 | 0.070 |
| Convent. algorithm | | | 0.027 |

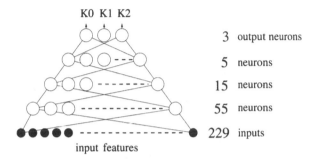

FIGURE 10.9. Dimensions of the best neural network of the second series of experiments.

ing set was higher than the error of the test set during the entire training. By tracking down the problem a pattern was found that had been mislabeled by a factor of ten. Sensitized by this discovery, the database was reviewed and cleaned of suspicious patterns.

For the second series, 145 experiments, all 229 color histogram features used by the conventional algorithm were used as inputs for the neural network. Additionally, each input was normalized by the accumulated weights used to weight the different pixels in the color histograms. The network output included all three corrective parameters K0, K1, and K2. The reason for this was the assumption that during training the network might profit from the information supplied by the other correction parameters. The number of neurons in the hidden layers had to be increased to account for the increased number of input and output values. The first hidden layer was varied in size between 35 and 70 neurons, the second one between 45 and 85 neurons. All of these modifications on the experiments resulted in a considerable increase of the performance. The best network achieved a performance comparable to that of the conventional algorithm (see Table 10.5).

TABLE 10.5. Summary of the second series of experiments.

| Network Configuration | Number of Weights | Mean Squared Error (MSE) | | | | |
| --- | --- | --- | --- | --- | --- | --- |
| | | Training Set | Test Set | | | |
| | | Global | Global | K0 | K1 | K2 |
| 229–50–50–3 | 14,203 | 0.023 | 0.029 | 0.030 | 0.025 | 0.033 |
| 229–55–15–5–3 | 13,588 | 0.024 | **0.028** | **0.029** | **0.023** | **0.032** |
| Convent. algorithm | | | 0.031 | 0.027 | 0.028 | 0.037 |

However, an even better result was obtained by a network with three hidden layers of 55, 15, and 5 neurons, respectively (see Table 10.5 and Figure 10.9). The size was found empirically. Theoretically, there is no need for three hidden layers because a two-hidden-layer network is able to perform every nonlinear function provided that its capacity is large enough. However, from a practical point of view the hierarchical structure probably supports the signal processing within the network better. The performance of the best network was, again, verified using cross-validation. For that purpose, the database was subdivided into 10 different subsets, each of them containing the same amount of photos of each class (flash, backlight shots, beach, and so on). The 10 networks were then trained over 400 epochs, which is 400 times the presentation of the entire training database. The results of the experiments were averaged and are shown in Figure 10.10.

Three of the curves show the decreasing mean squared error (MSE) of the output parameters K0, K1, and K2 for the test set during training. The fourth curve, named the test set global error, is the overall performance, which is the average of the three errors of K0, K1, and K2. For comparison, the performance of the conventional algorithm is displayed as dashed, horizontal lines. The results show a general improvement over the conventional algorithm. The error on the chromatic parameters K1 and K2 could be lowered remarkably, whereas the brightness error K0 remained slightly above the conventional algorithm. At first, an improvement of the global error from 0.031 to 0.028 does not seem to be much. However, one has to consider that this is the averaged performance. Most of the photos are corrected well by both algorithms, therefore the averaged performance difference is small. The improvements on individual photos can be much higher.

Note that the performance comparison of the neural network and the conventional algorithm is not completely fair. The error of the neural network was measured on a separate test set, which was not used for training. The performance of the conventional algorithm, on the other hand, was fine-tuned by using the entire database and therefore no independent test set was available anymore. Therefore, the presented performance comparison is expected to be slightly unfavorable for the neural network.

To get a better understanding of the corrective capability of the neural network, it is necessary to evaluate its performance according to different classes of photos. The pictures of the database are subdivided into 13 classes. Figure 10.11 shows the performance of the color and brightness correction in each of these classes. In color correction the neural network outperforms the conventional algorithm in almost every class. The results in brightness correction are less clear. On four classes the neural network did better than the conventional algorithm, on a few other classes the errors were comparable; and on four classes, especially class 0, the neural network clearly did poorer than the conventional algorithm. Those classes contain difficult illumination conditions, for example, an extremely large range of gray-levels. The reason for the bad performance is not only the difficult illumination but also the available number of examples in the database, which is, compared to the other classes, relatively small. For instance, classes 0, 5, 6, and 7 only contain 440, 809, 190, and 567 pictures, respectively. Most of the other classes have a few thousand pictures each.

To bring down the error, some experiments were carried out, where the difficult patterns were weighted four times more than the other patterns or were trained more often. However, the performance improvement of the brightness correction was not significant whereas the overall error increased. This effect shows that the network cannot derive more information from the few pictures even if they are weighted more. The underrepresentation of the four classes does not allow the network to generalize sufficiently. The performance is expected to increase only if the size of the difficult classes in the picture database is increased.

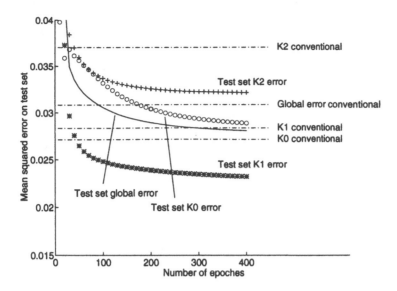

FIGURE 10.10. The performance of the best network for the correction of color photos (229 inputs, 55, 15, and 5 node in the hidden layers and 3 output nodes). About 12 weeks of CPU time on a 30-processor MUSIC system were required to reach this result, which is approximately equivalent to 3 years CPU time on a Sun SPARCstation 10.

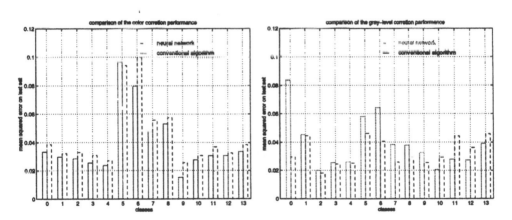

FIGURE 10.11. Arrangement of the results according to different picture classes. Left: Color correction. Right: Brightness correction. The classes (listed in alphabetic order) are backlight shot, beach/water, bulb light, bulb-light overcorrection, color dominant, density dominant, flash, member of a series, neon light, portrait/skin, snow, special flash, start of series, and vegetation. The exact assignment of the classes is confidential.

**Interpretation of the Results.** Even though the experiments show clear results, their interpretation is difficult because the calculated error only pretends to be an exact measurement. In reality, the decision of whether a photo is corrected well or not is subjective. Furthermore, some motifs, for instance, a house or a car, tolerate a larger deviation from the optimal correction than others, such as a portrait. On the other hand, the human expert who labeled the database has a certain tolerance range as well. Besides the fact that different experts would correct the same picture slightly differently, the correction of a single expert also depends on the expert's daily mood. Nevertheless, a rough bound can be given. An average photo is considered well corrected if the error is less than 0.025–0.030. Most of the pictures are corrected well by both the neural network and the conventional algorithm.

However, the neural network has the advantage of requiring less computation than the conventional algorithm. For example, the best network with 229–55–15–5–3 neurons and 13,588 weights (connections) requires less than 1 ms evaluation time on a 20 MHz C40 signal processor compared to approximately 10 ms required by the conventional algorithm. On a real-time system like the photo printers this difference can be essential. The large computational power for the neural network is only required during training.

The experiments demonstrate that neural networks are able to learn complex tasks, like the correction of photos, which cannot be expressed by a mathematical model. The knowledge was acquired only from examples during the training. Nevertheless, the correction performance is comparable to the correction algorithm of state-of-the-art photo printers, which are fine-tuned with a large amount of expert knowledge. To our knowledge, this is the first time that neural networks were applied to photo correction.

The training experiments could have never been carried out without the use of a fast hardware platform, such as the MUSIC system. For all training a 30-processor MUSIC system has been used. In average, this system was about 13 times faster than a Sun SPARC-station 10 for the experiments carried out. The loss in speedup compared to MUSIC's peak performance results from the fact that the size of the layers usually decreases from layer to layer and the system becomes less efficient for the simulation of small layers. However, even a speedup of 13 is evident for the real training. Table 10.6 demonstrates how quickly the computational demand adds up when applying neural networks to real problems.

TABLE 10.6. Time required for the training of 248 neural networks.

|  | Consisting of | CPU Time | | Unit |
|---|---|---|---|---|
|  |  | MUSIC-30 | SPARCstation 10 |  |
| 1 Pattern: |  | 0.0033 | 0.043 | sec |
| 1 Epoch: | 30,000 patterns | 1.6 | 21 | min |
| 1 Experiment: | 300 epochs | 8 | 104 | h |
| **Entire Search**: | **248 experiments** | **12** | **156** | **weeks** |

The entire search for the best network required about 12 weeks on the MUSIC computer. This is an equivalent of 3 years on a workstation like the Sun SPARCstation 10.

*10.6.1.3  Detection of Picture Sequences.*  People often take many pictures in a row of the same object. The photo printer might correct each of these pictures in a slightly different way. Viewed in isolation each of the pictures usually looks well, but if lined up next to each other small differences in color and brightness can be observed. The human eye is much more sensitive to color differences than to absolute colors. Therefore, people complain about even very small color differences of the same motif in different pictures. This is a well-known problem in photofinishing. Because such pictures always appear in series, they are also called serial photographs.

A step toward a solution is the detection of such series. If this can be achieved, then pictures within a series can be corrected with the same parameters resulting in equal colors on the prints. However, it is hard to find an appropriate measure for similarity, not only in terms of mathematical expressions but also for us humans. What are similar photos? Two photos showing the same motif? This common definition of serial photos is very weak and depends on the interpretation of each person. This can easily be demonstrated by looking at Figure 10.12. Are these pictures similar? Can picture (c), showing the backside of the

(a)                    (b)                    (c)

FIGURE 10.12. Illustration of the difficulty of defining serial pictures. Do all pictures contain the same motif?

gate, be considered as containing the same motif as pictures (a) and (b), which show the front side of the gate?

This example demonstrates that there are no exact rules that can be used to implement an automated detection system. This is where neural networks have an advantage. They can learn from examples without requiring explicit definitions.

The definition of serial photos (that is, pictures showing the same motif) brings up the idea of using object recognition. However, object recognition is not a good solution for several reasons. The same motif on two serial photos can widely vary in size, orientation, location on the picture, and even in shape, depending on the angle of view from which the picture was taken. The example of the gate in Figure 10.12 illustrates this fact. It can make it extremely difficult to identify the same object in two different pictures. For example, the windows in picture (a) and (b) differ in size, location, shape, and even in orientation (in the photo printer the negatives are all scanned with the same orientation). Moreover, even if the objects could be reliably recognized, there is still the problem of the interpretation of similarity. Therefore, the information used by a detection algorithm has to be based on a more general comparison of the pictures, which avoids the identification of single objects on the pictures. A possible solution is the use of color histograms, such as the those used for automated image indexing and image retrieval systems [17, 18]. Color histograms do not put the context of a picture into account and therefore provide a more general representation of the picture.

The pictures of the previously used database were classified by a human expert into three classes: "beginning of a series", "member of a series", "not belonging to a series." Nevertheless, two test persons who reclassified a few hundred pictures obtained a classification rate of only 75 percent compared to the labels in the database. This leads to the conclusion that a large percentage of the photographs cannot be classified precisely as serial or nonserial pictures. The human classification rate of 75 percent is considered to be an upper bound for the neural network performance. The lower bound is represented by a "silly" network having a constant output. Because 60 percent of the pictures in the database are classified as nonserial in such a network, voting always for nonserial will achieve a classification rate of 60 percent.

To find a neural network that detects similar photos, three different types of input features for the networks were explored: the unprocessed color scans of two pictures, two color histograms, and the difference of the color histograms of two pictures.

TABLE 10.7. Performance comparison of different feature preprocessing.

| Method | Network Configuration | Performance | | Number of Free Parameters |
|---|---|---|---|---|
| | | Training set | Test set | |
| Constant output ("silly" net) | (1) | 60% | 60% | 0 |
| No preprocessing | (6084-250-20-1) | 95% | 60% | 1,526,291 |
| Histograms | (246-35-14-1) | 76% | 67% | 9,164 |
| Histogram difference | (123-30-12-1) | 74% | 73% | 4,105 |
| Humans | | 75% | 75% | |

**Unprocessed Color Scans.** In a first approach, the neural network used directly the unprocessed color scans of two pictures as the input. This is an equivalent of 6,084 input values fed to the network. The entire database requires more than 365 MBytes of space. This amount exceeds by far the 90 MBytes memory of a 30-processor MUSIC system. Therefore the MUSIC disk array was used, consisting of four parallel disks, which allowed access to the training data over the fast communication ring directly from the disks. Retrieving a single pattern from the disk array is about five times slower than accessing it from the memory using the communication network. This factor can be cut down to about 1.5 when loading several patterns at once each time and using the MUSIC memory as a cache.

The best neural network found consisted of two hidden layers with 250 and 20 neurons, respectively, and one output node for the classification. This network showed, not surprisingly, a poor generalization because of its excessive amount of free parameters (more than 1.5 million weights), which allows the network to "memorize" the training patterns instead of generalizing (see Table 10.7). However, the obtained classification rate of 60 percent on the test set (95 percent on the training set) is not only a result of overcapacity but also of the bad input representation. Other experiments with a different number of nodes in both hidden layers led to similar results.

**Two Color Histograms.** To reduce the amount of input data, *color histograms* were built and used as input for the neural network. These color histograms were designed much simpler than the sophisticated ones developed by GRETAG Imaging, Inc. The basic idea for the choice of a simple histogram is intuitive: Similar photos have similar color distributions and therefore just the number of pixels belonging to each color has to be counted and compared. Therefore, the color space was subdivided into 123 cells using higher resolution on the chromatic plane (hue, saturation) than along the brightness axis.

The histograms of two pictures were fed into the neural networks. Compared to the first approach the input dimension was reduced from 6,084 to $2 \times 123 = 246$ input values. The neural networks trained consisted of two hidden layers ranging from 25 to 70 and five to 14 neurons, respectively. The best network found (246–35–14–1) showed a classification rate of 67 percent on the test set and about 76 percent on the training set (see Table 10.7). The performance of the other networks was only slightly below, which showed again that the performance of a neural network is not very sensitive to the exact number of neurons. According to the reduced input space, the capacity of the network could be lowered from 1.5 million to about 9,000 free parameters (weights). As the results show, this had a positive influence on the generalization of the network.

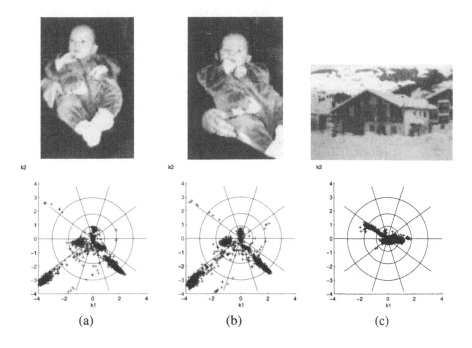

FIGURE 10.13. Color distribution of the pixels projected on the k1/k2 color plane. (a) and (b) the color distribution of two similar photographs of a baby. (c) the color distribution of a house in the mountains. The color histograms are built by counting the number of pixels belonging to each sector. When building the difference of the histograms of (a) and (b), the histograms will annihilate each other. This is not the case if the difference between the histogram of (c) and one of (a) or (b) is taken.

**Difference of Color Histograms.** In the previous experiments the networks always had "to figure out by themselves" that the input consists of two sources, which had to be compared. The task could definitively be simplified for the network if this comparison is already performed by the preprocessing. Therefore, the difference of the two color histograms was calculated and used as input data for a third set of neural networks. The difference of two histograms of similar pictures generates small values because both histograms annihilate each other. Nonsimilar pictures will produce a histogram difference with large values clustered at different centers. (See Figure 10.13).

Using the 123 numbers of the histogram difference as input features, different neural networks were trained for 400 epochs whereas the number of neurons in both hidden layers was varied from 15 to 60 for the first hidden layer and from four to 12 for the second hidden layer, respectively. Again, the networks showed about the same performance. The best configuration found consisted of one output node and two hidden layers with 30 and 12 nodes, respectively, which is an equivalent of 4,105 weights. The network classified more than 73 percent of the test set and about 74 percent of the training set correctly. This result is considered to be excellent not only because the classification rate is very close to the performance of the test persons but also because of the very good generalization, which is demonstrated by the fact that the error rate of both the training set and the test set are very similar.

Table 10.8 analyzes the results of the network (123-30-12-1) in more detail. The 73 percent classification rate consists of 27 percent correctly determined serial photos and

46 percent nonserial photos. This means that 27 percent of all pictures can potentially be corrected better using the neural network. Also 16 percent of all pictures are nonrecognized serial photos. These photos will be corrected individually as it is done by today's corrective algorithm resulting in neither an increase nor a decrease of performance. In addition, 11 percent of the photos, the misclassified nonserial photos, are potentially badly corrected pictures because their colors will be equalized although they are not similar. To verify this conclusion these photos were inspected manually. However, it turned out that, besides a few mislabeled pictures, lots of these picture pairs, 9 percent, are photos showing not the same but similar motives, for example, different persons but in the same room. Therefore, performing the same color correction on these photos will not affect the quality. Only 2 percent of the picture will probably be corrected worse compared to today's correction.

TABLE 10.8. Detailed analysis of the classification rates and their impact on the color correction.

| Classification rate | Serial Classified as | | Nonserial Classified as | |
|---|---|---|---|---|
| | Serial | Nonserial | NonSerial | Serial |
| Relative to class | 64% | 36% | 80% | 20% |
| Relative to all | **27%** | **16%** | **46%** | **11%** |
| | | | 9% | 2% |
| | Improved correction | Conventional correction | | No Possible quality loss |

The 39 experiments carried out to find a good network architecture and a suitable feature representation required about two weeks of MUSIC CPU time. The same experiments would have taken about six months on a SPARCstation 10 (see Table 10.9).

TABLE 10.9. Time required for the training of 39 neural networks.

| | Consisting of | Time on | | Unit |
|---|---|---|---|---|
| | | MUSIC-30 | SPARCstation 10 | |
| 1 pattern: | | 0.0034 | 0.044 | sec |
| 1 epoch: | 30,000 patterns | 1.7 | 22.4 | min |
| 1 experiment: | 300 epochs | 8.6 | 112 | h |
| **Entire search**: | **39 experiments** | **2** | **26** | **weeks** |

*10.6.1.4 Conclusion.* The experiments demonstrate that neural networks are able to learn complex tasks for which no exact model exists. Provided that a suitable input representation for the networks is found, multilayer perceptrons can successfully be trained for both difficult function approximations and classification tasks.

An example of the first category is the neural network, which reaches the performance of a state-of-the-art correction algorithm. The latter is demonstrated by a network trained to detect a photo series with a performance comparable to humans. Many other applications— for example, the automatic classification of the pictures to one of the classes such as flash or backlight shot— are conceivable. Photofinishing is a field full of tasks which cannot be described by exact models but where a large amount of training examples can be collected.

On the other hand, this work also demonstrates that the training of neural networks can easily exceed the computational power of a modern workstation. Without the use of the MUSIC parallel supercomputer, the experiments could not have been carried out in a reasonable time. Using multiple independent workstations instead of a parallel supercomputer would be of only limited help because the setup of most experiments incorporated the results of the preceding experiment. In the presented work, a total of 287 entire training experiments were carried out with an average duration of a half a day each. The networks were trained for an average of 300 epochs (300 is the presentation of the entire training set). The total CPU time spent for the different training experiments was approximately 14 weeks. This is equivalent to about 3.5 years of CPU time on a workstation (Sun SPARCstation 10).

### 10.6.2 The Truck Backer-Upper

In this section we present a solution for the so-called truck backer-upper problem using the parallel supercomputer MUSIC to accelerate the training process of the neural network. Its task is to back up a truck with a trailer to a loading dock with no forward movements being permitted.

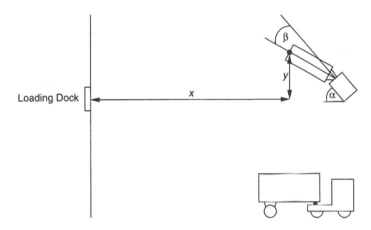

FIGURE 10.14. Start position of the truck.

Figure 10.14 shows the truck with the trailer and the loading dock. The position of the truck in relation to the loading dock can be described by the coordinates $(x, y)$ of the rear end of the trailer, the angle $\alpha$ between a horizontal and the direction of the cab, and the angle $\beta$ between the trailer and the cab. A solution to this problem was described by Widrow and associates [19]. Widrow used two neural networks, one that emulates the kinematics of the truck (the emulator) and one that controls the steering wheel angle (the controller).

Because of the large amount of training experiments, we carried out the training on the MUSIC system. A complete training session then only takes 10 minutes compared to about 60 minutes on a Sun SPARCstation 10.

After being able to reproduce Widrows results, the goal was to solve the problem for a real truck model in order to examine the influence of a variety of real-world parameters such as slippage, errors in the position measurement, and nonprecise mechanical components.

*10.6.2.1  Design and Training of the Neural Networks.*   The first network to be trained is the emulator network (Figure 10.15). Its only goal is to model the nonlinear truck kinematics. It takes the current truck position (including cabin and trailer angles) and the current steering wheel angle as input and predicts the next truck position after a specific short amount of backing up. The emulator network contains two hidden layers with 25 neurons each, which have a nonlinear output function (the hyperbolic tangent). The actual output is not the absolute truck position but only the position changes ($\Delta x, \Delta y, \Delta \alpha, \Delta \beta$). These position changes are independent of the absolute position of the truck. The $(x, y)$ coordinates therefore do not need to be fed into the network, which significantly reduces the complexity of the problem as well as the necessary network size and training time.

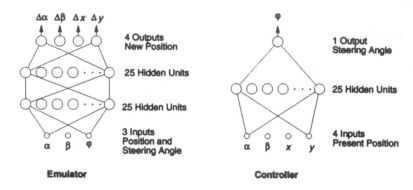

FIGURE 10.15. The emulator and controller neural networks.

The emulator network is trained with examples from the truck kinematics. After the output reaches the desired values within a chosen error range, the weights are frozen. Note that 1,000 training epochs, each epoch with totally 10,000 training examples, were necessary to achieve an error of less than 0.05 percent of the truck length.

Once the emulator network is fully trained it can be used to train the controller network. The controller network (Figure 10.15) contains one hidden layer with 25 neurons, which also have a nonlinear output function (hyperbolic tangent). Its purpose is to control the steering wheel angle or, in other words, "to drive the truck."

The training of the controller network is as follows. First, an initial position of the truck is chosen randomly. The controller network then chooses a steering wheel angle. Now the emulator network computes the new truck position after backing up a specific short distance, after which the controller network chooses a new steering wheel angle and so on (see Figure 10.16). This is repeated until either

- the truck reaches the end of the driving area or

- the angle between truck and trailer becomes larger then 90 degrees (jack-knife position).

In the first case, the difference between the end position of the truck and the desired position at the loading dock is calculated. It serves as network error, which is now backpropagated multiple times through the emulator and controller network in the reverse order of how they were used in the actual run (compare Figure 10.16). Only the weights of the controller network are updated. The ones of the emulator network remain frozen. However, the fact that we have a neural network that emulates the truck kinematics accurately allows us to use the standard backpropagation algorithm (backpropagation through time).

In the second case ("pivot crash"), the training run is discarded as it contains no useful information.

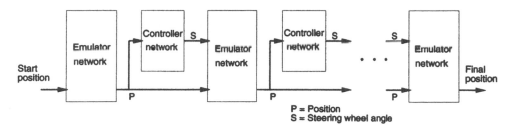

FIGURE 10.16. Information flow through the controller and emulator networks during a training run.

The training runs are repeated with various random start positions until the final error falls below a chosen error range. The complete training is subdivided into several "lessons." In the first lesson a set of "easy" start positions is chosen, which are closed to the loading dock and where the trailer angle is aligned to the dock. The training runs of each lesson are continued until fewer than 10 percent of the runs end with a pivot crash. Once this goal is reached the next lesson starts, which allows more difficult start positions. This is continued until in the last lesson any arbitrary start position and initial truck and trailer angles are allowed. A successful training setup is shown in Table 10.10.

TABLE 10.10. Training setup.

| Number of lessons | | 73 |
|---|---|---|
| Number of initial positions per lesson | | 100 |
| Average of training runs per lessons | | 220 |
| Total number of initial positions | Single processor system | 13,000 |
| | Multiprocessor system | 25,800 |
| Learning rate $\eta$ | | 0.01 |

At the end of a complete training session, the average error of the final position is about 5 percent of the total truck length. It has been observed that the controller is not able to learn from start positions with truck angles greater than 75 percent of the maximum values. A solution for a better training session will be presented in Section 10.6.2.3.

*10.6.2.2 Training Results.* The training is either carried out on a single-processor workstation (Sun SPARCstation 10) or on the parallel MUSIC system. In the case of the workstation, the weights of the controller are updated after each training run (continuous weight update). On the MUSIC system, on the other hand, pure continuous weight update is not feasible because of the small network dimensions. Therefore, each processing element performs one individual run from a different start position. After all processing elements have finished, the weight updates are averaged (partial batch learning with a batch size equal to the number of processing elements). If all training runs would be of the same length, a computational speedup close to the number of processing elements is expected. Unfortunately, the lengths of the training runs vary, especially for advanced lessons with more difficult start positions. This causes a performance degradation caused by unequal processing loads.

A comparison of the training times between the Sun SPARCstation 10 and the MUSIC system is found in Table 10.11. The numbers reflect the total training times including parallelization losses and losses attributed to the application of partial batch learning.

TABLE 10.11. Comparison of total training times.

| Sun SPARCstation 10 | 3240 sec |
|---|---|
| 30-processor MUSIC system | 614 sec |

The unequal processing loads caused by the different lengths of the training runs is the major limiting factor of the learning speed in this case. On the other hand, parallelizing the networks and letting all processing elements work on the same training run at a time is not feasible because of the small network dimensions. It would result in a very poor performance. Finally, one could increase the batch size and let each processing element work on several training runs before exchanging the weight updates in order to average out some of the differences in the training run lengths. However, experiments have shown that the convergence time for batch sizes larger than 60 increases to a nonacceptable level.

Figure 10.17 shows the performance of the controller network in different levels of training.

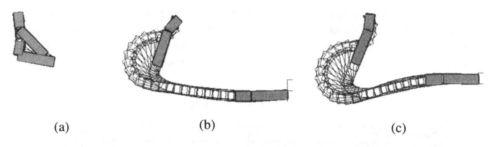

(a)  (b)  (c)

FIGURE 10.17. Performance examples of (a) an untrained, (b) a partially trained, and (c) a well-trained controller network. With the untrained controller, the truck crashes after only a few steps.

An interesting experiment is to see what happens if some of the controller information is destroyed, that is, some of the weights are set to zero. If this is done for less than 10 percent of the weights, then the controller still finds its way to the loading dock. However, the truck navigates less precisely and the driving trajectory becomes less optimal. If more than 20 percent of the weights are set to zero, the truck totally loses its orientation and crashes after only a few steps.

*10.6.2.3 Improving the Training.* So far, training runs with a pivot crash have been ignored because no error measure can be derived from them (the distance of the final truck position to the loading dock). However, avoiding pivot crashes is crucial. The training controller therefore has been extended with an initial phase where the neural network only learns to avoid pivot crashes:

- Choose a start position with the angle $\beta$ between cabin and trailer being difficult ($\pm 89$ degrees).

- Back up until the truck crashes.

- Tell the controller that the angle $\beta$ is too large by backpropagating an empirically chosen constant error.

- Repeat this until the controller learns how to avoid pivot crashes.

The complete first training phase needs only about 2,000 trials or less than one minute on the 30-processing element MUSIC system. The second phase of the training remains the same as described in Section 10.6.2.1 but now with a reduced pivot crash rate of less than 3 percent. This results in a controller that is able to drive the truck from any arbitrary starting position.

*10.6.2.4 Maneuvering Around Obstacles.* As a last experiment, the controller was improved to become capable of driving the truck around obstacles. The first idea was to use the same training concept as before. Once the controller is completely trained, a few obstacles are placed in the driving area and then the controller is retrained. If the truck touches one of the obstacles, a correction value is determined. This value says that the correct route is more toward one or the other side of the obstacle. However, trained in this way the network was not able to avoid the obstacles and hit the loading dock. Avoiding the obstacles and hitting the loading dock was somehow contradictory training information. The better the controller learned to pass an obstacle, the worse became its capability to find the loading dock.

One improved idea is to subdivide the driving area into regions. Each obstacle and the loading dock lay in a separate region and for each of them a separate network is trained. Once the truck leaves one region and enters the next, the networks are switched. This solution seems to be simple and straightforward. On the other hand, it requires a lot of training experiments and was therefore not implemented.

The final solution was to overlay the driving area with a vector field. All vectors of the field are flowing around the obstacles and pointing to the loading dock, which has the lowest potential in the driving area. The task of the controller is only to align the truck to the vectors of the field. To do this, the controller is trained with a homogeneous vector field. The $x$- and $y$- inputs of the controller (compare Figure 10.15) are replaced by the angle $\gamma$ of the vector field. The controller therefore has no more information about the absolute position of the truck. This has two benefits. On one hand, it simplifies the controller structure and results in faster learning; on the other hand, the vector field can be computed or changed on-line because the controller is independent of the obstacles. The controller therefore might even be able to drive the truck around (slow) moving obstacles. Figure 10.18 shows an example of the truck navigating through a field of obstacles.

*10.6.2.5 The Real Truck.* The real truck consists of a remote-controlled 1-m long truck model, an ultrasonic positioning system and an interface to the computer, which simulates the neural network (see Figure 10.19 and 10.20). The main problem is the implementation of the positioning system.

Three ultrasonic transducers, mounted on the cabin and the front and rear end of the trailer, periodically send out ultrasonic chirps with a length of 1 ms. Three ultrasonic receivers situated in a line near the driving area receive the chirp signals at different times. A digital correlation system detects the exact time when the signals are received. The two delay differences are then sent to the computer, which calculates the exact location (coordinates) of the sending transducer. After determining the positions of all three transducers, the exact location of the truck is known. The neural network controller then selects the necessary steering wheel angle, which is transmitted to the trucker with conventional remote-control equipment.

Simulations have shown that a sample rate of the truck position of 10 samples per second and a position error of 5 mm or less are necessary for successful operation of the truck. At this time, the positioning system is still insufficient in precision. More advanced signal processing and more qualified ultrasonic transducers that are currently being investigated

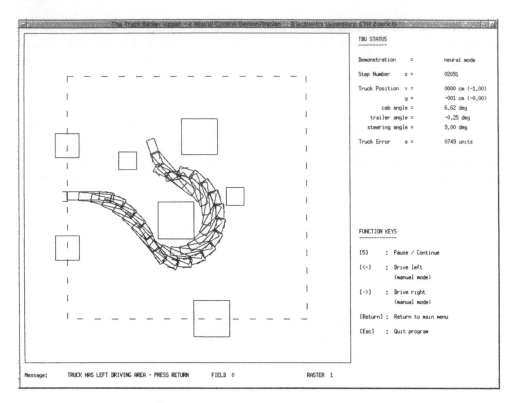

FIGURE 10.18. Driving around obstacles.

promise to bring the accuracy to the desired level. A retraining of the controller using the real truck model will be done in order to reduce the influence of a variety of real-world parameters such as slippage, position errors, and nonprecise mechanical components. It is expected that the retrained controller is able to compensate such real-world nonidealities.

*10.6.2.6 Conclusions.* Finding a good solution for the truck backer-upper problem requires hundreds of training experiments. The MUSIC system was of fundamental support for carrying out these experiments. However, it required additional programming time to implement the partial batch learning that was specifically used for these experiments. Table 10.12 compares the performance benefits as well as the programming costs of using the MUSIC system for this research work.

TABLE 10.12. Comparison of the computation times and programming cost.

| | |
|---|---|
| Total number of experiments | 1,400 |
| Total computation time on the MUSIC | 700 hours |
| Additional effort to implement the parallel functions | 240 hours |
| Total time spent on MUSIC (CPU and programming time) | 940 hours |
| Estimated computation time on a Sun SPARCstation 10 | 4,200 hours |

Table 10.12 shows that the execution time of all training experiments on the MUSIC system is about four weeks. It would take a conventional workstation (SPARCstation 10) almost half a year to complete the same experiments. Even when including the additional

Ultrasonic Receivers

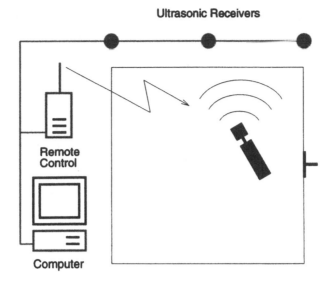

FIGURE 10.19. Diagram of the remote-controlled system.

FIGURE 10.20. Photo of the truck model with ultrasonic transducers.

time needed to program the MUSIC system (about four weeks), the speed advantage is enormous.

## 10.7 Analysis of RISC Performance for Backpropagation

Future generations of the MUSIC system will be based on reduced instruction set computer (RISC) processors, which today have a significant performance advantage compared to floating-point digital signal processors (DSP). This section analyzes the backpropagation performance of various RISC processors.

Modern superscalar RISC processors can issue several instructions each clock cycle (instruction stream parallelism) and use other sophisticated methods resulting in an impressive improvement of their peak performance. However, in order to make full use of these features, new programming techniques have to be applied. A straightforward implementation can lack performance even with the best optimizing compilers, but by rearranging the C source code, performance improvements of up to a factor of eight have been measured.

A nice property of RISC processors is that they allow almost maximum performance without the need of hand Assembly coding. In case of the backpropagation algorithm, for example, the C performance is only 10 to 30 percent lower than the Assembler performance. For the DSP 96002, on the other hand, there is a gap of about a factor of four between handwritten Assembly code and optimized C code for the same algorithm. This is mostly because of many DSP features, like multiple arithmetical and load/store operations in one instruction, which are difficult to be used by a compiler.

Another nice property of RISC processors is that code which has been optimized for one processor runs at optimum or close to optimum speed on other RISC processors as well. This makes the investment in code optimization cost-effective.

### 10.7.1 Introduction

During program optimization, two considerations turned out to be of special importance. On one side, to allow parallel execution, data dependencies between consecutive instructions have to be eliminated. On the other side, memory traffic needs to be minimized. In fact, the memory and cache bandwidth is more critical than the computational performance in many cases.

The speed benefit of numerous optimization techniques such as loop enrolling, jump elimination, data conversion, memory addressing, and (re)scheduling has been measured on different RISC processors. It turned out that the following optimization strategies are a good approach.

- Linearization of the instruction stream ($\times 1.9$ speedup)

- Reduction of the number of load/store operations ($\times 1.9$ speedup)

- Improvement of the internal instruction stream parallelism ($\times 1.5$ speedup)

The speedup is approximate because the effects of the optimizations are not independent. For example, the efficiency of loop unrolling highly depends on the elimination of jumps.

### 10.7.2 Linearization of the Instruction Stream

The loop overhead, which consists of up to three instructions (increment loop counter, compare, and branch), can be reduced by unrolling the loops. This means that the instructions inside the loop are repeated several times and the number of loop cycles is reduced accordingly. This reduces the amount of times the loop overhead is executed.

Furthermore, the number of instructions between branches increases (linearization of the instruction stream). This often results in better opportunities to resolve data dependencies and to rearrange the code in order to allow parallel execution of consecutive instructions.

Figure 10.21 illustrates the unrolling of the innermost loop of a perceptron simulation in the forward path. An additional regular loop is necessary for the iterations, which at the end do not fit completely within the unrolled loop.

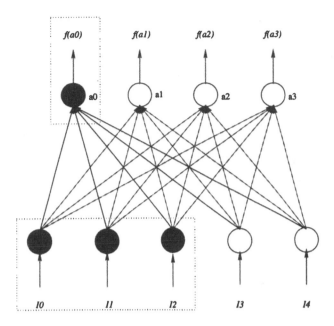

FIGURE 10.21. Unrolling of the innermost loop of a perceptron forward path simulation.

### 10.7.3  Reduction of Load/Store Operations

The high clock frequencies and superscalarity of modern RISC processors typically allow a higher rate of register-to-register operations than the rate of load/store operations. For data intensive applications, such as neural networks simulations, the memory and cache access therefore become a bottleneck and one target of software optimization is to reduce memory traffic.

One consequence of this is to avoid multiple operations on memory variables, such as, for instance, accumulating the weighted inputs in an array element (e. g., out[k] = weights[k][i] * in[i]). It is much better to do the accumulation in a temporary local variable (sum = weights[k][i] * in[i]) and write the result back to memory at the end of the loop (out[k] = sum).

In case of perceptron simulation, there is an additional and probably less obvious way to save memory accesses. The straightforward implementation is to calculate the weighted sums in the forward path (10.1) one by one, for example:

```
for (k = 0; k < nneurons; k++)
  for (i = 0; i < ninputs; i++)
    sum += weights[k][i] * in[i];
```

In case of a layer with $n$ neurons and $m$ inputs, each thus requires $n \cdot m$ load operations for weights and as many for inputs. Each input, however, is used $n$ times within the computation (once for each neuron) and there is no reason to load it from the memory/cache each time. To reduce the number of load operations for input values, the weighted sums of several neurons can be computed at once, for example:

```
for (k = 0; k < nneurons; k += 4)
  for (i = 0; i < ninputs; i++)
  {
```

335

```
    x = in[i];
    sum0 += weights[k][i] * x;
    sum1 += weights[k+1][i] * x;
    sum2 += weights[k+2][i] * x;
    sum3 += weights[k+3][i] * x;
}
```

This is equivalent to unrolling the outer loop, as illustrated in Figure 10.22. In the preceding case the number of load operations for input values is reduced by a factor of four. The optimum number of weighted sums to be computed at once depends on the number of registers of the processor.

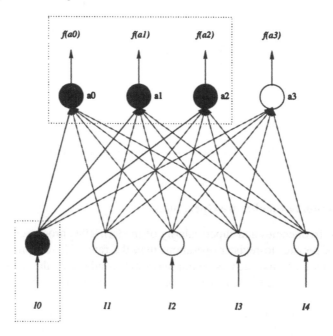

FIGURE 10.22. Unrolling of the outer loop of a perceptron forward path simulation.

Unrolling the outer loop furthermore increases the amount of instructions in the innermost loop, similar to unrolling the innermost loop itself. This, again, helps to resolve data dependencies. Generally, there is no need to unroll both loops.

The same techniques can be applied to the backward path for backpropagating the errors.

### 10.7.4   Improvement of the Internal Instruction Stream Parallelism

The maximum performance of modern RISC processors can only be achieved if multiple instructions can be issued each clock cycle, that is, all execution units of the processor are busy. This requires data dependencies to be resolved as well as consecutive instructions to be in the order in which the execution units fetch data from the instruction pipeline.

*10.7.4.1   Data Dependencies.*   Data dependencies appear whenever any operand of an instruction depends on the result of a previous instruction, for example:

```
for (...)
```

```
{
  a = b + c;
  w[i] - w[i] + a * in[i];
}
```

In this case, the second instruction has to wait for the result of the first instruction to become available before it can be executed. The latency of an instruction depends on the number of stages in the instruction pipeline. The processor automatically stalls until the necessary data becomes available, while actually other instructions could be executed in between. Therefore, data dependencies can be resolved if dependent instructions are separated in the code sequence, as illustrated in the following example:

```
for (...)
{
  a1 = b1+c1;    w1 = w[i1];    i1 = in[j1];
  a2 = b2+c2;    w2 = w[i2];    i2 = in[j2];
  a3 = b3+c3;    w3 = w[i3];    i3 = in[j3];
  a4 = b4+c3;    w4 = w[i4];    i4 = in[j4];
  w[i] = w1 + a1*i1;
  w[i] = w2 + a2*i2;
  w[i] = w3 + a1*i3;
  w[i] = w4 + a2*i4;
}
```

Note that modern compilers are capable of rearranging code themselves in order to resolve data dependencies. However, their scope is limited and the careful writing of the source code still has a great impact on the performance. The same is true for the scheduling, which is discussed in the following section.

*10.7.4.2 Scheduling.* RISC processors typically have more than one execution unit, for example, an integer unit, a load/store unit, and a floating-point unit, which can operate in parallel. If, for example, several load operations follow each other, this parallelism cannot be exploited. The purpose of scheduling is to rearrange the operations for optimal use of the execution units. Figure 10.23 shows two example sequences in pseudo Assembly code. The sequence was initially a part of an unrolled loop and has been compiled with an optimizing compiler.

```
1: load   reg1, mem[a0]        1: load   reg1,  mem[a0]
2: load   reg2, mem[a1]        2: fmul   reg9,  reg13,reg5
3: load   reg3, mem[a2]        3: load   reg2,  mem[a1]
4: load   reg4, mem[a3]        4: fmul   reg10, reg14,reg6
5: fmul   reg9 ,reg13,reg5     5: load   reg3,  mem[a2]
6: fmul   reg10,reg14,reg6     6: fmul   reg11, reg15,reg7
7: fmul   reg11,reg15,reg7     7: load   reg4,  mem[a3]
8: fmul   reg12,reg16,reg8     8: fmul   reg12, reg16,FR8
```

FIGURE 10.23. Examples in pseudo Assembly code to demonstrate scheduling.

On an Alpha 21064 (a first-generation Alpha processor), the code on the left side of Figure 10.23 will execute in almost sequential order consuming at least seven clock cycles. The Alpha 21064, however, is capable of issuing a load/store operation in parallel with a floating-point operation on each clock cycle, but this can only be exploited for the last load instruction on line 4 and the first floating-point multiplication on-line.

The rearranged instruction sequence on the right side of Figure 10.23, on the other hand, perfectly meets the dual issue rules of the Alpha 21064. In this case two consecutive instructions can be issued each clock cycle and the execution time is reduced to four clock cycles. Note that in both examples we assume a 100 percent cache hit rate.

The detailed scheduling can only be done on the Assembly level. However, the knowledge about scheduling helps to arrange the high-level code such that the load of the different execution units remains balanced in average. The detailed scheduling can then be performed well by most compilers or even by the hardware if the processor supports out-of-order execution.

### 10.7.5 Results

Table 10.13 summarizes the results of the optimized backpropagation C code (no parts were coded in Assembly language) on various RISC processors. The code has been optimized individually for each processor. Nevertheless, the necessary modifications to optimize the code of one processor for another were only minor, such as a different amount of loop unrolling.

Even when left unchanged, the optimal C code from one processor runs at almost optimal speed on another. For example, the C code that was optimized for the MIPS R8000 processor was recompiled unchanged for the HP PA-RISC 7100. The resulting performance, 17.4 MCUPS (million connection updates per second), was only slightly below the one reached by the optimal C code, 19.2 MCUPS.

All tested processors showed speedup factors between three and eight or even higher (Table 10.13). The only exception is the Pentium, which is probably not a pure RISC architecture.

TABLE 10.13. Comparison of backpropagation performance.

| | Forward Path [MCPS] | | Speedup Factor | Learning [MCUPS] | | Speedup Factor |
|---|---|---|---|---|---|---|
| PowerPC 601/75 MHz | 5.0 $\longrightarrow$ | 28.5 | ×5.7 | 2.5 $\longrightarrow$ | 7.5 | ×3.0 |
| Sun SuperSPARC II/85 MHz | 6.2 $\longrightarrow$ | 29.6 | ×4.7 | 2.5 $\longrightarrow$ | 15.0 | ×6.0 |
| HP PA-RISC 7100/99 MHz | 8.2 $\longrightarrow$ | 58.6 | ×7.1 | 3.0 $\longrightarrow$ | 19.2 | ×6.4 |
| Alpha 21064/275 MHz | 12.2 $\longrightarrow$ | 75.0 | ×6.1 | 5.0 $\longrightarrow$ | 25.0 | ×5.0 |
| MIPS R8000/75 MHz | 10.5 $\longrightarrow$ | 91.3 | ×8.7 | 3.5 $\longrightarrow$ | 32.9 | ×9.3 |
| Pentium/100 MHz | 5.5 $\longrightarrow$ | 9.9 | ×1.8 | 2.1 $\longrightarrow$ | 4.3 | ×2.0 |

The reference C version, against which the speedup has been measured, is a straightforward but not inefficient C implementation. The core part of the forward path is listed in Figure 10.24.

```
for (j = 0; j < nneurons; j++) {
    *a = 0;
    for (i = 0; i < ninputs; i++)
        *a += *weights++ * inputs[i];
    *a += *weights++;              /* add bias */
    *o++ =squash(*a++);
}
```

FIGURE 10.24. Innermost loops of the forward path of the reference C code.

Finally, the performance of the optimized C code was compared with the performance of hand-optimized Assembly code in case of the PowerPC 601 processor. The performance of the assembly code is slightly better but not by several factors and by far less than the speedup that has been achieved by C-only optimizations.

TABLE 10.14. Comparing the Assembler and the C version on the PowerPC 601.

| PowerPC 601/75 MHz | Forward Path [MCPS] | | Speedup Factor | Learning [MCUPS] | | Speedup Factor |
|---|---|---|---|---|---|---|
| C version | 5.0 $\longrightarrow$ | 28.5 | ×5.7 | 2.5 $\longrightarrow$ | 7.5 | ×3.0 |
| Assembler version | 6.2 $\longrightarrow$ | 29.6 | ×4.7 | 2.5 $\longrightarrow$ | 15.0 | ×6.0 |

The high computational power of modern RISC processors, the fact that code can be well optimized in a high-level language, and the fact that most optimizations are portable between different processor types make RISC processors more attractive than floating-point DSPs for neural networks simulation today.

## 10.8  Conclusions

A high-performance parallel computer architecture, along with its DSP-based implementation (the MUSIC system) and its application in practical research work in the field of neural networks, has been presented. It shows that it is possible to obtain a very high simulation speed of orders of magnitudes higher compared to a straightforward implementation on a workstation using parallel computers or optimized code on modern RISC processors, and that this speedup is not restricted to demonstration applications, but is actually applicable to real research work. However, it also shows what programming effort is involved in order to obtain these results.

The MUSIC environment has played an important role in a variety of neural networks and other research projects. It allowed experimental research to a depth that was unthinkable with current workstations only. Research projects that have been supported by MUSIC computers, besides the ones described here, include the classification of auditory signals with cellular neural networks (CNNs) [20], simulations in chemistry (molecular dynamics) [21], simulations in plasma physics, analysis of EEG signals, and computer graphics.

A next-generation parallel computer is being developed at the Electronics Laboratory [22]. It uses more modern hardware components, such as the DEC Alpha 21066 processor, but retains the same programming and communication model.

### Acknowledgements

The authors would like to thank the members of the Electronics Laboratory for their countless and very valuable contributions and excellent support. We would also like to thank the many students who helped us to realize the project during their graduate work.

# References

[1] B. E. Boser, E. Säckinger, J. Bromley, Y. L. Cun, and L. D. Jackel, "An analog neural network processor with programmable topology," *IEEE Journal of Solid-State Circuits*, vol. 26, December 1991.

[2] A. Gunzinger, U. A. Müller, W. Scott, B. Bäumle, P. Kohler, H. V. Mühll, F. Müller-Plathe, W. F. van Gunsteren, and W. Guggenbühl, "Achieving super computer performance with a DSP array processor," in *Supercomputing '92* (R. Werner, ed.), pp. 543–550, IEEE/ACM, IEEE Computer Society Press, November 16–20, 1992, Minneapolis, Minnesota 1992.

[3] U. A. Müller, A. Gunzinger, and W. Guggenbühl, "Fast neural net simulation with a DSP processor array," *IEEE Transactions on Neural Networks*, vol. 6, pp. 203–213, January 1995.

[4] P. Kohler and A. Gunzinger, "An efficient communication scheme for distributed parallel processor systems," in *International Conference on Massively Parallel Processing Using Optical Interconnections (MPPOI'95)*, pp. 196–202, 1995.

[5] D. E. Rumelhart, G. E. Hinton, and R. J. Williams, "Learning internal representation by error propagation," in *Parallel Distributed Processing: Explorations in the Microstructure of Cognition* (D. E. Rumelhart and J. L. McClelland, eds.), vol. 1, pp. 318–362, Cambridge MA: Bradford Books, 1986.

[6] D. A. Pomerleau, G. L. Gusciora, D. S. Touretzky, and H. T. Kung, "Neural network simulation at warp speed: How we got 17 million connections per second," in *IEEE International Conference on Neural Networks*, pp. II.143–150, July 24–27, San Diego, California 1988.

[7] M. Witbrock and M. Zagha, "An implementation of backpropagation learning on GF11, a large SIMD parallel computer," *Parallel Computing*, vol. 14, no. 3, pp. 329–346, 1990.

[8] X. Zhang, M. Mckenna, J. P. Mesirov, and D. L. Waltz, "An efficient implementation of the back-propagation algorithm on the Connection Machine CM-2," in *Advances in Neural Information Processing Systems (NIPS-89)* (D. S. Touretzky, ed.), (2929 Campus Drive, Suite 260, San Mateo, CA 94403), pp. 801–809, Morgan Kaufmann Publishers, 1990.

[9] A. Singer, "Exploiting the inherent parallelism of artificial neural networks to achieve 1300 million interconnects per second," in *International Neural Network Conference, Paris 90*, vol. 2, (Dordrecht and Boston and London), pp. 656–660, The International Neural Network Society (INNS) and IEEE Neural Network Council Cooperating Societies, Kluwer Academic Publishers, 1990.

[10] S. Shams and K. W. Przytula, "Implementation of multilayer neural networks on parallel programmable digital computers," in *Parallel Algorithms and Architectures for DSP Applications* (M. A. Bayoumi, ed.), (Boston/Dordrecht/London), pp. 225–253, Kluwer Academic Publishers, 1991.

[11] N. Morgan, J. Beck, P. Kohn, J. Bilmes, E. Allman, and J. Beer, "The Ring Array Processor: A multiprocessing peripheral for connectionist applications," *Journal of Parallel and Distributed Computing*, vol. 14, pp. 248–259, March 1992.

[12] H. Yoon, J. H. Nang, and S. R. Maeng, "Parallel simulation of multilayered neural networks on distributed-memory multiprocessors," *Microprocessing and Microprogramming*, vol. 29, pp. 185–195, October 1990.

[13] U. A. Müller, *Simulation of Neural Networks on Parallel Computers*, vol. 23 of *Series in Microelectronics*. Konstanz, Germany: Hartung-Gorre, 1993. Ph.D. Thesis at the Swiss Federal Institute of Technology (ETH), Zürich.

[14] X. Liu and G. L. Wilcox, "Benchmarking of the CM-5 and the Cray machines with a very large backpropagation neural network," in *IEEE International Conference on Neural Networks (ICNN'94)* (S. K. Rogers, ed.), pp. 22–27, June 28–July 2, Orlando, FL 1994.

[15] P. Kohn, J. Bilmes, N. Morgan, and J. Beck, "Software for ANN training on a Ring Array Processor," in *Advances in Neural Information Processing Systems 4 (NIPS-91)* (J. E. Moody, S. J. Hanson, and R. P. Lippmann, eds.), (2929 Campus Drive, Suite 260, San Mateo, California 94403), Morgan Kaufmann, 1992.

[16] Adaptive Solutions, Inc., 1400 N.W. Compton Drive, Suite 340, Beaverton, OR 97006, *CNAPS Server, Pereliminary Data Sheet*, 1992.

[17] M. A. Stricker and M. Swain, "The capacity of color histogram indexing," in *Proceedings 1994, IEEE Computer Society Conference on Computer Vision and Pattern Recognition, (Cat. No. 94CH3405-8), IEEE Compt. Soc. Press, Los Alamitos, CA, USA*, pp. xvi+1009 pp., p. 704–8, 1994.

[18] M. A. Stricker, "Bounds for the discrimination power of color indexing techniques," *Proceedings of the SPIE, The International Society for Optical Engineering*, vol. 1994, pp. 15–24, 1994.

[19] D. H. Nguyen and B. Widrow, "The Truck Backer-Upper: An example of self-learning in neural networks," in *INNC 90 Paris*, (Dordrecht and Boston and London), pp. 399–407, The International Neural Network Society (INNS) and IEEE Neural Network Council Cooperating Societies, Kluwer Academic Publishers, 1990.

[20] J. A. Osuna, G. S. Moschytz, and T. Roska, "A framework for the classification of auditory signals with cellular neural networks," in *Procedings of 11. European Conference on Circuit Theory and Design (ECCTD)* (H. Dedieux, ed.), pp. 51–56 (volume 1), Elsevier, August 30 – Sept. 3 1993.

[21] W. Scott, A. Gunzinger, B. Bäumle, P. Kohler, U. A. Müller, H.-R. V. Mühll, A. Eichenberger, W. Guggenbühl, N. Ironmonger, F. Müller-Plathe, and W. F. van Gunsteren, "Parallel molecular dynamics on a multi signalprocessor system," *Computer Physics Communications*, vol. 75, pp. 65–86, 1993.

[22] Björn Tiemann, H. Vonder Mühll, I. Hasler, E. Hiltebrand, A. Gunzinger, and G. Tröster, "Architecture and implementation of a single-board desktop supercomputer," in *Proceedings of High-Performance Computing and Networking (HPCN Europe)* (B. Hertzberger and G. Serazzi, eds.), pp. 481–487, May 1995.

# Chapter 11

# Training Neural Networks with SPERT-II

**Krste Asanović**
**James Beck**
**Brian Kingsbury**
**Nelson Morgan**
University of California at Berkeley
Department of Electrical Engineering and Computer Sciences
Berkeley, CA 94720-1776, USA
International Computer Science Institute
1947 Center Street, Suite 600
Berkeley, CA 94704-1105, USA
**David Johnson**
International Computer Science Institute
1947 Center Street, Suite 600
Berkeley, CA 94704-1105, USA
**John Wawrzynek**
University of California at Berkeley
Department of Electrical Engineering and Computer Sciences
Berkeley, CA 94720-1776, USA

## 11.1   Introduction

Applying artificial neural networks (ANNs) to the problem of computer-based speech recognition has been a research and development focus at the International Computer Science Institute (ICSI) since 1988. This work is characterized by two parallel tasks: adjusting the neural net algorithms to improve recognition scores and building special-purpose hardware and software to speed up net training. The task of improving speech recognition also requires research on the nonneural network steps of the process, which will not be covered in this chapter. See [1] for further information on our complete speech recognition effort.

Our first effort to build a training accelerator was called RAP, for ring array processor. Based on a commercial floating-point digital signal processor (DSP), the RAP uses the simplest communication scheme possible between nodes, a unidirectional ring. A total of nine RAP installations in the United States and Europe were placed in service starting in mid-1990. RAP users collaborate on code development, and the machines have primarily been used for training neural networks for speech recognition. The largest RAP assembled at one time contained 40 nodes and was benchmarked at a rate of 341 MCPS (millions of connections per second) and 45 MCUPS (millions of connection updates per second) on a neural network we commonly use in our recognition work (234–1024–61 nodes on the input, hidden and output layers, respectively). On larger networks with equal numbers of units in each layer, the same RAP configuration was measured at up to 573 MCPS and

345

102 MCUPS. RAP systems in use at customer sites vary in size from eight to 16 nodes. The architectural details and programming model for the RAP are similar to the MUSIC system developed at ETH Zentrum (see Chapter 10) and will not be detailed here. Full information on the RAP system is available in [2].

In early 1991, we were considering a follow-up project. Commercial DSP performance was not advancing rapidly, and RAP systems were expensive to replicate and proved inefficient on smaller neural networks. Rather than proceed with a second generation RAP using commercial DSPs, we entered into a collaboration with the Electrical Engineering and Computer Sciences Department of the University of California at Berkeley with the goal of designing a full-custom single-chip microprocessor to accelerate neural network algorithms. The result was the T0 vector microprocessor. The first systems built around T0, called SPERT-II, were delivered to customers beginning in the fall of 1995. At the time of writing, 25 SPERT-II systems have been installed at eight sites in the United States and Europe. We estimate that SPERT-II performance for online backprop training of large networks is roughly equivalent to that possible with 20 nodes of a hypothetical RAP-II redesigned to use 1995-era commercial DSPs, at about one-fifth the cost. Performance on smaller networks is even more competitive.

This chapter first describes how the algorithms used in our speech recognition research evolved together with our computing systems. We then discuss the design decisions that led to the T0 vector microprocessor. In Section 11.4 we outline the SPERT-II accelerator board and its software environment. The next two sections detail how we mapped two neural net training algorithms, backprop, and Kohonen self-organizing feature maps to SPERT-II and present the resulting performance before concluding.

## 11.2 Algorithm Development

In 1987, Hervé Bourlard showed that in principle, neural networks trained as classifiers using common error criteria would produce estimates of the posterior (class) probabilities [3]. He further showed that these estimates could in principle be used to derive emission probabilities for use with Hidden Markov Models in sequence recognition problems such as speech recognition. In the following years, researchers learned a number of practical lessons about this approach, and developed systems that exploited this principle [4–7]. Our speech recognition group at ICSI has been very active in this area.

From an algorithmic perspective, this approach appeared to offer numerous advantages: no strong reliance on feature distributions, potential for combining binary and continuous features, straightforward incorporation of long-term windows of feature vectors, and the availability of a simple discriminative training algorithm.

From a computational perspective, however, the method was inherently more complex during training than the dominant training methods used in speech recognition research. More standard approaches trained density estimates for each class separately, so that each training pattern only affected a small portion of the parameters. In order to share parameters over classes so that the training was discriminative, the neural network approach typically required modification of all parameters for each input pattern. Thus, training was computationally intensive, requiring months of computation on 1990-era workstations for our common tasks.

Initially, this was a major concern, so we limited our networks by using only binary input vectors. For instance, one could match an input spectrum to one of 256 possible spectra and use as network input a single "1" and 255 "0"s. In practice we used nine such vectors, as well as binary vectors associated with temporal derivatives, plus a few other features. This led to over 5,000 inputs, but because nearly all of them were zeroes, the computational load was small and consisted mainly of additions. Furthermore, in practice we found that a hidden layer was not useful for this case, so the net was really quite trivial— a single layer of sigmoidal units with the inputs pointing to weights that should be added in to the presigmoid total. The computational load of this system was so small that it permitted us to work on large problems using conventional workstations.

When some early experiments with continuous inputs showed improved recognition performance, we abandoned the binary inputs method. Moving to continuous inputs, however, meant that we needed a system that could perform the required arithmetic at a high enough speed to facilitate our research. Most of the computational load of this research became the backpropagation training that was used for the multilayered neural networks. Although we learned to train these networks with a very small number of passes over the data, each pass still often required trillions of arithmetic operations. Large networks (from 100,000 to 2,000,000 parameters) proved to be better at the overall task than smaller ones, and the data required to train these large networks often consisted of millions of feature vectors.

Once the RAP was developed, such trainings became routine in our institute, and we were able to share results and divide labor between collaborating labs on an international basis. The RAP achieved good efficiencies, typically 20 to 90 percent of peak on our larger networks, but performance on our smaller networks was much worse. As we looked forward to building a new system, we wanted to have one that was both cheaper (so that we could have many of them) and more efficient for smaller networks.

## 11.3   T0: A Vector Microprocessor

During our initial design studies, it became clear that no existing or planned commercial processor would meet our design criteria, so we decided to develop our own programmable VLSI processor. Competing with commercial microprocessors is a daunting challenge, especially for an academic research group with limited resources and no access to advanced semiconductor processes. However, neural network algorithms are massively parallel and require only moderate arithmetic precision, and we can exploit these features to improve performance.

Fast digital arithmetic units, multipliers and shifters in particular, require chip area proportional to the *square* of the number of operand bits. In modern microprocessors and digital signal processors, a single floating-point multiply-add unit takes up a significant fraction of the chip area. High-precision arithmetic units also require high memory bandwidth to move the large operands. Studies by ourselves and others indicated that fixed-point arithmetic would suffice for backpropagation training, with 16-bit weights and 8-bit activation values providing classification performance similar to a 32-bit single-precision floating point [8,9]. The small size of these reduced precision functional units would allow multiple parallel data paths to be integrated on a single die.

In considering the organization of our processor, we were very sensitive to Amdahl's Law [10], namely that if we accelerate only certain portions of the computation then our overall speedup will be limited by those we do not. Although backpropagation training execution time is dominated by weight matrix operations on conventional workstations, a complete net training system has to perform many other tasks. These tasks include managing training and cross-validation databases, data format conversion, control of the learning schedule, checkpointing, and status reporting. Furthermore, neural algorithms are often just one component within real-world applications. For example, our speech recognition system must execute various signal processing steps on the raw audio signal to extract spectral features to feed into the neural network used for phoneme estimation, and it then must perform dynamic programming using the output of the network to find the most likely word sequence. Finally, our algorithms continually evolve as our research progresses, requiring that the processor perform well even for algorithms invented after its design was completed. Together, these considerations led us to design a very general-purpose architecture.

We began with the industry-standard MIPS-II RISC instruction set architecture (ISA) and extended this with a fixed-point vector coprocessor; we call the resulting vector ISA "Torrent." The Torrent ISA is very similar to that of a traditional vector supercomputer [11], including vector registers, vector length control, strided and scatter/gather vector memory instructions, and conditional operations.

The combination of a fast scalar processor and a tightly coupled vector coprocessor has proved very successful in attacking a wide range of scientific and engineering problems when implemented in the form of a vector supercomputer. We believe such vector architectures are also very suited to attacking a wide range of neural network, multimedia, and other signal processing tasks when implemented in the form of inexpensive vector microprocessors. In particular, a vector ISA provides a succinct abstraction of data parallelism, one that is both easy to program and enables straightforward implementations controlling multiple parallel and pipelined functional units.

T0 (for Torrent-0) is the first implementation of the Torrent ISA, and the main components are shown in Figure 11.1. They include a MIPS-II compatible RISC CPU with a 1 KB on-chip instruction cache, a vector unit coprocessor, an external memory interface, and an 8-bit wide serial host interface port (TSIP). The external memory interface supports up to 4 GB of memory over a 128-bit wide data bus. The system coprocessor provides a 32-bit counter/timer and registers for host synchronization and exception handling.

The vector unit contains a vector register file and the VP0, VP1, and VMP vector functional units. The vector register file contains 16 vector registers, each holding 32 elements of 32 bits each. VP0 and VP1 are vector arithmetic functional units that can perform 32-bit integer arithmetic and logic operations and also support fixed-point scaling, rounding, and saturation. Multiplication is supported only in VP0, with 16-bit $\times$ 16-bit multiplies producing 32-bit results. Division is performed in software by iterative long division, using an estimate of the divisor's reciprocal to obtain 12 quotient bits per iteration. The vector memory unit (VMP), handles all vector load/store operations, scalar load/store operations, and the vector insert/extract operations.

Vectors are addressed in external memory with three types of load/store options: unit stride, nonunit stride, and indexed access. In unit stride addressing, vector elements occupy consecutive memory locations. In nonunit stride, elements are separated by a constant distance. With indexed access, a vector register provides a set of pointers to the elements of the operand vector. This option efficiently implements parallel table-lookup functions for function approximation and also supports sparse vector and matrix operations.

All three vector functional units are composed of eight parallel pipelines, and each unit can produce up to eight results per cycle. The T0 memory interface has a single memory address port, limiting nonunit stride and indexed memory operations to a rate of one element transfer per cycle. All vector pipeline hazards are fully interlocked in hardware, and so instruction scheduling is only needed to improve performance, not to ensure correctness. The elements of a vector register are striped across all eight pipelines. With the maximum vector length of 32, a vector functional unit can accept a new instruction every four cycles. T0 can saturate all three vector functional units by issuing one instruction per cycle to each in turn, leaving a single issue slot open every four cycles for the scalar unit. In this manner, T0 can sustain up to 24 operations per cycle while issuing only a single 32-bit instruction per cycle.

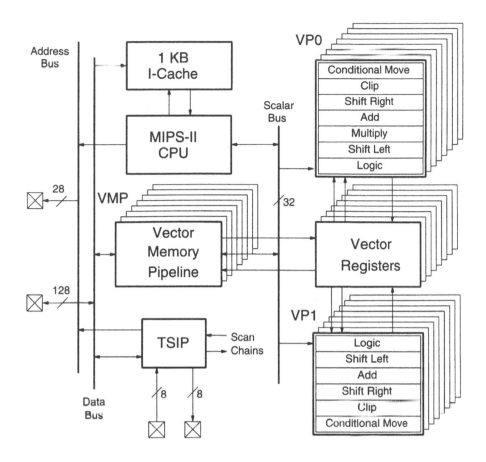

FIGURE 11.1. Block diagram of T0 microarchitecture.

T0 was fabricated in Hewlett-Packard's CMOS26G process using $1.0\,\mu m$ scalable CMOS design rules and two layers of metal. The die measures $16.75\,mm \times 16.75\,mm$ and contains 730,701 transistors. At a clock frequency of 40 MHz, the device consumes less than 12 W of power from a 5 V supply. The first silicon was received in April 1995 and is fully functional with no known bugs. Full details of the Torrent ISA and the T0 implementation are available in [12, 13].

## 11.4   The SPERT-II Workstation Accelerator

The SPERT-II hardware is a double slot SBus card for use in Sun-compatible workstations. The board contains a 40-MHz T0 vector microprocessor with 8 MB of off-chip SRAM and a Xilinx FPGA device for interfacing with the host (see Figure 11.2).

The SPERT-II software environment was designed to be similar to that of conventional workstations to ease the task of porting existing applications and to provide a comfortable environment for developing new code. For a process running on the SPERT-II board, its "operating system" comprises two programs: a small kernel that runs on T0 and a user-level server running on the host. To run a program on SPERT-II, a user invokes the server, passing the name of the SPERT executable as an argument. The server resets T0, loads

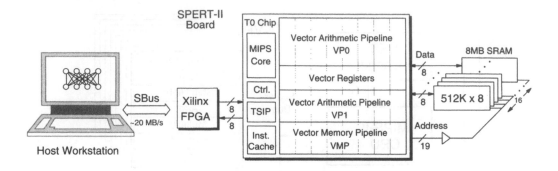

FIGURE 11.2. SPERT-II System Organization.

the kernel and SPERT executable, and then waits to handle I/O requests on behalf of the SPERT program. The software structure is shown in Figure 11.3.

By basing our design on a MIPS scalar architecture, we gain access to a wealth of existing software support, mostly taken from the popular GNU tool set. We use an unmodified version of gcc, an optimizing scalar C and C++ cross-compiler. Although T0 does not include a hardware floating-point unit, MIPS-II floating-point instructions are trapped and emulated by the kernel, simplifying porting. We have modified the gdb symbolic debugger to debug T0 programs remotely from the host and to give access to the vector coprocessor registers. We extended the gas assembler to include support for the new vector instructions and added an optimizing scheduler to avoid vector instruction interlocks. We also employ the GNU linker and other binary utility programs such as library archivers.

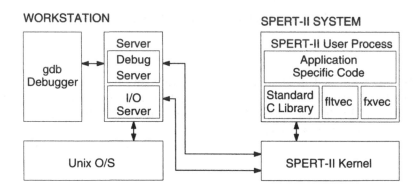

FIGURE 11.3. SPERT-II Software Environment.

Currently, the only access we provide to the vector unit is either via library routines or by coding directly in the assembler. We have developed an extensive set of optimized vector library routines, including many fixed-point matrix and vector operations. Vectorizable floating-point code can make use of our vectorized IEEE single precision floating-point emulation library, which can achieve up to 14 MFLOPS. Another group is developing a vectorizing compiler for T0 [14].

## 11.5 Mapping Backpropagation to SPERT-II

For our speech recognition work, we mostly use a simple feed-forward multilayer perceptron (MLP) with three layers. Typical MLPs for this task have 100 to 400 input units. The input layer is fully connected to a hidden layer of 100 to 4,000 hidden units. The hidden layer is fully connected to an output layer that contains one output per phoneme, typically 56 to 61. The hidden units incorporate a standard sigmoid nonlinearity, usually $f(x) = 1/(1 + e^{-x})$. The output units compute either a sigmoid or a "soft-max" activation function:

$$f(x) = \frac{e^x}{\sum_i e^{x_i}}.$$

We can classify backpropagation training techniques according to the number of patterns that are presented between weight updates. An *on-line* procedure updates weights after every pattern presentation. An *off-line* or *batch* procedure accumulates weight updates over the entire training database before updating the weights. Batch-mode training is easier to parallelize and tends to give greater raw MCUPS numbers. However, for large realistic problems such as speech or image recognition, the data sets tend to be quite redundant, and we have found that a single pass of on-line training tends to accomplish much more than a single pass of batch training.

Although some researchers have found slow convergence using backprop to train smaller networks with smaller data sets, we experience relatively fast convergence using on-line backprop to train large networks with large real-world data sets. We have found that when training large nets (40,000 to more than a million weights) using up to several million pattern presentations and starting with random weights, only three to 10 passes are required to obtain convergence. In some cases, when adapting a previously initialized network, only a single pass over a new training set is needed.

The most compute-intensive operations in on-line backpropagation training are those involving the weight matrices. Three operations are performed: forward propagation, error backpropagation, and weight update. On T0, we store weight matrices in *input-major* form, where element `weight[i][j]` holds the weight connecting input i to neuron j. The three on-line backprop matrix operations then correspond to three standard linear algebra routines in the T0 library: vector-transpose × matrix multiply, matrix × vector multiply, and scaled outer-product accumulation, respectively. We chose our weight matrix orientation to favor forward propagation because this is performed more often than backpropagation; error backpropagation is not required on the input-to-hidden weight matrix during training, and our cross-validation procedure monitors network convergence by running forward propagation on a separate test database once per epoch.

On-line forward propagation uses the vector-transpose × matrix multiply library routine. This routine processes large matrices 128 columns at a time, with matrix elements read using unit stride. Each 16-bit element from the source vector is loaded into a scalar register, then it is multiplied by 128 16-bit elements loaded from one row of the source matrix, with the products accumulated into 128 32-bit sums held in four vector registers. To reduce memory bandwidth further, two 16-bit source vector values are read at once using a single 32-bit scalar load. This loop requires one cycle to read two source vector elements, then 32 cycles to read the 2 × 128 matrix elements. The multiplies and adds can be overlapped with the memory accesses, giving a peak throughput of 310 MCPS, or nearly 97 percent of peak. After processing all elements in each of the 128 columns, the accumulated 32-bit sums are stored to memory at the rate of four per cycle, and the next set of 128 columns are processed. When fewer than 128 columns remain, the routine switches to a different loop that processes up to a single vector register full of columns at a time.

This loop also fetches two 16-bit source vector operands in one cycle, and takes nine cycles to process up to 64 multiplies and adds, achieving up to 284 MCPS, or nearly 89 percent of peak.

On-line error backpropagation uses the matrix $\times$ vector multiply library routine. The matrix is now accessed in a transposed manner compared to vector-transpose $\times$ matrix multiply, with dot-products calculated across the rows of the matrix. One approach would be to stride down a column to collect the source matrix elements that are multiplied by each source vector element. However, nonunit-stride accesses only run at the rate of 1 element per cycle on T0 and so this approach would yield only 1/8 of peak performance. Instead, the library routine operates on 12 rows of the source matrix at a time, using 12 vector registers to hold 32 partial sums for each row. The source vector is now accessed with a unit-stride vector load and is multiplied element-wise with 12 vectors of 32 matrix elements. This loop takes four cycles to load the 32 16-bit source vector elements, then $12 \times 4$ cycles to load the $12 \times 32$ 16-bit matrix elements. Again, multiplies and adds can be fully overlapped, giving a peak performance of 384 multiply-adds every 52 cycles, or 92 percent of peak for large matrices. However, there is an additional overhead at the end of each set of 12 rows. The 12 vector registers contain 32 partial sums that must be reduced to single 32-bit values before they are stored in the result vector. This process can take up to 140 cycles for all 12 vectors and is a considerable overhead for matrices with few columns. When there are fewer than 12 rows remaining, the routine drops down to perform 4, 2, and finally 1 row at a time, with corresponding decreases in performance.

The most time-consuming routine in on-line backpropagation training is weight update. This maps to a vector outer-product and matrix accumulate operation. The routine operates on eight rows of the matrix at a time, first loading eight 16-bit elements from the first source vector into eight scalar registers. These values are reused across the entire width of the matrix. The matrix is updated in blocks of eight rows by 32 elements. First, 32 16-bit elements are read from the second source vector into a vector register. These values are then multiplied by each of the eight scalar values in turn with the products summed in to each 32 element section of each of the eight matrix rows. The routine is dominated by the time taken to read the 16-bit weights in from memory and write them back out. The process takes 68 cycles to perform 256 multiply-adds, and so runs at up to 47 percent of peak.

For on-line backpropagation training of large three-layer neural networks with 16-bit weights and equal numbers of units in the input, hidden, and output layers, we can calculate that the maximum asymptotically achievable performance will be 310 MCPS and 86 MCUPS. The measured performance on several real matrix sizes is given below. Note that the rate depends on the ratio of input to output units; with fewer output units, less time is spent on error backpropagation and the achievable MCUPS rate will be higher. With fewer output units, the maximum achievable performance approaches 101 MCUPS.

Although the $O(n^2)$ matrix operations dominate performance for large networks, the other $O(n)$ operations required to handle input and output vectors and activation values would cause significant overhead on smaller networks if they were not also vectorized.

The sigmoid activation function is implemented using a library piecewise-linear function approximation routine. This routine makes use of the vector gather operations to perform the table lookups. Although T0 can only execute vector gather operations at the rate of one element transfer per cycle, the table lookup routine can simultaneously perform all the arithmetic operations for index calculation and linear interpolation in the vector arithmetic units, achieving a rate of one 16-bit sigmoid result every 1.5 cycles. Similarly, a lookup-table-based vector `logadd` routine is used to implement the soft-max function, producing one result every 2.25 cycles.

We have standardized on the IEEE floating-point format to store our training databases on disk. T0 uses vector library routines to convert single precision IEEE floating-point format to the internal 16-bit fixed-point representation. These conversion routines operate at the rate of 2.4 cycles per element converted.

We compared SPERT-II performance against two commercial RISC workstations. One was a SPARCstation-20/61 containing a single 60-MHz SuperSPARC+ processor with a peak performance of 60 MFLOPS, 1 MB of second level cache, and 128 MB of DRAM main memory. The other was an IBM RS/6000-590, containing the RIOS-2 chip-set running at 66.7 MHz with a peak performance of 266 MFLOPS, 256 KB of primary cache, and 768 MB of DRAM main memory. The SPERT-II system contains a single T0 processor running at 40 MHz with a peak performance of 640 million fixed-point arithmetic operations per second and 8 MB of SRAM main memory, mounted in a SPARCstation-5/70.

Figure 11.4 shows the performance of the three systems for a set of three-layer networks on both forward propagation and backpropagation training. Table 11.1 presents performance results for two speech network architectures. We used three-layer neural networks with total connectivity between adjacent layers. In Figure 11.4, for ease of presentation, we use networks with the same number of units per layer. The networks presented in the table have a different number of units per layer, as indicated there. The sigmoid function was the hidden layer activation function, and the soft-max function was the output layer activation function.

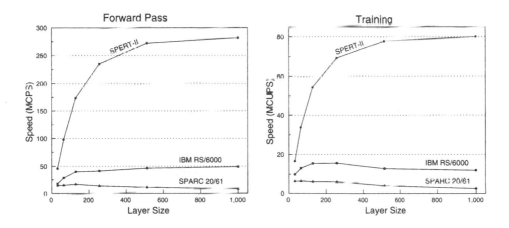

FIGURE 11.4. Performance evaluation results for on-line backpropagation training of three-layer networks, with equal numbers of units in the input, hidden, and output layers. The workstations perform all calculations in single precision IEEE floating point, whereas SPERT-II uses 16-bit fixed-point weights.

The workstation version of the code performs all input and output and all computation using IEEE single-precision floating-point arithmetic. We extensively hand optimized the matrix and vector operations within the backpropagation algorithm using manual loop unrolling with register and cache blocking. The following SPERT-II timings include the time for conversion between floating-point and fixed-point for input and output.

The SPERT-II system clearly performs better even for the smallest networks, such as those with only 32 units per layer. For large networks, the SPERT-II system performed 30 times better than the SPARCstation-20/61 and about six times better than the IBM

TABLE 11.1. Performance Evaluation for Selected Net Sizes.

| Net Type | Net Size (In–Hidden–Out) | SPERT-II | SPARC-20/61 | IBM RS/6000-590 |
|---|---|---|---|---|
| Forward Pass (MCPS) | | | | |
| Small Speech Net | 153–200–56 | 181.0 | 17.6 | 43.0 |
| Large Speech Net | 342–4000–61 | 276.0 | 11.3 | 45.1 |
| Training (MCUPS) | | | | |
| Small Speech Net | 153–200–56 | 57.1 | 7.00 | 16.7 |
| Large Speech Net | 342–4000–61 | 78.7 | 4.18 | 17.2 |

RS/6000-590. On-line backpropagation training exhibits poor temporal locality. Every other weight is touched in between accesses to any single weight and so if the weight matrices are too large to fit in cache, there is marked drop in performance. With more modern workstations, such as the Sun Ultra-1/170, we have observed an even more extreme drop off due to the increased gap between floating-point performance and sustainable memory bandwidth.

In [8, 15], we report on various experiments that show that the fixed-point trained net matches the floating-point net performance for frame-level phoneme classification. However, we have discovered that, in some cases, when we subsequently try to use the fixed-point network to generate probabilities for use in word or utterance level recognition, we attain noticeably poorer recognition scores compared with the floating-point trained network. We determined that the problem is due to loss of small weight updates through underflow caused by the limited range of the 16-bit weights.

Our solution to this problem was to extend the weight representation with a second 16-bit weight matrix holding low-order bits. The forward and error backpropagation routines are unchanged and operate on the upper 16-bit weight matrices as before. A new weight update routine is provided that concatenates the two 16-bit halves to form a full 32-bit weight, adds in the update, then stores the updated weight back into its two component matrices. Using this technique we have found that word level recognition accuracy is now indistinguishable from nets trained with the IEEE single-precision floating point. However, this routine is slower than before, requiring twice as much memory traffic for each weight update. The inner loop updates weight matrices 1 row by 32 elements at a time and requires 17 cycles to update 32 weights. This represents only 23 percent of peak arithmetic performance.

When using the 32-bit weight updates, the maximum achievable forward propagation rate is unchanged at 310 MCPS. The asymptotic maximum achievable training rate for equal numbers of input, hidden, and output units drops to 54 MCUPS. With small output layers, the maximum rate is 59 MCUPS.

Between the two extremes of on-line and off-line training lies what we refer to as *bunch*-mode training, where we update weights after every group, or bunch, of patterns. In our initial experiments we found that bunches of between 32 to 1,000 patterns appear to give comparable results with comparable convergence speed to the on-line approach, while permitting an amortization of many sources of per-pattern overhead. We retain the same weight matrix format as before, but now the three steps in backpropagation training can be formulated as variants of matrix × matrix multiply. Bunch-mode is also more efficient for large weight matrices on cached workstations, allowing reuse of cached weight values and correspondingly improving training performance [16]. We note, however, that bunch-mode backpropagation training is not always possible. For example, recurrent neural network architectures have interpattern dependencies that prevent this optimization [4].

Bunch-mode forward propagation is equivalent to a matrix × matrix multiply. The inner loop of the T0 matrix × matrix multiply library routine computes a 4-row by 32-element block of the destination matrix. Each iteration of the inner loop reads four 16-bit values into scalar registers from the first source matrix and 32 16-bit elements from the second source matrix into a vector register. Now four vector × scalar products can be calculated and accumulated into the four vector registers holding the 32-bit sums. This loop is dominated by the multiplies and adds and runs at the peak speed of 320 MCPS.

Bunch-mode error backpropagation is equivalent to a matrix × matrix-transpose multiply. The inner loop of the T0 library routine computes the sums for a 12-row by 32-element block of the destination matrix. The first matrix is accessed with scalar loads, whereas the second matrix is accessed with a nonunit stride vector load. The overhead of the strided vector access is amortized over 12 vector multiplies and adds. Each loop iteration requires 53 cycles to calculate 384 multiply-add, and so achieves 91 percent of peak. Although the peak rate is slightly lower, this loop is more efficient than the on-line backpropagate routine in practice, because it avoids the reduction step.

The bunch-mode weight update is equivalent to a matrix-transpose × matrix multiply accumulated into the destination matrix. Because the overhead of loading and storing the two halves of each 32-bit weight is now amortized over the patterns in a bunch, we have coded only the 32-bit weight update version of this routine. The inner loop is similar to the matrix × matrix multiply routine, with the order in which scalar values are loaded from the first source matrix transposed. Again, the routine is multiply-add dominated and the inner loop achieves 100 percent of peak.

The maximum achievable rates for bunch-mode training with 32-bit weight updates, for large bunches and for large matrices with equal numbers of input, hidden, and output units, is 320 MCPS and 125 MCUPS. For small output layers, the maximum achievable training rate increases to 160 MCUPS. The bunch-mode routines have less overhead than the on-line routines and perform better on smaller weight matrices. In addition, the amount of data operated on by each call to the $O(n)$ routines is increased by the bunch size, reducing the overhead per element.

## 11.6  Mapping Kohonen Nets to SPERT-II

Kohonen self-organizing feature maps (KSOFM) are a form of neural network that can learn to cluster data into topological maps with no external supervision [17]. They have been used in a wide range of applications including image classification and data compression [18].

In practice, Kohonen nets are quite small [18], and the neighborhood radius shrinks rapidly so that it is less than a few neurons wide for most of the training process. This makes training difficult to parallelize efficiently— first, because of the need to find the minimum distance neuron and, second, because only a few neurons' weights are updated at any time step. The algorithm can be modified to run in bunch mode, with weights updated less frequently to allow a higher update rate on parallel implementations, but this can lead to much slower convergence giving longer run times overall [19].

We have implemented two vectorized library routines for KSOFMs with a Euclidean distance measure. The first routine, forward, takes an input vector and a weight matrix and finds the neuron with the minimum squared Euclidean distance from the input vector. The matrix is stored in input-major form, as in our backpropagation routines, and the routine works on 32 columns at a time. Each 16-bit input vector element is read into a scalar register, then subtracted from a vector of up to 32 16-bit weights loaded from one row of the matrix. The differences are squared and accumulated into a vector register. This inner loop is dominated by the three arithmetic operations per connection and takes six cycles to compute 32 connections, giving an asymptotic peak of 213 MCPS. To locate the winning neuron, the routine keeps an index for each vector register element in a vector register that is initialized from memory at the start of the routine. These indices are incremented by 32 using a vector add as the routine steps over the columns of the matrix. Two global vector registers hold the 32 minimum sums seen so far and the 32 indices of these minima. At the end of the columns, the new sums are compared to the global sums at each element position, and if smaller, the sums and indices at each element position are copied into the global vector registers. At the end of the routine, the 32 global minimum sums and indices must be reduced to a single minimum sum and index, which takes 45 cycles. The forward routine works for any neural map topology, including 1-D, 2-D, and 3-D grids. It is the responsibility of the calling routine to convert the column index of the minimum sum neuron back into coordinates in the neural map. This can be easily achieved using precomputed lookup tables. Table 11.2 gives the measured performance of the forward pass routine on T0 for various sized networks taken from [18]. Performance is given in MCPS (millions of connections per second).

TABLE 11.2. Performance of SPERT-II KSOFM forward pass on real-world networks from [18].

| Application | Neuron Topology | Input Dimension | SPERT-II (MCPS) |
|---|---|---|---|
| Speech coding | $10 \times 10$ | 12 | 100.1 |
| | $16 \times 16$ | 12 | 132.9 |
| | $20 \times 20$ | 12 | 134.0 |
| Radar clutter classification | $10 \times 10$ | 11 | 93.4 |
| | $20 \times 20$ | 11 | 130.9 |
| Gas concentration | $12 \times 12$ | 32 | 159.3 |
| Binocular receptive fields | $16 \times 16$ | 256 | 208.9 |

The second routine, update, modifies weights for some number of neurons located in contiguous columns in the array. One input argument is a vector of update factors, one per neuron, that give the strength of the update for each neuron. The update routine is typically called multiple times to update all neurons in the neighborhood of the winner. For example, in a 2-D grid, it would be called once for each row in the neighborhood. In this manner, the routine can support any shape of neighborhood on any map topology. The routine works on one neuron at a time, accessing the weights using strided vector memory operations. The weights are subtracted from the input vector elements to find the element distances, then multiplied by the update factor for this neuron, before being added back into the weight, which is then stored back. The routine requires one cycle to load the factor, then $2N$ cycles to load and store $N$ weights. Though all arithmetic can be overlapped, this routine runs at only 9.4 percent of peak arithmetic performance. Fortunately, training neighborhoods shrink rapidly in practice, so only a small fraction of the neurons need to be updated.

To measure training performance, we used a benchmark supplied by EPFL, Switzerland [19], which uses a KSOFM to implement speech coding with vector quantization. This benchmark has 12-dimensional input vectors mapped to a 2-dimensional neuron grid.

EPFL supplies the training data already converted to a 16-bit fixed-point representation. Over time, the adaptation rate of the weights varies as

$$\alpha(t) = \frac{\alpha_0}{1 + K_\alpha \cdot t}$$

where $t$ is the number of patterns presented to the network, $\alpha_0$ is the initial adaptation rate, and $K_\alpha$ is a time constant that controls how fast the adaptation rate decreases.

The size of the neighborhood decreases over time according to

$$R(t) = 1 + \frac{R_0}{1 + K_R \cdot t}$$

where $R_0$ defines the initial radius, and $K_R$ is a time constant that controls the rate at which the radius shrinks. Within the neighborhood, the adaptation rate drops linearly, from $\alpha(t)$ at the winning neuron to 0 for neurons outside radius $R(t)$. The benchmark uses the Manhattan distance on the 2-D grid to determine how far a neuron is from the winner.

Computing the change in neighborhood parameters at every pattern can be time consuming. Fortunately, updating the parameters more slowly seems to have little effect on convergence. For the following timings, we updated the adaptation rates and radius every 100 patterns. We calculate the parameters using a software-emulated floating point on T0, convert to a fixed point, and cache them in an array. We have found no significant difference between floating-point and fixed-point trained nets in either convergence rate or final quantization distortion.

Table 11.3 shows training performance on the EPFL speech coding benchmark. Training time is given over all 30,000 patterns. These are small networks and small training databases, with total run times of around one second, yet T0 still achieves high performance. On larger networks and with larger training sets, the performance will asymptotically approach the peak forward pass rate of 213 MCUPS.

TABLE 11.3. Performance of SPERT-II on the EPFL benchmark for KSOFM training for all 30,000 training patterns. The neighborhood is updated after every 100 patterns with the initial radius, $R_0$, set to half the grid dimensions. The other training parameters are $\alpha_0 = 0.1$, $K_\alpha = 0.0025$, and $K_R = 0.02$.

| Neuron Topology | $R_0$ | SPERT-II Time (s) | SPERT-II (MCUPS) |
|---|---|---|---|
| 10×10 | 5 | 0.795 | 45.2 |
| 16×16 | 8 | 1.072 | 86.0 |
| 20×20 | 10 | 1.431 | 100.6 |

## 11.7  Conclusions

We have presented a workstation accelerator based on a unique custom vector microprocessor and have described how we have vectorized several neural network training tasks. We have evaluated the training and forward propagation performance of the system for a range of neural network sizes and showed that SPERT-II is efficient in practice, even on smaller networks common in real applications.

By adopting a vector architecture, we have not had to sacrifice either generality or a convenient software environment to achieve this high efficiency. We have also achieved promising results in a wide range of other important application areas, including image and audio signal processing, audio synthesis, image compression, and cryptography. This leads us to believe that vector processors will be an important class of processors in the future.

## Acknowledgments

Thanks to Bertrand Irissou for his work on the T0 chip, John Hauser for Torrent libraries, John Lazzaro for his advice on chip and system building, and Jerry Feldman. Primary support for this work was from ONR URI Grant N00014-92-J-1617, ARPA contract number N0001493-C0249, NSF Grant No. MIP-9311980, and NSF PYI Award No. MIP-8958568NSF. Additional support was provided by ICSI. IBM donated the RS/6000.

# Figures

FIGURE 11.5. Photograph of T0 on board.

FIGURE 11.6. Photograph of top of SPERT-II board.

FIGURE 11.7. Photograph of bottom of SPERT-II board.

# References

[1] N. Morgan and H. Bourlard, "Neural networks for statistical recognition of continuous speech," in *Proceedings of the IEEE*, pp. 742–770, May 1995.

[2] N. Morgan, et. al., "The ring array processor (RAP): A multiprocessing peripheral for connectionist applications," *Journal of Parallel and Distributed Computing*, vol. 14, 1992. Special Issue on Neural Networks.

[3] H. Bourlard and C. J. Wellekens, "Links between Markov models and multilayer perceptrons," in *Advances in Neural Information Processing Systems 1* (D. J. Touretzky, ed.), pp. 502–510, San Mateo: Morgan Kaufmann, 1989.

[4] A. Robinson and F. Fallside, "A recurrent error propagation network speech recognition system," *Computer, Speech and Language*, vol. 5, pp. 257–286, 1991.

[5] M. Cohen, et. al., "Hybrid neural network/hidden Markov model continuous speech recognition," in *Proc. of Intl. Conference on Speech and Language Processing*, (Banff, CANADA), pp. 915–918, 1992.

[6] S. Renals, et. al., "Connectionist probability estimators in HMM speech recognition," *IEEE Transactions on Speech and Audio Processing*, pp. 161–174, January 1994.

[7] N. Morgan and H. Bourlard, "Continuous speech recognition: An introduction to the hybrid HMM/connectionist approach," *Signal Processing Magazine*, pp. 25–42, May 1995.

[8] K. Asanović and N. Morgan, "Experimental determination of precision requirements for back-propagation training of artificial neural networks," in *Proceedings of the 2nd International Conference on Microelectronics for Neural Networks*, (Munich), pp. 9–16, 1991.

[9] T. Baker and D. Hammerstrom, "Modifications to artificial neural network models for digital hardware implementation," Tech. Rep. CS/E 88-035, Department of Computer Science and Engineering, Oregon Graduate Center, 1988.

[10] G. M. Amdahl, "Validity of the single processor approach to achieving large scale computing capabilities," in *AFIPS Conference Proceedings*, vol. 30, pp. 483–485, 1967.

[11] R. M. Russel, "The Cray-1 computer system," *Communications of the ACM*, vol. 21, pp. 63–72, January 1978.

[12] K. Asanović and D. Johnson, "Torrent architecture manual," Tech. Rep. CSD-97-930, University of California at Berkeley, Computer Science Division, 1997.

[13] K. Asanović and J. Beck, "T0 engineering data," Tech. Rep. CSD-97-930, University of California at Berkeley, Computer Science Division, 1997.

[14] D. D. Vries and C. G. Lee, "A vectorizing SUIF compiler," in *Proceedings of the First SUIF Compiler Workshop*, (Stanford University), pp. 59–67, January 1996.

[15] J. Wawrzynek, et. al., "SPERT-II: A vector microprocessor system," *IEEE Computer*, vol. 29, pp. 79–86, March 1996.

[16] J. Bilmes, K. Asanović, C. Chin, and J. Demmel, "Using PHIPAC to speed error back propagation," in (to appear) *in International Conference on Acoustics, Speech, and Signal Processing*, 1997.

[17] T. Kohonen, "Self-organizing formation of topologically correct feature maps," *Biological Cybernetics*, vol. 43, no. 1, pp. 59–69, 1982.

[18] G. Myklebust and J. G. Solheim, "Parallel self-organizing maps for actual applications," in *Proceedings of the IEEE International Conference on Neural Networks*, (Perth), 1995.

[19] T. Cornu and P. Ienne, "Performance of digital neuro-computers," in *Proceedings Fourth International Conference on Microelectronics for Neural Networks and Fuzzy Systems*, pp. 87–93, September 1994.

# Chapter 12

# Concluding Remarks

**N. Sundararajan**
**P. Saratchandran**
School of Electrical and Electronic Engineering,
Nanyang Technological University,
Singapore, 639798.

In this chapter, we take stock of all the work reported in the previous chapters and draw some overall conclusions and future directions for this area.

In general, if a computing platform has to offer an effective solution for neural computation, it should exhibit the following characteristics:

- Considerable computational power

- Sufficient capacity for handling large-scale neural networks

- Sufficient flexibility to handle various neural network configurations

- The potential to simulate a variety of neuron models including new models

Parallel computing architectures exhibit these characteristics and hence are natural candidates for solving neurocomputing problems.

Through the various chapters of the book, we have covered in detail the theoretical and implementation aspects of parallelization of popular ANN models on several parallel hardware architectures. Part I provides useful insights into the theoretical aspects and Parts II and III provide implementation details on various hardware platforms. The value of the theoretical analysis is that it provides useful insight into the strengths and weaknesses of different methods of parallelization without implementing and testing them in actual hardware. However, no amount of analysis can highlight the nuances of practical implementation, which can only be learned from actual implementation on real machines.

In Part I, the first two chapters develop a theoretical model for parallel implementations of backpropagation (BP) neural networks on a heterogeneous ring of processors. Chapter 3 covers network-based parallelism, and Chapter 4 covers training-set-based parallelism and experimental results have been provided to validate the developed models. Using the models, finding the optimal mapping (in the sense of minimizing the training time) of the neural network onto the processor array is shown to lead to a mixed integer optimization problem. Solving this optimization problem by using the conventional mixed integer programming and also the genetic algorithms was presented. The study also indicated that the location of the processors in the heterogeneous array is not critical.

Chapters 5 describes how the real time recurrent learning (RTRL) algorithm for training fully recurrent networks can be efficiently mapped onto a distributed memory ring multiprocessor architecture. This method uses space-time-mapping techniques, originally developed for translating sequential algorithms with static dependencies to very large scale integration (VLSI) arrays. The proposed scheme has been verified with an experimental setup consisting of a Transputer ring array. It has been demonstrated for the case of 152 neurons that the parallely implemented 19 Transputer T-800 array was 15 times faster than a SPARC-2-based Sun workstation.

Parallel algorithms for simulating large-size ART1 networks on ring architectures were covered in Chapter 6. Based on the performance results, it is clear that the point-to-point latency and not the bandwidth is the important parameter for optimizing communications. One of the main results emerging from the study is that because of the nature of the ART1 algorithm, allocation of processes to processors should be done independently along layers F1 and F2, as this choice facilitates pipelining and provides the freedom to allocate additional resources to F1 processes that can exploit them without introducing long communication paths between a smaller number of F2 processes.

In the current literature on parallel implementations, the focus has been mainly on experimental results and any progress in developing a theoretical framework for this area (as in Part I) should be of immense use to the researchers as it eliminates the need for expensive experimental setups.

Large general-purpose parallel machines are extremely useful for parallelization of the training phase for a wide range of applications. Part II of this book is thus devoted to implementation on such a machine (Fujitsu AP 1000) and the results shown for several applications amply justify the use of such implementations. However, these machines are not very convenient to use in the recall phase, especially for applications in which the ANN may be have to work in conjunction with other signal processing software or hardware.

Parallel machines designed with special hardware architectures and software environments customized for mapping ANNs are good for both the training and the recall phase. Part III of the book was devoted to implementations on such machines for several practical applications. The unique feature of these architectures is the flexibility in them that permits the mapping of different ANN models of varying sizes and complexity and also realizing them in VLSI environment.

The TLA and PLA architectures of Fujimoto, for example, provide a solution to the connectivity problem and the performance degradation due to the data transmission bottleneck in large-scale neural networks. The main building block for these architectures is the 2-D lattice, and these architectures are among the most efficient two-dimensional processor configurations that can be realized by the current state of wafer scale integration (WSI). The results from the traveling salesman problem and the identity mapping problem have clearly demonstrated the power of these architectures, which provide great flexibility for various configurations of neural networks and neuron models.

The DREAM architecture of Shams and Gaudiot allows dynamic reconfiguration of the processing elements and provides a parallel-computing environment, which allows mapping for any ANN problem, whether big or small, in an efficient manner. The architecture utilizes a variable-length ring to realize this efficient implementation. The results given for the image compression, Nettalk, and the traveling salesman problem show the capability of the DREAM Machine in solving these benchmark problems.

The MUSIC Machine developed at ETH, Zurich, consists of an array of floating-point processing elements (DSPs) with distributed memory and a ring communication network. With its "intelligent communication" and flexible parallel environment (NeuroBasic) MUSIC has been shown to produce great savings in training and recall times in a practical photo-finishing example in which the neural network is used to enhance the quality of photo correction. It is worth mentioning that the MUSIC Machine has been used by several ANN research groups throughout the world.

The SPERT-II built at ICSI, Berkeley, is a vector microprocessor system that brings parallelism to the chip level. It is primarily designed for mapping ANNs used in the speech recognition research. Results from BP and self organizing map (SOM) used in the speech recognition and speech coding applications show that this system produces impressive speedup for both the training and recognition phases of the ANN.

## 12.1 Future Trend

As the applications of neural network start gaining momentum in the industry, the need for a computing medium best suited for both the training and the recall phase will be felt more than ever. This raises the important question as to what is the best medium for hardware implementation of neural networks? Finding the answer to this question is difficult because it is impossible to predict precisely the future developments in computing technology or the direction of neural network research. However what is certain is that the rapid developments in VLSI technology with associated cost savings will greatly impact the design of neurocomputers. From this view point it seems likely that neurocomputers of the future will be realized in the form of VLSI chips employing a hybrid implementation of neural networks with parallelism enshrined in them.

In conclusion, we have attempted to bring together, in a single volume, all the different parallel implementation aspects of artificial neural networks. We realize that it is impossible to cover comprehensively these topics in a single volume because the technologies of both parallel processing and neural networks are expanding rapidly. However, we feel that this book will be a valuable contribution to the research community in consolidating the developments in this field and in spurring further activities leading to real-world applications of artificial neural networks.

# Index

**A**

Activation of neurons
    ART1 networks, 159–160, 162, 163, 165, 166
    competitive learning, 292
    Hopfield network simulation, 239, 241
    multilayer perceptron simulation, 242–245, 250
    sigmoid activation function, 8, 281–282, 352
Adaptive Resonance Theory (ART) networks, 16–17, 157–158
    *See also* ART1 networks
Algorithmic mapping
    DREAM Machine, 284–285
    optimal mapping on heterogeneous networks, 79–83, 120–124
    overview, 29
    *See also* Heuristic mapping
Allocation of neurons. *See* Neurons, mapping to processors
All-to-all broadcast, ART1 networks, 169
Amdahl's law, 3, 347
Analog chip technologies, 46
Anderson, J., 5
AP1000 computer. *See* Fujitsu AP1000 computer
Application adaptable mapping heuristic
    convergence, 200–201, 207–215, 218–219
    execution time, 199, 204–206
    image compression application, 221–225
    mapping degrees of parallelism, 189–196
    memory requirements, 201
    Nettalk benchmark application, 201–216, 219–221
    overview, 185, 188
    performance, 204–206, 221
    sonar return application, 216–221
    speech recognition application, 221
    total training time, 196–201, 215–216
    training speed, 202–204
Applications of artificial neural networks, 49–53
Architectures, parallel
    DREAM machine, 279–283
    extended ring architecture, 164, 172–173

fixed-ring systolic architecture, 274–278
lattice architectures (TLA, PLA), 237
MUSIC system, 304–306
neurocomputers, 233–234
palindrome ring architectures, 169–170, 172–173
T0 vector microprocessor, 347–349
Array topology, backpropagation implementations, 32
    *See also* DREAM (dynamically reconfigurable extended array multiprocessor); Fixed-ring systolic architecture
ART (Adaptive Resonance Theory) networks, 16–17, 157–158
    *See also* ART1 networks
ART1 networks
    learning algorithm, 17
    network architecture, 158–161
    overview, 157–158
    parallel ring algorithm, 164–169
    partitioning, 169–170, 172–173
    performance and scalability, 171–173
    serial learning algorithm, 161–164, 173
    Transputer implementation, 170
Associative networks, 13–15
Attentional subsystem, ART1 networks, 158–159
Azema-Barac, M. E., 32

**B**

Backpropagation learning
    application adaptable mapping heuristic, 189–201
    bunch-mode training, 354–355
    color correction application, 318–322, 327
    communication overhead, 68, 104–105, 111
    computation time, 101–104, 129–130
    convergence, 10–11, 200–201, 207–215, 218–219, 220–221
    degrees of parallelism, 26–29, 189–196, 307–310
    DREAM Machine implementation, 288
    learning algorithm, 8–10
    learning performance, 11–13, 48
    memory requirements, 105–106, 130–131

on multilayer perceptron, 306–307
MUSIC system implementation, 306–310, 312
network parallelism, 67–68, 70–75
optimal distribution of neurons, 79–96
optimal distribution of training sets, 120–128
optimization for RISC-based systems, 333–339
parallel implementations, 29–46
sensitivity to initial parameters, 197, 213–215
training-set parallelism, 111–112, 112–119
truck backer-upper application, 327–333
vector processing, 351–355
weights, updating, 7–8, 10–11, 11–13, 103–104, 188
*See also* Application adaptable mapping heuristic; Network-parallel backpropagation; Training-set-parallel backpropagation
Backpropagation through time (BPTT) algorithm, 135–136
Bade, S. L., 38
BASIC interpreter (NeuroBasic), 312–316
Batch learning
communication overhead, 111
convergence, 67, 351
DREAM Machine, 291–292
on-line learning *vs.,* 67, 351
parallelizing, 308–310
system utilization, 291
*See also* Learning by epoch
Benchmark applications. *See* Encoder benchmark application; Nettalk benchmark application
Bias, 8
Bidirectional communication. *See* Palindrome ring architecture
Bill recognition application, 52
Blelloch, G., 32
Block structured networks, 289–291, 295
Bourlard, H., 346
BPTT (backpropagation through time) algorithm, 135–136
Brightness adaptation, 317
Bunch-mode training, 354–355

C
Carpender, G., 16, 157, 158
Carpintero, A., 52
Cell bodies, 236
*See also* Neurons
Cell processors
computational load, 250
functions of, 237
Hopfield network simulation, 239, 241
multilayer perceptron simulation, 242–245
Cells, AP1000 computer, 186
Character recognition application, 51, 52
Chinn, G., 30
Cho, K. B., 51
Circuit switching, 3

CNAPS-1064 computer, 43
CNS-1 computer, 42
Coarse-grained parallelism, 5, 141
Coin recognition application, 52
Color correction application, 317, 318–322, 327
Color histograms, 323, 324–326
Communication, interprocessor
DREAM Machine, 282–283
fixed-ring systolic architecture, 274–275
heterogeneous networks, 68, 70, 79–80, 104–105, 121
MUSIC system, 304–306
process synchronization graphs, 114
ring parallel algorithm, ART1 networks, 164–165
timing diagrams, 74–75
Communicational upper bound, 310–311
Communication constraints, optimal mapping problems, 79–80, 121
Communication overhead
Fujitsu AP1000 computer, 192, 199
heterogeneous networks, 70, 71
homogeneous networks, 97–98
interprocessor message passing, 79–80, 104–105
network-parallel backpropagation, 68, 104–105
overview, 3
palindrome ring architecture, 172–173
real-time recurrent learning algorithm (RTRL), 143, 148–149
training-set-parallel backpropagation, 111
Competitive learning
DREAM Machine implementation, 292–293
finding global maximum, 282–283
self-organizing map networks, 17–18
Compression. *See* Image compression applications
Computational upper bound, 310
Computation times
delta values, 102–103
hidden layer neurons, 101–102, 103–104, 200
network-parallel backpropagation algorithm, 101–104
output layer neurons, 102, 103–104, 199–200
real-time recurrent learning algorithm (RTRL), 139, 143, 148–149
training-set-parallel backpropagation algorithm, 129–130
weight updates, 103–104, 200
Concurrency
ART1 networks, 158, 165–169
locally sequential globally parallel partitioning (LSGP), 149
Occam-2 programming language, 171
real-time recurrent learning algorithm (RTRL), 143, 148–149
represented in process synchronization graphs, 112, 114
T-800 Transputer operation, 150–152

Conditional masking instruction, DREAM
  Machine, 292
Connection Machines, 31–32
Connections per second (CPS), 2
Connection updates per second (CUPS), 2, 12
Continuous Hopfield networks, 15
  *See also* Hopfield networks
Continuous weight update. *See* Learning by
  pattern
Controller network, truck backer-upper
  application, 327–329, 330, 331
Convergence
  application adaptable mapping heuristic,
    207–215, 218–219
  continuous Hopfield networks, 15
  discrete Hopfield networks, 14–15
  estimating number of iterations, 200–201,
    220–221
  genetic algorithms, 86, 124, 197
  Kohonen self-organizing feature maps, 355
  on-line *vs.* batch learning, 67, 351
  real-time recurrent learning algorithm
    (RTRL), 149
  relation to weight update frequency, 10–11,
    207–215
  sensitivity to initial parameters, 197, 213–215
CPS metric (connections per second), 2, 294
Crossover operation, genetic algorithm, 85, 124
Crowl, L. A., 2
CUPS metric (connection updates per second),
  2, 12, 205, 294

**D**
Data dependencies, minimizing, 336–337
Data driven computers, 34
Data fusion structured networks, 289–291
Data integrity, 116–117
Data parallelism. *See* Training-set parallelism
Degrees of parallelism
  backpropagation learning algorithm, 307–310
  dimensions of, 29
  distributing among processors, 26–28,
    188–196
  overview, 26
Delayed weight update learning, 11
  *See also* Learning by pattern
Delta values
  memory requirements, 105
  predicting computation time, 102–103
Dendrites, 236
Dependency graphs
  partitioning large recurrent neural
    networks, 149–150
  real-time recurrent learning algorithm
    (RTRL), 141–144, 144
  transforming to signal flow graphs, 141
Diep, T. A., 52
Digital chip technologies, 46
Digital neurocomputers, 43–46
Discrete Hopfield networks, 13–15
  *See also* Hopfield networks

2D-lattice topology, 35
  *See also* Planar lattice architecture (PLA)
DREAM (dynamically reconfigurable
    extended array multiprocessor)
  algorithmic mapping, 284–285
  architecture, 279–283
  backpropagation learning, 35, 288
  batch learning, 291–292
  block structured networks, 289–291, 295
  competitive learning, 292–293
  conditional masking instruction, 292
  fully connected single layer networks,
    295–297
  interprocessor communication, 282–283
  lookup table hardware support, 281–282
  multilayer networks, 287–288, 294–295
  processor-memory interface, 280–281
  variable length ring architecture, 285–287,
    287–288
  virtual processors, 291
  *See also* Fixed-ring systolic architecture
DREAM Machine. *See* DREAM (dynamically
    reconfigurable extended array
    multiprocessor)
DSPs (digital signal processors), backpropaga-
    tion implementations, 41–43
2D-torus topology, 34, 39
  *See also* Toroidal lattice architecture (TLA)
Dynamically reconfigurable extended array
    multiprocessor. *See* DREAM (dynam-
    ically reconfigurable extended array
    multiprocessor)

**E**
Edge summing, 192
Efficiency. *See* System utilization
Embedded ring structures
  backpropagation implementations, 35
  DREAM Machine, 285
  multilayer neural networks, 287–288
Emulator network, truck backer-upper
    application, 327–329, 330, 331
Encoder benchmark application
  optimal mapping on heterogeneous
    networks, 76–79, 87, 119–120, 125
  optimal mapping on homogeneous
    networks, 97–98
  overview, 76
Energy functions, Hopfield networks, 14–15
Epochs (training epochs)
  computational steps, 112–113
  process synchronization graph, 114–116
  time per epoch, 117–120
  variable synchronization graph, 116–117, 118
  *See also* Batch learning; Learning by
    epoch; Training iterations
Excitatory connections, 159, 160
Execution times
  application adaptable mapping, 199, 204–206
  backpropagation, MUSIC system
    implementation, 309–310

backpropagation, SPERT-II implementation, 353
block structured networks, 289–291, 295
DREAM Machine, 285–287
fixed-ring systolic architecture, 277, 278, 295
fully connected single layer network,
295–297
Kohonen self-organizing feature maps,
356–357
multilayer neural networks, 278, 294–295
neuron parallelism, 294
using virtual processors, 291
Extended ring architecture
ART1 networks, 164, 172–173

**F**
Face recognition application, 50
Fahlman, S., 11
Fast learning model, 162
Feature detection structured networks, 291
Feed-forward networks
applications, 49–53
backpropagation learning algorithm, 7–13,
306–310
parallelization, 25–29
testing, 13
*See also* Application adaptable mapping
heuristic
Field programmable gate arrays (FPGAs), 38
Financial forecasting application, 53
Fine-grained parallelism, 5, 28
Fitness, genetic algorithms, 85, 124
Fixed-ring systolic architecture
deficiencies of, 278
execution rates, 277, 278, 295
mapping neurons to processors, 274–276
multilayer neural networks, 278
system utilization factor, 276–277, 278
weighted sum operation, 274–276
*See also* DREAM (dynamically reconfigur-
able extended array multiprocessor)
Flynn's classification, 3
Foo, S. K., 40
FPGAs (field programmable gate arrays), 38
Franzi, E., 47
Fujimoto, Y., 39
Fujitsu AP1000 computer
architecture, 186
communication overhead, 192, 199
floating point performance, 199
neural network implementations, 187
programming, 186–187
Fully connected multilayer networks, 294–295
Fully connected single layer networks, 295–297

**G**
Gain control subsystem, ART1 networks, 158,
160
Garris, M. D., 52
Garth, S. C. J., 47

G-bus, DREAM Machine, 282–283, 292–293
General asynchronous dynamics, 14
General neuron model, 235–237
Genetic algorithms
improving backpropagation convergence, 197
optimal mapping to heterogeneous
networks, 83–86, 87, 124–125
Gorman, R. P., 52, 217
Gradient descent, 16, 137–138
Grain size, 5
Gray-level correction application, 317, 318–322,
327
Grossberg, S., 5, 16, 158

**H**
Hammerstrom, D., 53
Hardware implementations of neural networks,
46–47, 347–349
Hebb, D., 5
Heterogeneous networks
communication overhead, 70, 71
optimal neuron distribution, 79–96
optimal training set distribution, 120–128
overview, 69–70
processor configurations, 77–78, 94–96,
127–128
processor speed, 96
Heuristic mapping
application adaptable mapping, 196–201
overview, 29, 48
*See also* Algorithmic mapping
Hidden layer neurons
color correction application, 318, 319
Encoder application, 76
homogeneous networks, 97–98
image compression application, 221–225
memory required, 105
Nettalk application, 76
predicting computation time, 101–102,
103–104, 200
Homogeneous networks, 97–98
Hopfield, J., 13, 15
Hopfield networks
continuous Hopfield networks, 15
discrete Hopfield networks, 13–15
planar lattice architecture (PLA)
simulation, 241
toroidal lattice architecture (TLA)
simulation, 238–240
traveling salesman problem, 258
Human visual perception, 317
Hutchings, B. L., 38
Hwang, J., 141
Hypercube topology, 31, 36, 41

**I**
IBM GF 11 computer, 31
Identity mapping problem, 258
Image compression applications
application adaptable mapping, 221–225

DREAM Machine implementation, 295
neural network implementations, 51
Image processing applications
    color correction application, 318–322, 327
    neural network implementations, 50–52
    photofinishing process, 316–317
    picture sequence detection application,
        322–326, 327
Inhibitory connections, 159, 160
Initial population, genetic algorithms, 83–84, 124
Input/output processors, 237
Input processors, 237, 238–239, 241
Instruction stream
    linearizing, 334
    parallelizing, 336–338
    T0 microprocessor, 348
Interconnected workstations, 33
Interconnection density, 276–277
Interprocessor communication
    DREAM Machine, 282–283
    fixed-ring systolic architecture, 274–275
    heterogeneous networks, 68, 70, 79–80,
        104–105, 121
    MUSIC system, 304–306
    process synchronization graphs, 114
    ring parallel algorithm, ART1 networks,
        164–165
    timing diagrams, 74–75
Iterations (training iterations)
    computational steps, 70–71
    defined, 25
    time per iteration, 70–79, 87, 97–98,
        199 200
    timing diagrams, 72–75
    See also Convergence; Training epochs

**K**
Kang, Y.-I., 51
Kerckhoffs, E., 31
Kohonen, T., 5, 17
Kohonen self-organizing feature maps, 355–357
Kuga, M., 187
Kumar, V., 32
Kung, S., 141

**L**
Lattice architectures (TLA, PLA)
    Hopfield network simulation, 238–240,
        241, 258
    load balancing, 250–251, 261–263
    multilayer perceptron simulation, 242–245,
        255–259
    performance, 251–255, 258, 263–265
    physical node processor implementation,
        245–250
    Transputer implementation, 255, 258
    virtual processor implementation, 237
Lbe. See Learning by epoch (lbe)
Lbp. See Learning by pattern (lbp)
Learning algorithms

ART1 networks, 17, 161–164
backpropagation, 8–10, 70–71, 112–113,
    288, 306 310
backpropagation through time (BPTT),
    135–136
competitive learning algorithm, 292–293
Hopfield networks, 13–15
real-time recurrent learning algorithm
    (RTRL), 16, 136–139
self-organizing map networks, 17–18,
    355–357
Learning by block (lbb), 8, 26
Learning by epoch (lbe)
    backpropagation algorithm, parallelizing,
        308–310
    convergence, 7, 11, 351
    learning performance, 11–13
    overview, 7–8, 26
    See also Training epochs; Weight update
        interval
Learning by pattern (lbp)
    backpropagation algorithm, parallelizing,
        308–310
    convergence, 11
    learning performance, 11–13
    overview, 7, 26
    See also Weight update interval
Learning phase, real time recurrent learning
    algorithm (RTRL)
    computational steps, 138–139
    computation time, 148–149
    parallel implementation, 143–149
    partitioning recurrent neural networks, 150
Learning rate
    effect on convergence, 197
    selecting, 10, 208–209, 219–221
Levels of parallelism. See Degrees of
    parallelism
Load balancing
    application adaptable mapping, 189, 195
    homogeneous networks, 97–98
    lattice architectures (TLA, PLA), 250–251,
        261–263
    MUSIC system, 304
    overview, 3
Load/store operations, reducing, 335–336
Locally parallel globally sequential
    partitioning (LPGS), 149
Long-term memory processes (LTM), ART1
    networks, 159–160
Lookup table mechanism, DREAM Machine,
    281–282
Loops, unrolling, 334
Loss factors, speedup model, 311–312
LPGS (locally parallel globally sequential
    partitioning), 149
LSGP (locally sequential globally parallel
    partitioning), 149
LTM (long-term memory) processes, ART1
    networks, 159–160

**M**

Magnetic character reader application, 53
Mapping neurons to processors
    ART1 networks, 169–170, 171–172
    DREAM Machine, 283–293
    lattice architectures (TLA, PLA), 245–250
    multilayer neural networks, 278
    network-parallel backpropagation, 79–96,
        97–98
    real-time recurrent learning algorithm
        (RTRL), 140–143, 143–149, 149–150
    ring systolic architecture, 274–276
    system utilization factor, 276–277, 278
    variable length ring structures, 285–288
    *See also* Application adaptable mapping
        heuristic
Mapping training sets to processors, 112–128
MasPar MP-1 computer, 30
Massively parallel computers, 260
    *See also* Application adaptable mapping;
        Lattice architectures (TLA, PLA)
McCulloch, W. S., 5
McKenna, S. J., 51
MCPS metric (million connections per
    second), 294
MCUPS metric (million connection updates
    per second), 205, 258, 294
Medical imaging application, 51
Meiko Computing Surface systems
    ART1 network implementation, 170–171
    recurrent neural network implementation,
        150–152
Memory constraints, optimal mapping
    problem, 81, 122
Memory operations, reducing, 335–336
Memory-processor interface, DREAM
    Machine, 280–281
Memory requirements
    backpropagation algorithm, 105–106,
        130–131, 201
    partitioned recurrent neural networks, 154
    real-time recurrent learning algorithm
        (RTRL), 143, 147
Mesh topology, 30, 33, 34–35, 37, 39
    *See also* Lattice architectures (TLA, PLA)
Microprocessors, 347–349
Million connections per second (MCPS), 294
Million connection updates per second
    (MCUPS), 205, 258, 294
MIMD (multiple instruction multiple data)
    computers, 3
    Fujitsu AP1000 computer, 186
    MUSIC system, 304–306
    Transputer systems, 76, 150–152, 170, 258
Minsky, M., 5
MISD (multiple instruction single data)
    computers, 3
Models. *See* Neural network models
Møller, M., 11

Momentum term
    backpropagation algorithm, 10
    effect on convergence, 197
Muller, U. A., 42
Multilayer feed-forward networks, 306–310
Multilayer neural networks
    DREAM Machine implementation, 294–295
    fixed-ring systolic architecture, 278
    variable length ring architecture, 287–288
Multilayer perceptron
    color correction application, 318–322, 327
    identity mapping problem, 258
    image sequence detection application,
        322–326, 327
    on MUSIC system, 306–307
    partitioning virtual processor matrices,
        250–251
    performance, 251–255, 263–265
    SPERT-II implementation, 351–355
    toroidal lattice architecture implementation,
        242–245, 255–259
Multiplication operation overhead, 38
MUSIC (MUlti Signal processor system with
    Intelligent Communication)
    architecture, 304–306
    backpropagation implementations, 41,
        306–310, 312
    color correction application, 318–322, 327
    image sequence detection application,
        322–326, 327
    NeuroBasic parallel simulation
        environment, 312–316
    performance, 310–311
    RISC processors, 333–339
    speedup, 311–312
    truck backer-upper application, 327–333
MUSIC system. *See* MUSIC (MUlti Signal
    processor system with Intelligent
    Communication)
Mutation, genetic algorithms, 85, 124
MY-NEUPOWER neurocomputer, 44

**N**

Nang, J. H., 38
Neighborhood function, 18
Nettalk benchmark application
    application adaptable mapping heuristic,
        201–216
    backpropagation implementations, 30, 31,
        32, 33, 40, 48
    DREAM Machine implementation, 294–295
    optimal mapping on heterogeneous
        networks, 76–79, 87, 125
    optimal mapping on homogeneous
        networks, 97–98
    overview, 50, 76
Network contention, 192
Network-parallel backpropagation
    communication overhead, 68, 104–105

mapping to heterogeneous networks, 67–69
mapping to homogeneous networks, 97–98
memory requirements, 81, 105–106
optimal distribution of neurons, 79–96
time per iteration, 70–79, 87, 97–98
*See also* Training-set-parallel
   backpropagation
Network paralysis, 10–11
Network topologies, 3, 4, 18, 19
*See also Names of specific topologies*
Neural network models
   classification of, 5–6
   hardware implementations, 46–47, 347–349
   history of, 5
   processor topologies, 3, 4, 18, 19
   survey of applications, 49–53
   universal characteristics, 272–274
   *See also Names of specific architectures;
      Names of specific neural network
      models*
NeuroBasic parallel simulation environment,
   312–316
Neurocomputers
   backpropagation implementations, 43–46,
      47–48
   classification of, 260
   defined, 2
   parallel architectures, 233–234
   toroidal lattice architecture (TLA), 255–259
Neuron activation
   ART1 networks, 159–160, 162, 163, 165, 166
   competitive learning, 292
   Hopfield network simulation, 239, 241
   multilayer perceptron simulation, 242–245,
      250
   sigmoid activation function, 8, 281–282, 352
Neuron parallelism
   application adaptable mapping, 189, 192, 196
   backpropagation implementations, 30, 31,
      33, 34, 36, 41, 47–48
   dimension of, 29
   distributed processing, 27–28
   MUSIC system, 308–310
   optimum execution rate, 294
   overview, 26
   *See also* Degrees of parallelism; Network-
      parallel backpropagation
Neurons
   general neuron model, 235–237
   representation in approximate linear
      heuristic solution, 87
   representation in genetic algorithm, 83
   weighted sum operation, 274–276
Neurons, mapping to processors
   ART1 networks, 169–170, 171–172
   DREAM Machine, 283–293
   lattice architectures (TLA, PLA), 245–250
   multilayer neural networks, 278
   network-parallel backpropagation, 79–96,
      97–98

real-time recurrent learning algorithm
   (RTRL), 140–143, 143–149,
   149–150, 150
ring systolic architecture, 274–276
system utilization factor, 276–277, 278
variable length ring structures, 285–287
*See also* Application adaptable mapping
   heuristic; Degrees of parallelism
Node parallelism
   in application adaptable mapping, 189, 192,
      195
   in backpropagation implementations, 30,
      31, 34, 36, 37, 39, 41
   distributed processing, 27–28
   overview, 26
   *See also* Degrees of parallelism; Network-
      parallel backpropagation
Normalization, genetic algorithms, 86

**O**

Object inspection applications, 51
Object recognition applications, 323
Obstacle recognition applications, 51, 331
Occam-2 programming language, 171
Omatu, S., 52
Onda, H., 51
One-to-all broadcast, ART1 networks, 169
On-line learning, 67, 111, 351
   *See also* Learning by pattern (lbp)
Optical character recognition application, 52
Optimal mapping problems
   approximate linear heuristic solution, 86–87,
      87
   communication constraints, 79–80, 121
   genetic algorithm solution, 83–86, 87,
      124–125
   heterogeneous networks, 79–96, 120–128
   homogeneous networks, 97–98
   linear mixed integer programming problem,
      123–124
   memory constraints, 81, 122
   neuron assignment constraints, 82
   nonlinear mixed integer optimization
      problem, 82–83
   pattern assignment constraints, 123
   processor configurations, 77–78, 94–96,
      120, 127–128
   statistical validation of solutions, 88,
      125–126
   temporal dependence constraints, 80–81,
      121–122
   time required to obtain optimal solution,
      91–94, 126–127
   wait time constraints, 82, 123
Optimization for RISC-based systems, 333–339
Optoelectronic chip technologies, 46
Orienting subsystem, ART1 networks, 158,
   159–160
Output layer neurons
   allocating to processors, 76, 97–98

in application adaptable mapping, 189, 192, 195
memory requirements, 105
predicting computation time, 102, 103–104, 199–200
updating, 13, 15
Output processors, 237

**P**
Packet switching, 3
Palindrome ring architectures, 169–170, 172–173
Papert, S., 5
Parallel architectures
DREAM machine, 279–283
extended ring architecture, 164, 172–173
fixed-ring systolic architecture, 274–278
lattice architectures (TLA, PLA), 237
MUSIC system, 304–306
neurocomputers, 233–234
palindrome ring architectures, 169–170, 172–173
T0 vector microprocessor, 347–349
Parallel computers (Flynn's classification), 3
Parallelization in layer space. *See* Pipelining
Parallelization in neuron space. *See* Neuron parallelism
Parallelizing instruction stream, 336–338
Parent selection, genetic algorithms, 85
Partitioning ART1 networks, 169–170, 172–173
Partitioning lattice architectures (TLA, PLA), 245
Partitioning recurrent neural networks, 149–150
Partitioning virtual processor matrices, 250–251
Pattern assignment constraints, optimal mapping problems, 122–123
Patterns. *See* Learning by pattern (lbp); Training-set-parallel backpropagation; Training sets
Paugam-Moisy, H., 10, 39, 209
Perception, visual, 316–317
Perceptron, multilayer
color correction application, 318–322, 327
identity mapping problem, 258
image sequence detection application, 322–326, 327
on MUSIC system, 306–307
partitioning virtual processor matrices, 250–251
performance, 251–255, 263–265
SPERT-II implementation, 351–355
toroidal lattice architecture implementation, 242–245, 255–259
Performance
Amdahl's law, 3, 347
application adaptable mapping heuristic, 204–206, 221
ART1 networks, 171–173
backpropagation, basic learning algorithm, 11–13, 48

backpropagation on RISC processors, 338–339
backpropagation on SPERT-II, 346, 353
color correction application, 320, 321–322, 327
communicational upper bound, 310–311
computational upper bound, 310
CPS metric, 2
CUPS metric, 2, 12
Kohonen self-organizing feature maps, 356–357
lattice architectures (TLA, PLA), 251–255, 258, 263–265
MCPS metric, 294
MCUPS metric, 205, 258, 294
MUSIC system, 310–311
NeuroBasic programming environment, 316
ring parallel ART1 algorithm, 171–173
ring systolic architecture, 277, 278
truck backer-upper application, 329–330, 332–333
Photofinishing applications
color correction application, 318–322, 327
picture sequence detection application, 322–326, 327
process overview, 316–317
Physical node processors, lattice architectures
load balancing, 250–251, 261–263
mapping virtual processors to, 245–250
Picture sequence detection application, 322–326, 327
Pipelining
application adaptable mapping, 189, 192, 195
backpropagation implementations, 33, 34, 36–37, 39, 41, 47–48
dimension of, 29
distributed processing, 26–27
multilayer neural networks, 278
MUSIC system, 308
overview, 26
ring-parallel ART1 algorithm, 169–170, 172–173
Pitts, W., 5
PLA. *See* Planar lattice architecture (PLA)
Planar lattice architecture (PLA)
backpropagation implementations, 39
Hopfield network simulation, 241
load balancing, 250–251, 261–263
performance, 251–255, 258
physical node processor implementation, 245–250
virtual processor implementation, 237
Process control application, 53
Processes
in process synchronization graphs, 114–116
in timing diagrams, 72–75
Processor-memory interface, DREAM Machine, 280–281
Processors, in variable synchronization graphs, 116–117, 118

Processor speed, 96
Process synchronization graphs (PSG), 114–117
Programming environments
    NeuroBasic interpreter, 312–316
    SPERT-II workstation accelerator, 349–350
PSG. *See* Process synchronization graphs (PSG)

**Q**
Quickprop (quick-propagation) algorithm, 11

**R**
RAP (ring array processor), 42, 345
Real-time recurrent learning algorithm
        (RTRL)
    convergence, 149
    learning algorithm, 16, 136–139
    learning phase, 138–139, 143–149
    matrix formulation, 139–140
    overview, 136
    parallel implementation, 140–149
    retrieving phase, 138–139, 140–143
    Transputer-based implementation, 150–152
Recurrent neural networks
    Hopfield networks, 13–15
    multilayer recurrent networks, 15–16
    overview, 135–136
    partitioning onto ring architectures, 149–150
RENNS (REconfigurable Neural Network
        Server), 42–43
Resonance of neurons, 17, 160
Retrieval phase, Hopfield networks, 14
Retrieving phase, real-time recurrent learning
        algorithm (RTRL)
    computational steps, 138–139
    computation time, 143
    parallel implementation, 140–143
    partitioning RNNs, 149–150
Ring architectures
    ART1 networks, 164–173, 169–170,
        171–173
    backpropagation implementations, 39–40
    fixed-ring systolic architecture, 274–278
    heterogeneous networks, 69–70
    partitioning large recurrent neural networks,
        149–150
    real-time recurrent learning algorithm
        (RTRL), 140–149
    variable length rings, 285–288
Ring parallel algorithm, ART1 networks,
        164–170
RISC (reduced instruction set computer)
        processors
    MUSIC system, 333–339
    T0 vector microprocessor, 347–349
RNNs. *See* Recurrent neural networks
Road and obstacle recognition application, 51
Root processors, toroidal lattice architecture, 255
Rosenberg, C., 32, 207
RRANN (Run-time Reconfiguration ANN), 38

RTRL. *See* Real-time recurrent learning
        algorithm (RTRL)
Rumelhart, D. E., 5, 10, 207
Run-time Reconfiguration ANN (RRANN), 38

**S**
Satellite image processing application, 50
Scalability
    ring parallel ART1 algorithm, 171–173
    Transputer-based recurrent neural
        networks, 150–152
Scheduling, for RISC processors, 336–338
Sejnowski, T. J., 207
Selection, genetic algorithms, 124
Self-organizing map networks, 17–18, 355–357
Semaphores, 116–117
Sequence detection (picture sequence
        detection application), 322–326, 327
SFG. *See* Signal flow graphs (SFG)
Shared weights-receptive fields (SW-RF)
        networks, 41
Shiotani, S., 51
Short-term memory processes (STM), ART1
        networks, 159–160
Sigmoid activation function
    function, 8
    lookup table implementation, DREAM
        Machine, 281–282
    vector implementation, T0 microprocessor,
        352
Signal flow graphs (SFG)
    generating from dependency graphs, 141
    partitioning large RNNs, 150
    real-time recurrent learning algorithm
        (RTRL), 141–144, 144
SIMD (single instruction multiple data)
        computers, 3
    DREAM Machine, 279–280
    SIMD mesh-connected computers, 37
Similarity test (vigilance test), ART1 networks,
        157–158, 163, 164–165, 167
Simple asynchronous dynamics, 14
Single layer recurrent networks. *See* Hopfield
        networks
SISD (single instruction single data)
        computers, 3
Smoothing term, backpropagation learning
        algorithm, 10
SNAP (SIMD numerical array processor),
        45–46
SOM. *See* Self-organizing map networks
Sonar return application, 52, 216–221
Speech recognition networks, 49, 187, 221,
        351–355
Speech synthesis application, 50
Speedup
    backpropagation algorithm on RISC
        processors, 338–339
    loss factors, 311–312

MUSIC system, 311–312
neuron distribution in homogeneous
    networks, 97–98
partitioned RNNs, 152
ring parallel ART1 algorithm, 171–173
weights computed twice *vs.* communicated,
    309–310
SPERT-II workstation accelerator
backpropagation implementation, 351–355
Kohonen self-organizing feature map
    implementation, 355–357
performance, 346, 353
T0 vector microprocessor integration,
    349–350
SPMD (single programs operating on multiple
    data) computers, 3
Stability-plasticity dilemma, 16
STM (short-term memory) processes, ART1
    networks, 159–160
Storage phase, Hopfield networks, 13
Supercomputers, 33
Symult S2010 computer, 33
SYNAPSE-1 computer, 44–45
Synapse parallelism
in application adaptable mapping, 189, 195
backpropagation implementations, 30, 32
dimension of, 29
distributed processing, 28–29
overview, 26
Synapse processors
computational load, 250
functions of, 237
Hopfield network simulation, 238–239, 241
multilayer perceptron simulation, 242–245
Synapses, 236, 273
*See also* Synapse parallelism; Synapse
    processor
System throughput
DREAM Machine, 285–287
ring systolic architecture, 277
System utilization
batch learning, 291
relation to interconnection density, 276–277,
    278
*See also* Application adaptable mapping
Systolic array topology, 36–37
*See also* DREAM (dynamically reconfigur-
    able extended array multiprocessor);
    Fixed-ring systolic architecture

**T**
Table lookup mechanism, DREAM Machine,
    281–282
Takeda, F., 52
Tank, D. W., 15
Temporal dependence constraints, optimal
    mapping problems, 80–81, 121–122
Temporal inhibition, 236
Temporal junctions
in process synchronization graphs, 114

in timing diagrams, 74–75
in variable synchronization graphs, 117
Threshold function, 236
Time per epoch, 117–120
Time per iteration
application adaptable mapping heuristic,
    199–200
network-parallel backpropagation, 70–79,
    87, 97–98
TLA. *See* Toroidal lattice architecture (TLA)
Topologies, network, 3, 4, 18, 19
*See also Names of specific topologies*
Topology preservation, 17
Toroidal lattice architecture (TLA)
backpropagation implementations, 39
Hopfield network simulation, 238–240
load balancing, 250–251, 261–263
multilayer perceptron simulation, 242–245
performance, 251–255, 258, 263–265
physical node processor implementation,
    245–250
Transputer implementation, 255, 258
virtual processor implementation, 237
Torrent ISA microprocessor, 347–349
Total training time, minimizing, 196–201,
    215–216
Training epochs
computational steps, 112–113
process synchronization graph, 114–116
time per epoch, 117–120
variable synchronization graph, 116–117, 118
*See also* Batch learning; Learning by
    epoch; Training iterations
Training iterations
computational steps, 70–71
defined, 25
time per iteration, 70–79, 87, 97–98,
    199–200
timing diagrams, 72–75
*See also* Convergence; Training epochs
Training-session parallelism, 26, 195–196
Training-set-parallel backpropagation
communication overhead, 111
memory requirements, 130–131
optimal distribution of training sets,
    120–127
overview, 111–112
time per epoch, 117–120
*See also* Network-parallel backpropagation
Training-set parallelism
in application adaptable mapping, 189, 192
dimension of, 29
distributed processing, 26
implementations, 30, 31, 32, 34, 39, 40, 41,
    47–48
overview, 26
*See also* Degrees of parallelism; Training-
    set-parallel backpropagation
Training sets
defined, 25

mapping to processors, 120–128
memory requirements, 105, 130
Training speed, 202–204
Training time, minimizing, 196–201
Transputers
ART1 network implementation, 170
lattice architecture (TLA, PLA) implementations, 255, 258
network-parallel backpropagation implementation, 69–70, 76–79, 97–98
processor configurations, 77–78, 94–96, 119–120, 127–128
recurrent neural network (RNN) implementation, 150–152
training-set-parallel backpropagation implementation, 119–120
T-805 series, timing for elemental operations, 106–107
Traveling salesman problem
DREAM Machine implementation, 295–297
Hopfield networks, 258
Truck backer-upper application, 327–333
Trunk processors, toroidal lattice architecture, 255
Tsinas, L., 51
T0 vector microprocessor
architecture, 347–349
backpropagation implementation, 351–355
SPERT-II workstation accelerator integration, 349–350

U
Unrolling loops, 334

V
Variable-length ring architectures. See DREAM (dynamically reconfigurable extended array multiprocessor)
Variable synchronization graphs (VSGs), 116–117, 118
Vector microprocessor (T0), 347–349
Vector processing
backpropagation algorithm, 351–355
Kohonen self-organizing feature map implementation, 355
Vertical slicing. See Neuron parallelism
Vigilance test, ART1 networks, 157–158, 163, 164–165, 167
Virtual processors
DREAM Machine, 291
lattice architectures (TLA, PLA), 237, 245–250, 250–251

Visual perception, 316–317
VSG. See Variable synchronization graphs (VSGs)

W
Wait time constraints, optimal mapping problems, 122–123
Wait times
heterogeneous networks, 72–74, 79–81, 82
homogeneous networks, 97
in process synchronization graphs, 114–116
in timing diagrams, 72–75
Warp computer, 32
Weather recognition application, 52
Weighted sum operation, 274–276
Weight parallelism. See Synapse parallelism
Weights, updating
in application adaptable mapping, 192
ART1 networks, 17, 160, 167, 169
backpropagation, 8–9, 103–104, 188
bunch-mode training, 355
competitive learning algorithm, 292–293
computing twice vs. communicating, 308–310
discrete Hopfield network, 13
gradient descent, 16, 137–138
learning performance, 11–13
MCUPS metric, 294
memory required, 106
multilayer perceptron, 244–245
on-line learning, 351
parallelizing backpropagation algorithm, 307–310
predicting computation time, 103–104, 200
real-time recurrent learning algorithm (RTRL), 16
self-organizing map networks, 18
strategies, 7–8, 25–26
Weight update intervals
effect on convergence, 10–11, 207–215
effect on total training time, 216–217
overview, 26
Widrow, B., 5
Williams, R. J., 136
Willshaw, D., 5

Y
Yoon, H., 38

Z
Zhang, X., 31
Zipser, D., 136

## IEEE

# COMPUTER SOCIETY

## Press Activities Board

Lightning Source UK Ltd.
Milton Keynes UK
UKOW07n1922070515

251079UK00001B/17/P